HIT PARADE

HIT PARADE

An Encyclopedia of the Top Songs of the Jazz, Depression, Swing, and Sing Eras

DON TYLER

QUILL
William Morrow
New York

To Doris, Scot, Matt, and Patrick

Library of Congress Cataloging-in-Publication Data

Tyler, Don.
  Hit parade.

  Includes index.
  1. Music, Popular (Songs, etc.)—United States—
Dictionaries. 2. Music, Popular (Songs, etc.)—United
States—Chronology. I. Title.
ML102.P66T9 1985   784.5′00973   85-12375
ISBN 0-688-06149-4 (pbk.)

Printed in the United States of America

First Edition

1 2 3 4 5 6 7 8 9 10

BOOK DESIGN BY RICHARD ORIOLO

P R E F A C E

This is a chronology of the most popular songs in the United States from 1920 and the start of the jazz age to 1955, when rock began its rise to dominance. For each year, it describes the top hits created by leading composers and lyricists, popular singers, noteworthy Broadway musicals, and big box-office movie musicals.

I have divided the years into eras corresponding to shifts in musical tastes and often to historical developments as well. "The Jazz Age" covers the Roaring Twenties of the flapper and her beau (during the twenties all popular music was called jazz). "The Depression Years" includes the songs of 1930 to 1934, the years of the Great Depression. "The Swing Era" refers to the time of the big bands; it covers 1935 to 1945, and includes World War II. From the end of the war to the advent of rock and roll lies "The Sing Era," in which singers were more important than bands.

Sometimes it was difficult to verify which songs actually were the top hits of their years. Only since 1958 have million-selling recordings been certified by the Recording Industry Association of America. Before 1958, often the company or recording artist estimated the sales figures. Beginning in 1935, *Your Hit Parade* radio program compiled and featured a list of the top songs of every week. And after 1940 there were weekly charts published in *Variety* and *Billboard* of the best-selling recordings of popular songs.

Lists compiled by *Variety* magazine also suggested which songs should be included. On its fiftieth anniversary in 1956, *Variety* published a "Fifty Year Hit Parade" covering 1905 to 1955. Although it lists the songs alphabetically rather than by popularity, it indicates the most famous songs of these years. In January 1981, *Variety* published "The Top Ten, 1941 to 1980," which ranks each year's top ten by popularity. *Variety* also published its list of "Golden 100 Tin Pan Alley Songs, 1915–1935," which helps greatly in a period where factual information is difficult to obtain. *Variety,* however, did not disclose how it determined which songs to include in the list.

Another source of outstanding hits was the "ASCAP (American Society of Composers, Authors and Publishers) All-Time Hit Parade," sixteen songs chosen by this performing-rights organization on its fiftieth anniversary in 1964 as the greatest hits during those fifty years.

Other songs have been included because of their longevity. Their popularity has stood the test of time.

The selections have not been influenced by my preferences or opinions about the qualities of the songs.

Brief biographies of many of the composers, lyricists, and performers are at the end of the book.

C O N T E N T S

T · H · E
JAZZ AGE: 1920 to 1929

The twenties—characterized by flappers and "jazz babies"—were known as the jazz age. Suitable theme songs for the era might include "Ain't We Got Fun?," "Let's Do It," and "Runnin' Wild!" The flapper and her beau would do practically anything as long as it was fun: They supposedly kissed indiscriminately, wore provocative clothing, used profanity, drank plenty of liquor, danced whenever they had the chance, sang their favorite songs with gusto, and laughed and giggled with abandon.

The Lost Generation flapper bobbed her hair and wore skirts that flirted with exposing the knee. She danced to the Charleston and the black bottom and twirled her ever-present pearl necklace. The "in" sayings of the day included "the cat's pajamas," "the bee's knees," "twenty-three skiddoo," "oh, you kid," and "stew in your own juice." Millions were entertained by playing Mah-Jongg or the Ouija board.

When the United States is prosperous and politically stable, people are generally happy. When people are happy and successful, they sing and dance to fast, hot music. Although the twenties were not all smooth sailing, the country sang and danced its way through the decade as if it had nothing to worry about but having a good time. A popular expression of the time sums up that outlook: "Goin' to hell in a handbasket."

The popular music of the decade included revivals of hits from the past ("Rock-a-Bye Your Baby with a Dixie Melody"), silly songs ("Barney Google"), girl songs ("Sweet Sue"), boy songs ("Sonny Boy"), mammy songs ("My Mammy"), baby songs ("Yes Sir, That's My Baby"), and blues songs ("The Wang, Wang Blues"), and of course, there was jazz ("Jazz Me Blues").

The Emergence of Jazz

Actually jazz had been around for years. In New Orleans, by 1880, the basic format of the jazz ensemble (two cornets, tuba, clarinet, and drums) had developed. Early jazz flourished in the Storyville section (the "sporting district") until it was closed down in 1917. Jazzmen sought new territory at cities along the Mississippi River, eventually reaching Chicago.

The prevailing style of jazz in the twenties was Dixieland, usually characterized as hot, loud, and fast. The Original Dixieland Jazz Band was one of the first nationally popular jazz bands. But compared with to-day, jazz had a small following.

True jazz, as black musicians played it, was rare on the top-seller lists. There was symphonic jazz, with its leader, the so-called King of Jazz Paul Whiteman, and sweet jazz, which retained many of the nuances of jazz but was appropriate for dancing. Many of the most popular tunes of the twenties are "jazzy" only in the sweet sense. Pure primitive jazz was refined into music more palatable to white middle-class and work-ing-class ears.

Legendary names associated with this period in jazz include clarinetists Sidney Bechet, Johnny Dodds, and Jimmie Noone; cornetists Johnny Dunn, Jabbo Smith, and, of course, the king, Louis Armstrong; trombon-ists Jimmy Harrison, Bennie Morton, and Claude Jones; pianists Jelly Roll Morton, James P. Johnson, and Fats Waller.

The Dance Bands

Paul Whiteman's was by far the most popular dance band of the twenties. It featured a symphonic string section; sweet, lush arrangements; and a danceable beat. Whiteman was called the King of Jazz, but his music sounds rather unjazzy to modern ears. Some magnificent soloists in his band emerged as genuine jazz artists, notably Bix Beiderbecke and the Dorsey brothers. It was Whiteman who commissioned George Gershwin to write a jazz concerto to prove that jazz was an idiom that commanded respect; the result was *Rhapsody in Blue* At least ten of the most important songs of the decade were popularized by Whiteman's orchestra.

Other sweet bands that emerged in the twenties in-cluded Ben Selvin and his Novelty Orchestra, Isham Jones and his orchestra, the Buddy Rogers orchestra, Art Landry and his Call of the North Orchestra, Lew Gold and his Club Wigwam Orchestra, Ted Fiorito and his orchestra, Ted Weems and his orchestra, Harry Richman and his orchestra, Ted Lewis's band, and toward the end of the decade Guy Lombardo and his Royal Canadians and Rudy Vallee and his Connecti-cut Yankees.

Musical Theater Enthusiasts

The twenties may be known as the jazz age, but the decade should really be remembered for producing wonderful music for the theater. Composers like George Gershwin, Irving Berlin, Richard Rodgers, Vincent Youmans, Rudolf Friml, Sigmund Romberg, Ray Henderson, and Walter Donaldson were at their peak, while Victor Herbert was still around for a few more bows and Cole Porter was just beginning his string of successful musicals.

The twenties may have expressed themselves most completely in the musical comedy and revue. Despite the overused formula for success—bring on the chorus at the beginning and the end of each act, empty the stage instantly by asking, "Anyone for tennis?," in-sert at least one big sidesplitting drunk scene, have the juvenile leads break into a tap dance or soft-shoe shuffle at the end of their duet—the big musicals of the decade yielded some of the great standards of all times.

Sigmund Romberg's *Blossom Time* in 1921 inspired a revival of interest in the operetta style. Operettas of the next few years included Victor Herbert's *Orange*

Blossoms (1922), Rudolf Friml's *Rose Marie* (1924), Sigmund Romberg's *The Student Prince in Heidel-berg* (1924), Friml's *The Vagabond King* (1925), and Romberg's *The Desert Song* (1926).

The Broadway musicals introduced the greatest number of giant hits. *Irene*, which opened in 1919, set the style of the musical of the decade and spawned the hit "In My Sweet Little Alice Blue Gown." More than 400 shows were produced on Broadway during the decade, introducing such hit songs as "Look for the Silver Lining," "The Love Nest," "My Mammy," "Toot, Toot, Tootsie!," "Indian Love Call," "I Want to Be Happy," "Tea for Two," "The Desert Song," "Can't Help Lovin' Dat Man," "'S Wonderful," "I Wanna Be Loved by You," and "More Than You Know," to name only a few.

The stars of these musicals were Al Jolson, Marilyn Miller, Eddie Cantor, Fred and Adele Astaire, Dennis King, Helen Morgan, Ed Wynn, Julia Sanderson, Edith Day, Gertrude Lawrence, and Beatrice Lillie.

Of all the significant musicals, a Jerome Kern and Oscar Hammerstein II collaboration had the greatest impact; they remodeled Edna Ferber's novel *Show Boat* into one of the classics of the Broadway stage. The music was stunning; the lyrics were pertinent; the story was touching; the effect of the whole production was stupendous.

The plush Broadway revue was in its full glory in the twenties. Gorgeous, long-limbed chorines in sequins and ostrich-feathered headdresses were a major attraction of such revues as *George White's Scandals*, Irving Berlin's *The Music Box Revue*, and Florenz Ziegfeld's *Follies*. The *Ziegfeld Follies*, the yardstick by which revues were measured, had passed its heyday, but it remained one of the ultimate stage entertainments of the era. The *Follies of 1921* introduced "My Man" and "Second Hand Rose," sung by Fanny Brice, and showcased the interpolation by Van and Schenck of "The Wang, Wang Blues." Comedians Gallagher and Shean stole the 1922 show with a topical song "Gallagher and Shean." Van and Schenck scored again in the 1923 *Follies* with "That Old Gang of Mine." Eddie Cantor's big song of 1927 was an interpolation of Walter Donaldson's "My Blue Heaven" into the last edition of the *Follies* of the twenties.

In 1919 a rival challenged the supremacy of Ziegfeld in the field of revues. *George White's Scandals* contributed several memorable songs to the decade: "Stairway to Paradise" (1922), "Last Night on the Back Porch" (1923), "Somebody Loves Me" (1924), plus "Birth of the Blues" and "Black Bottom" (1926). Other important revues included *The Century Revue and the Midnight Rounders, Earl Carroll's Vanities, The Greenwich Village Follies, The Music Box Revue, The Passing Show, Make It Snappy, Gay Paree,* and *Charlot's Revue.*

White Broadway audiences first heard jazz in all-black revues like 1921's *Shuffle Along*, 1928's *Lew Leslie's Blackbirds*, and 1929's *Hot Chocolates.*

The World's Greatest Entertainer

Many of the musicals of the period were tailor-made for certain stars, and no one more than Al Jolson. Jolson never sang a note from the score of the numerous musicals in which he appeared. Instead, at a particular point in each act, he would step entirely out of character, move to the front of the stage, and perform whatever song he chose to sing at that performance. What gall! But the audiences loved it. Jolson was billed as the World's Greatest Entertainer.

Jolson always appeared in blackface as the servant Gus. He became a star in 1912 and continued his enormous successes into the twenties. Some of Jolson's most famous Broadway show appearances were in 1916's *Robinson Crusoe, Jr.,* 1918's *Sinbad,* 1921's *Bombo,* and 1925's *Big Boy.*

The Sound Motion Picture

Because of his extraordinary popularity, Jolson had a hand in the first sound motion picture in 1927. In the film *The Jazz Singer,* which actually had only partial sound, Jolson sang six of his favorite songs. The phenomenal success of what was first regarded as a mere novelty launched the sound age in the movies. Next came *The Singing Fool,* again starring Jolson. This 1928 film featured Jolson singing "I'm Sittin' on Top of the World," "There's a Rainbow 'Round My Shoulder," and "Sonny Boy." The sound process was improved in 1928, and as the decade closed, "All-Talking! All-Singing! All-Dancing!" films like *Broadway Melody* and *The Hollywood Revue* arrived.

Theme songs for major nonmusical pictures also became popular. Even a few silent films had theme songs (example: "Charmaine" for *What Price Glory?* in 1927). But soon virtually every picture had a hackneyed theme song, which caused a backlash.

The Early Record Industry

At the beginning of the twenties sheet music was the main source of profit in music. As early as the late 1870s recorded music had been possible, but at the turn of the century a record was still a toy. By the end of World War I, though, many of America's stage stars were entering living rooms via records. The recording industry had become a reality by 1920, and by the middle twenties 130 million records were being sold annually.

At first, these records were played on the gramophone. It had to be wound up, and the needle had to be changed for every record. By the end of the decade, electric automatic record changers and long-lasting tungsten needles had been introduced. The disks were weighty ten- or twelve-inch records, which played at seventy-eight or eighty revolutions per minute.

The Birth of Radio

On November 2, 1920, station KDKA, installed at the Westinghouse plant in East Pittsburgh, Pennsylvania, went on the air with the news that Warren Harding had been elected president of the United States. A year later there were 8 more stations. Within two years there were 564—and a shortage of wavelengths. Millions of Americans made new friends with radio personalities.

In 1922, $60 million worth of radio sets were sold in the United States. By 1929, $842 million had been sold. Radio quickly traveled from infancy to maturity. Many bands and singers of the decade owe their fame to the radio. Paul Whiteman and his orchestra appeared regularly on radio, as did Rudy Vallee and his Yale Collegians. Vaughn De Leath was one of the first female singers to gain national recognition over radio. Wendell Hall became the singing star of *The Eveready Hour,* one of radio's earliest variety programs. Others who may have owed their stardom to radio included Little Jack Little, Whispering Jack Smith, Lanny Ross, Jessica Dragonette, Baby Rose Marie (she later dropped the "Baby" to become the Rose Marie who starred for many seasons on the Dick Van Dyke television series), and the "Sweethearts of the Air," Peter De Rose and the Ukulele Girl, May Singhi Breen.

The radio microphone and perhaps the intimacy it afforded was uniquely suited for the birth of the crooning style of singing. The singers who adapted their singing style to the gentle, relaxed, soft crooning style became the most successful radio singers.

The torch singer, the thrush of the speakeasy, was the rage. Perched on a piano, singing in a throaty, heartbreaking, breastbeating fashion, Libby Holman, Ruth Etting, and Helen Morgan were the epitome of the torch singer.

The twenties was one of the most difficult periods to obtain factual data on actual hits. Although *Variety* began publishing in 1905, it did not chart popular song hits until the forties. Two lists from *Variety,* "Golden 100 Tin Pan Alley Songs" and "Fifty Year Hit Parade," formed the basis for inclusion as the biggest hits of this era. However, in a few instances, songs that were not included on those lists were included here because of their popularity in subsequent years.

Never had popular music been so diverse and so lucrative or had such national impact. An examination of the most popular tunes of each year of the decade will give an even clearer picture of an era that can be only remotely connected with reality at one moment and so enduringly memorable at another.

1 9 2 0

Avalon
COMPOSER-LYRICISTS: **Vincent Rose and Al Jolson**

Borrowing tunes from the classics became very popular and highly profitable if the borrowers were not sued in the 1920s. Vincent Rose, collaborating with Al Jolson, wrote "Avalon," and Jolson helped skyrocket it to popularity. The melody was borrowed from the aria "E lucevan le stelle" from Puccini's opera *Tosca,* although the key of "Avalon" was changed from minor to major. Puccini's publishers brought suit and were awarded damages of $25,000 and all future royalties. Jolson interpolated "Avalon" into the 1918 musical *Sinbad* after the New York opening. The 1946 recording by Jolson became a million seller, partly because of the release of his film biography, *The Jolson Story.*

"Avalon" was chosen for *Variety*'s "Fifty Year Hit Parade."

Daddy, You've Been a Mother to Me
COMPOSER-LYRICIST: **Fred Fisher**

This sentimental waltz tells of a father who, after his wife's death, gives up going out with the guys to be mother and father to his child. This Fred Fisher product was used in his film biography, *Oh, You Beautiful Doll,* in 1949.

Dardanella
COMPOSERS: **Felix Bernard and Johnny S. Black**
   LYRICIST: **Fred Fisher**

This rag-style fox-trot novelty number is the song for which composer Fred Fisher is probably best remembered. Published in 1919, within its first year "Dardanella" had sold almost 2 million copies of sheet music. It was a million-selling record for Ben Selvin's Novelty Orchestra in 1920. Within a few years it is said to have sold 6.5 million records on various labels without the benefit of any radio or motion-picture plugs.

The tune was a piano rag by Johnny S. Black, "Turkish Tom Tom," which Fisher plagiarized, writing his own lyrics and then publishing it himself. As lyricist and publisher of "Dardanella," Fisher is believed to have earned more than $1 million. After "Dardanella" had become successful, Felix Bernard, a vaudevillian, claimed *he* had written the tune but had renounced his rights for a cash settlement of $100. After a court fight, later sheet music publications carried Fisher's name as lyricist and Black and Bernard as composers.

Dardanella is an Oriental beauty the singer wants to see again to capture her heart. The song is best remembered as an instrumental, so the lyrics are not well known.

"Dardanella" was selected for *Variety*'s "Fifty Year Hit Parade" for 1919.

Feather Your Nest
COMPOSER-LYRICISTS: **James Kendis, James Brockman, and Howard Johnson**

This 1920 song was cynical about materialism. The birds are singing it; the whole world is saying, "Go feather your nest!" It was popularized by Eddie Cantor and interpolated into the musical *Tip-Top* by the Duncan Sisters.

I'll Be with You in Apple Blossom Time
COMPOSER: **Albert Von Tilzer**
   LYRICIST: **Neville Fleeson**

"I'll Be with You in Apple Blossom Time" was popularized by Nora Bayes, "Queen of the Two-a-Days," in vaudeville. *Variety* chose this number as one of its "Fifty Year Hit Parade" selections.

I Never Knew I Could Love Anybody Like I'm Loving You
COMPOSER-LYRICISTS: **Tom Pitts, Ray Egan, and Roy Marsh**

Jane Green inserted this *Variety* "Fifty Year Hit Parade" selection into the revue *The Century Revue and the Midnight Rounders of 1921.* However, it was popularized by Paul Whiteman and his orchestra in 1920. It was successfully revived in 1941 and was performed in several motion pictures.

I Used to Love You but It's All Over Now
COMPOSER: **Albert Von Tilzer**
   LYRICIST: **Lew Brown**

Albert Von Tilzer composed two hits of 1920: "I'll Be with You in Apple Blossom Time" and this number. Von Tilzer made an attempt to bridge the generation gap by using syncopation fairly frequently in this song, but the new jazz age musical language was not his forte.

The Japanese Sandman
COMPOSER: **Richard A. Whiting**
   LYRICIST: **Raymond B. Egan**

The Western image of Oriental music gives the melody and harmony of this *Variety* "Fifty Year Hit Parade" selection a distinct Far Eastern flavor. During the twenties, transportation was still primitive enough that to most people the Orient was excitingly exotic and distant. Tin Pan Alley adapted authentic Far Eastern music to appeal to Americans, who accepted it as genuine.

Nora Bayes popularized "The Japanese Sandman" in vaudeville, and Paul Whiteman and his orchestra made a hit record for Victor. Backed by "Whispering," the Whiteman disc sold nearly 2 million by 1921 and helped establish the Whiteman orchestra as the most popular sweet-style orchestra of the twenties.

Lena from Palesteena
COMPOSER: **Con Conrad**
   LYRICIST: **J. Russel Robinson**

Con Conrad came to songwriting from the vaudeville stage, on which he had been appearing since 1907, when he was still in his teens. "Lena from Palesteena" (or "Palesteena") was introduced and made popular by the Original Dixieland Jazz Band. It was also popularized by Eddie Cantor.

Variety chose this jazz classic for its "Fifty Year Hit Parade."

Look for the Silver Lining
COMPOSER: **Jerome Kern**
LYRICISTS: **Buddy De Sylva and Clifford Grey**

Jerome Kern's *Sally* got the musical theater of the twenties off to a superb start. The musical tells a Cinderella story of a waif who is propelled into dancing stardom in the *Ziegfeld Follies.* In the show a young millionaire, played by Irving Fisher, gives advice to Marilyn Miller as Sally, a dishwashing waif. The story sounds more typical of the Depression than the twenties, but life is hard for the down-and-out of any era.

Sally in 1920 and *Sunny* in 1925 set the stage for Kern's greatest accomplishment, *Show Boat,* in 1927.

"Look for the Silver Lining" was a *Variety* "Fifty Year Hit Parade" selection.

The Love Nest
COMPOSER: **Louis A. Hirsch**
LYRICIST: **Otto Harbach**

The musical comedy *Mary* primarily owed its run on Broadway to its hit song, "The Love Nest." This was the greatest song success of composer Louis Hirsch, who had his first successful song included in a 1911 stage production. The song was for many years the theme for the Burns and Allen radio and television series.

The plot of *Mary* concerns building "portable houses" to sell for $1,300 each. "The Love Nest" was sung by Jack (played by Jack McGowan) to Mary (played by Janet Velie), detailing his plans for the love nest that will make him rich. Little did anyone in 1920 know to what proportions the mobile home and trailer business would later grow.

Variety selected "The Love Nest" for its "Fifty Year Hit Parade."

Margie
COMPOSERS: **Con Conrad and J. Russel Robinson**
LYRICIST: **Benny Davis**

"Margie" was written about Marjorie, the five-year-old daughter of Eddie Cantor, but it sounds more like an upbeat love song. Cantor introduced and made popular this *Variety* "Fifty Year Hit Parade" selection, interpolating it into the revue *The Midnight Rounders of 1921.*

My Mammy
COMPOSER: **Walter Donaldson**
LYRICISTS: **Joe Young and Sam Lewis**

William Frawley introduced this song in vaudeville, but it grew into a hit when Al Jolson sang it in *Bombo* in 1921.

One of the best-remembered of Jolson's routines was his singing this song and falling on his knees, pleading with his mammy to forgive him. Jolson's 1946 recording became a million seller, as did a 1967 recording by the Happenings.

Variety listed this song in its "Fifty Year Hit Parade" for 1921.

Rose of Washington Square
COMPOSER: **James F. Hanley**
LYRICIST: **Ballard MacDonald**

This song was copyrighted in 1920, but it was introduced by Fanny Brice in the *Ziegfeld Midnight Frolic of 1919.* She repeated the performance in the 1920 edition, and the song became one of her musical trademarks. It provided the title for a 1939 screen musical that was loosely based on Brice's career. The song recalls a time when beauty was appreciated from afar; beautiful women were "seen but not heard."

Variety chose "Rose of Washington Square" for its "Fifty Year Hit Parade."

When My Baby Smiles at Me
COMPOSER: **Bill Munro**
LYRICISTS: **Andrew B. Sterling and Ted Lewis**

Ted Lewis introduced this song, which became his theme, in 1918 before interpolating it into *The Greenwich Village Follies* of 1919. It was still a top song in 1920 when it was finally copyrighted. The last few words are the most famous: "I sigh, I cry, it's just a glimpse of Heaven, when my baby smiles at me."

"When My Baby Smiles at Me" was a selection in *Variety*'s "Fifty Year Hit Parade."

Whip-poor-will
COMPOSER: **Jerome Kern**
LYRICIST: **Buddy De Sylva**

Along with "Look for the Silver Lining," "Whip-poor-will" was a principal hit from *Sally.* It had been written for the unproduced musical *Brewster's Millions.* "Whip-poor-will," the airy recollection of birds singing, was introduced by Marilyn Miller and Irving Fisher. The melody and harmony of "Whip-poor-will" are clever and inventive, and the song contains a liberal sprinkling of syncopation. Could it be that Kern was experimenting with the music of the jazz age and abandoning the composing principles that had been in fashion namely, the waltz and European-inspired operetta?

Whispering

COMPOSERS: John Schonberger and Vincent Rose
LYRICIST: Richard Coburn

"Whispering" and "The Japanese Sandman" were the two sides of a disc that established Paul Whiteman and his orchestra as major show business personalities. The disc had sold nearly 2 million by 1921. Considering the number of record players in use in 1920, an equivalent sale today would be about 20 million.

The Whiteman orchestra began playing the song, which became a *Variety* "Fifty Year Hit Parade" selection, during an engagement at the Ambassador Hotel in Los Angeles early in 1920. Later the same year it was recorded for Victor.

The song has a basic stepwise melody, simple harmony, and no syncopation, which is common for the major hits of these years. The harmony lends itself to banjo and guitar accompaniment, and the melody encourages group singing, a prevalent form of entertainment. During pre-Victrola years families often gathered in parlors around player pianos for singing sessions. Widespread in the first decade of the century, the tradition was still being carried on by many families. Even though the new jazz age music had arrived, it did not immediately replace the older style. In this period the adults, not the young, made the hits, and jazz was the music of the flaming youth of the twenties.

The World Is Waiting for the Sunrise

COMPOSER: Ernest Seitz
LYRICIST: Eugene Lockhart

Listed by *Variety* in its "Fifty Year Hit Parade" as a top song of 1920, this 1919 song reflects the hope of a return to better days.

The lyricist, Eugene Lockhart, is better known to movie fans as Gene Lockhart.

"The World Is Waiting for the Sunrise" had the optimism that people needed in the aftermath of World War I, which had ended in 1918—a word of cheer about the loveliness of things like a rose, the song of a thrush, and love. Les Paul and Mary Ford revived the song and had a million seller in 1951; their rhythmic version was much different from the original slow ballad.

1 9 2 1

Ain't We Got Fun?

COMPOSER-LYRICIST: Richard A. Whiting

Richard Whiting's song would have made a good theme song for those hellbent on seeking the fun typical of the era. This *Variety* "Fifty Year Hit Parade" song was introduced by George Watts in vaudeville and was popularized there by Ruth Roye and Van and Schenck. It was featured in the 1952 movie musical *I'll See You in My Dreams*, in 1953's *By the Light of the Silvery Moon,* and in the 1974 film *The Great Gatsby.*

Any Time

COMPOSER-LYRICIST: Herbert Happy Lawson

This 1921 song became Eddie Fisher's first million-selling recording in 1951, after it had been a million seller for country star Eddy Arnold in 1948.

Perhaps because of Arnold's recording, the song is mostly remembered today as a country song. "Any Time" certainly fits the stereotype of the country song about broken romance: "Any time you say you want me back again . . . I'll come back home to you."

April Showers

COMPOSER: Louis Silvers
LYRICIST: Buddy De Sylva

This "ASCAP All-Time Hit Parade" song became a specialty of Al Jolson, who introduced it in the Winter Garden musical extravaganza *Bombo.* There was the merest hint of a plot in *Bombo.* Jolson played his blackface servant boy Gus, but this time "Gus" was named Bombo and served none other than Christopher Columbus.

The official score for the extravaganza was by Sigmund Romberg, but the hits were all interpolations. In *Bombo,* Jolson introduced three of his greatest songs: "April Showers," "Toot, Toot, Tootsie!" (1922), and "California, Here I Come" (1924). Jolson thus interjected new songs for three years, even after the show had left New York and gone on tour. Of course, he was famous for his impromptu concerts, whatever the production.

"April Showers," which enthralled most of the opening night audience, was, as one critic noted, not even on the program. Another critic reported that Jolson "sang with his old-time, knee-slapping, breast-beating, eye-rolling ardor, sang with a faith that moved mountains and audiences. You should have heard them cheer." Jolson recorded "April Showers" for Columbia in the fall of 1921.

After a decline in popularity in the late thirties, Jolson won renewed fame when the movie musicals *The Jolson Story* and *Jolson Sings Again* became big box-office successes in the forties. As a result of 1946's *The Jolson Story*, "April Showers" became a million-selling record (backed by "Swanee").

Down Yonder

COMPOSER-LYRICIST: **L. Wolfe Gilbert**

"Down Yonder" was introduced by the composer at the Orpheum Theater in New Orleans. One of the few hits of the era born outside of Broadway, vaudeville or Tin Pan Alley, it traveled to vaudeville and was sung by several headliners, including Jolson, Cantor, Sophie Tucker, and Belle Baker. When Gilbert founded his own publishing house and issued the song, it did not do well. It lay forgotten for a dozen years until Gid Tanner and his Skillet Lickers, a hillbilly quartet, recorded the tune and sold 4 million records. Another seventeen years passed before Del Wood, a female country pianist, revived it and had a million-selling recording.

The melody and rhythm remind one of "Waiting for the *Robert E. Lee*" (1912), not surprisingly since L. Wolfe Gilbert was lyricist for that standard as well. In addition, it may have tried to capitalize on the success of Jolson's "My Mammy" ("Ev-'ry day, my mammy land, . . . there's Daddy and Mammy").

I'm Just Wild About Harry

COMPOSER-LYRICISTS: **Noble Sissle and Eubie Blake**

Blake and Sissle, two black entertainers, had been a vaudeville team since 1915 and had appeared as the number two attraction or top headliners for several years. (In vaudeville the headline act, the prestige position, was next to closing. The number two spot was the next most preferred spot on the evening's fare. But by the late 1910s billing did not reflect merit.)

In 1921 Blake and Sissle wrote the songs for the first successful all-black revue produced in New York, *Shuffle Along*. Although blacks had performed on Broadway and all-black shows had played in principal houses, in some respects discrimination was more severe after World War I than before, so it was a remarkable accomplishment that *Shuffle Along* was such an outstanding success.

In the script Harry Walton (played by Roger Matthews) announces he is a reform candidate for mayor of Jimtown, and every citizen responds, "I'm just wild about Harry." Originally conceived as a waltz, the song was much more natural at a faster tempo and with a fox-trot rhythm. The foot-stomping score for the entire show had audiences shouting for more. Almost single-handedly *Shuffle Along* made black shows popular with white audiences.

Variety selected this Sissle-Blake standard for its "Fifty Year Hit Parade."

Jazz Me Blues

COMPOSER: **Tom Delaney**

This tune illustrates people's fascination with both jazz and the blues in the twenties. The blues, although largely unknown to the public before the decade, can be traced back to the field hollers and call-and-response work songs of the slaves on the southern plantations. The harmony of blues, consisting of the three primary chords of a key (tonic, subdominant, and dominant), is decidedly European.

Authentic blues has a twelve-bar form. Its most common characteristic is so-called blue notes (the flatted third, fifth, and seventh tones of the scale), which are used only melodically. The unflatted notes remain in the harmony, sounding out of tune, as if they were searching for a quarter tone that does not exist in the semitone system.

The traditional blues text is a rhymed couplet in iambic pentameter in which the first line is repeated. Actually only about half the twelve bars is sung, while the rest of the bars are filled with instrumental improvisation. Today the blues remain an active and vital source of inspiration to many musicians, especially jazz musicians. Some modern singers, like Janis Joplin, were greatly influenced by the early blues and those who sang them.

Jazz developed mainly from blues but also from ragtime, brass band marches, and the string bands that played for dances in the South in the early years of this century. By the 1920s the jazz bands' main role was to supply music for dancing, a pastime that became immensely popular.

"Jazz Me Blues" was introduced on records by Lucille Hegamin, but the Original Dixieland Jazz Band had the most success with the song. Bix Beiderbecke recorded Tom Delaney's tune in his first recording with the Wolverines.

Variety selected "Jazz Me Blues" for its "Fifty Year Hit Parade."

Ka-lu-a

COMPOSER: Jerome Kern
LYRICIST: Anne Caldwell

Jerome Kern's *Good Morning, Dearie* was the source of this 1921 hit. The show was one of the best of the season, but its plot was typical of the Cinderella stories then in vogue. Of its songs, only "Ka-lu-a" has remained a standard. It is reminiscent of the exotic melodies conjured up by Hollywood composers for some of Bing Crosby's road pictures and, to a degree, of "Pagan Love Song" (1929). "Ka-lu-a" seems to be trying to capture the atmosphere of the Hawaiian Islands, but never quite does. In 1921 the relative remoteness of such places added mystery and fascination to them.

Introduced by Oscar Shaw and the chorus, "Ka-lu-a" was involved in a plagiarism suit instituted by Fred Fisher (who was in turn involved in a suit over "Dardanella" in 1920). Fisher claimed that Kern had appropriated the use of a repetitive rolling bass from "Dardanella." It was the first time an infringement involved the bass part, not the melody. The court ruled in favor of Fisher and set damages at $250. The court might have ruled in Kern's favor, but it is possible that Kern alienated the judge by his hostile and sarcastic remarks during the trial.

Kitten on the Keys

COMPOSER: Zez Confrey

Zez Confrey, pianist, bandleader, and composer, wrote this piano solo. It is one of his novelty rags that have become standards. Unlike many of Tin Pan Alley's best-known composers, including one of the most famous of all, Irving Berlin, who were self-trained and actually had few technical skills, Confrey studied piano in college and cut many early piano rolls. He introduced this tune at the Paul Whiteman Aeolian Hall concert on the same program with George Gershwin's *Rhapsody in Blue*.

Ma—He's Making Eyes at Me

COMPOSER: Con Conrad
LYRICIST: Sidney Clare

This comedy number was written by Conrad and Clare for Eddie Cantor, who introduced it in *The Midnight Rounders of 1921*. The text exclaims to Ma: "he's making eyes . . . he's awful nice . . . he wants to marry . . . he's kissing me." A male singer clapping his hands as he jumped and skipped around the stage, singing "Ma—He's Making Eyes at Me" the way Cantor did was a showstopper.

Variety chose this Eddie Cantor specialty for its "Fifty Year Hit Parade."

My Man

COMPOSER: Maurice Yvain
LYRICIST: Channing Pollock

This French song ("Mon Homme") was introduced in the United States by Irene Bordoni. Mistinguett had made it a hit in France and had planned to use it in her American debut in the *Ziegfeld Follies of 1921*. Channing Pollock had written English lyrics for Mistinguett's *Follies* appearance, but Ziegfeld lost interest in her and dropped her from the show.

Although Fanny Brice had previously been used as a comedienne in the *Follies*, Ziegfeld selected her to do the number, perhaps because of the strong parallel between the subject of the ballad and Brice's ill-fated marriage to the gangster Nicky Arnstein. Brice, dressed in tattered clothes and leaning against a lamppost, created a classic in her poignant rendition. In a newspaper article a few years later Arnstein blamed the song for ruining his marriage.

Brice sang "My Man" in her talking film debut, *My Man* (1928), and in *The Great Ziegfeld* (1936). It became a hit for a new generation when Barbara Streisand performed it in the film *Funny Girl* (1968), the movie version of the Broadway smash of 1964, which loosely chronicled Fanny Brice's career. "My Man" was not used in the original Broadway production, but as often happens in Hollywood, several of Brice's famous songs were inserted into the film.

My Sunny Tennessee

COMPOSER: Harry Ruby
LYRICISTS: Bert Kalmar and Herman Ruby

"My Sunny Tennessee" was introduced by Eddie Cantor in *The Midnight Rounders of 1921* and was further popularized by Sophie Tucker in vaudeville.

Harry Ruby and Bert Kalmar were such famous songwriters that their careers were depicted in *Three Little Words*. In the screen biography Fred Astaire and Red Skelton sing this first big hit, which is about their "Dixie paradise."

Peggy O'Neil

COMPOSER-LYRICISTS: Harry Pease, Ed. G. Nelson, and Gilbert Dodge

This slow waltz was a hit in vaudeville. Singing a fast patter on the second chorus became very popular at family and community sings. The tune and lyrics are nostalgically reminiscent of 1890s songs like "The Sidewalks of New York."

Variety selected "Peggy O'Neil" for its "Fifty Year Hit Parade."

Say It with Music
COMPOSER-LYRICIST: **Irving Berlin**

Broadway saw a new, exquisitely beautiful theater open in 1921, the Music Box, with the first of five revues. The theater and revue were Irving Berlin products. It was built as a showcase for Irving Berlin music.

In Irving Berlin's 1921 *Music Box Revue,* this *Variety* "Fifty Year Hit Parade" song classic was introduced by Wilda Bennett and Paul Frawley. Berlin seemed to be trying to please his audience, which he assumed preferred a rather simple, unsyncopated melody, but at the same time he could not completely resist a few interruptions of jazz syncopation.

Second Hand Rose
COMPOSER: **James F. Hanley**
LYRICIST: **Grant Clarke**

Fanny Brice introduced this comedy number, which became one of her hallmarks, in the *Ziegfeld Follies of 1921*. Barbra Streisand revived the song in the movie of the Broadway musical *Funny Girl* in 1968. Brice also used this number in her first starring role in talking pictures, *My Man* (1928). In a bittersweet Yiddish accent, Rose sings that everything she has, even her boyfriend, is a hand-me-down.

Variety's "Fifty Year Hit Parade" included "Second Hand Rose" as one of the outstanding songs for 1921.

The Sheik of Araby
COMPOSER: **Ted Snyder**
LYRICISTS: **Harry B. Smith and Francis Wheeler**

This song was inspired by the silent motion-picture classic *The Sheik,* which starred the new romantic male star Rudolph Valentino. It was introduced in the musical *Make It Snappy* (1922). It was also used in the 1940 film *Tin Pan Alley* and was used in the sound track of *The Great Gatsby* (1974).

Song of Love
COMPOSER: **Sigmund Romberg**
LYRICIST: **Dorothy Donnelly**

The Broadway season of 1921 had its biggest hit in Sigmund Romberg's *Blossom Time*. This musical bi-

ography of Franz Schubert employed the composer's melodies for its songs. The evening's hit wass "Song of Love" taken from the Unfinished Symphony's first movement. It was introduced by Bertram Peacock, who played Schubert.

It has been estimated that Romberg earned more than $100,000 in royalties from this one song, whereas Schubert's earnings from his output of symphonies, songs, quartets, operas, sonatas, and other musical works amounted to the equivalent of about $500.

Tuck Me to Sleep in My Old 'Tucky Home
COMPOSER: **George W. Meyer**
LYRICISTS: **Sam Lewis and Joe Young**

"Tuck Me to Sleep" is one of composer George Meyer's most important songs after 1917.

It is one of *Variety*'s "Fifty Year Hit Parade" selections, but has not maintained its popularity in subsequent years.

Wabash Blues
COMPOSER: **Fred Meinken**
LYRICIST: **Dave Ringle**

Recorded by Isham Jones and his orchestra, featuring Louis Panico on trumpet, "Wabash Blues" was one of the biggest hits of 1921–22. It sold nearly 2 million copies, while the version by the Benson orchestra of Chicago sold more than 750,000 records. The Jones orchestra became the pride of Chicago and one of the most popular bands of the 1920s.

"Wabash Blues" is a good example of a commercial blues, written in Tin Pan Alley for the general market. Harmonic changes are few, approximately every two measures, allowing improvisation. The text is not an authentic blues couplet and sounds contrived. It is better known as an instrumental.

"Wabash Blues" was chosen for inclusion in *Variety*'s "Fifty Year Hit Parade."

The Wang, Wang Blues
COMPOSER: **Henry Busse**
LYRICISTS: **Gus Mueller and Buster Johnson**

Henry Busse—composer, trumpeter, conductor, and radio and recording artist—joined the Paul Whiteman orchestra in 1918 and stayed for ten years. "The Wang, Wang Blues" was Busse's first important composition, written in collaboration with Gus Mueller and

Buster Johnson, clarinetist and trombonist respectively with the orchestra. Recordings of this song by Whiteman and his orchestra and by Busse's own band are estimated to have sold more than a million.

Variety selected this song for its "Fifty Year Hit Parade."

Yoo-hoo
COMPOSER: **Al Jolson**
LYRICIST: **Buddy De Sylva**

Still another song that owes its popularity to the Jolson magic, "Yoo-hoo" was heard in *Bombo* (see "April Showers," page 17).

1 9 2 2

Carolina in the Morning
COMPOSER: **Walter Donaldson**
LYRICIST: **Gus Kahn**

The Passing Show of 1922's gift to posterity was "Carolina in the Morning." This schottische was introduced by the Howard brothers (Willie and Eugene). The text—"Nothing could be finer than to be in Carolina in the morning"—is world-famous, even though the melody for those words is two notes monotonously alternating back and forth.

This Donaldson-Kahn classic was selected as a *Variety* "Fifty Year Hit Parade" number.

Chicago
COMPOSER-LYRICIST: **Fred Fisher**

A million seller in sheet music in 1922, Fred Fisher's standard found new fame as a best-selling recording by the Tommy Dorsey orchestra in the late thirties and was a million-selling disc for Frank Sinatra in 1957. Although vaudeville was being replaced by other forms of entertainment, "Chicago" was first popularized in vaudeville by Blossom Seeley. "Chicago, Chicago, that toddling town" has been background music for several nonmusical films and has been performed in numerous movie musicals.

"Chicago" was a *Variety* "Fifty Year Hit Parade" selection.

China Boy
COMPOSER-LYRICISTS: **Dick Winfree and Phil Boutelje**

This *Variety* "Fifty Year Hit Parade" song was first popularized in a recording by the Paul Whiteman orchestra. Revived by Benny Goodman in the thirties, it became one of his specialties. The unusual opening chord structure that alternates between major and

augmented chords gives "China Boy" a distinctive sound.

Crinoline Days
COMPOSER-LYRICIST: **Irving Berlin**

Grace La Rue introduced this Irving Berlin tune in *The Music Box Revue of 1922*. As she sang, a stage elevator lifted her higher and higher while her hoop skirt kept growing fuller and wider until the dress engulfed the entire stage. The lyrics look nostalgically at days gone by, when "rosy complexions weren't bought in a store."

"Crinoline Days" was chosen for *Variety*'s "Fifty Year Hit Parade."

Do It Again
COMPOSER: **George Gershwin**
LYRICIST: **Buddy De Sylva**

This Gershwin-De Sylva song was introduced by Irene Bordoni in the musical *The French Doll*. The amusing lyrics play on a double entendre, the "It" in the title refers to kissing but is left ambiguous, so listeners can interpret the "It" however they wanted. For this reason, the song was banned from radio.

Surprisingly "Do It Again" was not included in *Variety*'s "Fifty Year Hit Parade."

Dreamy Melody
COMPOSER-LYRICISTS: **Ted Koehler, Frank Magine, and C. Naset**

Art Landry, bandleader and violinist, recorded this waltz with his Call of the North Orchestra. It sold about 1.5 million copies.

The wide range of the melody and, to a degree, its chromatic melody suggest an instrumentally conceived melody that was intended to be played as an instrumental rather than sung.

Georgette
COMPOSER: Ray Henderson
LYRICIST: Lew Brown

This is one of Ray Henderson's earliest song successes. Henderson worked first as a song plugger and later as a staff pianist and arranger for various music publishers. Louis Bernstein, of Shapiro-Bernstein, arranged for Henderson to write the music with a young but already experienced lyricist, Lew Brown. Their first hit, "Georgette," was introduced by Ted Lewis and his band in the revue *The Greenwich Village Follies of 1922*. Henderson and Brown joined forces with Buddy De Sylva in 1925 to produce many hits.

Hot Lips
COMPOSERS: Henry Busse, Henry Lange, and Lou Davis

Trumpeter Henry Busse composed this showcase tune for trumpet. The distinctive sound of Busse's vibrato on soft, muted trumpet with Paul Whiteman and later with his own group became his trademark.

"Hot Lips" was a *Variety* "Fifty Year Hit Parade" selection.

I Wish I Could Shimmy Like My Sister Kate
COMPOSER-LYRICIST: Armand J. Piron

This song helped promote the shimmy, a dance made famous by Gilda Gray, Bea Palmer, and Ann Pennington at the Winter Garden, in vaudeville, and in nightclubs. The shimmy, a ragtime dance noted for the shaking of the shoulders and hips, was the dancing fad of the early twenties. By the end of 1922 it had been eclipsed by the Charleston.

A Kiss in the Dark
COMPOSER: Victor Herbert
LYRICIST: Buddy De Sylva

Orange Blossoms was the last show Victor Herbert wrote before his death in 1924. Actually Herbert's great musical career had ended with World War I. His had been the age of the waltz, and his music sounded out of place in the postwar world of ragtime and jazz. He had had numerous operetta successes before the first decade of the new century. Then he scored with five successes between 1900 and 1919.

Orange Blossoms was not a huge financial or artistic success, but it did boast "A Kiss in the Dark," which was introduced by Edith Day. The heroine sings the song to her godfather as she recalls a kiss in the dark from a stranger while on vacation in Deauville.

Variety chose "A Kiss in the Dark" for inclusion in its "Fifty Year Hit Parade."

Lady of the Evening
COMPOSER-LYRICIST: Irving Berlin

Irving Berlin's "Lady of the Evening" was introduced by one of the greatest revue tenors, Irish-brogued John Steel, in the second edition of *The Music Box Revue*. Steel sang this serenade, one of Berlin's personal favorites, in a simple rooftop setting. There is nothing in the lyrics that is as suggestive of prostitution as the title.

"Lady of the Evening" was selected by *Variety* for its "Fifty Year Hit Parade."

L'Amour-Toujours-l'Amour—Love Everlasting
COMPOSER: Rudolf Friml
LYRICIST: Catherine Chisholm Cushing

This Rudolf Friml song became a favorite of sopranos and tenors in both concert hall and vaudeville. Despite the French title, it was sung with English words.

The 6/4 time signature is unusual. Also, a range of an octave and a sixth usually suggests an instrumental performance, but this song is by an operetta composer and was a concert specialty for the operatic singer whose range is larger.

Variety selected this number for its "Fifty Year Hit Parade."

Lovin' Sam, the Sheik of Alabam'
COMPOSER: Milton Ager
LYRICIST: Jack Yellen

This *Variety* "Fifty Year Hit Parade" selection was introduced by Grace Hayes in the musical *The Bunch and Judy*, where it was an interpolation. It was popularized by Anna Chandler.

In 1922 Milton Ager helped found the song publishing house of Ager, Yellen & Bornstein, which published "Lovin' Sam." With this hit Ager began an association with lyricist Jack Yellen, with whom he wrote several outstanding songs during the twenties.

Mister Gallagher and Mister Shean
COMPOSER-LYRICISTS: Ed. Gallagher and Al Shean

This *Variety* "Fifty Year Hit Parade" number was introduced by the clowns Gallagher and Shean in the *Ziegfeld Follies of 1922*. This edition of the *Follies* highlighted the shimmy sensation Gilda Gray and folk humorist Will Rogers. Unfortunately, the musical score was undistinguished, and the only memorable song was this comedy patter performed by a pair of dialect comedians who had been recruited from vaudeville. Their act—billed as "By, About and for Themselves"—featured this number, which they wrote. Incidentally Shean was the uncle of the Marx Brothers.

Gallagher and Shean recorded the song in the summer of 1922. It was issued by Victor.

My Buddy
COMPOSER: **Walter Donaldson**
LYRICIST: **Gus Kahn**

In 1922 Walter Donaldson began working with the lyricist Gus Kahn. They initiated the partnership with a smash hit: "My Buddy." Al Jolson sang it to national popularity. It was picked up by several ballad singers in vaudeville, who also helped make it popular.

"My Buddy" is quite a tearjerker: "Nights are long since you went away . . . my buddy . . . your buddy misses you." This tender, sentimental ballad is in triple meter, which generally suggests a waltz, but this song is usually sung with enough rubato to destroy the waltz feel.

"My Buddy" was selected by *Variety* for its "Fifty Year Hit Parade."

My Honey's Lovin' Arms
COMPOSER: **Joseph Meyer**
LYRICIST: **Herman Ruby**

"My Honey's Lovin' Arms" was composer Joseph Meyer's first hit and his first published song. It is what might be called a white jazz song, influenced greatly by the black man's jazz. The Gotham Stompers had an important recording of "My Honey's Lovin' Arms." It was revived successfully in 1963 by Barbra Streisand.

Oh Me, Oh My, Oh You
COMPOSER: **Vincent Youmans**
LYRICIST: **Ira Gershwin (under the pen name Arthur Francis)**

In 1922 Vincent Youmans wrote his first complete score for the Broadway stage, *Two Little Girls in Blue.* It was also the first Broadway musical for which Ira Gershwin, brother of George, wrote all the lyrics, even though it was under the pseudonym Arthur Francis. The principal hit from the production was "Oh Me, Oh My, Oh You," which was introduced by Oscar

Shaw and Marion Fairbanks. The song has an ingratiating tune, but it is difficult to sing.

Runnin' Wild!
COMPOSER: **A. Harrington Gibbs**
LYRICIST: **Joe Grey and Leo Wood**

Art Hickman and his orchestra helped popularize this song, which voices the reckless abandonment of the decade's youth. Hickman was one of the earliest of the dance orchestra leaders. The tune became a standard for Red Nichols and the Five Pennies in the late twenties and early thirties. It was also featured in the 1959 movie *Some Like It Hot,* in which it was sung by Marilyn Monroe.

Stairway to Paradise
COMPOSER: **George Gershwin**
LYRICISTS: **Ira Gershwin and Buddy De Sylva**

Between 1920 and 1924 George Gershwin wrote the complete scores for five editions of *George White's Scandals.* In songs for these productions he first revealed his musical genius. Gershwin had his first hit song, "Swanee," in 1919. It sold more than 2 million records and 1 million copies of sheet music.

By 1922 Gershwin's skill as a composer was very evident in "Stairway to Paradise," which he wrote with his brother, Ira (using the pen name Arthur Francis), and Buddy De Sylva. The song was originally called "A New Step Every Day," but De Sylva suggested revisions in the lyrics that gave him equal billing with Ira as lyricist. George's melodic and harmonic genius is evident in the unexpected flatted thirds and sevenths, the subtle enharmonic changes, and daring jazz accentuations.

Winnie Lightner, Pearl Regay, Colette Ryan, Olive Vaughn, George White, Jack McGowan, Richard Bold, Newton Alexander, and the chorus, accompanied by Paul Whiteman's orchestra, introduced this *Variety* "Fifty Year Hit Parade" selection as the Act One finale of the 1922 edition of *Scandals.*

Stumbling
COMPOSER-LYRICIST: **Zez Confrey**

This *Variety* "Fifty Year Hit Parade" song comments in lyrics and syncopated melody on the intricacy of the social dances that were popular during the first years of the twenties. The tune was used as a leitmotiv in the 1967 movie musical *Thoroughly Modern Millie.*

Three o'Clock in the Morning
COMPOSER: **Julian Robeldo**
LYRICIST: **Dorothy Terriss (pseudonym for Theodora Morse)**

Another million-selling record for Paul Whiteman and his orchestra, this waltz by Julian Robeldo was first published in New Orleans in 1919. Lyricist Dorothy Terriss later set it to words that changed it from a ribald drinking song to a ballad. It was introduced in the closing scene of the revue *The Greenwich Village Follies of 1921* by Rosalinde Fuller and Richard Bold. A distinctive feature of "Three o'Clock in the Morning" is its middle strain, which echoes a chiming clock. Whiteman's recording sold 3.5 million while the sheet music sales surpassed 1 million copies.

Toot, Toot, Tootsie!
COMPOSER-LYRICISTS: **Gus Kahn, Ernie Erdman, Dan Russo, and Ted Fiorito**

Bombo (see "April Showers," page 17) began its run in the Winter Garden in late 1921, and this song was added in 1922. An exuberant farewell, "Toot, Toot, Tootsie!" became one of Jolson's specialties.

This hit was selected by *Variety* for its "Fifty Year Hit Parade."

'Way Down Yonder in New Orleans
COMPOSER: **J. Turner Layton**
LYRICIST: **Henry Creamer**

Spice of 1922 ran for only about eight weeks, but it introduced the classic " 'Way Down Yonder in New Orleans." The song was inserted in *Spice* after it had been discarded from the score of *Strut Miss Lizzie*, which had lasted for only four weeks. This *Variety* "Fifty Year Hit Parade" song was popularized by vaudeville star Blossom Seeley. In addition to selling 1 million copies of sheet music, it became a million-selling record when it was revived by Freddy Cannon in 1959.

" 'Way Down Yonder in New Orleans" is a direct descendant of ragtime and shows considerable blues influence. A clever textual and melodic correlation occurs on the word *Stop*, for the song—melody and accompaniment—actually stops: "Stop!—Oh, won't you give your lady fair a little smile, Stop!—you bet your life you'll linger there a little while."

Wonderful One
COMPOSERS: **Paul Whiteman and Ferde Grofé**
LYRICIST: **Dorothy Terriss (pseudonym for Theodora Morse)**

"Wonderful One" is the second Dorothy Terriss lyric to receive recognition in 1922, the first being "Three o'Clock in the Morning." The melody for this fine lyric was written by Paul Whiteman and his pianist-orchestrator Ferde Grofé. They adapted the melody from a theme by Marshall Neilan, a film director. The song was introduced and played by the Whiteman orchestra in nightclubs, concerts, and in a best-selling recording.

This waltz is gushy and sentimental but is a lovely conception of what love can be: "Like you? I adore you, my life I live for you, my wonderful, wonderful one."

1 9 2 3

Bambalina
COMPOSER: **Vincent Youmans**
LYRICISTS: **Otto Harbach and Oscar Hammerstein II**

Wildflower opened in early 1923. This operetta had the longest run of any Youmans musical—586 performances. "Bambalina," which was the show's hit, established Youmans as a major figure in the musical theater. "Bambalina," however, has a rather monotonous fiddle tune and does not exhibit the genius Youmans shows in later hits. The lyric relates how the caller and fiddler, Bambalina, calls a stop in a square dance so that the dancers can embrace. The song was introduced by Edith Day, one of the era's female musical stars.

"Bambalina" was chosen for *Variety*'s "Fifty Year Hit Parade."

Barney Google
COMPOSER: **Con Conrad**
LYRICIST: **Billy Rose**

This *Variety* "Fifty Year Hit Parade" song, inspired by a popular cartoon character, helped feed the twenties' constant appetite for crazy songs. Some of the many nonsense songs became hits while others died the deaths they deserved. Examples include "Who Ate

Napoleons with Josephine When Bonaparte Was Away?," "Does the Spearmint Lose Its Flavor on the Bedpost Overnight?," "Diga Diga Doo," "Who Takes Care of the Caretaker's Daughter—While the Caretaker's Busy Taking Care?," "I Faw Down an' Go Boom," "I Got a 'Code' in My 'Doze,' " and "Yes! We Have No Bananas."

Conrad and Rose wrote this comical song for Eddie Cantor (perhaps there is a correlation between Barney "goo-goo-googlie eyes" and Cantor's bug-eyed singing). Cantor introduced "Barney Google" in 1923, but it is now identified with Olsen and Johnson, who became so popular doing this number that they became vaudeville headliners. Spike Jones and his City Slickers had a popular recording of "Barney Google."

Charleston
COMPOSER-LYRICISTS: **Cecil Mack and Jimmy Johnson**

Black musical comedy had its greatest success since 1921's *Shuffle Along* with *Runnin' Wild* in 1923. One number in the show, "Charleston," a gawky, zesty, irresistible dance, dominated social dancing for the next several years. Although a number of dances —shimmy, black bottom, varsity drag,—were popular in the twenties, the Charleston is most identified with the era.

Variety chose "Charleston" for its "Fifty Year Hit Parade."

I Cried for You
COMPOSERS: **Gus Arnheim and Abe Lyman**
LYRICIST: **Arthur Freed**

"I Cried for You" was introduced by Abe Lyman and his orchestra. A best-selling recording was made by Cliff ("Ukulele Ike") Edwards and was revived in the thirties by Glen Gray and the Casa Loma Orchestra. Some experts in the field of popular music believe its melody ranks among the great melodic inventions of popular inspiration. Its opening is instantly beguiling, and the entire melody retains interest.

I Love You
COMPOSER: **Harry Archer**
LYRICIST: **Harlan Thompson**

The biggest Broadway hit in 1923 was *Little Jessie James*. "I Love You" was the most successful song to come out of any musical during the year, and its great popularity probably lengthened the show's run considerably. Harry Archer's score, played by the Paul Whiteman orchestra in the pit, was not otherwise

noteworthy. Although Archer wrote the music for four other Broadway musicals in the twenties, none achieved distinction. This *Variety* "Fifty Year Hit Parade" selection, a straightforward declaration of love, was introduced by Ann Sands and Jay Velie in the show.

It Ain't Gonna Rain No Mo'
COMPOSER-LYRICIST: **Wendell Hall**

Hall, composer, author, poet, singer, guitarist, and radio, film, and television artist, appropriated this tune from a southern folk song of the 1870s. His recording, in which he accompanied himself on the ukulele, sold more than 2 million copies. It sold more than 5 million combined record and sheet music copies. Hall, known as the Red-Headed Music Maker, made the ukulele a popular instrument.

Wendell Hall's classic was chosen for *Variety*'s "Fifty Year Hit Parade."

Last Night on the Back Porch
COMPOSER: **Carl Schraubstader**
LYRICIST: **Lew Brown**

Lew Brown, normally lyricist for Ray Henderson, and Carl Schraubstader, wrote the words to this comical song. It was sung by Winnie Lightner in *George White's Scandals of 1923*. The lyrics of this *Variety* "Fifty Year Hit Parade" selection speak of a lover and his date kissing on the back porch: "Last night on the back porch I loved her best of all." It is doubtful anything risqué was implied.

Linger Awhile
COMPOSER: **Vincent Rose**
LYRICIST: **Harry Owens**

Another million-selling record for Paul Whiteman and his orchestra was this song, which is one of the best examples in all popular music for economical use of a small number of notes (forty-six). The recording featured the banjo playing of Mike Pingatore, who played with Whiteman for twenty-five years. Prior to Whiteman's success, "Linger Awhile" had been introduced by Lew Gold and his Club Wigwam Orchestra.

Variety chose "Linger Awhile" for its "Fifty Year Hit Parade."

Mexicali Rose
See page 94 (1938); the song was written in 1923 but was popular in 1938.

Nobody Knows You When You're Down and Out
COMPOSER-LYRICIST: **Jimmy Cox**

This song was introduced by its composer, Jimmy Cox, in vaudeville. It was first recorded by Bobby Baker in 1927, but Bessie Smith, the empress of the blues, triumphed with it when she recorded it in 1929. Smith had squandered her fortune, and her career was on the wane. Her plunge from the heights to the depths enabled her to sing this song with great conviction.

Oh! Gee, Oh! Gosh, Oh! Golly, I'm in Love
COMPOSER: **Ernest Breuer**
LYRICISTS: **Ole Olsen and Chick Johnson**

This comic song, a *Variety* "Fifty Year Hit Parade" selection, was introduced by Olsen and Johnson. It became identified with Eddie Cantor because of his many performances of it.

Sugar Blues
COMPOSER: **Clarence Williams**
LYRICIST: **Lucy Fletcher**

Clarence Williams, an early jazz writer and leader of the Blue Flame Orchestra, was the composer of this hit made famous by Clyde McCoy and his famous "wa-wa" trumpet styling. McCoy's 1936 recording was his only million seller.

Swingin' down the Lane
COMPOSER: **Isham Jones**
LYRICIST: **Gus Kahn**

The songs Isham Jones wrote and made popular were closely associated with an orchestra of violins, clarinets, saxophones, and muted brass. Jones wrote more than 200 tunes, and several of them became standards for dance bands. It's interesting that he used the same ending for "Swingin' down the Lane" as for "I'll See You in My Dreams."

"Swingin' down the Lane" was a *Variety* "Fifty Year Hit Parade" selection.

That Old Gang of Mine
COMPOSER: **Ray Henderson**
LYRICIST: **Billy Rose and Mort Dixon**

A gigantic success for Ray Henderson, "That Old Gang of Mine" was sung in the *Ziegfeld Follies of 1923* by Van and Schenck. The text speaks of barbershop quartet camaraderie ("I can't forget that old quartet that sang 'Sweet Adeline' ") and the days when sweethearts and pals were a part of "That old gang of mine."

This famous song was chosen by *Variety* for its "Fifty Year Hit Parade."

There'll Be Some Changes Made
COMPOSER-LYRICISTS: **Billy Higgins and W. Benton Overstreet**

Billy Higgins introduced this tune in vaudeville. It was first recorded by blues singer Ethel Waters. Then, in the mid-thirties, blues singer Mildred Bailey had a successful recording.

The "Changes" in the title may have referred to the changes in popular music as well as in the social scene during this era of the flapper and her boyfriend.

Variety chose this hit for its "Fifty Year Hit Parade."

Who's Sorry Now?
COMPOSER: **Ted Snyder**
LYRICISTS: **Bert Kalmar and Harry Ruby**

This hit, introduced by Van and Schenck, sold a million copies of sheet music when it was published in 1923. The song was revived in 1958 and became a million-selling record for Connie Francis, her first solo disc.

Yes! We Have No Bananas
COMPOSER-LYRICISTS: **Frank Silver and Irving Cohn**

This nonsense song, a *Variety* "Fifty Year Hit Parade" selection, became a sensation when Eddie Cantor introduced it into the 1922 revue *Make It Snappy* after the New York opening. The audience demanded that Cantor repeat the song for a quarter of an hour. The composers consciously or unconsciously borrowed a great deal of the tune from Handel's *Messiah* and Balfe's "I Dreamt That I Dwelt in Marble Halls."

You've Got to See Mamma Ev'ry Night (or You Can't See Mamma at All)
COMPOSER: **Con Conrad**
LYRICIST: **Billy Rose**

The "Last of the Red Hot Mamas," Sophie Tucker, was responsible for popularizing this song, which insists that "you've got to see your mamma ev'ry night or you can't see mamma at all."

Variety chose this Tucker specialty for its "Fifty Year Hit Parade."

1 9 2 4

All Alone
COMPOSER-LYRICIST: Irving Berlin

"All Alone" was introduced by Grace Moore and Oscar Shaw in the *Music Box Revue of 1924*. Irving Berlin had the pair, spotlit and holding telephones, sing his lovely song from opposite sides of the stage, but it is not just a gadget song. The lyrics are about one lover's loneliness and depression because the other lover has not telephoned. "All Alone" is one of several songs written under the inspiration of Berlin's love affair with Ellin MacKay (see "What'll I Do," page 30).

This Berlin love song was selected for *Variety*'s "Fifty Year Hit Parade."

Amapola
See page 104 (1941). That year it was one of the top ten songs.

California, Here I Come
COMPOSER: Joseph Meyer
LYRICISTS: Al Jolson and Buddy De Sylva

Even in 1924 songs were still being introduced into *Bombo,* which had opened in 1921: "California, Here I Come" was added by Jolson after the show had left New York and gone went on tour. It became a million-selling record for Jolson in 1946 following the release of the film *The Jolson Story.*

It is difficult to tell in retrospect whether Jolson actually wrote any of the songs for which he was given credit, but it was a fairly common practice to give entertainers of his caliber composer or lyricist credit for songs to get them to perform them. Jolson received royalties from songs practically guaranteed to be successful simply because he did them.

So many films have used this song to suggest going to California that it has become a cliché.

Variety selected this classic song for its "Fifty Year Hit Parade."

Charley, My Boy
COMPOSER: Ted Fiorito
LYRICIST: Gus Kahn

This *Variety* "Fifty Year Hit Parade" song was introduced by the Russo-Fiorito Oriole Orchestra at the Edgewater Beach Hotel in Chicago. The image conjured up by this song is that of the flapper with few brains singing of her love for Charley and dancing giddily to its upbeat tempo.

Deep in My Heart, Dear
COMPOSER: Sigmund Romberg
LYRICIST: Dorothy Donnelly

This beautiful duet was introduced by Howard Marsh and Ilse Marvenga in the Romberg operetta *The Student Prince in Heidelberg.*

Does the Spearmint Lose Its Flavor on the Bedpost Over Night?
COMPOSER: Ernest Breuer
LYRICISTS: Billy Rose and Marty Bloom

Billy Rose should be considered the champion of nonsense lyrics. This particular loony tune was introduced by Harry Richman (which in itself is odd since Richman always appeared to be sophisticated). The song had revived success in a 1959 recording by Britain's Lonnie Donegan, which sold a million discs in the United States by 1961.

Everybody Loves My Baby
COMPOSER-LYRICISTS: Jack Palmer and Spencer Williams

The first recording of this *Variety*'s "Fifty Year Hit Parade" song featured Louis Armstrong on trumpet with Clarence Williams's Blue Fire orchestra. The song is not much more than a riff (an ostinato phrase usually with instrumental improvisation) repeated three times. As important as jazz was during the decade, not many authentic jazz recordings are listed among its hits.

Ruth Etting, a major entertainer in the late twenties and early thirties, further popularized the song.

Fascinating Rhythm
COMPOSER: George Gershwin
LYRICIST: Ira Gershwin

Although George and Ira Gershwin's *Lady, Be Good!* was not the biggest smash of the 1924 Broadway season, it may well have been its most important musical. It was in this show that jazz was first used for an entire score. Gershwin had experimented with the style earlier with individual pieces in various shows, but the score for *Lady, Be Good!* broke out of the musical and operetta mold.

The unusual beat of "Fascinating Rhythm" made it one of the show's outstanding hits. In the context of Ira's lyrics, fascinate meant "to bewitch; to enchant; to influence in some wicked manner." It has been suggested that George perfected the rhythmic device that was first heard in Zez Confrey's "Stumbling," but it appeared so novel in Gershwin's skillful hands that one questions his need to borrow ideas.

Fred and Adele Astaire introduced this *Variety* "Fifty Year Hit Parade" song.

Hard-Hearted Hannah, the Vamp of Savannah
COMPOSER: **Milton Ager**
 LYRICISTS: **Bob Bigelow, Charles Bates, and Jack Yellen**

This vamp song was introduced by Frances Williams in the musical *Innocent Eyes*. It was further popularized by Margaret Young in vaudeville and successfully revived by Peggy Lee more than twenty years later.

How Come You Do Me Like You Do?
COMPOSER-LYRICISTS: **Gene Austin and Roy Bergere**

Singer and composer Gene Austin introduced "How Come You Do Me Like You Do?" Austin had a phenomenal career, especially with record sales. It was not until the 1950s that Elvis Presley exceeded Austin's recording sales total.

I'll See You in My Dreams
COMPOSER: **Isham Jones**
 LYRICIST: **Gus Kahn**

This *Variety* "Fifty Year Hit Parade" classic, introduced by Isham Jones and his orchestra, furnished the title for a 1951 film based on the life and songs of Gus Kahn.

This standard makes excellent use of a minimum of notes: fifty. Most really good melodies can stand alone—that is, they do not rely on harmony or rhythm for their interest. "I'll See You in My Dreams" is such a melody. It is strong enough to sound good a cappella.

Indian Love Call
COMPOSER: **Rudolf Friml**
 LYRICISTS: **Otto Harbach and Oscar Hammerstein II**

Rudolf Friml's operetta *Rose Marie* had the longest Broadway run of any of his musicals (557 performances). Set in the Canadian Rockies, the show was a resounding success, undoubtedly because of the tuneful score and perhaps because of its North American, instead of European, setting. It was not only the biggest hit of the season but the biggest grossing musical until *Oklahoma!* broke the record nearly twenty years later.

The show's most lasting song is unquestionably "Indian Love Call," which was introduced by Mary Ellis and Dennis King. However, it is most closely identified with Jeanette MacDonald and Nelson Eddy, who starred in the second film version of *Rose Marie* in 1936. Their duet recording was the first musical show tune to top the million mark. The distinctive call in the melody has become an operetta cliché. The song has been performed so often through the years, many times by singers who thought they had to put on airs, that it has become undeservedly comical.

Variety selected "Indian Love Call" for its "Fifty Year Hit Parade."

It Had to Be You
COMPOSER: **Isham Jones**
 LYRICIST: **Gus Kahn**

This beautiful ballad was introduced by composer Isham Jones's band. Cliff ("Ukulele Ike") Edwards had a best-selling recording. Author Alec Wilder has said that "It Had to Be You" would be a good choice if he had to pick only one song as his favorite. He further remarked that the song is so well known that we fail to appreciate the elements novel for its day.

Variety chose "It Had to Be You" for its "Fifty Year Hit Parade."

I Wonder What's Become of Sally?
COMPOSER: **Milton Ager**
 LYRICIST: **Jack Yellen**

Van and Schenck introduced this *Variety* "Fifty Year Hit Parade" waltz that is reminiscent of the barbershop quartets of the turn of the century.

Jealous
COMPOSER: **Jack Little**
 LYRICISTS: **Tommie Malie and Dick Finch**

Composer Little Jack Little introduced this *Variety* "Fifty Year Hit Parade" number. He was a particularly popular radio personality during the decade. The singer is jealous of "the moon . . . pretty flowers . . . birdies in the trees . . . the 'tick-tock' on the shelf" because they are close to you. He is "even getting jealous of" himself.

The opening melodic phrase is practically a chromatic scale, not typical popular song fare.

The Man I Love
COMPOSER: **George Gershwin**
LYRICIST: **Ira Gershwin**

This Gershwin classic was originally written for Adele Astaire to sing in the first act of *Lady, Be Good!*. However, it was removed from the show because the producers and director convinced Gershwin that it slowed the action of the opening act. It was next tried unsuccessfully in the original version of *Strike Up the Band* in 1927 and again in 1928's *Rosalie*. By the time the 1930 version of *Strike Up the Band* opened, the song, which had become successful in Britain and on the Continent, finally registered a hit. It was first identified with Helen Morgan as one of her specialties and has become one of the most treasured of Gershwin's standards. It is particularly interesting for the contrapuntal chromatic accompaniment figure against the blues-influenced tune.

The song, which was published in 1924, sold only 893 copies in the first two years. Eva Gauthier, accompanied by the composer, is credited with the first official performance of the song in 1925. The occasion was a repeat of the famous Aeolian Hall recital of November 4, 1923, this time in Derby, Connecticut. After a couple of years the song seemed to die. When it was resurrected in early 1928, it sold 60,133 copies of sheet music and 162,518 copies of various recordings. And that was only the beginning.

Nobody's Sweetheart
COMPOSERS: **Billy Meyers and Elmer Schoebel**
LYRICISTS: **Gus Kahn and Ernie Erdman**

This *Variety* "Fifty Year Hit Parade" song was introduced by Ted Lewis in the revue *The Passing Show of 1923*. It was revived in a 1931 recording, backed by "Tiger Rag," in the first million-selling record by a vocal quartet (the Mills Brothers). It was also an important recording for the Benny Goodman Trio in 1935. The song's lyrics tell about a sweet hometown girl who has changed into a woman of the world with "fancy hose, silken gown, . . . painted lips, painted eyes. . . ."

O, Katharina!
COMPOSER: **Richard Fall**
LYRICIST: **Fritz Lohner**

A revue conceived in Russia, revived in Paris, and brought to Broadway in 1922 proved to be a sensation. It was *Chauve Souris,* and from it came this song. L. Wolfe Gilbert wrote English words to replace the original German.

This *Variety* "Fifty Year Hit Parade" song is as timely today as it was then. It addresses the diet-conscious American woman, who is told by her lover that if she wants to keep his love, she has to be thinner.

The One I Love
COMPOSER: **Isham Jones**
LYRICIST: **Gus Kahn**

Another Isham Jones and Gus Kahn hit song was "The One I Love," which was introduced by the Isham Jones orchestra. It was also performed on best-selling discs by Bing Crosby and Ella Fitzgerald. The song is well-conceived popular music, memorable enough to have remained a standard for more than fifty years. Danny Thomas performed the song in the screen biography of Gus Kahn, *I'll See You in My Dreams.* The lyrics describe the plight of someone who is in love with a person in love with another.

Rhapsody in Blue
COMPOSER: **George Gershwin**

George Gershwin's significant serious jazz composition *Rhapsody in Blue* was almost not written. Paul Whiteman had been planning a serious concert hall performance devoted entirely to American popular music. He asked Gershwin to write a new work for him in a jazz style. Gershwin, burdened by other projects, forgot all about his promise until he happened to read a notice in the newspaper concerning the forthcoming concert. With just a few months to go, Gershwin began what became a jazz piano concerto that moved jazz from the speakeasy to the world of concert music. *Rhapsody* made Gershwin wealthy and gained him the world's admiration. The original Paul Whiteman orchestra recording was a best-selling record, and *Rhapsody in Blue* became the orchestra's theme.

The rhapsody is scored for solo piano and symphony orchestra. A rhapsody is a free-form piece and therefore did not have to conform to any particular structure. The opening clarinet portamento is magnetic and sets the tone. Two principal melodies are developed during the composition.

Rhapsody in Blue was selected by *Variety* for its "Fifty Year Hit Parade."

Rose Marie

COMPOSER: **Rudolf Friml**
  LYRICIST: **Otto Harbach and Oscar Hammerstein II**

Like "Indian Love Call" (page 28), this is a hit from *Rose Marie*. It was introduced by Dennis King and Arthur Deagon in the original show and sung by Nelson Eddy in the 1936 film version. The country singer Slim Whitman had a million-selling recording of "Rose Marie" in 1954.

This expressive operetta aria sings of the love the Canadian fur trapper Jim Kenyon and the Mountie Sergeant Malone have for Rose Marie la Flamme. Particularly potent is the closing: "Of all the queens that ever lived, 'I'd choose you/To rule me, my Rose Marie.'"

Serenade

COMPOSER: **Sigmund Romberg**
  LYRICIST: **Dorothy Donnelly**

Sigmund Romberg's score for *The Student Prince in Heidelberg* was his finest achievement. The producers, the Shubert brothers, were skeptical about the operatic score, apprehensive about the show's unhappy ending, and aghast that Romberg demanded a large male chorus rather than a chorus line of feminine lovelies. They almost threw Romberg and his music out of the show. But Romberg prevailed and made the Shuberts a handsome profit through the original 608 performances and nine touring productions. Dorothy Donnelly was lyricist for this masterpiece, which outranks Romberg's adaptation from Franz Schubert that became *Blossom Time* and seriously challenges *The Desert Song,* his 1926 hit, for the honor of being his best.

"Overhead the moon is beaming" begins this passionate song, which was introduced by a quartet and male chorus. "Serenade" was almost cut from the score by the Shuberts, but through Romberg's persistence it remained and went on to become one of the score's major successes. It is a tenor showpiece, with a range of almost two octaves climaxing on a high A flat as the singer pledges his eternal love.

"Serenade" was a *Variety* "Fifty Year Hit Parade" selection.

Somebody Loves Me

COMPOSER: **George Gershwin**
  LYRICISTS: **Buddy De Sylva and Ballard MacDonald**

George Gershwin's third big hit of 1924, in addition to *Rhapsody in Blue* and "Fascinating Rhythm," was "Somebody Loves Me," introduced by Winnie Lightner in *George White's Scandals of 1924*. Rich in jazz age harmonics, this cozy, intimate song became identified with Blossom Seeley because of her frequent outstanding performances. The slow, legato ballad begins with the statement "Somebody loves me" but asks, "I wonder who she can be?" It ends by suggesting that the lover may be you, the listener.

Variety selected this Gershwin classic for its "Fifty Year Hit Parade."

What'll I Do?

COMPOSER-LYRICIST: **Irving Berlin**

Irving Berlin's second hit of the year (see "All Alone," page 27) was introduced by Grace Moore and John Steel during the run of *The Music Box Revue of 1923*. In 1924 Berlin fell in love with Ellin MacKay, daughter of the Postal Telegraph tycoon, who did everything he could to break up the romance. It was at this time of frustration and hurt that Berlin wrote "What'll I Do?" and "All Alone." The singer asks what he will do when his love is far away and all he has to tell his troubles to is a photograph of her. More songs were written for Ellin MacKay in 1925 and 1926 prior to their secret marriage.

This Berlin love song for Ellin MacKay was selected for *Variety*'s "Fifty Year Hit Parade."

When My Sugar Walks down the Street

COMPOSER-LYRICISTS: **Irving Mills, Gene Austin, and Jimmy McHugh**

The second Gene Austin hit of the year (see "How Come You Do Me Like You Do?," page 28) was written for the Cotton Club, a Harlem nightclub.

1 9 2 5

Alabamy Bound
COMPOSER: **Ray Henderson**
LYRICISTS: **Buddy De Sylva and Bud Green**

Al Jolson introduced this song, before Eddie Cantor interpolated it into the musical *Kid Boots* after the New York opening in 1923. Only the interpolation of "Alabamy Bound" and the extraordinary "Dinah" kept *Kid Boots* going. "Alabamy Bound" sold more than 1 million copies of sheet music.

This bright march is another of the southern songs that were Jolson specialties. The singer is going to Alabama on a train, the twenties' ultimate means of fast, safe, and luxurious transportation. Several songs were inspired by the railroads, but "Alabamy Bound" is high on the list of standards.

"Alabamy Bound" was a *Variety* "Fifty Year Hit Parade" selection.

Always
COMPOSER-LYRICIST: **Irving Berlin**

This *Variety* Golden 100 song is an Irving Berlin love song written for his beloved Ellin MacKay (see "What'll I Do?," page 30). It is a pledge of love: "I'll be loving you always." This classic popular song was introduced by Gladys Clark and Henry Bergman in vaudeville. After Berlin had married Ellin MacKay in early 1926, he turned over all his rights to "Always" to her as a wedding gift. Ellin's father, Clarence MacKay, disinherited her and refused to have anything to do with her for years, but later they were reconciled. Berlin and Ellin have remained married for fifty-nine years.

Cecilia
COMPOSER: **Dave Dreyer**
LYRICIST: **Herman Ruby**

Whispering Jack Smith, a singer elevated to stardom by radio, popularized "Cecilia" in the twenties. The singer asks Cecilia about several things, then asks her for a kiss. Smith's quiet baritone voice also helped popularize " 'Gimme' a Little Kiss, Will 'Ya' Huh?" (1926) and a few other songs, but his audience had declined by the early thirties. "Cecilia" was probably most popular in the best-selling version by the Dick

Jurgens orchestra, with vocalist Ronnie Kemper, in 1940.

"Cecilia" was chosen for *Variety*'s "Fifty Year Hit Parade."

Collegiate
COMPOSER-LYRICISTS: **Moe Jaffe and Nat Bonx**

In the 1920s people had an extraordinary curiosity about things collegiate—not the life of the classroom but the extracurricular activities that took place on football fields, in fraternity and sorority houses, and at dances. There were college movies and musicals, dance bands, and songs inspired by college life and the typical collegiate. This preoccupation with campus life helped "Collegiate" to hit status. Fred Waring and his Pennsylvanians (a "collegiate" looking outfit) introduced the song, which was interpolated in the revue *Gay Paree* in 1926.

"Collegiate" was selected by *Variety* for its "Fifty Year Hit Parade."

A Cup of Coffee, a Sandwich and You
COMPOSER: **Joseph Meyer**
LYRICISTS: **Billy Rose and Al Dubin**

Jack Buchanan and Gertrude Lawrence included this song in *Charlot's Revue of 1926*. Lawrence was never famous as a great singer, but she had a fantastic stage personality that could sell any song. In this song, she sold the idea that she did not need the finer things of life, that all she required for happiness was "a cup of coffee, a sandwich and you."

The song was chosen for inclusion in *Variety*'s "Fifty Year Hit Parade."

Dinah
COMPOSER: **Harry Akst**
LYRICISTS: **Sam M. Lewis and Joe Young**

Eddie Cantor's interpolation of "Dinah" in *Kid Boots* helped save an otherwise mediocre show. It had been introduced by blues singer Ethel Waters in a revue at the Plantation Club in New York City.

The lyrics about the South were first set to a bouncy tune that the writers expected to be performed in a corny style, but Waters transformed it into a slow, sentimental classic.

Frances Rose Shore chose Dinah as her stage name because she used this *Variety* "Fifty Year Hit Parade" song as her signature tune over Nashville radio in the late thirties.

Five Foot Two, Eyes of Blue
COMPOSER: **Ray Henderson**
  LYRICISTS: **Sam M. Lewis and Joe Young**

This early Ray Henderson success is closely identified with the twenties because it seems to describe the typical flapper: "turned up nose, turned down hose . . . covered with fur, diamond rings and all those things." When the motion-picture industry wants to identify the era, one of its frequent choices for the background song is "Five Foot Two."

Here In My Arms
COMPOSER: **Richard Rodgers**
  LYRICIST: **Lorenz Hart**

While *The Garrick Gaieties,* for which Rodgers and Hart wrote "Manhattan," was still running, Rodgers and Hart collaborated on the musical *Dearest Enemy.* Its plot was based on an episode of American history. During the Revolution several patriotic ladies used their wiles to delay the British troops in New York long enough for George Washington's Continental Army to retreat. The hit from the score was "Here in May Arms," which was introduced by Helen Ford and Charles Purcell. The song is not Rodgers and Hart at their very best, but the public made it one of the hits of 1925.

If You Knew Susie
COMPOSER-LYRICISTS: **Buddy De Sylva and
    Joseph Meyer**

Al Jolson introduced this classic song in the musical *Big Boy,* then decided it was not his style, so he gave it to Eddie Cantor. Cantor first performed it at a New York benefit, it was a smash, and it became his specialty. The song, along with "Five Foot Two," is often used thematically to suggest a flapper in the movies about the twenties.

"If You Knew Susie" was selected for *Variety*'s "Fifty Year Hit Parade."

I'm Sitting on Top of the World
COMPOSER: **Ray Henderson**
  LYRICISTS: **Sam M. Lewis and Joe Young**

"I'm Sitting on Top of the World" was popularized by Al Jolson. Its optimistic text proclaims that this is the best of all possible worlds in the best of all possible times. It was sung by Jolson in his 1928 film *The Singing Fool* and was revived by Les Paul and Mary Ford in 1949.

I Want to Be Happy
COMPOSER: **Vincent Youmans**
  LYRICIST: **Irving Caesar**

No, No, Nanette was the most successful musical comedy of the 1925 season. The story was an undistinguished 1920s trifle, but it produced two hits: "I Want to Be Happy" and "Tea for Two." Vincent Youmans's score to Irving Caesar's lyrics was catchy and endearing. Louise Groody and Charles Winninger (Nannette and Jimmy Smith in the show) introduced "I Want to Be Happy," which has the theme that we achieve happiness by making others happy.

Variety selected this song for its "Fifty Year Hit Parade."

Manhattan
COMPOSER: **Richard Rodgers**
  LYRICIST: **Lorenz Hart**

In the spring of 1925 the "Junior Members" of the Theatre Guild staged a revue at the Garrick Theater entitled *The Garrick Gaieties.* The revue was a skillful production, even though it was small-scaled. The most lasting part of the evening proved to be the songs, seven of which were written by Rodgers and Hart.

Lyricist Lorenz ("Larry") Hart and composer Richard Rodgers first became known to the public through the hit "Manhattan" in the first edition of the *Gaieties* and through "Mountain Greenery" in the second (see page 36, 1926). Hart and Rodgers were opposites in personality, temperament, outlook, living and working habits, but their work carried them to the pinnacle of Broadway success.

The song "Manhattan" is a famous tribute to New York City. The lyrics mention major New York attractions: the zoo, Delancey Street, the subway, Mott Street, Greenwich Village, Coney Island, Central Park, Fifth Avenue, plus several others.

Moonlight and Roses
COMPOSER-LYRICISTS: **Ben Black and Neil Moret**

Tunesmiths of the twenties often borrowed from the classics, as in "Avalon" (1920) and "Song of Love" (1921). A prime example of tune lifting was Harry Carroll's "I'm Always Chasing Rainbows" (1918), which has the melody of Chopin's *'Fantaisie Impromptu.*

"Moonlight and Roses" came from an organ piece by Edwin H. Lemare (Andantino in D-flat, 1892). Ben Black and Neil Moret (pseudonym for Charles N. Daniels) were responsible for this song, which was identified with Lanny Ross, the Troubadour on the Moon, an early radio singer. Vic Damone successfully revived it in 1965. The lyrics to this sentimental ballad claim that "Moonlight and roses/Bring wonderful memories of you."

Variety chose this song for its "Fifty Year Hit Parade."

Oh, How I Miss You Tonight
COMPOSER: **Joe Burke**
  LYRICISTS: **Mark Fisher and Benny Davis**

Joe Burke had been an arranger in Tin Pan Alley before he became a composer. He waited ten years for his break, which came in 1925, when he teamed with Mark Fisher and Davis to write the dreamy waltz "Oh, How I Miss You Tonight." It was introduced by Benny Davis in vaudeville.

This song was selected by *Variety* for its "Fifty Year Hit Parade."

The Prisoner's Song
COMPOSER-LYRICIST: **Guy Massey**

Vernon Dalhart's recording of "The Prisoner's Song" was the largest-selling Victor record of the preelectric era. Estimates run as high as 7 million discs. Dalhart took his stage name from two towns (Vernon and Dalhart) near his hometown in Texas. After receiving formal music training, he went to New York to sing light opera. After hearing the Okeh recording of "The Wreck of the Old 97" by Henry Whitter, Dalhart concluded that there was big money in hillbilly music. He imitated the Whitter recording of "Wreck of Old 97" (for Edison Records) and then recorded it again, coupled with "The Prisoner's Song" (for Victor). Dalhart sang for thirty or more record companies and recorded "The Prisoner's Song" for at least twenty-eight labels (under seventy various names) for an estimated total of 25 million records. Hearing a Dalhart recording today makes one wonder how it could possibly have sold such a huge number of records because it sounds corny and shallow. Part of the sound can be attributed to the early recording equipment, but not all of it. Evidently enough early hillbilly music fans found it worthy to make it one of the most successful recordings of the early days of the recording industry.

"The Prisoner's Song" was selected for inclusion in *Variety*'s "Fifty Year Hit Parade."

Remember
COMPOSER-LYRICIST: **Irving Berlin**

The love affair of Irving Berlin and Ellin MacKay (see "What'll I Do?," page 30, and "Always," page 31) produced some of the most touchingly sentimental ballads that have ever been written. "Remember" is one. It was originally copyrighted under the title "You Forgot to Remember." It was introduced in vaudeville by Gladys Clark and Henry Bergman and became a special number for Ruth Etting. This poignant ballad, which speaks of fleeting love, was written in 1925 prior to Berlin's and MacKay's secret marriage in 1926.

Show Me the Way to Go Home
COMPOSER-LYRICISTS: **Reg Connelly and Jimmy Campbell**

Reg Connelly and Jimmy Campbell of London (using the pseudonym Irving King) adapted a Canadian folk song for this hit, still a favorite among those who imbibe. It was introduced in America by Vincent Lopez and his orchestra at New York's St. Regis Hotel. Many singers and bands have used the song, the sound of which recalls its folk song origin. The lyrics have a folk song feel, although the words were written for this version.

Variety chose this song for its "Fifty Year Hit Parade."

Sleepy Time Gal
COMPOSERS: **Ange Lorenzo and Richard A. Whiting**
  LYRICISTS: **Joseph R. Alden and Raymond B. Egan**

"Sleepy Time Gal" was a best-selling recording for Ukulele Ike (Cliff Edwards), Gene Austin, and Glen Gray and the Casa Loma Orchestra. This song is so well known, so much a part of the American popular music tradition that it could probably pass for a folk song. It is a favorite of sing-along groups, such as Mitch Miller's. But as easily singable as it is, the melody and harmony are the product of craft rather than of the folk tradition.

Song of the Vagabonds
COMPOSER: **Rudolf Friml**
  LYRICIST: **Brian Hooker**

Rudolf Friml brought a new operetta, *The Vagabond King,* to Broadway in 1925. It was his greatest box-office success after *Rose Marie*. From the lovely score came the hit "Song of the Vagabonds."

The romantic operetta about François Villon, the fifteenth-century French vagabond poet, was based on J. H. McCarthy's *If I Were King*. Dennis King introduced "Song of the Vagabonds," a rousing summon to arms.

"Song of the Vagabonds" was a *Variety* "Fifty Year Hit Parade" selection.

Sweet Georgia Brown
COMPOSER-LYRICISTS: **Ben Bernie, Maceo Pinkard, and Kenneth Casey**

Ben Bernie and his orchestra introduced this tune, which is today identified with the Harlem Globetrotters and their warm-up routine. In the late thirties the song was identified with the Benny Goodman Quartet. It was also featured in the 1976 all-black musical *Bubbling Brown Sugar*.

Tea for Two
COMPOSER: **Vincent Youmans**
LYRICIST: **Irving Caesar**

The Youmans hits from *No, No, Nanette* were "I Want to Be Happy" and "Tea for Two," which is one of his most memorable songs. "Tea for Two" was included as one of sixteen in the "ASCAP All-Time Hit Parade," which was selected to publicize the organization's golden anniversary in 1963. Louise Groody and John Barker introduced "Tea for Two" in the original Broadway show. The lyrics, intended to be temporary, were dashed off in five minutes but were never changed. This could be why even though the title is "Tea for Two," the only reference to tea occurs at the beginning with the rest of the lyric devoted to the happiness of marriage.

It was revived in a million-selling cha-cha version by Warren Covington with the Tommy Dorsey orchestra in 1958.

Ukulele Lady
COMPOSER: **Richard A. Whiting**
LYRICIST: **Gus Kahn**

This *Variety* "Fifty Year Hit Parade" song illustrates the popularity of the ukulele during the twenties. Cliff ("Ukulele Ike") Edwards, May ("The Ukulele Girl") Singhi Breen, and Wendell Hall playing the uke and singing "It Ain't Gonna Rain No Mo'" (see page 25) are further testimony to the popularity of this four-stringed instrument, which originated in Hawaii. A typical caricature of the jazz age male collegiate consists of a raccoon coat, a flask in the hip pocket, a college pennant in one hand, and a uke in the other.

He is probably dancing the Charleston.

This song was popularized by Vaughn De Leath, one of the first women singers to gain recognition on radio and the person who is often credited with originating the crooning style of singing.

Valencia
COMPOSER: **José Padilla**
LYRICISTS: **Jacques Charles, and Clifford Grey**

The Great Temptations, another of the Shuberts' Winter Garden revues, introduced one interpolation that has remained popular: José Padilla's "Valencia." It had first been sung by Mistinguett in the Moulin Rouge nightclub revue in Paris. Hazel Dawn, Halfred Young, and Charlotte Woodruff introduced it into the United States in *The Great Temptations*. It was also sung by Grace Bowman in the 1927 revue *A Night in Spain*. The form and melody of this *Variety* "Fifty Year Hit Parade" are more reminiscent of operettas of the period than of popular songs.

Who?
COMPOSER: **Jerome Kern**
LYRICISTS: **Otto Harbach and Oscar Hammerstein II**

In the first half of the twenties Jerome Kern had two extremely successful musicals: 1920's *Sally* and 1925's *Sunny*, both starring Marilyn Miller. In *Sally*, Miss Miller, the most adored musical-comedy actress of the twenties, introduced "Look for the Silver Lining," and in *Sunny* she introduced this breezy love duet with Paul Frawley. The word *who* is held for two measures each time it appears and starts various queries about the lover.

Sunny was the first Kern-Hammerstein collaboration, a partnership that eventually produced one of Broadway's all-time great musicals: 1927's *Show Boat*. George Olsen and his band had a million-selling recording of "Who?" in 1926.

Variety selected "Who?" for its "Fifty Year Hit Parade."

Yes Sir, That's My Baby
COMPOSER: **Walter Donaldson**
LYRICIST: **Gus Kahn**

The Walter Donaldson-Gus Kahn partnership that produced "My Buddy" and "Carolina in the Morning" continued with "Yes Sir, That's My Baby" in 1925. The song was written for and introduced by Eddie Cantor. Gus Kahn got the idea for the words in Cantor's living room, playing with a toy pig that belonged to Cantor's daughter. As the mechanical toy toddled around the room, he improvised the lines that became the song's beginning. Cantor insisted Kahn complete the lyrics, and he did. Donaldson wrote the melody and a popular music classic was born.

Gene Austin made a tremendously successful recording of this *Variety* "Fifty Year Hit Parade" song.

1 9 2 6

Baby Face
COMPOSER: **Harry Akst**
  LYRICIST: **Benny Davis**

"Baby Face" became a million-selling record for Art Mooney and his orchestra in 1948, but it was originally introduced in 1926 by Jan Garber and his orchestra with the lyricist, Benny Davis, doing the vocal. Along with "Five Foot Two" and "If You Knew Susie," "Baby Face" is one of the songs chosen by filmmakers to identify the 1920s flapper and her scatterbrained mentality.

The Birth of the Blues
COMPOSER: **Ray Henderson**
  LYRICISTS: **Buddy De Sylva and Lew Brown**

Introduced by Harry Richman as the first-act finale of *George White's Scandals of 1926*, this song was the first big hit for the team of Henderson, De Sylva, and Brown. The trio came together with considerable prior experience and then for the rest of the decade were without peer in capturing the spirit of the times in song. A second hit from the *Scandals of 1926* was "Black Bottom" (see below).

The setting for "The Birth of the Blues" was the gates of heaven, where a debate takes place between jazz and classical music. This song, a musical history lesson, was presented to Beethoven and Liszt as evidence that the blues are an important part of music. At the end of the scene the pearly gates open to accept blues and jazz into the musical heaven. "The Birth of the Blues" was one of sixteen songs selected in 1963 for the "ASCAP All-Time Hit Parade."

Black Bottom
COMPOSER: **Ray Henderson**
  LYRICISTS: **Buddy De Sylva and Lew Brown**

This Henderson, De Sylva, and Brown hit from the *Scandals of 1926* became a dance sensation of the late twenties. It was inspired by the muddy flats or bottom of the Suwanee River rather than from the slapping of the rump that was one of its movements. It also featured sluggish foot movements that suggested plodding through the mud. Alberta Hunter was credited with having invented the dance.

"Black Bottom" was selected for *Variety*'s "Fifty Year Hit Parade."

The Blue Room
COMPOSER: **Richard Rodgers**
  LYRICIST: **Lorenz Hart**

Sam White and Eva Puck sang this song that praises romantic seclusion in Rodgers and Hart's *The Girl Friend*, which Sandy Wilson used as the model for the 1953 musical *The Boy Friend*.

The singers are dreaming of the "blue room" they will have in their future home. In that room "every day's a holiday/Because you're married to me."

"The Blue Room" was one of *Variety*'s "Fifty Year Hit Parade" selections.

Breezin' Along with the Breeze
COMPOSER-LYRICISTS: **Haven Gillespie, Seymour Simons, and Richard A. Whiting**

This collaborative song was a hit for Al Jolson. It was Fred Waring's theme music for his radio program in the thirties.

Bye Bye Blackbird
COMPOSER: **Ray Henderson**
  LYRICIST: **Mort Dixon**

Following "Birth of the Blues" and "Black Bottom," Ray Henderson had a third hit in 1926 with "Bye Bye Blackbird." This time Henderson worked with lyricist Mort Dixon, with whom he had collaborated earlier on "That Old Gang of Mine" (1923).

"Blackbird" was first made popular by Eddie Cantor, then served as the theme song for vaudevillian Georgie Price. Gene Austin had a successful recording of this hit. The lyrics to "Bye Bye Blackbird" continued their popularity into the thirties because of the opening phrase: "Pack up all my cares and woe." The melody is narrow in range and moves in scale patterns, with few skips. These characteristics give the melody the character of a folk song.

Clap Yo' Hands
COMPOSER: **George Gershwin**
LYRICIST: **Ira Gershwin**

The third success, after "Someone to Watch over You" and "Do Do Do," from the score of *Oh, Kay!* was "Clap Yo' hands." In *Lyrics on Several Occasions* Ira Gershwin pointed out a curious thing about the text: The title does not appear in the song itself, but in the chorus it is heard as "clap-a yo' hands." Introduced by Harland Dixon, it projected a simple idea: Join the dance!

The Desert Song
COMPOSER: **Sigmund Romberg**
LYRICISTS: **Otto Harbach and Oscar Hammerstein II**

Sigmund Romberg's operetta *The Desert Song* is one of the most durable of all Broadway operettas, with lyrics and book by Otto Harbach and Oscar Hammerstein II. The authors tried to integrate modern news and literary events into the story. These included an uprising in Morocco, the exploits of Lawrence of Arabia, and the novel *The Sheik*, which had been turned into a film starring Rudolph Valentino.

At the end of Act One, the Red Shadow (played by Robert Halliday) comes to take Margot (played by Vivienne Segal) away with him into the desert and sweeps her off her feet with the impassioned title song, "The Desert Song," sometimes called "Blue Heaven."

"The Desert Song" was selected for *Variety*'s "Fifty Year Hit Parade."

Do-Do-Do
COMPOSER: **George Gershwin**
LYRICIST: **Ira Gershwin**

This lighthearted romantic duet was sung by Gertrude Lawrence and Oscar Shaw in *Oh, Kay!* Ira Gershwin has said that the brothers wrote the refrain (which is the most memorable part) in half an hour. He also insisted that kissing was all the couple in the song wanted to do again.

"Gimme" a Little Kiss, Will "Ya" Huh?
COMPOSER: **Maceo Pinkard**
LYRICISTS: **Roy Turk and Jack Smith**

One of the lyricists, Whispering Jack Smith, had great success with this song. Guy Lombardo and his Royal Canadians popularized " 'Gimme' a Little Kiss" during their stay at the Clairmont Café in Cleveland. The singer assures the girl that if she'll give him a kiss, he will give it right back.

I Know That You Know
COMPOSER: **Vincent Youmans**
LYRICIST: **Anne Caldwell**

Top comic talents Beatrice Lillie and Charles Purcell introduced this bouncy romantic duet in Vincent Youmans's *Oh, Please!* It is the one song from the score that has survived. The number uses a readily identifiable Youmans technique of a simple repeated series of notes over numerous harmonic changes.

The song was selected by *Variety* for its "Fifty Year Hit Parade."

In a Little Spanish Town
COMPOSER: **Mabel Wayne**
LYRICISTS: **Sam M. Lewis and Joe Young**

The "Doctor of Melody," Jimmy Carr, and his orchestra popularized "In a Little Spanish Town." Its success started a Tin Pan Alley vogue for Spanish-style songs. At the same time it launched Mabel Wayne on a career as a successful popular composer. A secondary title of this hit could easily be " 'Twas on a Night Like This," which appears more often than the title phrase.

Mountain Greenery
COMPOSER: **Richard Rodgers**
LYRICIST: **Lorenz Hart**

In the first *Garrick Gaieties*, Rodgers and Hart wrote a tribute to romantic New York in which a young city couple (Sterling Holloway, famous later for his voice in Disney cartoons, and June Cochrane) sang of their love dreams based on city life (see "Manhattan," page 32). In the second *Garrick Gaieties*, they switched things around, this time putting a young couple (Sterling Holloway and Bobbie Perkins) in a country setting for "Mountain Greenery." The song was interpolated into *The Girl Friend* and into Rodgers and Hammerstein's *Allegro* (1947).

Muskrat Ramble
COMPOSER: **Kid Ory**

Jazz trombonist Kid Ory composed this jazz classic. Ory began his career in New Orleans, learning from the legendary Buddy Bolden. After 1912 he had his own band in New Orleans, at times including cornetists King Oliver and Louis Armstrong and clarinetists Johnny Dodds, Sidney Bechet, Jimmie Noone, and George Lewis. Ory left New Orleans for the West Coast in 1919 but returned to Chicago to play with Armstrong and Oliver in the last half of the twenties. Ory's traditional tailgate style of trombone playing was his musical trademark. The first recording of "Muskrat Ramble" was by Louis Armstrong and his Hot Five. This tune was revived in the mid-fifties, and words were added by Ray Gilbert.

"Tailgate" was a style of trombone playing that was characteristic of Dixieland and consisted of a lot of slurs using the trombone's slide. It derived its name from the trombonist's position in the wagon as the early jazz ensembles toured the streets of New Orleans. The trombone normally was relegated to the tailgate of the wagon so his slide would not get in the way of the other musicians.

One Alone
COMPOSER: **Sigmund Romberg**
 LYRICISTS: **Otto Harbach and Oscar Hammerstein II**

"One Alone" was presented in the operetta *The Desert Song* as the third song in a musical debate concerning love (see "The Desert Song," page 36). A desert chieftain advocates brief, uninvolving flings, a lieutenant proposes a harem, but the Red Shadow rejects both in favor of the "one alone" philosophy. Robert Halliday, who portrayed the Red Shadow, introduced this gorgeous song.

"One Alone" was selected by *Variety* for its "Fifty Year Hit Parade."

The Ranger's Song
COMPOSER: **Harry Tierney**
 LYRICIST: **Joseph McCarthy**

This robust march in honor of the Texas Rangers was introduced by J. Harold Murray and a chorus of Rangers in Harry Tierney's *Rio Rita*. The show opened Florenz Ziegfeld's elaborate Ziegfeld Theater. The title song, "Rio Rita," is listed under 1928, when it was more popular (see page 45).

"The Ranger's Song" was a "Fifty Year Hit Parade" selection by *Variety*.

The Riff Song
COMPOSER: **Sigmund Romberg**
 LYRICISTS: **Otto Harbach and Oscar Hammerstein II**

"The Riff Song" is a battle call sung by the Red Shadow (Robert Halliday), Sid El Kar (William O'Neal), and their band of Riffians (bandits) in the opening scene of the operetta *The Desert Song* (see "The Desert Song," page 36).

This riding song was selected by *Variety* for its "Fifty Year Hit Parade."

Someone to Watch Over Me
COMPOSER: **George Gershwin**
 LYRICIST: **Ira Gershwin**

Another hit, besides "Do-Do-Do" and "Clap Yo' Hands," from the Gershwins' *Oh, Kay!* was "Someone to Watch over Me." It was introduced by Gertrude Lawrence in a romantic, plaintive scene in which she clutched a rag doll. George's melody was first conceived as fast and assertive, but he was not satisfied with it until he finally realized that what it needed was a slow tempo. Slowed down, the tune was given to Ira for setting the lyrics. He put together several contradictory proverbs, sayings, and clichés of wistfulness, which he joined together with consummate skill to create a lyric of rare beauty.

Tonight You Belong to Me
COMPOSER: **Lee David**
 LYRICIST: **Billy Rose**

Billy Rose, a champion of loony lyrics, also wrote "Tonight You Belong to Me," which became a million-selling recording for Patience and Prudence in 1956.

When the Red, Red Robin, Comes Bob, Bob, Bobbin' Along
COMPOSER-LYRICIST: **Harry Woods**

Harry Woods, a prominent composer of songs of the twenties and thirties, had his first big hit with "When the Red, Red Robin Comes Bob, Bob, Bobbin' Along." It was introduced by Sophie Tucker in Chicago. Al Jolson and Lillian Roth separately helped make the song a hit. In Roth's 1955 screen biography, *I'll Cry Tomorrow*, it was sung by Susan Hayward.

1 9 2 7

Ain't She Sweet?
COMPOSER: **Milton Ager**
  LYRICIST: **Jack Yellen**

Eddie Cantor, Sophie Tucker, and Lillian Roth adopted "Ain't She Sweet?" for their respective vaudeville acts after it was introduced by Paul Ash and his orchestra in Chicago. This song established its composer, Milton Ager, and its lyricist, Jack Yellen, as hit songwriters. This is another of the songs that is closely associated with the flapper. She prances down the street so all the guys can "look her over once or twice."

Among My Souvenirs
COMPOSER: **Horatio Nicholls (pseudonym for Lawrence Wright)**
  LYRICIST: **Edgar Leslie**

Thirty-two years after this British song had been written in 1927, it became a million-selling record for Connie Francis. It was originally introduced by Jack Hylton and his orchestra in England. Paul Whiteman and his orchestra introduced it to the United States.

The singer is living in memories, reviewing the souvenirs of a broken romance.

"Among My Souvenirs" was selected for *Variety*'s "Fifty Year Hit Parade."

At Sundown
COMPOSER-LYRICIST: **Walter Donaldson**

This Walter Donaldson hit song sold more than 2 million discs in various versions in the late twenties. Both Jimmy and Tommy Dorsey made hit recordings in the early thirties. It was also a favorite of Ruth Etting's.

Donaldson's lyrics sing of breezes "sighing of love undying." The singer hears love calling him home as the sun begins to fall. The opening notes on the phrase *Every little breeze* are enough for most popular music connoisseurs to identify the song.

The Best Things in Life Are Free
COMPOSER: **Ray Henderson**
  LYRICISTS: **Buddy De Sylva and Lew Brown**

The first book musical by Henderson, De Sylva, and Brown was a collegiate caper. *Good News* explores a burning issue often a part of twenties collegiana: Will

the star football player be allowed to play in the big game against the archrival school despite his failing grade in astronomy? The answer? Since college spirit is more important than grades, he plays . . . and wins.

In the plot, the rich football hero leads up to the song "The Best Things in Life Are Free" by trying to convince the poor heroine that money is not the answer to everything. This paean to the priceless things in life was introduced by John Price Jones and Mary Lawlor.

This song was a *Variety* "Fifty Year Hit Parade" selection.

Bill
COMPOSER: **Jerome Kern**
  LYRICIST: **P. G. Wodehouse**

"Bill" was introduced in *Show Boat* (see "Can't Help Lovin' Dat Man," page 39) by Helen Morgan, who starred as the mulatto Julie La Verne. Magnolia Hawks Ravenal gets a job at the Trocadero to help pay her husband Gaylord's gambling debts. She is replacing an alcoholic singer, Julie La Verne. Just before Magnolia arrives, Julie rehearses her evening's number, which reveals her devotion to her real-life man. Although "Bill" was not one of the most renowned of *Show Boat*'s songs, it provided one of the show's most touching moments.

The song, with a slightly different lyric, was originally intended to be used in 1918's *Oh, Lady! Lady!*, but it was dropped before the opening. Next, it was considered for Marilyn Miller in *Sally*, but it was dropped there, too. Although almost all the lyrics for *Show Boat* were written by Oscar Hammerstein II, "Bill," with lyrics by P. G. Wodehouse, was included in the score.

Blue Skies
COMPOSER-LYRICIST: **Irving Berlin**

The idea that love can turn gray skies to blue is aptly illustrated in this Irving Berlin song, introduced by Belle Baker in the musical *Betsy*. Although Rodgers and Hart wrote all the other songs for the musical, producer Florenz Ziegfeld insisted that this Berlin ballad be interpolated into the show.

"Blue Skies" proved to be the biggest hit of the

score. It is interesting to note that each of the three main sections of the piece begins with a "blue" variation—"blue skies," "bluebirds," and "blue days"—an example of excellent text writing technique. In the first sound film, *The Jazz Singer* (1927), Al Jolson included "Blue Skies" among several of his favorites.

Variety selected the song for its "Fifty Year Hit Parade."

Can't Help Lovin' Dat Man
COMPOSER: **Jerome Kern**
LYRICIST: **Oscar Hammerstein II**

Broadway history was made on December 27, 1927, when Florenz Ziegfeld presented Jerome Kern and Oscar Hammerstein II's *Show Boat*, which led the way toward a musical theater of increased scope and became the most lastingly effective and third-longest-running Broadway musical of the decade. Kern and Hammerstein had been determined to write a musical beyond the conventions of the musical comedy. They chose Edna Ferber's novel *Show Boat* for the experiment. Though the writing of the show entailed many difficulties, the result was an artistic and commercial triumph. The effort resulted in a new genre of musical play, integrating all the elements of the plot, music, and characters into one cohesive artistic concept.

Kern's score has become one of the best known of all Broadway musicals. "Can't Help Lovin' Dat Man" was introduced by Helen Morgan, Aunt Jemima (Tess Gardella), Norma Terris, Jules Bledsoe, and Arthur Campbell. As presented in the musical, it is supposed to be a traditional song of ardent love that only "colored folks" know.

Variety picked this Kern-Hammerstein song for its "Fifty Year Hit Parade."

Charmaine
COMPOSER: **Erno Rapee**
LYRICIST: **Lew Pollack**

Erno Rapee had the distinction of being the first to write a successful movie theme song. He took a melody that had been written in Hungary in 1913 and transformed it into the theme for the silent film *What Price Glory?* in 1926. It became a million sheet music seller and in 1951 became a million record seller for Mantovani and his orchestra. The title of the song could easily have been "I Wonder" since each phrase of the lyrics begins with those words. The singer wonders if the lover will return to the waiting Charmaine.

The song was chosen for *Variety*'s "Fifty Year Hit Parade."

Hallelujah!
COMPOSER: **Vincent Youmans**
LYRICISTS: **Clifford Grey and Leo Robin**

Hit the Deck was Vincent Youmans's second most memorable musical, after *No, No, Nanette*. Louise Groody played the proprietress of a coffee shop near a U.S. Navy installation. The nautical production boasts two all-time Youmans hits: "Hallelujah!" and "Sometimes I'm Happy."

"Hallelujah!" is a revival number featuring a male chorus and Lavinia (Stella Mayhew) in blackface. The melody was composed by Youmans during World War I but was first heard in *Hit the Deck!*

Variety selected "Hallelujah!" for its "Fifty Year Hit Parade."

I'm Looking over a Four Leaf Clover
COMPOSER: **Harry Woods**
LYRICIST: **Mort Dixon**

Harry Woods and Mort Dixon wrote this song hit, one of their most famous collaborations. It was perhaps even more popular in 1947, when it became a million seller for Art Mooney and his orchestra, featuring the banjo playing of Mike Pingatore, than it was when it was introduced. Pingatore also played with Paul Whiteman on his 1923 recording of "Linger Awhile."

It All Depends on You
COMPOSER: **Ray Henderson**
LYRICISTS: **B. G. De Sylva and Lew Brown**

Al Jolson added this Henderson, Brown, and De Sylva collaboration to the musical *Big Boy* after its opening. He also performed it in the 1928 movie musical *The Singing Fool*. Ruth Etting helped popularize the song, which in essence says that the singer's mood "depends on you."

Just a Memory
COMPOSER: **Ray Henderson**
LYRICISTS: **Buddy De Sylva and Lew Brown**

"Just a Memory," another Henderson, De Sylva, and Brown hit, was inserted into the musical *Manhattan Mary*. The musical was a vehicle for Ed Wynn, who was billed as "The Perfect Fool." With his faltering speech, silly laugh, fluttering hands, and outlandish apparel, Wynn played Crickets, a waiter who helps Mary Brennan (Ona Munson) get a job in *George White's Scandals*. The "memory" is of a former love affair. The singer remembers "days I knew with you" and wonders if they will "share the night, the moon, the stars above again."

"Just a Memory" was chosen for *Variety*'s "Fifty Year Hit Parade."

Make Believe

COMPOSER: **Jerome Kern**
 LYRICIST: **Oscar Hammerstein II**

"Make Believe" was sung in the historic musical *Show Boat* (see "Can't Help Lovin' Dat Man," page 39, and "Bill," page 38) at the first meeting of Magnolia Hawks (played by Norma Terris) and Gaylord Ravenal (played by Howard Marsh). They have noticed each other and are attracted but express their mutual interest in vague "make believe" terms.

"Make Believe" was selected for *Variety*'s "Fifty Year Hit Parade."

Me and My Shadow

COMPOSERS: **Dave Dreyer and Al Jolson**
 LYRICIST: **Billy Rose**

This 1927 hit was added to the 1975 movie *Funny Lady*, a sequel to *Funny Girl*. Since Billy Rose, Fanny Brice's second husband, had had a hand in writing the number, it was included in the film, which carried Brice's life beyond *Funny Girl*.

"Me and My Shadow" is most closely associated with Ted Lewis. He performed this number with "shadow" Eddie Chester, who duplicated Lewis's gestures behind a shadowy background while Lewis sang in a half-talking, lazy style.

My Blue Heaven

COMPOSER: **Walter Donaldson**
 LYRICIST: **George Whiting**

Lyricist George Whiting introduced this song in vaudeville; it was then reintroduced by Tommy Lyman. Eddie Cantor sang it in the *Ziegfeld Follies of 1927*. Cantor dominated the show with this song, as well as three by Irving Berlin. But it was singer Gene Austin who made the most lasting impression with the song. His recording of "My Blue Heaven" is reputed to have sold 5 million copies, and it made him rich and famous. His 1927 disc remained the top all-time seller until it was replaced by Bing Crosby's "White Christmas" fifteen years later.

Variety included "My Blue Heaven" in its "Fifty Year Hit Parade."

My Heart Stood Still

COMPOSER: **Richard Rodgers**
 LYRICIST: **Lorenz Hart**

This Rodgers and Hart song was introduced first in a 1927 English revue, *One Damn Thing After Another*,

then by William Gaxton and Constance Carpenter in the 1927 American musical *A Connecticut Yankee*. Rodgers and Hart got the idea in Paris from a French girl who was with them at the time of a near accident. She exclaimed, "Oh, my heart stood still!" Hart, thinking this would make a good title for a song, duly noted the sentence. Upon their return to London to resume work on the revue, Rodgers supplied a melody and Hart added words to go with the title.

A Connecticut Yankee was a musical version of Mark Twain's novel *A Connecticut Yankee in King Arthur's Court*.

This song was a *Variety* "Fifty Year Hit Parade" selection.

Ol' Man River

COMPOSER: **Jerome Kern**
 LYRICIST: **Oscar Hammerstein II**

In the plot of *Show Boat* (see "Can't Stop Lovin' Dat Man," page 39, "Bill," page 38, and "Make Believe," above) the sheriff warns Gaylord Ravenal that he is not wanted in town and should move on. Magnolia Hawks, who has been attracted to Gaylord, quizzes Joe, a black worker on the levee, about Gaylord. Joe refuses to tell her anything, if indeed he actually knows anything. In one of the show's most memorable hits, Joe suggests that if anyone can give her the answer, it must be "ol' man river," who sees all and knows all.

Variety selected this *Show Boat* classic for its "Fifty Year Hit Parade."

Ramona

COMPOSER: **Mabel Wayne**
 LYRICIST: **L. Wolfe Gilbert**

The most successful movie theme song of the twenties was "Ramona." It was commissioned by the film studio to help promote a movie of the same name and introduced by Paul Whiteman and his orchestra on a coast-to-coast radio broadcast before the picture opened. Gene Austin's recording sold 2 million copies, making it the first multimillion recording. The song also sold fantastically well on piano player rolls and in sheet music.

"Ramona" was chosen by *Variety* for its "Fifty Year Hit Parade."

Side by Side

COMPOSER-LYRICIST: **Harry Woods**

Harry Woods wrote both the music and lyrics to this song, which was a popular number in vaudeville in the late twenties. The text speaks of sticking together even though times may be rough. "Side by Side" was revived by Kay Starr about the same time that Frankie Laine and Keefe Brasselle performed it in the 1955 movie musical *Bring Your Smile Along*.

Sometimes I'm Happy
COMPOSER: **Vincent Youmans**
  LYRICIST: **Irving Caesar**

"Sometimes I'm Happy" was introduced by Louise Groody (as Loulou) and Charles King (as Bilge) in *Hit the Deck* (see "Hallelujah!," page 39). Its melody had been written earlier in a quicker tempo to the title "Come On and Pet Me." The lyricists for the original were William Cary Duncan and Oscar Hammerstein II, but Irving Caesar wrote this lyric for a never-opened musical, *A Night Out*. At a slower tempo "Sometimes I'm Happy" became a hit in *Hit the Deck*.

Variety included the song in its "Fifty Year Hit Parade."

The Song Is Ended
COMPOSER-LYRICIST: **Irving Berlin**

A year or so after Irving Berlin's marriage to Ellin MacKay he wrote "The Song Is Ended." The title was prophetic for Berlin. After he had completed this song, his creativity seemed to mysteriously disappear for a time. Whatever he tried to write seemed to him to be trite and repetitious, and he destroyed most of it. To make matters worse, Berlin's writer's block struck just after the stock market crash of 1929, when he could have used new hit songs financially as well as artistically. The road back began in 1932.

The lyrics tell of a melody that lingers on in the listener's mind after a song has ended.

Strike Up the Band
COMPOSER: **George Gershwin**
  LYRICIST: **Ira Gershwin**

This song came from a Gershwin musical of the same name that died in 1927 during its tryout period but was resurrected in 1930.

'S Wonderful
COMPOSER: **George Gershwin**
  LYRICIST: **Ira Gershwin**

The Gershwins created the songs for the musical *Funny Face*, which starred Fred and Adele Astaire, Allen Kearns, and Victor Moore. The top tune, made all the more memorable by the clever "shorthand" lyrics, was " 'S Wonderful." Ira's goal was to write rhymed

conversation. He had an unusually keen ear for the way people speak. When we speak, we elide words, slide into some, drop others, and communicate in ways that are almost impossible to put in writing. In " 'S Wonderful" we have a contraction with the elimination of *it* from *it's* and the elision of the remaining *s* with *wonderful*. Such usage is common in colloquial conversation.

This love duet was introduced by Adele Astaire (as Frankie Wynne) and Allen Kearns (as Peter Thurston), the lovers in the story. *Funny Face* was first dubbed *Smarty,* but the name was changed during pre-Broadway tryouts. The plot was shallow, but the show's main attractions were Gershwin's music and the Astaires.

" 'S Wonderful" was included by *Variety* in its "Fifty Year Hit Parade."

Thou Swell
COMPOSER: **Richard Rodgers**
  LYRICIST: **Lorenz Hart**

William Gaxton and Constance Carpenter introduced "Thou Swell" in *A Connecticut Yankee*. (See "My Heart Stood Still," page 40.) The combination of English from the time of King Arthur and American slang in the lyrics made this sprightly duet a classic.

"Thou Swell" was selected for *Variety's* "Fifty Year Hit Parade."

The Varsity Drag
COMPOSER: **Ray Henderson**
  LYRICISTS: **Buddy De Sylva and Lew Brown**

A second hit from the collegiate musical *Good News* (see "The Best Things in Life Are Free," page 38) was the Charleston number "The Varsity Drag." The song cue in the musical occurs when Zelma O'Neal (playing the coed Flo) tells the other students, "Let the professors worry about their dusty old books, we'll make Tait famous for the Varsity Drag!"

Variety listed "The Varsity Drag" in its "Fifty Year Hit Parade."

Why Do I Love You?
COMPOSER: **Jerome Kern**
  LYRICIST: **Oscar Hammerstein II**

In the landmark musical *Show Boat* (see "Can't Help Lovin' Dat Man," page 39, "Bill," page 38, "Make Believe," page 40, and "Ol' Man River," page 40), Magnolia and Gaylord eventually get married. After some time has passed, they sing this blissful duet. They are joyful and amazed that their love is still so strong.

You Are Love
COMPOSER: Jerome Kern
LYRICIST: Oscar Hammerstein II

"You Are Love" is the rapturous duet sung in *Show Boat* (see "Why Do I Love You?," page 41) by Magnolia and Gaylord as they pledge their love to each other and agree to marry.

The love song was included in *Variety's* "Fifty Year Hit Parade."

1 9 2 8

Angela Mia
COMPOSER: Erno Rapee
LYRICIST: Lew Pollack

Among the movie theme songs that swept the hit lists of the late twenties was this song, which served as the recurring theme in the synchronized score for the movie *Street Angel*, which starred Janet Gaynor. The singer believes that Angela is an angel sent from heaven in answer to his prayers.

Variety selected "Angela Mia" for its "Fifty Year Hit Parade."

Back in Your Own Backyard
COMPOSER-LYRICISTS: Dave Dreyer, Al Jolson, and Billy Rose

The next hit for the team of Dave Dreyer, Al Jolson, and Billy Rose, after 1927's "Me and My Shadow," was "Back in Your Own Backyard," which was popularized by Jolson. In fact, he revived it in the late forties by including it in the motion picture *Jolson Sings Again*.

The motif of the lyrics is that happiness can be found where we are. It is not necessary to travel all around, for happiness can be found "right under your eyes, back in your own backyard."

Button Up Your Overcoat
COMPOSER: Ray Henderson
LYRICISTS: Buddy De Sylva and Lew Brown

Henderson, DeSylva, and Brown's musical *Follow Thru* came to Broadway in 1928. Included in the score was "Button Up Your Overcoat," which had already become popular. *Follow Thru* was a commentary on country life and the swanky golf club hoi polloi that starred Jack Haley, Zelma O'Neal, and Eleanor Powell. This was Powell's first Broadway success and headed her career toward the successes she had in the screen musicals of the thirties. It was also the first starring role on Broadway for Jack Haley, who became immortal in his role as the Tin Man in the 1939 film *The Wizard of Oz*. Haley was particularly adept at playing the bewildered, inept, reluctant hero.

The lyrics of "Button Up Your Overcoat" are a catalog of health admonitions: Wear proper clothing, eat correct foods, be careful when you cross the street, do not stay up too late, and stay away from speakeasy liquor.

Variety picked the song for its "Fifty Year Hit Parade."

Carolina Moon
COMPOSER: Joe Burke
LYRICIST: Benny Davis

"Carolina Moon" was originally popularized by Guy Lombardo and his Royal Canadians. It became identified with Morton Downey because the song was his radio theme song. The first recording of this *Variety* "Fifty Year Hit Parade" selection was by Gene Austin.

"Carolina Moon" is a dreamy waltz that has remained a pop music staple over the years. The singer pleads with the moon that shines on Carolina to shine on the "one who waits for me" and let her know "I'm blue and lonely."

Diane
COMPOSER: Erno Rapee
LYRICIST: Lew Pollack

The theme song for the 1927 film *Seventh Heaven*, "Diane" was performed by an unidentified singer on the sound track that accompanied the silent film. The lyrics of this *Variety* "Fifty Year Hit Parade" selection request a smile from Diane. Something so simple puts the singer in heaven.

Diga Diga Doo
COMPOSER: Jimmy McHugh
LYRICIST: Dorothy Fields

Adelaide Hall introduced this song in her first starring role on Broadway in the all-black revue *Blackbirds of*

1928. It also was the broadway debut for the composer and the lyricist, Jimmy McHugh and Dorothy Fields.

In the presentation of the song, Hall was supported by a bevy of girls dressed in two-piece red sequin costumes with red feathers to typify Zulus. The "diga diga doo" of the title is the beat of a Zulu man's heart when he is in love.

Variety selected this song for its "Fifty Year Hit Parade."

Honey
COMPOSER: Richard A. Whiting
  LYRICISTS: Seymour Simons and Haven Gillespie

Rudy Vallee introduced and popularized "Honey" on his radio program and with his recording. It had sold more than a million copies of sheet music by 1930. In a "Name That Tune" game, the contestant would most likely recognize the sixteen measure chorus almost immediately.

Variety named "Honey" to its "Fifty Year Hit Parade."

I Can't Give You Anything but Love
COMPOSER: Jimmy McHugh
  LYRICIST: Dorothy Fields

In addition to "Diga Diga Doo" (see page 42) the second hit from *Blackbirds of 1928* was first introduced by Patsy Kelly in the 1927 revue *Harry Delmar's Revels.* "I Can't Give You Anything but Love" was then interpolated into *Lew Leslie's Blackbirds* by Aida Ward in her Broadway debut. She performed it with Willard Mclean and Bill Robinson. Later, during the run of the show, the song was taken over by Adelaide Hall.

The success of the song was partially due to jazz recordings by Louis Armstrong, Benny Goodman, and Fats Waller. By the mid-1960's there were more than 450 recordings of this tune, and it had sold a total of more then 2.5 million records.

This song was included in *Variety's* "Fifty Year Hit Parade."

I'll Get By
COMPOSER: Fred E. Ahlert
  LYRICIST: Roy Turk

"I'll Get By" was a leading song hit of the late twenties, selling more than a million copies of sheet music and approximately a million copies of various recordings. Unlike our day, when a song is identified with a specific performer, in this period it was generally the song, not a specific performance by a particular singer, that sold. Still, "I'll Get By" is often closely identified with Ruth Etting. In the mid-forties a revival of the song reached hit status after it had been used as a background theme in the 1943 film *A Guy Named Joe* and in the 1944 movie musical *Follow the Boys.* Recorded by Dick Haymes with Harry James and his orchestra, "I'll Get By" was the number three tune in 1944's top ten.

I Wanna Be Loved by You
COMPOSERS: Herbert Stothart and Harry Ruby
  LYRICIST: Bert Kalmar

"I Wanna Be Loved by You" is the "boop-boop-a-doop" song. Because Helen Kane introduced it in the musical *Good Boy,* she got the title "the Boop-Boop-a-Doop Girl." The one memorable number from the score was "I Wanna Be Loved by You." Delivered by Kane's dumb blond flapper in a unique squeaky delivery, the song became a hit worthy of inclusion in *Variety's* "Fifty Year Hit Parade."

Let a Smile Be Your Umbrella
COMPOSER: Sammy Fain
  LYRICISTS: Irving Kahal and Francis Wheeler

Two young vaudevillians, Sammy Fain and Irving Kahal, who liked to write lyrics, formed a writing partnership with Francis Wheeler that produced a hit, "Let a Smile Be Your Umbrella," in their first year together. The song was introduced in vaudeville by Fain and Artie Dunn and was sung in the 1929 film *It's a Great Life* by the Duncan Sisters. This popular sister act was an active vaudeville team during this period.

The lyrics were particularly appropriate for the Depression era, which started at the end of 1929. The idea of smiling through one's troubles seemed suited for the woes following the crash of the stock market.

Let's Do It
COMPOSER-LYRICIST: Cole Porter

This clever song was introduced by Irene Bordoni and Arthur Margetson in Cole Porter's *Paris.* The lyrics enumerate the mating habits of numerous flora and fauna. Porter became known almost immediately after *Paris* for his ingenious and imaginative lyrics.

E. Ray Goetz, the Broadway producer, encountered playboy Cole Porter at the Lido in Venice. Goetz, who knew of Porter's parties, at which he would perform some of his cute (and often sexy) songs for his guests, was planning the musical *Paris,* a vehicle to star his wife, Irene Bordoni. He decided to take a chance that someone as wealthy as Porter would work hard enough to produce the music for an entire Broadway musical. Not only did Porter complete the show, but he composed a remarkable musical score for a first attempt. From it came "Let's Do It," which convinced Porter and others that he should compose in earnest. *Fifty Million Frenchmen* and a long string of excellent scores for Broadway and the movies followed.

Love Me or Leave Me
COMPOSER: **Walter Donaldson**
LYRICIST: **Gus Kahn**

One of 1928's famous Broadway hit shows was *Whoopee.* Walter Donaldson was an established Tin Pan Alley composer, but this was his first complete Broadway score. The standout ballad of the show was "Love Me or Leave Me," which was sung by Ruth Etting. The song became so identified with her that Etting's 1955 movie biography was titled *Love Me or Leave Me,* with Doris Day playing the star.

Lover, Come Back to Me
COMPOSER: **Sigmund Romberg**
LYRICIST: **Oscar Hammerstein II**

Sigmund Romberg's *The New Moon,* which was the only show of the 1928 season to run for more than 500 performances, almost did not make it to Broadway. During tryouts it was canceled, but after being rewritten and recast, it reopened. All but one of the hits from the show were from the revision.

The New Moon marked the second collaboration between Romberg and Oscar Hammerstein II (the first was 1926's *The Desert Song*). The play was set in eighteenth-century New Orleans and was loosely based on the life and exploits of a French aristocrat, Robert Mission.

The biggest hit was "Lover, Come Back to Me," one of Romberg's best-known melodies, even though it was not completely an original. The middle section of the melody comes from Tchaikovsky's piano piece "June Barcarolle." It was introduced by Marianne (played by Evelyn Herbert), who pleads with Robert (played by Robert Halliday) to return her affection (Robert thinks Marianne has betrayed him into enemy hands).

There were two motion-picture adaptations of *The New Moon.* The first starred Grace Moore and Law-

rence Tibbett (1930), and the second starred Jeanette MacDonald and Nelson Eddy (1940).

Variety chose "Lover Come Back to Me" for its "Fifty Year Hit Parade."

Makin' Whoopee!
COMPOSER: **Walter Donaldson**
LYRICIST: **Gus Kahn**

Eddie Cantor, who starred with Ruth Etting in the musical *Whoopee,* introduced one of his all-time popular hits in the show. The lyrics to "Makin' Whoopee!" warn of the dangers of married life. Cantor played a shy hypochondriac who is induced to elope with Sally Morgan (played by Frances Upton) but ends up with the faithful nurse, Mary (played by Ethel Shutta). The movie adaptation of *Whoopee* was Cantor's talking-picture debut. Only three songs were used from the stage score, and several new ones, including "My Baby Just Cares for Me," were written for the movie.

Marie
COMPOSER-LYRICIST: **Irving Berlin**

This Irving Berlin classic was introduced in a 1928 film, *My Awakening,* and was the first Berlin song to appear in a movie. After its premiere "Marie" was popularized by Rudy Vallee over radio and in recordings. In 1937 the song was revived by Tommy Dorsey and his orchestra into a million-selling disc. It was one of Dorsey's first major recording successes. In this unique and catchy rendition, the bandsmen sang a patter chorus behind the melody. It reached the million record status again in 1954 for the Four Tunes.

Mississippi Mud
COMPOSER: **Harry Barris**
LYRICIST: **James Cavanaugh**

The Rhythm Boys, a trio consisting of Bing Crosby, Al Rinker, and Harry Barris, were a top attraction with Paul Whiteman and his orchestra. At this time they made a highly successful recording of Harry Barris's "Mississippi Mud" (1928). In the recording the Rhythm Boys were backed by jazz legend Bix Beiderbecke and future bandleaders Tommy and Jimmy Dorsey, who were then members of Whiteman's orchestra.

The lyrics to the song claim that "it's a treat to beat your feet on the Mississippi mud." The song describes a dance by the people who live adjacent to the river, in the delta where low tides leave mud.

One Kiss

COMPOSER: **Sigmund Romberg**
 LYRICIST: **Oscar Hammerstein II**

"One Kiss" was introduced in the operetta *The New Moon* by Evelyn Herbert (see "Lover, Come Back to Me," page 44). As Marianne, she vows that she loves just one man and that she saves her kisses for him. The melody of "One Kiss" is vaguely similar to Vincent Youmans's "No, No, Nanette."

Rio Rita

COMPOSER: **Harry Tierney**
 LYRICIST: **Joseph McCarthy**

"Rio Rita" is the principal love duet from the 1927 Broadway musical *Rio Rita*. This *Variety* "Fifty Year Hit Parade" song was introduced by J. Harold Murray and Ethelind Terry. Rio Rita is the girl whom Jim, the leader of the Rangers, loves. The song projects a Mexican flavor, but it needs the drumbeat and Mexican instruments to complete the image.

She's Funny That Way

COMPOSER: **Neil Moret**
 LYRICIST: **Richard A. Whiting**

This song is one of the few instances when Richard Whiting served as lyricist for someone else's music (Neil Moret). The male singer claims he is not very good-looking, but he is extremely happy to have "a woman, crazy for me." And if he went away, she would be unhappy because she is crazy about the guy: "She's funny that way."

Softly, as in a Morning Sunrise

COMPOSER: **Sigmund Romberg**
 LYRICIST: **Oscar Hammerstein II**

Romberg's operetta *The New Moon* introduced "Softly, as in a Morning Sunrise." (See "Lover, Come Back to Me," page 44). At a tavern Robert Mission's friend Philippe (played by William O'Neal) cautions Robert that while love steals in "Softly, as in a morning sunrise," its vows are always broken. This Romberg operetta aria was one of *Variety's* "Fifty Year Hit Parade" selections.

Sonny Boy

COMPOSER: **Ray Henderson**
 LYRICISTS: **Buddy De Sylva, Lew Brown, and Al Jolson**

While Al Jolson's second talking picture, *The Singing Fool*, was being rehearsed, "Sonny Boy" became a last-minute replacement for a song that had been judged unsuitable. Jolson telephoned Buddy De Sylva to urge the Henderson, De Sylva and Brown team to write a number that would fit into the specific spot in the film, and the next morning the song was ready. It has been suggested that the songwriters created "Sonny Boy" tongue in cheek. They did write it under the pen name Elmer Colby. Nevertheless, Jolson took it seriously and sang it into immortality. His recording was a two-time million seller: 1928 and 1946.

Variety placed "Sonny Boy" on its "Fifty Year Hit Parade."

Stout-Hearted Men

COMPOSER: **Sigmund Romberg**
 LYRICIST: **Oscar Hammerstein II**

Only "Stout-Hearted Men" was retained from the original version of *The New Moon* when it was revised and recast before it reached Broadway. (See "Lover, Come Back to Me," page 44.) Robert Mission (played by Robert Halliday) ignores his friend Philippe's warning and proclaims that given a band of "stout-hearted men," both love and liberty will always triumph.

Sweet Sue — Just You

COMPOSER: **Victor Young**
 LYRICIST: **Will J. Harris**

The "Sue" in the title of this song was Sue Carol (later Mrs. Alan Ladd), whose portrait appeared on the cover of the sheet music and to whom the song was dedicated.

A particularly impressive recording of "Sweet Sue" was Paul Whiteman's, featuring jazz immortal Bix Beiderbecke. By this time in Beiderbecke's career, alcoholism and declining health were depleting his considerable talent, but this recording hardly evidences any corrosion. Another significant recording was by the Benny Goodman Quartet in the late thirties.

Variety chose "Sweet Sue" for its "Fifty Year Hit Parade."

That's My Weakness Now

COMPOSER: **Sam H. Stept**
 LYRICIST: **Bud Green**

"That's My Weakness Now" was introduced at the Paramount Theater in New York by an unknown Helen Kane. She added a few "boop-boop-a-doops" to the chorus, which propelled her to stardom. The Boop-Boop-a-Doop Girl had established her trademark. And what was the "weakness"? The male singer had a weakness for whatever a particular girl had: "She's got eyes of blue/I never cared for eyes of blue/But she's got eyes of blue/And that's my weakness now."

"That's My Weakness Now" was selected for inclusion in *Variety's* "Fifty Year Hit Parade."

There's a Rainbow 'Round My Shoulder
COMPOSER: **Dave Dreyer**
LYRICISTS: **Billy Rose and Al Jolson**

In addition to "Sonny Boy," another Al Jolson specialty was introduced in the movie *The Singing Fool*. Jolson's 1928 recording of "Rainbow 'Round My Shoulder," coupled with "Sonny Boy," is estimated to have sold a million copies. The lyrics say that being in love gives one all the right things, including "a rainbow 'round my shoulder," which is symbolic of all the world's being in tune.

Variety selected this Jolson speciality for its "Fifty Year Hit Parade."

Wanting You
COMPOSER: **Sigmund Romberg**
LYRICIST: **Oscar Hammerstein II**

"Wanting You" is a beautifully tender song from *The New Moon* (see "Lover, Come Back to Me," page 44). Robert Mission and Marianne Beaunoir admit their longing for each other in this operetta duet.

You're the Cream in My Coffee
COMPOSER: **Ray Henderson**
LYRICISTS: **Buddy De Sylva and Lew Brown**

Henderson, De Sylva, and Brown's *Hold Everything*, a 1928 musical comedy that starred Bert Lahr in his first leading role on Broadway, introduced "You're the Cream in My Coffee." *Hold Everything* commented on the prizefight game and "clean sportsmanship." Bert Lahr was cast as a punch-drunk fighter, Victor Moore was his inept and victimized manager, and Jack Whiting was welterweight champion. Whiting introduced this love duet with Ona Munson, who played the object of his affection. The primary idea of the song is to point up what a necessity each is for the other. They consider necessities a few of the following: cream in coffee; salt in stew; starch in collar; lace in shoe. The bouncy melody and cute lyrics make the song an irresistible hit.

Variety selected "You're the Cream in My Coffee" for its "Fifty Year Hit Parade."

You Took Advantage of Me
COMPOSER: **Richard Rodgers**
LYRICIST: **Lorenz Hart**

This Rodgers and Hart song was introduced by Busby Berkeley and Joyce Barbour in the musical *Present Arms*. Rodgers and Hart had only minor Broadway success with several musicals between 1927's *A Connecticut Yankee* and the mid-thirties. *Present Arms* falls into this category and is remembered today only for its best song: "You Took Advantage of Me." Morton Downey had great success with this tune in the early thirties.

1 9 2 9

Ain't Misbehavin'
COMPOSERS: **Fats Waller and Harry Brooks**
LYRICIST: **Andy Razaf**

This famous Fats Waller song was introduced by Louis Armstrong in the all-black revue *Hot Chocolates*. Armstrong credited his appearance in the revue with the beginning of his international fame. His 1929 recording of "Ain't Misbehavin'" has become a jazz classic.

Waller's two most famous songs—"Ain't Misbehavin' " and "Honeysuckle Rose"—came in 1929. In 1978 Broadway honored Waller with a show, *Ain't*

Misbehavin', which featured many of his best works and other songs that were identified with him.

This Fats Waller classic was included in *Variety's* "Fifty Year Hit Parade."

Am I Blue?
COMPOSER: **Harry Akst**
LYRICIST: **Grant Clarke**

Ethel Waters introduced "Am I Blue?" in the 1929 motion-picture musical *On with the Show*. One of the world's most famous blues singers, Waters felt right at home with this commercial blues song. The singer laments the fact that every plan she has made with her lover has failed. Now they are sad, lonely, and blue.

"Am I Blue?" was included in *Variety's* "Fifty Year Hit Parade."

Broadway Melody
COMPOSER: **Arthur Freed**
LYRICIST: **Nacio Herb Brown**

Broadway Melody was the first successful "all-talking, all-singing, all-dancing" screen musical, and it won the Academy Award for best picture of 1928. It had a then-original plot of two stagestruck country girls (Bessie Love and Anita Page) trying to carve out careers on the Broadway stage. Vaudeville star Charles King appeared as the romantic lead. It also introduced the songwriting team of Nacio Herb Brown and Arthur Freed. Their score struck pay dirt with several hits: "Broadway Melody," "The Wedding of the Painted Doll," and "You Were Meant for Me."

The title number, "Broadway Melody," was introduced by Charles King. Gene Kelly sang it in the 1952 movie musical *Singin' in the Rain*.

Deep Night
COMPOSER: **Charlie Henderson**
LYRICIST: **Rudy Vallee**

"Deep night, stars in the sky above . . . deep in the arms of love" was introduced and popularized by Rudy Vallee. Vallee's appeal could sell love songs like "Deep Night," "I'm Just a Vagabond Lover," and "My Time Is Your Time."

Variety selected this Vallee specialty for its "Fifty Year Hit Parade."

Great Day
COMPOSER: **Vincent Youmans**
LYRICISTS: **Billy Rose and Edward Eliscu**

"Great Day" is a supercharged revival number that was introduced by the Jubilee Singers in the musical of the same name. This hymn to the "power of positive thinking" remained popular through the next several years. The people who lived during the Great Depression needed to hear, "When you're down and out/Lift up your head and shout/'There's gonna be a great day.' "

Happy Days Are Here Again
COMPOSER: **Milton Ager**
LYRICIST: **Jack Yellen**

Milton Ager and Jack Yellen wrote "Happy Days" for *Chasing Rainbows,* a screen musical. It was used in a scene in which World War I soldiers first receive the news that the war has ended.

Before the film was released, the writers published the song and took it to George Olsen for his orchestra. As fate would have it, Olsen introduced the song on "Black Tuesday," the day the stock market collapsed. It became the national anthem of those ruined by the crash and helped shore up the spirits of multitudes over the next several years of the Depression.

During the 1932 presidential election Franklin D. Roosevelt used it as his campaign song to underscore the promise of better times to come with a new administration. It has since been the unofficial anthem of the Democratic party and was used by Harry Truman and John F. Kennedy in their presidential campaigns.

The song was revived by Barbra Streisand in 1963. Her slow rendition of the normally fast tune helped bring her national recognition.

In 1963 ASCAP selected "Happy Days Are Here Again" as one of sixteen numbers on its "All-Time Hit Parade."

Honeysuckle Rose
COMPOSER: **Fats Waller**
LYRICIST: **Andy Razaf**

"Honeysuckle Rose" was introduced in a revue at Connie's Inn, a New York nightclub. It later was popularized on radio and through a recording by Paul Whiteman and his orchestra. Country singing star Willie Nelson successfully revived the song in 1980. In 1981 it was the title of a movie that starred Nelson.

If I Had a Talking Picture of You
COMPOSER: **Ray Henderson**
LYRICISTS: **Buddy De Sylva and Lew Brown**

The De Sylva, Brown, and Henderson team left Broadway for Hollywood in 1929. Their first assignment there was the screen musical *Sunny Side Up,* starring Janet Gaynor and Charles Farrell. Important songs from the score include "Aren't We All?," "Keep Your Sunny Side Up," and "If I Had a Talking Picture of You."

Since we have home movies and video cassette recorders, this song seems a bit outdated but the twenties were tremendously fascinated by the technological advances that had made the talking motion picture a reality.

I Guess I'll Have to Change My Plan
COMPOSER: **Arthur Schwartz**
LYRICIST: **Howard Dietz**

This casual acceptance of the end of a love affair was introduced by the great character actor Clifton Webb in the intimate revue *The Little Show* (see "Moanin' Low," below). It seems he has discovered that his lover is married. At first he is determined to call off the affair, change his plan as it were, but later in the song he changes his plan again as he decides it might be fun having an affair with someone who is married.

I Kiss Your Hand, Madame
COMPOSER: **Ralph Erwin**
LYRICISTS: **Sam M. Lewis and Joe Young**

"I Kiss Your Hand, Madame" originated in Europe. With English lyrics, the American version was introduced and popularized by Rudy Vallee. It became Lanny Ross's theme song on his Campbell soup radio show during the thirties. Bing Crosby sang it in the 1948 movie musical *The Emperor Waltz.*

"I Kiss Your Hand, Madame" was included in *Variety's* "Fifty Year Hit Parade" for 1928.

I'm Just a Vagabond Lover
COMPOSER-LYRICISTS: **Leon Zimmerman and Rudy Vallee**

Rudy Vallee introduced this song on radio and in a best-selling recording. He sang it in the film musical *Glorifying the American Girl,* which starred Mary Eaton, Eddie Cantor, and Helen Morgan. The success of the song led to the filming of another movie musical entitled *The Vagabond Lover* (also 1929), in which Vallee starred. The song was the object of several plagiarism suits, all of which were discredited.

Variety selected this song for inclusion in its "Fifty Year Hit Parade."

Indian Love Call
See page 28 (1924).

Liza
COMPOSER: **George Gershwin**
LYRICIST: **Ira Gershwin**

This minstrel number was sung by Nick Lucas and danced by Ruby Keeler and the chorus in the Gershwins' musical *Show Girl.* The show was, in a way, a jazzy version of 1920's *Sally* about a pretty, unknown girl who climbs to stardom. The hit that has outlived the show was "Liza."

A hundred beautiful girls were seated on steps that covered the entire stage. Ruby Keeler came dancing down the flight of stairs. At the opening performance in Boston, Al Jolson, who had recently married Miss Keeler, stood up from the audience and began singing the song. The incident received much publicity and helped the musical's box office.

Louise
COMPOSER: **Richard A. Whiting**
LYRICIST: **Leo Robin**

Maurice Chevalier, the debonair French entertainer, made his American stage debut in the last midnight revue produced by Florenz Ziegfeld on the roof of the New Amsterdam Theater in 1929. His bow on the American screen took place in 1929's *Innocents of Paris,* in which he introduced "Louise." His jaunty air, charm, and sex appeal immediately made him famous in America. He is particularly associated with two songs: "Louise" and 1932's "Mimi."

"Louise" was chosen for *Variety's* "Fifty Year Hit Parade."

Moanin' Low
COMPOSER: **Ralph Rainger**
LYRICIST: **Howard Dietz**

Torch singer Libby Holman, impersonating a mulatto, premiered "Moanin' Low" in *The Little Show.* The scene was a dingy, shabby tenement apartment. After rousing her lover (Clifton Webb) from a drunken stupor, the girl brings him to his feet, and they perform a sultry dance to the song. At the end of the number he strangles her.

"Moanin' Low" was included in *Variety's* "Fifty Year Hit Parade."

More Than You Know
COMPOSER: **Vincent Youmans**
LYRICISTS: **Billy Rose and Edward Eliscu**

"More Than You Know," a song of obsessive ardor, was introduced by Mayo Methot in the musical *Great Day.* The show was a failure, but Youmans was in top musical form. "More Than You Know" has become a standard and is particularly associated with Jane Froman because of her outstanding performances of the song.

Variety selected the song to be included in its "Fifty Year Hit Parade."

My Time Is Your Time
COMPOSER: **H. M. Tennant (using the pen name Leo Dance)**
LYRICIST: **R. S. Hooper (using the pen name Eric Little)**

Rudy Vallee's theme song, which he adopted for his first radio broadcast, is "My Time Is Your Time." It was an English song Vallee had heard in London in 1925 and to which he had secured the American rights. He had been expected to choose "Deep Night" or "I'm a Vagabond Lover" as his theme since he was already identified with both, but he picked "My Time Is Your Time" because he wanted to portray the feeling that he was "here to entertain you for the course of an hour."

Pagan Love Song
COMPOSER: **Nacio Herb Brown**
LYRICIST: **Arthur Freed**

"Pagan Love Song," the theme song for the movie *The Pagan*, was introduced by Ramon Novarro. Bob Hope used this piece in his debut act in vaudeville in New York at Proctor's Eighty-sixth Street Theater in 1929. He sang it straight, not comically, and, according to the *Variety* reviewer, performed it well.

The lyrics urge us to come away to Tahiti, where we can sing the "Pagan Love Song" to each other.

Singin' in the Rain
COMPOSER: **Nacio Herb Brown**
LYRICIST: **Arthur Freed**

Once again the team of Brown and Freed collaborated to produce a standard: "Singin' in the Rain." It was introduced by Cliff ("Ukulele Ike") Edwards in a film musical, *Hollywood Revue of 1929*. It has been revived several times in films, including Judy Garland's interpolation in 1940's *Little Nellie Kelly*. By far the most famous rendition came in the 1952 film *Singin' in the Rain* in an unforgettable performance by Gene Kelly. *That's Entertainment* saluted this song and Kelly's performance by highlighting it in this film cavalcade of great song-and-dance numbers from motion-picture musicals.

"Singin' in the Rain" was picked for *Variety's* "Fifty Year Hit Parade."

S'posin'
COMPOSER: **Paul Denniker**
LYRICIST: **Andy Razaf**

Rudy Vallee's first recording success came with "S'posin'," a contraction of the word *supposing*. The lyrics ask what would happen if . . . and conclude with the statement "I'm not s'posin', I'm in love with you."

Star Dust
COMPOSER: **Hoagy Carmichael**
LYRICIST: **Mitchell Parish**

Composer Hoagy Carmichael made a return visit to his alma mater, the University of Indiana, and during the nostalgic trip found himself at the "spooning wall." As he sat there, he reminisced about a college coed he had loved and lost. A melody suddenly came to mind, and he rushed to the nearest piano to write it down before he forgot it. A former fellow student and lyricist for Carmichael's "Georgia on My Mind," Stuart Gorrell, dubbed the piece "Star Dust" because he said "it sounded like dust from the stars drifting down through the summer sky."

The first version was a piano instrumental in a fast tempo. Don Redman and his orchestra introduced the fast version, but to mediocre success. An arranger, Jimmy Dale, was responsible for suggesting its appeal as a sentimental piece with a slow tempo. In this format, the song was presented in recordings by Isham Jones and his orchestra and by Emile Seidel and his orchestra with the composer, Hoagy Carmichael, at the piano.

At the insistence of publisher Irving Mills, lyrics were written for the melody by staff writer Mitchell Parish. The introduction of "Star Dust" with lyrics came at the Cotton Club in New York in 1929.

During the thirties the song was played by numerous bands and sung by many singers, until it became a standard through Artie Shaw's 1940 recording, which sold more than 2 million copies. Since then it has become one of the most recorded songs of all time (more than 1,000 American disc versions in at least forty-six different arrangements). It has been translated into at least forty different languages. It was revived by Billy Ward in 1957 in a hit single.

In 1963 "Star Dust" was selected as one of sixteen in the "ASCAP All-Time Hit Parade," one of five songs from the twenties and one of two from 1929 (see "Happy Days Are Here Again," page 47) to make this prestigious list.

Tip Toe Through the Tulips
COMPOSER: **Joe Burke**
LYRICIST: **Al Dubin**

The movie musical *Gold Diggers of Broadway* introduced "Tip Toe Through the Tulips." The song was revived in the late sixties by the unusual Tiny Tim into a best-selling record. Anyone who has heard Tiny Tim's rendition probably has a strange impression of the song, but it was not taken that way in its original 1920s form.

"Tip Toe" was selected by *Variety* for its "Fifty Year Hit Parade."

Why Was I Born?
COMPOSER: Jerome Kern
LYRICIST: Oscar Hammerstein II

Sweet Adeline was Kern and Hammerstein's attempt to duplicate the success of their incredible 1927 musical *Show Boat*. Although it was not as successful, it was a worthy show, full of flair, wit, and abundant melody. Described as "a musical romance of the Gay Nineties," it had a backstage setting, a heroine who becomes a singing star, and a hit torch song: "Why Was I Born?" The number is a carbon copy in tone and in theme of "Can't Stop Lovin' Dat Man" from *Show Boat*. Helen Morgan, the tragic Julie in *Show Boat,* was the star of *Sweet Adeline*. The title of the show, of course, comes from the 1903 sentimental ballad that is associated with barbershop quartets.

"Why Was I Born?," a poignant song of despair, became associated with Morgan after her introduction, but it also became a part of the tragic lives of blues singer Billie Holiday and Judy Garland.

Variety selected "Why Was I Born?" for its "Fifty Year Hit Parade."

With a Song in My Heart
COMPOSER: Richard Rodgers
LYRICIST: Lorenz Hart

The Rodgers and Hart score for *Spring Is Here* was outstanding, but the show lasted for only a disappointing 104 performances. The most enduring item from the score is "With a Song in My Heart," which was sung by John Hundley, who played Stacy, the losing suitor. Rarely has such a beautiful song gone to anyone but the hero or heroine.

Richard Rodgers conceived the basic idea for the song while he was visiting Jules Glaenzer's estate in Westhampton, Long Island. When Rodgers returned to the city, he composed the melody and presented it at a party at Glaenzer's city apartment.

The song was such a favorite of Jane Froman's that it became her theme song and the title of her screen biography.

Without a Song
COMPOSER: Vincent Youmans
LYRICISTS: Billy Rose and Edward Eliscu

"Without a Song," a powerful and emotional affirmation of the force of music in our lives, was introduced by baritone Lois Deppe and Russell Wooding's Jubilee Singers in the musical *Great Day*.

Variety selected this song for its "Fifty Year Hit Parade."

You Do Something to Me
COMPOSER-LYRICIST: Cole Porter

Cole Porter's second hit song came from *Fifty Million Frenchmen*. His first stage success was *Paris*, and this, his second musical success, was also set in Paris. (Porter continued this love affair with the city of light through his entire career.) The public usually left the theater singing the lovers' duet, "You Do Something to Me." Introduced by Peter (played by William Gaxton) and Looloo (played by Genevieve Tobin), the song has been one of Porter's many lasting successes.

Variety selected the song for its "Fifty Year Hit Parade."

You Were Meant for Me
COMPOSER: Nacio Herb Brown
LYRICIST: Arthur Freed

Broadway Melody, the Oscar-winning best picture of 1929, introduced "You Were Meant for Me" (see "Broadway Melody," page 47). In the film, a vaudeville act, loosely based on the Duncan Sisters, is split because the sisters love the same man. Charles King played the man in the middle. He was fortunate enough to introduce this popular song standard.

T · H · E
DEPRESSION YEARS: 1930 to 1934

The stock market crash on Black Tuesday, October 29, 1929, was the start of the Great Depression. During the early thirties every aspect of life, including popular music, was affected by the grave economic slump.

The twenties were a time to laugh, sing, and dance—an era hellbent on seeking fun. The thirties were a hell: a time of epidemic unemployment, dust storms, soup kitchens and breadlines, FDR, the NRA and WPA, living in shanties, scavenging for bits of food, facing eviction for not paying the rent, and lining shoes with cardboard to make them last longer. It was the time of Roosevelt's New Deal, which tried to cure the nation's economic ills.

The United States desperately needed a lift of spirit. For most people, the lift came in the popular songs of the day. The music and lyrics of the decade reflect the attitudes of the people and often comment on their social, economic, and political concerns.

The Musical Theater of the Thirties

The musicals of the thirties were decidedly different from those of the twenties. The Broadway stage began to show its ability to comment on the issues of the day. A lyric, a melody, a dance, or a bit of comedy could make stronger and more effective comments than any other form of theater because of the wide appeal of musical theater. Not all the musicals of the decade were satirical or thought-provoking, though; the theater was still capable of evenings that were escapes from reality, something the Depression generation desperately needed.

The satirical, intelligent musicals of the era were represented by George and Ira Gershwin's *Strike Up the Band* (1930) and *Of Thee I Sing* (1931) and by Irving Berlin's *As Thousands Cheer* (1933). More traditional subjects, such as show business, love, marriage, divorce, and college life, were still used for musical comedies, which contained more dance routines than before, dances that featured the fleet feet of Fred Astaire and Ginger Rogers (and their contemporaries).

The stage produced some of the best popular music of the era with hits like 1930's "I Got Rhythm," "Embraceable You," and "Body and Soul"; 1931's "Dancing in the Dark"; 1932's "April in Paris" and "Night and Day"; 1933's "Smoke Gets in Your Eyes," "Easter Parade," and "Yesterdays"; and 1934's "I Get a Kick Out of You."

The quality of the songs that came from the Broadway musicals reflects the genius of the composers and lyricists producing the scores. Some of the most illustrious were George and Ira Gershwin, Cole Porter, Jerome Kern, Irving Berlin, Vernon Duke, E. Y. Harburg, Howard Dietz, and Arthur Schwartz.

The decade belonged to the clown because of people's need to laugh in the face of adversity. The clowns poked fun at war and the makers of war; they kidded politicians and governments; they pricked the upper crust and exposed the foibles of all humankind.

The musical theater of the decade tried to raise the spirits of the nation. Americans sang "On the Sunny Side of the Street," "Life Is Just a Bowl of Cherries," "Rise 'n Shine," and "Get Happy" to shore up their sagging spirits. Songs also voiced the nation's despair with "I Gotta Right to Sing the Blues" and "Brother, Can You Spare a Dime?"

But the theater suffered during the Depression because people could not afford to attend productions. Other media could produce cheaper escapist entertainment.

The Cheapest Form of Entertainment

Radio was the most important entertainment medium of the decade. People could not afford to go out, so they sat at home and got music by twirling the radio dial. Therefore, many hit songs were made through exposure on the radio programs as sung or played by radio personalities. Important radio stars included Eddie Cantor, Jack Benny, Will Rogers, Fred Allen, Kate Smith, Bing Crosby, Ed Wynn, Lanny Ross, Fanny Brice, Jessica Dragonette, Rudy Vallee, Will Osborne, Russ Columbo, Morton Downey, Arthur Tracy, Maurice Chevalier, Gene Autry, and the Boswell Sisters. Bands that were popular on radio were those of Ben Bernie, Wayne King, Guy Lombardo, Fred Waring, and Paul Whiteman.

Radio could disseminate music to hundreds of thousands of listeners and make a hit overnight, but it also shortened the lives of hits. The public grew tired of hearing the songs over and over again.

The Record and Sheet Music Industry

Record and sheet music sales fell off drastically during the Depression. In the twenties a hit song would have sold between 750,000 and 1 million copies of sheet music. During the early thirties the maximum sheet music sale was about half a million. The industry never really recovered. Also, the publishers did not seem to be able to print the hits fast enough to keep up with the public's fancy now that radio made and killed hits so quickly.

Record sales were similarly affected. Where an international hit had sold between 1 million and 1.5 million discs, during the early thirties a big sale was about 25,000 records. In 1934 lower-priced records by popular entertainers entered the marketplace. Not until the end of the decade did record sales become an important part of the popular music industry again.

Dance Bands of the Early Thirties

Several dance bands emerged during the early thirties, and most continued into the swing era, which started in 1935. Joining the bands of the jazz age were those of Henry Busse, Hal Kemp, Glen Gray, Wayne King, Guy Lombardo, Will Osborne, Ted Weems, and Gus Arnheim.

These bands featured sweet, danceable music, generally not hot jazz. Jazz was kept alive by the black bands, like that of Fletcher Henderson. It was dormant, waiting for the nation to emerge from its economic doldrums.

People could not afford to go out, so the most successful bands were employed in radio or movies. Other bands merely survived with a fierce determination to wait for brighter days.

Movie Musicals

Motion pictures became even more important during the thirties than in the twenties. The screen burst with a plethora of musicals. The cinema offered people a chance to dream and fantasize. The songs from these escapist movie musicals are some of the decade's most enduring hits.

Starring in these classic movie musicals were Dick Powell, Ruby Keeler, Bing Crosby, Alice Faye, Shirley Temple, Maurice Chevalier, and especially Fred Astaire and Ginger Rogers.

The movie musical of the thirties used dance as it had never been seen before. Fred Astaire and Ginger Rogers emerged as the king and queen of the movie musicals. In films like *Flying Down to Rio* and *The Gay Divorcée,* their dancing was elegant. Several of their most famous films together came after 1934, but during the Depression they established themselves as the greatest dance team since Vernon and Irene Castle.

The Motion Picture Academy of Arts and Sciences had been giving screen awards since 1929. The name Oscar was concocted in 1931. But awards for a song were not made until 1934, when the first award went to "The Continental" from *The Gay Divorcée.*

Other hits from movies of the Depression years include "Beyond the Blue Horizon," "Three Little Words," "Cuban Love Song," "Forty-second Street," "Shuffle Off to Buffalo," "You're Getting to Be a Habit with Me," "Paradise," "Carioca," "It's Only a Paper Moon," "Let's Fall in Love," "Lover," "Shadow Waltz," "We're in the Money," "Temptation," "All I Do Is Dream of You," "I Only Have Eyes for You," "June in January," and "Stay as Sweet as You Are."

The major hits of the Depression years were basically as difficult to determine as were the ones of the twenties. The primary sources for those that should be included continued to be the same ones that were used in the twenties: *Variety*'s "Fifty Year Hit Parade" and "Golden 100 Tin Pan Alley Songs" lists; ASCAP's All-Time Hit Parade selections; plus, in 1934, the Academy Award-winning song.

The ultimate symbol of these early years of the thirties may be the three little pigs singing "Who's Afraid of the Big Bad Wolf?" Somehow Americans were able to keep smiles on their faces and beat the "big bad wolf" of Depression. Some of the loveliest melodies and lyrics ever written and some of the craziest tunes and verses of all time were on the lips of the people as they pulled together to overcome the dark days of the Depression.

1 9 3 0

Betty Co-Ed
COMPOSER-LYRICISTS: **J. Paul Fogarty and Rudy Vallee**

Not all college classics are on library shelves. This collegiate song was popularized by Rudy Vallee on his radio show and on an RCA Victor recording. The twenties' fascination with college life was still prevalent.

"Betty Co-ed is loved by every college boy,/But I'm the one who's loved by Betty Co-ed," say the lyrics. Betty's lips are red for Harvard, her eyes are Navy blue, and her hair is gold for Princeton.

The song was on the sound track of a 1946 film by the same name that starred Jean Porter, Shirley Mills, and William Mason.

Beyond the Blue Horizon
COMPOSER: **Richard A. Whiting**
LYRICIST: **Leo Robin**

This *Variety* "Fifty Year Hit Parade" song was introduced by Jeanette MacDonald in the movie *Monte Carlo.* MacDonald sang the song, which is about looking forward to the future, in a private compartment of a train. As the train moves along, shots out the window show peasants working in the fields and harmonizing with the song. Such was Hollywood's license for romantic unreality during the period.

MacDonald revived the song in the 1944 film *Follow the Boys*.

Bidin' My Time

COMPOSER: George Gershwin
LYRICIST: Ira Gershwin

This ensemble number from the stage musical *Girl Crazy* was introduced by a hillbilly quartet. The vocal style made the song amusing, and the intriguing lyrics of the verse quote popular song titles or phrases (for example, "singing in the rain," "swingin' down the lane," "cryin' for the Carolines," "tip toe through the tulips"). The song came in and out of the score during set changes.

The chorus lyrics sing about a guy who just sits around waiting for something to happen. For one thing, he doesn't get into trouble if he simply sits there "Bidin' [his] Time."

Body and Soul

COMPOSER: John Green
LYRICISTS: Edward Heyman, Robert Sour, and Frank Eyton

This song had been a hit in Europe in 1930 before it came to the United States, where it became a top song in 1931 and was later selected by *Variety* for its "Fifty Year Hit Parade." "Body and Soul" was written especially for Gertrude Lawrence, who sang it on British radio. Bert Ambrose, a major London bandleader, heard the broadcast and secured the song for his band to play and record. The exposure by Ambrose helped make it a hit in Britain. Max Gordon, a Broadway producer, then bought American rights for his revue *Three's a Crowd*, in which it was sung by torch singer Libby Holman and danced by Clifton Webb and Tamara Geva.

"Body and Soul" has become a classic popular song, as shown by its selection to *Variety's* "Golden 100 Tin Pan Alley Songs" list. It was a million-selling recording by jazz great Coleman Hawkins in 1939.

But Not for Me

COMPOSER: George Gershwin
LYRICIST: Ira Gershwin

Another song introduced by Ginger Rogers (see "Embraceable You," below), this sophisticated blues proved to be a lasting contribution from *Girl Crazy*. The lyrics speak of all the good things that can happen but aren't happening for the singer, especially getting the guy she wants. It has appeared in numerous films since its introduction, and when Ella Fitzgerald recorded it for the sound track of the Clark Gable film *But Not for Me*, she received a Grammy for the best female solo vocal performance of 1959.

Cheerful Little Earful

COMPOSER: Harry Warren
LYRICISTS: Ira Gershwin and Billy Rose

Harry Warren wrote the melody to an Ira Gershwin and Billy Rose lyric for the revue *Sweet and Low*. It was introduced by Hannah Williams, whose performance brought her at least temporary fame prior to her marriage to prizefighter Jack Dempsey.

And what is the "cheerful little earful"? It's that "well known 'I love you.'"

Dancing on the Ceiling

COMPOSER: Richard Rodgers
LYRICIST: Lorenz Hart

Rodgers and Hart wrote "Dancing on the Ceiling" for the Ziegfeld production *Simple Simon*, but it was dropped before the show opened in New York. Instead, it was premiered in the London musical *Evergreen* (1930). In a dream sequence, Jessie Matthews and Sonnie Hale, surrounded by the chorus, danced around a huge inverted chandelier.

Dancing with Tears in My Eyes

COMPOSER: Joe Burke
LYRICIST: Al Dubin

First performed by Rudy Vallee over the radio, this Burke and Dubin song had been written for the film *Dancing Sweeties* but had not been used. The Vallee rendition helped the song achieve hit status. This song and the previous one illustrate the thirties' fascination with dance. The reason for the tears was that the "girl in my arms isn't you."

Variety named the song to its "Fifty Year Hit Parade."

Embraceable You

COMPOSER: George Gershwin
LYRICIST: Ira Gershwin

This Gershwin standard, one of the top hits of 1930, was introduced by Ginger Rogers in her first Broadway starring role in *Girl Crazy*. The internal rhymes in the lyrics are interesting. Ira rhymes *embraceable* with *irreplaceable*, *tipsy* with *gypsy*, *charms* with *arms*, none of which is the end word of a phrase. The last words are always *you, me, you*.

These lyrics are one of four that Ira Gershwin regarded as his best. The others are "The Babbitt and the Bromide," "It Ain't Necessarily So," and "The Saga of Jenny."

Though "Embraceable You" suited perfectly the characters in *Girl Crazy*, the song had been written two years earlier for an Oriental operetta which Ziegfeld had considered but never staged. The slight Occidental sound of the melody is explained by its origin.

Girl Crazy was the 1930 Broadway season's best musical and biggest hit. In addition to introducing Ginger Rogers, the show presented another electrifying singing discovery, Ethel Merman, who went on to become Broadway's leading musical comedy star.

Exactly Like You
COMPOSER: **Jimmy McHugh**
LYRICIST: **Dorothy Fields**

This McHugh and Fields collaboration was introduced by Gertrude Lawrence and Harry Richman in *Lew Leslie's International Revue*. Incidentally, Ethel Merman sang this song, along with "Little White Lies," to audition for George Gershwin for the role in *Girl Crazy* that launched her career.

This was one of the "Golden 100 Tin Pan Alley Songs," and was chosen for *Variety*'s "Fifty Year Hit Parade," and was one of the biggest hits of 1930. The singer's prayers have finally been answered by "someone exactly like you."

Fine and Dandy
COMPOSER: **Kay Swift**
LYRICIST: **Paul James**

This title song from a Broadway show displays the optimism that became prevalent in the popular songs of the Depression. Introduced by comedian Joe Cook and Alice Boulden in *Fine and Dandy*, the song tried to promote a happy, hopeful attitude ("Even trouble has its funny side . . .").

Georgia on My Mind
COMPOSER: **Hoagy Carmichael**
LYRICIST: **Stuart Gorrell**

Hoagy Carmichael, talented composer of such hits as "Star Dust" and "The Nearness of You," first popularized this hit. Fats Waller and Frankie Laine made important recordings, while Mildred Bailey performed it often and is closely associated with it. In 1960 Ray Charles cut a million-selling disc that won the Grammy award for the best male vocal recording and the best pop single performance of the year. Country

singer Willie Nelson revived it in 1978 and won the Grammy award for the best country vocal performance, male, with his rendition, introducing the song to a new generation of listeners.

"An old sweet song keeps Georgia on my mind" is a familiar line from this Carmichael standard.

Get Happy
COMPOSER: **Harold Arlen**
LYRICIST: **Ted Koehler**

Ted Koehler set words to Harold Arlen's music and came up with a "Golden 100 Tin Pan Alley Songs" that remained popular long after the revue in which it debuted was forgotten (*9:15 Revue*). This rousing "hallelujah" song was introduced by Ruth Etting in a beach scene at the end of the first act.

During a break when Harold Arlen was a rehearsal pianist for the Vincent Youmans musical *Great Day*, he began improvising on one of the Youmans themes. Members of the cast and crew encouraged Arlen to turn his improvisation into a song.

"Get Happy" was also heard in the 1950 film musical *Summer Stock* and in Jane Froman's screen biography, *With a Song in My Heart* (1952).

I Got Rhythm
COMPOSER: **George Gershwin**
LYRICIST: **Ira Gershwin**

Ethel Merman stopped the show *Girl Crazy* with her brassy delivery of this Gershwin classic, which achieved "Golden 100 Tin Pan Alley" status and selection to *Variety*'s "Fifty Year Hit Parade." George had written the melody some years before in a slow tempo, but with these lyrics and an energetic tempo, it was a smash. When Ethel held a single note in the second chorus for sixteen measures, the audience reacted wildly and witnessed the inauguration of her reign as queen of the musical theater.

I've Got a Crush on You
COMPOSER: **George Gershwin**
LYRICIST: **Ira Gershwin**

This tune originated in the musical *Treasure Girl* (1928), introduced by Clifton Webb and Mary Hay. It was re-introduced by Gordon Smith and Doris Carson in *Strike Up the Band*. But it was soon practically forgotten. Though written as a spirited 2/4 number, a tempo that lent itself to the tongue-in-cheek humor of *Strike Up the Band*, a satire on war, "I've Got a Crush on You" has become popular in recent years as a slow ballad. Lee Wiley revived it in a slow tempo, as did Frank

Sinatra, who made one of his first successful recordings of it and interpolated it in the 1951 movie *Meet Danny Wilson*.

Little White Lies
COMPOSER-LYRICIST: **Walter Donaldson**

"Little White Lies" was probably the top hit of 1930 after "Happy Days Are Here Again." Walter Donaldson wrote it for Guy Lombardo and His Royal Canadians. Ethel Merman sang it for her audition for George Gershwin's *Girl Crazy*. Tommy Dorsey and his orchestra, with Frank Sinatra doing the vocal, had a best-selling recording, while Dick Haymes had a million-selling disc with the Four Hits and a Miss in 1948. The "little white lies" were those sighs when you said, "I love you."

Love for Sale
COMPOSER-LYRICIST: **Cole Porter**

This is one of the few songs in American popular music inspired by the "oldest profession in the world." For years radio banned the song because the words were considered wicked. Compared with the sexually explicit lyrics of songs of the eighties, "Love for Sale" seems tame. It was introduced by Kathryn Crawford and three other prostitutes in Cole Porter's *The New Yorkers*. Porter considered this song and "Begin the Beguine" his favorites. The show closed after twenty weeks of an unprofitable run because the nation was in the depths of the Depression.

The Stein Song (Maine Stein Song)
COMPOSER: **E. A. Fenstad**
LYRICIST: **Lincoln Colcord**

The University of Maine's "Stein Song" originated in 1901 as a band march. In 1910 a student at the university, A. W. Sprague, rewrote it and convinced his roommate, Lincoln Colcord, to write lyrics. For years it was the school song of the university and was virtually unknown by those not associated with the college. In 1920 NBC bought the rights to the song, which did not make much of a splash until Rudy Vallee sang it on his radio program in 1930. The collegiate rage was still in force, so the song quickly sold several thousand copies of sheet music and about half a million copies of Vallee's recording.

The 1952 film *With a Song in My Heart*, the screen biography of Jane Froman, used the "Maine Stein Song" in the sound track. *Variety* selected it for its "Fifty Year Hit Parade."

Mama Inez
COMPOSER: **Eliseo Grenet**
LYRICIST: **L. Wolfe Gilbert**

This Cuban number was one of the earliest rumba songs to be a hit in the United States. It was chosen by *Variety* for its "Fifty Year Hit Parade." Adapted from the Cuban song "Ay! Mama-Ines," it was introduced into the States by Maurice Chevalier. It was further popularized by Xavier Cugat.

My Baby Just Cares for Me
COMPOSER: **Walter Donaldson**
LYRICIST: **Gus Kahn**

Eddie Cantor introduced this song in the movie adaptation of the musical play *Whoopee*. It was written especially for the film and was not in the original Broadway score. It was also inserted into the 1932 film *Big City Blues*.

On the Sunny Side of the Street
COMPOSER: **Jimmy McHugh**
LYRICIST: **Dorothy Fields**

The second hit of *Lew Leslie's International Revue* (see "Exactly Like You," page 55), was another McHugh-Fields selection on *Variety*'s "Fifty Year Hit Parade" and *Variety*'s "Golden 100 Tin Pan Alley Songs" list. "On the Sunny Side of the Street" was introduced by Harry Richman. The lyric points out that if you walk "on the sunny side of the street," you'll have "gold dust at your feet." The "sunny side of the street" is a metaphor for optimism.

Tommy Dorsey and his band made a million-selling recording of "On the Sunny Side of the Street" in 1944. It was heard in at least seven films through the late fifties.

The Peanut Vendor
See page 61 (1931).

Something to Remember You By
COMPOSER: **Arthur Schwartz**
LYRICIST: **Howard Dietz**

"Body and Soul" and "Something to Remember You By" were the hits from the revue *Three's a Crowd*. Libby Holman, as a French girl, sang this tender good-bye to Fred MacMurray. It was among the top songs for 1931 and was chosen by *Variety* to appear on its "Fifty Year Hit Parade."

"Something to Remember You By" began in Britain, as did "Body and Soul." It was called "I Have No Words" when it was introduced as a fast fox-trot in the 1929 London musical *Little Tommy Tucker*. Even with a change in lyrics from "I Have No Words" to "Something to Remember You By," Schwartz and Dietz viewed it as a comedy number (*something* referred to a kick in the pants) until Libby Holman urged the writers to change the tempo and mood.

Fred MacMurray was still an unknown at this time, but his stage work had led to a movie contract and starring roles in films by 1935.

Strike Up the Band
COMPOSER: **George Gershwin**
LYRICIST: **Ira Gershwin**

The Gershwins' *Strike Up the Band* was the first musical political satire. Set mostly in a dream, it imagined a war between the United States and Switzerland over the earthshaking issue of tariffs on imported chocolate. The first version in 1927 was an uncompromising satire on war, big business, and politics that the twenties' mentality refused to accept. In the troubled world of the early thirties, the new version clicked. George Gershwin's score introduced a number of songs that quickly became popular standards: "I've Got a Crush on You" and the title song, "Strike Up the Band."

"Strike Up the Band" was the satirical, militaristic, first-act finale, sung by Jerry Goff and the company. One key to its success may have been Red Nichols's pit band, which included Benny Goodman, Gene Krupa, Glenn Miller, Jimmy Dorsey, and Jack Teagarden.

Ten Cents a Dance
COMPOSER: **Richard Rodgers**
LYRICIST: **Lorenz Hart**

Florenz Ziegfeld played havoc with the music of *Simple Simon*. He informed Rodgers and Hart during the Boston tryouts of the show that he needed a few more songs for Lee Morse, the female lead. So Rodgers and Hart wrote "Ten Cents a Dance" in less than an hour. The next day they found out that Lee Morse had been replaced by Ruth Etting, who then introduced it. She introduced it on top of a piano which was attached to a bicycle being pedaled by Ed Wynn. Even though this lament of a dime-a-dance ballroom hostess had little or nothing to do with the plot of *Simple Simon*, it proved to be the show's musical highlight.

Three Little Words
COMPOSER: **Harry Ruby**
LYRICIST: **Bert Kalmar**

The screen biography of Bert Kalmar and Harry Ruby was filmed in 1950 and starred Fred Astaire and Red Skelton. Entitled *Three Little Words*, it saluted one of their greatest hits.

This *Variety* "Fifty Year Hit Parade" selection was introduced by Bing Crosby (backed by Duke Ellington's orchestra) in the Amos and Andy film *Check and Double Check*, the first movie score by Kalmar and Ruby. The record by Crosby from the sound track helped the song achieve hit status. Rudy Vallee also helped by singing it on radio and recording it. Those "three little words" are, of course, the three biggest little words in our language: "I love you."

Time on My Hands
COMPOSER: **Vincent Youmans**
LYRICISTS: **Harold Adamson and Mack Gordon**

This song was introduced by Marilyn Miller and Paul Gregory in the Vincent Youmans musical *Smiles*. The lyrics say, in part, "with time on my hands and you in my arms and love in my heart all for you."

Two Hearts in Three-Quarter Time
COMPOSER: **Robert Stolz**
LYRICIST: **Joe Young**

This *Variety* "Fifty Year Hit Parade" waltz has German origins. Its German title, "Zwei Herzen im Dreivierteltakt," was also the name of the movie from which it came. The original lyrics were by W. Reisch.

Walkin' My Baby Back Home
COMPOSER-LYRICISTS: **Roy Turk, Fred E. Ahlert, and Harry Richman**

Harry Richman collaborated on, introduced, and popularized this song, which became closely identified with him. It was revived in 1952 in a best-selling recording by Johnnie Ray.

The lyrics describe some of the things that happen during a couple's old-fashioned walk, including walking arm in arm, stopping for a while, starting to pet, getting powder on his vest, "harmonizing a song, or I'm reciting a poem."

What Is This Thing Called Love?
COMPOSER-LYRICIST: **Cole Porter**

This torchy Porter ballad was introduced in *Wake Up and Dream* by Frances Shelley. Porter stated that he derived this "Golden 100 Tin Pan Alley Song" (and *Variety* "Fifty Year Hit Parade" selection) from the native dance music he heard in Marrakesh, Morocco, on one of his many trips. Porter called for a slow blues tempo in the original, but it is better known in a faster tempo. The song describes a vision of loveliness one wonderful day. It says that it is difficult to understand the mystery of love and why we do the things we do while under its spell.

When Your Hair Has Turned to Silver
COMPOSER: **Peter De Rose**
LYRICIST: **Charles Tobias**

Charles Tobias wrote the lyrics for this song in fifteen minutes after hearing Peter De Rose play the melody. Rudy Vallee's recording and his renditions on radio helped popularize it. The song sold more than 400,000 copies of sheet music, a considerable number for the Depression, when very few hits sold more than a half million copies. The lyrics reassure the loved one that even though she may be getting older, "I will love you just the same . . . I will love you as today."

You Brought a New Kind of Love to Me
COMPOSERS: **Pierre Norman and Sammy Fain**
LYRICIST: **Irving Kahal**

Maurice Chevalier introduced this *Variety* "Fifty Year Hit Parade" song in the musical movie *The Big Pond*. This was Sammy Fain's first movie song, but his songs appeared frequently in the next few years. He had songs in three films in 1933 and in nine films in 1934.

The lyrics are clever: "If the nightingales could sing like you/They'd sing much sweeter. . . . If the sandman brought me dreams of you/I'd want to sleep my whole life thru." Maurice Chevalier's rendition is a classic, remembered for his unique French-accented singing and his novel approach to a popular song.

1 9 3 1

All of Me
COMPOSER: **Gerald Marks**
LYRICIST: **Seymour Simons**

This was the theme song of the movie *Careless Lady*, which starred John Boles and Joan Bennett (1932). Frank Sinatra sang it in the film *Meet Danny Wilson* (1951) and made a recording that became one of his big sellers. The lyrics say that the loved one has taken "my heart, so why not take all of me?" As popular as this standard may be, it has never had the good fortune to be a million-selling recording. Few hits in the thirties became what is now known as a gold record. It furnished the title for a 1984 film that starred Steve Martin and Lily Tomlin.

As Time Goes By
COMPOSER-LYRICIST: **Herman Hupfeld**

Herman Hupfeld's best-remembered song was introduced by Frances Williams in the musical *Everybody's Welcome*. The lyrics champion romantic love and claim that whatever new there may be or whatever comes in the future, love will last "as time goes by." When Rudy Vallee recorded the song, it became moderately successful. When it was revived in the Humphrey Bogart classic *Casablanca* in 1942, its popularity skyrocketed and it achieved the status of a standard. Vallee's recording was rereleased and became a best seller. (A new recording could not be issued then because of an ASCAP ban on all recording.) *Variety* chose "As Time Goes By" for its list of "Golden 100 Tin Pan Alley Songs" and named it to its "Fifty Year Hit Parade" for 1943.

Cuban Love Song
COMPOSERS: **Jimmy McHugh and Herbert Stothart**
LYRICIST: **Dorothy Fields**

The first multiple recording in history was an overdubbing of Lawrence Tibbett for the sound track of the movie *Cuban Love Song*. Overdubbing did not become an important part of the recording industry until after Les Paul had made it fashionable in the late 1940s and early 1950s. Tibbett sang the song standing beside an image of his own ghost.

Without the native Cuban rhythms underneath the melody, this ¾ tune would not have a particularly exotic character. Other 1931 songs with Cuban influence were "Marta" and "The Peanut Vendor."

Variety chose "Cuban Love Song" for its "Fifty Year Hit Parade."

Dancing in the Dark
COMPOSER: Arthur Schwartz
  LYRICIST: Howard Dietz

Schwartz and Dietz's most famous hit, a *Variety* "Golden 100 Tin Pan Alley Songs" and "Fifty Year Hit Parade" listing, was introduced by John Barker in the revue *The Band Wagon*. Later in the production Tilly Losch danced to the tune on a tilted, mirrored stage, illuminated by continually changing lights. A curiosity in the lyrics is the line "We're waltzing in the wonder of why we're here," but the song is not in triple, or waltz, meter but in cut time (2/2). Artie Shaw's record ten years later sold a million copies.

Dream a Little Dream of Me
COMPOSERS: Wilber Schwandt and Fabian Andre
  LYRICS: Gus Kahn

Kate Smith featured this song on her first radio program on May 1, 1931. It is difficult to find anything distinctive about "Dream a Little Dream of Me." The melody and lyrics are so well known, and the song has been so enduringly popular that it is surprising that the tune and lyrics are not particularly novel ("say 'night-ie-night' and kiss me").

"Mama" Cass Elliott, formerly a member of The Mamas and Papas, revived the song in a solo recording in 1968.

Goodnight, Sweetheart
COMPOSER-LYRICISTS: Ray Noble, James Campbell, and Reg Connelly

Rudy Vallee introduced this *Variety* "Golden 100 Tin Pan Alley" tune on his radio show and promoted it into a best-selling recording. The Noble, Campbell, and Connelly song was featured in the 1931 edition of *Earl Carroll's Vanities*.

A year or two previously a hit song would have sold between 750,000 and 1 million copies of sheet music. But in the Depression economy of 1931 the maximum was about half a million. The only song to exceed that figure in 1931 was "Goodnight, Sweetheart," therefore, it qualifies as the top song of the year.

Heartaches
See page 131 (1947).

I Found a Million Dollar Baby
COMPOSER: Harry Warren
  LYRICISTS: Mort Dixon and Billy Rose

Billy Rose's revue *Crazy Quilt* introduced this *Variety* "Fifty Year Hit Parade" number. It was sung by Ted Healy, Phil Baker, Fanny Brice, Lew Brice, and Betty Jane Watson. The singer found the million-dollar baby in a five- and ten-cent store when he ducked in to escape an April shower.

I Love Louisa
COMPOSER: Arthur Schwartz
  LYRICIST: Howard Dietz

A second hit from *The Band Wagon* (see "Dancing in the Dark," above) was "I Love Louisa." The first-act finale in the revue, the number featured the first revolving stage in a Broadway musical. The gay Bavarian set was dominated by a merry-go-round. Part of the lyric of "I Love Louisa" is in German. The song was introduced by Fred and Adele Astaire and the company.

I Love a Parade
COMPOSER: Harold Arlen
  LYRICIST: Ted Koehler

Cab Calloway introduced this early Harold Arlen hit at the Cotton Club in Harlem. During a walk one cold day Arlen began to hum a marching tune to pep up his walking partner, lyricist Ted Koehler. It became a composer and lyricist game as they walked; they hummed and constructed lyrics respectively until by the end of the walk "I Love a Parade" was completed. The song was interpolated into the film *Manhattan Parade* (1932), which starred Winnie Lightner. *Variety* chose "I Love a Parade" for its "Fifty Year Hit Parade."

I Surrender, Dear
COMPOSER: Harry Barris
  LYRICIST: Gordon Clifford

"I Surrender, Dear" marks the start of Bing Crosby's career in the thirties. Crosby and the Rhythm Boys were fired by Paul Whiteman and joined Gus Arnheim and his orchestra in the early thirties. Crosby began doing solos, one of which was "I Surrender, Dear." The song brought him to the attention of radio executives, and his success in radio led to recordings and movies that made him a giant of the entertainment world. *Variety* chose "I Surrender, Dear" for its "Fifty Year Hit Parade."

Life Is Just a Bowl of Cherries
COMPOSER: Ray Henderson
  LYRICIST: Lew Brown

When Bing Crosby and the Boswell Sisters recorded this song, along with other hit numbers, on both sides of a twelve-inch record, it was one of the earliest attempts to reproduce the score of a Broadway musical on record. Ethel Merman had introduced this light-hearted view of life in *George White's Scandals of 1931*. Rudy Vallee's recording helped make this song a hit.

This is one of the most famous Depression philosophy songs. It reasons that one need not work and save because all can be gone in an instant. Whatever we have is a loan, so do not take life too seriously. Laugh at the mysteries of life, and don't worry too much. This Henderson and Brown standard was chosen by *Variety* for its "Fifty Year Hit Parade."

Love Is Sweeping the Country
COMPOSER: **George Gershwin**
    LYRICIST: **Ira Gershwin**

Just before a large political rally in Madison Square Garden in the Pulitzer prizewinning musical *Of Thee I Sing* (see "Of Thee I Sing," below), George Murphy, June O'Dea, and the chorus introduced this song. It was a warm-up for the appearance of presidential candidate John P. Wintergreen.

Gershwin originally intended this tune for the never-produced musical *East Is West,* which had an Oriental setting. Therefore, some parts of "Love Is Sweeping the Country" have an Eastern flavor.

Love Letters in the Sand
COMPOSER: **J. Fred Coots**
    LYRICISTS: **Nick and Charles Kenny**

Coots happened to read in the *New York Daily Mirror* a Nick Kenny poem that he immediately thought would make a great popular song. He obtained Kenny's permission to set it to music and after four different melodies composed the one we now know. Russ Columbo was the first singer to show interest in the song, which he recorded. George Hall and his orchestra further popularized the song on their fourteen broadcasts per week radio show. Hall later made it his theme song.

It was revived in 1957 into a million-selling recording by Pat Boone. He also sang it in the film *Bernardine,* (1957) in which he starred. It became the biggest hit of the year, selling almost 4 million copies.

Marta
COMPOSER: **Moises Simons**
    LYRICIST: **L. Wolfe Gilbert**

Arthur Tracy, known as The Street Singer, made this beautiful song his theme. He was a sentimental singer who achieved recognition over radio. He signed on and

off of his three-time-weekly radio show with "Marta," a Cuban song by Moises Simons, which had been given English lyrics by L. Wolfe Gilbert. It was also popularized in recordings by Roy Fox and Dick Haymes. *Variety* listed "Marta" in its "Fifty Year Hit Parade."

Minnie the Moocher
COMPOSER-LYRICISTS: **Irving Mills and Cab Calloway**

This was famed scat singer Cab Calloway's theme. Its "hi-de-ho" was his trademark. Calloway had his first shot at fame in the revue *Hot Chocolates* in 1929 but did not achieve fame until he fronted a hot band at Harlem's Cotton Club in 1931. He became famous for his frantic gyrations and for his vocals on swing and novelty numbers. Calloway recently performed "Minnie" in the 1980 film *The Blues Brothers*. He also used it in the 1932 *The Big Broadcast*.

Mood Indigo
COMPOSER: **Duke Ellington**
    LYRICISTS: **Irving Mills and Albany Bigard**

Jazz great Duke Ellington first wrote this mellow standard as an instrumental piece entitled "Dreamy Blues." The mood suggests the deep violet-blue of indigo. With lyrics and a title change it became one of Ellington's first popular hits.

Of Thee I Sing
COMPOSER: **George Gershwin**
    LYRICIST: **Ira Gershwin**

One of the greatest of all American musicals, the first musical awarded the Pulitzer Prize for drama, and the longest-running musical of the thirties was George and Ira Gershwin's *Of Thee I Sing*. The show took a barbed, witty, satirical look at American politics. Despite the Depression, the show lasted 441 performances on Broadway and had a road show tour.

"Of Thee I Sing" was John P. Wintergreen's campaign song for the presidency of the United States. It was introduced by William Gaxton and Lois Moran, who starred as Mr. and Mrs. Wintergreen.

Out of Nowhere
COMPOSER: **John Green**
    LYRICIST: **Edward Heyman**

Green and Heyman published this song as an independent number, not associated with a show or movie. This *Variety* "Fifty Year Hit Parade" selection was introduced by Guy Lombardo and His Royal Canadians. "Out of Nowhere" was Bing Crosby's first hit recording as a solo vocalist. Once the song had begun to gain in popularity, it was featured in the 1931 film *Dude Ranch.* "You came to me from out of nowhere," and if you leave and go "back to your nowhere, . . . I'll always wait for your return . . . hoping you'll bring your love to me" is the gist of the lyric.

The Peanut Vendor
COMPOSER: **Moises Simons**
  LYRICISTS: **L. Wolfe Gilbert and Marion Sunshine**

"The Peanut Vendor" was discovered by Herbert Marks, the son of the famous music publisher Edward B. Marks. Having heard it on his honeymoon in Havana, Herbert Marks learned it was written by Moises Simons, a local composer. Marks arranged to bring the song to the United States, where an English lyric was written by Louis Rittenberg. However, the publisher decided the Rittenberg lyric was unsuitable, so Marion Sunshine, who was married to the brother of Cuban bandleader Don Azpiazu, wrote a second lyric with L. Wolfe Gilbert. Azpiazu introduced the number at Keith's Palace Theater, recorded it, and promoted it into a tremendous hit, a million seller through subsequent years. One of the first Latin rhythm numbers to make the big time, it was featured in the film *Cuban Love Song* (1931).

Others who recorded "The Peanut Vendor" included Paul Whiteman, Guy Lombardo, and Xavier Cugat with their orchestras. The song was listed in *Variety*'s "Fifty Year Hit Parade" for 1930.

Penthouse Serenade
COMPOSER-LYRICISTS: **Will Jason and Val Burton**

Variety chose this song, the subtitle of which, "When We're Alone," gives a key to its character, for its "Fifty Year Hit Parade" even though it was not a monster hit for any performer. It was not among the top hits listed by *Variety* for 1931, nor was it ever a million-selling recording.

Prisoner of Love
See page 128 (1946).

River, Stay 'Way from My Door
COMPOSER: **Harry Woods**
  LYRICIST: **Mort Dixon**

Can you imagine a song being made popular by a mime? Well, this *Variety* "Fifty Year Hit Parade" song

was popularized by Jimmy Savo in a one-man mime revue, *Mum's the Word.* Savo's rendition, with accompanying pantomime, became his most famous routine.

Sleepy Time Down South
COMPOSER-LYRICISTS: **Leon and Otis Rene and Clarence Muse**

This *Variety* "Fifty Year Hit Parade" selection, sometimes entitled "When It's Sleepy Time Down South," became a speciality of Louis Armstrong. It was not, however, a million-selling record, nor was it listed by *Variety* as one of the top tunes of 1931. It is a famous tune, and Armstrong's performance was outstanding, but usually there is a more substantial reason for a song's being chosen for the "Fifty Year Hit Parade."

The lyrics sing about the "dear old Southland with its dreamy songs," and the singer wishes he could be "back there where I belong . . . When it's sleepy time down south."

Smile, Darn Ya, Smile
COMPOSER: **Max Rich**
  LYRICISTS: **Charles O'Flynn and Jack Meskill**

This *Variety* "Fifty Year Hit Parade" song became the theme of Fred Allen's radio show. This nice bit of anti-Depression philosophy in song stayed six weeks in the top ten during 1931 and peaked at number three in mid-March of the year.

The lyrics encourage the listener by saying that "Things are never black as they are painted. . . . Make life worth while/Come on and smile, darn ya, smile."

Sweet and Lovely
COMPOSER-LYRICISTS: **Gus Arnheim, Harry Tobias, and Jules Lemare**

Within a few months after its introduction by Gus Arnheim and his orchestra, "Sweet and Lovely" became one of the leading hits throughout the country. Arnheim, Harry Tobias, and Jules Lemare collaborated to write this hit while Arnheim's orchestra was appearing at the Cocoanut Grove in Los Angeles. Over the next several years it was popularized in recordings by Russ Columbo and Bing Crosby and was revived for the 1944 film *Two Girls and a Sailor,* which starred June Allyson and Van Johnson.

There is nothing distinctive about the song, but *Variety* chose it for its "Fifty Year Hit Parade." The orchestras that played it and the performers who sang it had a lot to do with its success.

Through the Years

COMPOSER: Vincent Youmans
LYRICIST: Edward Heyman

Vincent Youmans gave the title *Through the Years* to his musical play version of *Smilin' Through*. The romantic story leaps back and forth across forty-five years in the lives of Kathleen and Kenneth. In the title song, the singer is pledging her love and insists that no matter what may come the couple will stay together "through the years." Introduced by Natalie Hall, it has become a standard. Youmans often singled it out as his best song.

Time on My Hands

COMPOSER: Vincent Youmans
LYRICISTS: Harold Adamson and Mack Gordon

Smiles should have been a smash hit on Broadway in 1930. It had a Vincent Youmans score, starred Marilyn Miller and Fred and Adele Astaire, and was produced by Florenz Ziegfeld. But the show never clicked. Still, one Youmans classic, "Time on My Hands," came from the score. This beautiful "Fifty Year Hit Parade" love song was introduced by Marilyn Miller and Paul Gregory. In the show, Miller played a French waif who was adopted by three American soldiers during the war and afterward brought to the United States. Gregory played one of the young doughboys who adopted her. The singer had time on his hands and Miller in his arms and love in his heart; obviously the soldier had grown quite fond of the French waif.

The tune became the theme of *The Chase and Sanborn Hour* radio variety series. Marilyn Miller's biography featured the song as one of her specialites when *Look for the Silver Lining* was filmed in 1949.

When I Take My Sugar to Tea

COMPOSERS: Sammy Fain and Pierre Norman
LYRICIST: Irving Kahal

This cute song was interpolated in the motion picture *Monkey Business* (1931), which starred the Marx Brothers. It was also used in the 1951 film *The Mating Season*.

When the Moon Comes over the Mountain

COMPOSER-LYRICISTS: Kate Smith, Howard Johnson, and Harry Woods

This was Kate Smith's theme song, introduced on her first CBS radio show on May 1, 1931. "When the Moon Comes over the Mountain," a *Variety* "Fifty Year Hit Parade" selection, was second to "Goodnight, Sweetheart" in sheet music sales in 1931 with a sale of more than 400,000. (At the time the average hit sold around 200,000 copies.)

Kate Smith had an outstanding career, but she was most associated with her radio show and her introduction of Irving Berlin's "God Bless America" (see page 97). Her popular radio program helped many performers get their start. Abbott and Costello were boosted to fame by their appearances with Smith.

Where the Blue of the Night Meets the Gold of the Day

COMPOSER: Fred E. Ahlert
LYRICISTS: Roy Turk and Bing Crosby

This song became Bing Crosby's theme. He introduced it in his first major film role in *The Big Broadcast* (1932). Crosby used this *Variety* "Fifty Year Hit Parade" selection as the theme of his fifteen-minute radio show, which was broadcast several nights a week. In a short time the show was expanded to thirty minutes, then to sixty, and finally it became a weekly program.

You're My Everything

COMPOSER: Harry Warren
LYRICISTS: Mort Dixon and Joe Young

More than any other period the thirties belonged to the clown because people needed to laugh in the face of adversity. *The Laugh Parade,* an Ed Wynn comedy vehicle, presented one lasting hit, "You're My Everything," for the first time. Jeanne Aubert and Lawrence Gray introduced the hit in the musical.

The song has since appeared in numerous movie scores, including *You're My Everything* (1949) and *The Eddie Duchin Story* (1956).

1 9 3 2

April in Paris
COMPOSER: **Vernon Duke**
LYRICIST: **E. Y. Harburg**

Considering Cole Porter's love affair with Paris, one might guess that he wrote this song, but it was written instead by Vernon Duke and E. Y. Harburg for the Broadway revue *Walk a Little Faster*. The revue would have been forgotten had it not presented "April in Paris." The song describes the atmosphere of Paris in the spring: "chestnuts in blossom, holiday tables under the trees." The vocalist sings that he "never knew the charm of spring . . . never knew my heart could sing . . . till April in Paris."

This was Duke's first complete Broadway score. Evelyn Hoey introduced the song with laryngitis so bad she could barely be heard. For that reason or others, the song caught on slowly, but it became a classic, perhaps Duke's most famous song. *Variety* selected it as a "Golden 100 Tin Pan Alley Song" and for its "Fifty Year Hit Parade," and it was one of 1933's top three songs.

Brother, Can You Spare a Dime?
COMPOSER: **Jay Gorney**
LYRICIST: **E. Y. Harburg**

Sung by Rex Weber standing in a breadline in a scene in *New Americana,* this song became a theme for the Depression years. The lyrics illustrate Harburg's social consciousness, but they are slightly tongue-in-cheek. Bing Crosby helped popularize the song, and the nation quickly empathized with it. Because its lyrics spoke of a problem that was on the mind of every person, it probably would have been a hit regardless of who had sung it. It was chosen for *Variety*'s "Fifty Year Hit Parade."

Eadie Was a Lady
COMPOSERS: **Richard A. Whiting and Nacio Herb Brown**
LYRICIST: **Buddy De Sylva**

"Eadie Was a Lady," a narrative song, was written for Ethel Merman to sing in *Take a Chance*. The song had been salvaged from the flop show *Humpty Dumpty* (see "Rise 'n Shine," page 66) and was inserted for Merman when a song about drugs ("Poppy Smoke")

was dropped because of similarities to "Smokin' Reefers" from the already opened *Flying Colors*. In the lyrics Merman was mourning the death of a fellow prostitute, Eadie.

Forty-second Street
COMPOSER: **Harry Warren**
LYRICIST: **Al Dubin**

Broadway did not see *Forty-second Street* until 1981, but the 1932 original was a movie musical about backstage life on Broadway. Ruby Keeler and Dick Powell, a new song-and-dance team, were introduced in the film, and Keeler first performed the title number, a *Variety* "Fifty Year Hit Parade" selection. In addition to "Forty-second Street," the most popular songs were "Shuffle Off to Buffalo" and "You're Getting to Be a Habit with Me."

Forty-second Street started a movie musical renaissance that led to some of Hollywood's most triumphant musical successes. Depression movie audiences needed exactly what *Forty-second Street* offered: escapist entertainment that projected a little hope for the future into their lives.

What is so special about this street that a film would be named for it? New York's theater district centers on Broadway between Forty-second and Fiftieth streets. As the title song says, the street was filled with happy, dancing feet.

How Deep Is the Ocean?
COMPOSER-LYRICIST: **Irving Berlin**

Irving Berlin did not allow this song to be published for several years because he did not feel it was worthy. However, once it had been published, it became one of 1932's leading songs and was chosen for *Variety*'s "Fifty Year Hit Parade" and as a "Golden 100 Tin Pan Alley Song." The lyrics are full of rhetorical questions that reflect the vastness of love.

I Gotta Right to Sing the Blues
COMPOSER: **Harold Arlen**
LYRICIST: **Ted Koehler**

Although this song could be considered a commercial blues number, it has an authentic blues style. It was interpolated into *Earl Carroll's Vanities of 1932* by

Lillian Shade. Critics applauded several now-forgotten songs and practically overlooked this one, the only one that has survived. People easily empathized with its down-and-out feeling in Depression-weary 1932. It soon became Jack Teagarden's theme song and was one of Billie Holiday's most famous numbers.

I'm Getting Sentimental over You
COMPOSER: **George Bassman**
LYRICIST: **Ned Washington**

"I'm Getting Sentimental over You" was first popularized by the Dorsey brothers' band in 1932. After the brothers had split in 1935, it became the theme for Tommy Dorsey, "the Sentimental Gentleman of Swing" and his orchestra. Dorsey's recording sold at least half a million.

In a Shanty in Old Shanty Town
COMPOSER-LYRICISTS: **Joe Young, John Siras and Little Jack Little**

Radio star Little Jack Little collaborated with Joe Young and John Siras on this song, then introduced it. It was particularly popular as a Depression song that says poverty or a broken-down house does not exclude happiness and love. It was, along with "Paradise," the top song of 1932. Johnny Long revived it in 1940 and had a best-selling recording. *Variety* honored it by choosing it for its "Fifty Year Hit Parade."

It Don't Mean a Thing
COMPOSER: **Duke Ellington**
LYRICIST: **Irving Mills**

Duke Ellington originally wrote this tune as an instrumental. Later Irving Mills added the lyrics. It is one of the earliest uses in popular music of the term *swing,* which was to be the byword of most popular music of the late thirties and early forties. The lyrics insist that what makes a tune complete is not the melody, "it ain't the music,/There's something else. . . ." It's the rhythm that makes the song swing, and without it, "it don't mean a thing."

I've Got the World on a String
COMPOSER: **Harold Arlen**
LYRICIST: **Ted Koehler**

Aida Ward introduced "I've Got the World on a String" at the Cotton Club in Harlem. *Variety* selected the song for its "Golden 100 Tin Pan Alley Song" list. It is a good example of lyrics of the era which try to convince people that life is great.

I've Told Every Little Star
COMPOSER: **Jerome Kern**
LYRICIST: **Oscar Hammerstein II**

Jerome Kern claimed to have heard the basic melody for this number in the song of a finch. With words by Oscar Hammerstein II, this *Variety* "Fifty Year Hit Parade" love song was introduced by Walter Slezak in the musical *Music in the Air* as part of a choral society recital. A timid suitor asks why he has told everybody and everything of his love except the one he loves.

Just an Echo in the Valley
COMPOSER-LYRICISTS: **Harry Woods, Jimmy Campbell, and Reg Connelly**

Bing Crosby introduced this *Variety* "Fifty Year Hit Parade" selection in the movie musical *Going Hollywood.* According to *Variety,* it was the top song of the land for three weeks and stayed among the top ten for more than four months in 1932.

Let's Have Another Cup o' Coffee
COMPOSER-LYRICIST: **Irving Berlin**

As they dined at an Automat, Katherine Carrington and J. Harold Murray introduced this Berlin song in the musical *Face the Music.* The lyrics are a skillful compilation of chin-up clichés.

After a long dry period (see 1927's "The Song Is Ended," page 41) Berlin produced an excellent score for *Face the Music.* Perhaps part of Berlin's genius lay in his ability to mirror musically the decades in which he wrote. His pre-twenties style is different from his 1920s work, and his music and lyrics for the thirties are again different. The more subdued atmosphere of the thirties is reflectd in the tenuous melodic lines and subtler chord structure of his new style.

Let's Put Out the Lights and Go to Bed
COMPOSER-LYRICIST: **Herman Hupfeld**

This *Variety* "Fifty Year Hit Parade" song was a Depression favorite. When Rudy Vallee introduced the number at the Atlantic City Steel Pier, he was amazed that the audience burst into more than usual enthusiastic applause. When he used it on his radio program, the network insisted that he change the word *bed* to *sleep,* and it is best known that way. It has been suggested that the song was so popular because the people of Depression America indeed did not have money to go out, so they were simply turning out the lights at home and going to bed.

A Little Street Where Old Friends Meet
COMPOSER: **Harry Woods**
LYRICIST: **Gus Kahn**

This *Variety* "Fifty Year Hit Parade" song was introduced by Freddie Berrens and his orchestra. According to *Variety*, it was the nation's top song during the late summer of 1932 for more than a month and stayed among the top ten hits for more than four months.

Louisiana Hayride
COMPOSER: **Arthur Schwartz**
LYRICIST: **Howard Dietz**

This song was the jubilant first-act finale of the revue *Flying Colors*. A huge hay wagon was backed up to a moving projection of a country road. Clifton Webb, Tamara Geva, and the chorus introduced the *Variety* "Fifty Year Hit Parade" number.

Lullaby of the Leaves
COMPOSER: **Bernice Petkere**
LYRICIST: **Joe Young**

This *Variety* "Fifty Year Hit Parade" selection was popularized by Connee Boswell with Victor Young and his orchestra. According to *Variety*'s list of top hits of 1932, "Lullaby of the Leaves" was one of the top ten hits for about five months, peaking at number two in May and June.

Masquerade
COMPOSER: **John Jacob Loeb**
LYRICIST: **Paul Francis Webster**

"Masquerade" is a *Variety* "Fifty Year Hit Parade" waltz which Paul Whiteman conducted at its introduction at the Lewisohn Stadium concerts in New York City. It is difficult not to confuse 1932's "Masquerade" with 1939's "The Masquerade Is Over," but the 1939 song is not a waltz. More confusion is possible because of George Benson's 1976 recording of "This Masquerade," a Leon Russell song that became the Grammy winner as Record of the Year.

According to *Variety,* "Masquerade" stayed among the top ten hits of 1932 for fourteen weeks, peaking at number two in early summer.

Mimi
COMPOSER: **Richard Rodgers**
LYRICIST: **Lorenz Hart**

The debonair Maurice Chevalier introduced this Rodgers and Hart song in the movie musical *Love Me Tonight.* He revived it in the film *A New Kind of Love*

in 1963. The song is so closely associated with Chevalier that it is difficult to imagine its being sung without his distinctive French inflections.

My Silent Love
COMPOSER: **Dana Suesse**
LYRICIST: **Edward Heyman**

This melody for "My Silent Love" was adapted from Dana Suesse's instrumental "Jazz Nocturne." This song was among the top half dozen most popular songs for 1932 (because *Variety* and *Billboard* were not charting the hits as they did in the forties, it is difficult to determine the exact position). The singer wishes he could reveal his "silent love."

Night and Day
COMPOSER-LYRICIST: **Cole Porter**

Cole Porter wrote "Night and Day" for Fred Astaire's very limited vocal range. Fred, sans his sister, Adele, for the first time, was starring in Porter's *Gay Divorce.* Porter said that his inspiration was Muslim calls to prayer in Morocco. The song proved so popular that the show's box-office success was probably directly attributable to it.

"Night and Day" defies some of Tin Pan Alley's songwriting taboos. The introduction is built on a rhythmic variation of a two-note minor-key motif. When the chorus begins and the lyrics shift from meditative to cheery, the song shifts to the major key, which gives it a lighter air. The chorus is also not the typical thirty-two-bar AABA formula but instead is forty-eight measures.

Tommy Dorsey and his orchestra, with Frank Sinatra on the vocal, had an important recording of this song in the early forties. It was one of sixteen songs included by ASCAP in its "All-time Hit Parade" and was also a *Variety* "Fifty Year Hit Parade" and "Golden 100 Tin Pan Alley Song." Along with "Lazybones," "Smoke Gets in Your Eyes," and "Stormy Weather," it was one of 1933's most popular songs.

Paradise
COMPOSER-LYRICISTS: **Gordon Clifford and Nacio Herb Brown**

This waltz was the theme of the nonmusical motion picture *A Woman Commands.* It became one of the theme songs of Russ Columbo, was one of the two top songs of 1932, and was chosen by *Variety* for its "Fifty Year Hit Parade." The humming (actually "bumming," in the case of Columbo's recording) built into the melody for "Paradise" is very unusual and takes up a considerable part of the first (A) theme. After a repeat of the primary theme, the singer whistles instead of hums.

Bing Crosby is the singer who is famous for his buh-buh-buhs, but Columbo may have invented them. At that time, Crosby, Columbo, and Vallee were the three top male singers, and Crosby and Columbo sounded remarkably alike. Many people have speculated how Columbo would have fared had he not met a tragic accidental death in 1934.

Please
COMPOSER: **Ralph Rainger**
LYRICIST: **Leo Robin**

This was one of the songs with which Bing Crosby made his debut in a full-length movie, *The Big Broadcast*. It was also the song in which his buh-buh-buhs first became popular. (See "Paradise," above, for more about Crosby's buh-buh-buhs.) This song was among the top half dozen songs for 1932.

The song opens dramatically with the word *Please* on a high note for the first measure. The singer is pleading to be told "that you love me too."

Rise 'n Shine
COMPOSER: **Vincent Youmans**
LYRICIST: **Buddy De Sylva**

The musical *Humpty Dumpty* was completely rewritten and became *Take a Chance*. Two songs were kept, and Vincent Youmans was called in to provide some new songs. His most important contribution was "Rise 'n Shine," which was introduced by Ethel Merman. In the 1933 movie version it was sung by Lillian Roth.

"Rise 'n Shine" was another of the chin-up, look-at-the-bright-side-of-life songs that were an important part in the lives of people during the Depression.

Say It Isn't So
COMPOSER-LYRICIST: **Irving Berlin**

This was one of Berlin's first major song successes of the thirties after a number of years of artistic frustration, and it helped restore his self-confidence. Rudy Vallee's introduction on his radio show and his recording were largely responsible for its initial popularity. It was one of the top three songs of 1932 and was a *Variety* "Fifty Year Hit Parade" selection.

Shuffle Off to Buffalo
COMPOSER: **Harry Warren**
LYRICIST: **Al Dubin**

"Shuffle Off to Buffalo" was introduced by Ruby Keeler, Clarence Nordstrom, Ginger Rogers, and Una Merkel in the movie musical *Forty-second Street*. It was one of the top three songs of 1933 and a *Variety* "Fifty Year Hit Parade" honoree. The honeymoon couples were shuffling (a dance step) off to Buffalo and other cities en route to the city of their dreams, Hollywood.

Snuggled on Your Shoulder
COMPOSER-LYRICISTS: **Carmen Lombardo and Joe Young**

This *Variety* "Fifty Year Hit Parade" selection was introduced by Guy Lombardo and His Royal Canadians and further popularized by Bing Crosby. According to *Variety*'s list of hits of 1932, the song never made it into the top ten.

The lyrics say that the singer wants to dance forever and "dream about your charms,/Snuggled on your shoulder,/Cuddled in your arms."

Soft Lights and Sweet Music
COMPOSER-LYRICIST: **Irving Berlin**

The year 1932 brought Berlin back to the Broadway theater after several years' absence. His *Face the Music*, a topical musical comedy about the Depression and some of the humorous effects it had on American life, produced two hits: "Let's Have Another Cup o' Coffee," a jaunty ditty that sounds like a commercial for coffee, and the eloquent ballad "Soft Lights and Sweet Music."

The ballad praises the value of beautiful music in a romantic setting. Katherine Carrington and J. Harold Murray introduced it, and it became the top song in the country for a month in 1932.

The Song Is You
COMPOSER: **Jerome Kern**
LYRICIST: **Oscar Hammerstein II**

Tullio Carminati introduced "The Song Is You" in *Music in the Air*. In the 1934 movie adaptation of the musical John Boles sang it. Kern heightened the drama of the song by expanding the bridge section of the chorus and using a clever change of key that allowed the primary melodic idea to reach an even higher climax in its last statement. Such devices help make a song refreshingly different and intriguing to listen to time after time.

You're an Old Smoothie
COMPOSER: Richard A. Whiting
LYRICIST: Buddy De Sylva

Another hit from *Take a Chance* was "You're an Old Smoothie" (see "Rise 'n Shine," page 66). This *Variety* "Fifty Year Hit Parade" song was introduced by Ethel Merman and Jack Haley. The song was a second salvage job from *Humpty Dumpty*. It says that

"you're a smoothie, . . . I'm a softie . . . like putty in the hand of a girl like you."

You're Getting to Be a Habit with Me
COMPOSER: Harry Warren
LYRICIST: Al Dubin

Bebe Daniels introduced this song in the movie musical *Forty-second Street*. Doris Day performed it in the 1951 movie musical *Lullaby of Broadway*. The lyrics say your kisses and hugs act like a drug, for the singer is "addicted to your charms."

1 9 3 3

The Boulevard of Broken Dreams
COMPOSER: Harry Warren
LYRICIST: Al Dubin

This Warren-Dubin hit was introduced by Tullio Carminati in the 1934 movie *Moulin Rouge*. Tony Bennett revived it successfully in 1950, and it helped him get a good recording contract with Columbia.

The lyrics describe walking along the street where Gigolo and Giogolette live out their shattered dreams.

Carioca
COMPOSER: Vincent Youmans
LYRICISTS: Gus Kahn and Edward Eliscu

Flying Down to Rio was the movie musical that started the Fred Astaire-Ginger Rogers cycle of singing and dancing movies. Astaire was supposed to have performed the song with Dorothy Jordan, but she married the picture's executive producer and dropped out of the film. Her replacement was Rogers. The primary stars of the film were Dolores Del Rio and Gene Raymond, but Astaire and Rogers's charisma together dazzled so brightly they practically upstaged the stars.

"Carioca," which was introduced in an unforgettable dance routine on top of seven white pianos, was nominated for the first musical Academy Award in 1934. "Carioca" is not a foxtrot or a polka . . . it has a metre that is tricky." This Oscar nominee was selected by *Variety* for its "Fifty Year Hit Parade."

Did You Ever See a Dream Walking?
COMPOSER: Harry Revel
LYRICIST: Mack Gordon

Jack Haley introduced this song in the movie *Sitting Pretty*. It became a big hit in 1934, spending five weeks

at number one and was later honored by being named to *Variety*'s "Fifty Year Hit Parade."

The plot of *Sitting Pretty* concerned two songwriters (played by Haley and Jack Oakie) hitchhiking to Hollywood. The lyrics ask several questions: "Did you ever see a dream walking? . . . talking? . . . dancing? . . . romancing? Well, I did!"

Don't Blame Me
COMPOSER: Jimmy McHugh
LYRICIST: Dorothy Fields

Jimmy McHugh and Dorothy Fields wrote this lovely ballad, which was popularized by Walter Woolf King in Chicago and was used as a promotional song for the film *Dinner at Eight*. Sarah Vaughan later successfully recorded it.

What is it the lyricist does not want to be blamed for? "For falling in love with you . . . I can't help it . . . blame all your charms, that melt in my arms but don't blame me."

Easter Parade
COMPOSER-LYRICIST: Irving Berlin

Clifton Webb and Marilyn Miller led a stylish parade down Fifth Avenue in the first-act finale of *As Thousands Cheer* and introduced "Easter Parade," one of Irving Berlin's personal favorites. He had used the melody in 1917 for a lyric entitled "Smile and Show Your Dimple." As might be expected from the title, that song was a failure and was quickly forgotten. During the writing of music for *As Thousands Cheer*, Berlin rediscovered the tune and wrote the words for the parade scene.

Harry James's recording in 1942 and Guy Lombardo's in 1947 each sold a million copies. Bing Crosby sang it in the 1942 movie musical *Holiday Inn,* and Judy Garland sang it in 1948's movie musical *Easter Parade.*

With "Always" (1925), "God Bless America" (1939), "There's No Business Like Show Business" (1946), and "White Christmas" (1942), Berlin considered "Easter Parade" among the best of his songs. *Variety* chose it to appear in its "Fifty Year Hit Parade" and in its "Golden 100 Tin Pan Alley Song" list.

Flying down to Rio
COMPOSER: **Vincent Youmans**
LYRICISTS: **Gus Kahn and Edward Eliscu**

This was the title song from the movie musical that first matched Fred Astaire with Ginger Rogers. Their magic helped several songs become hits in this and later movie musicals.

Perhaps the exoticism of Rio de Janeiro helped the public find the song fascinating, but lyrics like "my Rio by the sea-o" could not have helped. The rest of the lyrics are just as contrived and silly, but the Astaire-Rogers magic overcame even that.

"Flying Down to Rio" was named to *Variety*'s "Fifty Year Hit Parade."

Heat Wave
COMPOSER-LYRICIST: **Irving Berlin**

Ethel Waters, as a lively and vivacious weather reporter, introduced "Heat Wave" in the revue *As Thousands Cheer.* She explains how the record hot spell came to New York from Martinique. A certain young lady "started the heat wave by making her seat wave."

Berlin's writing style is difficult to pinpoint because he has the ability to write in whatever style he chooses. Thus "Heat Wave" does not appear to have come from the same composer as "White Christmas," "What'll I Do?," and "Easter Parade." Berlin's genius for adapting to any music or lyric style is phenomenal.

Later generations probably associate "Heat Wave" with the 1946 movie *Blue Skies* or even more likely with Marilyn Monroe's performance of it in the 1954 film *There's No Business Like Show Business.*

I Cover the Waterfront
COMPOSER: **John Green**
LYRICIST: **Edward Heyman**

Johnny Green wrote this tune to exploit the motion picture by the same name which starred Claudette Colbert and Ben Lyon. The song was written after the film had been completed. But when it was introduced

by Ben Bernie and his orchestra on radio, it became such a hit that it was included on later prints of the film. Frank Sinatra and Artie Shaw helped popularize the number.

The singer is waiting on the waterfront, patiently hoping, longing, and waiting for the return of the loved one.

It's Only a Paper Moon
COMPOSER: **Harold Arlen**
LYRICISTS: **Billy Rose and E. Y. Harburg**

The incidental music for the nonmusical Broadway play *The Great Magoo* included this song. The song, then called "If You Believe in Me," served as a recurring theme throughout the play. After it had acquired a new title, it was interpolated in the film version of *Take a Chance.*

The lyrics are full of make-believe: a paper moon; a cardboard sea; a canvas sky; a muslin tree. The whole world is phony, a Barnum and Bailey world, "but it wouldn't be make believe if you believed in me."

Nat "King" Cole's 1945 recording was a best seller, and Ella Fitzgerald also recorded it successfully. This was the first song by Harold Arlen to appear in a film.

It's the Talk of the Town
See "The Talk of the Town," page 71.

The Last Round-up
COMPOSER-LYRICIST: **Billy Hill**

"The Last Round-up" is a popular song in the style of a cowboy ballad. Joe Morrison introduced it at the Paramount Theater in New York, and Don Ross used it in the *Ziegfeld Follies of 1934.* (Willie and Eugene Howard offered a comic version of the song in the same *Follies.*) It was one of Bing Crosby's earliest successful recordings. Roy Rogers had an even more successful recording; it was largely responsible for his getting a movie contract. Rogers used it again in his 1945 film *Don't Fence Me In.* Gene Autry sang it in 1941's *The Singing Hills* and 1947's *The Last Roundup.*

Variety reported that it sold 650,000 copies in various recordings in 1935. *Variety* selected it for its "Fifty Year Hit Parade" for 1933.

Lazybones
COMPOSER: **Hoagy Carmichael**
LYRICIST: **Johnny Mercer**

Hoagy Carmichael is sometimes called the lazy man's songwriter because he wrote lazy hits like "Rockin'

Chair," "Lazy River," "Two Sleepy People," and "Lazybones."

"Lazybones, loafin' thru the day," should be working, spraying for "tater bugs," but instead, he is "sleeping in the noonday sun . . . and he never heard a word. . . ." Johnny Mercer set these lyrics to the tune later. Carmichael had written the melody earlier and called it "Washboard Blues." Rudy Vallee and Ben Bernie first popularized the song (the lyric version) on the radio, in nightclubs, and through recordings and made it one of 1933's top songs.

"Lazybones" was chosen for *Variety*'s "Fifty Year Hit Parade."

Let's Fall in Love
COMPOSER: **Harold Arlen**
LYRICIST: **Ted Koehler**

After Harold Arlen's "It's Only a Paper Moon" had been interpolated into a film, he got his first assignment for a film score. He wrote "Let's Fall in Love," which was introduced by Ann Sothern, for the film musical of the same name. The *Variety* "Fifty Year Hit Parade" song asks, "why shouldn't we fall in love?" The song has since been heard in numerous movie musicals.

Love Is the Sweetest Thing
COMPOSER-LYRICIST: **Ray Noble**

This *Variety* "Fifty Year Hit Parade" number was introduced in the British film *Say It with Music*. It was premiered in the United States by Julia Sanderson. In 1945 it was interpolated into the motion picture *Confidential Agent*. According to *Variety*, it was the nation's biggest hit for three weeks during 1933.

Lover
COMPOSER: **Richard Rodgers**
LYRICIST: **Lorenz Hart**

Jeanette MacDonald introduced this *Variety* "Fifty Year Hit Parade" waltz in the movie musical *Love Me Tonight*. Peggy Lee sang it in the 1953 version of *The Jazz Singer*, and her recording of "Lover" was a million seller in 1953.

Composers generally do not separate syllables of words with rests, but Rodgers placed a rest between the syllables of *lov-er, soft-ly, glanc-ing, danc-ing,* and several other key words. The effect is memorable.

The names Jeanette MacDonald and Nelson Eddy now seem inseparable. The popularity of the team in several operetta-style movie musicals is unequaled. But they did not start their series of successful movie mu-

sicals until *Naughty Marietta* in 1935, so MacDonald made this song a hit on her own.

Mine
COMPOSER: **George Gershwin**
LYRICIST: **Ira Gershwin**

"Mine" was introduced by William Gaxton and Lois Moran at a political rally in the musical *Let 'Em Eat Cake* (1932). The number has a distinctive countermelody chorus, a patter sung independently against the main melody. Because of its political theme, it was interpolated in the 1952 revival of *Of Thee I Sing*.

My Moonlight Madonna
COMPOSER: **William Scotti**
LYRICIST: **Paul Francis Webster**

William Scotti adapted the melody for this song from Zdenko Fibich's "Poème." Paul Francis Webster added lyrics. This *Variety* "Fifty Year Hit Parade" song was introduced by Rudy Vallee. It was made popular in recordings by the rich baritone voice of Conrad Thibault, the soft-voiced tenor Jack Fulton with the Paul Whiteman orchestra, and Arthur Tracy, radio's "Street Singer." In addition, it was recorded by Freddy Martin under the pseudonym Albert Taylor and by bandleader and composer Victor Young.

Orchids in the Moonlight
COMPOSER: **Vincent Youmans**
LYRICISTS: **Gus Kahn and Edward Eliscu**

Another hit from *Flying Down to Rio,* in addition to "Caricoa," was "Orchids in the Moonlight." This *Variety* "Fifty Year Hit Parade" selection was introduced by the newly formed song-and-dance partnership of Fred Astaire and Ginger Rogers. Vincent Youmans composed his first film score for *Flying Down to Rio* after numerous successful Broadway scores.

Kahn and Eliscu's lyrics tell us that the orchids bloom in the moonlight as the lovers vow to be true, but they fade in the sunlight as the vows are shattered.

Play, Fiddle, Play
COMPOSER: **Emery Deutsch**
LYRICIST: **Jack Lawrence**

Gypsy violinist Emery Deutsch wrote this song, which *Variety* included in its "Fifty Year Hit Parade." It was his radio theme song with the A & P Gypsies. This waltz sounds antiquated today.

Shadow Waltz
COMPOSER: **Harry Warren**
LYRICIST: **Al Dubin**

After the success of Warren and Dubin's musical score for *Forty-second Street*, Warner Brothers hired them to produce music for what became a series of films, *Gold Diggers*, 1933–37.

Gold Diggers, a stage play by Avery Hopwood, was first filmed in 1923. Next came the 1929 musical version called *Gold Diggers of Broadway*. Warner Brothers revived the idea with *Gold Diggers of 1933*, which had the same basic concept as the previous efforts: a group of girls in search of rich husbands. In the 1933 version Dick Powell played a songwriter with wealthy parents. They disapprove of his musical inclinations (being a songwriter was not "working for a living"), and they also strongly oppose his intentions to marry a chorus girl (played by Ruby Keeler).

Powell and Keeler introduced "Shadow Waltz," a *Variety* "Fifty Year Hit Parade" song, in *Gold Diggers of 1933*. Busby Berkeley's ingenious staging of the number featured sixty chorus girls playing illuminated violins arranged in patterns until at the climax they form an enormous violin.

Smoke Gets in Your Eyes
COMPOSER: **Jerome Kern**
LYRICIST: **Otto Harbach**

This lovely ballad was introduced by Tamara in Jerome Kern's *Roberta*. She performed this song, which reflects on love gone up in smoke, seated on an empty stage, accompanying herself on a guitar, and wearing a peasant dress and babushka.

Kern originally wrote the melody as a march for the theme of a radio program that never materialized. By slowing the tempo and sentimentalizing the melody, he adapted it for Act II of *Roberta*. The song became a hit even though Harbach's lyrics were difficult for the audience to comprehend quickly ("so I chaffed them and I gaily laughed . . .").

In 1958 the Platters' recording of "Smoke Gets in Your Eyes" sold more than 1 million copies and was the number four song in 1959. (It had been one of the top four songs of 1933.)

Roberta was not treated kindly by the critics, but it had a successful run, thanks largely to the score. Kern was reaching the end of his Broadway career, but he was still composing classics. (Bob Hope made his first major appearance in *Roberta* and provided its few comic moments.)

Kern's ballad was chosen for *Variety*'s "Fifty Year Hit Parade" and for its "Golden 100 Tin Pan Alley Song" list.

Sophisticated Lady
COMPOSER: **Duke Ellington**
LYRICISTS: **Mitchell Parish and Irving Mills**

One of Duke Ellington's masterpieces, "Sophisticated Lady" originated as an instrumental composition for his orchestra. When lyrics were added, it became one of Ellington's most successful songs and a *Variety* "Fifty Year Hit Parade" honoree. According to the composer, the song was a portrait of three schoolteachers he remembered who spent nine months teaching but toured Europe during the summer months. To the boy Ellington, such a life was the epitome of sophistication.

Key changes within the song make it a little difficult to sing. The lyrics are a little strained in places.

Stars Fell on Alabama
COMPOSER: **Frank Perkins**
LYRICIST: **Mitchell Parish**

This *Variety* "Fifty Year Hit Parade" song is identified with trombonist Jack Teagarden, who was noted for his blues-influenced, deceptively lazy trombone playing. His recorded renditions of "Basin Street Blues," "Stars Fell on Alabama," and "The Sheik of Araby" are jazz classics. "Stars Fell on Alabama" was number one for three weeks in 1934. The melody is lovely and is most often heard as an instrumental—which is just as well since the lyrics do not make much sense.

Stormy Weather
COMPOSER: **Harold Arlen**
LYRICIST: **Ted Koehler**

Jerome Kern's "Smoke Gets in Your Eyes" and this torch song seem spiritually akin to each other and to the music Kern wrote for *Show Boat*, especially "Can't Help Lovin' Dat Man." They share a breastbeating, down-and-out feeling.

"Stormy Weather" was written for Cab Calloway to introduce in a Cotton Club revue, but since it seemed more suitable for a female singer, the writers chose Ethel Waters. In the interim, Leo Reisman and his orchestra recorded the number, with Harold Arlen doing the vocal. It became a best seller, so by the time the Cotton Club revue opened the song was already quite a hit: the biggest one of 1933.

Ethel Waters sang "Stormy Weather" with all of her soul. She seemed to be expressing the anguish of people who found nothing but gloom and misery in their own lives because of the Depression.

Variety selected "Stormy Weather" for its "Fifty Year Hit Parade" and as a "Golden 100 Tin Pan Alley Song."

The Talk of the Town
COMPOSER: **Jerry Livingston**
LYRICISTS: **Marty Symes and Al J. Neiburg**

"The Talk of the Town," a *Variety* "Fifty Year Hit Parade" song, was popularized by Glen Gray and the Casa Loma Orchestra. According to *Variety*, the song was number one for one week in 1933 and was among the top ten hits for more than a third of the year.

What was the talk of the town? "Everybody knows you left me" just before the wedding day.

Temptation
COMPOSER: **Nacio Herb Brown**
LYRICIST: **Arthur Freed**

Bing Crosby introduced this song in the movie musical *Going Hollywood*. With this film, Crosby rose to the top ten box-office attractions list. The song became one of his biggest hits.

"Temptation" normally is played with a beguine beat. The "temptation" is a person of the opposite sex: "you came, I was alone . . . I'm just a slave . . . to you." Crosby's best-selling recording helped the song become number one and stay there for three weeks in 1934. Perry Como had a million seller with it in the mid-forties, and Jo Stafford (as Cinderella G. Stump) with Red Ingle and the Natural Seven had a million seller with a hick version of it in 1947 pronounced "Tim-tayshun."

The Touch of Your Hand
COMPOSER: **Jerome Kern**
LYRICIST: **Otto Harbach**

"The Touch of Your Hand" was an emotional trade of good-byes sung by Stephanie (Tamara) and Ladislaw (William Hain) in Kern's *Roberta*. According to *Variety*, it never made the top spot but peaked at number three toward the end of the year. *Variety* selected it for its "Fifty Year Hit Parade."

Try a Little Tenderness
COMPOSER-LYRICISTS: **Harry Woods, Jimmy Campbell, and Reg Connelly**

Before it was fashionable for women and men to be equal partners in a love relationship, this love song encouraged men to remember that women need ten-

derness. The song can make a man with guilt pangs feel like a heel.

In the 1964 film *Dr. Strangelove*, the song received more exposure when it was used under the opening titles. Its use was ironic because the film chronicled the events leading to the final nuclear holocaust. The reviewer for the *New York Times* thought the choice of music was a sick joke.

We're in the Money
COMPOSER: **Harry Warren**
LYRICIST: **Al Dubin**

In addition to "Shadow Waltz," a second hit from the movie musical *Gold Diggers of 1933* was "We're in the Money," which is sometimes called "The Gold Diggers' Song." Introduced by Ginger Rogers, dressed in an outfit made of silver dollars, and a chorus of gold diggers, the song has become a standard.

The lyrics bid good-bye to blues and tears because "old man depression" is through. No more breadlines! No more money problems! Everyone will now be able to pay the rent!

Variety chose "We're in the Money" for its "Fifty Year Hit Parade."

Who's Afraid of the Big Bad Wolf?
COMPOSER-LYRICISTS: **Frank E. Churchill and Ann Ronell**

This delightful ditty was introduced in the Walt Disney animated cartoon *The Three Little Pigs*. It is probable that the people of 1933 consciously or unconsciously identified with this song because the big bad wolf, the Depression, had them by the throats. It may have dispelled their fears to sing about laughing in the face of danger. President Roosevelt had reminded the nation in his 1933 inaugural address that it had nothing to fear but fear itself. Yet people needed a morale boost, and "Who's Afraid of the Big Bad Wolf?," with all its frivolity, did the trick. *Variety* honored the song by selecting it for its "Fifty Year Hit Parade."

Barbra Streisand made her professional debut with this song in a Greenwich Village nightclub in 1961 and had good success with a recorded version.

Yesterdays
COMPOSER: **Jerome Kern**
LYRICIST: **Otto Harbach**

"Yesterdays" is often confused with the Beatles' more recent "Yesterday." Kern and Harbach's "Yesterdays" was introduced by Aunt Minnie (Fay Templeton) in Jerome Kern's *Roberta*. This beautiful song recalls the fond memories of "days of mad romance and love" during youth. It was featured in the movie adaptation of *Roberta* in 1935 and in another adaptation in 1952 entitled *Lovely to Look At*. When Kern's biography, *Till the Clouds Roll By*, was filmed in 1946, "Yesterdays" was included in the sound track performed by the chorus.

You Gotta Be a Football Hero
COMPOSER: **Al Sherman**
LYRICISTS: **Al Lewis and Buddy Fields**

This song is often revived in the fall as attention is turned to gridiron warriors. The lyrics suggest that if a guy wants the beautiful girls, then he must be a football hero.

1 9 3 4

All I Do Is Dream of You
COMPOSER: **Nacio Herb Brown**
LYRICIST: **Arthur Freed**

"All I Do Is Dream of You" was introduced by Gene Raymond in the 1934 Hollywood film *Sadie McKee*. It appeared again in 1935 in the Marx Brothers' farce *A Night at the Opera*, in which it was played by Chico. It may be best remembered in performances by Debbie Reynolds in 1952's *Singin' in the Rain* (she sings it after coming out of a large cake) and in 1953's *The Affairs of Dobie Gillis*.

The singer dreams of his love all day, all night, even if there were "more than twenty-four hours a day,/They'd be spent in sweet content dreaming away."

Anything Goes
COMPOSER-LYRICIST: **Cole Porter**

Anything Goes was one of the most successful musicals of the mid-thirties and the toast of Broadway in 1934. Producer Vinton Freedley conceived the idea of a show that would present an assortment of comic characters in a shipwreck, but the sinking of the SS *Morro Castle* in September 1934 forced him to revise the script. The new plot, though still taking place on a ship, eliminated the wreck. The story revolved around nightclub singer Reno Sweeney, her friend Billy Crocker (who stows away to be near Hope Harcourt), and Moon Face Mooney, alias Reverend Dr. Moon, currently Public Enemy No. 13. Ethel Merman became a star of major proportions as Reno.

Anything Goes, Porter's most popular musical score to date, was revived on Broadway in 1962 with the addition of several of Porter's most famous songs from other musicals.

In the title song, the thirties' moral climate is cataloged. As Reno, the nightclub singer turned evange-

list for ulterior motives, Merman described the decaying moral climate of the times. The list included women's short skirts, authors' four-letter words, nudist parties, and grandmothers going out with gigolos.

Baby, Take a Bow
COMPOSER: **Jay Gorney**
LYRICIST: **Lew Brown**

Shirley Temple, at the age of five, was on the set during the shooting of the movie musical *Stand Up and Cheer*. While the music from the film was being recorded, she began to do a number of dance steps. As she danced, the director of the film, Hamilton Mc-Fadden, scribbled a dummy lyric on the back of an envelope. He asked Shirley to learn the lines immediately and perform them. When she performed the song, everyone was so impressed that she was signed to a contract then and there. She was given a starring role in *Stand Up and Cheer* and performed the song "Baby, Take a Bow." Her success in the film catapulted her to stardom. She was presented a Special Academy Award (a minature statuette) in recognition of her extraordinary contribution to motion picture entertainment in 1934.

Blue Moon
COMPOSER: **Richard Rodgers**
LYRICIST: **Lorenz Hart**

This is the only Rodgers and Hart song that became a hit without having been introduced in a stage or movie musical. But it had to go through quite a metamorphosis before it achieved that status. It was first called "The Prayer" and was intended for a movie, next it was rewritten as "The Bad in Every Man," then it became "Act One," and finally it was revised again to "Blue Moon." Published in this form, it was Rodgers and Hart's biggest-selling song to date.

Surprisingly not until Elvis Presley's recording in 1961 did a recording achieve a million in sales. In the lyrics, the singer tells the moon he is alone and without a love.

Cocktails for Two
COMPOSER: **Sam Coslow**
  LYRICIST: **Arthur Johnson**

This *Variety* "Fifty Year Hit Parade" song was introduced in the 1934 movie musical *Murder at the Vanities*. However, it may be best remembered in the million-selling Spike Jones and his City Slickers recording of 1944. Jones specialized in incorporating strange sounds into songs. In this one, he included the sounds of hiccups and shattering cocktail glasses among others.

The Continental
COMPOSER: **Con Conrad**
  LYRICIST: **Herb Magidson**

"The Continental" won the first Academy Award for a best song from a film. Ginger Rogers introduced the *Variety* "Fifty Year Hit Parade" song in *The Gay Divorcée*, the film version of Cole Porter's 1932 musical *Gay Divorcée*, which retained only one song from the original Broadway production: "Night and Day." After Miss Rogers sings the lyrics, Fred and Ginger join a large dance ensemble in a twenty-two-minute production number of "The Continental." Erik Rhodes, who played a co-respondent (the person named in a divorce as guilty of adultery with the defendant), hired to help Rogers obtain a divorce, also sang the number during the lengthy segment.

The lyrics begin, "Beautiful music! Dangerous rhythm!" A new dance, the continental, was born, compliments of Fred, Ginger, and a large troup of dancers. Other nominees for that first Oscar for Best Song included "Carioca" (see 1933) and "Love in Bloom" (see page 74).

Incidentally, Betty Grable appeared in the film and was featured in the number "Let's K-nock K-nees."

Deep Purple
COMPOSER: **Peter De Rose**
  LYRICIST: **Mitchell Parish**

"Deep Purple" originated as a piano solo by Peter De Rose. A year later it was arranged for orchestra by Domenico Savino. *Variety* selected it as one of the hits for 1935 in its "Fifty Year Hit Parade." However, it may have reached higher on the hit list when lyrics were added by Mitchell Parish in 1939 (see page 97).

The lyrics and melody seem inseparable, yet it is doubtful that anyone could detect that the melody came before the lyrics of "Deep Purple." The "deep purple," by the way, is the curtain of darkness.

"Deep Purple," popularized by Larry Clinton and his orchestra and by Bing Crosby, became a million seller in a 1963 record by Nino Tempo and April Stevens.

Hands Across the Table
COMPOSER: **Jean Delettre**
  LYRICIST: **Mitchell Parish**

This *Variety* "Fifty Year Hit Parade" selection was introduced by Lucienne Boyer in the revue *Continental Varieties of 1934*. According to *Variety*, the song was one of the top ten hits of 1934 for nine weeks, but it never reached the number one slot.

If There Is Someone Lovelier Than You
COMPOSER: **Arthur Schwartz**
  LYRICIST: **Howard Dietz**

Schwartz and Dietz wrote this song for the 1933 radio serial *The Gibson Family*. Later it was interpolated into the musical *Revenge with Music*. Schwartz considered it one of his best.

The singer confesses that he cannot imagine anyone lovelier, and if there is, "then I am blind, a man without a mind."

I Get a Kick Out of You
COMPOSER-LYRICIST: **Cole Porter**

Anything Goes did not reflect the mood of the times, but it was nevertheless a tremendous hit during the Depression (see "Anything Goes," page 72). One reason for its success was the extraordinary Porter score, out of which came the sophisticated love song "I Get a Kick Out of You."

In this excerpt from *Anything Goes*, Reno, played by Ethel Merman, claims that the only thing that gives her a kick is the sight of Billy's face. She's bored by such stimulants as champagne, cocaine, and riding in a plane. Reno sang the song to Billy, played by William Gaxton, early in the first act.

Cole Porter never was satisfied with writing just a simple love song. This song probably sums up the playboy's jaded outlook on life.

"I Get a Kick Out of You" was selected for *Variety*'s "Fifty Year Hit Parade."

I'll Follow My Secret Heart
COMPOSER-LYRICIST: **Noel Coward**

This *Variety* "Fifty Year Hit Parade" song came from England's Noel Coward. It was introduced in London by Coward and Yvonne Printemps in the musical *Conversation Piece*.

According to *Variety,* "I'll Follow My Secret Heart" was one of the top ten hits of 1934 for a month and a half, but it stopped at number two (in November), never making it to the top spot.

The singer will follow his secret heart until he finds love, or so the lyrics say.

I'll String Along with You
COMPOSER: **Harry Warren**
LYRICIST: **Al Dubin**

Dick Powell and Ginger Rogers introduced this Harry Warren-Al Dubin song in the movie musical *Twenty Million Sweethearts*. The singer says, in part, that regardless of what human frailties and faults you, his loved one, possesses, "I'll string along with you."

I Only Have Eyes for You
COMPOSER: **Harry Warren**
LYRICIST: **Al Dubin**

Harry Warren and Al Dubin were hot commodities in Hollywood. After their success with *Forty-second Street* in 1932 and the beginning of the *Gold Diggers* series in 1933, they furnished songs for *Twenty Million Sweethearts* and *Dames* in 1934.

Choreographic genius Busby Berkeley set this beautiful song in a dream that the character played by Dick Powell has on a New York subway. In the sequence everywhere he looks he sees his loved one, played by Ruby Keeler. Even the advertisements inside the subway become her face. The lyrics say, "I don't know if it's cloudy or bright . . . or if we're in a garden" because "I only have eyes for you."

This song spent a month as the top song in 1934 and was revived in a best-selling recording by the Flamingos in 1956. *Variety* selected it as a "Fifty Year Hit Parade" song for 1934.

Isle of Capri
COMPOSER: **Will Grosz**
LYRICIST: **Jimmy Kennedy**

This is an English song that became a leading hit in the United States. It was a successful song for Xavier Cugat and his orchestra in nightclub appearances and on records. The song sold 500,000 copies in various recordings in 1935. The lyrics of this tango say that the singer found the woman of his dreams on the Isle of Capri only to discover as he kissed her hand that "she wore a plain golden ring on her finger."

Variety chose "Isle of Capri" for its "Fifty Year Hit Parade."

June in January
COMPOSER: **Ralph Rainger**
LYRICIST: **Leo Robin**

The American branch of Decca Records was formed in 1934, joining the main companies of the early thirties: Victor, Columbia, and Brunswick. Decca, a European outfit, opened its American branch and quickly pulled off a major coup by luring Bing Crosby away from Brunswick. Crosby's first recording for Decca was "June in January," which he introduced in the movie musical *Here Is My Heart*.

How can it be June in January? The answer is that it's always "spring in my heart . . . because I'm in love with you."

"June in January" was selected for inclusion in *Variety's* "Fifty Year Hit Parade."

Lost in a Fog
COMPOSER: **Jimmy McHugh**
LYRICIST: **Dorothy Fields**

"Lost in a Fog" was one of the top songs of 1934, when it spent six weeks at the top of the charts. The melody was written in 1934 as a theme for the Dorsey brothers and was introduced during their debut at the Riviera Café in New Jersey with the composer doing the vocal. The band consisted of Tommy and Jimmy Dorsey, Glenn Miller, Paul Weston, Alex Stordahl, Ray McKinley, Charlie Spivak, and vocalist Bob Crosby, all of whom later became bandleaders.

The song was performed in the 1934 film *Have a Heart*.

Love in Bloom
COMPOSER: **Ralph Rainger**
LYRICIST: **Leo Robin**

"Love in Bloom" was introduced by Bing Crosby in *She Loves Me Not*. However, it was not in the film or through Crosby's recording that the song achieved its greatest exposure. It was to become the theme song over radio and television for Jack Benny. This *Variety* "Fifty Year Hit Parade" number is most famous today in the "horrible" violin version that began

Benny's shows, but of course, that was not the way it was originally popular.

The lyrics ask, "Can it be the trees that fill the breeze with rare and magic perfume?" And they answer, "Oh, no, it isn't the trees,/It's love in bloom!"

Love Thy Neighbor
COMPOSER: **Harry Revel**
LYRICIST: **Mack Gordon**

Bing Crosby was very busy in 1934. Movie musicals he made that were released in 1934 include *She Loves Me Not, Here Is My Heart*, and *We're Not Dressing*, in which he introduced "Love Thy Neighbor." He further popularized it in a Decca recording. *Variety* selected it for its "Fifty Year Hit Parade." According to *Variety*, it was the top song in the nation for a month and spent three months in the top ten in 1934.

Mr. and Mrs. Is the Name
COMPOSER: **Allie Wrubel**
LYRICIST: **Mort Dixon**

Dick Powell was second only to Bing Crosby as the year's male movie musical star and introducer of hit songs, starring in *Dames, Twenty Million Sweethearts*, and *Flirtation Walk* in 1934. *Flirtation Walk* was his second musical film with costar Ruby Keeler, and they introduced "Mr. and Mrs. Is the Name." The patriotic film was set at West Point.

The Old Spinning Wheel
COMPOSER-LYRICIST: **Billy Hill**

Billy Hill wrote several nostalgic cowboy ballad songs that reached hit status. He had written "The Old Spinning Wheel" several years earlier, but it had not been published. After the success of 1933's "The Last Round-up," Hill pulled "The Old Spinning Wheel" out of mothballs. *Variety* reported sales of 800,000 records in 1935 and later named it to the "Fifty Year Hit Parade."

Solitude
COMPOSER: **Duke Ellington**
LYRICISTS: **Eddie DeLange and Irving Mills**

"Solitude" received the ASCAP award as the best popular song of 1934. The singer's "reveries . . . memories" prey on his mind in "Solitude." Ellington did a superb job of writing a lonely piece of music, and the words match its mood.

Stay as Sweet as You Are
COMPOSER: **Harry Revel**
LYRICIST: **Mack Gordon**

In the movie musical *College Rhythm*, Lanny Ross introduced "Stay as Sweet as You Are" and helped move it to the top of the charts for a month toward the end of the year.

The lyrics plead with the girl to remain as she is, lovely, charming, sweet, "young and gay or old and gray,/Near to me or afar,/Night and day I pray/That you'll always stay as sweet as you are."

Ross was one of the singing stars of the *Hit Parade* on radio in the late thirties. He was called the Troubadour of the Moon.

Tumbling Tumbleweeds
COMPOSER-LYRICIST: **Bob Nolan**

Bob Nolan's "Tumbling Tumbleweeds" conjures up an image of a group of cowhands singing around a campfire. Gene Autry introduced the song in his first full-length film, *Tumbling Tumbleweeds*. He sang it again in *Don't Fence Me In* in 1945.

The Sons of the Pioneers recorded "Tumbling Tumbleweeds" and helped popularize it. They performed it in the 1945 movie musical *Hollywood Canteen*. The Sons of the Pioneers consisted of composer Nolan, Tim Spencer, and Leonard Slye, who achieved celebrity status after 1937 as Roy Rogers, who in turn sang it in *Silver Spurs* (1943). It has become so well known that many people think it is an authentic western folk song, but it was written by Bob Nolan, a Canadian who became fascinated by the desert after he and his family had moved to Arizona.

The years 1933 and 1934 were particularly important for songs with a western character. Songs by Billy Hill and Bob Nolan, plus "El Rancho Grande" and "The Cattle Call," which were not as high on the hit list as "Tumbling Tumbleweeds" "Wagon Wheels," "The Last Roundup" or "The Old Spinning Wheel," illustrate the western song mania.

Two Cigarettes in the Dark
COMPOSER: **Lew Pollack**
LYRICIST: **Paul Francis Webster**

Gloria Grafton introduced this *Variety* "Fifty Year Hit Parade" selection in the nonmusical motion picture *Kill That Story* (1934).

Smoking was more fashionable in the thirties than it has been since being linked to cancer. Many of the sex symbols of the decade's movie industry were almost always pictured smoking. "Two Cigarettes in the Dark" compares "striking a match" to "the spark that thrilled me" and the glow of the cigarette to "love was the flame," while "the smoke rings seemed to signify/A story old yet new."

"Two Cigarettes in the Dark" was one of Bing Crosby's earliest recordings for the newly formed Decca Records.

Wagon Wheels
COMPOSER: **Billy Hill**
LYRICIST: **Peter De Rose**

"Wagon Wheels" was introduced by Everett Marshall in the *Ziegfeld Follies of 1934,* along with another western song, "The Last Round-up." Its basic two-part form gives the song a folk song feel. The chorus is sung first; then comes the verse, followed by the chorus with a slightly different ending. Most folk music and gospel songs have a verse and chorus two-part form pattern.

The lyrics ask the "Wagon wheels" to "keep on a-turning . . . roll along,/Sing your song . . . carry me home."

According to *Variety,* "Wagon Wheels" was the top song in the nation for three weeks and spent ten weeks in 1934's top ten. *Variety* selected it for its "Fifty Year Hit Parade."

What a Diff'rence a Day Made
COMPOSER: **Maria Grever**
LYRICIST: **Stanley Adams**

This popular Spanish song ("Cuando Vuelva a Tu Lado") was written by Maria Grever. The lyrics were translated into English by Stanley Adams in 1934. The difference made by "twenty-four little hours" is romance. Without it "yesterday was blue," but "it's heaven when you" find it.

Dinah Washington revived the number successfully in 1958. She won the best rhythm and blues recording of the year Grammy for her recording. *Variety* selected "What a Diff'rence a Day Made" as a "Golden 100 Tin Pan Alley Song."

With My Eyes Wide Open I'm Dreaming
COMPOSER: **Harry Revel**
LYRICIST: **Mack Gordon**

This *Variety* "Fifty Year Hit Parade" honoree was introduced by Dorothy Dell and Jack Oakie in the film *Shoot the Works.* It was revived in 1949 by Patti Page, who reaped her first million seller with her version. It was revived again in 1952, when Dean Martin performed it in the film *The Stooge.*

Variety reported that the song was the nation's top hit for two weeks, and it spent three months in the top ten during 1934.

You and the Night and the Music
COMPOSER: **Arthur Schwartz**
LYRICIST: **Howard Dietz**

In addition to "If There Is Someone Lovelier Than You," a second hit from the musical *Revenge with Music* was the smoldering duet "You and the Night and the Music," which was introduced by Georges Metaxa and Libby Holman. Conrad Thibault popularized it on the radio. The singer claims that the three ingredients that "fill me with flaming desire" are you, the night, and the music.

This song was honored by *Variety,* which selected it for the "Fifty Year Hit Parade."

You Oughta Be in Pictures
COMPOSER: **Dana Suesse**
LYRICIST: **Edward Heyman**

Jane Froman introduced this "Fifty Year Hit Parade" song in an interpolation into the *Ziegfeld Follies of 1934.* Mary Martin and Fred MacMurray reintroduced it in the film *New York Town* in 1941. Doris Day next revived it in the 1951 film *Starlift.* It is a classic song of the film industry along with "Hooray for Hollywood."

You're the Top
COMPOSER-LYRICIST: **Cole Porter**

During the thirties Cole Porter was relatively untouched by the Depression. He continued to live in his customary wealthy style and to produce songs of remarkable quality.

"You're the Top," a "Fifty Year Hit Parade" selection, was introduced by Reno and Billy in the musical *Anything Goes* (see "Anything Goes," page 72). Porter's clever lyrics itemize the praises of the lovers for each other. The exchange of compliments is filled with urbane allusions: "a Bendel bonnet to a Shakespeare sonnet," "from Mickey Mouse to a symphony by Strauss," "Mahatma Gandhi and Napoleon Brandy," "Fred Astaire and Camembert," and several other lovely bits of wordplay.

In the 1936 movie adaptation of the musical, "You're the Top" was sung by Ethel Merman and Bing Crosby. In the 1956 screen version it was performed by Bing Crosby and Mitzi Gaynor. In Cole Porter's movie biography, *Night and Day* (1946), it was sung by Ginny Simms and Cary Grant.

T · H · E

SWING ERA: 1935 to 1945

By the midyears of the thirties the country had recovered from the worst of the Depression, but only a few years of relative calm lay between the economic debacle of the early thirties and the holocaust of World War II. By 1937 Hitler was in power in Germany, Mussolini had brought fascism to Italy, the Spanish Republic was under attack by Francisco Franco, and Japan had begun systematic attacks upon China. The United States was being inexorably drawn into another major war.

As Americans got more money in their pockets, their musical tastes began to change.

The Big Bands

Swing-style big bands were not the important agents of the year's biggest hits until the last few years of the thirties. The swing era, also called the era of the big bands, has been dated variously from 1935 to 1945 or 1939 to 1949. No style comes to immediate prominence to the exclusion of all other styles. As one style is beginning, another is declining in popularity. It is impossible, therefore, to say that the swing era began at a particular moment, but Benny Goodman's engagement at the Palomar Ballroom in Los Angeles in August 1935 was one of the early indications that a change was happening. Goodman decided to feature his swing repertoire rather than the society style of dance music that his band had been playing. The audience, particularly the youth, gave enthusiastic approval.

Swing was the music of youth, just as much as rock and roll was in the fifties. In the swing era, the adults, not the youth, made the hits. Kids did not yet have the buying power they were to acquire by the rock era. Swing had to make inroads into the establishment before it was capable of producing hits.

The trend toward recognition of the swing consciousness beginning is shown by the 1936 movie title *Swing Time* (see "A Fine Romance" page 86).

The roots of swing can be traced to jazz and the sweet bands of the twenties and early thirties. True jazz, as the black bands played it, was kept alive by aficionados, and the general public knew very little about it. Sweet music was the dominant style on radio and on records. The swing style was a direct result of Goodman (and other white bandleaders) imitating the black bands and using the arrangements of black arrangers like Fletcher Henderson, Don Redman, and Jimmy Mundy. Goodman was able to introduce the swing sound to a broad audience through radio, hotel and ballroom engagements, and recordings. He became King of Swing, and danceable jazz was the music of the day.

The black musicians were the innovators and the ones who brought the hot sound of swing into the dance bands, but the white bands sold. Of course, this seems grossly unfair today. But Goodman was also responsible for breaking the color barrier in bands by being the first to have whites and blacks play together in the same band.

Many bands, or orchestras as they were called, began about 1935. The Dorsey brothers—Jimmy and Tommy—formed theirs in 1934. Tommy withdrew in 1935 to lead his own group. Clarinetist Artie Shaw formed an orchestra with strings in 1936 but abandoned it in the face of Goodman's popularity and formed what he called the "loudest band in the world" in 1937. Woody Herman took over the Isham Jones orchestra in 1936.

The sweet bands had reigned supreme for several years, but they became edgy as the country became increasingly "swing-crazy." The major sweet bands included those of Larry Clinton, Eddie Duchin, Shep Fields, Horace Heidt, Sammy Kaye, Hal Kemp, Wayne King, Andy Kirk, Kay Kyser, Guy Lombardo, Vincent Lopez, Glenn Miller, Russ Morgan, Ray Noble, Leo Reisman, and Lawrence Welk.

In the swing category, the important bands included those of Louis Armstrong, Charlie Barnet, Count Basie, Bunny Berigan, Jimmy Dorsey, Tommy Dorsey, Duke Ellington, Benny Goodman, Glen Gray, Erskine Hawkins, Fletcher Henderson, Earl Hines, Harry James, Jimmie Lunceford, Artie Shaw, and Chick Webb.

There were a few other bands that featured singers or a leader who could not be identified with either sweet or swing. In this category belong the bands of Ben Bernie, Cab Calloway, Bob Crosby, Little Jack Little, Will Osborne, Rudy Vallee, and numerous others that were not as popular.

Many of the big bands also featured small combos that played more authentic jazz with superb improvisation.

By the end of the decade the trend toward less boisterous music had become evident. The popularity of Glenn Miller's soft, sweet sound was an indication that the public wanted to dance to dreamy music. The swing hysteria had passed.

The first peacetime military draft in U.S. history was instituted in 1940 because of the war in Europe. The draft caused the bands to juggle their personnel and to look for replacements. Keeping together a band that could play the complex arrangements became more difficult.

A trend toward the use of a vocalist or vocal groups with the band began in the early forties. Important singers with the bands included Tex Beneke, Doris Day, Bob Eberly, Ray Eberle, Ella Fitzgerald, Helen Forrest, Connie Haines, Kitty Kallen, Helen O'Connell, and, of course, Frank Sinatra. Important vocal groups included the Andrews Sisters, the Merry Macs, the Mills Brothers, the Modernaires, the Pied Pipers, and the Song Spinners.

Wartime shortages, particularly of gasoline, caused problems for the bands. Neither they nor their fans could travel. And a levied amusement tax made it very expensive for people to go out. These, and other factors, contributed to the demise of the big bands. The singers became the important ingredient, leading to the sing era.

The Hit Parade

On April 20, 1935, *Your Hit Parade* began broadcasting its weekly program of the top songs in the country. Millions of Americans sat in front of their radios each Saturday evening, awaiting the announcement of the top ten hits in the nation, especially the number one song. The songs were rated by sheet music and record sales and by the number of performances on jukeboxes. For the next twenty-five years the program served as an excellent barometer of the nation's taste in popular music.

The Popularity of Movie Musicals

The movie musicals of the swing era are distinctive types: the dance musical, the revue, the operetta, and the animated musical.

The nine films that Fred Astaire and Ginger Rogers made together were filled with incomparable dance routines. They danced to some of the era's most popular music composed by some of its best composers. Their films during the era included *Roberta, Top Hat, Follow the Fleet, Swing Time, Shall We Dance?, Carefree,* and *The Story of Vernon and Irene Castle.* Of course, there were other movie musicals, and there were important stars other than Astaire and Rogers. Some of the most important movie musicals of the era included *Broadway Melody of 1936,* which was nominated for the best picture Oscar in 1935; the Oscar winner for best picture of 1936, *The Great Ziegfeld;* 1938's *Alexander's Ragtime Band;* 1939's Academy Award nominee for best picture, *The Wizard of Oz;* 1940's Crosby, Hope, and Lamour *Road* film *Road to Singapore;* 1941's *Road* film *Road to Zanzibar;* 1942's *Yankee Doodle Dandy,* with James Cagney portraying George M. Cohan; Mickey Rooney and Judy Garland's *Babes on Broadway;* 1943's *Road* film *Road to Morocco;* and 1944's best picture Oscar winner, *Going My Way.*

The revue films were nothing new, but several of this type were very popular, especially as the industry began to turn out entertainment for servicemen. After the 1941 bombing of Pearl Harbor, most of the movie musicals were patriotic to aid the war effort and escapist to help the country forget the problems war was creating. A few of the revue type of musical films included *The Big Broadcast of 1938, Stars over Broadway, The Goldwyn Follies, Hit Parade of 1941, Buck Privates, Stage Door Canteen,* and *Stars on Parade.*

Jeanette MacDonald and Nelson Eddy teamed for eight movie versions of operettas beginning with 1935's *Naughty Marietta* and including *Rose Marie, Maytime, Rosalie, Sweethearts, New Moon, Bitter Sweet,* and *The Chocolate Soldier.* There were other operettas and other performers, but MacDonald and Eddy were the biggest stars of the operetta-style movie musicals. There also were several movie versions of Broadway musicals, including *Roberta, Babes in Arms, This Is the Army, Panama Hattie, Du Barry Was a Lady,* and *Knickerbocker Holiday.*

A new kind of movie musical was created during this era: the animated musical, which, of course, was the exclusive product of the Disney studios. Important movie musicals of this type included *Snow White and the Seven Dwarfs, Pinocchio, Fantasia, Dumbo,* and *Bambi.*

Some of the important stars of the movie musicals of the swing era were Alice Faye, Frances Langford, Judy Garland, Al Jolson, Bing Crosby, Gene Kelly, Eleanor Powell, Betty Hutton, Martha Raye, Betty Grable, Mary Martin, Dan Dailey, Kathryn Grayson, Gloria De Haven, Dick Haymes, Jane Powell, and June Allyson.

The Musical Theater

The stage continued to produce many beautiful and enduring popular songs. With composers like Cole Porter, Richard Rodgers, and Irving Berlin turning out fabulous scores, Broadway produced more than its share of major hits.

The era began with Cole Porter's *Jubilee* and George Gershwin's incredible folk opera *Porgy and Bess.* It also saw the premieres of *Red, Hot and Blue,* Rodgers and Hart's *Babes in Arms,* and Kurt Weill's *Knickerbocker Holiday* and *Lady in the Dark.* The outstanding musical event of the decade came in 1943 with *Oklahoma!,* the first musical collaboration between Richard Rodgers and Oscar Hammerstein II.

Oklahoma! became one of the greatest Broadway musicals of all time, eventually running for 2,248 performances. The Rodgers and Hammerstein team dominated musical theater for the next ten years.

Some of the most important hits from the Broadway stage during this era include "Begin the Beguine," "Just One of Those Things," "Summertime," "These Foolish Things," "My Funny Valentine," "September Song," "All the Things You Are," "Bewitched, Bothered and Bewildered," "Oh, What a Beautiful Mornin'," "People Will Say We're in Love," and "I'll Be Seeing You."

The Record Industry

The record industry began to recover from the Depression and was booming by the early forties. But the boom was short-lived. Members of the American Federation of Musicians had become worried as recordings began to replace live music on radio and on jukeboxes. They demanded that the record companies establish a fund for unemployed musicians, and they called a strike against companies to emphasize the point. Vocalists filled the vacuum left by the instrumentalists (a good example of this is Dick Haymes's and the Song Spinners' recording of "You'll Never Know" in 1943). Toward the end of 1944 the recording companies agreed to pay a royalty on each disc for the benefit of unemployed members. However, the passage of the Taft-Hartley Act in 1947 made the agreement illegal. This resulted in another ban on making records, but the companies had stockpiled enough recordings that they were not as vulnerable as they had been the first time.

Record production also declined in the early forties because there was a shortage of shellac, which was used in making records, because it was needed for the war effort. The industry launched a drive to get the public to turn in old records that could be melted and reused to make new records. The drive robbed us of many rare recordings, but fortunately many people kept their records.

The ASCAP Ban

As the forties opened, before the attack on Pearl Harbor, record sales soared. That prompted ASCAP, the performing rights society, to propose a new contract with radio stations that demanded twice the annual fee the stations had paid in the old contract for playing records made from the work of ASCAP members. Radio executives refused to discuss the proposed contract. As a result, all ASCAP music was banned from the airwaves. To protect its interests, radio formed a new performing rights organization: Broadcast Music Incorporated (BMI), which sought out songwriters and publishers from fields that ASCAP had ignored: foreign music and country and western (then called hillbilly) music, and from places outside the metropolitan areas of New York and Los Angeles. Within a decade BMI was licensing eighty percent of all the music played on radio.

Because of the absence of ASCAP music on radio, public domain songs, like Stephen Foster's "I Dream of Jeannie with the Light Brown Hair," were played too often for their own good. But some imported tunes got a hearing, and some relative unknown songwriters and performers got their big breaks.

ASCAP retreated in its demands in 1941. In the new agreement, it agreed to accept even less each year from the radio stations than under the previous contract.

The End of an Era

The riots caused by Frank Sinatra in the early forties clearly signaled the end of an era. By 1942 Sinatra had decided to break loose from singing with a band and make it as a solo act. For the first few months he seemed to be going nowhere. Then a series of explosive appearances skyrocketed him to the top. The first came in November 1942 in Newark, New Jersey. The predominantly teenage audience squealed, screamed, and howled when Sinatra began to sing. A couple of months later, at the Paramount Theater in New York, he created even more pandemonium among the youngsters in the audience. Then, in 1944, at the Paramount the most volcanic riot occurred. Ten thousand youths waited in line for tickets, and many thousands more wandered in the streets near the theater. When the box office opened, the booth was destroyed by the rush, people were trampled, and a few girls fainted. Sinatra had already become a lead singer on *Your Hit Parade* radio program in 1943. His high recognition because of his *Hit Parade* appearances and the new fame created by the riots caused his career to soar.

This marked the end of the swing era. The next several years were dominated by the singers. The drawing power of the bands had declined. Several survived to accompany the singers, but their roles were now secondary.

Determining the biggest hits of each year becomes easier during subsequent years. *Your Hit Parade* (also called the *Hit Parade* and *The Lucky Strike Hit Parade*) began featuring the weekly top hits on April 20, 1935. The list of hits from these charts helped tremendously.

The pop charts of *Variety* and *Billboard* began in the early forties. *Variety* published a top ten for each year from 1941 to 1980 in their January 1981 edition, which was most valuable. Other lists, including *Variety*'s "Fifty Year Hit Parade" and "Golden 100 Tin Pan Alley Songs," plus ASCAP's "All-Time Hit Parade" continued their usefulness.

1 9 3 5

About a Quarter to Nine
COMPOSER: HARRY WARREN
LYRICIST: Al Dubin

Harry Warren and Al Dubin wrote "About a Quarter to Nine" for the musical motion picture *Go into Your Dance* (1935). "The World's Greatest Entertainer," Al Jolson, introduced the song in the film and also sang it for the sound track of *The Jolson Story* in 1946.

Alone
COMPOSER: Nacio Herb Brown
LYRICIST: Arthur Freed

Kitty Carlisle and Allan Jones introduced this "Fifty Year Hit Parade" song in the Marx Brothers film *A Night at the Opera*. It was interpolated into 1940's *Andy Hardy Meets a Debutante* and 1942's *Born to Dance*.

"Alone" was the top song on *Your Hit Parade* for five weeks in early 1936.

Begin the Beguine
COMPOSER-LYRICIST: Cole Porter

This Cole Porter classic—on both the ASCAP "All-Time Hit Parade" and *Variety* "Fifty Year Hit Parade"—was introduced by June Knight in the musical *Jubilee*. The song made little impression at first. It might have been forgotten had it not been for Artie Shaw. In 1936 Shaw was contracted to record his first disc, a swing version of Rudolf Friml's "Indian Love Call." Shaw signed the contract with the stipulation that he be permitted to record the relatively unknown "Begin the Beguine" for the flip side. The disc sold 2 million copies to become one of the largest-selling instrumental recordings by an American band.

Porter composed the score for *Jubilee* while he was on a world cruise. The inspiration for "Begin the Beguine" came at Kalabahi in the Dutch East Indies. An Indonesian war dance spurred his musical imagination.

"Begin the Beguine" was one of Porter's personal favorites (another was 1930's "Love for Sale"). Porter's career began in the late twenties, but during the thirties and forties he was "King Cole" on Broadway.

A famous rendition of "Begin the Beguine" was

Fred Astaire and Eleanor Powell's dance to it in *Broadway Melody of 1940*.

Bess, You Is My Woman
COMPOSER: George Gershwin
LYRICISTS: Ira Gershwin and DuBose Heyward

George Gershwin's last musical was his crowning achievement in the theater. The music, lyrics, and libretto of *Of Thee I Sing* are predictable musical fare, but *Porgy and Bess* is a step beyond. The inspired music, lyrics, and libretto are as unlike other Gershwin musicals as his *Rhapsody in Blue* is unlike other instrumental writing for 1924. *Porgy and Bess* is called a folk opera, not a musical comedy, but several of the songs from the score have become hits.

Gershwin had been planning to write a musical setting of DuBose Heyward's novel *Porgy* since early in 1926. In 1927 Heyward and his wife, Dorothy, adapted the novel into a play that the Theatre Guild produced. In 1928 a capsule musical version of the play was included in the revue *Blackbirds of 1928*. In the early thirties the Theatre Guild considered a version of *Porgy* starring Al Jolson with music and lyrics by Jerome Kern and Oscar Hammerstein II. Heyward preferred to wait for Gershwin. Finally, in late 1933, the project began, and eleven months later the score had been written.

The story concerns the people of Catfish Row in Charleston, South Carolina. Porgy, a crippled goat-cart beggar, and Bess, who is the woman of a brutal man named Crown, fall in love. One of the show's hits is the duet by Porgy and Bess announcing their love for each other. "Bess, You Is My Woman" was sung in the original cast by Porgy (Todd Duncan) and Bess (Anne Brown). In the 1959 movie adaptation, the song was dubbed by Robert McFerrin for Sidney Poitier and by Adele Addison for Dorothy Dandridge.

Variety chose "Bess" for its "Fifty Year Hit Parade."

Broadway Rhythm
COMPOSER: Nacio Herb Brown
LYRICIST: Arthur Freed

Eleanor Powell introduced this *Variety* "Fifty Year Hit Parade" song in the movie musical *Broadway Melody of 1936,* an updated imitation of 1929's *Broadway Melody.* Other films in the series followed in 1938 and 1940. There was to have been another in 1944, but the title was changed to *Broadway Rhythm.* The *New York Times* reviewer was particularly taken with Eleanor Powell, calling her the distaff Fred Astaire with the most eloquent feet in show business.

Cheek to Cheek
COMPOSER-LYRICIST: **Irving Berlin**

Irving Berlin provided the score for the delightful musical film *Top Hat,* which starred Fred Astaire and Ginger Rogers. The musical score, one of Berlin's best, included "Cheek to Cheek" and "Top Hat, White Tie and Tails."

Astaire, the dancing master, and Rogers, his ideal partner, brought all their joyous talent to *Top Hat,* and Berlin contributed some charming songs. The two stars introduced the romantic adagio "Cheek to Cheek." It got an Academy Award nomination for best song and became one of Berlin's greatest commercial successes. It was number one on *Your Hit Parade* for five weeks and was a *Variety* "Fifty Year Hit Parade" honoree.

Darling, Je Vous Aime Beaucoup
COMPOSER-LYRICIST: **Anna Sosenko**

This was Hildegarde's theme song, written by her manager, Anna Sosenko. It was even more successful when Nat "King" Cole made a successful recording in the fifties.

Deep Purple.
See page 73 (1934).

I Feel a Song Comin' On
COMPOSER: **Jimmy McHugh**
LYRICIST: **Dorothy Fields**

Jimmy McHugh and Dorothy Fields produced two hit songs for the score of the motion picture *Every Night at Eight:* "I'm in the Mood for Love" and "I Feel a Song Comin' On."

"I Feel a Song Comin' On" was introduced by Frances Langford. This rollicking tune is a great opening number for a nightclub act or a choir concert because of its suggestion that "a victorious, happy and glorious" song is about to be sung. It is such an upbeat, tuneful song that it puts audiences in a good mood immediately.

I Got Plenty o' Nuttin'
COMPOSER: **George Gershwin**
LYRICISTS: **Ira Gershwin and DuBose Heyward**

Porgy, played by Todd Duncan, introduced "I Got Plenty o' Nuttin' " in George Gershwin's folk opera *Porgy and Bess* (see "Bess, You Is My Woman," page 81). The lyrics express Porgy's contentment with the simple things of life. This Gershwin classic was selected by *Variety* for its "Fifty Year Hit Parade."

I Loves You, Porgy
COMPOSER: **George Gershwin**
LYRICISTS: **Ira Gershwin and DuBose Heyward**

Nina Simone had a million-selling record of "I Loves You, Porgy," in 1959. It was introduced in the 1935 Broadway production by Anne Brown and Todd Duncan (see "Bess, You Is My Woman," page 81). In the song, Bess and Porgy pledge their love when Bess is afraid Crown is coming to take her away.

I'm Gonna Sit Right Down and Write Myself a Letter
COMPOSER: **Fred E. Ahlert**
LYRICIST: **Joe Young**

This song has been a hit twice: first in 1935 for Fats Waller and then even greater (2 million records sold) for Billy Williams when he revived it in 1956–57. The simple chord structure of the song is more common to that of the fifties than to the complicated, lush chords common to the music of the thirties.

I'm in the Mood for Love
COMPOSER: **Jimmy McHugh**
LYRICIST: **Dorothy Fields**

Jimmy McHugh and Dorothy Fields are the writers of this *Variety* "Fifty Year Hit Parade" and "Golden 100 Tin Pan Alley Song" that by 1965 had been recorded more than 400 times with a total sale of more than 3 million. Frances Langford introduced the song in the motion picture *Every Night at Eight,* and it became her biggest hit. The singer is in a loving mood "simply because you're near me."

It Ain't Necessarily So
COMPOSER: **George Gershwin**
LYRICISTS: **Ira Gershwin and DuBose Heyward**

Performed by Sportin' Life (John Bubbles in the original cast) in *Porgy and Bess* (see "Bess, You Is My Woman," page 81) this song takes a skeptical view of several biblical tales. Sportin' Life performs the song in high style during a picnic at Kittiwah Island. Sammy Davis, Jr., performed it in the 1959 movie version. *Variety* honored this *Porgy and Bess* excerpt by including it in its "Fifty Year Hit Parade."

I Won't Dance
COMPOSER: **Jerome Kern**
 LYRICISTS: **Otto Harbach and Oscar
  Hammerstein II**

Jerome Kern wrote two additional hit songs for the movie version of his 1933 musical *Roberta:* "Lovely to Look At" and "I Won't Dance."

Fred Astaire asked Kern to write a rhythmic, electrifying dance number to which he could perform a dynamic tap dance. Astaire proceeded to demonstrate the type of dance steps he had in mind. Kern went to work and produced "I Won't Dance," one of his best rhythmic compositions. The movie scene is a classic that shows off the dance talents of Astaire and Ginger Rogers.

Just One of Those Things
COMPOSER-LYRICIST: **Cole Porter**

A second hit (see "Begin the Beguine," page 81) from Cole Porter's *Jubilee* was "Just One of Those Things," which was introduced by June Knight and Charles Walters. Porter wrote the song overnight while the show was in pre-Broadway tryouts in Ohio. Since then it has been interpolated into at least five films and was selected as a *Variety* "Fifty Year Hit Parade" and "Golden 100 Tin Pan Alley Song." It describes a debonair man's approach to the end of a romance. There are, after all, other worlds to be conquered.

Little Girl Blue
COMPOSER: **Richard Rodgers**
 LYRICIST: **Lorenz Hart**

"Little Girl Blue" was introduced by Gloria Grafton in the Rodgers and Hart musical extravaganza *Jumbo*. In a blue-tinted scene, the girl dreams of a childhood in a circus but laments the absence of a "little boy blue." In the adaptation for Hollywood, it was sung by Doris Day. Mabel Mercer and Nina Simone featured it in their individual nightclub acts. Miss Simone's recording, which uses "Good King Wenceslas" as a counterpoint accompaniment, is particularly inventive.

Rodgers and Hart called *Jumbo* a musical extravaganza, and what a spectacle it was, combining a circus with musical comedy, not unlike the first New York Hippodrome extravaganza, *A Yankee Circus on Mars*, in 1905. Three Rodgers and Hart classics came

from the score: "My Romance," "The Most Beautiful Girl in the World," and "Little Girl Blue."

Lovely to Look At
COMPOSER: **Jerome Kern**
 LYRICISTS: **Jimmy McHugh and Dorothy Fields**

The musical *Roberta* was written by Jerome Kern in 1933. The movie version in 1935 starred Fred Astaire. For the film, Kern wrote two additional hit songs: "Lovely to Look At" introduced by Irene Dunne's cool soprano voice and "I Won't Dance" (see page 000).

The movie's producers believed that "Lovely to Look At" was not hit material because the refrain was only sixteen measures long and the last four measures were unusually complex and subtle. Kern refused to change anything. The song became a huge hit, so much so that the second film version of *Roberta* in 1952 was called *Lovely to Look At.*

"Lovely to Look At" was the first number one song on *Your Hit Parade's* first broadcast on April 29, 1935. It also received an Oscar nomination for the year's best song.

Lullaby of Broadway
COMPOSER: **Harry Warren**
 LYRICIST: **Al Dubin**

With "Cheek to Cheek" and "Lovely to Look At" as competition, "Lullaby of Broadway" won the Oscar as the best song from motion pictures in 1935. It was the number two song on the first broadcast of *Your Hit Parade*, second to "Lovely to Look At." *Variety* chose "Lullaby of Broadway" for its "Fifty Year Hit Parade."

Harry Warren and Al Dubin continued their string of successes after *Forty-second Street* with the score for *Gold Diggers of 1935*. In 1935, they also wrote the music for six other movie musicals.

Busby Berkeley directed *Gold Diggers of 1935*. "Lullaby of Broadway" was staged as part of a charity show that was produced at a New England summer resort hotel. Berkeley considered it his favorite among the numerous ones he staged for various movie musicals.

As the sequence begins, Wini Shaw's face is only a small speck on the otherwise black screen. It grows larger during the song. After her face is close-up size and the song is finished, her profile turns into the Manhattan skyline. Then more than 100 dancers flood the screen in a frenzied sequence. The number ends in reverse, as we watch Shaw's face recede from close-up to speck to black screen.

The Most Beautiful Girl in the World
COMPOSER: **Richard Rodgers**
 LYRICIST: **Lorenz Hart**

This waltz was introduced by Donald Novis and Gloria Grafton in the Rodgers and Hart musical extravaganza *Jumbo*. In the film version, it was sung by Stephen Boyd.

"The most beautiful girl in the world picks my ties out, eats my candy, drinks my brandy," say the famous lyrics. The song is seventy-two measures, unusually long, and is packed with lovely words and a melody that is a delight to sing and a pleasure to hear.

The Music Goes 'Round and 'Round
COMPOSERS: **Edward Farley and Michael Riley**
 LYRICIST: **Red Hodgson**

"The music goes 'round and 'round and it comes out here" refers to a French horn's wound-up tubing. This syncopated music lesson was introduced and popularized by Farley and Riley. Their recording in 1934 for the newly formed Decca Records was the first release to show a profit for the company. It was chosen for *Variety*'s "Fifty Year Hit Parade" and was the nation's top hit on *Your Hit Parade* for three weeks in early 1936.

My Lucky Star
COMPOSER: **Nacio Herb Brown**
 LYRICIST: **Arthur Freed**

Eleanor Powell introduced this *Variety* "Fifty Year Hit Parade" song in the movie musical *Broadway Melody of 1936*. The *New York Times* reviewer was particularly impressed with the song "Sing Before Breakfast," which did not become a hit, but he was also enchanted with "My Lucky Star" (also called "You Are My Lucky Star"). He practically ignored the hit "Broadway Rhythm."

"My Lucky Star" was subsequently inserted into at least four other Hollywood films through the early fifties. The most famous was 1952's *Singin' in the Rain*. The song stayed at the number one position on *Your Hit Parade* for three weeks.

My Romance
COMPOSER: **Richard Rodgers**
 LYRICIST: **Lorenz Hart**

"My Romance" is a duet espousing a love so great it does not need romantic trappings. This *Variety* "Fifty Year Hit Parade" selection was introduced by Donald Novis and Gloria Grafton in the Rodgers and Hart musical extravaganza *Jumbo*. In the 1962 movie adaptation the song was performed by Doris Day.

Red Sails in the Sunset
COMPOSER: **Will Grosz (using the pen name Hugh Williams)**
 LYRICIST: **Jimmy Kennedy**

An English import, "Red Sails in the Sunset" became a hit in the United States in 1935, selling more than a million copies of sheet music and staying at number one on *Your Hit Parade* for four weeks. It was one of the most frequently represented songs on *Your Hit Parade* from 1935 to 1940. *Variety* recognized its accomplishments by selecting it for its "Fifty Year Hit Parade." Ray Noble and his orchestra introduced the song, before it was interpolated in the revue *The Provincetown Follies*.

The singer is hoping that those "red sails in the sunset" will bring a "loved one home safely to me."

Star Dust
See page 49 (1929). Named to *Variety*'s "Fifty Year Hit Parade" for 1935.

Summertime
COMPOSER: **George Gershwin**
 LYRICISTS: **Ira Gershwin and DuBose Heyward**

"Summertime" is a beautiful lullaby that is sung by Clara (Abbie Mitchell) as the folk opera *Porgy and Bess* opens. (See "Bess, You Is My Woman," page 81). In the 1959 adaptation for the screen, it was sung by Loulie Jean Norman for Dorothy Dandridge.

In addition to its popularity in connection with *Porgy and Bess*, Bob Crosby (Bing's brother) chose it for the theme for his orchestra. *Variety* selected it for its "Golden 100 Tin Pan Alley Song" list.

Tell Me That You Love Me
COMPOSER: **Cesare A. Bixio**
 LYRICIST: **Al Stillman**

This *Variety* "Fifty Year Hit Parade" song came to America from Italy. The original lyrics by Ennio Neri were titled "Parlami d'Amore, Mariù." Frank Parker introduced the song, with English lyrics by Al Stillman, in the United States. It was one of the top ten hits on *Your Hit Parade* in 1935 but never made it to the top.

These Foolish Things
(Remind Me of You)
COMPOSERS: **Jack Strachey and Harry Link**
 LYRICIST: **Holt Marvell (a pseudonym for Eric Maschwitz)**

This bittersweet nostalgic song comes from the musical *Spread It Abroad*, and it was introduced by Dorothy Dickson. Lyricist Maschwitz tried to imitate Cole Porter's complex rhyme scheme, as in "You're the Top," to enumerate the fleeting memories of young love. Some of the things that call forth memories include "a cigarette that bears a lipstick's traces, . . . an airline ticket . . . A tinkling piano . . . The winds of March,/A telephone that rings" It is a "Golden 100 Tin Pan Alley Song."

Top Hat, White Tie and Tails
COMPOSER-LYRICIST: **Irving Berlin**

Fred Astaire, fortified with a chorus of gentlemen, introduced this *Variety* "Fifty Year Hit Parade" song in the Berlin musical movie *Top Hat*. A top hat, white tie, tails, and Fred Astaire just seem to go together. Ironically, in Astaire's autobiography, he reveals that he was not particularly fond of the attire.

When I Grow Too Old to Dream
COMPOSER: **Sigmund Romberg**
LYRICIST: **Oscar Hammerstein II**

This *Variety* "Fifty Year Hit Parade" selection is one of Sigmund Romberg's most famous waltzes. He wrote it to Oscar Hammerstein II's lyrics for the movie musical *The Night Is Young*. It was introduced by Evelyn Laye and Ramon Novarro.

The movie and its music were not particularly well received. The only song that survived was "When I Grow Too Old to Dream." Romberg wrote much more interesting music; this song seems to have been dashed off without a lot of thought. Perhaps this is because the pressure to provide songs quickly was far greater in Hollywood than on Broadway, with less regard for worth.

You Are My Lucky Star
See "My Lucky Star," page 84.

Zing! Went the Strings of My Heart
COMPOSER-LYRICIST: **James F. Hanley**

This *Variety* "Golden 100 Tin Pan Alley Song" was introduced by Hal LeRoy and Eunice Healey in the revue *Thumbs Up*. It was interpolated into the musical shows *Listen, Darling* (1938) and *Lullaby of Broadway* (1951) and the film *Thumbs Up* (1943). Judy Garland's performance of the number helped get her a movie contract at MGM.

The singer's heartstrings went "zing" because "you smiled at me." Consequently, "I heard a melody, . . . Started a symphony/ . . . In perfect harmony . . . /A rhapsody divine."

1 9 3 6

Did I Remember?
COMPOSER: **Walter Donaldson**
LYRICIST: **Harold Adamson**

An Academy Award nominee in 1936, "Did I Remember? was featured in *Suzy*, which starred Jean Harlow and Cary Grant. Virginia Verrill's voice was dubbed into the sound track for Harlow for "Did I Remember?" It was reprised by Cary Grant in a rare attempt at singing. That sequence from the film is included in 1974's *That's Entertainment*. Grant's singing was charming and adequate for the circumstances.

The song was number one on *Your Hit Parade* for six weeks. The singer asks if she has remembered to tell you "I adore you, . . . I'm lost without you . . . and pray forevermore you are mine."

Easy to Love
COMPOSER-LYRICIST: **Cole Porter**

Reginald Gardiner is seen conducting an invisible orchestra in Central Park in Ponchielli's "Dance of the

Hours" in the movie musical *Born to Dance*. Suddenly and magically it becomes "Easy to Love." Frances Langford also performed this Cole Porter tune in the same film. (Another "Easy to Love" was written by Ralph Rainger and Leo Robin in 1937 for a movie, *Easy to Love*.)

"You'd be so easy to love" that it's too bad that "you can't see your future with me," say the lyrics.

Empty Saddles
COMPOSER-LYRICIST: **Billy Hill**

Bing Crosby introduced this Billy Hill western song in the movie musical *Rhythm on the Range*. The public enjoyed cowboy films and songs, so Hollywood turned them out. Even stars who had little western inclinations sang western songs in films. This was the first of two westerns starring Crosby. The other was 1969's *Stagecoach*.

Variety selected "Empty Saddles" for its "Fifty

Year Hit Parade,'' even though it made the top ten on *Your Hit Parade* for only one week in the year.

A Fine Romance
COMPOSER: Jerome Kern
  LYRICIST: Dorothy Fields

Jerome Kern and Dorothy Fields wrote this song for Fred Astaire and Ginger Rogers to perform in the movie musical *Swing Time*. Subtitled "A Sarcastic Love Song," it ridicules a romance "with no kisses . . . you won't nestle . . . you won't wrestle . . . you're as cold as yesterday's mashed potatoes . . . I might as well play bridge with my old maid aunts!"

Rogers first sang this clever song to Astaire during a snowstorm, complaining about his seeming lack of romanticism. He sings his answer.

Goody Goody
COMPOSER-LYRICISTS: Matt Malneck and Johnny Mercer

"Goody Goody" is a Johnny Mercer and Matt Malneck composition that Benny Goodman popularized in the late thirties. The Goodman recording helped the song become number one on *Your Hit Parade* for four weeks. The "King of Swing," clarinetist Benny Goodman, in this instance exemplifies the dawn of the swing era.

I Can't Get Started with You
COMPOSER: Vernon Duke
  LYRICIST: Ira Gershwin

Bob Hope first sang this song to try to break down Eve Arden's resistance in a scene from the *Ziegfeld Follies of 1936*. Hope is convinced that the song got him a film contract. The singer explains that he has done almost anything anyone could want to do in life, including flying around the world in a plane and even selling short just before the stock market crash, but he's downhearted because he "can't get started with you."

I'm an Old Cowhand
COMPOSER-LYRICIST: Johnny Mercer

Bing Crosby introduced this *Variety* "Fifty Year Hit Parade" cowboy song in the movie musical *Rhythm on the Range*. He further popularized it in a recording. Roy Rogers revived it in 1943's *The King of the Cowboys*.

Although his "legs ain't bowed and . . . his cheeks ain't tanned" and he's never seen a cow or roped a steer, he's "an old cowhand from the Rio Grande," say Mercer's satirical lyrics.

Variety called the public's apparent enchantment with western songs "hillbilly mania."

In the Chapel in the Moonlight
COMPOSER-LYRICIST: Billy Hill

The famous hillbilly songsmith Billy Hill wrote this song, which was a best-selling record for Shep Fields and his orchestra. It was even more of a hit in 1954, when Kitty Kallen's version sold a million copies. Dean Martin revived it in 1967 into a best seller.

In this song of a broken romance, the singer dreams about strolling down the aisle for a wedding "in the chapel in the moonlight."

Indian Love Call
See page 28 (1924). This famous duet sold a million records in 1936 because of the release of the film version of Rudolf Friml's *Rose Marie*, which starred Jeanette MacDonald and Nelson Eddy. Their recording of "Indian Love Call" was the first musical show tune to top the million mark.

Is It True What They Say About Dixie?
COMPOSER: Gerald Marks
  LYRICISTS: Sammy Lerner and Irving Caesar

Rudy Vallee and Al Jolson helped popularize this *Variety* "Fifty Year Hit Parade" tune over radio and in recordings. It was *Your Hit Parade*'s top song for five weeks in 1936. "Does the sun really shine all the time?" it asks; in other words, are all the nice things that one hears about the South really true?

It's a Sin to Tell a Lie
COMPOSER-LYRICIST: Billy Mayhew

Kate Smith introduced this Billy Mayhew song in 1936, but it may have been an even greater hit when it was revived in 1955 by Something Smith and the Redheads in a best-selling recording. *Variety* selected it for its "Fifty Year Hit Parade" for 1936.

The lyrics warn that we should "be sure it's true when you say 'I love you'," for "millions of hearts have been broken, Just because these words were spoken."

It's De-Lovely
COMPOSER-LYRICIST: Cole Porter

This clever song is by the master of intricately rhymed comic songs Cole Porter. Ethel Merman and Bob Hope introduced it in *Red, Hot and Blue*. The verse and four choruses trace the blissful saga of a boy and girl from the night they fall in love, through marriage, to the birth of their first child.

I've Got You Under My Skin
COMPOSER-LYRICIST: **Cole Porter**

Virginia Bruce introduced this Academy Award nominee in the movie musical *Born to Dance*. Even though the singer knows that the "affair never will go so well," she cannot stop seeing her loved one " 'cause I've got you under my skin."

Cole Porter uses inner rhymes very effectively in this song, for example, in the phrase "But each time I do, just the thought of you makes me stop." And he puts a rest immediately following the word *stop*, so the singer emphasizes it.

The song was selected by *Variety* for its "Fifty Year Hit Parade" and as a "Golden 100 Tin Pan Alley Song." "I've Got You Under My Skin" was featured in Cole Porter's screen biography, *Night and Day* (1946), and as a comedy number for Tony Randall and Debbie Reynolds in the 1959 film *The Mating Game*.

Let's Face the Music and Dance
COMPOSER-LYRICIST: **Irving Berlin**

Fred Astaire and Ginger Rogers introduced this Irving Berlin song in the movie musical *Follow the Fleet*. The song was first sung by Astaire and then danced by him and Rogers as the finale of their fund raiser for restoration of a schooner. For the routine, Rogers wore a costume that was dreadfully heavy. With every turn Astaire feared being slammed by a flying sleeve. At one point a sleeve did hit him in the mouth and eye, leaving him a little stunned. The accident happened while the camera was on Rogers, and Astaire recovered without ruining the take.

Moon over Miami
COMPOSER: **Joe Burke**
LYRICIST: **Edgar Leslie**

This *Variety* "Fifty Year Hit Parade" selection was number one on *Your Hit Parade* for one week and stayed in the top ten for more than two months.

The singer is asking the "moon over Miami" to "shine on my love and me." He says the moon knows that they are "waiting for, A little love, a little kiss,/ On Miami shore."

The Night Is Young and You're So Beautiful
COMPOSER: **Dana Suesse**
LYRICISTS: **Billy Rose and Irving Kahal**

Billy Rose opened his Casa Manana Theater in Fort Worth during the Frontier Days Celebration in 1936. This song was introduced during the opening of a then unique theater-in-the-round. The singer blames his being "overamorous" on the girl's beauty and because "I'm in love with you!"

Pennies from Heaven
COMPOSER: **Arthur Johnston**
LYRICIST: **Johnny Burke**

Bing Crosby introduced this nominee for the Academy Award in the movie musical *Pennies from Heaven*. Crosby further popularized it in a recording. *Variety* selected "Pennies from Heaven" as a "Golden 100 Tin Pan Alley Song." It was number one for four weeks at the end of 1936 and the beginning of 1937. The song contends that we "must have showers" in our life if we "want the things we love," but those showers contain "pennies from heaven, for you and me."

It was inserted into the 1935 film *Cruisin' down the River*, 1954's *From Here to Eternity*, and 1960's *Pepe*. Comedian Steve Martin starred in the 1981 film of the same title, which saluted movie musicals and the Depression, but had no relation to the 1936 film.

San Francisco
COMPOSER: **Bronislaw Kaper**
LYRICIST: **Gus Kahn**

Several songs have been written about the City by the Bay, but this is one of the most famous. It was sung under the titles of *San Francisco* and used as a recurrent theme for the film, which starred Jeanette MacDonald and Clark Gable.

Say Si, Si
COMPOSER: **Ernesto Lecuona**
LYRICIST: **Al Stillman**

This *Variety* "Fifty Year Hit Parade" selection originated in Cuba with the Spanish title "Para Vigo Me Voy." The original Spanish lyrics were by Francia Luban. It was introduced to the United States by Xavier Cugat and his orchestra, with Lina Romay doing the vocal. The Andrews Sisters had a best-selling record of "Say Si Si" in 1940, and Gene Autry sang it in the 1940 film *Carolina Moon*. According to *Your Hit Parade*, it never made the top ten.

Sing, Sing, Sing
COMPOSER: **Louis Prima**

Drummer Gene Krupa joined the Benny Goodman band in 1935 and was featured in the first extended jazz drum solo on a record in the best-selling disc of

"Sing, Sing, Sing," which the Goodman band recorded in 1936.

Stompin' at the Savoy
COMPOSERS: **Benny Goodman, Chick Webb, and Edgar Sampson**
LYRICIST: **Andy Razaf**

Another celebrated recording for the Benny Goodman band in 1936 was "Stompin' at the Savoy." The Savoy, a famous ballroom, was the scene of a lot of "rompin' and stompin' " by the youth of the era as their happy feet danced "while the band is swingin'."

There's a Small Hotel
COMPOSER: **Richard Rodgers**
LYRICIST: **Lorenz Hart**

Originally intended for *Jumbo* but dropped from the production, this tune resurfaced in *On Your Toes*. Rodgers and Hart wrote this dream of a perfect honeymoon. It was introduced by Ray Bolger and Doris Carson. *On Your Toes* was revived on Broadway in 1982 starring Leslie Caron.

The Way You Look Tonight
COMPOSER: **Jerome Kern**
LYRICIST: **Dorothy Fields**

The best-remembered song from the movie musical *Swing Time* is the 1936 Oscar winner "The Way You Look Tonight." It was the top song on *Your Hit Parade* for a month and a half during the year.

Even though "The Way You Look Tonight" is a love song and as such has become a standard, it was conceived as a comical song. Fred Astaire was kidding Ginger Rogers about her appearance while she was shampooing her hair.

The other Academy Award nominees were "Did I Remember?" from *Suzy*, Cole Porter's "I've Got You Under My Skin" from *Born to Dance*, "A Melody from the Sky" from *The Trail of the Lonesome Pine*, and "When Did You Leave Heaven?" from *Sing, Baby, Sing*.

When Did You Leave Heaven?
COMPOSER: **Richard A. Whiting**
LYRICIST: **Walter Bullock**

Tony Martin introduced this Oscar-nominated song in the movie musical *Sing, Baby, Sing*. It made the top of *Your Hit Parade* for a couple of weeks. The melody and lyrics seem naïve and sentimental today, but their saccharine sweetness fitted the band singers who helped popularize it.

The Whiffenpoof Song
COMPOSER: **Guy Scull (sometimes credited to Tod B. Galloway)**
LYRICISTS: **Meade Minnigerode and George S. Pomeroy**

This song originated in 1909, when the Whiffenpoof Society, a branch of the Yale Glee Club, was formed. Words were added by members of the 1910 class at Yale. The word *whiffenpoof* comes from an imaginary character in the Victor Herbert operetta *Little Nemo* (1908). Other lines from the song were adapted from Rudyard Kipling's poem "Gentlemen Rankers."

Rudy Vallee had heard the song during his collegiate days at Yale. In 1936 he was reintroduced to it when the society singers performed it on a radio program they shared. Vallee adapted it and featured it on his own program. This radio exposure and Vallee's recording built the song into a national hit. In 1947 Robert Merrill's recording gave the song renewed prominence, which may have brought it to Bing Crosby's attention. His subsequent 1947 recording backed by Fred Waring's Glee Club (later called the Pennsylvanians) had become a million seller by 1950.

You Turned the Tables on Me
COMPOSER: **Louis Alter**
LYRICIST: **Sidney D. Mitchell**

Alice Faye introduced "You Turned the Tables on Me" in the movie musical *Sing, Baby, Sing* (see "When Did You Leave Heaven?," above). It became a favorite with jazz ensembles, especially those of Louis Armstrong and Benny Goodman. ASCAP periodically rewarded unusually creative songs with special awards, and this song received one for 1936.

1 9 3 7

Caravan
COMPOSERS: Duke Ellington and Juan Tizol
LYRICIST: Irving Mills

This 1937 Duke Ellington composition was perhaps a bigger hit in 1949 and 1952, when million-selling records were made. Billy Eckstine sang the song to gold status in 1949, and trumpeter Ralph Marterie and his orchestra sold a million of their recording in 1952.

The lyrics speak of a desert caravan where "my dream of love is coming true." The scene depicted is reminiscent of the Rudolph Valentino sheik films that were popular in earlier years.

The Dipsy Doodle
COMPOSER-LYRICIST: Larry Clinton

This nonsense song was written by Larry Clinton for Tommy Dorsey. Dorsey's rendition helped make Clinton famous enough that he started his own band. Then Clinton's band further popularized it and used it as its theme song. The lyrics make little sense, but perhaps "that's the way the dipsy doodle works": "You'll think you're crazy, the things that you'll say, like rhythm got I and hot am I,/ That's the way the dipsy doodle works!"

The Donkey Serenade
COMPOSER: Rudolf Friml
LYRICISTS: Bob Wright and George ("Chet") Forrest

This song was based on "Chansonette" by Friml and Sigmund Spaeth, which in turn was based on an early Friml piano piece entitled "Chanson." Herbert Stothart arranged the song for the film, while Bob Wright and Chet Forrest contributed lyrics. It appeared in the movie adaptation of the Friml operetta *The Firefly*, in which it was sung by Allan Jones, who also made it into a best-selling recording. Friml wrote *The Firefly* in 1912, but the film version bears little or no relation to the original. The 1937 movie costarred Jeannette MacDonald and Allan Jones.

A Foggy Day
COMPOSER: George Gershwin
LYRICIST: Ira Gershwin

Damsel in Distress, a 1937 motion-picture musical starring Fred Astaire, introduced "A Foggy Day." The George and Ira Gershwin song originally had a longer title, "A Foggy Day in London Town." Frank Sinatra successfully used the song in nightclubs and in a recording.

The song paints the atmosphere of London. In the movie, Astaire crooned that the British fog depressed him, but then he "saw you there/And through foggy London town the sun was shining ev'rywhere."

Harbor Lights
Written in 1937, but see page 142 (1950), when it was a top hit.

I Can Dream, Can't I?
COMPOSER: Sammy Fain
LYRICIST: Irving Kahal

This ballad about wishful thinking was introduced by Tamara in the musical *Right This Way*. Its popularity increased during World War II, when the lyrics seemed particularly apropos for those who were "oceans apart." Patty Andrews had a million-selling record of "I Can Dream, Can't I?" in 1949, when the song was one of the year's top songs. The Carpenters successfully revived it in the seventies.

I'll Take Romance
COMPOSER: Ben Oakland
LYRICIST: Oscar Hammerstein II

Ben Oakland and Oscar Hammerstein II wrote this song for Grace Moore to sing in the movie musical *I'll Take Romance* (1938). The film seemed to be just an excuse to feature several operatic excerpts. It had very little plot and apart from the title song has been practically forgotten. Tony Martin further popularized the song in his nightclub appearances. It was featured in at least three other films through 1949.

In the Still of the Night
COMPOSER-LYRICIST: Cole Porter

Cole Porter's second Hollywood assignment was *Rosalie* (the first had been 1936's *Born to Dance*). Nelson Eddy introduced one of Porter's most lyrical songs, "In the Still of the Night," as he portrayed a college football hero smitten with Princess Rosalie of Romanza, who is attending college in America.

The suave melody sets a mood of mystery that fits the dreamy words.

"In the Still of the Night" had already become a standard by 1956, when the Five Satins' recording became a million seller. Della Reese also had a successful recording of the song in 1949.

I've Got My Love to Keep Me Warm
COMPOSER-LYRICIST: **Irving Berlin**

Irving Berlin wrote this song for the movie musical *On the Avenue* (1937). The film was a standard backstage musical and would have been exceedingly boring without Berlin's songs. Dick Powell and Alice Faye introduced "I've Got My Love to Keep Me Warm," but it was most popular when it was revived in a best-selling recording by Les Brown and his orchestra in 1949.

Johnny One Note
COMPOSER: **Richard Rodgers**
LYRICIST: **Lorenz Hart**

Rodgers and Hart wrote *Babes in Arms* in 1937. A group of stage apprentices decide to put on a musical show to avoid being sent to a work farm. Sound familiar? Well, it was novel in 1937. The show was a success, helped by four distinguished Rodgers and Hart songs: "Where or When," "Johnny One Note," "The Lady Is a Tramp," and *Variety*'s "Golden 100 Tin Pan Alley Song" "My Funny Valentine."

"Johnny One Note" is an account of the vocal feat of a singer who could sing one note so long and so loud that his fame spread far and wide. The song was introduced by Baby Rose (played by Wynn Murray) and the chorus.

The Lady Is a Tramp
COMPOSER: **Richard Rodgers**
LYRICIST: **Lorenz Hart**

Billie Smith (played by Mitzi Green) introduced this song in Rodgers and Hart's *Babes in Arms* (see "Johnny One Note," above). The song asserts that a girl is branded a tramp if she refuses to go along with social conventions, like having dinner at eight and arriving at the theater late. Buddy Greco and his orchestra had a gold record of this song in 1961.

Judy Garland performed it in the 1939 movie adaptation, while Lena Horne sang it in 1948's Rodgers and Hart screen biography, *Words and Music*. It was also added to the 1957 film version of the musical *Pal Joey*, in which it was sung by Frank Sinatra.

Let's Call the Whole Thing Off
COMPOSER: **George Gershwin**
LYRICIST: **Ira Gershwin**

This George and Ira Gershwin song was introduced by Fred Astaire and Ginger Rogers in the movie musical *Shall We Dance?* The clever lyrics compare American and British pronunciations, like "potayto—potahto, tomayto—tomahto." The song is perfectly suited to a moment that seems to occur in all Astaire-Rogers films: the bicker-reconciliation scene.

My Funny Valentine
COMPOSER: **Richard Rodgers**
LYRICIST: **Lorenz Hart**

Mitzi Green introduced this *Variety* "Golden 100 Tin Pan Alley Song" in Rodgers and Hart's *Babes in Arms* (see "Johnny One Note," above). It is a common misconception that the song's lyrics are about a comical female sweetheart, but the song was sung by Billie Smith about Valentine ("Val") Lamar, whom she loves despite his imperfections.

Judy Garland sang it in the film version in 1939, and the song became one of her specialties. It was also inserted into 1957's *Gentlemen Marry Brunettes* and 1957's *Pal Joey*.

Nice Work If You Can Get It
COMPOSER: **George Gershwin**
LYRICIST: **Ira Gershwin**

"Nice Work" had its beginnings in George Gershwin's manuscript book in the summer of 1930. In that idea book there appeared a nine-bar theme with the lyric "If the truth you're telling, then I'm yelling/There's no stopping us now." "There's No Stopping Us Now" was later developed into "Nice Work If You Can Get It."

In the movie musical *A Damsel in Distress* it is sung in Totleigh Castle by a trio of girls. Fred Astaire joined them on the chorus and reprised it later in the film while he pounded on several percussion instruments. Gershwin was convinced that Hollywood should reprise key songs in film musicals the way Broadway does. The reprise of "Nice Work If You Can Get It" was unusual in a film of this vintage.

The lyrics and music have a normal structure until the final hook "and if you get it—won't you tell me how?," which made George add two additional measures of music. The B-theme lyric (bridge) contains a quote of another Gershwin lyric: "Who could ask for anything more?" (the same line that appears in 1930's

"I Got Rhythm"), but it is set to a different melody, of course.

Once in a While
COMPOSER: **Bud Green**
LYRICIST: **Michael Edwards**

"Once in a While" may have been as big a hit when Harry James revived it in the 1950 movie musical *I'll Get By* as it was when it first appeared in 1937. Still, *Metronome* picked this song as one of the "best sides" (records) of 1937, when it was number one on *Your Hit Parade* for seven weeks.

The singer asks the loved one to "try to give one little thought to me," even though another "may be nearer your heart." That way the performer can be "contented with yesterday's memory," knowing that he is thought of "once in a while."

The One Rose That's Left In My Heart
COMPOSER-LYRICISTS: **Del Lyon and Lani McIntire**

This *Variety* "Fifty Year Hit Parade" selection, one of only half a dozen for 1937, originated in Hawaii in 1936. It spent six weeks in the top ten in 1937 but never made it to the top, rising no higher than number six.

Rosalie
COMPOSER-LYRICIST: **Cole Porter**

The final version of "Rosalie" was the seventh re-write that Porter presented to the studio brass when he was writing the score for the musical *Rosalie*. He thought that several of the previous six were better songs than the one finally used, but it nevertheless was good enough to make number one for two weeks. *Variety* selected "Rosalie" for its 1937 list in its "Fifty Year Hit Parade," one of only six songs chosen for the year.

The lyrics and melody of "Rosalie" do not have the brittle rhymes and haunting melody that are Porter trademarks. However, he is still the master of the inner rhyme scheme: "Won't you make my life thrilling,/And tell me you're willing to be mine, Rosalie, mine!"

Nelson Eddy, playing a college football hero, and Eleanor Powell, playing Princess Rosalie of Romanza, introduced the title song in an elaborate song and dance number (Eddy and the chorus sang, while Powell danced) that seemed to employ every actor and actress who could be found. In 1974 *That's Entertainment* featured this number. With wages what they are today, such extravagance will never be seen again.

September in the Rain
COMPOSER: **Harry Warren**
LYRICIST: **Al Dubin**

"September in the Rain" was introduced in the 1935 movie musical *Stars over Broadway*. It was heard there only as instrumental background music. Budget cuts eliminated Busby Berkeley's planned scene for the song.

James Melton, who starred in *Stars over Broadway,* reintroduced "September in the Rain" in the 1937 movie musical *Melody for Two.*

Warren and Dubin wrote this reverie of a September that love made worth remembering. It was number one for five weeks in 1937. George Shearing had his first successful recording with the song in 1949.

So Rare
COMPOSER: **Jerry Herst**
LYRICIST: **Jack Sharpe**

Jimmy Dorsey popularized this number in the late thirties when it was the top song on *Your Hit Parade* for one week. In the late fifties, Lee Carlton of Fraternity Records felt the tune had hit potential. He hired Lou Douglas to write a new arrangement and hired Jimmy Dorsey to cut a new recording. The new "So Rare" stayed on the charts for thirty-eight weeks and became the seventh biggest hit of 1957, twenty years after Dorsey had originally recorded it. Jimmy died of cancer shortly after he was awarded a gold record for "So Rare" in June of 1957.

It seems rather strange that a big band tune would be such a hit in the early years of rock, but it happened. Although the new arrangement had more of a rock backbeat than the original 1937 recording, it still sounded like a big band playing the piece. Perhaps it was nostalgia, similar to the rebirth in the seventies of numerous fifties hits and the personalities that made them hits.

Jerry Herst and Jack Sharpe wrote this song, which catalogs the reasons why the loved one and the love are "So Rare."

Sweet Leilani
COMPOSER-LYRICIST: **Harry Owens**

The Academy Award for the best song from films went to "Sweet Leilani" in 1937. Bing Crosby introduced it in the movie musical *Waikiki Wedding*. The *Variety* "Fifty Year Hit Parade" song was written by Harry Owens, the leader of the Royal Hawaiians orchestra, and has an authentic Hawaiian flavor.

Crosby's recording was the first of his twenty-two

discs to sell 1 million. He sold more than 400 million records and made more than 2,600 recordings during his long career.

The other Academy Award nominees for 1937 were "Remember Me?," by Harry Warren and Al Dubin, from *Mr. Dodd Takes the Air*; "That Old Feeling," by Sammy Fain and Lew Brown, from *Vogues of 1938*; "They Can't Take That Away from Me," by George and Ira Gershwin, from *Shall We Dance?*; and "Whispers in the Dark," by Frederick Hollander and Leo Robin, from *Artist and Models*.

Thanks for the Memory
COMPOSER: **Ralph Rainger**
LYRICIST: **Leo Robin**

"Thanks for the Memory" became Bob Hope's theme song after he had introduced it in his screen debut in the movie musical *The Big Broadcast of 1938*. The tongue-in-cheek lyrics, a catalog of "thanks," fitted Hope's comic style perfectly. It won the Academy Award for the best film song of 1938. A recording by Bob Hope and Shirley Ross was a best seller in 1938, when it hit the top of *Your Hit Parade* for three weeks.

The song was written and released in 1937, and appeared on *Variety*'s "Fifty Year Hit Parade." (See "Jeepers Creepers," page 94, for the other Oscar nominees for 1938.)

That Old Feeling
COMPOSER: **Sammy Fain**
LYRICIST: **Lew Brown**

An Academy Award nominee in 1937, this *Variety* "Fifty Year Hit Parade" song was introduced in the movie musical *Vogues of 1938*. The film was primarily a fashion show with a shallow plot and a few songs.

"That Old Feeling" tries to rekindle an old romance by suggesting that "that old feeling/Is still in my heart." Jane Froman had success with the song,

so it was used in her film biography, *With a Song in My Heart*, in 1952. It held the top spot on *Your Hit Parade* of 1937 for four weeks.

They Can't Take That Away from Me
COMPOSER: **George Gershwin**
LYRICIST: **Ira Gershwin**

Fred Astaire, singing to Ginger Rogers on a ferry to Hoboken, New Jersey, introduced this song in the film *Shall We Dance?* Ira Gershwin used a popular expression of the day as the title and central theme of his lyric. "They Can't Take That Away from Me" is the only Gershwin song to have been nominated for an Academy Award.

As originally sketched out in Gershwin's manuscript idea book, this song had a nine-bar theme similar to the beginning of Beethoven's Fifth Symphony, except that the fourth note rose, instead of descended. George and Ira eventually broke the first three notes into five: three-eights, one-quarter, and one-eighth. The last four measures of the song are a tag, restating the lyric of the previous four bars, but with a new musical theme.

Where or When
COMPOSER: **Richard Rodgers**
LYRICIST: **Lorenz Hart**

Billie Smith (Mitzi Green) and Val Lamar (Ray Heatherton) introduced this *Variety* "Fifty Year Hit Parade" song in the Rodgers and Hart musical *Babes in Arms* (see "Johnny One Note," page 90). They sing that this moment seems to have happened before, although neither can recall "where or when."

In the 1939 film version of the musical it was sung by Betty Jaynes and Douglas MacPhail, while Lena Horne sang it in the Rodgers and Hart screen biography, *Words and Music* (1948).

1 9 3 8

A-Tisket A-Tasket
COMPOSER-LYRICISTS: **Ella Fitzgerald and Al Feldman**

"The First Lady of Jazz," Ella Fitzgerald, achieved her first million seller with this song, which was the top tune on radio for the year and spent several weeks at the head of *Your Hit Parade*.

Leonard Bernstein, in the 1973 Norton Lectures at Harvard, said that research indicates that the melodic motif of "A-Tisket A-Tasket" is the same all over the world, wherever children tease each other. On every continent, in every culture, it is one of the few musical universals.

Ella and Al Feldman adapted an old nursery rhyme

into the song. "A-Tisket A-Tasket,/A green and yellow basket,/I bought a basket for my mommie,/On the way I dropped it" are the lyrics that come practically without change from the nursery rhyme. "She was truckin' on down the avenue" is an example of a phrase added by Ella and Al.

Variety listed this song as one of eight in its "Fifty Year Hit Parade" for 1938's biggest hits.

Bei Mir Bist Du Schoen
COMPOSER: **Sholom Secunda**
LYRICISTS: **Sammy Cahn and Saul Chaplin; original lyrics by Jacob Jacobs**

English lyrics were added to this 1932 Yiddish popular song in 1937. It sold a million records for the Andrews Sisters, the first gold record earned by a female group. It was number one on *Your Hit Parade* for two weeks and the number three sheet music seller of 1938. The lyrics explain that "Bei mir bist du schoen means that you're grand . . . the fairest in the land."

Variety selected this song as one of only eight in its "Fifty Year Hit Parade" for 1938.

Boogie Woogie
COMPOSER: **Clarence ("Pinetop") Smith**

Tommy Dorsey and his orchestra had a million-selling record of "Boogie Woogie" in 1938. Clarence ("Pinetop") Smith composed the piece and first recorded it in 1928 under the title "Pinetop's Boogie Woogie."

The form is similar to a classic passacaglia, in which a bass melody is repeated over and over while the upper voice melody and chord structure change above it.

Falling in Love with Love
COMPOSER: **Richard Rodgers**
LYRICIST: **Lorenz Hart**

Rodgers and Hart found the idea of basing a musical on a Shakespeare play fascinating, so in 1938 they produced *The Boys from Syracuse* derived from *The Comedy of Errors*. Set in Ephesus, in ancient Greece, the plot involves the attempt by Antipholus and his servant Dromio of Syracuse to find their long-lost twins. Complications arise when the wives of the Ephesus twins mistake the twins from Syracuse for their husbands.

"Falling in Love with Love" is a doleful waltz introduced by Adriana, wife of Antipholus of Ephesus, and her maids as they weave a tapestry. Muriel Angelus played Adriana on Broadway. Author Alan Jenkins suggests that the lyric sums up better than any other poetry of the decade the urban attitude toward love in the troubled thirties: "Falling in love with love is falling for make-believe . . ."

In the movie adaptation in 1940, Hollywood, as it often does, switched things around and gave the song to Allan Jones to sing.

The Flat Foot Floogee
COMPOSER-LYRICISTS: **Slim Gaillard, Slam Stewart, and Bud Green**

This "hep" swing era lyric was introduced by two of its writers, Slim and Slam. It was listed by *Variety* as one of only eight songs in its "Fifty Year Hit Parade" for 1938. One needs a jive dictionary to translate the lyrics ("Flat foot floogee with the floy, floy"). The flat foot floogee was a dance: "When you're feelin' low down . . . Here's the dance . . . to do." The song has had more longevity in jazz than in the popular field.

Heart and Soul
COMPOSER: **Hoagy Carmichael**
LYRICIST: **Frank Loesser**

Hoagy Carmichael published "Heart and Soul" as an independent number (not intended for a specific movie or Broadway show). It then was interpolated into the 1938 movie short *A Song Is Born* by Larry Clinton and his orchestra. In 1939 Gene Krupa and his orchestra used it in the film *Some Like It Hot*. It is not a slow dreamy love song, which the title might suggest, but rather a lilting love ballad.

Hooray for Hollywood
COMPOSER: **Richard A. Whiting**
LYRICIST: **Johnny Mercer**

This paean to the movie industry's capital city premiered in the movie musical *Hollywood Hotel*. The film was Busby Berkeley's last directing job with the Warner Brothers studio before he moved to MGM.

Heigh-Ho
COMPOSER: **Frank Churchill**
LYRICIST: **Larry Morey**

The seven dwarfs' song from Walt Disney's first full-length cartoon, *Snow White and the Seven Dwarfs,* is one of several songs from the score that rate mention for their creativity and longevity. "Heigh-ho, heigh-ho . . . makes your troubles go," sang the dwarfs. That type of philosophy was still music to the ears of the people who had survived the troubled years of the early thirties.

I'll Be Seeing You

See page 115 (1944) when it was the top hit of the year.

I've Got a Pocketful of Dreams

COMPOSER: **James V. Monaco**
 LYRICIST: **Johnny Burke**

Bing Crosby introduced this song in the movie musical *Sing, You Sinners*. In the film Crosby played a singer who loves to gamble on the horses. Crosby also had a best-selling recording of the song, which says everything is okay as long as one can dream. "I've Got a Pocketful of Dreams" was the number one sheet music seller in 1938 and spent four weeks at the top of *Your Hit Parade*.

Jalousie

COMPOSER: **Jacob Gade**

Arthur Fiedler and the Boston Pops' 1938 recording of "Jalousie" became the first million-selling record of a light orchestral piece. "Jalousie" was written in 1926 by the Danish composer Jacob Gade as "Tango Tzigane." More than 200 recordings of it have been made.

Jeepers Creepers

COMPOSER: **Harry Warren**
 LYRICIST: **Johnny Mercer**

Louis Armstrong introduced this Academy Award-nominated song in the movie musical *Going Places*. "Jeepers Creepers" became one of his specialties. The song seems frivolous, in a style similar to Eddie Cantor's. It was the number six top radio tune and stayed at number one on *Your Hit Parade* for five weeks in 1939.

The Oscar was awarded to "Thanks for the Memory" (see page 92) in 1938. The other nominations were "Change Partners," by Irving Berlin, from *Carefree*; "Jeepers Creepers," by Harry Warren and Johnny Mercer, from *Going Places*; "My Own," by Jimmy McHugh and Harold Adamson, from *That Certain Age*; "A Mist over the Moon," by Ben Oakland and Oscar Hammerstein II, from *The Lady Objects*; and "Now It Can Be Told," by Irving Berlin, from *Alexander's Ragtime Band*.

Love Walked In

COMPOSER: **George Gershwin**
 LYRICIST: **Ira Gershwin**

This was one of George Gershwin's last songs, one he wrote for the movie musical *The Goldwyn Follies*. He also partially completed "Our Love Is Here to Stay"

before he collapsed from a brain tumor. Gershwin died in 1937 following exploratory brain surgery.

Dead at thirty-nine, but what he had achieved in those years! Had his life not ended at such a young age he surely would have accomplished even more fantastic musical feats. He seemed to be always pushing back the horizons of music.

"Love Walked In" was introduced by Kenny Baker in *The Goldwyn Follies*. It was on *Your Hit Parade* for fourteen weeks and was number one for four weeks. It was also among the four top sheet music sellers for the year.

Ira's lyrics say everything is sunny since "love walked in" when you appeared.

Mexicali Rose

COMPOSER: **Jack Tenny**
 LYRICIST: **Helen Stone**

"Mexicali Rose" was written by Jack Tenny and Helen Stone in 1923. It was popularized on radio in 1926 by the Cliquot Club Eskimos. *Variety* lists "Mexicali Rose" in its "Fifty Year Hit Parade" in 1938, when it was popularized by Bing Crosby. Gene Autry used it in the film *Mexicali Rose* in 1939 and also sang it in *Barbed Wire* in 1952. Roy Rogers used it in *Song of Texas* in 1943. Its frequent use in western films made it a stereotype of songs about Mexico and its women.

Music, Maestro, Please

COMPOSER: **Allie Wrubel**
 LYRICIST: **Herb Magidson**

This was the number two sheet music seller and was number one on *Your Hit Parade* for four weeks in 1938. The song was introduced by Frank Parker and Frances Langford on radio. *Variety* included it in its "Fifty Year Hit Parade" as one of only eight songs it listed for the year.

My Heart Belongs to Daddy

COMPOSER-LYRICIST: **Cole Porter**

Cole Porter's *Leave It to Me!* was a musical satire on communism and United States diplomacy. The musical introduced Mary Martin to Broadway audiences. She in turn introduced "My Heart Belongs to Daddy," in which the word *daddy* denotes a "sugar daddy." Even though Martin's role was a minor one, she stole the show with this number. Martin sang the number in a babylike, flapper voice, while she simulated a striptease. She performed it again in the 1946 film *Night and Day*, and Marilyn Monroe sang it in *Let's Make Love*, a 1960 film.

My Reverie

COMPOSER: **Claude Debussy, adapted by Larry Clinton**

LYRICIST: **Larry Clinton**

Bandleader and composer Larry Clinton adapted the French impressionist composer Claude Debussy's famous "Revierie" into the popular song "My Reverie" and had his first major success as a recording artist. The song was number one on *Your Hit Parade* for eight weeks at the end of 1938 and the beginning of 1939. It was among the most played radio tunes and number two in sheet music sales for 1938. The melody is gorgeous, but the lyrics are far less appealing. Phrases like "only a poor fool never schooled in the whirlpool/Of romance could be so cruel" and "My dreams are as worthless as tin to me" are not classic examples of the lyricist's art.

One O'Clock Jump

COMPOSER: **Count Basie**

One of the all-time great jazz pianists and bandleaders, Count Basie wrote "One O'Clock Jump" in 1937. Trumpeter Harry James and his orchestra had their first million-selling record with the tune in 1938. It is unusual for a song without lyrics to become and remain popular, but this is a notable exception.

More than fifty years later it was revived by the country group Asleep at the Wheel and earned the 1978 Grammy Award for best country instrumental performance of the year.

One Song

COMPOSER: **Frank Churchill**

LYRICIST: **Larry Morey**

Walt Disney produced his first full-length animated cartoon in 1938. Frank Churchill and Larry Morey wrote several memorable songs for the score of *Snow White and the Seven Dwarfs,* including "One Song."

"One Song," according to *Variety* and *Your Hit Parade* charts, may have been one of the year's top songs, but it seems the least popular in subsequent years. In this love song "my heart keeps singing . . . only for you."

Our Love Is Here to Stay

COMPOSER: **George Gershwin**

LYRICIST: **Ira Gershwin**

"Our Love Is Here to Stay," George Gershwin's last song, was introduced by Kenny Baker in the movie musical *The Goldwyn Follies.* (See "Love Walked In,"

page 94.) Actually it was unfinished at Gershwin's death and was completed by Vernon Duke. Duke started with twenty bars of an incomplete lead sheet, but fortunately George had played it for friends enough that it could be pieced together.

Gene Kelly and Leslie Caron performed it in the 1951 movie musical *An American in Paris.*

Says My Heart

COMPOSER: **Burton Lane**

LYRICIST: **Frank Loesser**

Harriet Hilliard (of Ozzie and Harriet) introduced "Says My Heart" in the movie musical "The Coconut Grove." She played a singer who pretends to be a schoolteacher. "Fall in love, says my heart," but the schoolteacher's brain keeps wanting the head to rule the heart.

The song stayed at number one on *Your Hit Parade* for four weeks and was the number four sheet music seller and the third-ranked radio tune of the year.

September Song

COMPOSER: **Kurt Weill**

LYRICIST: **Maxwell Anderson**

"September Song" was one of only sixteen songs selected by ASCAP for its "All-Time Hit Parade, and *Variety* named it to its "Fifty Year Hit Parade."

It was written for *Knickerbocker Holiday,* one of the first musicals on Broadway to be based on a historical subject that commented on contemporary issues. The theme of democracy versus totalitarianism is presented in the reign of Governor Peter Stuyvesant in New Amsterdam in 1647. Walter Huston played Stuyvesant and acted it so well, especially when he sang "September Song," that audiences found themselves pulling for the wrong side. Stuyvesant confesses his fears of growing old in this tender ballad sung to the young girl he intends to marry.

Jazz great Stan Kenton and his orchestra had a best-selling recording of "September Song," as did Bing Crosby in 1946.

Small Fry

COMPOSER: **Hoagy Carmichael**

LYRICIST: **Frank Loesser**

"Small Fry" was sung by Bing Crosby to thirteen-year-old Donald O'Connor, who was making his screen debut, in *Sing, You Sinners.* The song was popularized in recordings by Crosby and Johnny Mercer.

Some Day My Prince Will Come
COMPOSER: **Frank Churchill**
LYRICIST: **Larry Morey**

In *Snow White and the Seven Dwarfs,* "Some Day My Prince Will Come" was sung by Snow White dreaming of the day when her knight in shining armor would come to sweep her off her feet.

The entire score received an Academy Award nomination for best score in 1937. In 1938 the Motion Picture Academy awarded Walt Disney a special Oscar for "significant screen innovation which has charmed millions and pioneered a great new entertainment field for the motion picture cartoon."

There's a Gold Mine in the Sky
COMPOSER-LYRICISTS: **Charles and Nick Kenny**

This *Variety* "Fifty Year Hit Parade" selection provided the title for a 1938 film that starred Gene Autry, who, of course, performed the song in the movie.

"Gold Mine" was one of the top ten hits on *Your Hit Parade* for fourteen weeks toward the end of 1937 and the beginning of 1938.

Ti-Pi-Tin
COMPOSER: **Maria Grever**
LYRICIST: **Raymond Leveen**

"Ti-Pi-Tin" was a Spanish popular song by Maria Grever. English lyrics were added by Raymond Leveen, and it was introduced in America by Horace Heidt and his Brigadiers. "Ti-Pi-Tin" was the number two radio tune (most plays), was tied for the number one sheet music seller, and was number one on *Your Hit Parade* for six weeks in 1938. A vintage recording reveals a soft-voiced male singer crooning lyrics too superficially silly for contemporary tastes. Even though there are numerous lyrics in any age that are silly, this drivel was not intended to be so. It is now out of place and time.

Two Sleepy People
COMPOSER: **Hoagy Carmichael**
LYRICIST: **Frank Loesser**

Bob Hope and Shirley Ross, who introduced "Thanks for the Memory" in *The Big Broadcast of 1938,* introduced "Two Sleepy People" in the film *Thanks for the Memory.* "Two sleepy people" are "too much in love to say goodnight," say the lyrics in this conversational song.

Whistle While You Work
COMPOSER: **Frank Churchill**
LYRICIST: **Larry Morey**

"Whistle While You Work" was introduced by the dwarfs in the Walt Disney animated cartoon feature film *Snow White and the Seven Dwarfs.* They found that their work was much easier and less exhausting when they whistled.

Columnist Westbrook Pegler claimed that this Disney product was the "happiest thing that has happened in the world since the armistice." The pleasing fantasy started the entire nation singing, whistling, and/or humming "Heigh-Ho, Heigh-Ho" and "Whistle While You Work." It also was a blessing to some toy manufacturers, who, along with much of the nation, were suffering a bleak business year because of an economic recession. Over three million rubber reproductions of the seven dwarfs from the film were snatched up by toy buyers. The factory worked twenty-four hours a day and could not keep up with the demand.

Variety selected this Disney song for its "Fifty Year Hit Parade" representing 1938.

You Go to My Head
COMPOSER: **J. Fred Coots**
LYRICIST: **Haven Gillespie**

This *Variety* "Golden 100 Tin Pan Alley Song" was introduced by Glen Gray and the Casa Loma Orchestra, with Kenny Sargent doing the vocal. The song is a little longer than most songs of the day, and the melody jumps around, with several octave intervals. Frank Sinatra had a successful recording, and it was the theme for Mitchell Ayres and his orchestra.

You Must Have Been a Beautiful Baby
COMPOSER: **Harry Warren**
LYRICIST: **Johnny Mercer**

Dick Powell introduced this *Variety* "Fifty Year Hit Parade" song (listed in 1939) in the movie *Hard to Get.* The song topped the *Hit Parade* for one week in 1938 and two weeks in 1939. Bobby Darin revived the song in a 1961 best-selling recording.

Everyone knows that the lyrics compare present beauty with that of infancy: "You must have been a beautiful baby, 'cause, baby, look at you now."

1 9 3 9

And the Angels Sing
COMPOSER: **Ziggy Elman**
LYRICIST: **Johnny Mercer**

Trumpeter Ziggy Elman's orchestra introduced this number, but it became famous through the Benny Goodman orchestra recording that has a vocal rendition by Martha Tilton and trumpet solo by Elman. The song was the number one top radio tune for three weeks, the number one jukebox tune for eight weeks, and number one on *Your Hit Parade* for four weeks. This song offers more than normal harmonic variety, changing chords as often as seven times in two measures.

At the Balalaika
COMPOSER: **George Posford**
LYRICISTS: **Bob Wright and George ("Chet")**
Forrest

This *Variety* "Fifty Year Hit Parade" selection originated in England. The original music by George Posford was adapted by Herbert Stothart, and the original lyrics by Eric Maschwitz were discarded for new ones by Bob Wright and Chet Forrest. The revised version of "At the Balalaika" was introduced by Ilona Massey and the Russian Art Choir in the film *Balalaika*, (1939). The song spent nine weeks among the top ten on *Your Hit Parade* in 1940 but never reached number one (number three, February 17, 1940).

Beer Barrel Polka
COMPOSER: **Jaromir Vejvoda**
LYRICIST: **Lew Brown**

This was a popular Czech song written by Jaromir Vejvoda and given English words by Lew Brown in 1934. Its original Czech title, "Skoda Lasky," means "lost love." Will Glahe and his orchestra recorded a million seller of the English version in 1938. Sammy Kaye and his orchestra helped popularize the tune with their recording. The Andrews Sisters also had a best-selling recording. It was the number five sheet music seller and the number one jukebox song of 1939, staying on top of that chart for twenty weeks. The song was particularly popular during World War II. It seems like a folk or drinking song from oral tradition rather than a composed song.

Variety selected "Beer Barrel Polka" for its "Fifty Year Hit Parade."

Brazil
See page 111 (1943).

Darn That Dream
COMPOSER: **James Van Heusen**
LYRICIST: **Eddie De Lange**

Benny Goodman and his orchestra introduced this song in the musical *Swingin' the Dream*. The musical was a swing version of Shakespeare's *A Midsummer Night's Dream*. The singer dreams of his beloved, but when he awakes, she is not there, and he curses the dream.

Deep Purple
Even though "Deep Purple" was written in 1934 (see page 73), it was one of the top hits of 1939 as well. Jimmy Dorsey's recording was on *Metronome*'s best sides of 1939, was the number one top radio tune for three weeks, the number two sheet music seller, and the number three jukebox selection of the year, and it was six weeks on the top of *Your Hit Parade* in 1939. *Variety* selected the song for its "Fifty Year Hit Parade" twice, 1935 and 1939.

Friendship
COMPOSER-LYRICIST: **Cole Porter**

Ethel Merman and Bert Lahr introduced this mock hillbilly number in Cole Porter's musical *Du Barry Was a Lady*. It is a catalog song, listing the acts that reinforce a friendship. The show was the third-longest-running Broadway book musical of the thirties. Kay Kyser and his orchestra had the most notable recording of "Friendship."

God Bless America
COMPOSER-LYRICIST: **Irving Berlin**

Irving Berlin wrote this song in 1918 for a production number in the all-soldier show *Yip, Yip, Yaphank* but decided to delete it from the show.

In 1938 Kate Smith was planning a patriotic program for her radio show on Armistice Day. She asked

Berlin to write an appropriate song. Failing to come up with anything that pleased him enough, he resurrected "God Bless America." Kate introduced it on November 10, 1938, the last peacetime Armistice Day in America prior to the beginning of World War II.

Both major political parties used it as their key song for the presidential nominating conventions of 1939. As the United States drew closer to war, the song's popularity grew astronomically.

Berlin refused to capitalize on patriotism, so he copyrighted the song in the names of Gene Tunney, Mrs. Theodore Roosevelt, Jr., and A. L. Berman, making them a committee to administrate a God Bless America fund. All proceeds were assigned to the Boy Scouts and Girl Scouts. By 1981 more than $1 million had been turned over to the Scouts.

In a national poll in the late fifties "God Bless America" was second to the national anthem as the nation's favorite patriotic song. It is a *Variety* "Golden 100 Tin Pan Alley Song," a "Fifty Year Hit Parade" selection for 1940, and, perhaps more significant than these because only sixteen were chosen, an "ASCAP All-Time Hit Parade" selection.

Berlin considered "God Bless America" one of his five best songs, along with "Always," "Easter Parade," "There's No Business Like Show Business," and "White Christmas."

I Didn't Know What Time It Was
COMPOSER: **Richard Rodgers**
 LYRICIST: **Lorenz Hart**

Rodgers and Hart's *Too Many Girls* was a 1939 musical about collegiate matters, especially football. Consuelo (played by Marcy Wescott) and Clint Kelley (acted by Richard Kollmar) introduced this song about naive romance.

If I Didn't Care
COMPOSER-LYRICIST: **Jack Lawrence**

"If I Didn't Care" was popularized by the Ink Spots, who had been porters at New York's Paramount Theater before their singing career gained momentum. They were heard by an agent who arranged for them to record their first big hit, "If I Didn't Care." The chorus was spoken over a vocal background, one of the Ink Spots' trademarks.

I'll Never Smile Again
COMPOSER-LYRICIST: **Ruth Lowe**

The tale concerning the origin of this song may be apocryphal, but it is interesting. Ruth Lowe, a pianist

with Ina Ray Hutton's all-girl orchestra, wrote the song while mourning the death of her husband a few months after they had been married.

Percy Faith and his orchestra introduced the number on Canadian radio. Tommy Dorsey and his orchestra, with the vocal by Frank Sinatra, made the song an outstanding hit, the number one jukebox tune for sixteen weeks in 1940. It was the first number one on the first *Billboard* best seller chart in 1940. It was also Sinatra's first best-selling recording. Up to this time a big band usually limited the singer to one chorus. In this recording, Sinatra was featured, backed by the Tommy Dorsey Orchestra. More and more in the next few years, bands featured the singers, leading to the end of the swing era and the opening of the sing era, when the vocalists, not the bands and their leaders, were kings.

In the Mood
COMPOSER: **Joe Garland**
 LYRICIST: **Andy Razaf**

This tune became a Glenn Miller specialty and is responsible for his first success as a bandleader. Miller and his orchestra played the song in *Sun Valley Serenade,* a 1941 movie musical. It was a million seller for them, as well as the top jukebox tune of 1940, spending twenty-one weeks at the top of the chart. The tempo direction in the score reads "In the Groove," which means "cool, with it" in swing era jive talk.

The Lamp Is Low
COMPOSER: **Maurice Ravel, adapted by Peter De Rose**
 LYRICIST: **Mitchell Parish**

"The Lamp Is Low" is another example of a popular song derived from a famous composition by a classical composer. Peter De Rose adapted "Pavane pour une Infante Défunte" by Maurice Ravel, and Mitchell Parish added words to make "The Lamp Is Low." Ravel's impressionistic chords and exquisite melody required little adaptation to become a successful popular song. Larry Clinton and his orchestra introduced the number.

Moonlight Serenade
COMPOSER: **Glenn Miller**
 LYRICIST: **Mitchell Parish**

Glenn Miller wrote the music for this song, which he and his orchestra made into a million-selling recording. "Sunrise Serenade" appeared on the flip side.

"Moonlight Serenade" became the orchestra's theme

song, featuring Miller's distinctive arranging and his trombone. Miller and his orchestra had four million-selling discs in 1939: "Little Brown Jug," "In the Mood," and the two serenades, "Sunrise" and "Moonlight."

Moon Love
COMPOSER: **Peter I. Tchaikovsky, adapted by André Kostelanetz**
LYRICISTS: **Mack Davis and Mack David**

André Kostelanetz based this song on a theme from Tchaikovsky's Fifth Symphony. The lyricists added, "Will this be moon love . . . will you be gone when the dawn comes stealing through? . . . Say it's not moon love,/Tell me it's true love." The marriage of melody and lyrics was number one on *Your Hit Parade* for four weeks in 1939 and was one of the top radio tunes of the year.

Tchaikovsky and Chopin are the nineteenth-century Romantic composers whose melodies have most often been adapted into popular songs.

My Prayer
COMPOSER: **Georges Boulanger, adapted by Jimmy Kennedy**
LYRICIST: **Jimmy Kennedy**

Another tune based on a work by a classical composer, "My Prayer" was based on Georges Boulanger's "Avant de Mourir." The famous English songwriter Jimmy Kennedy was the adapter and lyricist. The song was on *Your Hit Parade* for fourteen weeks in 1939, reaching the second spot by the end of the year, and it was one of the top radio tunes of the year. Sammy Kaye and his orchestra were probably the chief agents for popularizing the tune. In 1956 it was revived by the Platters, who had a million-selling recording that was the number ten hit of the year and spent twenty-three weeks on the best-selling chart.

Our Love
COMPOSER: **Peter I. Tchaikovsky, adapted by Larry Clinton**
LYRICISTS: **Larry Clinton, Buddy Bernier, and Bob Emmerich**

Larry Clinton appropriated the theme for this hit from Tchaikovsky's *Romeo and Juliet.* Clinton and his orchestra introduced the song and helped make it number one on *Your Hit Parade* for two weeks during the year as well as a top radio tune. The original romantic Tchaikovsky theme was perfect for a popular hit.

Over the Rainbow
COMPOSER: **Harold Arlen**
LYRICIST: **E. Y. Harburg**

This "ASCAP All-Time Hit Parade" and *Variety* "Fifty Year Hit Parade" selection was the Academy Award winning song in 1939. "Over the Rainbow" is so well known that it is easily recognized after the first three notes (an octave skip up, followed by a half step down). Judy Garland introduced it in *The Wizard of Oz,* and her recording with Victor Young and his orchestra was a million seller. Garland was only sixteen when she starred in the film classic. The film has been an annual presentation on network television for years so that each new generation has been introduced to Dorothy, Toto, the Tin Man, the Scarecrow, and the Cowardly Lion plus the glorious musical score.

The other Academy Award nominations for best song from a motion picture for 1939 were "Faithful Forever," by Ralph Rainger and Leo Robin from *Gulliver's Travels;* "I Poured My Heart into a Song," by Irving Berlin, from *Second Fiddle;* and "Wishing," by Buddy De Sylva, from *Love Affair.*

Penny Serenade
COMPOSER: **Melle Weersma**
LYRICIST: **Hal Halifax**

Guy Lombardo and his Royal Canadians introduced this *Variety* "Fifty Year Hit Parade" selection for 1939. Written in England in 1938, it was the first-ranking jukebox tune for eleven weeks during 1939. It spent ten weeks in the top ten and stayed in the second spot for five weeks in the spring.

Scatterbrain
COMPOSERS: **Frankie Masters, Kahn Keene, and Carl Bean**
LYRICIST: **Johnny Burke**

This nonsense song was performed by Kay Kyser and his orchestra in the 1939 movie musical *That's Right, You're Wrong* and was a big production number in the Judy Canova film *Scatterbrain* (1940). The song stayed at the top spot on *Your Hit Parade* for six weeks at the end of 1939 and the beginning of 1940. Frankie Masters and his orchestra helped popularize the song, which became their theme. Benny Goodman and Freddy Martin also contributed to its success. The song was one of the top radio tunes of 1939. In 1940 it was a top sheet music seller and spent a dozen weeks at the number one position on the jukebox chart.

South of the Border
COMPOSER-LYRICISTS: Jimmy Kennedy and Michael Carr

English songwriters Jimmy Kennedy and Michael Carr wrote this song for Gene Autry, whose recording sold 3 million copies in two years. It was number one on *Your Hit Parade* for five weeks toward the end of 1939 and was chosen by *Variety* for its "Fifty Year Hit Parade" representing 1939. It was also the top-ranking sheet music seller and the fifth best-selling record of the year. It continued to be popular in 1940, selling enough sheet music to be the top seller, and it was the top jukebox tune for twelve weeks as well. Shep Fields and his Rippling Rhythm made a successful recording of this hit. The singer "fell in love . . . south of the border down Mexico way." The song has a Mexican style only when accompanied by the appropriate instruments and played with typical Mexican rhythms.

Sunrise Serenade
COMPOSER: Frankie Carle
LYRICIST: Jack Lawrence

Frankie Carle introduced this *Variety* "Fifty Year Hit Parade" song. It has lyrics (it was thought most songs had to have lyrics to be popular), but it is principally known as an instrumental. The wide interval leaps (frequent octaves and major sevenths, plus a few minor sixths and diminished fifths) make it difficult to sing and better suited to instruments.

Tara's Theme
COMPOSER: Max Steiner

Gone with the Wind was one of the most successful motion pictures ever filmed, and it had one of the best musical scores. "Tara's Theme" became famous in instrumental versions apart from the film. Tara was the home to which Scarlett O'Hara returns after the Civil War. The orchestral theme that accompanied the scene of her return was so powerful that the song transcended incidental music status and became a hit.

Three Little Fishies
COMPOSER-LYRICIST: Saxie Dowell

This nonsense song was popularized by Kay Kyser and his orchestra. It had become Kyser's first million-sell-ing disc by 1941. Hal Kemp and his orchestra introduced the song, which spent four weeks as the top sheet music seller of 1939. *Variety* selected it for its "Fifty Year Hit Parade."

The Very Thought of You
COMPOSER-LYRICIST: Ray Noble

This *Variety* "Fifty Year Hit Parade" choice for 1939 was written by Ray Noble in 1934. *Variety* reported that it was one of the top ten songs in the nation for fifteen weeks during 1934 but did not mention its popularity in 1939.

It was used as the title for and was featured prominently in a 1944 motion picture that starred Faye Emerson and Dennis Morgan. Again, in 1950 it was featured in the movie musical *Young Man with a Horn*, in which it was sung by Doris Day.

Wishing
COMPOSER-LYRICIST: Buddy De Sylva

Buddy De Sylva wrote both words and music for this song, which topped 1939's hit list for four weeks. It was introduced in the nonmusical film *Love Affair*. It was a nominee for the Oscar and was made popular in a recording by the Glenn Miller orchestra. It was the fourth best-selling record and the third best sheet music seller for the year. *Variety* named it to its "Fifty Year Hit Parade."

De Sylva was a very successful lyricist with the Henderson, Brown, and DeSylva team. This was one of the rare occasions when he wrote both words and music.

Woodchopper's Ball
COMPOSER: Woody Herman
LYRICIST: Joe Bishop

Clarinetist and bandleader Woody Herman wrote and popularized this fast blues. It was his first million-selling disc. It was revived in 1947, and the Herman orchestra recording sold substantially again.

You Must Have Been a Bautiful Baby
See page 96 (1938).

1 9 4 0

All the Things You Are
COMPOSER: **Jerome Kern**
   LYRICIST: **Oscar Hammerstein II**

During the first two months of 1940, "All the Things You Are" was the top song in the nation for a couple of weeks. It came from the 1939 musical *Very Warm for May,* in which it was introduced by Hollace Shaw, Frances Mercer, Hiram Sherman, and Ralph Stuart. Kern was convinced the song was too sophisticated to be popular, but he was mistaken. It was the top hit for two weeks in early 1940 and stayed in the top ten for almost three months at the end of 1939 and the beginning of 1940.

"All the Things You Are" seems too much in the operetta style for the swing era, but for seven weeks it was the top jukebox song in recordings by Tommy Dorsey, Artie Shaw, and Freddy Martin and their orchestras. In a poll conducted by the *Saturday Review* in 1964, more composers picked this song as their favorite than any other. This song was selected by *Variety* for its "Fifty Year Hit Parade."

The singer compliments the loved one with these lyrics: "You are the promised kiss of springtime/That makes the lonely winter seem long." He hopes for the day when his "happy arms will hold you. . . ./When all the things you are, are mine!"

Bewitched, Bothered and Bewildered
COMPOSER: **Richard Rodgers**
   LYRICIST: **Lorenz Hart**

Dick Rodgers and Larry Hart wrote this *Variety* "Golden 100 Tin Pan Alley Song" selection for the 1940 musical *Pal Joey* (see "I Could Write a Book," page 102). Vivienne Segal introduced the song as a middle-aged woman who is cynical about falling in love again. It was not an immediate hit, probably because it could not be played on the radio because of the AS-CAP ban (see page 80). The only million-seller version was by pianist Bill Snyder and his orchestra in 1950 (see page 141).

Blueberry Hill
COMPOSER-LYRICISTS: **Al Lewis, Larry Stock, and Vincent Rose**

Today this song is particularly associated with Fats Domino, and most people probably think he com-

posed it during the fifties. It is, however, a tune that Gene Autry introduced in the 1941 film *The Singing Hill.* It was featured in the forties by Glenn Miller and his orchestra with vocalist Ray Eberle, by Kay Kyser and his orhestra, and by Russ Morgan and his orchestra. It was the top jukebox song for eleven weeks. Louis Armstrong also made it one of his specialties. But Domino's 1957 gold record, on which he sings about finding his thrill on "Blueberry Hill," is the most memorable to most people.

The Breeze and I
COMPOSER: **T. Camerata (adapted from Ernesto Lecuona)**
   LYRICIST: **Al Stillman**

Jimmy Dorsey and his orchestra made an important recording of this song, which was adapted from Ernesto Lecuona's "Andalucia." *Variety* listed the song as one of the top ten of 1940 in its "Fifty Year Hit Parade," but other information makes it appear not that important. *Billboard* reported that recordings by Dorsey's, Charlie Barnet's, and Freddy Martin's orchestras made the song the number one jukebox record for seven weeks during the year. The song that stayed on top the longest in that category stayed there for twenty-one weeks, and twenty-seven songs were on top longer than "The Breeze and I."

Cabin in the Sky
COMPOSER: **Vernon Duke**
   LYRICIST: **John Latouche**

The Broadway musical *Cabin in the Sky* became a great triumph for Ethel Waters. The story concerned a battle between the Lawd's general and Lucifer, Jr., for the soul of Little Joe Jackson. Waters played Petunia, Joe's wife. In the title song she described what life must be like in heaven.

Ferryboat Serenade
COMPOSER: **Eldo di Lazzaro**
   LYRICIST: **Harold Adamson**

The Andrews Sisters' recording of this Italian song helped it stay nine weeks at number one on the jukebox charts and rate among the top fifteen sheet music sellers for the year.

The singer loves to ride the ferry, the music is good, couples are dancing and romancing, and everyone is happy.

Fools Rush In
COMPOSER: **Rube Bloom**
LYRICIST: **Johnny Mercer**

Johnny Mercer set words to Rube Bloom's composition "Shangri La" to make "Fools Rush In." The second-strain lyrics are "Fools rush in where wise men never go, but wise men never fall in love, so how are they to know?"

"Fools Rush In" was the top jukebox song for eight weeks in 1940. It was made popular through recordings by Mildred Bailey and by Glenn Miller and his Orchestra. Rick Nelson revived it in 1963 in a successful recording.

How High the Moon
COMPOSER; **Morgan Lewis**
LYRICIST: **Nancy Hamilton**

Frances Comstock and Alfred Drake introduced this song in the revue *Two for the Show*. It was popularized by Benny Goodman's orchestra with singer Helen Forrest. Les Paul and Mary Ford revived it in a million-selling record in 1951.

"Somewhere there's music . . . somewhere there's heaven" is sung twice with different responses. The singer is searching for music and heaven but will not be able to find them until "you love me as I love you."

I Could Write a Book
COMPOSER: **Richard Rodgers**
LYRICIST: **Lorenz Hart**

Rodgers and Hart's *Pal Joey* was considered daring because the lead, Joey, was an antihero. Gene Kelly had his first leading role as Joey.

A wealthy older woman, Vera, gets Joey's attention away from the younger Linda by agreeing to build him a nightclub. Joey has been an entertainer in a Chicago nightclub but would do anything to own his own club. His schemes and dirty dealings get him in deep trouble. Even when Joey sings the beautiful "I Could Write a Book" to the naïve chorus girl, he isn't as sweet as he sounds.

I'll Never Smile Again
See page 98 (1939).

Imagination
COMPOSER: **James Van Heusen**
LYRICIST: **Johnny Burke**

Fred Waring and his Pennsylvanians introduced "Imagination." Recordings by Glenn Miller, Tommy Dorsey, Ella Fitzgerald, and Kate Smith helped popularize the song. It was on top of the jukebox charts for seven weeks.

Indian Summer
COMPOSER: **Victor Herbert**
LYRICIST: **Al Dubin**

The tune originated in 1919 as a piano composition by Victor Herbert. But not until Al Dubin furnished it with lyrics in 1939 did it become a hit. Recordings by Tommy Dorsey and Glenn Miller helped the song become the number one music machine recording for twelve weeks in 1940. One of operetta's great composers, Victor Herbert, wrote this melody, which has a wide range in comparison to most other popular songs of the period.

In the Mood
See page 98 (1939).

It's a Big Wide Wonderful World
COMPOSER-LYRICIST: **John Rox**

The revue *All in Fun* introduced this number. The lyrics are a catalog of the ways, often rather outlandish, a person feels when in love. It was introduced by Wynn Murray, Walter Cassel, Marie Nash, and Bill Johnson.

The Last Time I Saw Paris
COMPOSER: **Jerome Kern**
LYRICIST: **Oscar Hammerstein II**

The Nazis occupied Paris in June 1940. This invasion inspired Oscar Hammerstein II to write this lyric. He shared it with Kern, who wrote the tune. It is the only Jerome Kern song for which the lyric came before the music and which was not written for stage or screen.

Kate Smith introduced it on her radio program, and because she had a six-week option on the song, nobody else could perform it during those weeks. By the time the option ended the ASCAP strike had started, keeping it off the airwaves. Therefore, it was first featured by Hildegarde, Noel Coward, and Sophie Tucker in nightclubs.

Ann Sothern interpolated the song into the 1941

movie musical *Lady Be Good*. Even though all the other songs in the film were George Gershwin's numbers from the original 1924 Broadway musical, Kern's tune walked off with the Academy Award. Kern felt that the song was not eligible for the Oscar because it had not been written for the film. As a result of this incident, the rules were changed so that subsequent songs had to be expressly written for the motion picture in which they appeared to be eligible for the award.

Make Believe Island
COMPOSER-LYRICISTS: **Nick Kenny, Charles Kenny, Will Grosz, and Sam Coslow**

"Make Believe Island" spent nine weeks at the top of the music machine charts in 1940. The public in the early forties was just as interested in unreality as we are today with *Fantasy Island*. "Make Believe Island" was widely heard in recordings by Mitchell Ayres, Dick Todd, and Dick Jurgens.

Maybe
COMPOSER: **George Gershwin**
LYRICIST: **Ira Gershwin**

This George and Ira Gershwin song came from the 1926 Broadway musical *Oh, Kay!* The Ink Spots' 1940 recording of "Maybe" was number one for eleven weeks on the jukebox charts and spent three weeks on the top of *Your Hit Parade*. "Maybe" has a style and lyrics typical of the twenties, but perhaps the forties' audience was nostalgic about the jazz age.

The Nearness of You
COMPOSER: **Hoagy Carmichael**
LYRICIST: **Ned Washington**

Hoagy Carmichael considered this one of his best songs (along with "Star Dust," "Rockin' Chair," and "One Morning in May"). He collaborated with Ned Washington to write it for the movie musical *Romance in the Dark*. It was made popular by Glenn Miller and his orchestra.

Oh Johnny, Oh Johnny, Oh!
COMPOSER: **Abe Olman**
LYRICIST: **Ed Rose**

"Oh Johnny, Oh Johnny, Oh!" was written in 1917 and interpolated into the musical *Follow Me*. Twenty-two years later it was revived by Wee Bonnie Baker with the Orrin Tucker orchestra and again became a big hit. It stayed at the top of the jukebox charts for

a dozen weeks in 1940 and was the second best sheet music seller for the year.

Playmates
COMPOSER-LYRICIST: **Saxie Dowell**

Novelty songwriter Saxie Dowell (see "Three Little Fishies," page 100) wrote "Playmates." Recordings by Kay Kyser and his orchestra and Mitchell Ayres and his orchestra in 1940 made it number one on the jukebox chart for eleven weeks and sixth biggest hit of the year.

Scatterbrain
See page 99 (1939).

Sierra Sue
COMPOSER-LYRICIST: **Joseph Buell Carey**

"Sierra Sue" was written in 1916. Elliott Shapiro revised it in 1940, when Bing Crosby sang the new version. In 1941 Gene Autry sang it in a film that used the song title as its title. It probably was revived because of the popularity of other western songs in the late thirties.

South of the Border
See page 100 (1939).

Tuxedo Junction
COMPOSERS: **Erskine Hawkins, William Johnson, and Julian Dash**
LYRICIST: **Buddy Feyne**

Erskine Hawkins and his orchestra introduced "Tuxedo Junction" at the Savoy Ballroom in New York, but Glenn Miller and his orchestra popularized it. Recordings by Hawkins, Miller, Jan Savitt, and the Andrews Sisters helped make the song one of the top three on the jukebox chart for 1940. It stayed on top for fifteen weeks during the year. The Miller recording was a million seller by 1945.

Tuxedo Junction is a railroad junction in Alabama.

We Three
COMPOSER-LYRICISTS: **Sammy Mysels, Dick Robertson, and Nelson Cogane**

The Ink Spots and Tommy Dorsey and his orchestra made recordings of "We Three" that helped it stay on top of the jukebox chart for eight weeks during the year. *Your Hit Parade* top ten listed it on top in the last month of 1940 with sales in the "going strong" category into 1941.

The "we three" in the title is "my echo, my shadow, and me."

When You Wish upon a Star
COMPOSER: **Leigh Harline**
LYRICIST: **Ned Washington**

Cliff ("Ukulele Ike") Edwards sang this Academy Award winner on the sound track of the Walt Disney full-length animated film *Pinocchio*. "When You Wish upon a Star" was among the top sheet music sellers of 1940 and was on top of the jukebox charts for eight weeks. It was recorded by Glenn Miller, Guy Lombardo, and Horace Heidt and his Musical Knights.

The Oscar-nominated songs for 1940 included "Down Argentine Way," by Harry Warren and Mack Gordon, from *Down Argentine Way;* "I'd Know You Anywhere," by Jimmy McHugh and Johnny Mercer, from *You'll Find Out;* "It's a Blue World," by Chet Forrest and Bob Wright, from *Music in My Heart;* "Love of My Life," by Artie Shaw and Johnny Mercer, from *Second Chorus;* "Only Forever," by James Monaco and Johnny Burke, from *Rhythm on the River;* "Our Love Affair," by Roger Edens and Georgie Stoll, from *Strike Up the Band;* "Waltzing in the Clouds," by Robert Stolz and Gus Kahn, from *Spring Parade;* and "Who Am I?," by Jule Styne and Walter Bullock, from *Hit Parade of 1941*.

The Woodpecker's Song
COMPOSER: **Eldo di Lazzaro**
LYRICIST: **Harold Adamson**

This Italian import is not to be confused with 1947's "Woody Woodpecker." A host of recordings by Glenn Miller, the Andrews Sisters, Will Glahe, and Kate Smith helped make this a hit. It was on top of the jukebox chart for sixteen weeks, tied with "I'll Never Smile Again," and second to "In the Mood" for the year. It was also among the top sellers of sheet music and spent seven weeks at the top spot on *Your Hit Parade*. It's "tick-a-tick-tick, tick-a-tick-tick" lyrics were almost as contagious as the hand-clapping chorus from 1941's "Deep in the Heart of Texas."

You Are My Sunshine
COMPOSER-LYRICISTS: **Jimmie Davis and Charles Mitchell**

Jimmie Davis used the popularity of this song to launch a film and political career. He made several movies, even after he had become governor of Louisiana. "You Are My Sunshine" was introduced in the film *Take Me Back to Oklahoma* by cowboy star Tex Ritter. In 1942 it was added to *In the Groove*, a film which starred Donald O'Connor and Martha Tilton.

Because Davis's musical background was in gospel music, he used the verse and chorus form (also called two-part or AB form) that is prevalent in gospel songs but very rare during this time of the AABA (three-part) form. (Many of the songs from the seventies and eighties are two-part [verse and chorus] form.)

1 9 4 1

Amapola
COMPOSER: **Joseph M. Lacalle**
LYRICIST: **Albert Gamse**

The first million-selling record for Jimmy Dorsey was a revival of this 1924 hit. Albert Gamse added English lyrics to Lacalle's original Spanish song. In this form it was introduced by Deanna Durbin in the film *First Love* in 1939 and was inserted in the 1942 movie musical *The Fleet's In* by Jimmy Dorsey and his orchestra. The performance catapulted the song into a hit.

The Anniversary Waltz
COMPOSER: **Dave Franklin**
LYRICIST: **Al Dubin**

"The Anniversary Waltz" was popularized by Bing Crosby. This song is often confused with Al Jolson's "Anniversary Song" (1946), but Jolson's song is in cut time while this waltz is, of course, in triple.

Dave Franklin and Al Dubin's waltz was included in *Variety*'s "Fifty Year Hit Parade."

Blues in the Night
COMPOSER: Harold Arlen
LYRICIST: Johnny Mercer

The mood and style of this song are as true to blues as any Tin Pan Alley song can be. Arlen and Mercer had written the number for a film called *Hot Nocturne.* The song was so effective in William Gillespie's jail scene that the producers decided to change the name of the film to *Blues in the Night.*

Jimmie Lunceford and his orchestra had a hit recording of the song even before the film was released. Dinah Shore's first million-selling recording was "Blues in the Night."

Boogie Woogie Bugle Boy
COMPOSER: Don Raye
LYRICIST: Hughie Prince

The Andrews Sisters introduced this song in the Abbott and Costello film *Buck Privates.* This famous World War II vintage number was an Academy Award nominee, but it was not listed among the top songs of the year. However, when people think back to the war years, "Boogie Woogie Bugle Boy" is one of the songs they call to mind. It was revived by Bette Midler in 1972–73, when it climbed to the top of the charts.

Chattanooga Choo Choo
COMPOSER: Harry Warren
LYRICIST: Mack Gordon

The top song of 1941 was Harry Warren and Mack Gordon's "Chattanooga Choo Choo." It was featured in the movie *Sun Valley Serenade,* in which Glenn Miller and his orchestra shared top billing with ice skating star Sonja Henie.

Miller's recording had sold a million copies by 1942. The first gold disc ever (a gold-lacquered facsimile) was given to him by RCA Victor for this recording on their Bluebird label. The presentation was made over the Chesterfield radio program on February 10, 1942; the recording had sold 1.2 million copies by then. The song stayed on the best-selling chart for twenty-three weeks.

Daddy
COMPOSER-LYRICIST: Bobby Troup

Sammy Kaye and his orchestra had a best-selling record of "Daddy," which was introduced in the 1941 film *Two Latins from Manhattan* by Joan Davis and Jinx Falkenburg. *Variety* listed it as the number five song of the year.

Elmer's Tune
COMPOSER-LYRICISTS: Elmer Albrecht, Sammy Gallop, and Dick Jurgens

The seventh-ranking top tune of 1941 was "Elmer's Tune." Dick Jurgens and his orchestra introduced it, but it was Glenn Miller and his orchestra, with Ray Eberle and the Modernaires doing the vocal, that had the best-selling recording. Peggy Lee made her first recording as vocalist with the Benny Goodman ensemble with "Elmer's Tune." It was inserted into the film *Strictly in the Groove* in 1942.

Frenesi
COMPOSER: Alberto Dominguez
LYRICISTS: Ray Charles and S. K. Russell

"Frenesi" was the first song by any Mexican writer to sell a million records. The song was popularized by Artie Shaw. His recording, a million seller, stayed at number one for thirteen weeks and for twenty-three weeks on the best sellers. *Variety* listed it as the second best song of 1941.

According to the lyric, "Frenesi" meant "please love me."

Green Eyes
COMPOSER: Nilo Menendez
LYRICISTS: E. Rivera and Eddie Woods; original lyrics, Adolfo Utrera

Several of the songs of 1941 were BMI tunes that were discovered during the ASCAP ban. "Frenesi," from Mexico, is a good example, as is "Green Eyes," which had been written by Nilo Menendez and Adolfo Utrera in 1929. Jimmy Dorsey and his orchestra (with the vocal by Helen O'Connell and Bob Eberly) popularized the song and had a milion-selling recording, which helped make it the year's number three record.

The opening of "Green Eyes" might be described as a rocket launch covering an octave and a half in the first seven notes. The song is recorded now and then, but when a melody has a range of two notes less than two octaves, only a few singers can successfully negotiate it. In other words, it was meant to be an instrumental.

How About You?
COMPOSER: Burton Lane
LYRICIST: Ralph Freed

Ralph Freed's lyric to "How About You?" pays a compliment to another songwriter, George Gershwin

("I like a Gershwin tune, how about you?"). Mickey Rooney and Judy Garland introduced the number in the movie musical *Babes on Broadway*. They sang and danced "How About You?" to an Academy Award nomination for best song from a film for 1942.

The Hut Sut Song
COMPOSER-LYRICISTS: **Leo Killian, Ted McMichael, and Jack Owens**

This 1939 novelty song found success in 1941, when it was sung in the movie *San Antonio Rose* by the Merry Macs. Freddy Martin and his orchestra had been playing this nonsense song for a couple of years. The Merry Macs were a four-part modern harmony vocal group consisting of the McMichael brothers—Joe, Ted, and Judd—and Cherry MacKay.

This song was selected by *Variety* for its "Fifty Year Hit Parade."

I Don't Want to Set the World on Fire
COMPOSER-LYRICISTS: **Bennie Benjamin, Eddie Durham, Eddie Seiler, and Sol Marcus**

This hit was written three years before its publication in 1941, but once it was published, it was one of the year's leading songs. The lyrics say, in part, that the singer is not interested in setting the world on fire but "I just want to start a flame in your heart."

This ardent love song was introduced by Harlan Leonard and his Kansas City Rockets and was popularized by the Mills Brothers. It spent four weeks at the top of *Your Hit Parade* and was picked by *Variety* for its "Fifty Year Hit Parade."

I Don't Want to Walk Without You
COMPOSER: **Jule Styne**
LYRICIST: **Frank Loesser**

Jule Styne and Frank Loesser became hot properties in Hollywood with this song about a broken romance, which they wrote for the movie musical *Sweater Girl*. The film was a typical campus frolic that involved a group of collegians producing a musical revue.

"I Don't Want to Walk Without You" was introduced by Johnnie Johnston in the film and was popularized in recordings by Harry James and his orchestra and by Bing Crosby. The song reappeared in 1944's *You Can't Ration Love* and was revived by Barry Manilow in 1979–80.

"I Don't Want to Walk Without You" was Jule Styne's most successful song before he teamed up with Sammy Cahn in 1942.

I Got It Bad and That Ain't Good
COMPOSER: **Duke Ellington**
LYRICIST: **Paul Francis Webster**

Between "Solitude" in 1934 and the early forties Duke Ellington was rather quiet, but 1941 brought "I Got It Bad and That Ain't Good." It was introduced by Ivy Anderson in the revue *Jump for Joy*, which was produced on the West Coast by the American Revue Theater. The best recordings were by Ivy Anderson with Duke Ellington and his orchestra and by Ella Fitzgerald.

I Hear a Rhapsody
COMPOSER-LYRICISTS: **George Fragos, Jack Baker, and Dick Gasparre**

This 1940 song was featured in several nonmusical motion pictures and was on a best-selling recording by Jimmy Dorsey and his orchestra. The lovers' call, their sparkling eyes, and whispers of love make music of rhapsodic sweetness. This is another example of an early BMI property that achieved hit status, in this instance 1941's tenth-ranked song of the year.

I'll Remember April
COMPOSER-LYRICISTS: **Don Raye, Gene de Paul, and Pat Johnston**

Dick Foran introduced "I'll Remember April" in the Bud Abbott and Lou Costello film *Ride 'Em Cowboy*. It was popularized by Woody Herman and his orchestra.

The Last Time I Saw Paris
See page 102 (1940).
The other nominees for the Academy Award for Best Song in 1941 included "Baby Mine," by Frank Churchill and Ned Washington, from *Dumbo*; "Be Honest With Me," by Gene Autry and Fred Rose, from *Ridin' On a Rainbow*; "Blues in the Night," by Harold Arlen and Johnny Mercer, from *Blues in the Night*; "Boogie Woogie Bugle Boy," by Hugh Prince and Don Raye, from *Buck Privates*; "Chattanooga Choo Choo," by Harry Warren and Mack Gordon, from *Sun Valley Serenade*; "Dolores," by Lou Alter and Frank Loesser, from *Las Vegas Nights*; "Out of the Silence," by Lloyd B. Norlind, from *All American Co-ed*; and

"Since I Kissed My Baby Goodbye," by Cole Porter, from *You'll Never Get Rich*.

Oh, Look at Me Now
COMPOSER: **Joe Bushkin**
LYRICIST: **John De Vries**

This song was introduced and first recorded by Tommy Dorsey and his orchestra, with the vocal by Frank Sinatra and Connie Haines.

Joe Bushkin, a mainstream swing and jazz pianist, played keyboard for the Tommy Dorsey band when he wrote "Oh, Look at Me Now." Although he and Johnny De Vries collaborated on several other songs, none reached the status of this one.

Rose O'Day
COMPOSER-LYRICISTS: **Charles Tobias and Al Lewis**

Charles Tobias reportedly wrote the lyrics to this number while dining at Eddie Cantor's home. When Tobias asked the serving maid her name, she replied, "Rose O'Day." The name set Tobias's creative brain into action, and in practically no time the lyric was done. Al Lewis helped Tobias finish the product. Eddie Cantor introduced it, but it was made into a hit by a million-selling disc by Kate Smith. "Rose O'Day" is a fast waltz sung with patter effects.

This song was selected by *Variety* for its "Fifty Year Hit Parade."

This Love of Mine
COMPOSERS: **Sol Parker and Henry Sanicola**
LYRICIST: **Frank Sinatra**

Frank Sinatra is responsible for the lyrics and for popularizing "This Love of Mine" in a recording with the Tommy Dorsey orchestra. *Variety*'s top ten for 1941 listed the song as the year's number eight tune. The singer insists his love will continue even though his lover is gone.

Tonight We Love
COMPOSERS: **Ray Austin and Freddy Martin**
LYRICIST: **Bobby Worth**

The basic melody and harmony of "Tonight We Love" come from Russian composer Peter I. Tchaikovsky's Piano Concerto No. 1 in B Flat Minor. Ray Austin and bandleader Freddy Martin were the adapters, while Bobby Worth supplied the words. With Clyde Rogers doing the vocal, the Martin orchestra's recording achieved a million in sales. The success sparked sixteen different versions of the Tchaikovsky melody. "Tonight We Love" was number four in *Variety*'s year's top ten.

This song was selected by *Variety* for its "Fifty Year Hit Parade."

You and I
COMPOSER-LYRICIST: **Meredith Willson**

This song was Meredith Willson's first major success. In addition to being featured by Glenn Miller and his orchestra, the song was the theme for the *Maxwell House Coffee Time* radio program.

You Made Me Love You—I Didn't Want to Do It
COMPOSER: **James V. Monaco**
LYRICIST: **Joe McCarthy**

This *Variety* "Golden 100 Tin Pan Alley Song" selection originated in 1913, when Al Jolson introduced the song in the Winter Garden extravaganza *The Honeymoon Express*. The song's next success came in 1938, when the young Judy Garland (fifteen years old) sang it to a photograph of Clark Gable in the film *Broadway Melody of 1938*.

Harry James further enhanced his reputation as one of the most popular bandleaders with a million-selling recording of "You Made Me Love You" in 1941. James featured this song in the motion pictures *Syncopation* and *Private Buckaroo*, also in 1941.

One of the song's greatest honors came in 1963, when ASCAP selected it as one of sixteen numbers for its "All-Time Hit Parade."

1 9 4 2

Der Fuehrer's Face
COMPOSER-LYRICIST: **Oliver Wallace**

"Der Fuehrer's Face" was a wartime morale booster with its madcap musical portrait of Hitler. It was the comedy musical hit of World War II. "Der Fuehrer's Face" was written for the Donald Duck cartoon *In Nutzy Land*. Once the song had become a hit, the cartoon was retitled *Der Fuehrer's Face*. Spike Jones and his City Slickers, the kings of comedy music, had a million-selling record of the song.

Don't Sit Under the Apple Tree
COMPOSER: **Sam H. Stept**
LYRICISTS: **Charles Tobias and Lew Brown**

This melody was written in 1939 to a text entitled "Anywhere the Bluebird Goes." The lyricists changed the lyric to its present form when the song was used in the 1939 Broadway musical *Yokel Boy*. Then, in 1942, the Andrews Sisters used it in the film *Private Buckaroo*. In the film the sisters joined Harry James and his orchestra to put on a show for servicemen. The Andrews Sisters' skillfully harmonized trio rendition of "Don't Sit Under the Apple Tree (with Anyone Else but Me)" was one of the musical highlights of the film.

Other best-selling recordings came from Kay Kyser and from Glenn Miller. The GI's of World War II considered the song a favorite because it expressed their sentiments about the girls back home.

This song was picked by *Variety* for its "Fifty Year Hit Parade."

I Left My Heart at the Stage Door Canteen
COMPOSER-LYRICIST: **Irving Berlin**

Irving Berlin's all-soldier revue *This Is the Army* was a benefit for the Army Emergency Relief Fund. Among its scenes were a military minstrel show and the show at the Stage Door Canteen (including impersonations of theatrical personalities), where "I Left My Heart at the Stage Door Canteen" was introduced by Earl Oxford.

The Stage Door Canteen, located in the basement of the Forty-fourth Street Theater in New York City, was one of the most famous of the places where off-duty service personnel could eat and relax. Operated by the American Theater Wing exclusively for the Allied forces, the canteen offered both free food and the world's greatest entertainers. Not only did the entertainers perform, but they served food, washed dishes, and talked to the GI's—whatever would help the war effort and boost the morale of the soldiers. Many of the female stars and starlets danced with the guys (they were forbidden to date the servicemen).

The song speaks of the fleeting love that many felt when they had to leave the canteen, never to see these beautiful women again. Sammy Kaye and his orchestra had a best-selling recording of the song.

I've Got a Gal in Kalamazoo
COMPOSER: **Harry Warren**
LYRICIST: **Mack Gordon**

"I've Got a Gal in Kalamazoo" was written for the movie *Orchestra Wives*. Glenn Miller and his orchestra with Tex Beneke, Marion Hutton, and the Modernaires captured America's musical tastes in the early forties with their performance of the song in the film. They also had a million-selling disc of the song, which was number three in *Variety*'s top ten of 1942.

Jersey Bounce
COMPOSERS: **Bobby Plater, Tiny Bradshaw, Edward Johnson, and Robert B. Wright**
LYRICISTS: **Buddy Feyne and Robert B. Wright**

"Jersey Bounce" was originally a successful instrumental composition in 1941; lyrics were not added until 1946. As an instrumental it was performed by Benny Goodman and Glenn Miller. It held the number nine spot in 1942's top ten.

This is an example of a tune that was popular without lyrics. At a moderate tempo and with chords changing every couple of measures some improvisation was possible even within the context of a big band arrangement.

Jingle, Jangle, Jingle
COMPOSER: **Joseph J. Lilley**
LYRICIST: **Frank Loesser**

A group of horseback riders in the film *The Forest Rangers* introduced this song, which became the number two hit in 1942's top ten. Both Kay Kyser and his orchestra and the Merry Macs popularized this simple, catchy tune with successful recordings. The Kyser disc, a million seller, was number one for eight weeks and spent thirteen weeks on the best-selling chart. An unusual feature was a round on the second chorus.

This song was selected by *Variety* for its "Fifty Year Hit Parade."

Moonlight Becomes You
COMPOSER: **James Van Heusen**
LYRICIST: **Johnny Burke**

This song was introduced by Bing Crosby in the movie musical *Road to Morocco,* one of a series of *Road* pictures that starred Crosby, Bob Hope, and Dorothy Lamour. Crosby's Decca recording helped popularize the tune even more. Harry James's recording sold a million copies. John McAfee, saxophonist of the James orchestra, was the vocalist on the record.

Variety chose "Moonlight Becomes You" for its "Fifty Year Hit Parade."

Moonlight Cocktail
COMPOSER: Lucky Roberts
LYRICIST: Kim Gannon

The fourth-ranked song in 1942's top ten was "Moonlight Cocktail." Glenn Miller and his orchestra made the most successful recording. The piece was adapted from Lucky Roberts's early ragtime piece called "Ripples of the Nile."

This recipe song outlines a mixed drink that combines a "coupla jiggers of moonlight," a star, the blue of a June night, a guitar, a couple of dreamers, flowers, and a drop of dew. You stir for a couple of hours (the number of kisses is up to you), then you serve it under starlight. As cute as the lyrics are, it is, like big band tunes, most familiar as a melody sans words.

Praise the Lord and Pass the Ammunition!
COMPOSER-LYRICIST: Frank Loesser

This was the first major hit to come out of the direct involvement of the United States in World War II. During the Japanese attack on Pearl Harbor Navy Chaplain William Maguire spoke the words that inspired the song. It was the first hit for which Loesser wrote both words and music (up to 1942 he had mainly written lyrics). He wrote it shortly after Pearl Harbor and, as was his habit, furnished the text with a dummy tune to try out the lyrics. When he sang the song for some friends, they insisted that he keep the folk melody rather than get another composer to write a new one.

Kay Kyser's recording was a million seller. The song in various recorded versions sold more than 2 million, and it also sold a million copies of sheet music. It was the tenth-ranked song in 1942's top ten.

This song was chosen by *Variety* for its "Fifty Year Hit Parade."

Sleepy Lagoon
COMPOSER: Eric Coates
LYRICIST: Jack Lawrence

This 1930 song became a major hit in 1942, when it was popularized by Tommy Dorsey and his orchestra and by Harry James and his orchestra. A Judy Canova movie in 1943 bore the *Sleepy Lagoon* title.

"Sleepy Lagoon" is another example of a melody which has lyrics but is by far better known without them.

The lyrics are reminiscent of the fascination during the late twenties and early thirties for faraway places. "A tropical moon, a sleepy lagoon and you!" sums up the text. It was the number six tune in 1942's top ten.

A String of Pearls
COMPOSER: Jerry Gray
LYRICIST: Eddie De Lange

Glenn Miller and his orchestra had a best-selling recording of this song in 1942, as did Benny Goodman. The text is less familiar than the melody, but it is interesting to note that the string of pearls was "a la Woolworth." It was number eight in 1942's top ten.

Tangerine
COMPOSER: Victor Schertzinger
LYRICIST: Johnny Mercer

"Tangerine" was introduced by Jimmy Dorsey and his orchestra with Helen O'Connell and Bob Eberly doing the vocal in the movie musical *The Fleet's In.* Their recording reached the best sellers' list and was the number seven song on 1942's top ten. In this song Tangerine is not the small bright orange-colored citrus fruit, but the name of a girl from Argentina.

That Old Black Magic
COMPOSER: Harold Arlen
LYRICIST: Johnny Mercer

This song was introduced by Johnnie Johnston (and danced by Vera Zorina) in the movie musical *Star Spangled Rhythm,* which starred Bing Crosby, Bob Hope, and Dick Powell.

Composer Arlen has given Mercer's lyrics credit for the song's success, contending that the words sustain the listener's interest, make sense, contain memorable phrases, and tell a story. Such ingredients add up to a successful lyric.

Many people will remember Frank Sinatra's successful disc of the song, but Billy Daniels achieved the greatest success with it in his nightclub act and on records. His Liberty recording sold more than 2 million copies. In 1958 jazz trumpeter and vocalist Louis Prima and singer Keely Smith had a gold record with "That Old Black Magic," which also earned them the Grammy for best vocal (group) performance of 1958.

There's a Star-Spangled Banner Waving Somewhere
COMPOSER-LYRICISTS: **Paul Roberts and Shelby Darnell and coauthored with Bob Miller**

This song was one of the most timely hits of the early war years. Elton Britt, a hillbilly singer from Marshall, Arkansas, made a recording of the song which had sold a million discs by 1944 and was the first country recording to receive an official gold record.

The song was named by *Variety* to its "Fifty Year Hit Parade."

This Is the Army, Mr. Jones
COMPOSER-LYRICIST: **Irving Berlin**

This sanguine introduction to military life was premiered in Berlin's all-soldier revue *This Is the Army*. It was introduced by a group of new inductees.

Berlin had written a successful all-soldier wartime revue, *Yip, Yip, Yaphank* in 1918, so the idea was revived for World War II. Berlin wrote a score that was a nonstop succession of various views of army life, seen in the lives of the men.

This song was selected by *Variety* for its "Fifty Year Hit Parade."

White Christmas
COMPOSER-LYRICIST: **Irving Berlin**

This Irving Berlin classic is the second most popular Christmas song next to "Silent Night." Bing Crosby introduced "White Christmas" in the movie musical *Holiday Inn*. Crosby's recording with the Ken Darby Singers and John Scott Trotter's orchestra sold 1 million copies within four years. By 1968 it had established a world record for sales for a single disc: 30 million. Sales of all recordings by the end of 1970 added up to the astronomical total of 68 million. By the end of the seventies the total had grown to more than 90 million. Other million-selling discs were made by Freddy Martin and his orchestra (1942) and by Frank Sinatra with the Ken Lane Singers and an orchestra directed by Axel Stordahl (1944).

The "White Christmas" copyright is the world's most valuable song property because the song returns every year to sell an average of 120,000 copies of sheet music and almost innumerable versions on Christmas records. It has been translated into numerous languages and had sold 43 million discs in foreign countries by the end of the seventies. The seventy-two weeks that the song spent on the best-seller charts in the United States is still a record.

In addition to all its other honors, "White Christ-

mas" won the Academy Award for 1942. The other nominees included "Always in My Heart," by Ernesto Lecuona and Kim Gannon, from *Always in My Heart;* "Dearly Beloved," by Jerome Kern and Johnny Mercer, from *You Were Never Lovelier;* "How About You?," by Burton Lane and Ralph Freed, from *Babes On Broadway;* "It Seems I Heard That Song Before," by Jule Styne and Sammy Cahn, from *Youth on Parade;* "I've Got a Gal in Kalamazoo," by Harry Warren and Mack Gordon, from *Orchestra Wives;* "Love Is a Song," by Frank Churchill and Larry Morey, from *Bambi;* "Pennies for Peppino," by Edward Ward, Chet Forrest, and Bob Wright, from *Flying With Music;* "Pig Foot Pete," by Gene de Paul and Don Raye, from *Hellzapoppin';* and "There's a Breeze on Lake Louise," by Harry Revel and Mort Greene, from *The Mayor of 44th Street.*

In 1963 ASCAP selected "White Christmas" as one of sixteen numbers in its "All-Time Hit Parade." Irving Berlin considered it one of his greatest creations.

Who Wouldn't Love You?
COMPOSERS-LYRICISTS: **Billy Carey and Carl Fischer**

Kay Kyser and his orchestra made a million-selling disc of this song in 1942. *Variety* listed it as the number five hit of the year. A slow ballad, "Who Wouldn't Love You?" speaks of a loved one who is so enchanting, so much like a breath of spring, so much the answer to a prayer that no one could keep from falling in love with her or him.

You'd Be So Nice to Come Home To
COMPOSER-LYRICIST: **Cole Porter**

Cole Porter wrote this number for the movie musical *Something to Shout About*. It was introduced in the film by Janet Blair and Don Ameche. "You'd Be So Nice to Come Home To" is a slow ballad, not as inventive and special as most of Porter's Broadway songs. The final line of the song sums up the lyric's intent: "You'd be so nice, you'd be paradise to come home to and love."

The song was picked by *Variety* for its "Fifty Year Hit Parade."

You Were Never Lovelier
COMPOSER: **Jerome Kern**
LYRICIST: **Johnny Mercer**

Fred Astaire introduced this song in the movie musical *You Were Never Lovelier*, in which he starred with Rita Hayworth. Astaire always has been more dancer than singer, but he had a marvelous way of interpreting popular songs. He did not possess a beautiful voice, nor did he have a wide range, but somehow his showmanship and savoir faire covered up any vocal shortcomings. Kern's operetta style did not make it any easier for Astaire, but as usual, he engagingly performed the number and danced with his costar with his normal flair.

1 9 4 3

All or Nothing at All
COMPOSER-LYRICISTS: **Jack Lawrence and Arthur Altman**

Frank Sinatra recorded "All or Nothing at All" with Harry James and his orchestra in 1940, but it did not stir any enthusiasm when it was first released. Sinatra's meteoric rise to fame in 1943 caused the record to be rereleased, and it subsequently sold a million copies.

The singer pleads not to be tempted by lips, a kiss, a touch of a hand. It is better to say "No!" than to be caught by unfulfilled love.

Variety selected this song for its "Fifty Year Hit Parade."

As Time Goes By
See page 58 (1931, when *Variety* listed the song on its "Fifty Year Hit Parade").

Brazil
COMPOSER: **Ary Barroso**
LYRICIST: **Bob Russell**

This Brazilian samba was composed by Ary Barroso in 1939 and Bob Russell added English lyrics. It was interpolated into Walt Disney's full-length animated film *Saludos Amigos* (1942), *The Gang's All Here* (1943), *Jam Session* (1944), *Brazil* (1944), and *The Eddie Duchin Story* (1956). Recordings by Eddie Duchin, by Xavier Cugat, and by Jimmy Dorsey, with Helen O'Connell and Bob Eberly, helped make "Brazil" the number five song in 1943's top ten.

The samba beat is the most distinguishing and intriguing feature of the song. It begins with a pickup of an interval of a sixth and holds the next note for more than two measures while the chords change underneath. Several other times during the song, notes are held for an extended time while chords change similarly. It would be a boring song if not for the samba rhythm.

This is an example of a foreign song discovered for radio to fill the void during the ban of ASCAP songs.

"Brazil" was selected by *Variety* for its "Fifty Year Hit Parade."

Comin' in on a Wing and a Prayer
COMPOSER: **Jimmy McHugh**
LYRICIST: **Harold Adamson**

The idea for this song came from a letter by an air force pilot (a former football star named Sonny Bragg). He told composer Jimmy McHugh of a close call he'd had on a flying assignment to North Africa; he'd made it back to his base on one engine and a prayer. Eddie Cantor introduced the song at an air force base.

Variety chose this song for its "Fifty Year Hit Parade."

Don't Get Around Much Anymore
COMPOSER: **Duke Ellington**
LYRICIST: **Bob Russell**

Duke Ellington's instrumental composition "Never No Lament" (1942) furnished the melody for this song, to which Bob Russell furnished lyrics. Ellington and his band introduced "Don't Get Around Much Anymore" and made a successful recording. Jimmy Savo did a burlesque treatment of the song in his nightclub act.

In the lyrics, the person does not go to the Saturday dance, to the club, or out on dates, because he is without his love.

The song was chosen by *Variety* for its "Fifty Year Hit Parade."

I Had the Craziest Dream
COMPOSER: **Harry Warren**
LYRICIST: **Mack Gordon**

This song was introduced by Harry James and his orchestra in the 1942 movie musical *Springtime in the Rockies*. With the vocal performed by Helen Forrest, the recording had sold a million copies by 1943.

The GIs' favorite pinup girl, Betty Grable, married bandleader Harry James in 1943. She also starred in *Springtime in the Rockies*, sharing the musical spotlight with her future husband.

I'll Be Home for Christmas
COMPOSER-LYRICISTS: Walter Kent, Kim Gannon, and Buck Ram

This traditional Tin Pan Alley Christmas favorite was introduced by Bing Crosby, who also had a million-selling recording. It has always been especially appealing to those in the service and others who must be away from home for the holidays because the text says they will be home for Christmas even if only in their dreams.

I've Heard That Song Before
COMPOSER: Jule Styne
LYRICIST: Sammy Cahn

Jule Styne and Sammy Cahn began their successful composer-lyricist partnership with this hit. The number was introduced by Bob Crosby and his orchestra in the 1942 movie musical *Youth on Parade*. Harry James and his orchestra recorded the tune in Hollywood in July 1942 and had a million seller by 1943; Helen Forrest did the vocal on the disc.

The lyrics comment on how certain songs help us reminisce about an old flame.

"I've Heard That Song Before" was an Academy Award nominee for 1942 (losing out to "You'll Never Know," page 114) and was the number two song of 1943.

A Lovely Way to Spend an Evening
COMPOSER: Jimmy McHugh
LYRICIST: Harold Adamson

Frank Sinatra introduced this song in the 1944 movie musical *Higher and Higher*. He further popularized the tune in a Capitol recording.

Higher and Higher had been a 1940 stage musical by Rodgers and Hart. The movie changed the script considerably and included a new musical score. McHugh and Adamson wrote eight songs for the film, and Sinatra sang five of them, including "A Lovely Way to Spend an Evening" and "I Couldn't Sleep a Wink Last Night" (see page 115).

Mairzy Doats
COMPOSER-LYRICISTS: Milton Drake, Al Hoffman, and Jerry Livingston

Every time has its crazy songs. The nonsense song hit of 1943 was "Mairzy Doats." The Al Trace orchestra introduced this unusual lyric, while the Merry Macs featured it in a best-selling record.

Milton Drake got the idea for the song when his four-year-old daughter came home from kindergarten one day jabbering, "Cowzy tweet and sowzy tweet and liddle sharsky doisters." That kind of gibberish inspired "Mairzy Doats."

Variety named "Mairzy Doats" to its "Fifty Year Hit Parade."

Oh, What a Beautiful Mornin'
COMPOSER: Richard Rodgers
LYRICIST: Oscar Hammerstein II

"Oh, What a Beautiful Mornin' " is the lazy waltz that opens Rodgers and Hammerstein's blockbuster musical *Oklahoma!* Alfred Drake, who played Curly McLain, introduced the song.

Oklahoma! held the record for the longest-running musical in Broadway history for fifteen years (until 1961).

The basic concept for the musical came from Theresa Helburn of the Theatre Guild, who suggested to Richard Rodgers a musical based on Lynn Riggs's play *Green Grow the Lilacs*. Larry Hart, Rodgers's lyricist since 1919, was uninterested, so Rodgers turned to Oscar Hammerstein II for the lyrics.

The birth of the Rodgers and Hammerstein partnership was fortunate, for their collaboration gave us not only *Oklahoma!* but other Broadway classics, including *Carousel, South Pacific, The King and I,* and *The Sound of Music.*

The story is set in the Oklahoma Territory a few years before statehood in 1907. Two ranch hands, Curly and Jud, are rivals for their boss's niece, Laurey. To spite Curly, Laurey goes to a dance with Jud. To prove his affection, Curly bids all he owns on a picnic basket that Laurey has made. Curly and Laurey marry. Jud challenges Curly to a fight and is accidentally killed by his own knife. Curly is tried for murder but is acquitted just in time to celebrate Oklahoma's being admitted to the Union as a state.

The exceptional score spawned at least two hit songs: The primary love song, "People Will Say We're in Love," stayed on the charts for thirty weeks, and a recording by Bing Crosby with "Oh, What a Beautiful Mornin' " on the flip side was the number ten hit record of 1943.

The score of *Oklahoma!* was put on 78 rpm discs, the first time an entire score was put on record. The original cast album, still available, has sold more than 3 million, with the sound track album made from the 1955 movie version selling more than 1 million copies.

Oklahoma! is one of the most important productions in Broadway theater history: a literate, believable story, enhanced by a gorgeous musical score that does not interrupt the action. It also makes use of ballet in the development of the plot.

"Oh, What a Beautiful Mornin' " was selected by *Variety* for its "Fifty Year Hit Parade."

Paper Doll
COMPOSER-LYRICIST: **Johnny S. Black**

"Paper Doll" was written twelve years before it was published. The Mills Brothers' 1943 recording sold a million copies and is said to have signaled the demise of the big band era. "Paper Doll" became the biggest hit of 1943 and was one of the biggest hits of the decade. It was on *Billboard*'s best-selling charts for thirty consecutive weeks, twelve weeks at the top. It appeared on *Your Hit Parade* for twenty-three weeks, a record eventually topped by only seven other songs. It eventually sold more than 6 million copies in the Mills Brothers' version alone.

The singers want to buy a paper doll so they can have a doll of their own and not have to bother with the real-live types, who are, in their opinion, too fickle.

"Paper Doll" was selected by *Variety* for its "Fifty Year Hit Parade."

People Will Say We're in Love
COMPOSER: **Richard Rodgers**
LYRICIST: **Oscar Hammerstein II**

"People Will Say We're in Love" is the principal love song of *Oklahoma!* (see "Oh, What a Beautiful Mornin' " page 112). Curly (sung by Alfred Drake) and Laurey (sung by Joan Roberts) want to convince other people and themselves that they are not in love. Of course, they are but are hesitant to admit it.

A recording by Bing Crosby, with "Oh, What a Beautiful Mornin' " on the flip side, was the number ten hit of the year. *Variety* chose the song for its "Fifty Year Hit Parade."

Pistol Packin' Mama
COMPOSER-LYRICIST: **Al Dexter**

A big novelty hit of 1943 was Al Dexter's "Pistol Packin' Mama." Two million-selling records were issued: Al Dexter and his Troopers and Bing Crosby with the Andrews Sisters and Vic Schoen's orchestra.

The song was inspired by a tale about a Texas roadside café owner, Molly Jackson. In earlier days Molly, with a pistol for protection, would ride out into the Kentucky hills to bring her bootlegger husband home for the weekends. When she approached his still, she would call out to her husband to come down. He would call back, "Lay your pistol down, Ma, or we ain't comin'." Dexter frequently ate at Molly's and she often treated him to meals when he was broke. He repaid her by writing this song inspired by her tale.

The song was named by *Variety* to its "Fifty Year Hit Parade."

Speak Low
COMPOSER: **Kurt Weill**
LYRICIST: **Ogden Nash**

This love duet came from *One Touch of Venus*, Kurt Weill's longest-running Broadway musical. The story was a fantasy about a statue of Venus that comes to life and falls in love with a barber named Rodney. Mary Martin played Venus, in her first starring Broadway role.

Ogden Nash got the idea for the lyrics from a line in Shakespeare's *Much Ado About Nothing*: "Speak low, if you speak love."

The song was popularized in a recording by Guy Lombardo and his Royal Canadians. It was selected by *Variety* for its "Fifty Year Hit Parade."

Sunday, Monday, or Always
COMPOSER: **James Van Heusen**
LYRICIST: **Johnny Burke**

Bing Crosby sang this song in the 1943 movie musical *Dixie*. Crosby played Daniel Decatur Emmett, a singer in the Virginia Minstrels who composed such classics as "Dixie," "Blue Tail Fly," and "Old Dan Tucker." The fictional plot was about the transformation of Emmett's "Dixie" from a slow ballad to the rousing song we know today. Crosby's recording of "Sunday, Monday, or Always" had notable sales, but the song is even more identified with Frank Sinatra, whose recording was a best seller. It was the fourth-rated song in 1943's top ten.

Variety selected it for its "Fifty Year Hit Parade."

There Are Such Things
COMPOSER: **George W. Meyer**
LYRICISTS: **Abel Baer and Stanley Adams**

The recording of "There Are Such Things" by the Tommy Dorsey orchestra, with Frank Sinatra and the Pied Pipers, took two years to become a million seller. The lyrics strike a note of optimism: Two people can fulfill their dream even though the world is torn apart by war. A particularly philosophical phrase from the lyrics is "not caring what you own but just what you are."

This 1942 composition was the number three song

in 1943's top ten. It was picked by *Variety* for its "Fifty Year Hit Parade."

They're Either Too Young or Too Old
COMPOSER: **Arthur Schwartz**
  LYRICIST: **Frank Loesser**

In World War II the only men left at home were "either too young or too old" for military service. This song, a female's wartime lament about that problem (especially a dilemma for marriageable women), was introduced by Bette Davis in the 1943 movie musical *Thank Your Lucky Stars*. It was typical of the seemingly hundreds of films that were turned out in assembly-line fashion for one purpose: to entertain the soldiers and those left behind during the war.

Variety selected the song for its "Fifty Year Hit Parade."

Tico-Tico
COMPOSER: **Zequinha Abreu**
  LYRICIST: **Ervin Drake**

Disney's *Saludos Amigos* introduced "Tico-Tico," a Brazilian popular song by Zequinha Abreu; English lyrics were added by Ervin Drake (American copyright 1943). Xavier Cugat and his orchestra helped popularize the tune through a recording and in nightclub appearances. Cugat is best known as a bandleader whose group specialized in Latin American dance songs. The English lyrics to this samba identify Tico as a cuckoo in a clock that advises in matters of amour.

"Tico-Tico" was chosen by *Variety* for its "Fifty Year Hit Parade."

You'll Never Know
COMPOSER: **Harry Warren**
  LYRICIST: **Mack Gordon**

The Academy Award winner for 1943 and the year's number six song in the top ten was Warren and Gordon's "You'll Never Know." It was written for the movie musical *Hello, Frisco, Hello* and sung by Alice Faye. Dick Haymes and the Song Spinners had a gold disc of the song in 1943.

The idea behind the lyrics is that with all the things done and said to prove love, if the loved one does not know by now, he or she never will.

The 1943 list of nominees for the Academy Award is one of the longest. The other nominees were "Change of Heart" by Jule Styne and Harold Adamson from *Hit Parade of 1943;* "Happiness Is a Thing Called Joe" by Harold Arlen and E. Y. Harburg from *Cabin in the Sky;* "My Shining Hour" by Harold Arlen and Johnny Mercer from *The Sky's the Limit;* "Say a Pray'r for the Boys Over There" by Jimmy McHugh and Herb Magidson from *Hers to Hold;* "That Old Black Magic" by Harold Arlen and Johnny Mercer from *Star Spangled Rhythm;* "They're Either Too Young or Too Old" by Arthur Schwartz and Frank Loesser from *Thank Your Lucky Stars;* "We Mustn't Say Goodbye" by James V. Monaco and Al Dubin from *Stage Door Canteen;* and "You'd Be So Nice to Come Home To" by Cole Porter from *Something to Shout About.*

Variety chose "You'll Never Know" for its "Fifty Year Hit Parade."

1 9 4 4

Bell Bottom Trousers
COMPOSER-LYRICIST: **Moe Jaffe**

Navy trousers during World War II had belled cuffs. Moe Jaffe set new lyrics to a sea chantey for this popular song. Vincent Lopez and his orchestra helped popularize it, and Tony Pastor and his orchestra had a best-selling record.

This song was included in *Variety*'s "Fifty Year Hit Parade."

Besame Mucho
COMPOSER: **Consuelo Velázquez**
  LYRICIST: **Sunny Skylar**

Originally composed in 1941 by a Mexican, Consuelo Velázquez, this song got English lyrics by Sunny Skylar in 1944. A recording by Jimmy Dorsey and his orchestra, with Kitty Kallen and Bob Eberly, caught on immediately and sold a million or more copies. It was number one for seven weeks and was number seven in 1944's top ten. *Besame mucho* translates as "kiss me much," but the English lyrics' only reference to kissing is "each time I cling to your kiss I hear music divine."

This song was on *Variety*'s "Fifty Year Hit Parade."

Holiday for Strings
COMPOSER: **David Rose**

This brilliant and original composition and orchestral scoring by David Rose made him famous and gave him his first million-selling record.

"Holiday for Strings" was the number nine hit of 1944 and was selected by *Variety* for its "Fifty Year Hit Parade."

I Couldn't Sleep a Wink Last Night
COMPOSER: **Jimmy McHugh**
LYRICIST: **Harold Adamson**

Frank Sinatra introduced this song in his 1944 film *Higher and Higher* (see "A Lovely Way to Spend an Evening," page 112). McHugh and Adamson's song was an Academy Award nominee (the winner was "Swinging on a Star," page 117), and hit the top of the Hit Parade early in 1944.

I'll Be Seeing You
COMPOSER: **Sammy Fain**
LYRICIST: **Irving Kahal**

This torch ballad was introduced by Tamara in the 1938 musical *Right This Way*. "I'll Be Seeing You" became particularly popular during World War II, when it seemed apropos to the soldier and his girl friend. Its popularity was aided by performances by Hildegarde and Frank Sinatra. Bing Crosby sang it in the 1944 film *I'll Be Seeing You*. It became the number one song of 1944. It was number one for ten weeks on 1944's *Your Hit Parade*. Liberace used it as the closing theme for his television show in the fifties. *Variety* selected it as "Golden 100 Tin Pan Alley Song."

I'll Get By
See page 43 (1928).

I'll Walk Alone
COMPOSER: **Jule Styne**
LYRICIST: **Sammy Cahn**

"I'll Walk Alone" was nominated for the Academy Award (but lost to "Swinging on a Star," page 117) after it appeared in the 1944 film *Follow the Boys*. Di-

nah Shore introduced and recorded the song. Frank Sinatra helped popularize it by recording it also. Don Cornell's version in 1952 was among the best sellers. The song had great success during the war years because of its lyrics, which suggest that the lovers who are separated will "walk alone" until they can walk together. Those parted by military service found this idea appealing.

I Love You
COMPOSER-LYRICISTS: **Edvard Grieg, Robert Wright, and George ("Chet") Forrest**

Robert Wright and Chet Forrest borrowed Edvard Grieg's music and took liberties with his life story to create *Song of Norway*, a 1944 Broadway musical. The show's most famous hits were "I Love You" and "Strange Music" (see page 116).

"I Love You" comes from the art song "Ich Liebe Dich." Grieg was a nineteenth-century Romantic composer, and the emotion and passion for which the Romantics are famous come through in "I Love You." Bing Crosby's recording of the song on the flip side of "I'll Be Seeing You" helped send the record to the top of the year's top ten.

I Love You
COMPOSER-LYRICIST: **Cole Porter**

The *other* "I Love You" also came from a Broadway show during 1944. Cole Porter wrote this "I Love You" for his show *Mexican Hayride*, in which it was sung by Wilbur Evans.

Porter wrote the song when a friend bet him he could not write a successful song with such a trite title as "I Love You." Porter accepted the challenge, wrote the song, and won the bet. He maintained, however, that it was the song's melody, not the lyric, that made it popular. However, it is interesting how Porter builds the lyric: the April breeze, the echoing hills, the birds sing "I love you."

Is You Is or Is You Ain't My Baby?
COMPOSER: **Louis Jordan**
LYRICIST: **Billy Austin**

This unusual song was interpolated by the composer, Louis Jordan, into the 1944 movie musical *Follow the Boys*. It was also sung by the Delta Rhythm Boys in the 1945 film *Easy to Look At*.

Jazz critic Leonard Feather has suggested that if one traced rock and roll to its hub, Louis Jordan would be at that hub. The rhythmic character of his band had a tremendous influence on the course of popular music. Melodically this song foreshadows the endless repetitiveness of some rock pieces.

Long Ago and Far Away
COMPOSER: **Jerome Kern**
LYRICIST: **Ira Gershwin**

Jerome Kern collaborated with Ira Gershwin to write this song for the movie musical *Cover Girl,* in which it was sung by Gene Kelly. The number was set in a dingy Brooklyn nightclub. The film concerned a nightclub dancer, played by Rita Hayworth, who deserts her lover, played by Gene Kelly, to become a model. In a series of flashbacks we find that Hayworth's grandmother followed the same course, hence the song "Long Ago and Far Away."

In addition to receiving an Academy Award nomination, the song climbed to the top of the charts and stayed there for more than a month in midyear.

Moonlight in Vermont
COMPOSER: **Karl Suessdorf**
LYRICIST: **John Blackburn**

This song was the first million seller for singer Margaret Whiting, the daughter of the famous songwriter Richard Whiting.

"Moonlight in Vermont" conjures up a romantic setting of a log cabin in snow-covered mountains. Inside the cabin with a glowing fireplace two lovers are completely lost in each other.

My Heart Tells Me
COMPOSER: **Harry Warren**
LYRICIST: **Mack Gordon**

Betty Grable introduced "My Heart Tells Me" in the 1943 movie musical *Sweet Rosie O'Grady.* Grable was cast as Madeleine Marlowe, a musical comedy star. This song was filmed with Grable, the GIs' favorite pinup girl, in a bathtub.

"My Heart Tells Me" was popularized by Glen Gray and the Casa Loma Orchestra with a vocal by Eugenie Baird in a recording that made it the number six hit in 1944's top ten. The flip side of the record was "My Shining Hour" (below).

My Shining Hour
COMPOSER: **Harold Arlen**
LYRICIST: **Johnny Mercer**

Fred Astaire introduced "My Shining Hour" in the 1943 movie musical *The Sky's the Limit.* Astaire portrayed a Flying Tiger war hero.

Subsequently this Arlen-Mercer song received an Academy Award nomination and was successfully recorded by Glen Gray and the Casa Loma Orchestra. With "My Heart Tells Me" on the flip side, the record was the number six hit in 1944's top ten.

One for My Baby
COMPOSER: **Harold Arlen**
LYRICIST: **Johnny Mercer**

Fred Astaire introduced "One for My Baby (and One More for the Road)" in the 1943 movie musical *The Sky's the Limit.* Astaire has said that he considers "One for My Baby" the best song ever written specially for him.

Shoo-Shoo Baby
COMPOSER-LYRICIST: **Phil Moore**

Phil Moore was employed at the MGM studios in Hollywood, where he had the habit of using the term *shoo-shoo.* At a rehearsal with Lena Horne, which had not gone well, he kept trying to relax her by saying, "Shoo, shoo, Lena, take it easy. . . ." After several days of this he decided to improvise a lyric around the phrase and then set it to music. It was sung by Horne and by Georgia Gibbs in their nightclub acts before it was published. It was interpolated into the 1943 movies *Three Cheers for the Boys* and *Follow the Boys,* as well as into several other films. Recorded by the Andrews Sisters and by Ella Mae Morse, the song made the top ten songs of 1944.

"Shoo-Shoo Baby" was selected by *Variety* for its "Fifty Year Hit Parade."

Spring Will Be a Little Late This Year
COMPOSER-LYRICIST: **Frank Loesser**

Deanna Durbin introduced "Spring Will Be a Little Late This Year" in the 1944 film *Christmas Holiday.* Spring will be late because "you have left me," says the lyric.

Strange Music
COMPOSER-LYRICISTS: **Edvard Grieg, Robert Wright, and George "Chet" Forrest**

"Strange Music" came from Edvard Grieg's "Wedding Day at Troldhaugen" and from "Nocturne." Wright and Forrest borrowed the melodies and used them in the Broadway musical *Song of Norway* (see "I Love You," page 115). This duet was introduced in the musical by Grieg (played by Lawrence Brooks) and Nina (played by Helena Bliss), his wife. The "strange music" is the "strange, new music of love."

Swinging on a Star
COMPOSER: James Van Heusen
LYRICIST: Johnny Burke

The winner of the 1944 Academy Award for the best song from a film went to James Van Heusen and Johnny Burke's "Swinging on a Star." Bing Crosby introduced it in the film *Going My Way,* one of Crosby's best and most remembered performances. He was cast as Father O'Malley, a young Catholic priest, who has been sent to replace Father Fitzgibbon, played by Barry Fitzgerald. Crosby performed "Swinging on a Star" with a group of children at St. Dominic's Church.

Crosby's recording with the John Scott Trotter orchestra became a gold disc. One of the most popular songs of modern times, this whimsical ditty owed its birth to Crosby. Burke and Van Heusen were visiting in Crosby's home when one of Crosby's sons misbehaved. Bing reprimanded him for acting "like a mule." Burke expanded the incident into the lyrics "By the way, if you hate to go to school, you may grow up to be a mule."

The number two song in 1944's top ten has an interesting side note. The vocal background for Bing's recording was by the Williams Brothers, who included future singing star Andy Williams.

This song was selected by *Variety* for its "Fifty Year Hit Parade."

The list of 1944 Academy Award nominees for Best Song is the longest of all. The other nominees were "I Couldn't Sleep a Wink Last Night" by Jimmy McHugh and Harold Adamson from *Higher and Higher;* "I'll Walk Alone" by Jule Styne and Sammy Cahn from *Follow the Boys;* "I'm Making Believe" by James V. Monaco from *Sweet and Lowdown;* "Long Ago and Far Away" by Jerome Kern and Ira Gershwin from *Cover Girl;* "Now I Know" by Harold Arlen and Ted Koehler from *Up in Arms;* "Remember Me to Carolina" by Harry Revel and Paul Francis Webster from *Minstrel Man;* "Rio de Janeiro" by Ary Barroso and Ned Washington from *Brazil;* "Silver Shadows and Golden Dreams" by Lew Pollack and Charles Newman from *Let's Dance;* "Sweet Dreams Sweetheart" by M. K. Jerome and Ted Koehler from *Hollywood Canteen;* "Too Much Love" by Walter Kent and Kim Gannon from *Song of the Open Road;* and "The Trolley Song" by Ralph Blane and Hugh Martin from *Meet Me in St. Louis.*

Too-Ra-Loo-Ra-Loo-Ral
COMPOSER-LYRICIST: J. R. Shannon

"Too-ra-loo-ra-loo-ral," a hit from the Bing Crosby movie musical *Going My Way* (see "Swinging on a Star," above), was actually a revival of a popular song from 1914. In an especially touching scene from the film, Bing, as the young Father O'Malley, sings this "traditional" Irish ballad to Barry Fitzgerald, the sickly, elderly Father Fitzgibbon. Crosby's recording with the Victor Young orchestra was another million seller.

The Trolley Song
COMPOSER-LYRICISTS: Ralph Blane and Hugh Martin

Ralph Blane and Hugh Martin wrote "The Trolley Song" for the 1944 movie musical *Meet Me in St. Louis.* Judy Garland introduced the song in the film and also had a best-selling recording. Garland played Esther, the Smith sister who has developed a crush on the boy next door. She sang about that crush in two of the film's best-remembered songs: "The Trolley Song" and "The Boy Next Door."

The Pied Pipers also had a best-selling recording of "The Trolley Song." It received an Academy Award nomination for the year's best song (the winner was "Swinging on a Star," above). The "clang, clang, clang" in the lyric imitating the trolley bell is a distinctive feature.

Variety picked "The Trolley Song" for its "Fifty Year Hit Parade."

You Always Hurt the One You Love
COMPOSER-LYRICISTS: Doris Fisher and Allan Roberts

The Mills Brothers popularized this song, and their recording sold more than a million discs. The tune, with "Till Then" on the flip side of the Mills Brothers' recording, was the fifth-ranked hit of 1944. The tender lyric and the Mills Brothers' rendition caught the fancy of the public.

T · H · E

SING ERA: 1945 to 1955

As World War II ended, the people of the United States found far too often that the lives they had known before the war did not exist anymore.

The big bands had suffered during the war years because most of the musicians had been drafted or had enlisted in the military services. Once these bandsmen reentered civilian life, they found that the popular music scene had changed drastically. The bands were no longer the major hit makers. The top tunes now came from singers like Frank Sinatra, Dinah Shore, Perry Como, and Doris Day.

During the war, because rationing of gasoline and tires made traveling difficult, numerous clubs and ballrooms where the bands had once played had been forced to close. In addition, a twenty percent amusement tax had been imposed wherever there was dancing. That caused many clubs to cover their dance floors. Therefore, the bands that re-formed after the war had fewer places to perform. The era of the big bands became a memory. The singers were now the giants of the entertainment world.

The Expanding Record Industry

By the end of World War II there were several new record companies, and the recording industry was growing into the giant of today.

The records that were sold during the late forties were 78 rpm discs. In 1949 the Victor and Columbia record companies argued over the merits of the 45 and 33⅓ rpm speeds. Columbia unveiled the 33⅓ rpm long-playing record. Victor, however, favored the smaller 45 rpm discs and brought out a new three-speed player (78, 45, and 33⅓ rpms) in the early fifties. Capitol and Decca switched to the new speeds. In a few years the 78 rpm record practically disappeared from the market.

The number of million-selling records more than doubled from 1945 to 1955, and that was only the beginning of the big boom in record sales. In 1945 twenty-one records that would sell a million were launched. It usually took three to five years for a disc to become a million seller. In 1955 fifty records became million sellers, and the discs usually reached gold within their first year of release.

Some of the most successful sellers of records during this period were Perry Como, Bing Crosby, Billy

Eckstine, Frankie Laine, Jo Stafford, Nat ("King") Cole, Patti Page, the Ames Brothers, Teresa Brewer, Rosemary Clooney, Eddie Fisher, the Four Aces, Doris Day, Al Jolson (because *The Jolson Story* was re- leased in 1946), Mantovani and his orchestra, early rhythm and blues artist Fats Domino, and country singers Eddy Arnold and Hank Williams.

The Movies Spawn Hits

The fiftieth anniversary of motion pictures was observed in 1944, and movies were more popular than ever. Some very ambitious movie musicals premiered during the late forties and early fifties.

Several screen biographies of composers or performers were made in Hollywood. These included 1946's *The Jolson Story; Night and Day*, the Cole Porter musical biography; *Till the Clouds Roll By*, the musical biography of Jerome Kern; 1948's *Words and Music*, about Richard Rodgers and Lorenz Hart; 1950's *Three Little Words*, with Fred Astaire and Red Skelton portraying Burt Kalmar and Harry Ruby; and 1951's *The Great Caruso*, with Mario Lanza playing Enrico Caruso, the fabled opera singer.

Several nostalgic musicals were produced in the late forties and early fifties. These included 1949's *Look for the Silver Lining, In the Good Old Summertime,* and *Take Me Out to the Ball Game;* 1951's *On Moonlight Bay;* and 1953's *By the Light of the Silvery Moon.*

The Broadway stage was the source of several movie musicals, such as *Annie Get Your Gun, Show Boat, The Merry Widow, Roberta* (retitled *Lovely to Look At*), *The Band Wagon, Kiss Me Kate, Call Me Madam, Rose Marie, The Student Prince, Brigadoon, Kismet, Guys and Dolls, Hit the Deck,* and *Oklahoma!*

Singin' in the Rain (1952) is one of the most enduring movie musicals ever made. Gene Kelly, Debbie Reynolds, and Donald O'Connor star in this classic film musical.

Some of the most honored (by Academy Award nominations) and top moneymaking movie musicals of the last half of the forties are 1945's *Anchors Aweigh*, which features Gene Kelly in a dance sequence with the cartoon character Jerry the mouse; *The Dolly Sisters*, a fictionalized biography of two turn-of-the-century performers; *Rhapsody in Blue*, George Gershwin's movie biography, and *A Song to Remember*, the screen biography of Frédéric Chopin. In 1946 Hollywood released *The Jolson Story; Night and Day; Till the Clouds Roll By; The Harvey Girls*, a frontier musical that stars Judy Garland and Ray Bolger; *Road to Utopia*, one of the best of the Crosby, Hope, and Lamour *Road* films; *Blue Skies*, the Bing Crosby and

Fred Astaire entertainment; and *Ziegfeld Follies*, Florenz Ziegfeld's heavenly dream of another *Follies* presentation. The selection in 1947 included *Mother Wore Tights*, a nostalgic musical starring Betty Grable; *My Wild Irish Rose*, Chauncey Olcott's musical biography; *Good News*, June Allyson and Peter Lawford's campus musical; and *The Perils of Pauline*, Betty Hutton's romp as a movie serial actress. The year 1948 saw release of the Crosby, Hope, and Lamour *Road* film *Road to Rio; Easter Parade*, perhaps the year's best movie musical, starring Fred Astaire and Judy Garland; *A Date with Judy*, with Jane Powell and Elizabeth Taylor; *Words and Music*, the fictitious musical biography of Rodgers and Hart; and *When My Baby Smiles at Me*, starring Betty Grable and Dan Dailey. In 1949 there was *Jolson Sings Again; Look for the Silver Lining*, the musical biography of Marilyn Miller; *In the Good Old Summertime; Take Me Out to the Ball Game; Neptune's Daughter*, an Esther Williams combination of swimming and music; the movie version of Leonard Bernstein's *On the Town*; and *The Barkleys of Broadway*, another Fred Astaire and Ginger Rogers film after ten years' absence.

Top moneymaking and Academy Award-nominated movie musicals of the first half of the fifties include 1950's movie version of *Annie Get Your Gun*, Disney's *Cinderella*, and *Three Little Words*. In 1951 came *An American in Paris*, one of the most beautiful dance films ever made; the third version of Jerome Kern and Oscar Hammerstein II's *Show Boat; The Great Caruso; Royal Wedding*, in which Fred Astaire danced on the ceiling; *Here Comes the Groom*, which stars Bing Crosby and Jane Wyman; and *On Moonlight Bay*, which stars Doris Day and Gordon MacRae. The 1952 selection includes the sequel to Bob Hope's *Paleface, Son of Paleface; Singin' in the Rain; With a Song in My Heart*, the musical biography of Jane Froman; *Stars and Stripes Forever*, the screen biography of march king, John Philip Sousa; *Hans Christian Anderson*, Danny Kaye's starring role as the writer of fairy tales; and the screen biography of lyricist Gus Kahn, *I'll See You in My Dreams. Lili*, the film that inspired the Broadway musical *Carnival*, appeared in

1953, along with the Disney production of *Peter Pan;* *Gentlemen Prefer Blondes,* which stars Jane Russell and Marilyn Monroe; *Scared Stiff* and *The Stooge,* both Dean Martin and Jerry Lewis films; and yet another *Road* musical for Crosby, Hope, and Lamour, *Road to Bali.* In 1954 movie audiences could see *Seven Brides for Seven Brothers,* one of the most energetic dance films ever made; *White Christmas,* the top moneymaking film of the year, which stars Bing Crosby, Danny Kaye, Rosemary Clooney, and Vera-Ellen; *A Star Is Born,* Judy Garland's crowning achievement; *There's No Business Like Show Business,* starring Ethel Merman, Donald O'Connor, Marilyn Monroe, Dan Dailey, Johnnie Ray, and Mitzi Gaynor; and *The Glenn Miller Story,* the musical biography of one of the most popular of the big band leaders. Finally, in 1955 there were released *Love Me or Leave Me,* the screen biography of Ruth Etting; Disney's *The Lady and the Tramp;* and *Pete Kelly's Blues,* starring Jack Webb and Peggy Lee.

A few of the era's most popular songs that were introduced in the movie musicals include 1945's Oscar winner "It Might as Well Be Spring"; 1946's Academy Award honoree, "On the Atchison, Topeka and the Santa Fe"; 1947's winner, "Zip-a-Dee-Doo-Dah"; 1948's "Buttons and Bows," the Academy Award winner from *The Paleface;* 1949's Esther Williams and Ricardo Montalban duet, "Baby, It's Cold Outside," the Oscar winner from *Neptune's Daughter;* 1950's winner, "Mona Lisa"; 1951's Oscar winner "In the Cool, Cool, Cool of the Evening"; 1952's theme song from the western classic *High Noon;* 1953's "Secret Love"; 1954's title song from *Three Coins in a Fountain;* and 1955's "Love Is a Many-Splendored Thing."

As the decade closed, television was capturing much of the movie audience. That situation was worsened when McCarthy accused many in the motion-picture industry of Communist associations, which caused public skepticism about the movies in general.

Postwar Broadway Musicals

The thirties are often called the heyday of the musical theater, while the forties marked a transition from musical comedy to a more serious dramatic musical. There were no earthshaking musical developments on Broadway during the early fifties, but the theater did its share of producing hit musicals.

Richard Rodgers and Oscar Hammerstein II were the most important writers of hit musicals for the Broadway stage during the 1945–1955 period. As the era opened, their *Oklahoma!* was still running on Broadway and on the road, and they had a new hit with *Carousel.* In 1949 *South Pacific* opened and broke all kinds of records and was awarded a Pulitzer Prize. Rodgers and Hammerstein returned to Broadway in 1951 with *The King and I.*

The Antoinette Perry Awards (the Tonys) for "distinguished achievement in the theater" began honoring musicals of the year in 1949. Those honored during this period were *Kiss Me, Kate, South Pacific, Guys and Dolls, The King and I, Wonderful Town, Kismet, The Pajama Game,* and *Damn Yankees.*

Other significant musicals that were not selected for Tony Awards include 1946's *Annie Get Your Gun,* 1947's *Finian's Rainbow* and *Brigadoon,* 1948's *Where's Charley?,* and 1951's *Paint Your Wagon.*

Broadway was not the hit-making medium for popular songs that it had been, but it produced a few genuine hits and some songs that have become standards. Only 1949's "Some Enchanted Evening" and "Bali Ha'i" from *South Pacific* and 1954's "Hey There" from *The Pajama Game* were top ten hits, but some great songs came from the period's musicals. They include "You'll Never Walk Alone" from *Carousel,* "There's No Business Like Show Business" from *Annie Get Your Gun,* "Almost Like Being in Love" from *Brigadoon,* "How Are Things in Glocca Morra?" from *Finian's Rainbow,* "Another Op'nin', Another Show" from *Kiss Me, Kate,* "Once in Love with Amy" from *Where's Charley?,* "A Bushel and a Peck" from *Guys and Dolls,* "Hello, Young Lovers" from *The King and I,* "Stranger in Paradise" from *Kismet,* and "Heart" from *Damn Yankees.*

The Foreign Influence

The popular music industry in the forties and fifties imported more songs, particularly Latin American ones. The practice had started during the ASCAP ban in the early forties, when songs like "Frenesi," "Amapola," and "Brazil" were imported. The trend continued in the mid-forties and early fifties with the

English song "The Gypsy," the French "La Vie en Rose" and "C'est Si Bon," the Australian "Now Is the Hour," the German songs "You, You, You," "You Can't Be True, Dear" and "Glow-Worm," the Swiss songs "Oh! My Pa-pa" and "Forever and Ever," the Brazilian song "Delicado," the Italian song "Botch-a-Me," the Bahamian calypso trend of the early fifties, and the Austrian song "The Happy Wanderer." The industry was becoming more international.

Hillbilly Crossovers

In addition to embracing foreign popular music, the industry began to recognize the country artists and their songs. Eddy Arnold and Hank Williams garnered several million-selling records in this period. Other country stars who were able to cross over and have mainstream hits during the era were Jimmy Wakely, who had a hit duet with Margaret Whiting in 1949; Tex Williams, who had a top ten hit with "Smoke, Smoke, Smoke That Cigarette" in 1947; Red Foley, who had four million sellers in 1950 and 1951; and Cowboy Copas, who had a 1948 recording of "Tennessee Waltz,"

which was covered by Patti Page in 1950, when it became a multimillion seller. White mainstream singers released "cover versions" of country songs just as they did R&B songs.

There were several other hits that had a definite country feel, if not origin. Some of these include songs performed by Tennessee Ernie Ford, Guy Mitchell, Les Paul and Mary Ford, and even Frankie Laine.

The inroads that country made during these years laid the foundation for the astronomical success of Elvis Presley in the last half of the fifties.

TV—A New Medium of Entertainment

A new medium of entertainment began to challenge the supremacy of radio by the mid-forties. By the end of the forties fifty stations were broadcasting to 700,000 home television sets with a potential audience of approximately 4 million.

Still, not until the last years of the forties and the first few years of the fifties was radio seriously threatened. By that time TV had begun to take over the variety shows, the quiz programs, the soap operas, and the big stars.

Radio as we know it today, primarily dedicated to the dissemination of news and the playing of music (whether the station plays top forty, country, standard pop, soul, or whatever), originated when television usurped its place in the entertainment world. Now the disc jockey began to rule the airwaves. He became a power in the pop music industry, especially in metropolitan areas. A disc jockey could make or break a record, make unknown singers overnight sensations or send them into oblivion.

The Birth of Rock

In 1951, Alan Freed, a disc jockey in Cleveland, used the term *rock and roll* to describe his rhythm and blues program. Freed played only rhythm and blues records on his show. When he moved to New York in 1954, his rock and roll programming became even more influential, but white audiences were still hesitant to accept this new sound.

Then, in 1954, a white combo headed by Bill Haley gave new impetus to rock and roll. Haley and his Comets' frenzied rock music sold like wildfire. Their first big hit was "Shake, Rattle and Roll," followed closely by "Rock Around the Clock,"both discs recorded in 1954. "Rock Around the Clock" is now

practically a symbol of the rock era. The tune was included in the 1955 film *The Blackboard Jungle,* and Haley's version is estimated to have sold more than 16 million copies globally.

Some of the other early rock pioneers include Fats Domino (only Elvis Presley, the Beatles, the Rolling Stones, and the Supremes had more million-selling discs by the mid-seventies), Ivory Joe Hunter, Hank Ballard and the Midnighters, Joe Turner, and LaVern Baker.

The Crew Cuts' cover version of the Chords' "Sh-Boom" is now considered one of the first rock and roll hits. It proved to record executives that cover recordings were profitable. Soon many white singers and groups were making covers of rhythm and blues songs recorded by blacks.

As the rock and roll craze picked up momentum, new stars emerged. Out of country or rockabilly came Buddy Holly, Jerry Lee Lewis, and Carl Perkins. Out of the rhythm and blues tradition came Chuck Berry, Little Richard, the Penguins, the Platters, and B. B. King. A few whites began to have hits with rock material: Pat Boone with "Ain't That a Shame!" the McGuire Sisters with "Sincerely," and Georgia Gibbs with "Dance with Me, Henry."

But what rock needed was a charismatic superstar, and it found that in 1956 with Elvis Presley.

To verify the hits of the sing era, the same sources were used that had been used for the last portion of the swing era. The only addition came from a list of *Billboard*'s top hits of 1955 and *Billboard*'s list of the top forty hits from 1955 to 1982.

1 9 4 5

Ac-cent-tchuate the Positive
COMPOSER: **Harold Arlen**
  LYRICIST: **Johnny Mercer**

Bing Crosby introduced this song in the 1944 movie musical *Here Come the Waves*. Crosby played a singing idol, a parody of the crooners like Sinatra and himself. Crosby's recording helped popularize the song.

While Harold Arlen and Johnny Mercer were writing the music for the film, they got the idea for this song during a drive. Mercer reminded Arlen of a spiritual-sounding tune Arlen had been humming almost constantly. When Arlen began singing it again, Mercer remarked rather disgustedly, "You've got to accentuate the positive." Arlen then went about fitting the line into his melody. By the time they arrived at the studio they had the song practically written. It was such a hit in the film that it received an Academy Award nomination as the best song from a film for 1945, but it lost out to Rodgers and Hammerstein's "It Might as Well Be Spring" (see page 123).

Variety chose this song for its "Fifty Year Hit Parade."

Candy
COMPOSERS: **Joan Whitney and Alex Kramer**
  LYRICIST: **Mack David**

"Candy" was best known through recordings by Johnny Mercer, Jo Stafford and the Pied Pipers. The song climbed to the top of *Your Hit Parade* and stayed there for a month in the spring of 1945. The song is often sung by a male vocalist, with "Candy" a female. But the original lyrics sang of a male: "I wish that there were four of him so I could love much more of him . . . The day I take my 'Candy' and make him mine all mine."

Chickery Chick
COMPOSER-LYRICISTS: **Sidney Lippman and Sylvia Dee**

One of the big novelty hits of 1945 was "Chickery Chick." Sammy Kaye and his orchestra, with a vocal by Nancy Norman and Billy Williams, had a best-selling recording of the song. The lyrics to "Chickery Chick" are as nonsensical as 1943's "Mairzy Doats": "Chickery chick cha-la, cha-la, check-a-la romey in a bananika, bollika wollika;" etc.

Don't Fence Me In
COMPOSER-LYRICIST: **Cole Porter**

This 1944 number is far too plebeian to have been written by Cole Porter. It does not have the sophistication of most of his lyrics, nor does it seem especially clever or debonair. But Cole Porter wrote it for a never-released film, *Adios Argentina*. Some sources claim that Porter bought the rights to the lyrics from a Montana cowboy, Robert H. Fletcher. Porter used the title and a few phrases from the original poem in his lyrics. That could explain the un-Porter-like character of the lyrics.

It lay forgotten until Roy Rogers and the Andrews Sisters performed it in the 1944 movie musical *Hollywood Canteen*. Rogers sang it again in the 1945 film

Don't Fence Me In, and it was featured in the tribute to Porter's life and music, *Night and Day* (1946).

Kate Smith and Bing Crosby featured the song in their radio appearances. Crosby's recording with the Andrews Sisters sold more than a million copies. Eight weeks at the top of the charts in late 1944 and early 1945 qualified "Don't Fence Me In" as 1945's number four hit.

The number is a cowboy folk song style of song that repeats the title phrase four different times. The singer is a footloose and fancy-free kind of person who refuses to settle down.

Dream
COMPOSER-LYRICIST: **Johnny Mercer**

Johnny Mercer wrote this gorgeous song for his closing theme on the CBS Chesterfield radio show in 1945. A recording by the Pied Pipers became their first million seller. The lyric may be summarized with the last line: "Things never are as bad as they seem, so dream . . ."

A Hubba Hubba Hubba (Dig You Later)
COMPOSER: **Jimmy McHugh**
LYRICIST: **Harold Adamson**

Perry Como introduced this song in the 1945 movie musical *Doll Face.* His recording with the Satisfiers became a million seller.

I Can't Begin to Tell You
COMPOSER: **James V. Monaco**
LYRICIST: **Mack Gordon**

The 1945 movie musical *The Dolly Sisters* introduced "I Can't Begin to Tell You." First Betty Grable sang it; then it was reprised in the final scene by Grable and John Payne. Bing Crosby's recording helped make it popular. "I Can't Begin to Tell You" was an Academy Award nominee in 1946. (See "All Through the Day," 1946, page 126, for other 1946 nominees.)

If I Loved You
COMPOSER: **Richard Rodgers**
LYRICIST: **Oscar Hammerstein II**

Molnar's robust but tender fantasy *Liliom,* about a carnival barker who marries a factory girl, is killed in a robbery attempt, and then is allowed to return to earth for a brief time, was transformed by Rodgers and Hammerstein into the highly successful Broadway musical *Carousel.* The main romantic duet, "If I Loved You," was sung by Billy Bigelow (played by John Raitt) and Julie Jordan (played by Jan Clayton). The

dialogue that precedes the song prompted the Hammerstein lyric. In the scene Billy asks Julie, "But you wouldn't marry a rough guy like me—that is—uh—if you loved me?" Julie answers, "Yes, I would—if I loved you."

Perry Como had a 2 million seller with this hit from *Carousel. Variety* chose the song for its "Fifty Year Hit Parade."

I'm Beginning to See the Light
COMPOSER-LYRICISTS: **Don George, Johnny Hodges, Duke Ellington, and Harry James**

Harry James and his orchestra introduced "I'm Beginning to See the Light." Connie Francis had a best-selling record of the song in the early sixties.

It Might as Well Be Spring
COMPOSER: **Richard Rodgers**
LYRICIST: **Oscar Hammerstein II**

The Academy Award winner in 1945 was "It Might as Well Be Spring" from the Rodgers and Hammerstein movie musical *State Fair.* It was sung on the sound track by Louanne Hogan (for Jeanne Crain). The film was a musical remake of a 1933 nonmusical that starred Will Rogers and Janet Gaynor.

Lyricist Hammerstein wanted the girl, Marty, to appear to have spring fever, but the state fair was in the fall, so he had her sing that even though it was autumn, "it might as well be spring."

The list of nominations for the Best Song Academy Award for 1945 is a long one. The other nominees were "Accentuate the Positive" by Harold Arlen and Johnny Mercer from *Here Come the Waves;* "Anywhere" by Jule Styne and Sammy Cahn from *Tonight and Every Night;* "The Cat and the Canary" by Jay Livingston and Ray Evans from *Why Girls Leave Home;* "Endlessly" by Walter Kent and Kim Gannon from *Earl Carroll Vanities;* "I Fall in Love Too Easily" by Jule Styne and Sammy Cahn from *Anchors Aweigh;* "I'll Buy That Dream" by Allie Wrubel and Herb Magidson from *Sing Your Way Home;* "More and More" by Jerome Kern and E. Y. Harburg from *Can't Help Singing;* "Sleigh Ride in July" by Jimmy Van Heusen and Johnny Burke from *Belle of the Yukon;* and "So in Love" by David Rose and Leo Robin from *Wonder Man.*

It's Been a Long, Long Time
COMPOSER: **Jule Styne**
LYRICIST: **Sammy Cahn**

"It's Been a Long, Long Time" was introduced on the radio by Phil Brito, but Harry James and his orchestra, with a Kitty Kallen vocal, had the best-selling recording of the song. The most famous lines of the song are "Kiss me once, then kiss me twice,/Then kiss me once again,/It's been a long, long time." It was number one for five weeks and was the number nine song of 1945's top ten.

Variety named the song to its "Fifty Year Hit Parade."

It's a Grand Night for Singing
COMPOSER: **Richard Rodgers**
LYRICIST: **Oscar Hammerstein II**

"It's a Great Night for Singing" was a hit from Rodgers and Hammerstein's only original score for the screen, *State Fair*. In the 1945 film it was sung by the ensemble. In the 1962 remake it was sung by Pat Boone, Anita Gordon (dubbed for Pamela Tiffin), and Bobby Darin. This fast waltz-meter tune was one of the songs audiences left the theaters humming.

Variety picked this song for its "Fifty Year Hit Parade."

June Is Bustin' Out All Over
COMPOSER: **Richard Rodgers**
LYRICIST: **Oscar Hammerstein II**

"June Is Bustin' Out All Over" was the announcement of the arrival of summer in Rodgers and Hammerstein's musical *Carousel* (see "If I Loved You," page 123). The song was introduced by Nettie Fowler (played by Christine Johnson), Carrie Pipperidge (played by Jean Darling), and the chorus and was danced by Pearl Lang and the chorus.

This song is in *Variety*'s "Fifty Year Hit Parade."

Laura
COMPOSER: **David Raksin**
LYRICIST: **Johnny Mercer**

This David Raksin tune was the theme of the 1944 nonmusical motion picture *Laura*. The lyrics were added by Johnny Mercer a few months after the film's release. Johnnie Johnston first sang the song on radio, and Woody Herman's band had the most successful recording of the song. Their Columbia recording sold a million copies.

Variety chose this song for its "Fifty Year Hit Parade."

The More I See You
COMPOSER: **Harry Warren**
LYRICIST: **Mack Gordon**

Dick Haymes introduced this song in the 1945 movie musical *Billy Rose's Diamond Horseshoe*. The song

climbed to the top spot on the hit chart in the summer of 1945.

My Dreams Are Getting Better All The Time
COMPOSER: **Vic Mizzy**
LYRICIST: **Mann Curtis**

The number seven hit in 1945 was this song. It had been introduced in the Abbott and Costello 1944 film *In Society* by Marion Hutton. A best-selling recording by Les Brown and his orchestra featured Doris Day on the vocal.

My Heart Sings
COMPOSER-LYRICISTS: **Jamblan and Herpin**

Harold Rome adapted a 1944 French popular song, "Ma Mie," by Jamblan and Herpin into "My Heart Sings," which Kathryn Grayson introduced in the 1945 movie musical *Anchors Aweigh*.

"My Heart Sings" was listed in *Variety*'s "Fifty Year Hit Parade."

On the Atchison, Topeka and the Santa Fe
COMPOSER: **Harry Warren**
LYRICIST: **Johnny Mercer**

The number three hit in 1945's top ten and the 1946 Academy Award winner was "On the Atchison, Topeka and the Santa Fe." Harry Warren and Johnny Mercer wrote this song for the 1946 movie musical *The Harvey Girls*. The Harvey Girls were a group of waitresses taken to the Wild West by restaurateur Fred Harvey. In the film, "On the Atchison, Topeka and the Santa Fe" was performed by Judy Garland, Ray Bolger, and a train full of Harvey Girls.

The song was popularized in a recording by Johnny Mercer and the Pied Pipers. A unique feature of the song is the imitation of the train whistle. The subject is also unusual. Most popular songs are love songs, but this is a song about anticipating the arrival of a train. (See "All Through the Day," 1946, page 126, for other 1946 nominees.)

Variety picked the song for its "Fifty Year Hit Parade."

Rum and Coca-Cola
COMPOSER: **Lionel Belasco**
ADAPTORS: **Jeri Sullivan and Paul Baron**
LYRICISTS: **Morey Amsterdam**

The number five hit in 1945 was the Andrews Sisters' recording of "Rum and Coca-Cola." Morey Amsterdam heard this calypso melody during a Trinidad vacation. He assumed it was a folk melody in the public domain, so he had Jeri Sullivan and Paul Baron adapt it for American audiences. He then published it with his own lyrics. It was introduced by Sullivan at a nightclub in New York and was popularized by the Andrews Sisters. Their recording with Vic Schoen and his orchestra was a million seller. When the song became famous, it was involved in a plagiarism suit. The original tune was not in the public domain, but was Lionel Belasco's "L'Année Passée," which had been written in Trinidad in 1906.

Saturday Night Is the Loneliest Night in the Week
COMPOSER: **Jule Styne**
LYRICIST: **Sammy Cahn**

Jule Styne and Sammy Cahn wrote this song in 1944. It was introduced and popularized by Frank Sinatra.

Variety chose it for its "Fifty Year Hit Parade."

Sentimental Journey
COMPOSER-LYRICISTS: **Bud Green, Les Brown, and Ben Homer**

The top hit of 1945 was a recording of "Sentimental Journey" by Les Brown and his orchestra (with a Doris Day vocal). The recording was a million seller and helped them earn the top spot in a poll as band of the year. Brown adopted it as his theme song.

"Sentimental Journey" was a *Variety* choice for its "Fifty Year Hit Parade."

That's for Me
COMPOSER: **Richard Rodgers**
LYRICIST: **Oscar Hammerstein II**

"That's for Me" is a hit from the movie musical *State Fair* (see "It Might as Well Be Spring," page 123). It was introduced by Vivian Blaine and Dick Haymes. In the 1962 remake it was sung by Pat Boone.

Variety named the song to its "Fifty Year Hit Parade."

There! I've Said It Again
COMPOSER-LYRICISTS: **Redd Evans and Dave Mann**

In 1941 Redd Evans and Dave Mann wrote the words and music to "There! I've Said It Again." Evans convinced the still-unknown Boston bandleader Vaughn Monroe to use the song, but it was not until 1945 that Monroe recorded it. It turned out to be a million seller and established Monroe as a star. It was the number six hit in 1945's top ten.

The song was revived in 1964 by Bobby Vinton and was picked by *Variety* for its "Fifty Year Hit Parade."

Till the End of Time
COMPOSER: **Ted Mossman, adapted from Frédéric Chopin**
LYRICIST: **Buddy Kaye**

Ted Mossman used Chopin's melody from Polonaise in A Flat Major to write "Till the End of Time." Perry Como's recording with the Russ Case orchestra became a million seller and was 1945's number two song.

A rhythmic version of the same polonaise by pianist Carmen Cavallaro and his orchestra also sold a million copies and was the number ten hit of the year. Concert pianist José Iturbi, who played the polonaise for the 1944 film *A Song to Remember,* supposedly based on the life of the great Polish composer, sold another million copies.

The lyrics for "Till the End of Time" insist that "long as stars are in the blue, long as there's a spring," in other words, "till the end of time," you will be loved.

The song was chosen for the *Variety* "Fifty Year Hit Parade."

You Belong to My Heart
COMPOSER: **Augustín Lara**
LYRICIST: **Ray Gilbert**

The Spanish-Cuban influence in songs continued in 1945 with "You Belong to My Heart." It was introduced by Dora Luz in the 1945 Walt Disney production *The Three Caballeros*. Recordings by Bing Crosby and by Xavier Cugat and his orchestra became big sellers.

Variety selected this song for its "Fifty Year Hit Parade."

You'll Never Walk Alone
COMPOSER: **Richard Rodgers**
LYRICIST: **Oscar Hammerstein II**

"You'll Never Walk Alone" is an inspirational number from the Rodgers and Hammerstein musical *Carousel* (see "If I Loved You," page 123). It was introduced by Nettie (played by Christine Johnson) as she was trying to give Julie (played by Jan Clayton) courage after her husband, Billy, was killed in a robbery attempt. In the musical's finale, the song is reprised by the entire ensemble as Billy, on a visit to earth after death, watches his daughter graduate from high school.

Variety selected "You'll Never Walk Alone" as a "Golden 100 Tin Pan Alley Song."

1 9 4 6

All Through the Day
COMPOSER: **Jerome Kern**
   LYRICIST: **Oscar Hammerstein II**

Jerome Kern and Oscar Hammerstein II wrote "All Through the Day" for the 1946 movie musical *Centennial Summer*. It was introduced by Larry Stevens, Cornel Wilde, and Louanne Hogan (who dubbed for Jeanne Crain). Kern's music was the highlight of an otherwise lackluster film. The composer died shortly after completing this project.

Kern's melody is not as operatic as his earlier songs had been. Even this master had difficulty spanning the gap between the operettas he had written in his youth and the music that was now fashionable.

Kern and Hammerstein's song was one of the nominated songs for the 1946 Academy Award for Best Song, which was captured by "On the Atchison, Topeka and the Santa Fe" (listed in 1945 because it was one of the top hits of that year, see page 124). The other nominated songs were "I Can't Begin to Tell You" by James V. Monaco and Mack Gordon from *The Dolly Sisters;* "Ole Buttermilk Sky" by Hoagy Carmichael and Jack Brooks from *Canyon Passage;* and "You Keep Coming Back Like a Song" by Irving Berlin from *Blue Skies.*

The Christmas Song
COMPOSER-LYRICISTS: **Mel Tormé and Robert**
   Wells

Mel Tormé (in collaboration with Robert Wells) wrote and introduced this seasonal favorite in 1946. However, Nat ("King") Cole's version was the most popular. The song has remained an important seasonal song. The lyrics conjure up lovely images: "Chestnuts roasting on an open fire . . . Yuletide carols being sung by a choir . . . tiny tots with their eyes all aglow." No authoritative sales figures are available, but since it returns year after year and is included on numerous Christmas albums, it either is or will be one of the world's best sellers.

Come Rain or Shine
COMPOSER: **Harold Arlen**
   LYRICIST: **Johnny Mercer**

This love duet from the stage musical *St. Louis Woman* was written by Harold Arlen and Johnny Mercer. It was introduced by Ruby Hill and Harold Nicholas at the opening of Act II. The melody and lyrics have a distinctly blues feel. *St. Louis Woman* had an all-black cast which included Pearl Bailey and Rex Ingram.

Doin' What Comes Natur'lly
COMPOSER-LYRICIST: **Irving Berlin**

"Doin' What Comes Natur'lly" is a comic song sung by Annie Oakley (played by Ethel Merman) in the musical comedy *Annie Get Your Gun* (see "There's No Business Like Show Business," page 129). It expresses Annie's idea of the way life should be: natural. She claims we do not need education to create children; we have no need to learn to write our names to cash checks if we have millions; we need no special training to attract the opposite sex, etc. Dinah Shore had a best-selling record of this hit.

Variety chose this song for its "Fifty Year Hit Parade."

Five Minutes More
COMPOSER: **Jule Styne**
   LYRICIST: **Sammy Cahn**

The sixth-rated hit in 1946's top ten was Jule Styne and Sammy Cahn's "Five Minutes More." It was first published independently (that is, not written for a musical or movie), but it was later interpolated into the 1946 movie musical *The Sweetheart of Sigma Chi,* in which it was sung by Phil Brito. Frank Sinatra's best-selling recording helped it reach the top of *Your Hit Parade* and stay there for a month in late 1946.

The song is a date's plea for five more minutes to enjoy "your charms."

Full Moon and Empty Arms
COMPOSER-LYRICISTS: **Buddy Kaye and Ted**
   Mossman, adapted from Sergei
   Rachmaninoff

Buddy Kaye and Ted Mossman adapted the melody for this beautiful ballad from Russian composer Sergei Rachmaninoff's Second Piano Concerto. The theme from the third movement furnished the melody. Rachmaninoff's luscious harmonies and warm, passionate melodies made excellent popular song material. "Full Moon and Empty Arms" was a popular recording by Frank Sinatra.

The Girl That I Marry
COMPOSER-LYRICIST: **Irving Berlin**

"The Girl That I Marry" was introduced by Frank Butler (played by Ray Middleton) in Irving Berlin's *Annie Get Your Gun* (see "There's No Business Like Show Business," page 129). He sang the number to illustrate to hickster Annie that she definitely was not the kind of girl he intended to marry.

The song was a *Variety* choice for its "Fifty Year Hit Parade."

The Gypsy
COMPOSER-LYRICIST: **Billy Reid**

English composer Billy Reid wrote this song in 1945, and it was popularized in the United States in 1946 by a million-selling disc featuring the Ink Spots and a best-selling recording with Dinah Shore. The Ink Spots' disc was the year's top hit, while Shore's recording (with "Laughing on the Outside, Crying on the Inside" on the flip side) was number eight in the year's top ten.

The song describes seeking a Gypsy fortune teller's advice on romance.

Variety chose this song for its "Fifty Year Hit Parade."

I Got the Sun in the Morning
COMPOSER-LYRICIST: **Irving Berlin**

Annie Oakley (played by Ethel Merman) introduced this hit in the musical *Annie Get Your Gun* (see "There's No Business Like Show Business," page 129). She sang it to enumerate some of life's simple pleasures. "Got no diamonds, got no pearls, but still I think I'm a lucky girl," because I have the "sun in the morning and the moon at night."

Variety picked this song for its "Fifty Year Hit Parade."

I'm Always Chasing Rainbows
COMPOSER: **Harry Carroll, adapted from Frédéric Chopin**
LYRICIST: **Joseph McCarthy**

In 1918 Harry Carroll lifted the middle section from Chopin's Fantasie Impromptu in C Sharp Minor for this hit. In *Oh Look!*, a 1918 Broadway success, it was introduced by Harry Fox. Perry Como revived it successfully in 1946 and made a million-selling recording. The song appeared in a number of movie musicals, including 1945's *The Dolly Sisters*, which may have again brought it to the attention of the public.

The lyrics suggest that the singer is a daydreamer who never accomplishes anything worthwhile.

Laughing on the Outside (Crying on the Inside)
COMPOSER: **Bernie Wayne**
LYRICIST: **Ben Raleigh**

"Laughing on the Outside (Crying on the Inside)" tries to cover up the singer's sad feelings with a light-hearted air. It was introduced by Sammy Kaye and his orchestra and popularized by Doris Day.

Let It Snow! Let It Snow! Let It Snow!
COMPOSER: **Jule Styne**
LYRICIST: **Sammy Cahn**

Jule Styne and Sammy Cahn wrote this seasonal hit in 1945. It was popularized by Vaughn Monroe in a recording in 1946 and tied with "Symphony" for the number ten hit. The lyrics say that even though the weather is unbearable outside, two can keep cozy and warm together by the fire, so why go out?

Variety selected this song for its "Fifty Year Hit Parade."

Oh! What It Seemed to Be
COMPOSER: **Bennie Benjamin**
LYRICISTS: **George Weiss and Frankie Carle**

This number as recorded by Frankie Carle and his orchestra and by Frank Sinatra gained the top spot on the charts and remained there for two months in the spring of 1946. That helped put it among the top ten hits of the year (number seven).

The song was selected for the *Variety* "Fifty Year Hit Parade."

The Old Lamplighter
COMPOSER: **Nat Simon**
LYRICIST: **Charles Tobias**

Charles Tobias got the idea for this song from his memories of boyhood days in Worcester, Massachusetts, and the lamplighter there. Recordings by Kay Kyser and his orchestra, with a Michael Douglas vocal (the same Douglas who became a talk show host), and by Sammy Kaye and his orchestra, with a Billy Williams vocal, put the number in the number four spot in 1946's top ten.

The lamplighter makes his nightly rounds, lighting the lamps in the park, but he will leave a lamp unlit near two lovers sitting on a park bench because of his memories of a time when he too had a love.

Ole Buttermilk Sky
COMPOSER-LYRICISTS: **Hoagy Carmichael and Jack Brooks**

It had been six years since Hoagy Carmichael created a big hit, but in 1946 he and Jack Brooks collaborated to produce the Academy Award nominee "Ole Buttermilk Sky" (see "On the Atchison, Topeka and the Santa Fe," 1945, page 124, and 1946 nominees listed under "All Through the Day," page 126). Carmichael introduced it in the nonmusical film *Canyon Passage.* Kay Kyser and his orchestra had the most successful recording of the song.

The singer asks the "ole buttermilk sky" to make a lovely setting for a rendezvous with the one he loves.

The song is included in *Variety*'s "Fifty Year Hit Parade."

Personality
COMPOSER: **James Van Heusen**
  LYRICIST: **Johnny Burke**

There have been two tunes with the title "Personality." James Van Heusen and Johnny Burke wrote one (copyright 1945), and Harold Logan and Lloyd Price wrote the second (1959). The Van Heusen-Burke tune was introduced by Dorothy Lamour in the 1946 movie musical *Road to Utopia,* another in the Crosby, Hope, and Lamour *Road* series. Johnny Mercer, a songwriter himself, made the song popular in a recording with the Pied Pipers. Part of the song's success was due to its double entendres.

Prisoner of Love
See page 61 (1931). Perry Como's million-selling recording helped the song become the number three hit in 1946's top ten.

Shoofly Pie and Apple Pan Dowdy
COMPOSER: **Guy Woods**
  LYRICIST: **Sammy Gallop**

This novelty became a hit in 1946 in records by Dinah Shore and by Guy Lombardo and his Royal Canadians. It was a million seller for Stan Kenton and his orchestra with a June Christy vocal.

Variety chose the song for its "Fifty Year Hit Parade."

Sioux City Sue
COMPOSER: **Dick Thomas**
  LYRICIST: **Ray Freedman**

Written in 1945, this song was introduced by Gene Autry in the 1946 film *Sioux City Sue.* A recording by Dick Thomas helped popularize it. Sue, with "hair of gold and eyes of blue," has captured the heart of the singer.

"Sioux City Sue" is in *Variety*'s "Fifty Year Hit Parade."

South America, Take It Away
COMPOSER-LYRICIST: **Harold Rome**

Harold Rome wrote this song two years before it was introduced in the 1946 musical *Call Me Mister.* A satirical look at the Latin American dances like the rumba and samba that were invading the United States, it became the hit of the show. It was introduced by Betty Garrett in a serviceman's canteen scene. Bing Crosby and the Andrews Sisters with Vic Schoen and his orchestra had a million seller. A similar subject was the idea behind "Who's Got the Pain?" from 1955's *Damn Yankees.*

Variety selected the song for its "Fifty Year Hit Parade."

Symphony
COMPOSER: **Alex Alstone**
  LYRICIST: **Jack Lawrence; French lyrics by André Tabet and Roger Bernstein**

Freddy Martin and his orchestra with a vocal by Clyde Rogers had a best-selling recording of this song, which climbed to top ten status for 1946 (tied with "Let It Snow!") and stayed at the top of the charts for almost two months at the beginning of the year.

Variety picked "Symphony" for its "Fifty Year Hit Parade."

Tenderly
COMPOSER: **Walter Gross**
  LYRICIST: **Jack Lawrence**

"Tenderly" is one of the most beautiful romantic ballads ever written. It was first recorded by Clark Dennis, then used on the sound track of the 1953 film *Torch Song.* Rosemary Clooney had a successful recording in 1955.

The lyrics—"Your arms opened wide and closed me inside: You took my lips, you took my love so tenderly"—express feelings with which most lovers readily identify. Although "Tenderly" did not reach top ten status, it has become a standard.

Variety selected "Tenderly" as a "Golden 100 Tin Pan Alley Song."

There's No Business Like Show Business
COMPOSER-LYRICIST: **Irving Berlin**

This song is the unofficial anthem of the theater. Irving Berlin wrote it for the 1946 musical *Annie Get Your Gun*. It was introduced by Annie Oakley (played by Ethel Merman), Frank Butler (played by Ray Middleton), Buffalo Bill Cody (played by William O'Neal), and Charlie Davenport (played by Marty May). Annie actually sings only toward the end of the song, after the three others have convinced her how great their Wild West Show is going to be.

Annie Get Your Gun is based on the life of sharpshooter Annie Oakley. The idea originated with Dorothy Fields, who intended to write the score with composer Jerome Kern, who died before the project began. Rodgers and Hammerstein had agreed to be the producers (the only musical they produced that was not their own). After Kern's death, they signed Irving Berlin to write both music and lyrics. The show became the second book musical to exceed the magical 1,000-performance figure on Broadway (*Oklahoma!* was the first).

A 1950 film version was made, and numerous road companies and revivals have been produced through the years, making *Annie Get Your Gun* one of Broadway's most successful musicals.

They Say It's Wonderful
COMPOSER-LYRICIST: **Irving Berlin**

"They Say It's Wonderful" is Annie Oakley and Frank Butler's contemplation of what they have heard love is supposed to be in the musical *Annie Get Your Gun* (see "There's No Business Like Show Business," above). Perry Como had a best-selling recording of the song, and it was at the top of *Your Hit Parade* for a month in the summer of 1946.

Variety chose the song for its "Fifty Year Hit Parade."

To Each His Own
COMPOSER-LYRICISTS: **Jay Livingston and Ray Evans**

The first major success for the songwriting team of Jay Livingston and Ray Evans was "To Each His Own," which boasted sales of 3 million recordings in 1946. The Ink Spots' disc climbed to the number one spot and remained there for eleven weeks in 1946. Tony Martin's version had reached gold status by 1955, while Eddy Howard and his orchestra's version had reached 2 million sales by 1957.

The song was written for a film with the same title but was not used there. The beautiful lyrics use analogies to say that everyone must do what he must do and be what he must be, but "I've found my own, one and only you."

"To Each His Own" is included in the *Variety* "Fifty Year Hit Parade."

Winter Wonderland
COMPOSER: **Felix Bernard**
LYRICIST: **Dick Smith**

This seasonal favorite was written in 1934. Guy Lombardo and his Royal Canadians and the Andrews Sisters made a million-selling disc of the song in 1946. It was backed by "Christmas Island." Collective sales of "Winter Wonderland" are more than 40 million.

This perennial Yuletide favorite tells of two lovers who enjoy some of the pleasantries of winter, including building a snowman they pretend is a minister who will marry them.

1 9 4 7

Almost Like Being In Love
COMPOSER: **Frederick Loewe**
LYRICIST: **Alan Jay Lerner**

This romantic duet is a chief hit from Lerner and Loewe's *Brigadoon*. It was introduced by American hunter Tommy Albright (played by David Brooks) and the Scottish maid Fiona MacLaren (played by Marion Bell).

Lerner's lyrics express the feelings that suggest one

is in love: "A rare mood . . . a smile on my face . . . I could swear I was falling . . . in love."

Brigadoon was Lerner and Loewe's third Broadway musical, but their first unqualified hit. The musical is about a town in Scotland that is resurrected for twenty-four hours once each century. On the day the town, Brigadoon, reawakens in the twentieth century, it is discovered by two Americans, Tommy and Jeff. Tommy quickly falls in love with Fiona, but when he learns the town's secret, he anguishes over whether to return home or to remain with his newfound love. In the end, love triumphs, of course.

The Scottish-flavored score did not produce many hits, but it contained an ample supply of beautiful songs that have remained favorites, including the tender "Come to Me, Bend to Me," "The Heather on the Hill," and "There but for You Go I."

Anniversary Song
COMPOSER: **Saul Chaplin, adapted from J. Ivanovici**
LYRICIST: **Al Jolson**

This song became an international hit because it was included in the fabulous 1946 film *The Jolson Story*. Saul Chaplin adapted the melody of Ivanovici's "Danube Waves," and Al Jolson added words. Backed by 1920's "Avalon," Al Jolson's recording from the film sound track quickly sold more than a million copies.

In the few years preceding the release of the movie and for a period between 1946's *The Jolson Story* and the 1949 film *Jolson Sings Again*, Jolson was introduced to a new generation and had a remarkable comeback. His million-selling singles included "April Showers," "Swanee," "Rock-a-bye Your Baby with a Dixie Melody," "California, Here I Come," "You Made Me Love You," "Ma Blushin' Rosie," "Sonny Boy," and "My Mammy." Both *The Jolson Story*, one of the first sound track albums, and the album *Songs He Made Famous* had enormous success.

The similarity of titles between 1941's "The Anniversary Waltz" and Jolson's "Anniversary Song" has sometimes caused confusion. The waltz is in 3/4 time, while the song is in cut time. The song is much more familiar to most fans of popular music. It speaks of the couple dancing on the night of their wedding and vowing their love would remain true. Jolson's recording was number nine among the year's top ten hits.

Variety chose this song for its "Fifty Year Hit Parade."

Ballerina
COMPOSER: **Carl Sigman**
LYRICIST: **Bob Russell**

By 1948 "Ballerina (Dance, Ballerina, Dance)," recorded by Vaughn Monroe, had sold a million copies. It was 1947's number two top ten hit. Nat "King" Cole successfully revived the song in 1955.

The lyrics encourage the ballerina to dance her best even though her heart is breaking and the man she loves is not sitting in the second row watching as thousands of other people watch her steal the show.

Variety picked the song for its "Fifty Year Hit Parade."

Civilization
COMPOSER: **Carl Sigman**
LYRICIST: **Bob Hilliard**

Carl Sigman scored again (see "Ballerina," above) in 1947 with "Civilization," which he wrote with Bob Hilliard. It was interpolated into the Broadway revue *Angel in the Wings*, in which it was introduced by Elaine Stritch.

The things that civilization brings are chronicled in the song, supposedly to convince a native of its value, but once "bright lights, false teeth, door bells, landlord" are itemized, civilization appears less attractive. The song was popularized by the Mills Brothers and by Danny Kaye with the Andrews Sisters.

Variety chose "Civilization" for its "Fifty Year Hit Parade."

Feudin' and Fightin'
COMPOSER: **Burton Lane**
LYRICISTS: **Al Dubin and Burton Lane**

This comic hillbilly number was introduced by Pat Brewster in the Broadway revue *Laffing Room Only* in 1944 but did not become well known until 1947 because the producers of the revue were involved in a bitter dispute with ASCAP and refused to release the broadcasting rights to the musical score from the show. The composer, Burton Lane, acquired the rights in 1947 and gave permission to Dorothy Shay to sing "Feudin' and Fightin'." She introduced it on a Bing Crosby radio program and had a best-selling record.

For Me and My Gal
COMPOSER: **George W. Meyer**
LYRICISTS: **Edgar Leslie and E. Ray Goetz**

This 1917 classic was the flip side of Arthur Godfrey's million-selling disc in 1947. The A side of the disc was "Too Fat Polka." Godfrey's record was the number eight hit of the year.

Originally "For Me and My Gal" was popularized in vaudeville by such outstanding personalities as Eddie Cantor, Sophie Tucker, and Al Jolson.

Variety selected it for its "Fifty Year Hit Parade" for 1917.

For Sentimental Reasons
COMPOSER: William Best
LYRICIST: Deke Watson

"For Sentimental Reasons" (1945) was popularized by recordings in 1947 by Eddy Howard, the King Cole Trio, Dinah Shore, and Charlie Spivak and his orchestra. "I love you for sentimental reasons, I hope you do believe me, I've given you my heart," says this ballad, which rises above mediocrity with a tender and passionate feeling in the melody and text. It was the top song on *Your Hit Parade* for seven weeks in the first three months of 1947.

A Gal in Calico
COMPOSER: Arthur Schwartz
LYRICIST: Leo Robin

This song was written for the 1946 movie musical *The Time, the Place and the Girl*. An Academy Award nominee (see "Zip-a-dee-doo-dah," page 133), "A Gal in Calico" was introduced by Jack Carson, Dennis Morgan, and Martha Vickers in the film. Tex Beneke and his orchestra had a best-selling recording, which climbed to the top of *Your Hit Parade* in early 1947.

The Gentleman Is a Dope
COMPOSER: Richard Rodgers
LYRICIST: Oscar Hammerstein II

Lisa Kirk introduced this song in *Allegro*. The musical was Richard Rodgers and Oscar Hammerstein II's third collaboration. It dealt with the theme of the corruption in an institution. The story covers a doctor's schooldays, marriage, success, and disillusionment with working in a large city hospital. He eventually returns to his small hometown.

In the song, Lisa Kirk, playing Emily West, tries vainly to hail a taxi in a rainstorm, while she mumbles about the way her boss, the doctor, is being led around by his wife. The song eventually reveals how much she loves the doctor even after she has itemized his faults.

Heartaches
COMPOSER: Al Hoffman
LYRICIST: John Klenner

Al Hoffman and John Klenner wrote this song in 1931. A recording by Ted Weems and his orchestra became a million seller, but it took fourteen years. The Weems disc was not particularly successful when it was released in 1933. In 1947 a Charlotte, North Carolina, disc jockey found the record, liked it, and played it

every day for a week. Record dealers in the South were suddenly swamped with requests for the record. It scored on *Your Hit Parade* and stayed at number one for a dozen weeks, making it the number three hit in 1947's top ten.

How Are Things in Glocca Morra?
COMPOSER: Burton Lane
LYRICIST: E. Y. Harburg

Finian's Rainbow, a fantasy musical, introduced this wistful ballad. The song is sung by Sharon McLonergan (played by Ella Logan) in America, wondering about her homeland, Ireland. Her reminiscence is prompted by the song of a bird, "the same skylark music we have back in Ireland."

Finian's Rainbow was written by Burton Lane and E. Y. Harburg. Harburg wanted to satirize the American economic system. Finian, a simple Irish immigrant, believes that a buried pot of gold in America will grow and make him rich. He happens to bury the pot at Fort Knox. Also included in the plot are comments on union versus labor, the Social Security system, and integration. In many respects, the musical was ahead of its time.

The 1968 film version starred Fred Astaire as Finian, Petula Clark as Sharon, and Tommy Steele as the leprechaun, Og. In the original, Finian did not sing or dance, but Astaire was given songs to sing and to feature his dancing.

The song was included in *Variety*'s "Fifty Year Hit Parade."

I Wish I Didn't Love You So
COMPOSER-LYRICIST: Frank Loesser

This Frank Loesser song was introduced by Betty Hutton (called the Blonde Bombshell) in the 1947 movie musical *The Perils of Pauline*. Both Dinah Shore and Vaughn Monroe had best-selling recordings. Betty Hutton, singing with the Joe Lilley orchestra, had a million-seller recording of the song, which was also an Academy Award nominee (see "Zip-a-dee-doo-dah," page 133).

I Wonder Who's Kissing Her Now
COMPOSERS: Joe E. Howard and Harold Orlob
LYRICISTS: Will M. Hough and Frank R. Adams

This 1909 song was a hit in 1947 for the second time. It had been introduced in the 1909 musical *The Prince of Tonight* and sold more than 3 million copies of sheet music. Then, in 1947, Joe E. Howard's film biography, *I Wonder Who's Kissing Her Now,* was made. The film helped the song to become popular again, and it climbed to number one on the charts. Its renewed popularity resulted in Harold Orlob's going to court to prove that he had composed the song. He asked for no financial reward, simply for credit for his creation. He proved that he had written the number for Howard, who paid him for the job. At the time (1909) it was considered legitimate for Howard to publish the song as his own since he had compensated Orlob.

In this waltz, the singer contemplates about who must be doing the things he once did with the girl who is no longer his.

ASCAP chose it as one of only sixteen numbers to appear in its "All-time Hit Parade." It was also in *Variety*'s "Fifty Year Hit Parade" in 1909 and was also included as a "Golden 100 Tin Pan Alley Song."

Linda
COMPOSER-LYRICISTS: **Jack Lawrence and Ann Ronell**

"Linda" (1944) was introduced in the 1945 film *The Story of G.I. Joe.* Then Buddy Clark with Ray Noble and his orchestra had a 1947 best-selling recording that kept the tune at the top of the charts for a month in the late spring and early summer of the year. That allowed it to be number seven in 1947's top ten.

The singer "doesn't count sheep" when he goes to sleep but counts "all the charms about Linda."

Variety chose the song for its "Fifty Year Hit Parade."

Mam'selle
COMPOSER: **Edmund Goulding**
LYRICIST: **Mack Gordon**

"Mam'selle" was introduced in a French café scene in the 1946 film *The Razor's Edge.* Art Lund popularized the song with a million-selling record that enjoyed three weeks on the top of the charts in mid-1947.

The lyrics speak of a rendezvous in a small café between the singer and Mam'selle, but there is a hint of sadness because the singer feels Mam'selle will say good-bye.

"Mam'selle" is in *Variety*'s "Fifty Year Hit Parade."

Near You
COMPOSER: **Francis Craig**
LYRICIST: **Kermit Goell**

The top hit of 1947 was pianist Francis Craig's "Near You," which sold 2.5 million discs. There were also several other successful recordings, notably those by the Andrews Sisters, Larry Green, Elliott Lawrence, and Alvino Rey. The song became Milton Berle's signature tune.

Craig's recording of "Near You" was a happenstance. He had organized a band after World War I and had played for more than twenty years at Nashville's Hermitage Hotel. He was also a staff member of a Nashville radio station for twenty-five years and was on NBC for twelve years. After he had retired, he approached the owner of Bullet Records, Jim Bulleit, about recording his orchestral tune "Red Rose." Bulleit reminded Craig that he needed two songs for the record. Craig selected "Near You" for the second side.

Craig regrouped his band for the session. He himself played the piano, and Bob Lamm provided the vocal. The recording was made in station WSM's studio and piped by telephone line across the street to a recording studio.

Milton Berle singing "There's just one place for me, near you" was familiar to many TV viewers since he used the song as his theme during the many years his program was on television.

"Near You" was selected by *Variety* for its "Fifty Year Hit Parade."

Open the Door, Richard
COMPOSERS: **Jack McVea and Don Howell**
LYRICISTS: **Dusty Fletcher and John Mason**

The title of this novelty song practically became a nuisance because it was sung by so many people whenever they wanted a door opened. Fletcher and Mason used the phrase as a part of a comedy routine in the thirties and forties. They turned it into a 1947 hit song recorded by Fletcher. The recording eventually sold more than a million. Several other artists— notably Louis Jordan and his Tympany Five, the Three Flames, Jack McVea, and Count Basie and his orchestra—also had hit recordings.

Variety chose this song for its "Fifty Year Hit Parade."

Papa, Won't You Dance with Me?
COMPOSER: **Jule Styne**
LYRICIST: **Sammy Cahn**

Jule Styne and Sammy Cahn wrote this polka in the style of the turn-of-the-century song-and-dance number. It was introduced by Nanette Fabray and Jack McCauley in the 1947 Broadway musical *High Button Shoes.*

Peg o' My Heart
COMPOSER: Fred Fisher
LYRICIST: Alfred Bryan

José Collins introduced the song in the *Ziegfeld Follies of 1913* as an interpolation. The writers dedicated the song to Laurette Taylor, the star of a 1912 Broadway comedy *Peg o' My Heart*. In 1933 it was featured in the film *Peg o' My Heart*. It was also prominent in Fred Fisher's 1949 screen biography, *Oh, You Beautiful Doll*.

"Peg o' My Heart" was a big hit in 1947. The Harmonicats' recording was the year's number four hit, while the Three Suns' disc was the number ten hit and went gold by 1950. Peggy Lee also had a successful recording.

Smoke, Smoke, Smoke That Cigarette
COMPOSER-LYRICISTS: Tex Williams and Merle Travis

One of the top country and western songs of the year also became the fifth-ranked hit of 1947. Tex Williams and Merle Travis wrote this comic patter song, which Tex Williams recorded with his band, the Western Caravan. It sold more than 2.5 million copies and was number one for six weeks. It became Capitol Records' first million seller.

That's My Desire
COMPOSER: Helmy Kresa
LYRICIST: Carroll Loveday

Irving Berlin published this song in 1931, but it remained reasonably forgotten until Mills Music, Inc., acquired the copyright sixteen years later. Frankie Laine revived the number in his nightclub act, and it was heard by a Mercury Records executive who signed him to record it. The disc brought commercial success to both Laine and Mercury.

Too Fat Polka
COMPOSER-LYRICISTS: Ross MacLean and Arthur Richardson

Arthur Godfrey had been a famous entertainer since he entered vaudeville in 1924, but this novelty song was his first million-seller record. The comical lyrics say "she's too fat for me." The flip side of the Godfrey record was 1917's "For Me and My Gal." The two songs, both hits, caused the disc to rank among the year's top ten (number eight).

You Call Everybody Darling
COMPOSER-LYRICISTS: Sam Martin, Ben Trace, and Clem Watts (pseudonym for Al Trace)

Written in 1946, this song was a million seller for Jack Smith with the Clark Sisters in 1947 and was a best-selling disc for Al Trace and his orchestra.

The lyrics claim that if you go around calling everybody darling and you're called that in return, "love won't come a-knockin' at your door."

Zip-A-Dee-Doo-Dah
COMPOSER: Allie Wrubel
LYRICIST: Ray Gilbert

This Academy Award winner of 1947 from Disney's 1946 cartoon-live action feature *Song of the South* is a gem. It was sung in the film by Uncle Remus, James Baskett. It was popularized by Johnny Mercer and the Pied Pipers in a best-selling recording.

How *does* a lyricist come up with such an unusual term as *zip-a-dee-do-dah*? It expresses jollity and carefree spirits. Wrubel's bright, bouncy melody helped the lyrics project the idea of a wonderful, sunshiny day when "ev'rything is 'satisfactch'll."

Variety chose this song for its "Fifty Year Hit Parade."

The other nominees for the 1947 Academy Award for Best Song were "A Gal in Calico" by Arthur Schwartz and Leo Robin from *The Time, the Place and the Girl;* "I Wish I Didn't Love You So" by Frank Loesser from *The Perils of Pauline;* "Pass That Peace Pipe" by Ralph Blane and Hugh Martin from *Good News;* and "You Do" by Josef Myrow and Mack Gordon from *Mother Wore Tights*.

1 9 4 8

All I Want for Christmas Is My Two Front Teeth
COMPOSER-LYRICIST: **Don Gardner**

Don Gardner wrote this seasonal favorite in 1946. It was introduced by the Satisfiers on Perry Como's radio show. Spike Jones and his City Slickers popularized the song in 1948 through a recording that was a million seller.

Another Op'nin', Another Show
COMPOSER-LYRICIST: **Cole Porter**

Cole Porter wrote the musical *Kiss Me Kate,* transforming Shakespeare's *Taming of the Shrew* into a modern tale. The musical is a play within a play. A group of actors are performing the Shakespearean play, but offstage a modern "taming" is in progress as a husband tries to tame his former wife. The actors play two roles: the Shakespeare characters and their offstage persons. Porter's sophisticated lyrics and beautiful melodies were never better, mixing Elizabethan dialogue and American slang to create a unique and colorful production.

"Another Op'nin', Another Show" is the first musical number. It was introduced in the musical by the maid, Hattie (played by Annabelle Hill).

Along with Irving Berlin's "There's No Business Like Show Business," "Another Op'nin', Another Show" is the best-known ode to show business and the theater.

"A"—You're Adorable
COMPOSER-LYRICISTS: **Buddy Kaye, Fred Wise, and Sidney Lippman**

" 'A'—You're Adorable," sometimes called "The Alphabet Song," was written in 1948, and became a hit through the best-selling recordings by Jo Stafford and Gordon MacRae and by Perry Como and the Fontane Sisters.

"A" is adorable; "B," beautiful; "C," cutie full of charms, etc. The lyrics itemize what, alphabetically speaking, "you mean to me."

Variety selected the song for its "Fifty Year Hit Parade."

Buttons and Bows
COMPOSER-LYRICISTS: **Jay Livingston and Ray Evans**

The Academy Award winner in 1948 was introduced by Bob Hope and Jane Russell in the movie *The Paleface.* Dinah Shore's recording was a million seller, as was the Dinning Sisters' with the Art Van Damme orchestra. Bob Hope's recording was a best seller. The song stayed ten weeks on the top of the charts and became 1948's top hit.

"Buttons and Bows" has a distinct western flavor in lyrics and melody. The song makes several allusions to Hope's film character, an eastern dude dentist: "I'll love ya longer, stronger where yer friends don't tote a gun. My bones denounce the buckboard bounce."

Variety chose "Buttons and Bows" for its "Fifty Year Hit Parade."

Paleface was not a movie musical, but it did feature the song that garnered the Oscar. The other nominees were "For Every Man There's a Woman" by Harold Arlen and Leo Robin from *Casbah;* "It's Magic" by Jule Styne and Sammy Cahn from *Romance on the High Seas;* "This Is the Moment" by Frederick Hollander and Leo Robin from *That Lady in Ermine;* and "The Woody Woodpecker Song" by George Tibbles and Ramez Idriss from *Wet Blanket Policy.*

Golden Earrings
COMPOSERS: **Jay Livingston and Ray Evans**
LYRICIST: **Victor Young**

This 1946 song was introduced by Marlene Dietrich in the 1947 movie *Golden Earrings.* Peggy Lee had the most popular recording of the song, which climbed to the top of the charts early in 1948.

It was included in the *Variety* "Fifty Year Hit Parade."

Hair of Gold, Eyes of Blue
COMPOSER-LYRICIST: **Sunny Skylar**

This folk song style piece was introduced by Jack Emerson, but it was Gordon MacRae who had a best-selling recording of the number. It was included in *Variety*'s "Fifty Year Hit Parade."

I'm Looking Over a Four Leaf Clover

See page 39 (1927). Art Mooney and his orchestra's million-selling recording caused the song to rank as the number seven hit in 1948's top ten.

It's a Most Unusual Day
COMPOSER: **Jimmy McHugh**
LYRICIST: **Harold Adamson**

Jane Powell introduced this number in the 1948 movie musical *A Date with Judy*. "It's a Most Unusual Day" is a happy song that could have served well as a Depression era song with its everything-is-great philosophy.

It's Magic
COMPOSER: **Jule Styne**
LYRICIST: **Sammy Cahn**

Doris Day's first film, *Romance on the High Seas*, produced this hit and made her an internationally known singer and actress. Her recording of "It's Magic" was a million seller.

What's magic? "Without a golden wand or mystic charms, fantastic things begin to happen when I am in your arms . . . the magic is my love for you."

Variety chose "It's Magic" for its "Fifty Year Hit Parade."

Little White Lies

See page 56 (1930). Dick Haymes with Four Hits and a Miss had a million-selling disc of this song in 1948.

Mañana
COMPOSER-LYRICISTS: **Peggy Lee and Dave Barbour**

Peggy Lee wrote "Mañana" in cooperation with guitarist Dave Barbour. Her recording produced a million seller and the number three hit in 1948's top ten. "Mañana" was Lee's first gold record.

Variety picked the song for its "Fifty Year Hit Parade."

My Darling, My Darling
COMPOSER-LYRICIST: **Frank Loesser**

Frank Loesser wrote the musical *Where's Charley?*, which premiered in 1948. One of the theater's most durable farces, *Charley's Aunt*, furnished the story. The action takes place at Oxford in 1892, when two undergraduates, Jack and Charley, wish to entertain their women friends, Amy and Kitty, but have to have a chaperone. Charley disguises himself as his aunt to fit the bill. Complications develop.

The show's hits were "My Darling, My Darling" and "Once in Love with Amy." "My Darling, My Darling" was Jack's salutation on a letter to his beloved Kitty. Doris Day and Buddy Clark and Jo Stafford and Gordon MacRae had successful recordings.

My Happiness
COMPOSER: **Borney Bergantine**
LYRICIST: **Betty Peterson**

This song was written in 1933, but it was first popular in 1948 as a result of million-selling discs by the Pied Pipers and by John and Sandra Steele. Ella Fitzgerald also had a successful recording. "My Happiness" enjoyed a comeback in 1959, when Connie Francis made it a million seller again.

Its 1933 birth explains lyrics such as "whether skies are gray or blue, anyplace on earth will do," anti-Depression era philosophy.

Nature Boy
COMPOSER-LYRICIST: **eden ahbez**

The year 1948 saw Nat "King" Cole become a major disc personality. "Nature Boy," his first million-selling record and the fifth-ranked hit in 1948's top ten, made him internationally famous.

"Nature Boy" was written by a Brooklyn yogi, eden ahbez, who believed that only divinities deserved capital letters. He left the song at the stage door of a California theater where Cole was playing. Cole recorded it, and it leaped into immediate popularity.

The "Nature Boy" of the song was a "strange, enchanted" lad who espoused this philosophy to the singer one day: "The greatest thing you'll ever learn is just to love and be loved in return."

Variety selected "Nature Boy" for its "Fifty Year Hit Parade."

Now Is the Hour
COMPOSER: **Clement Scott**
LYRICISTS: **Maewa Kaihan and Dorothy Stewart**

The sixth-ranked hit in 1948's top ten was written in New Zealand as a Maori tribal farewell song. In 1913 Clement Scott and Maewa Kaihan adapted the tribal song, and it became a favorite in New Zealand. Words for the English version were written by Dorothy Stewart. It was first recorded by Gracie Fields in Great Britain. Bing Crosby with the Ken Darby Choir recorded it in the United States and enjoyed a million seller.

Variety chose this song for its "Fifty Year Hit Parade."

On a Slow Boat to China
COMPOSER-LYRICIST: **Frank Loesser**

This Frank Loesser number had two million-seller recordings in 1948 and was the year's number nine hit in the top ten.

Benny Goodman's band, with Al Hendrickson doing the vocal, had one million-selling version, while Kay Kyser and his orchestra, with the vocal by Harry Babbitt and Gloria Wood, had the other.

The year 1948 was a great one for Frank Loesser, with this song capturing the top spot on *Your Hit Parade* for two weeks and his "My Darling, My Darling" (see page 135) in second place on the parade at the same time in early 1949.

The singer wants to get his love "on a slow boat to China," all to himself. He feels he must get the girl away from her other suitors and try to melt her "heart of stone."

Variety named the song to its "Fifty Year Hit Parade."

Once in Love with Amy
COMPOSER-LYRICIST: **Frank Loesser**

"Once in Love with Amy" is one of the big hits from the musical *Where's Charley?* (see "My Darling, My Darling," page 135). Ray Bolger, as Charley, sings the praises of his beloved Amy and eventually makes the song an audience participation number. A soft-shoe song, "Amy" was a show stopper that has continued to be identified with Bolger.

Red Roses for a Blue Lady
COMPOSER-LYRICISTS: **Sid Tepper and Roy Brodsky**

Vaughn Monroe and Guy Lombardo and his Royal Canadians first popularized "Red Roses for a Blue Lady." Bert Kaempfert and his orchestra revived it in 1965 and made it a million seller. Other recordings by Wayne Newton and Vic Dana were also well received.

Variety chose the song for its "Fifty Year Hit Parade" for 1949.

So in Love
COMPOSER-LYRICIST: **Cole Porter**

The biggest hit from Cole Porter's musical *Kiss Me Kate* (see "Another Op'nin', Another Show," page 134) was "So in Love," which climbed to number three on the charts by early 1949. The love ballad is sung first by Lilli Vanessi (played by Patricia Morison) and reprised toward the end of the musical by Fred Graham (played by Alfred Drake). Lilli and Fred have been divorced and are at each other's throats but are eventually reconciled.

Tennessee Waltz
COMPOSER-LYRICISTS: **Redd Stewart and Pee Wee King**

Redd Stewart and Pee Wee King wrote this hit in 1948, and country and western singer Cowboy Copas had a million seller with it in that year. The song was more popular in 1951 (see page 148).

A Tree in the Meadow
COMPOSER-LYRICIST: **Billy Reid**

Written by England's Billy Reid, this number was Margaret Whiting's second million seller. Her first had been a recording of "Moonlight in Vermont" with the Billy Butterfield orchestra in 1944. "A Tree in the Meadow" was the year's fourth-ranked hit in the top ten and spent ten weeks at the top of *Your Hit Parade* in the fall of 1948.

The song lyrics explain that the tree in the meadow is special because "you carved on that tree I love you till I die." However, the singer sees a silhouette of the loved one kissing someone else down lover's lane. Still, he wants her to know "I love you till I die."

Variety chose this song for its "Fifty Year Hit Parade."

Twelfth Street Rag
COMPOSER: **Euday L. Bowman**
LYRICIST: **Andy Razaf**

This ragtime classic was published as a piano rag in 1914. Lyrics were added to the music in 1916 by James S. Sumner. New lyrics were added by Spencer Williams in 1929 and by Andy Razaf in 1942. Pee Wee Hunt and his orchestra decided to do the number during one of their Capitol recording dates. When it was released, it surprisingly became one of the biggest hits Capitol had had to date. It sold a million by 1951 and was number two in 1948's top ten.

Variety named "Twelfth Street Rag" to its "Fifty Year Hit Parade," listing it in 1914.

The Woody Woodpecker Song

COMPOSER-LYRICISTS: **George Tibbles and Ramez Idriss**

The infectious *ha ha ha ha ha* phrase, for which the cartoon character Woody Woodpecker is famous, is the principal ingredient of this 1947 song. It was introduced in the 1948 cartoon *Wet Blanket Policy*, sold a million copies of Kay Kyser's (see "Buttons and Bows," page 134) recording, was nominated for the Academy Award for the year's best song from films, and was the year's tenth-ranked hit.

You Can't Be True, Dear

COMPOSER: **Hans Otten**
LYRICISTS: **Gerhard Ebeler and Hal Cotton**

A recording of this song by organist Ken Griffin and vocalist Jerry Wayne was a first. Griffin made the recording early in 1948, primarily as music to accompany ice skaters on public rinks. It became so popular with the skaters that publisher Dave Dreyer decided to dub in a vocal. He signed Jerry Wayne to do the vocal. The lyrics were written by Hal Cotton while Wayne was waiting to do the recording. The resulting disc was the first big success for a recording made by superimposing a voice on an already existing recording. It became one of the top sellers of 1948 (eventually selling 3 million) and was number eight in the year's top ten.

The song was originally written in 1935 in Germany, its original title being "Du Kannst Nicht Treu Sein," by Hans Otten and Gerhard Ebeler. Dick Haymes and Vera Lynn both had successful recordings of the song, too.

1 9 4 9

Again

COMPOSER: **Lionel Newman**
LYRICIST: **Dorcas Cochran**

Ida Lupino originally sang this song in the 1948 film *Road House*. Vic Damone recorded it and achieved his first million seller with it. It climbed to number one on the charts, stayed there for a couple of weeks in the late spring of 1949, and was among the year's top ten hits (number ten, tied with Blue Barron's recording of "Cruising down the River").

The lyrics say that this once-in-a-lifetime thrill "couldn't happen again," and when it "doesn't happen again/We'll have this moment forever/But never, never again."

"Again" is in *Variety*'s "Fifty Year Hit Parade."

Baby, It's Cold Outside

COMPOSER-LYRICIST: **Frank Loesser**

Frank Loesser wrote this clever song to perform at parties, never thinking it would become a hit. However, in 1948 he decided to use it in the film *Neptune's Daughter* (1949); it was sung by Esther Williams and Ricardo Montalban and reprised, comically, by Red Skelton and Betty Garrett. The song won the Academy Award in 1949.

The other nominees were "It's a Great Feeling" by Jule Styne and Sammy Cahn from *It's a Great Feeling;* "Lavender Blue" by Eliot Daniel and Larry Morey from *So Dear to My Heart;* "My Foolish Heart" by Victor Young and Ned Washington from *My Foolish Heart;* and "Through a Long and Sleepless Night" by Alfred Newman and Mack Gordon from *Come to the Stable.*

"Baby, It's Cold Outside" was a million-seller recording for Esther Williams and Ricardo Montalban and best-selling discs for Dinah Shore and Buddy Clark and for Johnny Mercer and Margaret Whiting.

In the duet the woman tells the man that she can't stay, but he says it's too cold to go out. For every reason she finds to leave, he finds a reason for her to stay.

Bali Ha'i

COMPOSER: **Richard Rodgers**
LYRICIST: **Oscar Hammerstein II**

The next colossal Rodgers and Hammerstein musical success, *South Pacific,* opened in 1949. Hammerstein and Joshua Logan adapted James A. Michener's Pulitzer prizewinning novel, *Tales of the South Pacific,* for the musical's plot. They combined "Fo'Dolla" (Four Dollar), a short story about U.S. Captain Joe Cable's romance with a Polynesian girl, with "Our Heroine," which dealt with the unlikely love between Emile de Becque, a worldly French planter and Nellie

Forbush, a naïve navy nurse from Little Rock, Arkansas. The common ingredient of both stories is the power of love to break down barriers. It was also built around World War II, which was still very much in the minds of Americans (it had ended in 1945).

Bloody Mary (played by Juanita Hall), a Polynesian con artist in a grass skirt, introduced "Bali Ha'i." Bali Ha'i is an island that is off limits to servicemen, but Bloody Mary lures Cable there to meet her daughter, Liat. "Bali Ha'i" creates a mood of mystery, of a world where dreams come true. Perry Como made a successful recording of the song.

Careless Hands
COMPOSER-LYRICISTS: **Bob Hilliard and Carl Sigman**

This song was made popular both by Sammy Kaye and his orchestra in a best-selling record and by Mel Tormé in a successful disc. The singer lets his "heart fall into careless hands," which breaks his "heart in two."

Variety chose the song for its "Fifty Year Hit Parade."

Cruising down the River
COMPOSER: **Nell Tollerton**
LYRICIST: **Eily Beadell**

This popular song was written by two middle-aged British women, Eily Beadell and Nell Tollerton, in 1945. It won a nationwide song contest in Great Britain.

Two recordings in 1949 sold a million copies, making the song the sixth- and tenth-ranked hits of 1949. A recording by Russ Morgan and his orchestra, with the Skylarks, was on the top of the charts for eight weeks in the spring of 1949; their disc was the number six hit of the year. The Blue Barron and his orchestra's version was number one for two weeks and the number ten hit of the year, tied with Gordon Jenkins and his orchestra's record of "Again."

This waltz seems out of place in the late forties. Its style is reminiscent of songs written forty to fifty years earlier. The carefree Sunday afternoon spent cruising down the river is a scene associated with the 1890s and early 1900s. In that sense the song could be considered a nostalgic hit. But we must remember that in 1949 adults, not youths, still made the hits. Adults might very likely feel sentimental about a more uncomplicated time. Only with the coming of rock did the making of hits become the province of the young.

The song was included in the *Variety* "Fifty Year Hit Parade."

Dear Hearts and Gentle People
COMPOSER: **Sammy Fain**
LYRICIST: **Bob Hilliard**

Bing Crosby, accompanied by Perry Botkin's String Band, had a million-selling disc with this Sammy Fain and Bob Hilliard number. Dinah Shore also had a best-selling recording.

The title comes from a phrase Stephen Foster scribbled on a piece of paper but never used before he died. Like "Cruising Down the River" (see above), it was a nostalgic hit. It tells of the love the singer has for "those dear hearts and gentle people/Who live in my home town."

Diamonds Are a Girl's Best Friend
COMPOSER: **Jule Styne**
LYRICIST: **Leo Robin**

Although Carol Channing introduced this song in the 1949 stage musical *Gentlemen Prefer Blondes,* it has probably become more associated with Marilyn Monroe, who sang it with Jane Russell in the 1953 film version.

The song advises women to get all they can get from a man because when all is said and done, diamonds, for one thing, will last much longer than romance. A 1974 revision of *Gentlemen Prefer Blondes* was a musical titled *Lorelei.*

Far Away Places
COMPOSER-LYRICISTS: **Joan Whitney and Alex Kramer**

"Far Away Places" was featured on popular recordings by Bing Crosby with the Ken Darby Choir and by Perry Como. It was number one on *Your Hit Parade* for three weeks in early 1949.

Of course, it is only speculation, but this song may have been a hit because of servicemen who yearned to return to places they saw during World War II, or because of the people at home who might have learned about many places they never knew existed from their loved ones who served there or from news reports from war zones.

The singer dreams of seeing "those far away places with the strange sounding names" that are "callin', callin' me."

Variety chose this song for its "Fifty Year Hit Parade."

Forever and Ever
COMPOSER: Franz Winkler
LYRICIST: Malia Rosa

This hit originated in Switzerland. English lyrics were written in 1948. Perry Como and Russ Morgan had recordings that popularized the song. In this waltz, the singer promises to be always true.

Variety picked the song for its "Fifty Year Hit Parade."

I Can Dream, Can't I?
COMPOSER: Sammy Fain
LYRICIST: Irving Kahal

Sammy Fain's second hit of 1949 (see "Dear Hearts and Gentle People," page 138) was composed in 1937 for the 1938 musical *Right This Way*. Patty Andrews, of the famous Andrews Sisters, recorded the song as a solo with Gordon Jenkins, his orchestra and chorus, and had a million seller by 1950. Not only did it sell a million, but it was 1949's number three hit. (For more on this song, see page 89).

I'm in Love with a Wonderful Guy
COMPOSER: Richard Rodgers
LYRICIST: Oscar Hammerstein II

Mary Martin introduced this *Variety* "Fifty Year Hit Parade" selection in the Rodgers and Hammerstein musical *South Pacific* (see "Bali Ha'i," page 137). Mary, who starred as Nellie Forbush, the navy nurse, is ecstatic as she announces to her fellow nurses that she is "in love with a wonderful guy."

I've Got My Love to Keep Me Warm
COMPOSER-LYRICIST: Irving Berlin

This is another revived song. Berlin originally wrote it for the 1937 movie musical *On the Avenue,* in which it was introduced by Dick Powell. Les Brown and his orchestra had a million-selling record of the song in 1949 (the disc was recorded in 1946 but not released until 1949).

A Little Bird Told Me
COMPOSER-LYRICIST: Harvey O. Brooks

The seventh-ranked hit in the top ten in 1949 was this 1947 song. It was introduced by Paula Watson, but Evelyn Knight with the Star Dusters made it well known with a million-selling disc (recorded in 1948), which stayed on the top of the charts for three weeks in early 1949.

And what did the little bird tell me? "That you love me" and that "we'd be happy."

Mule Train
COMPOSER-LYRICISTS: Johnny Lange, Hy Heath, and Fred Glickman

Frankie Laine hit the million sales figure with this rugged number that became the number nine hit of the year. The story of the mule train's cargo was brilliantly and dramatically portrayed. The pounding rhythm of the "clippety-clop" refrain is distinctive. The song provided the title for and was sung by Gene Autry in a 1950 film. Vaughn Monroe sang it in *Singing Guns,* also in 1950. "Mule Train" was nominated for the Academy Award in 1950 for its appearance in *Singing Guns* (see "Mona Lisa," page 143, for other nominees).

Powder Your Face with Sunshine
COMPOSER: Carmen Lombardo
LYRICIST: Stanley Rochinski

Stanley Rochinski brought Carmen Lombardo this lyric. Lombardo found it fascinating, so he set it to music. Guy Lombardo and his Royal Canadians introduced and helped popularize it. Evelyn Knight and the Star Dusters had a successful recording. The song was interpolated into the 1950 Gene Autry film *Cow Town.*

The song sounds like the anti-Depression songs of the early thirties. The cheerful lyrics promise that if we smile, others will smile, too. As a matter of fact, the song's subtitle is "Smile! Smile! Smile!"

Variety chose it for its "Fifty Year Hit Parade."

Riders in the Sky
COMPOSER-LYRICIST: Stan Jones

The biggest hit song of 1949 was "Riders in the Sky." Vaughn Monroe had a million seller. Burl Ives and Gene Autry also had hit records. It was featured in the 1949 Autry film *Riders in the Sky.* The song was on the top of the charts for eleven weeks, second only to "Goodnight, Irene," which stayed on top for thirteen weeks. (Four other songs tied with "Riders in the Sky" with eleven weeks at number one.)

"Riders in the Sky," "That Lucky Old Sun," and "Mule Train" gave 1949's top ten songs a rustic, outdoors bias.

"Riders in the Sky" is subtitled "A Cowboy Legend." It tells of a cowboy who witnesses "a mighty herd of red-eyed cows . . . A ploughin' thru the ragged skies . . . The ghost herd in the sky.''

Room Full of Roses
COMPOSER-LYRICIST: **Tim Spencer**

"Room Full of Roses" was popularized by Sammy Kaye and his orchestra with a vocal by Don Cornell; by Dick Haymes; by George Morgan; and by Eddy Howard and his orchestra. It was sung by Gene Autry in the 1950 film *Mule Train*.

Rudolph the Red-Nosed Reindeer
COMPOSER-LYRICIST: **Johnny Marks**

This Christmas favorite is Columbia Records' all-time best seller. The lyrics were based on Robert L. May's book. Gene Autry introduced and recorded the song. His disc had reached 1 million in sales by 1950 and went on to sell more than 7 million. Sales of more than 450 versions in the United States rose to more than 75 million by the end of the seventies, and the song continues to sell more every Christmas. Foreign sales have contributed another 36 million.

This song is runner-up to "White Christmas" as the top seasonal song. ASCAP selected it in 1963 as one of sixteen songs to appear in its "All-Time Hit Parade."

Slipping Around
COMPOSER-LYRICIST: **Floyd Tillman**

Margaret Whiting and Jimmy Wakely combined to record this Floyd Tillman tune, which sold almost 2 million copies. Their duet recording became 1949's number eight hit in the top ten.

Some Enchanted Evening
COMPOSER: **Richard Rodgers**
LYRICIST: **Oscar Hammerstein II**

"Some Enchanted Evening" was introduced by Ezio Pinza (as the French planter Emile de Becque) in the Rodgers and Hammerstein musical *South Pacific* (see "Bali Ha'i," page 137). Emile sings this passionate love song when he discovers that he has fallen in love with Nellie Forbush, the navy nurse. Pinza's recording and one by Perry Como made the song the second-ranked hit of 1949.

Variety selected "Some Enchanted Evening" as a "Golden 100 Tin Pan Alley Song."

That Lucky Old Sun
COMPOSER: **Beasley Smith**
LYRICIST: **Haven Gillespie**

Frankie Laine had two songs in 1949's top ten: "That Lucky Old Sun" was in fifth place; "Mule Train," in ninth. Laine's recording of "That Lucky Old Sun" was a million seller within a year of its release.

"That lucky old sun has nothin' to do but roll around heaven all day." The line is reminiscent of a Hoagy Carmichael "lazy lyric." It speaks of a man who is tired of working, of fussing with his woman and who longs for the day when the Lord will "send down that cloud with a silver linin',/Lift me to Paradise," so he can be like "that lucky old sun."

With My Eyes Wide Open I'm Dreaming
COMPOSER: **Harry Revel**
LYRICIST: **Mack Gordon**

This 1934 song was introduced in the movie musical *Shoot the Works*. Patti Page's first million-selling record was this revival. It also appeared in the 1953 Dean Martin and Jerry Lewis film *The Stooge*.

The song was selected for *Variety's* "Fifty Year Hit Parade," listed under "1934."

Younger Than Springtime
COMPOSER: **Richard Rodgers**
LYRICIST: **Oscar Hammerstein II**

"Younger Than Springtime" is a lovely, innocent love song that is sung by Lieutenant Cable (played by William Tabbert) to Liat (played by Betta St. John) on Bali Ha'i in the Rodgers and Hammerstein musical *South Pacific* (see "Bali Ha'i," page 137). Cable describes Liat in the song as "younger than springtime . . . softer than starlight . . . gayer than laughter . . . sweeter than music. . . ."

You're Breaking My Heart
COMPOSER-LYRICISTS: **Pat Genaro and Sunny Skylar, adapted from Ruggiero Leoncavallo**

This song was based on "Mattinata" ('Tis the Day) from Ruggiero Leoncavallo's opera *I Pagliacci*. Vic Damone's record made it the number four hit in 1949's top ten. It eventually sold more than 3 million copies.

The lyrics tell us that the singer's heart is breaking " 'cause you're leaving."

1 9 5 0

All My Love
COMPOSER: **Maurice Ravel, adapted by Paul Durand**
LYRICIST: **Mitchell Parish**

Once again a popular song is borrowed from the classics, this time "Boléro" by Impressionist composer Maurice Ravel. Patti Page had a 1950 million-selling recording of "All My Love," and *Variety* selected it for its "Fifty Year Hit Parade."

The very distinctive bolero rhythm of Ravel's original has probably been the key to its continuing popularity. The same melodic idea is repeated over and over, beginning very softly. With each repetition instruments are added, until the sound is almost deafening.

"Boléro" has found new popularity recently because in the highly successful movie *10*, the character played by Bo Derek chose it as lovemaking music.

Bewitched Bothered and Bewildered

See page 101 (1940). Pianist Bill Snyder had his only million-selling record with a 1950 recording of this *Pal Joey* number. His recording stayed on the best-seller charts for nineteen weeks and was number one on the "Easy Listening" list for five weeks.

Bibbidi-Bobbidi-Boo
COMPOSER-LYRICISTS: **Mack David, Al Hoffman, and Jerry Livingston**

Walt Disney's full-length animated *Cinderella* introduced this cute number. It was sung on the sound track by Verna Felton as the voice of Cinderella's fairy a75mother.

Perry Como's recording helped popularize the song, which was an Academy Award nominee in 1950 (see "Mona Lisa," page 143).

A Bushel and a Peck
COMPOSER-LYRICIST: **Frank Loesser**

This satirical *Variety* "Fifty Year Hit Parade" song was squeaked out by Vivian Blaine and the Hot Box girls during a floor show scene in Frank Loesser's *Guys and Dolls*.

Guys and Dolls garnered several outstanding honors, including the Tony Award for the best Broadway show of 1950. Based on Damon Runyan stories about Broadway night life, the show was an outstanding success. Marlon Brando, Frank Sinatra, Jean Simmons, and Vivian Blaine starred in the 1955 film version. Blaine re-created her role as Miss Adelaide, the Hot Box singer and dancer who has been engaged for fourteen years.

The two-part song is made up of several verses and a chorus, which are more characteristic of songs of the late seventies and eighties than of the fifties. A distinctive ingredient of the chorus is the "doo-dle oodle ooo."

Chattanoogie Shoe Shine Boy
COMPOSER-LYRICISTS: **Harry Stone and Jack Stapp**

One of the biggest country and western discs of 1950 became *Variety*'s ninth-ranked hit in the year's top ten. Red Foley's recording of "Chattanoogie Shoe Shine Boy" was this Country Music Hall of Famer's first million-selling record. The song was written by Harry Stone and Jack Stapp, employees at WSM radio in Nashville.

Even though the title is spelled "Chattanoogie," it is often pronounced "Chattanooga." *Variety* honored it by including it in its "Fifty Year Hit Parade."

The Cry of the Wild Goose
COMPOSER-LYRICIST: **Terry Gilkyson**

Frankie Laine recorded his fifth million seller when he sang "The Cry of the Wild Goose." It was also interpolated into the 1950 film *Saddle Tramp*. "The Cry of the Wild Goose" continued the style with which Laine had had such success in the late forties ("Mule Train" and "That Lucky Old Sun").

Enjoy Yourself (It's Later Than You Think)
COMPOSER: **Carl Sigman**
LYRICIST: **Herb Magidson**

Sigman and Magidson wrote this song in 1948, but it was not a hit until Guy Lombardo and his Royal Canadians' recording became a best seller in 1950. The lyrics encourage us to enjoy ourselves because it's later than we think.

Variety selected "Enjoy Yourself" as a "Fifty Year Hit Parade" song.

Frosty the Snowman
COMPOSER: **Jack Rollins**
  LYRICIST: **Steve Nelson**

This seasonal favorite was a million seller for cowboy star Gene Autry. Autry followed 1949's "Rudolph the Red-Nosed Reindeer" with "Frosty," which was number one during the Christmas season of 1950.

Network television has perpetuated the song with a cartoon version that shows yearly. The same writers also had great success with "Peter Cottontail" (also 1950).

Goodnight, Irene
COMPOSER-LYRICISTS: **Huddie Ledbetter and John Lomax**

The Weavers' recording of "Goodnight, Irene" with "Tzena, Tzena, Tzena" on the flip side sold more than two million copies. "Goodnight, Irene" is an adaptation by John Lomax of a folk song recorded by Huddie ("Leadbelly") Ledbetter in 1936. The Weavers recorded the disc with Gordon Jenkins and his orchestra. Other successful recordings were made by Frank Sinatra, Ernest Tubb, and Red Foley.

"Goodnight, Irene" had the longest stay at number one of any song from 1948 to 1975: thirteen weeks. That qualifies it to be the top hit of 1950, one of the biggest hits of the next quarter of a century, and a "Fifty Year Hit Parade" selection by *Variety*.

"Goodnight, Irene" has a two-part (verse and chorus) framework. Such a form is very common in songs of the late seventies and eighties, but was not so typical in the fifties.

Harbor Lights
COMPOSER: **Will Grosz**
  LYRICIST: **Jimmy Kennedy**

Although this song was written by English tunesmiths Will Grosz (under the pen name Hugh Williams) and Jimmy Kennedy in 1937, it had its greatest fame when it was revived in 1950. Sammy Kaye and his orchestra and Dinah Washington had successful recordings of the song. It spent two weeks on the top of the charts toward the end of the year, was the number six hit in 1950's top ten, and was selected by *Variety* for its "Fifty Year Hit Parade." The lyrics say that the "harbor lights . . . told me we were parting" because "you were on the ship and I was on the shore."

Hoop-Dee-Doo
COMPOSER: **Milton DeLugg**
  LYRICIST: **Frank Loesser**

This nonsense phrase was the title of a *Variety* "Fifty Year Hit Parade" selection. It was not a million seller but was a best seller for Perry Como.

I Can Dream, Can't I?
See page 89 (1937). The song was listed on *Variety's* "Fifty Year Hit Parade" for 1950 because of the Andrews Sisters' recording, which was released in 1949 and had sold a million copies by 1950.

If I Knew You Were Comin' I'd 'ave Baked a Cake
COMPOSER-LYRICISTS: **Al Hoffman, Bob Merrill, and Clem Watts**

An obscure Chicago publisher of hymns, Maurice Wells, bought this *Variety* "Fifty Year Hit Parade" song for $300 and persuaded some friends to sing it on the *Breakfast Club Radio Show*, which was broadcast early each morning. Before the day was over several publishers were seeking publishing rights to the song. Brooklyn-born Eileen Barton got to record the song, and it brought her her only gold disc.

Like a folk song, parts of the text repeat, and the melody has limited range and stepwise movement. A distinctive lyric in the song is "How ja do, how ja do, how ja do," meaning "How do you do?" The song has a contagious down-home friendliness.

It Isn't Fair
COMPOSER-LYRICISTS: **Richard Himber, Frank Warshauer, and Sylvester Sprigato**

This 1933 oldie was revived in 1950 by Don Cornell with Sammy Kaye's orchestra. It was chosen by *Variety* for its "Fifty Year Hit Parade" for 1950 and had sold a million records by 1952. Himber wrote the words and helped the others write the music. He had once been the bandleader for Sophie Tucker.

What isn't fair? "It isn't fair for you to want me . . . taunt me. . . ."

It's a Lovely Day Today
COMPOSER-LYRICIST: **Irving Berlin**

Irving Berlin's Broadway musical *Call Me Madam* introduced this duet, which was sung by the young

American attaché Ken Gibson (Russell Nype) and Princess Maria (Galina Talva) of Lichtenburg. It tells of the pleasures of companionship.

I Wanna Be Loved
COMPOSER: John Green
LYRICISTS: Billy Rose and Edward Heyman

This *Variety* "Fifty Year Hit Parade" selection for 1950 was introduced in 1932 in Billy Rose's Casino de Paree in New York. The Andrews Sisters popularized the song in a recording. It was revived in the early sixties by Jan and Dean, but why it was chosen for 1950 is a mystery.

"I Wanna Be Loved by You" was revived in 1950 in the movie biography of Bert Kalmar and Harry Ruby, *Three Little Words,* but that is not the song selected for the "Fifty Year Hit Parade."

Mysterious, but since it was named in 1950, it is included.

La Vie en Rose
COMPOSER: Louiguy
LYRICIST: Edith Piaf

This French song was written in 1946 by Louiguy and Edith Piaf. An English lyric was written by Frank Eyton in 1947, and another by Mack David in 1950.

Edith Piaf's recording has sold more than 3 million globally through the years. Although recorded earlier, it gained prominence in 1950. Tony Martin had the most successful recording of the song with Mack David's English lyrics.

Variety selected "La Vie en Rose" as one of the songs of 1950 for its "Fifty Year Hit Parade."

Mona Lisa
COMPOSER-LYRICISTS: Jay Livingston and Ray Evans

This song was introduced in the 1949 film *Captain Carey, U.S.A.* It was heard only in fragments and in Italian in the sound track, but it won the Oscar for the best song from a film in 1950.

Nat ("King") Cole agreed to record the song only after the writers almost begged. It stayed on the best-seller chart for twenty-seven weeks, eight weeks at number one and sold more than 3 million records. That qualified it to be the number 3 hit in 1950's top ten and a *Variety* "Fifty Year Hit Parade" selection.

Leonardo da Vinci's *Mona Lisa* was the inspiration for the song. The Mona Lisa of the song has a mystic smile—is it to tempt a lover or to hide a broken heart? The singer asks, "Are you warm, are you real, Mona Lisa, or just a cold and lonely, lovely work of art?" He was, of course, quizzing his love, not the painting.

The other nominees for the 1950 Academy Award for best song from a film were "Wilhelmina," by Josef Myrow and Mack Gordon, from *Wabash Avenue;* "Be My Love," by Nicholas Brodszky and Sammy Cahn, from *The Toast of New Orleans,* "Bibbidi-Bobbidi-Boo," by Mack David, Al Hoffman, and Jerry Livingston, from *Cinderella;* and "Mule Train," by Fred Glickman, Hy Heath, and Johnny Lange, from *Singing Guns.*

Music! Music! Music!
COMPOSER-LYRICISTS: Stephen Weiss and Bernie Baum

Singer Teresa Brewer had her first major hit with "Music! Music! Music!" This peppy tune requests us to "put another nickel in, in the nickelodeon" because "all I want is loving you and music, music, music." This disc became Brewer's first gold record, spent four weeks at the top of the charts, was the number five hit in the 1950's top ten, and is a *Variety* "Fifty Year Hit Parade" song.

My Foolish Heart
COMPOSER: Victor Young
LYRICIST: Ned Washington

This *Variety* "Fifty Year Hit Parade" selection was the title song of the 1949 nonmusical film *My Foolish Heart.* Sung by Susan Hayward on the sound track, it was an Academy Award nominee (see "Mona Lisa," above, for other nominees). Billy Eckstine had a million seller by 1951 with his recording. Gordon Jenkins and his orchestra also had a successful recording of the song. The tune spent nine weeks at number one in the spring and early summer of 1950.

The lyrics warn that it is difficult to tell apart "love and fascination . . . for they both give the very same sensation."

Nevertheless
COMPOSER: Harry Ruby
LYRICIST: Bert Kalmar

Quite a few songs that were hits in the late forties and early fifties were revivals. "Nevertheless" was written by Ruby and Kalmar in 1931. Bing Crosby and Rudy Vallee popularized the song in the thirties on their respective radio shows and with recordings. When Ruby and Kalmar's screen biography, *Three Little Words,* was released in 1950, "Nevertheless" found new life. It was performed in the film by Anita Ellis (her voice dubbed for Vera-Ellen) and Fred Astaire. The song climbed to the top spot on *Your Hit Parade* in December 1950 and was chosen by *Variety* for its "Fifty Year Hit Parade" for 1950.

The Old Master Painter
COMPOSER: **Beasley Smith**
LYRICIST: **Haven Gillespie**

This *Variety* "Fifty Year Hit Parade" song, written in 1949, was introduced by Snooky Lanson and popularized by Richard Hayes in a best-selling recording.

Peter Cottontail
COMPOSER: **Jack Rollins**
LYRICIST: **Steve Nelson**

This Easter cutie came from the same writers who penned "Frosty the Snowman" and from the same singer, Gene Autry, who recorded both "Frosty" and "Rudolph the Red-Nosed Reindeer." But this time Autry's record was not the most successful. It was a million seller, but country and western singer Merv Shiner's recording was a bigger success. This "hoppin' down the bunny trail" song has been presented annually in a cartoon version on television.

Steve Nelson and Jack Rollins were extraordinarily successful with "Frosty" and "Peter" with the sales of records, the television rights, book rights for stories about their characters, and novelty gifts deriving from the songs, these guys hit the big time quickly.

Play A Simple Melody
COMPOSER-LYRICIST: **Irving Berlin**

In another revival of an oldie, Bing and Gary Crosby, father and son, recorded "Play a Simple Melody," which was introduced by Sallie Fisher and Charles King in the 1914 Broadway revue *Watch Your Step*.

With Lew Quadling and Jack Elliott's "Sam's Song" (a *Variety* "Fifty Year Hit Parade" selection) on the flip side, the Crosby disc quickly sold a million copies. It was *Variety's* number four hit in 1950's top ten.

"Play a Simple Melody" is a delightful song. First, the father says, "Play a simple melody," like those that were popular when I was young. The son then says, No! Play a tune that is snappy (in 1914, Berlin was talking about ragtime, but in every age there has existed that generation gap, whether it was during the roaring twenties, the early rock years of the mid-fifties, or the eighties). Then the two melodies are combined and make beautiful contrapuntal harmonies,

probably musical propaganda to signify that the generations can "make beautiful music together."

Ethel Merman and Dan Dailey sang it also in the 1954 movie musical *There's No Business Like Show Business*.

Rag Mop
COMPOSER-LYRICISTS: **Johnnie Lee Wills and Deacon Anderson**

This bouncy, rhythmical song has only six notes. It throws in a few nonsense syllables for variety, and *voilà!* a million seller! The Ames Brothers' recording, backed with "Sentimental Me," was a big hit, number one for one week, and spent fourteen weeks on the best-selling records list.

Sam's Song
See "Play a Simple Melody," above.

The Thing
COMPOSER-LYRICIST: **Charles R. Grean**

The tune for this *Variety* "Fifty Year Hit Parade" hit was adapted by Charles Grean from an old Rabelaisian song, "The Tailor's Boy." The words never specify what "the thing" is; there is a period of silence followed by three booms on the drum. A film called *The Thing* had been released, and although not related, the disc may have capitalized upon the horror film's popularity.

The Third Man Theme
COMPOSER: **Anton Karas**

Anton Karas, a zither player from Vienna, was hired to furnish the sound track music for Orson Welles's *The Third Man*, which needed music appropriate to postwar Vienna. Karas composed the theme, which is variously called "The Third Man Theme" or "The Harry Lime Theme," for the main character in the film. Karas's recording from the sound track sold 4 million copies, and total disc sales for the song were estimated to have reached more than 40 million. Karas's disc was number 1 for eleven weeks. Guy Lombardo and the Royal Canadians' recording also reached the million plateau and was listed as the seventh-ranked hit for the year.

The two million sellers boosted the song to number two in 1950's top ten and qualified it for selection to *Variety's* "Fifty Year Hit Parade."

Tzena, Tzena, Tzena
COMPOSER: **Issachar Miron (Michrovsky)**
LYRICIST: **Mitchell Parish**

The Weavers with Gordon Jenkins and his orchestra (see "Goodnight, Irene," page 142) sparked a rebirth of interest in folk music that culminated in the folk song craze of the early sixties. Their recording of this Jewish song was almost as popular as the other side of the record, "Goodnight, Irene."

"Tzena, Tzena, Tzena" went through a metamorphosis before it got to this recording. Written in 1941, it was rewritten by Julius Grossman in 1947 and arranged by Spencer Ross to lyrics by Gordon Jenkins. This version was forced off the market by legal action. The next version had lyrics by Mitchell Parish and was recorded by the Weavers.

Variety chose it for its "Fifty Year Hit Parade."

1 9 5 1

The Aba Daba Honeymoon
COMPOSER-LYRICISTS: **Arthur Fields and Walter Donovan**

This 1914 oldie was revived for the 1950 movie musical *Two Weeks with Love*. Debbie Reynolds and Carleton Carpenter performed "The Aba Daba Honeymoon," the highlight of the film. Their recording from the movie sound track became a multimillion seller. This nonsense song about a monkey honeymoon sold more than 3 million records.

Ruth Roye introduced the song originally at the Palace Theater in New York in 1914. It was revived in the 1930 movie musical *The King of Jazz* before its inclusion in *Two Weeks with Love*.

Because of You
COMPOSER: **Dudley Wilkinson**
LYRICIST: **Arthur Hammerstein**

This 1940 song became popular in 1951, when it was featured in the film *I Was an American Spy*. It was also used as incidental music in the 1951 Claudette Colbert film *Let's Make It Legal*.

Tony Bennett had his first million seller with this song, which stayed on the top of *Your Hit Parade* for eleven weeks in 1951. It became the number one hit of the year and was selected to appear in *Variety's* "Fifty Year Hit Parade."

The lyrics say that "Because of you there's a song in my heart . . . my romance had its start . . . the sun will shine . . . my life is now worth while; and I can smile . . ."

Lyricist Arthur Hammerstein was the uncle of famed lyricist Oscar Hammerstein II.

Be My Love
COMPOSER: **Nicholas Brodszky**
LYRICIST: **Sammy Cahn**

The number six hit in 1951's top ten was "Be My Love" as recorded by Mario Lanza. Lanza and Kathryn Grayson introduced the *Variety* "Fifty Year Hit Parade" song in the 1950 movie musical *Toast of New Orleans*. In addition to an Academy Award nomination (see "Mona Lisa," page 143, for other nominees), the song helped Lanza achieve his first gold disc (recorded in 1950).

Most of the score for the film consisted of excerpts from operas, but the audiences seemed to be most impressed with this original song. Lanza's operatic tenor voice fitted the style of "Be My Love" nicely. The melody is dramatic and shows a voice's agility, range, and power.

Cold, Cold Heart
COMPOSER-LYRICIST: **Hank Williams**

In the early fifties a few country stars like Eddy Arnold began to bridge the gap between true country and western music and main-line popular music, and a few songs transcended their country music origin to become top popular songs. Such a song was "Cold, Cold Heart."

Hank Williams wrote the song and recorded it in 1951. His disc became his seventh million seller. The others were "Ramblin' Man," "Hey, Good Lookin'," "Moanin' the Blues," "Long Gone Lonesome Blues," "My Bucket's Got a Hole in It," and "Lovesick Blues."

Since his tragic death in a car accident in 1953, Williams has become a country-music legend. He was named to the Country Music Hall of Fame in 1961, and his screen biography, *Your Cheating Heart,* was filmed in 1964. His son, Hank, Jr., is a country music star.

Tony Bennett's cover version also sold a million. It stayed at the top of the charts for six weeks and helped qualify the tune as the number five hit in 1951's top ten. *Variety* selected it to appear on its "Fifty Year Hit Parade."

Come on-a My House
COMPOSER-LYRICISTS: **Ross Bagdasarian and William Saroyan**

This song launched Rosemary Clooney's career. "Come on-a My House" was an adaptation of an Armenian folk song that playwright William Saroyan and his cousin Ross Bagdasarian remembered from their childhoods. On an automobile trip through the western states in 1949 the two devised the song, which Saroyan used in his 1949 off-Broadway play *Son.* Kay Armen recorded it at that time. Mitch Miller, then recording director of popular music at Columbia, persuaded Rosemary Clooney to record the song. Released in 1951, it became her first gold record and the number eight hit in 1951's top ten. It was also selected for *Variety's* "Fifty Year Hit Parade."

In the recording an unusual effect suggested by Miller, was the use of a harpsichord to accompany Clooney.

Ross Bagdasarian was later responsible for the famous "Chipmunk" recordings, which began in 1958.

Down Yonder
COMPOSER-LYRICIST: **L. Wolfe Gilbert**

The composer L. Wolfe Gilbert introduced this song at the Orpheum Theater in New Orleans in 1921. Several important singers of the time used it in their acts, but when Gilbert published it, it never sold well. For a dozen years it was practically forgotten. Then, in 1934, Gid Tanner and his Skillet Lickers, a hillbilly quartet, revived it with a million-selling recording. Once again it disappeared for several years until country pianist Del Wood recorded it in 1951; her disc had sold a million copies by the mid-fifties. At about the same time, Champ Butler released another version, which also sold well. All this activity thirty years after the song had been written helped it achieve top ten status (number six) and remain on *Your Hit Parade* for eighteen consecutive weeks.

Variety chose "Down Yonder" to appear on its "Fifty Year Hit Parade" for 1951.

Hello, Young Lovers
COMPOSER: **Richard Rodgers**
LYRICIST: **Oscar Hammerstein II**

Rodgers and Hammerstein's giant Broadway success after *South Pacific* was 1951's *The King and I.* Set in Bangkok in the 1860s, the musical centers on an English governess, Anna, and the king of Siam. It is about mutual understanding between people of different cultures.

Anna (played by Gertrude Lawrence) introduces "Hello, Young Lovers" as she counsels the young lovers, Tuptin and Lun Tha, to be "brave and faithful and true."

The King and I, based on Margaret Landon's novel *Anna and the King of Siam,* ran for 1,246 performances. The film version in 1956 spawned a gold album.

Although there are many wonderful songs in the score of *The King and I,* only "Hello, Young Lovers" gained hit status. Other great songs include "I Whistle a Happy Tune," "March of the Siamese Children," "Getting to Know You," "We Kiss in a Shadow," "Something Wonderful," and "Shall We Dance?"

How Could You Believe Me When I Said I Loved You When You Know I've Been a Liar All My Life?
COMPOSER: **Burton Lane**
LYRICIST: **Alan Jay Lerner**

This song, with one of the longest titles, is sometimes known as just "The Liar Song." Burton Lane and Alan Jay Lerner concocted this novelty song in 1950 for the 1951 movie musical *Royal Wedding.* It was introduced by Fred Astaire and Jane Powell in the film, and their recording from the sound track sold a million copies over the next seventeen years.

How High the Moon
See page 102 (1940). Les Paul and Mary Ford's million-selling record helped this song become 1951's number four hit.

If
COMPOSER: **Tolchard Evans**
LYRICISTS: **Robert Hargreaves and Stanley J. Damerell**

Perry Como's ninth million-selling record was "If" by the English writing team of Hargreaves, Damerell, and

Evans. It was one of many revivals of a 1934 song. Como's 1951 recording spent ten weeks on the top of *Your Hit Parade*, became the year's number seven hit, and was selected by *Variety* for its "Fifty Year Hit Parade."

Another "If" was a hit by the group Bread in the seventies, but the two songs are not at all alike. This "If" is a waltz tempo song that says life would not be worth anything if it were not for loving and being loved.

I Get Ideas

COMPOSER: **Sanders**
  LYRICIST: **Dorcas Cochran**

An Argentine tango, entitled "Adios Muchachos," was transformed into the popular song "I Get Ideas." The singer gets ideas when he's dancing with his best girl. Tony Martin popularized the English version with a best-selling recording. *Variety* selected it for its "Fifty Year Hit Parade."

In the Cool, Cool, Cool of the Evening

COMPOSER: **Hoagy Carmichael**
  LYRICIST: **Johnny Mercer**

This Academy Award winner was introduced by Bing Crosby, this time in a duet with Jane Wyman in the movie musical *Here Comes the Groom*. Another title for the song might be "Tell 'Em I'll Be There," because the phrase is heard often in the lyrics. "In the cool, cool, cool of the evening,/Tell 'em I'll be there,/. . . When the party's getting a glow-on . . . just tell 'em I'll be there."

Other nominations for the 1951 Oscar for the best song from a film were "A Kiss to Build a Dream On," by Bert Kalmar, Harry Ruby, and Oscar Hammerstein II, from *The Strip*, "Never," by Lionel Newman and Eliot Daniel, from *Golden Girl*; "Too Late Now," by Burton Lane and Alan Jay Lerner, from *Royal Wedding*; and "Wonder Why," by Nicholas Brodszky and Sammy Cahn, from *Rich, Young and Pretty*.

It Is No Secret

COMPOSER-LYRICIST: **Stuart Hamblen**

Stuart Hamblen promoted this religious song to best-selling record status in 1951. Jo Stafford also had a best-selling disc of the song, which says, "It is no secret what God can do." It was selected for *Variety's* "Fifty Year Hit Parade."

Kisses Sweeter Than Wine

COMPOSER: **Huddie ("Leadbelly") Ledbetter, under the pseudonym Joel Newman**
  LYRICISTS: **The Weavers, under the pseudonym Paul Campbell**

Huddie Ledbetter and the Weavers (Pete Seeger, Lee Hayes, Fred Hellerman, and Ronnie Gilbert) adapted the Irish folk song "Drimmers' Cow" into the song "Kisses Sweeter Than Wine" in 1951. It was introduced by the Weavers in a 1951 Decca recording, but when it was revived by Jimmie Rodgers in 1957, it was a bigger hit. Rodgers's recording achieved gold status, as did two other of his singles in that year: "Honeycomb" and "Oh Oh I'm Falling in Love Again."

A Kiss to Build a Dream On

COMPOSER: **Harry Ruby**
  LYRICIST: **Bert Kalmar and Oscar Hammerstein II**

This 1935 composition was introduced in the 1951 movie musical *The Strip* and honored with an Academy Award nomination. Ruby and Kalmar wrote the first version of the song with the title "Moonlight on the Meadows," but when it was not found satisfactory, Oscar Hammerstein II was called in to revise the lyrics. The new version was the hit of the film and was reprised several times. A particularly interesting rendition was by Kay Brown and Louis Armstrong in the film. Armstrong's recording helped popularize the song.

The Loveliest Night of the Year

COMPOSER: **Juventino Rosas, adapted by Irving Aaronson**
  LYRICIST: **Paul Francis Webster**

Mario Lanza's second million seller (see "Be My Love," page 145) was this song from the movie musical *The Great Caruso*. Irving Aaronson adapted Juvenito Rosas's "Sobre las Olas," a waltz composed in the late nineteenth century, for this hit.

Enrico Caruso was one of the world's greatest operatic tenors, and Lanza fitted the title role both dramatically and vocally. Ann Blyth sang this song in the motion picture, but Lanza recorded it.

The lyrics say that "when you are in love, it's the loveliest night of the year."

Variety selected this song for its "Fifty Year Hit Parade."

Mockin' Bird Hill
COMPOSER-LYRICIST: **Vaughn Horton**

This Les Paul and Mary Ford disc was the first multitrack recording. Guitarist Les Paul and his then wife, Mary Ford, became famous for their new technique. The duo had three million sellers in 1951: "Mockin' Bird Hill," "How High the Moon," and "The World Is Waiting for the Sunrise." "Mockin' Bird Hill" was also a million seller for Patti Page in 1951. Both recordings propelled the song to the number four hit on the year's top ten and selection to *Variety's* "Fifty Year Hit Parade."

This waltz-tempo tune is a verse and chorus type of song that has a simple, easy chord structure (only G, C, and D7). It has a folk song character.

My Heart Cries for You
COMPOSER: **Percy Faith**
LYRICIST: **Carl Sigman**

In 1950 Carl Sigman and Percy Faith adapted the melody of "Chanson de Marie Antoinette" for this hit. The original was supposedly written by France's eighteenth-century queen Marie Antoinette. Guy Mitchell's 1950 gold recording helped the song become the number nine hit in 1951's top ten and secured its selection on *Variety's* "Fifty Year Hit Parade."

On Top of Old Smokey
COMPOSER-LYRICIST: **Unknown**

Folk singer Pete Seeger adapted this Appalachian folk song into one of 1951's big hits and a *Variety* "Fifty Year Hit Parade" selection. A million seller was recorded by the Weavers and Terry Gilkyson with chorus and orchestra conducted by Vic Schoen. The disc climbed as high as number two on the charts and spent more than four months on the best seller list. Gene Autry sang it in the 1951 film *Valley of Fire*.

Shrimp Boats
COMPOSER-LYRICISTS: **Paul Mason Williams and Paul Weston**

"Shrimp boats is a-comin', there's dancin' tonight," sang Jo Stafford in her million-selling disc of this charming bayou song. The song was most popular toward the end of 1951 and the beginning of 1952. *Variety* chose it for its 1952 list in its "Fifty Year Hit Parade." Stafford's disc was a million seller by 1952. Its high spot on the charts came at number two in

January and February 1952, and it stayed for seventeen weeks among the best sellers.

Sin
COMPOSER: **George Hoven**
LYRICIST: **Chester R. Shull**

Two gold records of this hit propelled it to top ten status for 1951 and selection on *Variety's* "Fifty Year Hit Parade." One million seller was by singer Eddy Howard, and the other was by the Four Aces.

Slow Poke
COMPOSER-LYRICISTS: **Pee Wee King, Redd Stewart, and Chilton Price**

Pee Wee King and his Golden West Cowboys had their first gold record in 1951 with "Slow Poke." Its lyrics say: "I wait and worry but you never seem to hurry . . . so guess I'll have to learn to be a slow-poke, too." King collaborated with Redd Stewart to revise and polish this song, which had been sent to him by Louisville, Kentucky's Chilton Price.

Sound Off
COMPOSER-LYRICIST: **Willie Lee Duckworth**

This song was originally used for close-order drill training by the U.S. armed forces. It was first published in *The Cadence System of Teaching Close Order Drill* by Colonel Bernard Lentz. In 1951 a best-selling recording by Vaughan Monroe propelled it onto the hit list. *Variety* chose it for its "Fifty Year Hit Parade" as a result.

Sparrow in the Tree Top
COMPOSER-LYRICIST: **Bob Merrill**

Even though a group known as the Pinetoppers first recorded this Bob Merrill song, it was not until Guy Mitchell teamed with Mitch Miller that it became a top ten hit and was selected for *Variety's* "Fifty Year Hit Parade." The Merrill, Mitchell, and Miller team was heard often on the airwaves during the spring of 1951 with "Sparrow in the Tree Top" and "My Truly, Truly Fair."

Tennessee Waltz
See page 136 (1948). This smash hit sold more than 6 million records in twenty years. Patti Page's disc, released in 1950, was the number two hit in 1951's top ten. Her recording was historic because it was one of the first multivoice recordings in which her voice was

148

THE SING ERA

coupled polyphonically with a tape of her own voice recorded previously.

In 1965 the state of Tennessee chose this Pee Wee King and Redd Stewart *Variety* "Fifty Year Hit Parade" waltz as its official song.

They Call the Wind Maria
COMPOSER: **Frederick Lowe**
LYRICIST: **Alan Jay Lerner**

Rufus Smith introduced this powerful western number in Lerner and Loewe's musical *Paint Your Wagon*. The lonesome prospector remembers the wife he left back east and asks the wind to "blow my love to me." The wind's name is pronounced "Mah-ri-ah," not "Mah-ree-ah." Harve Presnell and a male chorus sang the song in the 1969 film version.

Too Young
COMPOSER: **Sid Lippman**
LYRICIST: **Sylvia Dee**

Nat "King" Cole's gold record of this hit moved it to the number three position in 1951's top ten and to selection in *Variety's* "Fifty Year Hit Parade." Johnny Desmond introduced the song, but it was Cole's performance that caused it to climb to the top of the charts and stay there for a dozen weeks.

Several songs about the young were in vogue, and teenagers, even preteenagers, began to have more influence on the making of hits. It was probably this song that convinced record producers that the youth had the buying power to make songs hits.

The lyrics sing that adults try to tell the youth they are "too young to really be in love," but of course, that is not the opinion of the young lovers.

1 9 5 2

Auf Wiederseh'n, Sweetheart
COMPOSER: **Eberhard Storch**
LYRICISTS: **John Sexton and John Turner**

Total sales of this song, published in Germany in 1949, went over 2 million. Storch wrote the melody, to which English lyrics were added in 1952. Vera Lynn, a British singer, sold a million records or more with this tune, propelling it to the number four position on 1952's top ten. *Variety* selected it for its "Fifty Year Hit Parade."

Other "Auf Wiederseh'n" songs include Sigmund Romberg's "Auf Wiedersehen" in 1915 and "Auf Wiedersehen, My Dear" in 1932.

Be Anything (But Be Mine)
COMPOSER-LYRICIST: **Irving Gordon**

Eddy Howard popularized this *Variety* "Fifty Year Hit Parade" selection. It entered the top ten at number seven in May and peaked at number two in June. The lyrics tell the loved one he can be a beggar, a thief, a wiseman, a fool, an angel, or the devil. He can be whatever he wants to be as long as he continues to love the singer.

Because You're Mine
COMPOSER: **Nicholas Brodszky**
LYRICIST: **Sammy Cahn**

This Academy Award nominee (see "High Noon," page 150) became a gold record for Mario Lanza. Lanza introduced it in the film of the same title, in which he starred. Nicholas Brodszky and Sammy Cahn, who had written "Be My Love" for Lanza's *Toast of New Orleans* in 1951, also wrote this song. Once again Brodszky was able to write a melody that was operatic enough for Lanza's voice yet not so operatic that it would not have popular appeal.

Blue Tango
COMPOSER: **Leroy Anderson**
LYRICIST: **Mitchell Parish**

Leroy Anderson wrote semiclassical music that often featured unusual sound effects. Good examples are "The Syncopated Clock," with its jazzy tick-tocks; "Sandpaper Ballet," with the sound of sandpaper scraped together as if it were a dancer's feet; and "The Typewriter," with its typing sounds. His biggest popular hit does not rely on an unusual sound effect, however.

"Blue Tango" was Anderson's biggest hit (he was its composer, and his orchestra recorded it). It was 1952's second-ranked hit, with seven weeks at the top of the charts, thirty-eight weeks on the best-seller charts, and a 2 million seller in various recordings. *Variety* picked it for its "Fifty Year Hit Parade."

Botch-a-Me
COMPOSER: **R. Morbelli and L. Astore**
LYRICIST: **Eddie Y. Stanley**

This part-English, part-Italian version of a 1941 Italian song became a gold record for Rosemary Clooney. The original Italian song, "Ba-Ba Baciami Piccina," was written by Morbelli and Astore for the Italian film *Una Famiglia Impossibile*. Eddie Y. Stanley adapted the song and added English lyrics in 1952, changing the "baciami" to "botch-a-me." The lyrics become almost nonsensical: "Botch-a-me, bambino, ba-ba, bo-bo-booca piccolino . . . Beo, byo, beo boo."

Cry
COMPOSER-LYRICIST: **Churchill Kohlman**

Johnnie Ray cried himself to fame and fortune in 1952 with two big hits: "Cry," backed by "The Little White Cloud That Cried" (page 152). This disc was the year's biggest seller. "Cry" was a much bigger hit than "Little White Cloud," but both were million sellers. "Cry" was a *Variety* "Fifty Year Hit Parade" song.

Churchill Kohlman, a Pittsburgh dry cleaning plant watchman, entered this song in a 1951 amateur songwriting contest at the Copa Night Club in Pittsburgh. It was eliminated in the first round, while another Kohlman song made it to the finals. "Cry" never made an impression until Johnnie Ray recorded it.

Delicado
COMPOSER: **Waldyr Azevedo**
LYRICIST: **Jack Lawrence**

This Brazilian song, a *Variety* "Fifty Year Hit Parade" selection, was popularized by Percy Faith and his orchestra in a best-selling recording. Many songs are remembered when we hear them, but we may not always remember them by their title or by who performed them. Such is the case of "Delicado."

Glow-Worm
COMPOSER: **Paul Lincke**
LYRICIST: **Johnny Mercer**

"Glow-Worm," originally published in Germany in 1902, became a big seller at that time in Europe and the United States, selling more than 4 million sheet music copies. Lilla Cayley Robinson wrote English lyrics in 1907. Spike Jones and the City Slickers had a gold record comedy version of the song in 1946. Publisher Edward Marks signed Johnny Mercer to write new lyrics, which the Mills Brothers recorded and ultimately made into another million seller and 1952's number nine hit in the top ten.

One might not consider a song about a bug whose tail lights up to be the best popular song material, but the singer is requesting the "glow-worm" to "light the path . . . and lead us on to love."

"Glow-Worm" was named to *Variety's* "Fifty Year Hit Parade" for 1907.

Half as Much
COMPOSER-LYRICIST: **Curley Williams**

Rosemary Clooney had three gold records in 1952: the beautiful 1946 Walter Gross and Jack Laurence waltz "Tenderly" (see page 128), "Botch-a-me" (see above), and this Curley Williams song. Hank Williams also had a best-selling disc of this *Variety* "Fifty Year Hit Parade" song.

The chord structure is definitely simpler than that of music in the forties. The tune uses the tonic chord (D) for the first six and a half measures, then the dominant seventh (A7) for two measures before returning to tonic for the cadence. Only two other chords are used in the song. Music was gravitating toward amateurism, a trend even more apparent in the latter part of the decade and over the next several years.

Here in My Heart
COMPOSER-LYRICISTS: **Pat Genaro, Lou Levinson, and Bill Borrelli**

Al Martino's first big hit (and his first gold record) was "Here in My Heart." It ranked number eight in 1952's top ten. Martino's tenor voice suited the musical and lyrical style of "Here in My Heart."

High Noon
COMPOSER: **Dimitri Tiomkin**
LYRICIST: **Ned Washington**

The classic western *High Noon* introduced this hit as its theme. It won the Oscar for the best song from films in 1952 and was chosen for *Variety's* "Fifty Year Hit Parade."

It was sung on the sound track by cowboy movie star and singer Tex Ritter (father of John Ritter, who starred on TV's *Three's Company*). At previews neither the film nor its music found favor. Tiomkin asked for and received publication rights to the song, and since Ritter refused to record the theme song, Tiomkin talked Frankie Laine into it. The recording was released four months before the film and was such a hit that interest was heightened in the film. Once the Laine disc had become successful (and eventually a million seller), Tex Ritter reconsidered and recorded the theme. The film turned out to be profitable and achieved classic status among westerns perhaps because of its theme song, which went: "Do not forsake me, oh, my darling."

Other Oscar nominees for 1952 were "Because You're Mine," by Nicholas Brodszky and Sammy Cahn, from *Because You're Mine;* "Zing a Little Zong," by Harry Warren and Leo Robin, from *Just for You;* "Am I in Love," by Jack Brooks, from *Son of Paleface;* and "Thumbelina," by Frank Loesser, from *Hans Christian Andersen.*

I'm Yours
COMPOSER-LYRICIST: **Robert Mellin**

Singer Don Cornell had a hit with this song, which became his second million seller (his first was "It Isn't Fair" in 1950). Eddie Fisher also had a best-selling disc with the number. The song was number one on *Your Hit Parade* for three weeks in the summer of 1952. *Variety* selected it for its "Fifty Year Hit Parade."

The chord structure of this hit is complicated, more similar to the hits of the past than to the majority of those in the future. Chords like B flat diminished, F7, C diminished, and B flat augmented in the key of E flat make for variety, interest, and a lush harmonic scheme.

I Saw Mommy Kissing Santa Claus
COMPOSER-LYRICIST: **Tommie Connor**

This Jimmy Boyd disc broke records for Columbia, selling 248,000 in one day, 700,000 in ten days in early December, and more than 1 million before Christmas. Total sales exceeded 2.5 million. *Variety* honored this cute seasonal novelty song by choosing it for its "Fifty Year Hit Parade."

British songwriter Tommie Connor wrote the song, which had sold more than 11 million discs in all versions by the mid-sixties.

It's in the Book
COMPOSER-LYRICISTS: **Johnny Standley and Art Thorsen**

This is a comedy disc, not a song in the strict sense, but it was 1952's tenth-ranked hit according to *Vari-*

ety. Comedian Johnny Standley's parody of a fundamentalist peacher sermonizing on "Little Bo Peep" was the top disc for two weeks and produced a gold record. Standley wrote the routine in collaboration with Art Thorsen and recorded it with Horace Heidt and his Musical Knights.

I Went to Your Wedding
COMPOSER-LYRICIST: **Jessie Mae Robinson**

The number six hit in 1952's top ten was Patti Page's million seller "I Went to Your Wedding." The Jessie Mae Robinson song became Page's eighth gold record and was number one on the charts for six weeks in 1952.

This hit is a bore. Its slow tempo and "oom-pah-pah" guitar accompaniment sound simplistic and amateurish.

Jambalaya
COMPOSER-LYRICIST: **Hank Williams**

The Louisiana Cajun dish jambalaya furnished the title for this Hank Williams song about the bayou culture and language of the Creoles: "Jambalaya and a crawfish pie and fillet gumbo . . . tonight I'm gonna see my ma cher amio." The song was a million seller for composer Hank Williams and for Jo Stafford. Stafford's "Shrimp Boats" (see page 148) had a similar locale.

"Jambalaya" was selected for *Variety's* "Fifty Year Hit Parade."

Kiss of Fire
COMPOSER: **A. G. Villoldo, adapted by Lester Allen and Robert Hill**
LYRICISTS: **Lester Allen and Robert Hill**

An Argentine tango, "El Choclo," written by A. G. Villoldo in 1913, was adapted by Lester Allen and Robert Hill into the hit "Kiss of Fire." Georgia Gibbs's recording was a million seller and spent seven weeks on the top of *Your Hit Parade* in the late spring and early summer of 1952. Her sultry rendition of the lyrics—"I touch your lips, and all at once the sparks go flying . . . I must have your kiss although it . . . consumes me"—burned up the airwaves and jukeboxes, making it one of 1952's big hits.

Lady of Spain
COMPOSER: **Tolchard Evans**
LYRICIST: **Erell Reaves**

British writers Evans and Reaves wrote this song in 1931, but it was put back into circulation in 1952, when

Eddie Fisher's recording sold a million copies. "Lady of Spain" was selected for *Variety's* "Fifty Year Hit Parade" representing 1952.

Most of the song is simply a repetition of a musical phrase at different pitches. The key ingredient in "Lady of Spain" is its catchy, spirited Spanish rhythm.

The Little White Cloud That Cried
COMPOSER-LYRICIST: **Johnnie Ray**

Johnnie Ray wrote and popularized this *Variety* "Fifty Year Hit Parade" song. It was the flip side of "Cry," which made the disc the number one record of 1952 (it was recorded in 1951). "The Little White Cloud That Cried" was not nearly as popular as "Cry," but both songs sold more than a million copies. Ray's voice broke with emotion as he crooned (that he would remember forever "the little white cloud, that sat right down and cried." The cloud cried because it was lonesome and it felt that "no one cared" what happened to it. Then the cloud offered this Depression era-sounding philosophy that we should "have faith in all kinds of weather,/For the sun will always shine . . . the dark clouds pass with time."

Please, Mr. Sun
COMPOSER: **Ray Getzov**
LYRICIST: **Sid Frank**

This *Variety* "Fifty Year Hit Parade" selection was composed in 1951 and made popular in recordings by Tommy Edwards and by Johnnie Ray in 1952. It rose to number two on the charts in the early spring of 1952 and stayed on the best-seller chart for fourteen weeks.

Shrimp Boats
See page 148 (1951).

Wheel of Fortune
COMPOSER: **Bennie Benjamin**
LYRICIST: **George Weiss**

The third-ranked hit on the top ten of 1952 was Kay Starr's recording of "Wheel of Fortune." The song spent six weeks at the top spot on *Your Hit Parade* in the spring of 1952. It was chosen by *Variety* for its "Fifty Year Hit Parade."

The "wheel of fortune" suggests that love is a game of chance; if the wheel lands on your number, love will come your way.

Wish You Were Here
COMPOSER-LYRICIST: **Harold Rome**

The title song of the Broadway musical *Wish You Were Here* was introduced by Jack Cassidy (father of teenage heart throb David Cassidy, a singer and TV star of *The Partridge Family).* The hero longs for his absent heroine in this *Variety* "Fifty Year Hit Parade" selection.

Eddie Fisher's recording sold a million copies and his popularization of the song may have helped the Broadway show which still had lackluster success. On Broadway, 1952 was a poor season.

Why Don't You Believe Me
COMPOSER-LYRICISTS: **Lew Douglas, King Laney, and Roy Rodde**

Joni James had her first million seller with this hit. Her recording reached the number seven position in 1952's top ten, and the song spent five weeks at number one on *Your Hit Parade* at the end of 1952 and the beginning of 1953. *Variety* named it to its "Fifty Year Hit Parade" for 1952. James actually paid for the recording session herself, but the disc was purchased and released by MGM.

You Belong to Me
COMPOSER-LYRICISTS: **Pee Wee King, Redd Stewart, and Chilton Price**

Patti Page's "I Went to Your Wedding" (see page 151) was backed by "You Belong to Me." Jo Stafford's gold disc of "You Belong to Me" was 1952's number five hit in the top ten. Stafford's version spent nine weeks at number one on *Your Hit Parade* in the fall of 1952.

The writers of "Slow Poke" and "Tennessee Waltz" (see page 148), Pee Wee King and Redd Stewart (for a second time in collaboration with Chilton Price), wrote this hit.

The lyrics say that a loved one may travel all around the world and see many of the most famous sights, but "just remember 'til you're home again, you belong to me." *Variety* selected "You Belong to Me" for its "Fifty Year Hit Parade."

Your Cheatin' Heart
COMPOSER-LYRICIST: **Hank Williams**

Hank Williams had four different million-selling recordings in 1952: "Jambalaya" (see page 151), "Honky Tonk Blues," "I'll Never Get Out of This World Alive" (which may have been prophetic since he died in 1953), and "Your Cheatin' Heart," backed with "Kaw-Liga." "Your Cheatin' Heart" was also a million seller for Joni James in 1953.

The song has a typical country and western subject, a broken romance, but it transcended the boundaries of country and western to become a major hit.

1 9 5 3

And This Is My Beloved
COMPOSER-LYRICISTS: **Robert Wright and George "Chet" Forrest**

Wright and Forrest's chief claim to fame is ransacking the classics for musical stage scores. Their greatest success came in 1953 with *Kismet*, which used the music of Aleksandr Borodin, the Russian Romantic composer.

Kismet, a musical Arabian night, tells a romantic tale of a day in the life of Hajj, a handsome, poetic beggar in ancient Baghdad. Hajj determines that begging would bring in more money than his rhyming, so he tries it, only to be kidnapped by the bandit Jawan. Jawan intends to kill the beggar, because he thinks Hajj is the beggar who put a curse on him years earlier. Jawan blames the curse for the disappearance of his son. Hajj promises to find the son before the day ends in order to escape execution.

Jawan gives him a bag of gold for expenses and Hajj returns to the marketplace and gives his daughter, Marsinah, some of the gold to spend on finery. Hajj is arrested by the vizier's guards because the gold from Jawan had been stolen. Hajj is condemned to death, but once again escapes, this time saved by the vizier's wife, Lalume, who covets Hajj for herself. She convinces the vizier that Hajj cannot be killed because he is a prophet. By the end of the day, the caliph and Marsinah fall in love with each other and are married, and Hajj tricks the vizier into drowning and runs off into the desert with his wife.

"And This Is My Beloved" was based on the third movement of Borodin's String Quartet No. 2. The song was a quartet, with two conversations: Marsinah's father asks her about her lover the caliph and she sings her passionate reply, while the caliph tells the vizier of police about Marsinah. (Also see "Baubles, Bangles and Beads," below, and "Stranger in Paradise," page 156.)

April in Portugal
COMPOSER: **Paul Ferrão**
LYRICIST: **Jimmy Kennedy**

This *Variety* "Fifty Year Hit Parade" instrumental number, popularized by Les Baxter and his orchestra, was among the top ten hits of 1953. It originated as a 1947 Portuguese song by Paul Ferrão titled "Coimbra." Georgia Carr introduced it in America as "The Whispering Serenade." It became "April in Portugal" when the Chappel Publishing Company hired Jimmy Kennedy to write a new lyric. Baxter's version, however, did not use the lyrics.

Baubles, Bangles and Beads
COMPOSER-LYRICISTS: **Robert Wright and George "Chet" Forrest**

"Baubles, Bangles and Beads" was based on a theme from Borodin's String Quartet No. 2, like "And This Is My Beloved" (see above). The song is introduced in *Kismet* by Marsinah in a scene at the Baghdad bazaar in which she sings about rings and other jewelry. Peggy Lee and the Kirby Stone Four had successful recordings.

Changing Partners
COMPOSER: **Larry Coleman**
LYRICIST: **Joe Darion**

This disc became Patti Page's tenth million seller. Joe Darion later became famous as a lyricist for the Broadway stage, notably for *Man of La Mancha* in 1964–65, and for the Academy Award-winning song "Never on Sunday" in 1960.

This *Variety* "Fifty Year Hit Parade" waltz tells the sad tale of a lover who danced away "when they called out 'change partners.' " The singer is certain the lovers will continue "changing partners" until they have their loved one again and then they'll "never change partners again!"

Crying in the Chapel
COMPOSER-LYRICIST: **Artie Glenn**

This *Variety* "Fifty Year Hit Parade" tune has been a million seller three times, twice in 1953 and again in 1965. It was first introduced by composer Artie Glenn's son Darrell, who had a hit with it. Country and western vocalist Rex Allen garnered a gold record with his Decca version, and a rhythm and blues group, the Orioles, featuring Sonny Til, had a million seller with its Jubilee disc. June Valli also had a successful version on RCA Victor, but it was Elvis Presley's 1965 recording that became a million seller for RCA Victor.

In the song, a person searches for peace, and once it has been found, he thanks the Lord with tears of joy.

Doggie in the Window
COMPOSER-LYRICIST: **Bob Merrill**

Bob Merrill wrote this novelty hit in 1952; it became a million seller for Patti Page in 1953. It sold more than 3 million records in the next fourteen years. Page's disc garnered the number three spot in 1953's top ten and was honored by *Variety* by inclusion on the "Fifty Year Hit Parade." "How much is that doggie in the window?" sang Page, and the nation showed its empathy by buying the record.

Don't Let the Stars Get in Your Eyes
COMPOSER-LYRICISTS: **Slim Willet, Cactus Pryor, and Barbara Trammel**

The number four hit in 1953's top ten was Perry Como's recording of this 1952 song, which was subsequently selected for *Variety*'s "Fifty Year Hit Parade." Como's disc, recorded in 1952, was solid gold by 1953, when it spent five weeks at the top of the charts between January and March. Como's recording is a cover version since the song is country and western in flavor and origin.

First the chorus is sung; then two verses are interspersed between choruses. Two chords, the tonic and dominant seventh, constitute the sparse harmonic scheme.

Ebb Tide
COMPOSER: **Robert Maxwell**
LYRICIST: **Carl Sigman**

The beautiful melody of "Ebb Tide" was played by the Frank Chacksfield orchestra featuring a solo oboe,

against a background of waves hitting the shore. Chacksfield's recording was released in Britain on Decca and in the United States on the London label. Roy Hamilton had a successful disc with the song in 1954. Singer and organist Earl Grant had a million seller with "Ebb Tide" in 1961. Then Lawrence Welk and his orchestra had a successful recording in 1964, followed by the Righteous Brothers in 1965.

Sigman's lyrics draw a clever analogy between the sea and love: "Like the tide at its ebb, I'm at peace in the web of your arms."

Variety selected "Ebb Tide" for its "Fifty Year Hit Parade" representing 1953.

Hi-Lili, Hi-Lo
COMPOSER: **Bronislaw Kaper**
LYRICIST: **Helen Deutsch**

This lilting waltz was introduced in the film *Lili* by Leslie Caron and Mel Ferrer. The disc was taken from the sound track and sold a million copies in the next fifteen years. Bronislaw Kaper won an Oscar for his musical score for *Lili*.

I Believe
COMPOSER-LYRICISTS: **Ervin Drake, Irvin Graham, Jimmy Shirl, and Al Stillman**

This 1952 song has been a million seller three times. Frankie Laine's 1953 gold record helped push the song to top ten status (number nine) and eventually sold 3 million copies. Mahalia Jackson's 1958 recording of "I Believe," on the flip side of "He's Got the Whole World in His Hands," gained gold status. The vocal trio the Bachelors had another million seller with the song in 1964.

According to a survey compiled by the makers of Lucky Strike cigarettes, sponsors of *Your Hit Parade,* "I Believe" was 1953's most successful song. It was chosen by *Variety* for its "Fifty Year Hit Parade."

The lyrics allude to a belief in God but never actually say, "I believe in God." Therefore, many ministers object to its inclusion in worship. The nearest the song comes to affirming religious belief is "I believe . . . the smallest pray'r will still be heard."

I Love Paris
COMPOSER-LYRICIST: **Cole Porter**

Cole Porter had a lifelong love for Paris, and when he wrote a song that expressed that feeling for the 1953 Broadway show *Can-Can,* it achieved hit status. La

Mome Pistache (played by Lilo) introduced the song, which is in a minor key. In the 1960 movie version Frank Sinatra and Maurice Chevalier sang it. The movie sound track album won the Grammy award for the best sound track album in 1960. Les Baxter and his orchestra popularized it in 1953, while Michel Legrand had a successful recording in 1960.

I'm Walking Behind You
COMPOSER-LYRICIST: **Billy Reid**

British songwriter Billy Reid wrote this song, which Eddie Fisher popularized. It reached the number eight position in 1953's top ten and was number one for three weeks in the fall of 1953. *Variety* selected the song for its "Fifty Year Hit Parade" representing 1954.

The lyrics tell about watching the one you love get married. The singer wishes the bride well but promises that if things go wrong, he'll be there "walking behind you."

It's All Right with Me
COMPOSER-LYRICIST: **Cole Porter**

A second hit from the score of *Can-Can* (see "I Love Paris," page 154) was "It's All Right with Me." Peter Cookson introduced this fox-trot on Broadway, while Frank Sinatra sang it in the movie. Aristide Forestier (Cookson) is considering an affair with Claudine (played by Gwen Verdon) as he sings "tho' your face is charming it's the wrong face, it's not her face but such a charming face that It's All Right with Me."

Keep It a Secret
COMPOSER-LYRICIST: **Jessie Mae Robinson**

This *Variety* "Fifty Year Hit Parade" selection was a hit in best-selling recordings by Jo Stafford and by country star Slim Whitman in late 1952 and early 1953. It was one of the top ten songs on *Your Hit Parade* for fourteen weeks in 1953 but never made it to the top spot.

Many Times
COMPOSER: **Felix Stahl**
  LYRICIST: **Jessie Barnes (English lyrics)**

This *Variety* "Fifty Year Hit Parade" number was a Belgian song that was introduced in the United States by Percy Faith and his orchestra. It was on *Your Hit Parade*'s top ten for eleven weeks at the end of 1953 and the beginning of 1954, but it never made it past the number three spot.

No Other Love
COMPOSER: **Richard Rodgers**
  LYRICIST: **Oscar Hammerstein II**

Richard Rodgers first used this melody as a tango in the "Beneath the Southern Cross" section of the television documentary *Victory at Sea* in 1952. Then he transformed it into "No Other Love," which was introduced by Bill Hayes and Isabel Bigley in the musical *Me and Juliet*, a 1953 Broadway show. The lyrics, written by Oscar Hammerstein II, pledge undying faithfulness.

Perry Como's recording was number one for three weeks in the fall of 1953. *Variety* selected the song for its "Fifty Year Hit Parade."

Oh! My Papa
See page 159 (1954).

Pretend
COMPOSER-LYRICISTS: **Lew Douglas, Cliff Parman, and Frank Lavere**

Nat "King" Cole recorded "Pretend," which was in the top spot on *Your Hit Parade* for three weeks in the spring of 1953. Ralph Marterie also had a successful recording of the 1952 song. The singer encourages you to "pretend you're happy when you're blue."

Rags to Riches
COMPOSER-LYRICISTS: **Richard Adler and Jerry Ross**

The sixth-ranked hit in 1953's top ten was Tony Bennett's recording of "Rags to Riches." Before Adler and Ross composed the musicals *Pajama Game* (1954) and *Damn Yankees* (1955), they wrote this *Variety* "Fifty Year Hit Parade" hit as an independent song. Bennett's disc sold almost 2 million copies and spent two weeks on the top of *Your Hit Parade* in December 1953. Bennett sang that he would go from rags to riches if only the object of his affection would say that she cared.

Ricochet
COMPOSER-LYRICISTS: **Larry Coleman, Joe Darion, and Norman Gimbel**

Teresa Brewer had a gold record with this country-sounding song, which was written by Larry Coleman, Joe Darion (see "Changing Partners," page 153) and Norman Gimbel. Brewer sang in her shrill voice that she did not want a romance that would ricochet, or she would gladly set her lover free.

"Ricochet" was chosen by *Variety* for its "Fifty Year Hit Parade."

Secret Love
COMPOSER: **Sammy Fain**
LYRICIST: **Paul Francis Webster**

The Oscar for the best song from films in 1953 went to the *Variety* "Fifty Year Hit Parade" song "Secret Love" from the movie musical *Calamity Jane*, which starred Doris Day. The film was released in 1953, as were recordings of "Secret Love" by Doris Day and country singer Slim Whitman. Both discs sold enough to be gold records in 1954, and they boosted the song to the top of *Your Hit Parade* for seven weeks in early 1954 and to the tenth spot on the year's top ten.

Calamity sings about the love she feels for Wild Bill Hickok, which has been a secret, perhaps even to her until this moment. She has always been too rough and tough to let love enter her life.

The other songs nominated for the 1953 Academy Awards were "The Moon Is Blue," by Herschel Burke Gilbert and Sylvia Fine, from *The Moon Is Blue;* "My Flaming Heart," by Nicholas Brodszky and Leo Robin, from *Small Town;* "Sadie Thompson's Song (Blue Pacific Blues)" by Lester Lee and Ned Washington, from *Miss Sadie Thompson;* and "That's Amore" by Harry Warren and Jack Brooks, from *The Caddy.*

The Song from Moulin Rouge (Where Is Your Heart?)
COMPOSER: **Georges Auric**
LYRICIST: **William Engvick**

The screen biography of artist Henri Toulouse-Lautrec, *Moulin Rouge,* produced the number two hit in 1953's top ten. Two million-selling recordings boosted this *Variety* "Fifty Year Hit Parade" song to eight weeks at the top of the charts from May to July. Even though this was one of the year's biggest hits with film origins, it was ignored by the academy when Oscar nominations were made.

Percy Faith and his orchestra, with a vocal by Felicia Sanders, and Mantovani and his orchestra both had million-seller recordings of the theme from the film. Faith's recording sold 2 million copies; Mantovani's eventually sold a million.

The tune was by classical music composer Georges Auric with English words by William Engvick. The original title was "Le Long de la Seine" with words by Jacques Larue. The song's subtitle, "Where Is Your Heart?," expresses its lyric intent: "Your lips may be near, but where is your heart?"

Stranger in Paradise
COMPOSER: **Robert Wright**
LYRICIST: **George "Chet" Forrest**

"Stranger in Paradise," the most popular number from the Broadway show *Kismet* (see "And This Is My Beloved," page 153), was based on a theme from the "Polovtsian Dances" from Borodin's opera *Prince Igor.* The caliph and Marsinah sing this lovely song as a duet when they first meet.

Two million sellers helped promote "Stranger in Paradise" to hit status and to number one on *Your Hit Parade* for six weeks at the beginning of 1954. Tony Bennet had a gold record with his solo version in 1953, while the Four Aces achieved a million seller with their quartet version in 1954. It was selected for *Variety*'s "Fifty Year Hit Parade."

Till I Waltz Again with You
COMPOSER-LYRICIST: **Sidney Prosen**

Teresa Brewer performed this *Variety* "Fifty Year Hit Parade" hit in 1952 and had herself a gold record. It was the number five hit in 1953's top ten, spending a month on the top of *Your Hit Parade* in March and April 1953. The song suggests that the loved one waltz alone "till I waltz again with you." Ironically, the song is not a waltz.

Vaya con Dios
COMPOSER-LYRICISTS: **Larry Russell, Inez James, and Buddy Pepper**

The top hit in 1953's top ten was Les Paul and Mary Ford's recording of "Vaya con Dios." This *Variety* "Fifty Year Hit Parade" Spanish number had been introduced by Anita O'Day. "Vaya con Dios" is a salutation meaning "God be with you," which was the singers' wish as they said goodbye.

Where Is Your Heart
See "The Song from *Moulin Rouge,*" above.

You, You, You
COMPOSER: **Lotar Olias**
LYRICIST: **Robert Mellin**

The seventh slot in 1953's top ten was filled by the Ames Brothers' recording of this song by German composer Lotar Olias with English lyrics by Robert Mellin. The recording sold 2 million copies and stayed on top of *Your Hit Parade* for a month in the fall and early winter of 1953.

The repetition of the "You, You, You" ("Du, Du, Du" in German) of the title five times in the song is its most distinctive characteristic.

Variety named "You, You, You" to its "Fifty Year Hit Parade" representing 1953.

1 9 5 4

Count Your Blessings Instead of Sheep
COMPOSER-LYRICIST: **Irving Berlin**

Master songwriter Irving Berlin was still producing hits in 1952 at age sixty-four, when he wrote this Academy Award nominee (see "Three Coins in a Fountain," page 160). It was introduced by Bing Crosby and Rosemary Clooney in the 1954 movie musical *White Christmas*. The Berlin seasonal favorite "White Christmas" (see page 110) furnished the title for the film but had been introduced in the 1942 film *Holiday Inn*.

The lyrics suggest we count our blessings instead of sheep, and we'll fall asleep very quickly. Bing Crosby and Eddie Fisher both made popular recordings.

Cross over the Bridge
COMPOSER-LYRICISTS: **Bennie Benjamin and George Weiss**

Patti Page's eleventh million-selling recording was "Cross over the Bridge." Page's hit rose to number three and stayed for nineteen weeks on the best-seller chart. The singer advises us to leave our fickle pasts behind us and "cross over the bridge" to true romance. The song was named to *Variety*'s "Fifty Year Hit Parade."

Earth Angel
COMPOSER-LYRICIST: **Curtis Williams**

One of the great rhythm and blues songs of the fifties was "Earth Angel" written by Curtis Williams, the lead singer of the quartet that popularized the song, the Penguins. Their disc had become a million seller by 1957 and had sold almost 4 million by 1966. The Penguins' smooth harmony as they sang "Earth angel, will you be mine?" made this one of the classic early rhythm and blues hits.

Fanny
COMPOSER-LYRICIST: **Harold Rome**

Fanny was Harold Rome's 1954 Broadway musical based on Marcel Pagnol's film trilogy *Marius, César,* and *Fanny*. The title tune is a beautiful, touching solo sung by Marius (played by William Tabbert) to Fanny (played by Florence Henderson). He explains that he loves her but that he also loves the sea. He goes to sea, not knowing that Fanny is pregnant with his child. Fanny accepts the proposal of the middle-aged Panisse (played by Walter Slezak) to give the child a name.

The 1960 film used "Fanny" as its theme, but scuttled the rest of the score in favor of a dramatic movie version. The film starred Leslie Caron and Maurice Chevalier.

The Happy Wanderer
COMPOSER: **Friedrich Wilhelm Möller**
LYRICIST: **Antonia Ridge**

The Austrian popular song "Der Fröhliche Wanderer" became a hit in America in 1954 as "The Happy Wanderer." The *Variety* "Fifty Year Hit Parade" song was introduced by the Oberkirchen Children's Choir. Antonia Ridge added English lyrics to the song, which was popularized by Henri René and his orchestra. The "val-de-ri, val-de-ra" of the chorus is very distinctive and memorable.

Hernando's Hideaway
COMPOSER-LYRICISTS: **Richard Adler and Jerry Ross**

This comic tango comes from the 1954 Broadway show *The Pajama Game*. The musical was based on Richard Bissell's novel *7½*, about a small-town pajama factory that is threatened by a strike. Gladys (played by Carol Haney, who became known primarily as a choreographer) introduced this slinky tune, which was recorded for the popular music marketplace by Archie Bleyer and his orchestra (number one for one week in late summer 1954). *Variety* chose "Hernando's Hideaway" for its "Fifty Year Hit Parade."

Hey There
COMPOSER-LYRICISTS: **Richard Adler and Jerry Ross**

"Hey There" was the first Broadway song to reach the top-tune-of-the-year plateau since the yearly top ten had begun in the early forties. John Raitt, playing Sid Sorokin, the new superintendent of the Sleep Tite Pajama Factory, introduced this song in the musical *The Pajama Game* (see "Hernando's Hideaway" above). Sid sings the song into a Dictaphone as a memo to himself; then, as he plays it back, he interpolates comments and ends by singing a duet with himself.

Rosemary Clooney's recording of "Hey There" was a 2.5 million seller, spent ten weeks at the top of *Your Hit Parade* in the fall of 1954, and, coupled with the flip side recording of "This Ole House" (see page 160) became the number one hit of the year. Her recording also was a duet with herself through one of the earliest uses of multitrack recording.

The 1957 film version of *The Pajama Game* starred Doris Day and John Raitt.

Variety included "Hey There" in its "Fifty Year Hit Parade."

The High and the Mighty
COMPOSER: **Dimitri Tiomkin**
LYRICIST: **Ned Washington**

Dimitri Tiomkin had great success with the theme from the film *The High and the Mighty*. He had composed the 1952 Academy Award winner, "High Noon," with Ned Washington as lyricist. The two collaborated again for this theme song, which copped an Oscar nomination in 1954 (see "Three Coins in a Fountain" page 160). In the film John Wayne whistled the melody, so in the million-selling recording by Leroy Holmes and his orchestra, Fred Lowry did the whistling. Other successful recordings were by Victor Young and Les Baxter and their orchestras.

"The High and the Mighty" was chosen for *Variety*'s "Fifty Year Hit Parade."

Hold My Hand
COMPOSER-LYRICISTS: **Richard Myers and Jack Lawrence**

This song was written in 1950 and interpolated into the film *Susan Slept Here* in 1954. The Academy of Motion Pictures had ruled in 1940 that a song must be written for the specific movie in which it appears in order to receive a nomination for best song, but evidently the rule was not in force in 1954, when "Hold My Hand" received an Oscar nomination (see "Three Coins in a Fountain," page 160).

The singer who popularized the song to million-seller status was Don Cornell. He pleaded in the song for his loved one to hold his hand as they stood at the threshold of heaven.

Home for the Holidays
COMPOSER: **Robert Allen**
LYRICIST: **Al Stillman**

This Yuletide favorite was made into a hit by Perry Como. It is particularly meaningful to people who are away from their families during the holiday season.

If I Give My Heart to You
COMPOSER-LYRICISTS: **Jimmie Crane, Al Jacobs, and Jimmy Brewster**

This *Variety* "Fifty Year Hit Parade" song was popularized by Doris Day. She asked, "If I give my heart to you, will you handle it with care?" Her recording boosted the number to the number one spot for two weeks in the fall of 1954.

I Need You Now
COMPOSER-LYRICISTS: **Jimmie Crane and Al Jacobs**

Crane and Jacobs (see "If I Give My Heart to You," above) had an even greater hit with "I Need You Now," which was a gold record for Eddie Fisher (written 1953, recorded 1954). Fisher's recording climbed to number one on *Your Hit Parade* and became 1954's seventh-place hit on the top ten.

Little Things Mean A Lot
COMPOSER-LYRICISTS: **Edith Lindeman and Carl Stutz**

The number two hit in 1954's top ten was Kitty Kallen's recording of "Little Things Mean a Lot." A Richmond, Virginia, disc jockey, Carl Stutz, and the amusement editor for the Richmond *Times-Dispatch*, Edith Lindeman, wrote this song, which became a million seller for Miss Kallen, her first and last solo gold record. The song itemizes some of those little things: "Blow me a kiss . . . Say I look nice when I'm not . . . Give me your arm as we cross the street," etc.

Make Love to Me!
COMPOSERS: **Leon Roppolo, Paul Mares, Benny Pollack, George Brunies, Mel Stitzel, and Walter Melrose**
LYRICISTS: **Bill Norvas and Allan Copeland**

This blunt song seems too sexually suggestive to have been popular in the relatively conservative fifties.

Perhaps its roots in jazz explain its suggestiveness since many jazz lyrics are full of sexual innuendos. But the song was extremely popular and was a million seller for Jo Stafford. It became the number eight hit on 1954's top ten.

It began in 1923 as "Tin Roof Blues," written by five players in the New Orleans Rhythm Kings plus Walter Melrose, a composer, author, and publisher during the twenties. Melrose wrote the original lyrics. Bill Norvas and Allan Copeland wrote the new lyrics for the present version in 1953.

The song's tempo marking calls for a moderately slow shuffle with a beat. The predominance of dotted eighth- and sixteenth-note patterns gives the tune a bounciness that's catchy.

Mambo Italiano
COMPOSER-LYRICIST: **Bob Merrill**

Rosemary Clooney had three gold records in 1954: "Hey There," "This Ole House," and "Mambo Italiano."

The mambo is a type of rumba that originated in Cuba. It has quadruple (4) meter with a syncopated (accented) third beat. Its Spanish origins make "Mambo Italiano" sound like a misnomer.

The Man That Got Away
COMPOSER: **Harold Arlen**
LYRICIST: **Ira Gershwin**

Harold Arlen and Ira Gershwin wrote this song for the 1953 film *A Star Is Born*, which starred Judy Garland. It has a down-and-out feeling reminiscent of blues songs. Garland's recording from the sound track sold a million copies, and the song was nominated for the Oscar as the best song from a film in 1954 (see "Three Coins in a Fountain," page 160).

Mister Sandman
COMPOSER-LYRICIST: **Pat Ballard**

The number six hit in 1954's top ten was the Chordettes' recording of "Mister Sandman." The number was written by the music editor of *College Humor*, Pat Ballard. The Chordettes were the prototype of many groups that became famous in the next several years.

The singers are begging the sandman to bring them a dream of the cutest guy they have ever seen. Most of the melody is sung staccato. The song was number one on *Your Hit Parade* for eight weeks—four at the end of 1954 and four at the beginning of 1955.

Oh My Papa (Oh Mein Papa)
COMPOSER: **Paul Burkhard**
LYRICISTS: **John Turner and Geoffrey Parsons**

This song was a fantastic hit in 1954: it was the year's number four hit in the top ten and had two million sellers, one by Eddie Calvert and another by Eddie Fisher. *Variety* chose it to represent 1953 in its "Fifty Year Hit Parade."

The song, with German words, was written by Paul Burkhard in 1948, published in Switzerland, and used in a musical in Zurich (*Schwarze Hecht*). The show was revived in Hamburg, Germany, as *Feuerwerke* ("Fireworks") in 1953, when the song began to gain attention. Britain's John Turner (pen name for Jimmy Phillips) and Geoffrey Parsons translated the original into English.

Eddie Calvert is a trumpet player from Preston, England. He began recording in England in 1951 and switched to Columbia just before the release of "Oh! My Pa-pa" (1953), which sold a million by 1954.

Eddie Fisher's recording with the Hugo Winterhalter orchestra and chorus was far more popular in the United States than Calvert's was. Fisher's disc was number one for eight weeks. Fisher sang with heartfelt passion about his late father, who could "change my tears to laughter."

Papa Loves Mambo
COMPOSER-LYRICISTS: **Al Hoffman, Dick Manning, and Bix Reichner**

This was the second mambo to sell a million records in 1954 (see "Mambo Italiano," above). Perry Como's recording was a million seller even though it climbed only to the number four spot on *Your Hit Parade*.

Como sang that "Papa loves mambo, Mama loves mambo," and evidently the nation loved the mambo in 1954.

Shake, Rattle and Roll
COMPOSER-LYRICIST: **Charles Calhoun**

This Bill Haley and his Comets disc, along with "Rock Around the Clock" (1955), launched the rock and roll craze that dominated the second half of the decade. Haley was to sell more than 60 million records by 1970, but "Shake, Rattle and Roll" was his first million seller.

Other successful recordings of the song were made by Joe Turner, who actually introduced the song, and by Elvis Presley.

Sh-Boom
COMPOSER-LYRICISTS: **The Chords**

The Crew Cuts' version of "Sh-Boom" was one of the first rock and roll hits and one of a flood of cover version recordings. "Sh-Boom" was written and recorded by the Chords (James Keyes, Claude Feaster, Carl Feaster, Floyd F. McRae, and James Edwards) for Cat Records. The Chords' version sold well among blacks, so the Crew Cuts, a white group with the closely cropped hair, covered the song for Mercury. Their version zoomed to the top of the charts, which proved to record producers that cover versions could be extremely popular.

The song opens with nonsense lyrics: "Hey nonny ding dong alang alang alang/Boom badoh, badoo badoo." Then the lyrics open with the song's subtitle, "Life could be a dream." But the most memorable part of the song is an interlude of "sh-boom, sh-boom, ya-da-da" nonsense words.

"Sh-Boom" became the number five hit in 1954's top ten. *Variety* selected it for its "Fifty Year Hit Parade."

Teach Me Tonight
COMPOSER: **Gene De Paul**
LYRICIST: **Sammy Cahn**

This *Variety* "Fifty Year Hit Parade" song was the first collaboration between Gene De Paul and Sammy Cahn. Cahn had to give Warner Brothers first chance at the song because he was under contract. The studio turned it down, and Cahn got it published by a small company owned by several songwriters. The first recording, according to Cahn, was by "some young lady," and it sold three copies: The girl bought one, Cahn and De Paul bought the other two. Then the De Castro Sisters recorded it on Abbott Records, and it began to achieve hit status. It was further popularized by a best-selling disc by Jo Stafford.

That's Amoré
COMPOSER: **Harry Warren**
LYRICIST: **Jack Brooks**

This Academy Award nominee in 1953 from *The Caddy,* which starred Dean Martin and Jerry Lewis, was a million seller for Dean Martin and the number nine hit in 1954's top ten. The song became Martin's first gold record, and sold more than 4 million copies in the next ten years. (See "Secret Love," page 156, for the other 1953 Academy Award nominees.)

Martin sings in a slight Italian accent, "When the moon hits your eye like a big pizza pie . . . When the stars make you drool just like pasta fazool, that's amoré . . . you're in love."

This Ole House
COMPOSER-LYRICIST: **Stuart Hamblen**

Composer Hamblen was inspired to write this song when he discovered a dilapidated hunter's hut while on a hunting trip in Texas. Inside the house a man was dead. Moved by what he had seen, Hamblen wrote the song, published it himself, and introduced it. But it was Rosemary Clooney's recording on the flip side of "Hey There" (see page 157) that propelled the song to hit status. *Variety* honored Hamblen by selecting two of his songs for the "Fifty Year Hit Parade," this one and 1951's "It Is No Secret."

Three Coins in a Fountain
COMPOSER: **Jule Styne**
LYRICIST: **Sammy Cahn**

The Academy Award winner for best song from the movies in 1954 went to the theme song for the non-musical film *Three Coins in a Fountain.* Frank Sinatra sang the song on the sound track and his recording became a best seller. The Four Aces' disc was a million seller, which kept the song in the number one spot on *Your Hit Parade* for a month in the summer of 1954. *Variety* chose it for its "Fifty Year Hit Parade."

According to legend, whoever throws a coin into the water of the Trevi Fountain in Rome will return to the Eternal City. The three coins were for the three couples featured in the film and played by Clifton Webb and Dorothy McGuire, Jean Peters and Louis Jourdan, and Maggie McNamara and Rossano Brazzi.

The other songs nominated for the 1954 Academy Award for best song from a film were "Count Your Blessings Instead of Sheep," by Irving Berlin, from *White Christmas;* "The High and the Mighty," by Dimitri Tiomkin and Ned Washington, from *The High and the Mighty;* "Hold My Hand," by Jack Lawrence and Richard Myers, from *Susan Slept Here;* and "The Man That Got Away," by Harold Arlen and Ira Gershwin, from *A Star Is Born.*

Wanted
COMPOSER-LYRICISTS: **Jack Fulton and Lois Steele**

The number three hit in 1954's top ten was Perry Como's recording of "Wanted." It was so successful that the song was number one on *Your Hit Parade* for seven weeks in the late spring and early summer. "Wanted" was Como's twelfth gold record.

The word *wanted* is used in the song as if it were a police warning to be on the lookout for some suspicious character. In this case the singer wants the person "who kissed me and held me closely, then stole my heart." Several words in the song are police jargon: "hiding out," "jury may find her guilty," "a signed confession."

"Wanted" was chosen for *Variety*'s "Fifty Year Hit Parade."

Young and Foolish
COMPOSER: Albert Hague
LYRICIST: Arnold B. Horwitt

The Broadway show *Plain and Fancy* introduced "Young and Foolish" in 1955. It had been written in 1954 by Albert Hague and Arnold B. Horwitt and was introduced by David Daniels as he recalled his youth.

Young at Heart
COMPOSER: Johnny Richards
LYRICIST: Carolyn Leigh

The tune for this *Variety* "Fifty Year Hit Parade" song originated in 1939 as "Moonbeam" by Johnny Richards. Carolyn Leigh supplied new lyrics in 1953. Frank Sinatra's 1953 disc sold a million copies, and the song held down the number one spot for two weeks in the spring of 1954. It was then used as the title and theme song for a 1954 film starring Sinatra and Doris Day.

Sinatra sang that if we are among the young at heart, "fairy tales can come true," and among other things, we can laugh as our dreams fall apart at the seams.

1 9 5 5

Ain't That a Shame!
COMPOSER-LYRICISTS: Fats Domino and Dave Bartholomew

New Orleans rhythm and blues pianist and singer Antoine ("Fats") Domino is estimated to have sold more than 65 million records (among the top dozen in record history). Domino had a string of million sellers, beginning with "The Fat Man" in 1948. By 1960 he had twenty-three gold records.

As popular as Domino's version of "Ain't That a Shame!" was, it was not as big a hit as Pat Boone's version.

Autumn Leaves
COMPOSER: Joseph Kosma
LYRICIST: Johnny Mercer

The number three hit in 1955's top ten began as a French popular song, "Les Feuilles Mortes," by Joseph Kosma in 1947. Johnny Mercer supplied the English lyrics in 1955. Twelve recordings, none successful, were made of this song by such artists as Bing Crosby and Jo Stafford in the first few years of the fifties. Then pianist Roger Williams recorded it in 1953 (released in late 1954), and it subsequently sold more than 2 million copies globally. Nat ("King") Cole sang it in the 1956 film *Autumn Leaves* as a theme at the beginning and end of the film.

Variety selected "Autumn Leaves" for its "Fifty Year Hit Parade."

Ballad of Davy Crockett
COMPOSER: George Bruns
LYRICIST: Tom Blackburn

George Bruns, a trombonist on Walt Disney's music staff, and Tom Blackburn wrote this song for the Disney television series *Davy Crockett*. The series, the recording of the theme song by Bill Hayes, and more than 100 merchandise items, including coonskin caps, created "Crockett-mania." Bill Hayes had his only million seller with this song, and Fess Parker, the star of the TV series, also had a disc that sold almost a million. Such sales figures pushed the song to the number seven position on 1955's top ten and to nine weeks at number one on *Your Hit Parade*. *Variety* selected it for its "Fifty Year Hit Parade."

A ballad typically tells a story, and indeed, this ballad chronicles some of the exploits of the legendary Crockett, who was "king of the wild frontier." It sounds like a folk song, with a narrow range, reasonably simple chord structure, and an easy tune to sing.

Cherry Pink and Apple Blossom White
COMPOSER Louiguy
LYRICIST: Mack David

The top hit on 1955's top ten was this million seller by the Perez ("King of the Mambo") Prado and his orchestra. Prado's recording was also the second biggest hit of the second half of the fifties, and according to *Billboard*, the second-biggest single between 1955 and 1982.

The song had been written by Louiguy and Jacques Larue and published in Paris in 1950 as "Cerisier Rose et Pommer Blanc." In 1951 Mack David wrote English lyrics for the song. Prado's version with Billy Regis featured on trumpet was used in the 1955 film *Underwater.* Prado had recorded the song in 1951, but when the song was selected for inclusion in *Underwater,* he was chosen to cut a new version for the film.

Alan Dale had a gold record with the song as a vocal in 1956. *Variety* honored the song by including it in its "Fifty Year Hit Parade."

Cry Me a River
COMPOSER-LYRICIST: **Arthur Hamilton**

This was actress and singer Julie London's only million-selling record. Arthur Hamilton wrote the words and music in 1953.

Julie sang to an imaginary beau that he could cry a river for her now because she had cried enough for him.

Dance with Me, Henry
COMPOSER-LYRICISTS: **Johnny Otis, Hank Ballard, and Etta James**

Hank Ballard had a hit with his "Work with Me, Annie" in 1954, but the lyrics were too suggestive, so it was banned by many radio stations. Etta James recorded the tune as "Roll with Me, Henry," but her version was still too raunchy. Georgia Gibbs's cover version altered the suggestive lyrics and was marketed as "Dance with Me, Henry." Her disc sold a million copies.

Heart
COMPOSER-LYRICISTS: **Richard Adler and Jerry Ross**

The Broadway show *Damn Yankees* spawned this hit. Four baseball players and the manager introduce this song in the musical. The down-and-out players are trying to shore up their spirits by claiming that "all you really need is heart" to become a winning team. Eddie Fisher helped popularize the song with a best-selling recording.

How Important Can It Be?
COMPOSER-LYRICISTS: **Bennie Benjamin and George Weiss**

This disc by Joni James became her fourth gold record. Bennie Benjamin and George Weiss wrote this

Variety "Fifty Year Hit Parade" song that spent fifteen weeks on the best-seller chart. Sara Vaughan also had a successful recording of the song.

I'll Never Stop Loving You
COMPOSER: **Nicholas Brodszky**
LYRICIST: **Sammy Cahn**

The movie musical *Love Me or Leave Me* was the biography of Ruth Etting, the famous *Follies* star and nightclub performer, who was particularly popular during the twenties and thirties. Most of the music for the film was old songs, especially those associated with Etting's career, but Nicholas Brodszky and Sammy Cahn wrote "I'll Never Stop Loving You," which Doris Day introduced, especially for it.

Ko-Ko-Mo
COMPOSER-LYRICISTS: **Forrest Wilson, Jake Porter, and Eunice Levy**

The original rhythm and blues version of this *Variety* "Fifty Year Hit Parade" number was by Gene and Eunice for Combo No. 64 records. However, as was often the case, the cover version, by Perry Como, sold best.

Learnin' the Blues
COMPOSER-LYRICIST: **Dolores Vicki Silvers**

"Learnin' the Blues," a *Variety* "Fifty Year Hit Parade" selection, was a million seller for Frank Sinatra in 1955. His disc had a sale of 900,000 in the United States and topped the million mark with sales around the world. The song reached number two on the top ten and spent about five months on the best-seller chart.

Let Me Go, Lover!
COMPOSER-LYRICIST: **Jenny Lou Carson (lyrics adapted by Al Hill)**

Jenny Lou Carson originally wrote this song under the title "Let Me Go, Devil" in 1953 as a song against alcohol. Mitch Miller suggested that the lyrics be revised, as they were by Al Hill in 1954. Eighteen-year-old Joan Weber recorded the song and gained her only gold record with it in 1954. Then, in 1955, Teresa Brewer achieved her fifth million seller with the song. These two gold records helped elevate "Let Me Go, Lover!" to the number ten spot in 1955's top ten and to selection in *Variety*'s "Fifty Year Hit Parade." Brewer's shrill, high voice belted out "Let me go, lover . . . let me be, set me free. . . . "

Love and Marriage
COMPOSER: James Van Heusen
LYRICIST: Sammy Cahn

"Love and Marriage" was introduced by Frank Sinatra in the musical adaptation of Thornton Wilder's *Our Town* for television in 1955. Sinatra's recording eventually went gold. It became the first popular song ever to win an Emmy and received the Christopher Award from the Catholic Church, because it extolled the virtues of love and marriage, saying that they "go together like a horse and carriage."

Love Is a Many-Splendored Thing
COMPOSER: Sammy Fain
LYRICIST: Paul Francis Webster

The Academy Award winner for 1955 was this *Variety* "Fifty Year Hit Parade" theme song from the motion picture *Love Is a Many-Splendored Thing*. This passionate song defines love as "nature's way of giving a reason to be living," then describes a scene from the film when high on a windy hill, "in the morning mist two lovers kissed and the world stood still."

The Four Aces were about the only popular singers willing to record the song; most felt it was too heavy for wide popularity. Their recording spent two weeks at number one and became their fifth gold record. After the song had become popular, many big-name recording artists changed their minds and issued successful discs. It ranks as the sixth-place hit in 1955's top ten. This Academy Award winner, as recorded by the Four Aces, was also the thirtieth biggest hit single between 1955 and 1982, according to *Billboard*.

The other songs nominated for the 1955 Oscar were "I'll Never Stop Loving You," by Nicholas Brodszky and Sammy Cahn, from *Love Me or Leave Me;* "The Tender Trap," by James Van Heusen and Sammy Cahn, from *The Tender Trap;* "Something's Gotta Give," by Johnny Mercer, from *Daddy Long Legs;* and "Unchained Melody," by Alex North and Hy Zaret, from *Unchained.*

Marianne
COMPOSER-LYRICISTS: Terry Gilkyson, Frank Miller, and Richard Dehr

Terry Gilkyson, one of the original Weavers and the lead vocalist on the million-selling "On Top of Old Smokey" disc, added a soft calypso beat to this Bahamian folk song in 1955. In the calypso craze of the later fifties, "Marianne" climbed into the top ten and became a million seller for Gilkyson (1957).

Melody of Love
COMPOSER: H. Engelmann
LYRICIST: Tom Glazer

The tune for this *Variety* "Fifty Year Hit Parade" hit came from "Melodie d'Amour" by Engelmann in 1903. Billy Vaughn and his orchestra had a million seller with the song in 1955. Recordings by the Four Aces, Dinah Shore, and Tony Martin also helped popularize the song, which had been given new lyrics by Tom Glazer in 1954.

Moments to Remember
COMPOSER: Robert Allen
LYRICIST: Al Stillman

The Four Lads had their first gold record with this nostalgic song. They were the background singers for Johnnie Ray's "Cry" in 1951.

The song is a graduation type of number which reminisces about several different occurrences that are fun to remember.

Only You
COMPOSER-LYRICISTS: Buck Ram and Ande Rand

A male quartet plus one girl constituted the Platters, a black rhythm and blues group that was one of the most successful of the prerock and early rock era. Their recording of "Only You" became their first number one record and launched their career. Buck Ram, who discovered and managed the group, wrote both "Only You" and the next big hit, "The Great Pretender." The Platters were the most popular vocal group of the fifties with four number one hits and sixteen gold records.

The Platters' distinctive sound singing "Only you and you alone can thrill me like you do" is often associated with the fifties. Four different versions of "Only You" made the top ten: The Platters' and the Hilltoppers' in 1955, Frank Pourcel's in 1949, and Ringo Starr's in 1974.

Rock Around the Clock
COMPOSER-LYRICISTS: Max C. Freedman and Jimmy De Knight

In 1970 world sales figures of Bill Haley and his Comets' recording of this *Variety* "Fifty Year Hit Parade" song were estimated to have reached 16 million. The television series *Happy Days* has kept it before the public for years since. It has been featured in at least fourteen different films and has been recorded in thirty-five different languages with more than 140 versions around the globe. Collective sales figures are estimated at more than 25 million.

This phenomenal song was written in 1953, Bill Haley and his Comets waxed the song in 1954, and it and their "Shake Rattle and Roll" (see page 159) launched the rock era. The tune received even more impetus when it was included in the 1955 film *The Blackboard Jungle,* which helped the song become the number two hit on 1955's top ten. This Bill Haley classic is the seventh biggest hit of the second half of the fifties and, according to *Billboard,* the thirteenth highest-selling single from 1955 to 1982.

Sincerely

COMPOSER-LYRICISTS: **Harvey Fuqua and Alan Freed**

The three-sister singing group the McGuire Sisters had their first gold record with this *Variety* "Fifty Year Hit Parade" selection in 1955. The rhythm and blues number zoomed into the top ten, claimed the top spot for six weeks, and spent five months among the best sellers. The Moonglows had the original R & B version, which the McGuire Sisters covered for this hit.

The composer Alan Freed was most famous as a disc jockey and for originating the term *rock and roll* in the early fifties for his "Moon Dog's Rock and Roll Party" radio program. However, he occasionally contributed material to the rock milieu as he did with "Sincerely." The McGuire Sisters' recording of "Sincerely" was the fourth biggest hit of the second half of the fifties, and according to *Billboard,* the sixth biggest hit single from 1955 to 1982.

Sixteen Tons

COMPOSER-LYRICIST: **Merle Travis**

Tennessee Ernie Ford's biggest hit came in 1955 with "Sixteen Tons," which was his first gold record and became the number four hit in 1955's top ten. It was in top place for five weeks in 1955 and two weeks in 1956. "Sixteen Tons" was the tenth biggest hit of the second half of the fifties and, according to *Billboard,* the sixteenth biggest hit single of 1955 to 1982.

"Sixteen Tons" was written by Merle Travis, a Kentucky coal miner's son, in 1947. The lyrics' homey cynicism struck a chord with the record-buying public. People empathized with working hard but not really getting ahead, getting older "and deeper in debt."

That's All I Want from You

COMPOSER-LYRICIST: **M. Rotha**

Fritz Rotta, using the pseudonym M. Rotha, wrote this *Variety* "Fifty Year Hit Parade" song in 1954. It was popularized by Jaye P. Morgan in a best-selling recording in 1955.

Tweedle Dee

COMPOSER-LYRICIST: **Winfield Scott**

This 1954 song was Georgia Gibbs's second million seller of 1955 (see "Dance with Me, Henry," page 162). It also was a million seller for LaVern Baker, who recorded the rhythm and blues version. Baker's disc climbed to number twenty-two on the national charts, while Gibbs's disc made it to the top in March 1955. It was chosen by *Variety* to represent 1955 in its "Fifty Year Hit Parade."

Unchained Melody

COMPOSER: **Alex North**
LYRICIST: **Hy Zaret**

This was the theme for the film *Unchained* (1955). Two million-selling discs helped this song to reach the number nine spot on 1955's top ten. Les Baxter and his orchestra and chorus had one of the million sellers, while blind singer Al Hibbler had the other. Four versions of "Unchained Melody" made the top ten: Les Baxter's, Al Hibbler's, and Roy Hamilton's in 1955, and the Righteous Brothers' in 1965.

The song has an unusual structure: The chorus comes first ("Oh, my love, my darling, I've hungered for your touch . . ."), followed by a verse. Normally the pattern is verse and chorus. With this pattern the chorus is heard more than the verses.

Variety honored "Unchained Melody" by selecting it for its "Fifty Year Hit Parade."

Wake the Town and Tell the People

COMPOSER: **Jerry Livingston**
LYRICIST: **Sammy Gallop**

This hit, written in 1954, was popularized in 1955 recordings by Mindy Carson and by Les Baxter and his orchestra. The refrain suggests that we "wake the town and tell the people" to "tell them I'm in love with you."

Whatever Lola Wants

COMPOSER-LYRICISTS: **Richard Adler and Jerry Ross**

Satan's emissary in *Damn Yankees* (see "Heart," page 162) was Lola, played by Gwen Verdon in the original Broadway cast. She sang "Whatever Lola Wants (Lola Gets)" seductively to baseball player Joe Hardy (played by Stephen Douglas). Sarah Vaughan's recording was a best seller.

The Yellow Rose of Texas

COMPOSER-LYRICIST: **J. K. (adapted by Don George)**

The number five hit in 1955's top ten was this million seller by Mitch Miller, his orchestra and chorus. Miller's recording spent nine weeks at the top spot on *Your Hit Parade* in the fall of 1955. The hit was an adaptation of a song written in 1853 that became a Civil War march known as "The Gallant Hood of Texas." The composer-lyricist was identified only as "J.K." In 1955 Don George adapted it into "The Yellow Rose of Texas."

"The Yellow Rose of Texas" was chosen for *Variety*'s "Fifty Year Hit Parade." Mitch Miller's recording was also the thirty-ninth biggest hit single from 1955 to 1982.

SELECTED BIOGRAPHICAL SKETCHES

A

Harold Adamson
b. 1906, Greenville, New Jersey
d. 1980, Beverly Hills, California

Lyricist Harold Adamson had a long and successful career in the popular music field. He left Harvard in the late twenties to write songs. He wrote lyrics for several Broadway musicals and several important movie musicals.

Adamson's most famous lyrics include 1930's "Time on My Hands," from *Smiles;* 1933's "Everything I Have Is Yours," from the movie *Dancing Lady;* 1936's "Did I Remember?," from the movie *Suzy;* 1940's "The Woodpecker's Song"; 1943's World War II-inspired "Comin' In on a Wing and a Prayer"; 1944's "A Lovely Way to Spend an Evening" and "I Couldn't Sleep a Wink Last Night," from the movie *Higher and Higher;* 1948's "It's a Most Unusual Day," from the movie *A Date with Judy;* 1956's "Around the World," the theme from the film *Around the World in 80 Days;* and 1957's movie theme "An Affair to Remember." He is a member of the Songwriters' Hall of Fame.

Richard Adler
b. 1921, New York, New York

Composer, lyricist, and producer Richard Adler is best known for two Broadway musicals: 1954's *The Pa-*

jama Game and 1955's *Damn Yankees.* "Hey There," from *The Pajama Game,* was 1954's top hit. Adler's chief collaborator was Jerry Ross.

Milton Ager
b. 1893, Chicago, Illinois
d. 1979, Los Angeles, California

Milton Ager was an important composer of the twenties and thirties. His most famous songs include 1922's "Lovin' Sam," 1924's "Hard-Hearted Hannah" and "I Wonder What's Become of Sally," 1927's "Ain't She Sweet?," 1929's "Happy Days Are Here Again," and 1933's "If I Didn't Care."

In 1922 he helped organize an important publishing firm, Ager, Yellen & Bornstein. His chief lyricist was Jack Yellen. Ager was elected to membership in the Songwriters' Hall of Fame.

Fred E. Ahlert
b. 1892, New York, New York
d. 1953, New York, New York

Fred Ahlert was a famous composer of the twenties and thirties. Most of his songs were written independently of the Broadway stage and Hollywood musicals. His chief lyricist was Roy Turk. Ahlert is a member of the Songwriters' Hall of Fame.

His most popular hits include 1928's "I'll Get By"; 1929's "Mean to Me"; 1931's "I Don't Know Why,"

"Walkin' My Baby Back Home," and "Where the Blue of the Night Meets the Gold of the Day"; and 1936's "I'm Gonna Sit Right Down and Write Myself a Letter" (million seller in 1957).

Harry Akst
b. 1894, New York, New York
d. 1963, Hollywood, California

Harry Akst was a composer of popular songs during the twenties and thirties. His chief lyric collaborators were Sam M. Lewis, Joe Young, Bert Kalmar, Al Jolson, and Gus Kahn. His most famous songs were 1925's "Dinah," 1926's "Baby Face," and 1929's "Am I Blue?"

Rex Allen
b. 1924, Wilcox, Arizona

Movie star Rex Allen made thirty-two westerns from 1950 through 1957. In 1953 he recorded the popular hit "Crying in the Chapel." In recent years he has done a great deal of film and recording work for the Disney organization.

Louis Alter
b. 1902, Haverhill, Massachusetts
d. 1980, New York, New York

Louis Alter was an important composer of popular songs in the thirties and forties. He served as accompanist for the famous vaudeville entertainer Nora Bayes from 1924 through 1928. He composed his first successful popular song in 1926. His most famous composition, "Manhattan Serenade," was composed in 1928 as an instrumental. Harold Adamson added lyrics in 1942. "Manhattan Serenade" was the theme song for the Easy Aces' radio show in the thirties.

Alter wrote music for a few Broadway musicals and for several movie musicals. Popular Alter tunes include 1936's "You Turned the Tables on Me," from the movie *Sing, Baby, Sing;* 1941's "Dolores," from the movie *Las Vegas Nights;* and 1947's "Do You Know What It Means to Miss New Orleans?," from the movie *New Orleans.*

Arthur Altman
b. 1912, Brooklyn, New York

Altman has composed only a few popular songs that drew much attention—namely, "Play, Fiddle, Play" (1932) and "All or Nothing at All" (1943). His chief collaborators were Jack Lawrence and Hal David.

Ames Brothers
b. Malden, Massachusetts

The Ames Brothers (Ed, Gene, Joe, and Vic; real name: Urick) were a popular quartet in the late forties and fifties. They broke up in the late fifties, and Ed continued as a single. He is particularly remembered for his role as the Indian on the Daniel Boone television series. His recording of "Try to Remember" was popular.

Million-selling discs recorded by the quartet include 1950's "Rag Mop," backed by "Sentimental Me"; 1951's "Undecided," 1953's "You, You, You"; 1954's "The Naughty Lady of Shady Lane"; and 1957's "Melodie d'Amour."

Morey Amsterdam
b. 1912, Chicago, Illinois

Morey Amsterdam is primarily known as a comedian, but he wrote the lyrics for "Rum and Coca-Cola," adapting a calypso melody from Trinidad into one of the big hits of the mid-forties.

Ivy Anderson
b. 1904, Gilroy, California
d. 1949, Los Angeles, California

Ivy Anderson was the featured vocal soloist with Duke Ellington's orchestra from 1931 until the middle of 1942. In that position, she introduced and helped popularize numerous songs. When she left Ellington, she settled in California and played clubs as a single. She owned her own club in Los Angeles for several years.

Leroy Anderson
b. 1908, Cambridge, Massachusetts
d. 1975, Woodbury, Connecticut

Leroy Anderson was a noted composer of semiclassical and unusual descriptive pieces. His best-known works are 1952's "Blue Tango," 1948's "Fiddle Faddle," 1950's "Sleigh Ride," "A Trumpeter's Lullaby," "Sandpaper Ballet," "The Syncopated Clock," and "The Typewriter." Anderson led large orchestras in recording many of his compositions. His only million sellers were "The Syncopated Clock" and "Blue Tango," which he and his pops orchestra recorded in 1951.

Maxwell Anderson
b. 1888, Atlantic, Pennsylvania
d. 1959, Stamford, Connecticut

Playwright and lyricist Maxwell Anderson's best-known popular song is "September Song" from

Knickerbocker Holiday. He wrote the book and lyrics, while Kurt Weill contributed the music, for two Broadway shows: 1938's *Knickerbocker Holiday* and 1944's *Lost in the Stars*. As a playwright Anderson had several plays produced on Broadway, including *What Price Glory?*, *Saturday's Children*, *Key Largo*, and *The Bad Seed*.

Julie Andrews
b. 1935, Walton-on-Thames, England

Julie Andrews got her start in show business on the London stage as a child star. She came to the United States in the British musical *The Boy Friend* (1954). Her greatest success on the Broadway stage was as Eliza Doolittle in *My Fair Lady* (1956). Other successes followed in 1960's *Camelot* as Guenevere and in the movie musicals *Mary Poppins* and *The Sound of Music*.

Andrews Sisters
Patty b. 1920, Minneapolis, Minnesota
Maxine b. 1918, Minneapolis, Minnesota
LaVerne b. 1915, Minneapolis, Minnesota
d. 1967, Brentwood, California

The Andrews Sisters got their start in Minneapolis by winning a children's talent contest at the Orpheum Theater. Patty, Maxine, and LaVerne sang with bands and appeared in vaudeville and in nightclubs, but it was not until their 1937 recording of "Bei Mir Bist Du Schoen" that the trio became famous. Their only other million seller was 1944's "Rum and Cola-Cola." However, they combined with Bing Crosby for million sellers with "Pistol Packin' Mama" and "Jingle Bells" (1943), "Don't Fence Me In" (1944), and "South America, Take It Away" (1946). They joined Guy Lombardo and his Royal Canadians for a million seller in 1946 with "Christmas Island" backed by "Winter Wonderland." Their recording of "Boogie Woogie Bugle Boy" is one of their most famous numbers, but it was not a million seller. Bette Midler's recording of the song in 1973 was very similar to the Andrews Sisters' original and caused a revival of interest in their work. The sisters' collective disc sales through the years have been estimated at 60 million. They also appeared in seventeen films.

Harry Archer
b. 1888, Creston, Iowa
d. 1960, New York, New York

Harry Archer (real name: Harry Auracher) was an important bandleader and occasional composer dur-

ing the twenties and thirties. He wrote the scores for several Broadway musicals, including 1923's *Little Jesse James*. His most popular song, "I Love You," came from that 1923 musical.

Harold Arlen
b. 1905, Buffalo, New York

Harold Arlen (real name: Hyman Arluck) was a top composer from 1929 through the fifties with many excellent songs and a large number of hits. Arlen's first song success was "Get Happy" in 1930. His chief collaborator was lyricist Ted Koehler.

Arlen had famous hits with 1931's "Between the Devil and the Deep Blue Sea"; 1932's "I Love a Parade" and "I Gotta Right to Sing the Blues"; 1933's "Stormy Weather," "It's Only a Paper Moon," and "I've Got the World on a String"; 1934's "Let's Fall in Love"; 1939's "Over the Rainbow"; 1941's "Blues in the Night"; 1942's "That Old Black Magic"; 1943's "My Shining Hour," "One for My Baby," and "Happiness Is Just a Thing Called Joe"; 1944's "Ac-cent-tchu-ate the Positive"; 1946's "Come Rain or Come Shine"; and 1954's "The Man That Got Away." Arlen wrote songs for many films, but by far the most memorable was the excellent score for *The Wizard of Oz* in 1939. Arlen was elected to membership in the Songwriters' Hall of Fame.

Louis Armstrong
b. 1900, New Orleans, Louisiana
d. 1971, Queens, New York

Daniel Louis ("Satchmo") Armstrong was one of the most important jazz trumpeters in the popular music field. He learned to read music and play several instruments in the Colored Waif's Home for Boys in New Orleans. He got his professional start with King Oliver in 1922, joined Fletcher Henderson in New York in 1924, and played with several other bands until 1927, when he formed his own band. In 1929 he was featured in the revue *Hot Chocolates*. He appeared in several movies, including 1936's *Pennies from Heaven* and the very successful *High Society* (1956), with Bing Crosby, Frank Sinatra, and Grace Kelly. His first official million-selling recording came to him at age sixty-four with his raspy-voiced rendition of the title song from the Broadway musical *Hello, Dolly!*

In jazz circles, Armstrong was a staple since the twenties, and many of his trumpet solos and vocal renditions have become jazz classics.

Gus Arnheim

b. 1897, Philadelphia, Pennsylvania
d. 1955, Los Angeles, California

Gus Arnheim was the leader of a popular band during the twenties and thirties. He formed his band in the late twenties. They toured the United States and Europe and appeared in the 1929 film *The Street Girl*. Russ Columbo sang with the band from 1929 through early 1931. Bing Crosby, as a member of the Rhythm Boys, recorded with the band in early 1931.

Arnheim also composed several popular songs, including 1923's "I Cried for You" and 1931's "Sweet and Lovely."

He retired from the band after the mid-forties but returned in the mid-fifties for a brief time.

Eddy Arnold

b. 1918, Henderson, Tennessee

Eddy Arnold has been a top country and western singer, one of the first to bridge the gap between country and main-line popular music. Arnold worked with Pee Wee King and his band in the early forties and with them began to attract attention at the Grand Ole Opry. By the mid-forties he had begun to work as a single, but it was not until 1947 that he had his first big hit, "I'll Hold You in My Heart."

This Country Music Hall of Famer has collected several gold records, including 1947's "I'll Hold You in My Arms"; 1948's "Bouquet of Roses," "Any Time," and "Just a Little Lovin' Will Go a Long, Long Way"; 1951's "I Wanna Play House with You"; and 1955's "Cattle Call." Other hits that have been associated with Arnold include "That's How Much I Love You," "I Really Don't Want to Know," and "Make the World Go Away."

Fred Astaire

b. 1899, Omaha, Nebraska

Fred Astaire (real name: Frederick Austerlitz) began his career in 1916 with his sister, Adele, as a dancing couple, much like the famous Castles, Vernon and Irene, who had been popular in the 1910s. The Astaires started in vaudeville and climbed to Broadway stardom.

Adele retired from the act when she married Lord Charles Cavendish in 1932.

Fred has appeared as a solo dancer and with numerous dancing partners, but his most famous partner was Ginger Rogers, with whom he made several Hollywood movie musicals.

Astaire is the acknowledged King of the Movie Musicals, and is unrivaled as an elegant, sophisticated, virtuoso dancer. His small, limited voice has never hindered him or the musicals or films in which he appeared. He has a style with popular songs that is irresistible.

Important hits that were premiered by Astaire include: 1924's "Oh, Lady Be Good!" and "Fascinating Rhythm"; 1927's " 'S wonderful"; 1931's "Dancing in the Dark"; 1932's "Night and Day"; 1933's "Carioca"; 1934's Academy Award winner, "The Continental"; 1935's "I Won't Dance," the Academy Award winner "Cheek to Cheek," and "Top Hat, White Tie and Tails"; 1936's Academy Award winner, "The Way You Look Tonight," and "A Fine Romance"; 1937's "Let's Face the Music and Dance," "They Can't Take That Away from Me," and "A Foggy Day"; and 1938's "Change Partners." In the forties he continued to introduce important songs, but not to the extent he had in the thirties. One example worth mentioning is 1943's "One for My Baby." In all, Astaire starred in more than thirty movie musicals and in about a dozen Broadway musicals.

Gene Austin

b. 1900, Gainesville, Texas
d. 1972, Palm Springs, California

Gene Austin (real name: Eugene Lucas) began his recording career in the mid-twenties and had established himself as a major star before the end of the decade. In 1927 he recorded the hit "My Blue Heaven," which became a multimillion-selling disc and remained the biggest-selling record until Bing Crosby's "White Christmas" replaced it fifteen years later. By the early thirties, Austin's fame began to fade primarily because his soft voice could not compete with the bands that were becoming fashionable and microphones were not developed enough to help.

In addition to his performing, he composed several popular songs, including 1924's "How Come You Do Me Like You Do?" and "When My Sugar Walks down the Street" and 1929's "The Lonesome Road."

Austin's million-selling records included 1928's "Ramona," in addition to "My Blue Heaven."

Gene Autry

b. 1907, Tioga Springs, Texas

Gene Autry was the first big singing cowboy movie star. His first starring movie role came in the film *Tumbling Tumbleweeds* (1935). By the end of his career, in the early fifties, he had made about 100 movies. In addition, he was the star of the radio show

Melody Ranch from the early forties through the early fifties. He recorded extensively and made several hit records, particularly "Rudolph the Red-Nosed Reindeer," "Peter Cottontail," and "Frosty the Snowman," all of which are big sellers annually.

He was also the composer or co-composer of several hits in the country and western market, some of which became national hits. His most famous compositions include "That Silver-Haired Daddy of Mine," "Back in the Saddle," "Have I Told You Lately That I Love You?," and "Here Comes Santa Claus."

Autry's million-selling recordings include 1939's "That Silver-Haired Daddy of Mine," 1947's "Here Comes Santa Claus," 1949's "Peter Cottontail" and "Rudolph the Red-Nosed Reindeer," and 1950's "Frosty the Snowman."

In recent years he has been less active in show business, concentrating instead on his considerable business empire, which includes radio and television stations, recording and publishing firms, movie studios, and the California Angels baseball team.

Mitchell Ayres
b. 1910, Milwaukee, Wisconsin
d. 1969, Las Vegas, Nevada

Mitchell Ayres (real name: Mitchell Agress) was a bandleader who gained fame when he and his band backed Perry Como on his radio and television shows. During the thirties and forties Ayres led a popular sweet band. They appeared in a few minor films and recorded occasionally.

When Perry Como folded his television show, Ayres moved to the Hollywood Palace television show, on which he worked up to the time of his death.

B

Abel Baer
b. 1893, Baltimore, Maryland
d. 1976, New York, New York

Abel Baer was a composer and lyricist who was active as a songwriter especially during the twenties. His most famous song was 1942's "There Are Such Things."

Mildred Bailey
b. 1907, Tekoa, Washington
d. 1951, Poughkeepsie, New York

Jazz vocalist Mildred Bailey became famous with the Paul Whiteman orchestra and later with the Red Norvo band (she married Norvo). She was the sister of Al Rinker, who was one of the Rhythm Boys along with Bing Crosby.

Pearl Bailey
b. 1918, Newport News, Virginia

Pearl Bailey began her career in show business as a dancer but later became a famous popular singer in nightclubs, in vaudeville, in musicals, and with a few big bands. She appeared on Broadway in 1946's *St. Louis Woman* and in 1954's *House of Flowers*. She also appeared in several films, notably *Carmen Jones* and *Porgy and Bess*.

Bonnie Baker
b. circa 1918

Bonnie Baker (real name: Evelyn Nelson) is primarily known for her million-selling hit "Oh Johnny, Oh Johnny, Oh!" with the Orrin Tucker band. Called Wee Bonnie Baker, she rose to prominence as the tiny-voiced soloist with the band after she had joined them in 1936. She and the band were featured in the 1941 film *You're the One*. In the late forties, when she worked as a single, her career gradually declined.

Kenny Baker
b. 1920, Monrovia, California

Kenny Baker is a tenor best known for his work in films, beginning with 1936's *King of Burlesque* and concluding with 1947's *Calendar Girl*.

Baker held a spot on the popular Jack Benny radio show from 1935 through the remainder of the decade. He appeared on the *Texaco Star Theater* radio show in the late thirties and with Fred Allen on his popular radio show in the early forties. He had his own radio program in 1944.

He starred in the Broadway musical *One Touch of Venus* in 1943.

Hank Ballard
b. 1936, Detroit, Michigan

Hank Ballard and his group, the Midnighters, were one of the most consistent hit makers among the early rhythm and blues artists. Their string of gold records began in 1954 with "Work with Me, Annie," "Sexy Ways," and "Annie Had a Baby." The list continued in 1960 with "Finger Poppin' Time," "Let's Go, Let's Go, Let's Go," and the first version of "The Twist," which became the dance sensation of the sixties.

Harry Barris
b. 1905, New York, New York
d. 1962, Burbank, California

Harry Barris grew up in Denver but began to gain fame in 1926, when he joined Bing Crosby and Al Rinker to form the Rhythm Boys, a vocal trio that was hired by Paul Whiteman. They appeared with Whiteman's band in the 1930 film *King of Jazz*, then left him to join Gus Arnheim's band at the Los Angeles Cocoanut Grove. As Crosby began to do more solo work, the trio faded in importance and broke up. During the thirties and forties Barris often appeared in bit parts as a rehearsal pianist, jive-talking band musician, or bandleader in Crosby's films.

He also composed a couple of all-time pop standards—namely, 1928's "Mississippi Mud" (which the Rhythm Boys recorded with Whiteman) and 1931's "I Surrender, Dear."

Blue Barron
b. 1911, Cleveland, Ohio

Blue Barron was the leader of a sweet-style band in the mid-thirties. His style featured the trombone and sax sections. His theme song was "Sometimes I'm Happy" (1927). The band was led by singer Tommy Ryan while Barron was in military service during World War II, but he resumed leadership upon return to civilian life.

His only major hit was the million-selling disc of "Cruising down the River" in 1949.

Eileen Barton
b. circa 1928, Brooklyn, New York

Eileen Barton is chiefly remembered for her 1950 hit recording of "If I Knew You Were Comin' I'd 'ave Baked a Cake."

Her parents were vaudevillians, and as a child she appeared in vaudeville, on children's radio programs, and occasionally on major radio shows. At age nine she appeared on the Milton Berle radio program and toured with him. She did some dramatic work on radio, had an understudy role on Broadway, appeared in concerts and on radio with Frank Sinatra until 1950, when she had her big hit, which boosted her career for several more important bookings. By the late fifties, however, her fame had faded.

Count Basie
b. 1904, Red Bank, New Jersey
d. 1984, Hollywood, Florida

Count Basie (real name: William Basie) was one of the most famous bandleaders. As pianist and leader he had one of the most popular bands from the thirties into the seventies.

Basie began playing piano in New York in the early twenties and toured for several years in the vaudeville circuits. He played with Bennie Moten's band from 1929 until Moten's death in 1935. Basie began to form his own band in 1936, but it did not achieve popularity until 1938 at New York's Savoy Ballroom.

Basie's theme song, "One O'Clock Jump," was one of the best-liked big band themes.

Les Baxter
b. 1922, Mexia, Texas

Les Baxter started his musical career as a teenage concert pianist. Later he was a member of the vocal group Mel Tormé and the Mel Tones. After that stint he began concentrating on arranging and conducting. In the late forties he was musical director for Bob Hope's and Abbott and Costello's radio shows. In the fifties he was a producer and recording artist for Capitol Records.

His biggest record hits include the 1955 million-selling "Unchained Melody" and 1956's "Poor People of Paris." His orchestra and chorus backed Nat "King" Cole on the million-selling "Mona Lisa" (1950) and "Too Young" (1951). He also had important recordings of "The High and the Mighty" (1954), "Quiet Village" (1959), and "I'll Never Stop Loving You" (1955).

Phil Baxter
b. 1896, Navarro County, Texas
d. 1972, Dallas, Texas

Phil Baxter is primarily remembered as the composer of the novelty hits "Piccolo Pete" (1929) and "I'm a Ding Dong Daddy from Dumas" (1930). Otherwise, his musical activity was limited to leading bands that were more regional than national. After the thirties he stopped being active in music.

Nora Bayes
b. 1880, Joliet, Illinois
d. 1928, Brooklyn, New York

Nora Bayes (real name: Dora Goldberg) was called Queen of the Two-a-Days because of her fame on the vaudeville circuit. She also starred in several Broadway musicals from the early 1900s into the early 1920s. She and her second husband, Jack Norworth, wrote the 1908 popular classic "Shine On, Harvest Moon."

Most of her popularity was in an era not covered by this book, but she helped popularize several hits in the first few years of the twenties—notably "I'll Be with You in Apple Blossom Time" and "Japanese Sandman" (1920).

Tex Beneke
b. 1914, Fort Worth, Texas

Tex Beneke was the featured tenor sax soloist and occasional singer with the Glenn Miller band who assumed leadership after Miller's death. Billed as the Glenn Miller Band with Tex Beneke, they have perpetuated the Miller sound for several years.

Beneke's most famous recordings include 1941's "Chattanooga Choo Choo" and 1942's "I've Got a Gal in Kalamazoo," both million-selling discs, on which he was a featured vocalist with Marion Hutton and the Modernaires.

Bennie Benjamin
b. 1907, Christiansted, St. Croix, Virgin Islands

Bennie Benjamin and his chief collaborator, George Weiss, contributed several song hits to the forties and fifties. Their biggest successes include 1941's "I Don't Want to Set the World on Fire," 1942's "When the Lights Go on Again," 1946's "Oh, What It Seemed to Be," 1952's "Wheel of Fortune," 1954's "Cross over the Bridge," and 1955's "How Important Can It Be?"

Tony Bennett
b. 1926, Queens, New York

Singer Tony Bennett (real name: Anthony Dominick Benedetto) was most popular in the fifties, when he had five gold records: 1951's "Because of You" and "Cold, Cold Heart"; 1953's "Rags to Riches" and "Stranger in Paradise"; and 1957's "In the Middle of an Island." His biggest hit came in 1962 with "I Left My Heart in San Francisco."

A church minstrel show gave him his first public appearance at age seven, but he did not begin to make an impact until he appeared on an *Arthur Godfrey's Talent Scouts* show. That led to a television contract that helped Bennett become nationally famous. His first successful recording effort was a revival of "Boulevard of Broken Dreams."

Irving Berlin
b. 1888, Temun, Russia

Irving Berlin, (real name: Israel Baline) is one of the greatest writers of popular songs in the history of the industry. Some say, "Irving Berlin *is* American pop-

ular music!" His career stretches from just after the turn of the century into the sixties. He was elected to the Songwriters' Hall of Fame.

Baline came to the United States as a youngster when his family settled in New York. He left home as a teenager to earn a living playing and singing in saloons. Part of his early music career was spent as a song plugger. He changed his name to Irving Berlin and began his composing career shortly before 1910. His first big hit, "Alexander's Ragtime Band," came in 1911. Early in his composing career he collaborated with other writers, notably Ted Snyder, but later he wrote both music and lyrics.

Berlin's hit list is extensive, but the most famous early ones include 1914's "Play a Simple Melody" (a million-selling top ten hit for Bing and Gary Crosby in 1950), 1918's "Oh, How I Hate to Get Up in the Morning," and 1919's "A Pretty Girl Is Like a Melody" and "Mandy."

Berlin continued his string of hits in the twenties with 1921's "Say It with Music"; 1922's "Lady of the Evening" and "Crinoline Days"; 1924's "All Alone" and "What'll I Do?"; 1925's "Always" and "Remember"; 1927's "Blue Skies" and "The Song Is Ended"; and 1928's "Marie" (a million seller for Tommy Dorsey in 1937 and for the Four Tunes in 1954).

Some of Berlin's most popular hits of the thirties include 1930's "Puttin' on the Ritz"; 1932's "Soft Lights and Sweet Music," "Let's Have Another Cup o' Coffee," "Say It Isn't So," and "How Deep Is the Ocean?"; 1933's "Easter Parade" (a million seller for Harry James in 1942 and for Guy Lombardo in 1947) and "Heat Wave"; 1935's "Cheek to Cheek" and "Top Hat, White Tie and Tails"; 1936's "I'm Putting All My Eggs in One Basket" and "Let's Face the Music and Dance"; 1937's "I've Got My Love to Keep Me Warm"; and 1939's "God Bless America."

His hits in the forties include 1942's "This Is the Army, Mr. Jones," "I Left My Heart at the Stage Door Canteen," and "White Christmas" (a million seller for Bing Crosby and Freddy Martin in 1942 and for Frank Sinatra in 1944); 1946's "They Say It's Wonderful," "There's No Business Like Show Business," "Doin' What Comes Natur'lly," and several others from *Annie Get Your Gun;* 1948's "Steppin' Out with My Baby" and "A Couple of Swells"; and 1949's "Let's Take an Old-Fashioned Walk" and "Give Me Your Tired, Your Poor."

Berlin's last hits were 1954's "Count Your Blessings Instead of Sheep" and "Sisters." His "Puttin' on the Ritz" was revived in 1983 by Taco. His final important composing venture was the Broadway musical *Mr. President* in 1962.

In 1984 he was still living with his wife, Ellin, whom he married in 1926.

Berlin's personal favorites among his hits are "Easter Parade," "Always," "God Bless America," "There's No Business Like Show Business," and "White Christmas."

When ASCAP selected its "All-Time Hit Parade" on the organization's fiftieth anniversary in 1963, Berlin was honored by having "Alexander's Ragtime Band," "God Bless America," and "White Christmas" included in the list of only sixteen songs.

Ben Bernie
b. 1891, New York, New York
d. 1943, Beverly Hills, California

Ben Bernie (real name: Benjamin Anzelwitz) was a popular bandleader in the late twenties and thirties. He was known as the Ol' Maestro. He was also the co-composer of 1925's "Sweet Georgia Brown" and 1931's "Who's Your Little Whoozis?" His band appeared in the movies *Shoot the Works* (1934) and *Stolen Harmony* (1935).

Important recordings include "Au Revoir," "Pleasant Dreams," "Lazybones," and "Sweet Georgia Brown."

Vivian Blaine
b. 1921, Newark, New Jersey

Vivian Blaine (real name: Vivienne Stapleton) is best known for her role as Miss Adelaide in the Broadway and Hollywood versions of *Guys and Dolls*. She also appeared on Broadway in 1958's *Say, Darling* and in 1971's *Company*.

Eubie Blake
b. 1883, Baltimore, Maryland
d. 1983, New York, New York

Eubie Blake (real name: James Hubert Blake) was active in the popular music field for more than seventy years, beginning as a teenager playing the piano wherever he could find work and continuing well into the seventies, when he was still performing at age ninety. The Broadway show *Eubie* was a tribute to him.

Blake's first successful popular song, "Charleston Rag," came in 1899. In 1915 he joined with Noble Sissle for a vaudeville act, and they wrote songs for their performances. In 1921 they brought a show, *Shuffle Along,* to Broadway, with its hit song "I'm Just

Wild About Harry." It was the first show written, directed, performed, and produced by blacks and introduced the sound of the blues and jazz to Broadway audiences.

Blake died in 1983, five days after celebrating his hundredth birthday.

Ralph Blane
b. 1914, Broken Arrow, Oklahoma

Ralph Blane is a lyricist who primarily collaborated with composer Hugh Martin. His best-known lyrics are 1941's "Buckle Down, Winsocki" and 1944's "The Trolley Song" and "Have Yourself a Merry Little Christmas."

Ray Bolger
b. 1904, Dorchester, Massachusetts

Ray Bolger is so closely identified with his role as the rubbery-legged scarecrow in the 1939 film *The Wizard of Oz* that it may have hindered his career. He is primarily known as a dancer who specialized in comic routines, but he occasionally sang and introduced a number of hits.

His first supporting role on Broadway came in 1929, and his first starring role in 1934. *On Your Toes* in 1936 was his second leading role, but the first that introduced a hit, "There's a Small Hotel." His most notable Broadway performance was in 1948 in *Where's Charley?,* which introduced "Once in Love with Amy."

Pat Boone
b. 1934, Jacksonville, Florida

Pat Boone (real name: Charles Eugene Boone) was a very popular singer during the early rock years, probably the biggest singing star next to Elvis Presley.

Boone won the *Original Amateur Hour* and *Arthur Godfrey's Talent Scout* show and signed with Dot Records before he finished college. He married Shirley Foley, the daughter of famous country and western legend Red Foley. Boone appeared in several films and had his own television show. His daughter Debbie has also become a popular singer; she had fantastic success with "You Light Up My Life" in 1977.

Most of Boone's success came in a period not covered by this book, after 1955. Some of his biggest hits include 1955's "Ain't That a Shame!"; 1956's "I'll Be Home," "I Almost Lost My Mind," "Friendly Persuasion," and "Remember You're Mine"; 1957's "Love Letters in the Sand," "Don't Forbid Me," "Why, Baby, Why," and "April Love"; 1961's

"Moody River"; and the 1962 comedy number "Speedy Gonzales." Most of his energies in recent years have been put into religious recordings.

Boone was the clean-cut alternative to Presley. Even though he performed soft rock or rhythm and blues songs, parents did not object to Boone as much as they did to the blatant sexuality and greasy-haired black-leather-jacket image that Presley presented. During the early years of his popularity, Boone was still attending school, earning his master's degree in English. This ambitious, married, educated young man was much less a threat to the values of the older generation than most of the other early rock personalities.

Irene Bordoni
b. 1895, Corsica
d. 1953, New York, New York

Irene Bordoni was a charming French singer and actress who made her debut in Paris in 1907. Her first appearance in the United States was in 1912's *Broadway to Paris.* Her most famous Broadway appearance was in 1928's *Paris,* in which she introduced "Let's Do It."

Boswell Sisters
Connee, b. circa 1912, New Orleans, Louisiana
d. 1976, New York, New York
Martha, b. 1905, New Orleans, Louisiana
d. 1958, Peekskill, New York
Vet, b. New Orleans, Louisiana

The Boswell Sisters were a very popular trio in the early to mid-thirites. These New Orleans natives began to make records in 1931, and that led to appearances in several movie musicals, including *The Big Broadcast of 1932* and 1934's *Moulin Rouge* and *Transatlantic Merry-Go-Round.* The sisters disbanded the act in late 1935, but Connee continued as a single even though she performed from a wheelchair as the result of a handicap.

The Boswell Sisters' most famous contribution to popular music was their recording with Bing Crosby of "Life Is Just a Bowl of Cherries," along with other hits from *George White's Scandals of 1931,* one of the earliest efforts to reproduce the most important songs from the score of a Broadway musical on record.

Teresa Brewer
b. 1931, Toledo, Ohio

Teresa Brewer was an important singing star in the fifties. Her start came at the early age of five, when she appeared on the *Major Bowes Amateur Hour* on radio. She spent the next several years touring with the *Amateur Hour* troupe. Then, at age twelve, she joined the *Pick and Pat* radio show. At sixteen she won several radio talent shows, and her singing career moved into high gear when she had a big hit in 1950 with "Music, Music, Music." By 1956 she had accumulated six million sellers, including her 1950 hit and 1952's "Till I Waltz Again with You," 1953's "Ricochet," 1955's "I Gotta Go Get My Baby," and "Let Me Go, Lover!" and "A Tear Fell." By the sixties her career had begun to wane, but she continued to perform. A revival of interest in the music of the fifties caused her to make a comeback in the early seventies.

Fanny Brice
b. 1891, New York, New York
d. 1951, Los Angeles, California

Fanny Brice (real name: Fannie Borach) was a star comedienne of several *Ziegfeld Follies* and was immortalized in the 1964 Broadway musical *Funny Girl,* which was based on her life.

Brice was best known for her comic renditions of novelty and dialect songs, but occasionally she performed serious songs. Her two most famous numbers show both styles: "My Man," which she introduced to America in the 1921 *Follies,* is a serious song, while "Second Hand Rose," which she performed in the same revue, is more comic.

Later in her career she portrayed Baby Snooks on a popular radio program.

Phil Brito
b. 1915, Boomer, West Virginia

Phil Brito (real name: Philip Colombrito) is best remembered for his performance of "Five Minutes More" in 1946's movie musical *The Sweetheart of Sigma Chi.* He had been vocalist with the Al Donahue band from 1939 to 1942 and performed on several radio shows in the mid-forties. He remained active into the sixties but never had major successes.

Elton Britt
b. 1912, Marshall, Arkansas
d. 1972, Pennsylvania

Elton Britt was particularly known for his hit recording of the World War II song "There's a Star-Spangled Banner Waving Somewhere" (1942). Britt was a popular country singer who began his career at age fifteen, when he was discovered by talent scouts. He worked in California and New York on several radio shows until his 1942 hit. He recorded for more than twenty years for Victor but never experienced another large success. In the fifties and sixties he often appeared on the Grand Ole Opry in Nashville. He later raised cattle in Maryland and only occasionally worked in the music field.

Les Brown
b. 1912, Reinerton, Pennsylvania

Les Brown had one of the most popular bands, the Band of Renown, from the mid-thirties through the seventies. He and his band were one of only a few that survived the decline of the big bands in the mid-forties.

Brown and his band, with Doris Day singing, had an all-time hit with "Sentimental Journey," the biggest hit of 1945. The band's second million seller was a revival of Irving Berlin's 1937 song "I've Got My Love to Keep Me Warm" in 1949. In 1952 the band teamed with the Ames Brothers for another million seller with "Undecided."

Brown was the conductor on the Bob Hope radio and television shows from 1947 through 1962.

Lew Brown
b. 1893, Odessa, Russia
d. 1958, New York, New York

Lyricist Lew Brown (real name: Louis Brownstein) is most famous as one of the partners of Henderson, De Sylva, and Brown, who wrote several popular hits. His first hit came in 1912, when he wrote the lyrics to a song by Albert Von Tilzer. Brown teamed with Ray Henderson to write 1922's "Georgette." They joined Buddy De Sylva in 1925. The partnership lasted until the early thirties. After De Sylva left, Brown and Henderson continued their collaborations. (See also Henderson, page 203).

Nacio Herb Brown
b. 1896, Deming, New Mexico
d. 1964, San Francisco, California

Nacio Herb Brown, a Songwriters' Hall of Fame member, was an important composer of music for the movies from the early days of recorded sound through the early fifties.

After attending UCLA, he became a tailor and made a fortune in Beverly Hills real estate. He began to try his hand at composing in the early twenties, but success was scarce until 1929, when he became a top composer for early movie musicals.

His most famous songs include 1929's "Broadway

Melody," "You Were Meant for Me," "The Wedding of the Painted Doll," "Singin' in the Rain," and "Pagan Love Song"; 1932's "Eadie Was a Lady" and "You're an Old Smoothie"; 1933's "Temptation"; 1934's "All I Do Is Dream of You"; 1935's "You Are My Lucky Star"; 1941's "You Stepped Out of a Dream"; 1948's "Love Is Where You Find It"; and 1952's "Make 'Em Laugh."

Yul Brynner
b. 1915, Sakhalin, Russia

Yul Brynner (real name: Youl Bryner) is most famous as the bald king in 1951's *The King and I*.

Jack Buchanan
b. 1891, Helensburgh, Scotland
d. 1957, London, England

British dancing and singing star Jack Buchanan is remembered in America for two 1930 movie musical appearances, *Monte Carlo* and *Paris*, and for 1953's *The Band Wagon*. He performed 1929's "I Guess I'll Have to Change My Plans" in *The Band Wagon* in a memorable number with Fred Astaire.

He first appeared in the United States in *Charlot's Revue of 1924*. Then followed appearances in 1930's *Wake Up and Dream* and 1938's *Between the Devil*.

Buchanan introduced "A Cup of Coffee, a Sandwich and You" in *Charlot's Revue of 1926*.

Walter Bullock
b. 1907, Shelburn, Indiana
d. 1953, Los Angeles, California

Lyricist Walter Bullock contributed several songs to Hollywood movie musicals from the mid-thirties through the late forties. His most famous lyric was 1936's "When Did You Leave Heaven?" from the movie *Sing, Baby, Sing*.

Johnny Burke
b. 1908, Antioch, California
d. 1964, New York, New York

Johnny Burke was a prolific lyricist who wrote many songs for Hollywood films. He primarily collaborated with James V. Monaco and James Van Heusen on several songs for Bing Crosby films. His lyrics seemed to fit Crosby's easygoing style.

His most famous lyrics include 1936's "Pennies from Heaven"; 1939's "Scatterbrain" and "What's New?"; 1940's "Polka Dots and Moon Beams" and "Imagination"; 1942's "Moonlight Becomes You"; 1943's

"Sunday, Monday, or Always''; 1944's "Swinging on a Star'' and "It Could Happen to You''; 1947's "But Beautiful''; and 1955's "Misty.''

Joseph A. Burke
b. 1884, Philadelphia, Pennsylvania
d. 1950, Upper Darby, Pennsylvania

Joe Burke was an important composer from the late twenties through the forties. His biggest hits were 1929's "Tip Toe Through the Tulips,'' "Painting the Clouds with Sunshine'' and "Carolina Moon''; 1930's "Dancing with Tears in My Eyes''; 1935's "Moon over Miami''; and 1937's "It Looks Like Rain in Cherry Blossom Lane.'' Burke is a Songwriters' Hall of Fame member.

Henry Busse
b. 1894, Magdeburg, Germany
d. 1955, Memphis, Tennessee

Trumpeter Henry Busse is particularly remembered for his theme song, "Hot Lips,'' a showcase tune for trumpet. He played with Paul Whiteman and later with his own band. He was co-composer of "Hot Lips'' and 1921's "The Wang, Wang Blues.''

Busse's soft, muted trumpet styling was his trademark.

C

Irving Caesar
b. 1895, New York, New York

Irving Caesar, a Songwriters' Hall of Fame member, is a composer, author, and publisher who wrote several songs that were popular during the twenties. He was the lyricist for the 1924 Broadway musical *No, No, Nanette.*

His most famous contributions to popular music were 1919's "Swanee''; 1924's "Tea for Two'' and "I Want to Be Happy''; 1927's "Sometimes I'm Happy''; and 1936's "Is It True What They Say About Dixie?''

Sammy Cahn
b. 1913, New York, New York

Sammy Cahn, a Songwriters' Hall of Fame member, is a famous lyricist of popular songs. His chief collaborators were composers Jule Styne and James Van Heusen. Most of their hits came from films.

Cahn's most remembered song lyrics between the mid-thirties and the end of the forties include 1937's "Bei Mir Bist Du Shoen''; 1942's "I've Heard That Song Before''; 1944's "I'll Walk Alone,'' "I Should Care,'' and "Saturday Night Is the Loneliest Night of the Week''; 1945's "It's Been a Long, Long Time,'' "Day by Day,'' and "Let It Snow, Let It Snow, Let It Snow''; 1946's "The Things We Did Last Summer'' and "Five Minutes More''; and 1948's "It's Magic.''

The most famous Cahn lyrics from the fifties through the mid-sixties were 1951's "Be My Love''; 1952's "Because You're Mine''; 1954's Academy Award winner, "Three Coins in a Fountain,'' and "Teach Me Tonight''; 1955's "Love and Marriage'' and "I'll Never Stop Loving You''; 1957's Academy Award winner, "All the Way''; 1959's Academy Award winner, "High Hopes''; 1961's "The Second Time Around''; 1963's Academy Award winner, "Call Me Irresponsible''; and 1964's "My Kind of Town.''

Anne Caldwell
b. 1867, Boston, Massachusetts
d. 1936, Hollywood, California

Lyricist Anne Caldwell (full name: Anne Caldwell O'Dea) wrote songs for several Broadway musicals from 1907 through 1928. Most of her songs were so tied to the context of the show that they attained very little popularity. Only 1921's "Ka-lu-a'' achieved national attention. She was elected to the Songwriters' Hall of Fame.

Cab Calloway
b. 1907, Rochester, New York

Cab Calloway achieved phenomenal success in the mid-thirties as the King of Hi-de-ho for his rendition of the song "Minnie the Moocher.'' But as popular as "Minnie the Moocher'' was, Calloway's recording did not sell a million copies. Calloway achieved his only gold record for his 1939 version of "Jumpin' Jive,'' a dance disc that was particularly popular during World War II. He received an award for his work in the 1943 film *Stormy Weather,* was outstanding in the role of Sportin' Life in George Gershwin's *Porgy and Bess* in the early fifties, and appeared in the 1980 movie *The Blues Brothers,* in which he performed "Minnie the Moocher.''

Eddie Calvert
b. 1922, Preston, England

Calvert's only million-selling disc was the instrumental version of "Oh! My Pa-pa'' in 1953. This British trumpet player zoomed into popularity with this recording and faded almost as quickly.

James Campbell

James Campbell combined with fellow Briton Reginald Connelly to write some popular songs that gained substantial popularity in the United States. Campbell and Connelly usually collaborated with another composer. Their most famous hits include 1931's "Goodnight, Sweetheart" and 1933's "Try a Little Tenderness."

Eddie Cantor
b. 1892, New York, New York
d. 1964, Hollywood, California

Eddie Cantor (real name: Eddie Israel Iskowitz) was a world-famous entertainer. He began his show business career as a child when he appeared in Gus Edwards's vaudeville act, which featured young performers. Cantor made the leap to stardom in 1916, when he was first signed by Florenz Ziegfeld. He appeared in the 1917 edition of the *Ziegfeld Follies* and became a full-fledged Ziegfeld star. He appeared in the next several editions of the *Follies*. He also performed in *The Midnight Rounders of 1921* and 1922's *Make It Snappy*. He was a featured performer in the 1924 musical *Kid Boots* and the 1928 musical *Whoopee*.

Cantor began his movie career in the Depression years and made several popular films during the thirties and forties. He also did considerable radio and television work until the early fifties, when a heart attack caused him to retire.

Cantor is famous for his stage demeanor: His "banjo eyes" practically popping out of their sockets through large white horn-rimmed spectacles (with no glass), he clapped his hands as he jumped like a kangaroo around the stage.

He is associated with several songs because he either introduced them or helped popularize them with his extroverted performances: 1920's "Margie," 1925's "If You Knew Susie," 1922's "Oh! Gee, Oh! Gosh, Oh! Golly, I'm in Love," 1928's "Makin' Whoopee!" 1919's "Mandy," 1925's "Yes Sir, That's My Baby," 1917's "They Go Wild, Simply Wild over Me" (written in 1903), "Ida," and 1919's "You'd Be Surprised."

Frankie Carle
b. 1903, Providence, Rhode Island

Frankie Carle (real name: Francis Nunzio Carlone) is a well-known pianist, composer, and bandleader. He was leading his own band by the late thirties, then joined Horace Heidt and remained with him until 1943.

He organized a big band in 1944 and was very successful for the rest of the forties and early fifties. His theme song, 1939's "Sunrise Serenade," is his best-known composition, but 1946's "Oh, What It Seemed to Be" was also extremely popular.

Kitty Carlisle
b. 1914, New Orleans, Louisiana

Kitty Carlisle (full name: Kitty Carlisle Hart) was particularly active as a singer onstage, in movies, and on radio during the thirties and forties. She costarred with Bing Crosby in two important films and with Allan Jones in another. She is primarily remembered for her television work, especially as a panelist on *To Tell the Truth*, in the fifties and later.

Her recording output was slim. She recorded 1944's "I'll Remember April," 1928's "I'll Get By," 1934's "The Very Thought of You," and 1944's "Sweet Dreams, Sweetheart."

She introduced "Alone" with Allan Jones in the 1935 Marx Brothers' film *A Night at the Opera*.

She was married to playwright Moss Hart, who also wrote the book and lyrics for three Broadway musicals.

Hoagy Carmichael
b. 1899, Bloomington, Indiana
d. 1981, Rancho Mirage, California

Hoagy Carmichael, the "lazy man's songwriter," was a composer, an author, and an entertainer. He collaborated with some major lyricists, including Mitchell Parish, Johnny Mercer, Paul Francis Webster, Ned Washington, and Irving Mills, to name just a few.

Carmichael's most famous popular songs include 1929's "Star Dust"; 1930's "Rockin' Chair" and "Georgia on My Mind"; 1931's "Lazy River"; 1933's "Lazybones"; 1938's "Small Fry," "Two Sleepy People," and "Heart and Soul"; 1939's "I Get Along Without You Very Well"; 1940's "The Nearness of You"; 1946's "Ole Buttermilk Sky"; and the 1951 Academy Award winner, "In the Cool, Cool, Cool of the Evening." Carmichael is a member of the Songwriters' Hall of Fame.

Tullio Carminati
b. 1894, Zara, Dalmatia
d. 1971

Carminati was primarily famous for his success as a singer-actor in the Broadway musical *Music in the Air*, in which he introduced "The Song Is You." He also performed in the movie musicals *Moulin Rouge* and

One Night of Love in 1934 and in 1935's *Paris in Spring.*

Leslie Caron
b. 1931, Paris, France

Dancer and actress Leslie Caron is not known as a singer, yet she had a million-selling recording with Mel Ferrer of "Hi-Lili, Hi-Lo" from the 1953 film *Lili.* She is well known for her role in the film classic *An American in Paris* with Gene Kelly, but her biggest success was in *Gigi,* the 1958 film that garnered ten Academy Awards.

Carleton Carpenter
b. 1926, Bennington, Vermont

Actor, pianist, songwriter, dramatic coach, and soft-shoe virtuoso, Carleton Carpenter began his career with a magic act. At fourteen he toured with a carnival. He then quit school and landed a job in the chorus of *The Chocolate Soldier,* but later returned to school. In 1944 he landed the second comedy lead in *Bright Boy* in New York. After a stint in the Seabees he worked radio, TV, and Broadway. He signed with MGM and played opposite Debbie Reynolds in *Two Weeks with Love,* in which they performed "The Aba Daba Honeymoon." A single cut from the film's sound track became a million seller, Carpenter's only claim to recording history fame.

Earl Carroll
b. 1893, Pittsburgh, Pennsylvania
d. 1948, Mount Carmel, Pennsylvania

Earl Carroll produced and directed numerous revues on Broadway, notably *Earl Carroll's Vanities* of 1923, 1924, and 1925. In the late thirties he became a movie producer.

Harry Carroll
b. 1892, Atlantic City, New Jersey
d. 1962, Mount Carmel, Pennsylvania

Composer Harry Carroll composed several songs for various Broadway shows and a few that were not connected to shows. His most famous compositions are 1913's "The Trail of the Lonesome Pine," 1914's "By the Beautiful Sea," and the classic of 1918, "I'm Always Chasing Rainbows," which was revived by Perry Como in 1946. Carroll is a Songwriters' Hall of Fame member.

Jack Carson
b. 1910, Carmen, Manitoba, Canada
d. 1963, Encino, California

Jack Carson is primarily remembered for his roles in several movie musicals in the late forties. He introduced "A Gal in Calico" in 1946's *The Time, the Place and the Girl.* He often played the part of a wisecracker, and he usually costarred in the movie musicals with Dennis Morgan. In later years he acted in 1954's *A Star is Born* and 1958's *Cat on a Hot Tin Roof.*

Carmen Cavallaro
b. 1913, New York, New York

Pianist Carmen Cavallaro formed his own orchestra in 1939 and featured a sweet sound with numerous piano solos. His biggest hit came in 1945 with a rhythmic version of Frédéric Chopin's Polonaise in A. He also gained a great deal of attention with the piano recordings for the 1956 movie *The Eddy Duchin Story.*

Frank Chacksfield
b. 1914, Battle, England

Frank Chacksfield is a British arranger and orchestra leader who had two million-selling recordings in 1953: "Ebb Tide" and "*Limelight* Theme" from the film *Limelight.*

Carol Channing
b. 1921, Seattle, Washington

Carol Channing, the wide-eyed, gravel-voiced actress, became a Broadway star in 1949's *Gentlemen Prefer Blondes.* She introduced "Diamonds Are a Girl's Best Friend." Her biggest triumph came in 1964's *Hello, Dolly!,* in which she starred as Dolly Gallagher Levi.

Saul Chaplin
b. 1912, Brooklyn, New York

Composer Saul Chaplin is primarily remembered for three songs: 1936's "Until the Real Thing Comes Along," 1937's "Bei Mir Bist du Schoen," and 1947's "Anniversary Song." His chief collaborator was Sammy Cahn.

In addition to his composing career, he scored numerous Hollywood films, including 1946's *The Jolson Story,* 1949's *On the Town,* 1951's *An American in Paris,* 1953's *Kiss Me Kate,* 1954's *Seven Brides for Seven Brothers,* 1956's *High Society* and *The Teahouse of the August Moon,* and 1961's *West Side Story.*

Maurice Chevalier
b. 1888, Paris, France
d. 1972, Paris, France

Maurice Chevalier, the French entertainer, made his debut in the United States in the last midnight revue produced by Ziegfeld on the roof of the New Amsterdam Theater in 1929. His first American film role was in *Innocents of Paris,* in which he introduced "Louise." His jaunty air, French charm, and sex appeal immediately made him a star in the United States. In addition to "Louise," he is strongly associated with 1932's "Mimi."

His popularity declined from the mid-thirties until he starred in the 1958 movie musical *Gigi.* In the following ten years he was very busy with a dozen films and frequent television appearances.

The Chordettes
Jimmy Lochard
Carol Bushman
Nancy Overton
Lynn Evans

The Chordettes first gained attention when they won an *Arthur Godfrey's Talent Scout* show. They continued with Godfrey for four years. Then, in 1954, they hit the big time with a million-selling recording of "Mister Sandman." They had similar success with "Lollipop" in 1958 and then faded from the national spotlight.

Frank Churchill
b. 1901, Rumford, Maine
d. 1942, Castaic, California

Composer Frank Churchill was active during the thirties and early forties. His most famous song is 1933's "Who's Afraid of the Big Bad Wolf?" and the score from the 1938 feature-length cartoon *Snow White and the Seven Dwarfs.* He also wrote the scores for 1941's *Dumbo* and 1942's *Bambi.* His chief lyricists were Ann Ronell, Larry Morey, and Ned Washington.

Buddy Clark
b. 1912, Dorchester, Massachusetts
d. 1949, Los Angeles, California

Vocalist Buddy Clark (real name: Samuel Goldberg) was an important radio personality in the thirties and forties. He appeared on *Your Hit Parade* from 1936 to 1938. He was the vocalist for Benny Goodman on two recordings and on Goodman's *Let's Dance* radio show. Even though Clark performed on radio often and

on numerous recordings, often without label credit, he was not very well known until the forties.

His biggest hits came with 1947's "Linda" and in a duet with Doris Day on "Confess" and "Love Somebody." He also had good success with a duet with Dinah Shore of 1949's Academy Award winner, "Baby, It's Cold Outside."

Larry Clinton
b. 1909, Brooklyn, New York

Larry Clinton was an outstanding bandleader, arranger, and composer of the thirties and forties. He was particularly noted for adapting classics to popular music. Clinton arranged for many of the best big bands,—namely, Isham Jones, Glen Gray, and Tommy and Jimmy Dorsey. Several of his compositions reached *Your Hit Parade,* including 1937's "Dipsy Doodle," 1938's "My Reverie," and 1939's "Our Love" and "Moon Love." His orchestra helped make a hit of "Deep Purple" in 1939. His career began to wane after 1941, and although he tried a comeback in the late forties, he never regained his former popularity.

Rosemary Clooney
b. 1928, Maysville, Kentucky

Rosemary Clooney began her career as half of the Clooney Sisters' singing act with Tony Pastor's band in 1946. In 1949 she got her solo break when Mitch Miller helped her toward a career in records, television, nightclubs, and films. She became particularly known for her roles in the films *Here Come the Girls,* with Bob Hope, and *White Christmas,* with Bing Crosby.

Her first recording success was 1951's "Come on-a My House," which became her first million seller. In 1952 she had three million sellers with "Tenderly," "Botch-a-me," and "Half as Much." She had her biggest hit in 1954, when she recorded the Broadway show excerpt "Hey There," backed by "This Ole House"; the disc became the year's biggest seller. In addition, she had a million seller with "Mambo Italiano," her seventh gold record.

Nat "King" Cole
b. 1919, Montgomery, Alabama
d. 1965, Santa Monica, California

Nat ("King") Cole, the son of an ordained minister, was born in Montgomery, Alabama, but attended school and received his music training in Chicago. His first professional job was in the tour band for the revue *Shuffle Along* in 1936. Otherwise, he worked primarily as a nightclub pianist. Cole's singing career started by accident. On a particular evening an over-enthusiastic patron insisted that he sing "Sweet Lorraine." After he had complied, his relaxed style of singing became a major asset. For a while he performed in what was billed as the Nat Cole Trio, and he added the "King" to his name in 1940. The trio signed with Capitol Records in 1943, and Cole began to emerge as a solo attraction. In 1958 he starred in the film *St. Louis Blues* as the famous composer W. C. Handy.

Cole's first million-selling recording came with "Nature Boy" in 1948. Also in 1948, the trio had a gold record with "Little Girl." One of Cole's biggest hits came in 1950 with the million-selling version of "Mona Lisa." Next came "Too Young" (1951), "Answer Me, My Love" (1954), "A Blossom Fell" (1955), and the album and single of "Ramblin' Rose" (1962).

Russ Columbo
b. 1908, Philadelphia, Pennsylvania
d. 1934, Hollywood, California

Russ Columbo was a strong competitor of Bing Crosby and Rudy Vallee. The crooning of Crosby and Columbo was so similar that it was difficult to identify which one was singing. Columbo might have become a huge star, but a fatal accident cut his career short in 1934. A friend used a set of ancient dueling pistols as paperweights. Believing them to be unloaded, the friend struck a match against one pistol to light a cigarette. The gun fired, and the bullet ricocheted off a desk and struck Columbo in the head.

Columbo appeared in three films and had a hand in writing several songs he featured in his brief but spectacular career (1931–34). His best-known recording was "Prisoner of Love" (1931). He was also famous for his theme song, "You Call It Madness" (1931), and he recorded many of the most popular songs of the early thirties, including "Time on My Hands" (1930) and "Goodnight, Sweetheart," "All of Me," "You're My Everything," "Paradise," and "Sweet and Lovely" (1931).

Perry Como
b. 1913, Canonsburg, Pennsylvania

Perry Como (real name: Pierino Como) was one of the most dominant performers in the recording field from the mid-forties through the fifties. His amazingly popular career extended into the seventies, but his prime popularity came from the end of the big band era into the early years of rock.

Como was an established barber in his hometown before he successfully auditioned for Freddie Carlone's band and traveled with it for several years. He signed a recording contract in 1943 and had his first million-selling disc with "Till the End of Time" in 1945. His collective disc sales by the end of the sixties were estimated at more than 50 million.

The million-selling recordings of "Mr. C" include 1945's "Till the End of Time," "If I Loved You," backed by "I'm Gonna Love That Girl," "A Hubba Hubba Hubba (Dig You Later)," and "Temptation"; 1946's revivals of 1931's "Prisoner of Love" and 1918's "I'm Always Chasing Rainbows"; 1947's revival of 1898's "When You Were Sweet Sixteen"; 1948's revival of 1902's "Because"; 1951's "If"; 1952's cover version of the country song "Don't Let the Stars Get in Your Eyes"; 1954's "Papa Loves Mambo" and "Wanted"; 1956's "Hot Diggity" and "More," backed by "Glendora"; 1957's "Round and Round," backed by "Mi Casa Su Casa"; 1958's "Catch a Falling Star," backed by "Magic Moments," "Kewpie Doll," and "I May Never Pass This Way Again"; 1960's "Delaware"; 1970's "It's Impossible"; and the 1975 album *Perry Como's 40 Greatest Hits*.

Zez Confrey
b. 1895, Peru, Illinois
d. 1971, Lakewood, New Jersey

Pianist, bandleader, composer Zez Confrey (real name: Edward Elzear Confrey) wrote several solo piano pieces that became very popular in the twenties. His best-known works include "Kitten on the Keys," "Dizzy Fingers," and "Stumbling." He was pianist for many piano rolls for player pianos.

Reginald Connelly
See James Campbell, page 178.

Con Conrad
b. 1891, New York, New York
d. 1938, Van Nuys, California

Con Conrad (real name: Conrad K. Dober) was a composer, pianist, and publisher who wrote several popular songs from the twenties through the thirties. His chief lyricist collaborators were Buddy De Sylva, Vincent Rose, Leo Robin, Joe Young, and Herb Magidson. Conrad was elected to the Songwriters' Hall of Fame.

Conrad's most famous compositions include 1920's

"Margie" and "Lena from Palesteena," 1921's "Ma—He's Making Eyes at Me," 1923's "Barney Google" and "You've Got to See Mama Ev'ry Night or You Can't See Mamma at All," 1931's "Prisoner of Love" and "You Call It Madness, but I Call It Love," and 1934's "The Continental," the first Academy Award-winning song.

J. Fred Coots
b. 1897, New York, New York

J. Fred Coots is a composer who began his career as a song plugger and vaudeville performer but turned to songwriting. He collaborated with lyricists Benny Davis, Sam M. Lewis, Dorothy Fields, and Haven Gillespie. Coots is a Songwriters' Hall of Fame member.

Coots's most famous songs include 1931's "Love Letters in the Sand" (a million seller in 1957), 1934's "Santa Claus Is Coming to Town" and "For All We Know," and 1938's "You Go to My Head."

Cowboy Copas
b. 1913, Muskogee, Oklahoma
d. 1963, Camden, Tennessee

Cowboy Copas (real name: Lloyd Copas) was a famous country and western singer whose recording of "Tennessee Waltz" in 1948 became a million seller. His recording and its popularity influenced Mercury Records to chance a cover version by main-line pop songstress Patti Page in 1950.

Copas was killed in the same airplane crash that killed country music star Patsy Cline in 1963.

Don Cornell
b. 1921, New York, New York

Singer Don Cornell sang with several bands in the forties before he gained success with "It Isn't Fair" in 1950 with the Sammy Kaye orchestra. The recording became a million seller, as did 1952's "I'm Yours" and 1954's "Hold My Hand" from the movie *Susan Slept Here*.

Sam Coslow
b. 1902, New York, New York

Composer-lyricist Sam Coslow wrote several popular songs during the twenties and thirties. His best-known songs were 1930's "Sing You Sinners," 1931's "Just One More Chance," 1934's "Cocktails for Two," and "My Old Flame."

Coslow began writing after he had graduated from high school. He also became a partner in the publishing firm Spier and Coslow. In the late twenties he began to write for Hollywood films. He became involved in producing and in publishing and retired from the music field. He was elected to the Songwriters' Hall of Fame.

Francis Craig
b. 1900, Dickson, Tennessee
d. 1966, Sewanee, Tennessee

Francis Craig was a pianist and composer who wrote and recorded the top song of 1947. He and his orchestra, with vocalist Bob Lamm, recorded "Near You," a multimillion seller. Craig's only other nationally recognized recording was "Beg Your Pardon" in 1948.

The Crew Cuts
Rudi Maugeri
Pat Barrett
Roy Perkins
Johnnie Perkins

The Crew Cuts had their only million-selling recording with "Sh-Boom" in 1954. This male quartet from Toronto, Canada, made a cover version of the Chords' original rhythm and blues version. The Crew Cuts' recording is considered one of the first rock and roll hits.

Bing Crosby
b. 1904, Tacoma, Washington
d. 1977, Madrid, Spain

Harry Lillis Crosby acquired the nickname Bing in his childhood because of his attachment to the character Bingo in the comic *The Bingville Bugle*. During his college days at Gonzaga University, he teamed with Al Rinker to form a small band. In 1924 they quit school and went to Los Angeles to see if Rinker's sister Mildred Bailey could help them get started in show business. In 1927, after several jobs on the West Coast, they were hired by Paul Whiteman, who took them to New York. There Harry Barris joined the group, forming the Rhythm Boys. After three on and off years with Whiteman, the trio got a booking at the Cocoanut Grove in Los Angeles, where Crosby began to emerge as a soloist. In 1931 he signed a contract with CBS and began his radio career, which eventually brought him a film contract.

His extraordinary fame in films, on recordings, and on radio and television continued for many years.

Crosby made more than 2,600 recordings, which had amassed a total disc sales figure by 1975 of 400 million. Twenty-one of these recordings were million-selling singles, and he had one gold album. His gold records include 1937's "Sweet Leilani"; 1940's "San Antonio Rose"; 1942's "White Christmas" and "Silent Night" backed by "Adeste Fideles"; 1943's "I'll Be Home for Christmas," "Sunday, Monday, or Always," "Pistol Packin' Mama," and "Jingle Bells"; 1944's "Swinging on a Star," "Too-ra-loo-ra-loo-ral," and "Don't Fence Me In"; 1945's "I Can't Begin to Tell You"; 1946's "McNamara's Band" and "South America, Take It Away"; 1947's album *Merry Christmas,* plus singles of "Alexander's Ragtime Band" backed by "The Spaniard That Blighted My Life" with Al Jolson, and "The Whiffenpoof Song" with Fred Waring and his Glee Club; 1948's "Now Is the Hour" and "Galway Bay"; 1949's "Dear Hearts and Gentle People"; 1950's "Play a Simple Melody," backed by "Sam's Song," with his son Gary; and 1956's "True Love" with Grace Kelly from the film *High Society.*

Bob Crosby
b. 1913, Spokane, Washington

Bing Crosby's younger brother, Bob, led a successful band in the mid-thirties. He began his career as a singer with various bands, including the Dorsey brothers.

When Ben Pollack retired in 1934, several of the bandsmen reorganized as a corporation and hired Crosby as the front man and singer. The band had a Dixieland style, which was unusual for a big band. Their theme was Gershwin's "Summertime." A combo within the band, the Bob Cats, played even more Dixieland. The Crosby orchestra was very successful until the early forties, when it disbanded.

After that Crosby worked in several movies and led military big bands during World War II. After the war he worked on radio and early television. He remained active into the sixties and early seventies.

Xavier Cugat
b. 1900, Barcelona, Spain

Xavier Cugat and his orchestra are famous for the rumba and other Spanish and Latin American dances. He organized his band in the late twenties. They gained popularity in the early thirties and continued into the late forties.

Cugat's family moved to Cuba when he was young. He came to the United States as a violinist to play in symphony orchestras.

One of his wifes, Abbe Lane, was a singer with his band in the fifties. His latest wife was Charo.

D

Vernon Dalhart
b. 1883, Jefferson, Texas
d. 1948, Bridgeport, Connecticut

Vernon Dalhart (real name: Marion Try Slaughter) chose the names of two towns hear his hometown in Texas for his professional moniker. He went to New York seeking a career in opera. However, he soon became convinced that large amounts of money could be made in hillbilly music, so he made a dramatic career change. The beginning of his hillbilly career was a recording for Edison and then for Victor of "The Wreck of the 97" coupled with "The Prisoner's Song." This became the biggest selling record for the Victor company to that date. Estimates of sales are between 6 and 7 million.

He recorded "The Prisoner's Song" for at least twenty-eight record labels under various names, with an estimated total of 25 million copies sold. It has been speculated that Dalhart recorded for every American recording company east of the Mississippi. He sold a staggering quantity of records between 1924 and 1930, under his own name and under more than seventy pseudonyms. By the beginning of the Depression, his sales had slumped, and his career began to decline. He had a comeback on the Bluebird label in 1939, but it was short-lived.

Vic Damone
b. 1928, Brooklyn, New York

Vic Damone (real name: Vito Farinola) had a distinguished career as a singer in records, radio, television, and movies. Milton Berle helped him land his first singing job at La Martinique club. He graduated to the Paramount Theater and radio appearances and, in the late forties, to his own radio program. He began his recording career in the late forties and had his first million seller with "Again" in 1949. That success led to network radio spots, more prestigious nightclub appearances, and his film debut in 1951's *Rich, Young and Pretty.* After two years of military service, Damone resumed his singing career. He did some radio work, recorded occasionally, and appeared in several films, including 1955's *Hit the Deck* and *Kismet.* His other gold record came in 1956 with "On the Street Where You Live" from *My Fair Lady.*

Bebe Daniels

b. 1901, Dallas, Texas
d. 1971, London, England

Bebe Daniels was the singing star of several movie musicals in the late twenties and early thirties. She began her movie career in the silent era but, unlike many silent movie actors, made the transition to the talkies. She is especially remembered for her appearances with Harold Lloyd in several of his films and for her starring roles in the movie musicals *Rio Rita* (1929) and *Forty-second Street* (1933). She and her husband, film executive Ben Lyon, remained active in the entertainment business into the sixties, when Bebe suffered a stroke and had to retire. She died of cancer.

Mack David

b. 1912, New York, New York

Mack David was an important lyricist from the early thirties through the sixties. In addition to lyrics for popular songs, he wrote the lyrics for the themes of several television shows, including *Caspar, the Friendly Ghost, 77 Sunset Strip, Bourbon Street Beat,* and *Hawaiian Eye.* He collaborated with several of the best composers in the business, notably Jerry Livingston, Count Basie, Burt Bacharach, Ernest Gold, Elmer Bernstein, and Henry Mancini.

His best-known song lyrics are 1939's "Moon Love," 1947's "Chi-Baba, Chi-Baba," the lyrics for the 1949 Disney feature cartoon *Cinderella,* including "A Dream Is a Wish Your Heart Makes" and "Bibbidi-Bobbidi-Boo," 1949's "I Don't Care If the Sun Don't Shine," the English lyrics for "La Vie en Rose" (1950), the lyrics for Max Steiner's "Tara's Theme" from *Gone with the Wind* (1954's "My Own True Love," the movie was made in 1939), 1954's "Cherry Pink and Apple Blossom White," 1962's "A Walk on the Wild Side," 1964's "Hush, Hush, Sweet Charlotte," 1965's "The Ballad of Cat Ballou," and 1966's "Hawaii," the theme for the movie of the same name.

Benny Davis

b. 1895, New York, New York
d. 1979, Miami, Florida

Benny Davis was a lyricist who had a significant output of songs that became hits. His most productive years were in the twenties, but he was still producing in the sixties. His best-known song lyrics include 1920's "Margie," 1921's "I'm Nobody's Baby" (revived in 1940), 1926's "Baby Face," and 1929's "Carolina

Moon." Davis is a Songwriters' Hall of Fame member.

Jimmie Davis

b. 1902, Quitman, Louisiana

Jimmie Davis was governor of Louisiana for two terms, but he was also a country and western singer, composer, lyricist, and actor in Hollywood westerns. He began his recording career in the mid-thirties, often singing his own compositions, including 1940's "You Are My Sunshine." He was governor of Louisiana from 1944 through 1948 and again from 1960 to 1964. In more recent years he has concentrated on the gospel music field.

Doris Day

b. 1924, Cincinnati, Ohio

Doris Day (real name: Doris Von Kappelhoff) was offered her first job by bandleader Barney Rapp, who suggested she change her name. She was christened Day because of her rendition of the 1932 Schwartz-Deitz song "Day After Day," which she used to audition for Rapp. She continued to be known primarily as a band singer until 1948, when she became one of the top female movie box-office attractions after she had starred in *Romance on the High Seas.* Since then she has starred in numerous films.

Her first million seller was with Les Brown and his orchestra in 1945. Their disc of "Sentimental Journey" started her on the road to stardom in the record business. In 1947, with Buddy Clark, she had a million seller with "Love Somebody," backed by "Confess." This was followed by "It's Magic," which she sang in her first film. Her next gold record came in 1951 with "A Guy Is a Guy" with the Paul Weston orchestra. She joined Frankie Laine in 1952 for a happy recording of "Sugarbush." Her sixth million seller was her recording of the 1954 Academy Award winner "Secret Love," which she introduced in the 1953 film *Calamity Jane.* Her last gold record was the 1955 Academy Award winner, "Que Será, Será," which she had introduced in Alfred Hitchcock's *The Man Who Knew Too Much.*

Edith Day

b. 1896, Mineapolis, Minnesota
d. 1971, London, England

Edith Day was a Broadway star in the early twenties. She is remembered for introducing "In My Sweet Little Alice Blue Gown" in 1919's *Irene* and "A Kiss in the Dark" in 1922's *Orange Blossoms.* In the late twenties she moved to London, where she appeared in many American musicals.

Eddie De Lange
b. 1904, Long Island City, New York
d. 1949, Los Angeles, California

Eddie De Lange was a lyricist and popular bandleader during the thirties and forties. About 1934, after several years in show business, including bit parts in several movies, De Lange began to concentrate on writing lyrics. His most famous lyrics are 1934's "Moonglow" and 1935's "Solitude."

Vaughn De Leath
b. 1896, Mount Pulaski, Illinois
d. 1943, Buffalo, New York

Vaughn De Leath had a very successful singing career during the twenties and thirties. She is sometimes given credit for devising the crooning style of singing that became successful during the thirties. She was very popular on radio during the late twenties and early thirties, appeared occasionally on Broadway and in vaudeville, and recorded frequently. She was also composer or lyricist for several songs, none of which was especially successful. She is particularly remembered for popularizing 1925's "Ukulele Lady."

Gene De Paul
b. 1919, New York, New York

Gene De Paul composed several popular songs that were hits in the forties and fifties. He also teamed with Johnny Mercer for the score and lyrics for the 1954 movie *Seven Brides for Seven Brothers* and the 1956 Broadway musical *Li'l Abner.*

De Paul's best-remembered lyrics include 1942's "I'll Remember April," 1943's "Cow Cow Boogie," and 1954's "Teach Me Tonight."

Peter De Rose
b. 1900, New York, New York
d. 1953, New York, New York

Peter De Rose, a Songwriters' Hall of Fame member, was a composer who wrote the music for several popular songs in the thirties. His first published song came in 1918, and his last in 1953. He was also famous for a radio series with his wife, May Singhi Breen. They were billed as the Sweethearts of the Air for sixteen years (1923–39).

His most famous compositions were "When Your Hair Has Turned to Silver" (1930), "Wagon Wheels" (1934), and "Deep Purple" (1934.)

Buddy De Sylva
b. 1895, New York, New York
d. 1950, Hollywood, California

Buddy or B. G. De Sylva (real name: George Gard De Sylva) was one of the most prolific and successful popular song lyricists. In 1918 Al Jolson discovered De Sylva in California and took him to New York. He interpolated several of De Sylva's songs into *Sinbad.*

De Sylva teamed up with Lew Brown and Ray Henderson in 1925. The trio produced several outstanding popular hits for the rest of the decade. After leaving the team in the early thirties, De Sylva collaborated with several other outstanding composers and occasionally wrote both words and music for songs. He became a Broadway show and film producer (he produced several Shirley Temple films) and wrote songs for several pictures. He even was head of Paramount Pictures for several years. After that he became a music publisher and an executive in Capitol Records. He was elected to the Songwriters' Hall of Fame.

A list of his hits follows: 1920's "Avalon"; 1921's "April Showers," "Yoo-hoo," "Look for the Silver Lining," "Whip-poor-will" and "Down South"; 1922's "Stairway to Paradise" and "A Kiss in the Dark"; 1924's "Somebody Loves Me," "Alabamy Bound," and "California, Here I Come"; 1925's "If You Knew Susie"; 1926's "When Day Is Done" (see Henderson, De Sylva, and Brown for 1925–31 songs); and 1932's "Eadie Was a Lady," "You're an Old Smoothie," and "Rise 'n Shine."

Emery Deutsch
b. 1907, Budapest, Hungary

Deutsch was a prominent bandleader in the thirties and forties. He was particularly famous for his Gypsy violin style of playing. He composed and popularized "Play, Fiddle, Play" in 1933. He also wrote "When a Gypsy Makes His Violin Cry" (1935), which became his theme.

Al Dexter
b. 1919, Jacksonville, Texas

Al Dexter (real name: Albert Poindexter) wrote and recorded a million-selling disc of 1943's "Pistol Packin' Mama." Dexter had been a paperhanger by trade, but he joined a hillbilly band during the Depression for additional work. He was successful in the southwestern states and made several recordings for Columbia Records.

Dorothy Dickson
b. 1896, Kansas City, Missouri

Dancer and actress Dorothy Dickson made her first appearance on Broadway as a dancer. She moved to London in 1921 and became a musical star there. Her major claim to fame in the United States was introducing "These Foolish Things" in 1936's *Spread It Abroad.*

Marlene Dietrich
b. 1904, Weimar, Germany

Marlene Dietrich (real name: Maria Magdalene Dietrich von Losch) was a very successful star of American movies in the thirties and forties. Her half-talking, low, raspy singing voice was deemed extremely sexy. One of her most famous roles was in the German 1930 film *The Blue Angel,* in which she introduced "Falling in Love Again." Her first film in the United States was 1931's *Morocco.* She is especially remembered for her rendition of "See What the Boys in the Back Room Will Have" from the 1939 movie *Destry Rides Again.* She introduced "Golden Earrings" in the 1947 movie *Golden Earrings,* but it was Peggy Lee who popularized the song in recordings.

Howard Dietz
b. 1896, New York, New York
d. 1983, New York, New York

Howard Dietz was an important popular song lyricist from the twenties to the sixties. In the early years of his career, he collaborated primarily with composer Arthur Schwartz on Broadway shows. After his partnership with Schwartz had ended, he wrote with Jerome Kern, Vernon Duke, Jimmy McHugh, and Ralph Rainger. Dietz is one of the writers in the Songwriters' Hall of Fame.

Dietz's best-known lyrics include 1929's "I Guess I'll Have to Change My Plans" and "Moanin' Low," 1930's "Something to Remember You By," 1931's "Dancing in the Dark," 1932's "Louisiana Hayride" and "A Shine on Your Shoes," 1934's "You and the Night and the Music" and "If There Is Someone Lovelier Than You," 1938's "I See Your Face Before Me," and 1953's "That's Entertainment."

Dinning Sisters
Lou b. 1922, Kentucky
Ginger and Jean (twins) b. 1924, Braman, Oklahoma

The Dinning Sisters began singing together when they were five. In 1935 they started their professional ca-reer with Herbie Holmes and his orchestra, with whom they toured the Midwest. In 1939 they went to Chicago to audition successfully for a job in radio. They spent the next six years as featured singers on a coast-to-coast broadcast.

Their only million-selling hit was "Buttons and Bows," which they recorded with the Art Van Damme orchestra in 1948.

Mort Dixon
b. 1892, New York, New York
d. 1956, Bronxville, New York

Songwriters' Hall of Fame lyricist Mort Dixon was an important writer during the twenties and thirties. He began writing songs in the early twenties and achieved success with his first published effort, 1923's "That Old Gang of Mine." His chief composer collaborators were Ray Henderson, Harry Warren, Harry Woods, and Allie Wrubel.

Other famous lyrics include 1926's "Bye Bye Blackbird"; 1927's "I'm Looking over a Four Leaf Clover"; 1930's "Would You Like to Take a Walk?"; 1931's "I Found a Million Dollar Baby," "You're My Everything," and "River, Stay 'Way from My Door"; 1934's "Flirtation Walk" and "Mr. and Mrs. Is the Name"; and 1935's "The Lady in Red."

Fats Domino
b. 1928, New Orleans, Louisiana

Antoine ("Fats") Domino's estimated record sales are more than 65 million, ranking him among the top dozen recording stars of all time.

Domino was the first of the New Orleans rhythm and blues personalities to break into the national limelight. He recorded his first million-selling disc in 1948 with "The Fat Man." Next came "Goin' Home" in 1952 and four gold records in 1953 with "Going to the River," "You Said You Loved Me," "Please Don't Leave Me," and "I Lived My Life." In 1954 he had two more million sellers with "Love Me" and "Leave Me This Way." Despite all this success, not until he recorded "Ain't That a Shame!" in 1955 did he gain much national attention. Also in 1955, he had gold records with "Thinking of You," "All by Myself," "I Can't Go On," and "Poor Me." It was Pat Boone's recording of "Ain't That a Shame!" that was the big-gest hit nationally. In 1956 Domino had these million sellers: "Bo Weevil," "I'm in Love Again," "Blue Monday," and one of his most famous hits, the re-make of the 1940 song "Blueberry Hill." The next year he had three million sellers: "I'm Walking," "It's You

I Love,'' and "I Still Love You." Domino had gold records for "Whole Lotta Lovin'," (1958) and "Be My Guest" (1959). His last million seller came in 1960 with "Walkin' to New Orleans," backed by "Don't Come Knockin'."

Almost all his hits and million-selling recordings were written with Dave Bartholomew. The two reaped twenty-two million-selling singles as songwriters; they rank just behind the Beatles' John Lennon and Paul McCartney.

Walter Donaldson
b. 1893, Brooklyn, New York
d. 1947, Santa Monica, California

Songwriters' Hall of Fame composer Walter Donaldson was one of the top writers of popular songs, with a long list of famous hits. He was particularly active from 1925 through 1928. He wrote the score for the Broadway show *Whoopee* (1928), which starred Eddie Cantor. He formed his own publishing company, Donaldson, Douglas & Gumble.

His most famous early songs include 1918's "My Mammy," 1919's "How Ya Gonna Keep 'Em Down on the Farm?," 1921's "Down South," 1922's "Carolina in the Morning" and "My Buddy," 1925's "Yes Sir, That's My Baby," 1927's "At Sundown" and "My Blue Heaven," and 1928's "Makin' Whoopee!," "Love Me or Leave Me," and "My Baby Just Cares for Me."

Donaldson's hits of the thirties include 1930's "You're Driving Me Crazy" and "Little White Lies." He continued to write until 1943, when he composed songs for the movie *Nevada,* but had no major hits after 1930.

Jimmy Dorsey
b. 1904, Shenandoah, Pennsylvania
d. 1957, New York, New York

Jimmy Dorsey was one of the great bandleaders of the swing era. His primary instrument was the alto saxophone, but he was also a facile performer on the clarinet.

Jimmy and his brother, Tommy, formed a joint band in 1928 and stayed together until 1935, when they broke up to form separate units. Jimmy's band was immediately successful and remained so until the early fifties.

Jimmy Dorsey's theme song for his band was "Contrasts" (1935), a beautiful piece that showcased his sax styling.

The band built a good following in the thirties and

hit its peak in the early forties, when it popularized several Latin American songs, including 1941's "Green Eyes," "Maria Elena," "Amapola," and 1943's "Besame Mucho." Vocalist Helen O'Connell and Bob Eberly teamed with the band for several hits, including 1941's "Blue Champagne," "Embraceable You," and 1942's "Tangerine." In 1957, twenty years after it had been first recorded, "So Rare" became a million seller.

The Dorsey brothers starred in a biographical movie, *The Fabulous Dorseys,* in 1947.

Tommy Dorsey
b. 1905, Shenandoah, Pennsylvania
d. 1956, Greenwich, Connecticut

Tommy Dorsey was one of the most famous bandleaders and trombonists of the swing era.

When the Dorsey brothers split up in 1935, Jimmy kept the nucleus of the band, while Tommy took over the Joe Haymes band, which became the Tommy Dorsey orchestra. Over the next fifteen years they recorded extensively.

From 1940 to 1942 Frank Sinatra was the star vocalist with Tommy's band. Other famous vocalists who sang with the group included Connie Haines, Jo Stafford, the Pied Pipers, and Dick Haymes.

The theme song of the Tommy Dorsey orchestra was "I'm Getting Sentimental over You," which featured Dorsey's trombone styling. Some of their major hits included 1937's revival of 1928's "Marie," "Boogie Woogie" (recorded in 1938 and a big hit when reissued in 1943 during the recording ban), 1942's "There Are Such Things" (with Frank Sinatra and the Pied Pipers), 1944's "Opus No. 1" and a revival of 1930's "On the Sunny Side of the Street."

In the movie *New, York, New York,* starring Liza Minnelli and Robert DeNiro, several Tommy Dorsey favorites were featured.

Saxie Dowell
b. 1904, Raleigh, North Carolina
d. 1974, Scottsdale, Arizona

Saxie Dowell played tenor saxophone and occasionally sang with Hal Kemp's band in the twenties and thirties. He organized his own band in 1939 and popularized two novelty songs, which he wrote: 1939's "Three Little Fishies" and 1940's "Playmates." He remained in the business after a stint in the service during World War II and also worked in the music publishing business.

Alfred Drake
b. 1914, New York, New York

Singer Alfred Drake (real name: Alfred Capurro) is famous for his starring roles in three Broadway musicals: 1943's *Oklahoma!*, in which he introduced "Oh, What a Beautiful Mornin'," "People Will Say We're in Love," "Surrey with the Fringe on Top," and "Oklahoma!"; 1949's *Kiss Me Kate*, in which he introduced "Wunderbar" and "So in Love"; and 1953's *Kismet*, in which he introduced "And This Is My Beloved." He also introduced "How High the Moon" in 1940's *Two for the Show*.

Milton Drake
b. 1916, New York, New York

Composer Milton Drake is primarily remembered for 1941's "Java Jive" and 1944's novelty song "Mairzy Doats." He performed in vaudeville, in silent films and on radio while he was a child. Later he wrote music for several films and became research manager for McGraw-Hill.

Dave Dreyer
b. 1894, Brooklyn, New York
d. 1967, New York, New York

Dave Dreyer wrote several successful songs during the twenties and thirties. He began his career as pianist for publishing companies and as accompanist for such stars as Al Jolson and Sophie Tucker. He collaborated with several different lyricists to write 1925's "Cecilia," 1927's "Me and My Shadow," and 1928's "Back in Your Own Backyard" and "There's a Rainbow 'Round My Shoulder." Dreyer was elected to the Songwriters' Hall of Fame.

Al Dubin
b. 1891, Zurich, Switzerland
d. 1945, New York, New York

Al Dubin was one of the most prolific lyricists in popular music. He began his career in 1917 and produced hit lyrics until his death. His chief collaborator was Harry Warren, but he wrote lyrics for several other famous composers, including Jimmy McHugh. Dubin was inducted into the Songwriters' Hall of Fame.

His most famous lyrics include 1925's "A Cup of Coffee, a Sandwich and You"; 1929's "Tip Toe Through the Tulips"; 1930's "Dancing with Tears in My Eyes"; 1932's "Too Many Tears"; 1933's "Forty-second street," "Shuffle Off to Buffalo," "You're Getting to Be a Habit with Me," "We're in the

Money," and "Shadow Waltz"; 1934's "Boulevard of Broken Dreams" and "I Only Have Eyes for You"; 1935's "Lullaby of Broadway"; 1937's "September in the Rain"; 1939's "Indian Summer"; 1941's "The Anniversary Waltz"; and "Feudin' and Fightin'," written in 1945 but popular in 1947.

Vernon Duke
b. 1903, Parafianovo, Russia
d. 1969, Santa Monica, California

Vernon Duke (real name: Vladmir Dukelsky) was a composer of popular songs principally in the thirties and forties. He fled from Russia to the United States during the Revolution, but did not find much success here at first. He went to Europe in 1923 and wrote several musicals for the London stage. In 1929, he returned to the United States where he wrote music for several Broadway musicals, beginning with *The Garrick Gaieties of 1930*.

Duke's most famous songs include 1932's "April in Paris," 1935's "Autumn in New York," 1936's "I Can't Get Started," and 1940's "Taking a Chance on Love" (popularized in 1943). Duke was elected to the Songwriters' Hall of Fame.

Jimmy Durante
b. 1893, New York, New York
d. 1980, Santa Monica, California

Jimmy Durante, nicknamed "the Schnoz" because of his large nose, was one of the most popular comedians in show business, but he also starred in several Broadway and Hollywood musicals, in which he introduced several hit songs. His raspy, half-talking singing style was one of his trademarks. Another part of his act consisted of his slaughtering the English language.

Durante also composed and popularized "Inka Dinka Doo" in 1933.

Deanna Durbin
b. 1922, Winnipeg, Canada

Deanna Durbin (real name: Edna Mae Durbin) starred in several movie musicals from 1937 through the late forties. Her first film was a short with Judy Garland. Initially, because of her age, she played teenage roles, but later she matured into more romantic roles. She married a French film director in the late fifties and retired from the business to live in France.

She introduced "Amapola" in the 1939 film *First Love*. Her operatic soprano voice was best suited for dramatic songs and popular songs derived from the classics.

E

Ray Eberle
b. 1919, Hoosick Falls, New York

Ray Eberle was the featured male vocalist with the Glenn Miller band at the zenith of the big bands. His older brother, Bob Eberly, was the male vocalist for the Jimmy Dorsey orchestra. The spelling of the last name was changed by Bob, with Ray keeping the original family spelling.

Eberle's voice was featured on dozens of the Miller band's recordings and on their radio show. His two most famous solos with the band were "At Last" and "Moonlight Cocktail." Neither of the tunes was a million seller, but he was recording at a time when it was difficult to collect the million sales figure. He left the band shortly before Miller entered military service in 1942. Then he worked as a single. He led the Miller band in the late forties and fifties.

Bob Eberly
b. 1916, Mechanicville, New York
d. 1981, Glen Burnie, Maryland

Bob Eberly was the featured male vocalist of the Jimmy Dorsey band in the heyday of the big bands. He began singing with the Dorsey brothers orchestra just before their split. At the separation, Eberly stayed with Jimmy. Eberly and Helen O'Connell teamed up on several of the band's biggest hits, notably the 1941 million sellers "Amapola," "Green Eyes," and "Maria Elena" (Eberly without O'Conell) and the 1943 million seller "Besame Mucho," on which Eberly teamed with Kitty Kallen for the vocal. Other noteworthy vocal renditions for him were "Tangerine" (1942), "Blue Champagne" (1941), and "The Breeze and I" (1940).

Eberly left the band for military service in 1943 and never regained his popularity after the war. In the early fifties he and O'Connell appeared with Ray Anthony's band on a television series.

Buddy Ebsen
b. 1908, Orlando, Florida

Buddy Ebsen (real name: Christian Ebsen, Jr.) is most famous today for his roles as Jed Clampett in *The Beverly Hillbillies* and Barnaby Jones on television, but in the early years of his career he was a dancer. He and his sister, Vilma, appeared as a dance team in the

Broadway musicals *Flying Colors* (1932) and *Ziegfeld Follies of 1934* and in the movie *Broadway Melody of 1936*. After Vilma had quit performing, Ebsen continued in the movie musicals *Born to Dance* and *Captain January* (1936); *Broadway Melody of 1938, Girl of the Golden West,* and *My Lucky Star* (1938); *They Met in Argentina* (1941); and *Sing Your Worries Away* (1942).

During the forties his caeeer faltered, but he returned in the fifties as a dramatic actor and very occasionally in a movie musical.

Billy Eckstine
b. 1914, Pittsburgh, Pennsylvania

Singer Billy Eckstine (real name: William Clarence Eckstein) was a very successful entertainer during the late forties and early fifties. Often known by the nickname Mr. B, Eckstine began his career singing in small clubs in Washington, D.C., after he had attended college there. His first big break came when he became a singer with Earl Hines's band in the late thirties. Eckstine formed his own band in 1944. When the band folded in 1947, he continued his singing career as a single and became even more famous. He continued to work in the late fifties and sixties, even though his major popularity had declined.

Eckstine's most famous recordings included 1945's "Cottage for Sale" and "Prisoner of Love," 1947's "Everything I Have Is Yours," 1948's "Blue Moon," 1949's "Caravan," 1950's "My Foolish Heart," and 1951's "I Apologize." All these were million sellers.

Nelson Eddy
b. 1901, Providence, Rhode Island
d. 1967, Miami Beach, Florida

Nelson Eddy was a star of several operetta movies during the thirties and forties. When he teamed up with Jeanette MacDonald in a series of operetta musicals, they became top box-office attractions.

His most famous roles in movies came in *Naughty Marietta* (1935), *Rose Marie* (1936), *Rosalie* (1937), *Girl of the Golden West* and *Sweethearts* (1938), *Bitter Sweet* and *New Moon* (1940), and *Knickerbocker Holiday* (1944).

Cliff Edwards
b. 1895, Hannibal, Missouri
d. 1971, Hollywood, California

Cliff Edwards, known as Ukulele Ike, was a very popular singer in the 1920s and 1930s. He appeared in the Broadway musicals *Lady Be Good* (1924), *Sunny* (1925), *Ziegfeld Follies of 1927,* and *George White's*

Scandals of 1936. He had roles in more than twenty movies in the late twenties and early thirties, notably *The Hollywood Revue of 1929,* the film in which he introduced "Singin' in the Rain." Through the rest of the thirties and in the forties, he appeared in an additional forty-seven films, mostly musicals.

His voice is probably most familiar to modern audiences as the squeaky-voiced Jiminy Cricket in Disney cartoons, especially in the feature-length cartoon *Pinocchio.*

Raymond B. Egan
b. 1890, Windsor, Ontario, Canada
d. 1952, Westport, Connecticut

Songwriters' Hall of Fame lyricist Raymond B. Egan is remembered as the writer of a few hit songs from the twenties and thirties. His most famous creations include 1920's "The Japanese Sandman," 1921's "Ain't We Got Fun?" and 1925's "Sleepy Time Gal."

Edward Eliscu
b. 1902, New York, New York

Edward Eliscu is famous as a lyricist, actor, playwright, and producer, who was active on Broadway and in Hollywood. Musically he is remembered for his collaborations on several important songs, including 1929's "Great Day," "More Than You Know," and "Without a Song" and 1933's "Flying Down to Rio," "Carioca," and "Orchids in the Moonlight."

Duke Ellington
b. 1899, Washington, D.C.
d. 1974, New York, New York

Duke Ellington was one of America's musical giants: a composer, a bandleader, and an arranger. Most of his compositions were jazz works, but several that started as instrumental jazz compositions became lastingly popular songs. Duke was elected to the Songwriters' Hall of Fame.

Ellington began by leading a small band in 1918 in Washington, D.C., and he had a highly successful career for the next half century and more. His band recorded a large catalog of discs and appeared in seven movies.

His most famous songs are 1931's "Mood Indigo," 1932's "It Don't Mean a Thing," 1933's "Sophisticated Lady," 1935's "Solitude," 1936's "In a Sentimental Mood," 1937's "Caravan," 1941's "I Got It

Bad," 1942's "Don't Get Around Much Anymore," and 1958's "Satin Doll."

The Ellington band's theme was Billy Strayhorn's "Take the 'A' Train."

Ziggy Elman
b. 1914, Philadelphia, Pennsylvania
d. 1968, Van Nuys, California

Ziggy Elman (real name: Harry Finkelman) was one of the leading trumpeters of the big band era. Elman joined the Benny Goodman band in the fall of 1936. When trumpet star Harry James left at the end of 1938, Elman became the leading trumpet soloist. He in turn left the Goodman band in 1940 and joined Tommy Dorsey. He remained with Dorsey, except for military service and a short stint leading his own band, for most of the forties. Elman is particularly famous for his trumpet solo on the Goodman band's recording of Elman's compostion "And the Angels Sing" (1939).

Ruth Etting
b. 1903, David City, Nebraska
d. 1978, Colorado Springs, Colorado

Ruth Etting was a major singing star of the twenties and thirties. She got her big break in show business in the *Ziegfeld Follies of 1927.* Other Broadway shows that followed included *Whoopee* (1928), *Simple Simon* (1930), and the *Ziegfeld Follies of 1931.* She also appeared often on radio during the thirties and occasionally in movies, but by the late thirties her career had begun to wane.

Etting's film biography was the 1955 movie *Love Me or Leave Me,* which starred Doris Day.

Ray Evans
b. 1915, Salamanca, New York

Ray Evans is a lyricist of several popular songs from the forties and fifties. Most of his lyrics have been written for songs from movies. Evans is a member of the Songwriters' Hall of Fame.

Evans's most famous lyrics include 1946's "To Each His Own"; 1949's Academy Award winner, "Buttons and Bows"; 1950's Academy Award winner, "Mona Lisa"; 1951's "Silver Bells"; 1956's Academy Award winner, "Que Será, Será"; 1957's "Tammy"; and 1964's "Dear Heart."

F

Nanette Fabray
b. 1922, San Diego, California

Actress, dancer, and singer Nanette Fabray (real name: Nanette Fabares) began her career as a child star in the *Our Gang* films. She later graduated to minor roles in several movie musicals and a featured role in 1953's *The Band Wagon*. She also starred in several Broadway musicals, including 1947's *High Button Shoes* and 1962's *Mr. President*. She introduced "Papa, Won't You Dance with Me?" and "I Still Get Jealous" in *High Button Shoes*.

She was on television often during the late fifties into the eighties. She is most remembered for her appearances on *The Show of Shows* with Sid Caesar. Recently she was on the television series *One Day at a Time*.

Sammy Fain
b. 1902, New York, New York

Sammy Fain is an important composer of popular song melodies whose career spans from the twenties into the seventies. He collaborated with several lyricists, notably Paul Francis Webster, E. Y. Harburg, Jack Yellen, Mitchell Parish and Lew Brown.

His most famous compositions before 1940 include 1928's "Let a Smile Be Your Umbrella," 1929's "Wedding Bells Are Breaking Up That Old Gang of Mine," 1930's "You Brought a New Kind of Love to Me," 1931's "When I Take My Sugar to Tea," 1937's "That Old Feeling," and 1938's "I Can Dream, Can't I?" and "I'll Be Seeing You."

Since 1940 his most popular hits have been 1948's "The Dickey Bird Song"; 1949's "Dear Hearts and Gentle People"; 1952's "I'm Late," from the movie cartoon *Alice in Wonderland;* "Secret Love," the 1953 Academy Award song from *Calamity Jane;* 1954's "I Speak to the Stars"; "Love Is a Many-Splendored Thing," the 1955 Acadamy Award winner; 1957's "April Love"; and 1958's "A Certain Smile." Fain composed "Strange Are the Ways of Love" in 1972, but, it was not a great hit. He is a member of the Songwriters' Hall of Fame.

Percy Faith
b. 1908, Toronto, Canada
d. 1976, Los Angeles, California

Percy Faith's orchestra specialized in beautiful, interesting arrangements of popular tunes, but occasionally it had hits of its own. Faith held the post of musical director at Columbia Records and recorded with its studio orchestra.

In 1951 Faith and his orchestra backed Tony Bennett for the million selling discs "Cold, Cold Heart," "Rags to Riches," and "Stranger in Paradise." Faith and the orchestra struck gold on their own in 1953 with "The Song from *Moulin Rouge*" and again in 1960 with "Theme from *A Summer Place*."

In addition, Faith arranged and conducted the music for the 1955 Doris Day film *Love Me or Leave Me*, which was Ruth Etting's film biography. His song, written with Carl Sigman, "My Heart Cries for You" was a million seller for Guy Mitchell in 1950. Faith composed the theme for the television series *The Virginian* and remained active in studio recording work into the seventies.

Eddie Farley
b. 1905, Newark, New Jersey

Eddie Farley is the Farley of the Riley-Farley band, which gained fame in 1936 with the novelty hit "The Music Goes 'Round and 'Round." The two split in late 1936, and each organized his own group.

Alice Faye
b. 1915, New York, New York

Alice Faye (real name: Alice Jeanne Leppert) was a star performer in the movies from the mid-thirties to the mid-forties. She was in the chorus line at the Capitol Theater by age fourteen. She met Rudy Vallee when they both appeared in *George White's Scandals of 1931*, and he took charge of her career. He helped her get a role in his 1934 movie *George White's Scandals*. After three minor roles she shot to stardom in three 1935 films. She was married first to singer Tony Martin, then to bandleader and singer Phil Harris. In the mid-forties she retired but made occasional appearances in films, radio, and television.

She introduced several hits in her films, notably 1935's "I'm in the Mood for Love" and 1943's "You'll Never Know."

Dorothy Fields
b. 1905, Allenhurst, New Jersey
d. 1974, New York, New York

Dorothy Fields, the daughter of Lew Fields of the famous comedy team Weber and Fields, was an important lyricist of popular songs from the late twenties into the seventies. Her chief collaborator was composer Jimmy McHugh. She was elected to the Songwriters' Hall of Fame.

Fields's best-known lyrics include 1928's "I Can't Give You Anything but Love" and "Diga Diga Doo"; 1930's "On the Sunny Side of the Street" and "Exactly Like You"; 1931's "Cuban Love Song"; 1933's "Don't Blame Me"; 1934's "Lost in a Fog"; 1935's "Lovely to Look At," "I Won't Dance," "I'm in the Mood for Love," "I Feel a Song Comin' On," and "Hooray for Love"; 1936's Academy Award winner, "The Way You Look Tonight," and "A Fine Romance"; and 1965's "Big Spender."

Dorothy Fields was the first woman elected to the Songwriters' Hall of Fame.

Shep Fields
b. 1911, Brooklyn, New York

Shep Fields intended to be a lawyer but earned his way through school playing in bands. He decided to stay with music and organized his first professional band at age nineteen. It took several years of one-night stands before the group began to receive much national attention. Fame came only after he had created his "rippling rhythm" style reeds, a violin, and a muted trumpet played a staccato melody, while an accordion, piano, or muted viola filled in; each number opened with the effect of someone blowing through a straw into a glass of water near a microphone.

In 1943 Fields pioneered another style: an all-reed (no brass) ensemble, but he never recaptured the success he had had in the thirties. By the mid-fifties he had retired to Houston, where he worked as a disc jockey and occasionally as a bandleader.

One of Shep Fields and his Rippling Rhythm's biggest successes was with 1939's "South of the Border." Their theme song was called "Rippling Rhythm."

Ted Fiorito
b. 1900, Newark, New Jersey
d. 1971, Scottsdale, Arizona

Ted Fiorito was a pianist and bandleader who also occasionally composed popular songs. Film star Betty Grable sang with his band briefly in the early thirties, as did June Haver in the early forties. His most popular time was the mid-thirties, when he had a great deal of exposure on radio, records, and movies. In the forties his fame began to diminish. In the fifties and sixties he led bands in Chicago and Arizona.

His most famous songs include 1922's "Toot, Toot, Tootsie!" and 1924's "Charley, My Boy."

Doris Fisher
b. 1915, New York, New York

Songwriter Doris Fisher, the daughter of composer Fred Fisher, wrote a few hits with Allan Roberts. She also sang in nightclubs, on radio, and with Eddie Duchin and his orchestra in the early forties. She organized her own group called Penny Wise and Her Wise Guys, but they had only limited success. Her most remembered songs include 1944's "You Always Hurt the One You Love" and 1946's "Put the Blame on Mame," from the movie *Gilda*.

Eddie Fisher
b. 1928, Philadelphia, Pennsylvania

Eddie Fisher was the nation's number one singing idol of the fifties until the arrival of Elvis Presley. He had his first successful recording in 1950 with "Thinking of You," the first of more than thirty hits.

Fisher was twenty-one years old when he became the protégé of Eddie Cantor, who heard him sing at Grossinger's, the Catskills resort in New York State. Cantor featured him on his radio show in the late forties and promoted him toward a successful singing career.

Fisher was very popular for the first few years of the fifties, but his career was interrupted by military service in 1952 and 1953. After discharge he again reached stardom.

According to his autobiography, *Eddie: My Life, My Loves,* Fisher was not able to cope with the fishbowl existence of a celebrity. By his account, the press forced him into his first marrage with actress Debbie Reynolds. From that marriage came his daughter Carrie Fisher, who starred as Princess Leia in *Star Wars*. He divorced Debbie Reynolds to marry Elizabeth Taylor. Later he married Connie Stevens.

Fisher's first million-selling record came in 1951 with a revival of 1921's "Any Time." Other million sellers included 1952's "Lady of Spain," backed by "Outside of Heaven," and "Wish You Were Here"; 1953's "I'm Walking Behind You" and "Oh My Papa"; 1954's "I Need You Now"; and 1955's "Dungaree Doll."

Fisher has attempted comebacks but has never regained the popularity he had in the early years of the fifties.

Fred Fisher
b. 1875, Cologne, Germany
d. 1942, New York, New York

Fred Fisher was one of America's best-known songwriters from the early years of this century through the forties. He was educated in Germany and served in the German military and in the French Foreign Legion. He came to the United States in 1900 and began his songwriting career shortly thereafter. He eventually organized his own publishing firm. He was the father of Doris Fisher (see page 192). Fisher was inducted into the Songwriters' Hall of Fame.

Fisher's most famous songs include 1910's "Come, Josephine, in My Flying Machine," 1913's "Peg o' My Heart" (revived 1947), 1919's "Dardanella," 1920's "Daddy, You've Been a Mother to Me," and 1922's "Chicago" (million seller for Frank Sinatra in 1957).

Ella Fitzgerald
b. 1918, Newport News, Virginia

Ella Fitzgerald is one of the most famous jazz singers in the world, and she has also made her mark in popular music.

Fitzgerald won a Harlem amateur hour in 1934 and joined the Chick Webb band as part of the prize. Her first big popular success came with the hit "A-Tisket, A-Tasket," which she wrote with Webb in 1938. When Webb died in 1939, Fitzgerald took over leadership of the band until she broke away in 1942 to try her musical wings as a single. She appeared in several movies and performed often on television from the late fifties through the seventies. In 1944, Ella teamed with the Ink Spots for the million-selling record "Into Each Life Some Rain Must Fall."

Red Foley
b. 1910, Blue Lick, Kentucky
d. 1968, Fort Wayne, Indiana

Red Foley (real name: Clyde John Foley) was one of the most famous country singers of all time. He was particularly popular in the 1940s and 1950s. His daughter Shirley married singer Pat Boone.

Foley had million-selling records of "Chattanoogie Shoe Shine Boy," the spiritual "Steal Away," and the gospel song "Just a Closer Walk with Thee" in 1950 and "Peace in the Valley" in 1951.

Foley owned a publishing firm, composed many country songs, and appeared regularly at Nashville's Grand Ole Opry.

Dick Foran
b. 1910, Flemington, New Jersey
d. 1979, Los Angeles, California

Dick Foran acted in numerous western movies beginning in 1934. In many of them he displayed a beautiful Irish tenor voice, as he did in 1941's *Ride 'Em Cowboy,* in which he introduced "I'll Remember April."

Mary Ford
b. 1924, Pasadena, California
d. 1977, Los Angeles, California

Mary Ford began singing and playing guitar on country and western radio shows as a child. She joined Les Paul in 1942 for a radio show. They married in 1948 and later divorced. During their time together they had several major hits, including "Mockin' Bird Hill," "How High the Moon," and "The World Is Waiting for the Sunrise," which were popular in 1951, and "Vaya con Dios," which was 1953's number one hit.

Tennessee Ernie Ford
b. 1919, Bristol, Tennessee

Tennessee Ernie Ford (real name: Ernest Jennings) was a popular singer and television personality in the fifties and sixties. Ford specialized in gospel and country songs, but he had several popular hits. His first million-selling recording was 1950's "Shotgun Boogie," but it was not until "Sixteen Tons" in 1955 that his fame really spread. His 1956 album *Hymns,* was the largest-selling album up to that time ever recorded by a Capitol artist.

In later years Ford appeared often on Lucille Ball's television series, had his own summer television show, and a daily morning show in the fifties. He still performs occasionally on television.

George ("Chet") Forrest
b. 1915, Brooklyn, New York

Chet Forrest teamed up with Robert Wright on the music and lyrics for several popular songs, but they are best known for adapting classical material to popular songs. Their most famous adaptation was Aleksandr Borodin's music for the 1953 Broadway musical *Kismet.* They also adapted Norwegian composer Edvard Grieg's music for 1944's *Song of Norway.* One of their first transformations was Rudolf Friml's "Chansonette" to "Donkey Serenade" in 1937.

Other well-known songs that were Forrest-Wright collaborations are 1939's "At the Balalaika," 1940's "It's a Blue World," 1944's "Strange Music" and "I Love You," and 1953's "Stranger in Paradise," "Baubles, Bangles and Beads," and "And This Is My Beloved."

Helen Forrest
b. 1918, Atlantic City, New Jersey

Helen Forrest was a leading female vocalist during the big band era. She was a leading singer with the Artie Shaw, Benny Goodman, and Harry James bands. She first sang with Shaw in 1938, then, in late 1939, joined Goodman. In 1941 she sang with James's band on several hit recordings. By the late fifties she was less active in the music business, but she continued to perform occasionally into the seventies.

James and his orchestra's recordings of "I Had the Craziest Dream" and "I've Heard That Song Before," backed by "Moonlight Becomes You," featured Forrest vocals. They were million-selling recordings in 1942.

The Four Aces
Al Alberts
Dave Mahoney
Lou Silvestri
Sol Vocarro

The Four Aces were organized in 1949 by Al Alberts. At first they sang only part time, but later they graduated to full-time work and recording. Their first successful disc was "Sin," which they paid to record. It sold a million copies in 1951, as did "Tell Me Why." Next came success in 1954 with "Three Coins in a Fountain" and "Stranger in Paradise." Their last million seller came in 1955 with "Love Is a Many-Splendored Thing."

The Four Lads
Frank Busseri
Bernard Toorish
James Arnold
Corrie Codarini

The Four Lads, from Toronto, Canada, backed Johnnie Ray in 1951 on his big hit "Cry." In 1953 they started recording for themselves, but it was not until 1955 that they hit it big with "Moments to Remember." Their only other gold record was 1956's "No, Not Much."

Alan Freed
b. 1922, Johnstown, Pennsylvania
d. 1965, Palm Springs, California

Disc jockey Alan Freed originated the term rock and roll in 1951 on his *Moon Dog's Rock and Roll Party* over radio station WWJ in Cleveland. Freed moved in 1954 to New York's WINS, where his fame spread. Within a year he was earning high pay promoting rock records and selling the products that sponsored his program. In addition to his disc jockeying, Freed occasionally contributed material to the rock milieu, as with 1954's "Sincerely." The 1978 film *American Hot Wax* chronicled Freed's career.

Arthur Freed
b. 1894, Charleston, South Carolina
d. 1973, Los Angeles, California

Arthur Freed was an important song lyricist who collaborated chiefly with composer Nacio Herb Brown. Particulary noteworthy were his lyrics for the 1929 movie *Broadway Melody*. Freed was inducted into the Songwriters' Hall of Fame.

Later in his career Freed became a producer of many successful movies, including 1939's *Babes in Arms*, and *The Wizard of Oz*, 1946's *The Harvey Girls*, and *Till the Clouds Roll By*, 1948's *Easter Parade*, 1949's *On the Town*, 1950's *Annie Get Your Gun*, 1951's *Show Boat*, and *An American in Paris*, 1954's *Brigadoon*, 1953's *The Band Wagon*, 1958's *Gigi*, and 1960's *Bells Are Ringing*.

Freed's most famous song lyrics include 1923's "I Cried for You"; 1929's "Broadway Melody," "You Were Meant for Me," "Singin' in the Rain," and "Pagan Love Song"; 1930's "The Moon Is Low"; 1932's "Fit as a Fiddle"; 1933's "Temptation"; 1934's "All I Do Is Dream of You"; 1935's "Broadway Rhythm" and "You Are My Lucky Star"; 1939's "Good Morning"; and 1952's "Make 'Em Laugh."

Ralph Freed
b. 1907, Vancouver, Canada
d. 1973, Los Angeles, California

Lyricist Ralph Freed wrote several songs, the most popular ones for the movies of the thirties and forties. He began writing in 1934 and began working for films in 1937. His most remembered song is "How About You?," from the 1941 movie musical *Babes on Broadway*.

Cliff Friend
b. 1893, Cincinnati, Ohio
d. 1974, Las Vegas, Nevada

Cliff Friend was a successful popular songwriter from the early twenties through the mid-fifties. His best-known hits include 1924's "June Night," 1925's "Then I'll Be Happy," 1936's "When My Dream Boat Comes Home," and 1937's "The Merry-Go-Round Broke Down."

Rudolf Friml
b. 1879, Prague, Bohemia
d. 1972, Hollywood, California

Rudolf Friml was one of the most famous composers of music for the Broadway stage. Friml is a member of the Songwriters' Hall of Fame. He was educated in Prague and became a concert pianist. After two United States tours in 1901 and 1906, he decided to remain. His first break in the business of songwriting came in 1912, when he got to write the score to *The Firefly* after Victor Herbert had backed out. Friml soon became, along with Herbert and Sigmund Romberg, one of the leading composers of operettas. After the mid-thirties he was less active but appeared on several television shows that honored popular composers.

Friml's most important contributions to popular songs include 1912's "Giannina Mia" and "Sympathy," 1922's "L'Amour, Toujours l'Amour," 1923's "Chansonette" (later adapted into "Donkey Serenade," 1937), 1924's "Rose Marie" and "Indian Love Call," and 1925's "Song of the Vagabonds" and "Only a Rose."

Rose Marie became a successful movie in 1936 and again in 1954, as did *The Vagabond King,* in 1930 and 1956; and *The Firefly,* in 1937.

Jane Froman
b. 1907, St. Louis, Missouri
d. 1980, Columbia, Missouri

Jane Froman was a well-known singer in the thirties and the forties. She starred in several Broadway musicals, notably *Ziegfeld Follies of 1934, Keep Off the Grass* (1940), and *Artists and Models* (1943), and in the Hollywood movies *Stars over Broadway* (1935) and *Radio City Revels* (1938).

Froman was seriously injured in a 1943 plane accident while entertaining the U.S. military overseas.

The 1952 movie *With a Song in My Heart* was a tribute to Froman and her life; Susan Hayward played the starring role. By the mid-fifties Froman's career was more or less over.

"More Than You Know" (1929) became a Froman specialty, as did "That Old Feeling" (1938), "I Believe" (1952), and "With a Song in My Heart" (1929).

G

Slim Gaillard
b. 1916, Detroit, Michigan

Slim and Slam (Bulee and Slam Stewart Gaillard) formed a combo that won popularity with the 1938 novelty hit "The Flat Foot Floogee." Gaillard composed several novelty songs with jive lyrics, but the only one that gained national popularity was "The Flat Foot Floogee."

Gallagher and Shean
Ed Gallagher
Al Shean, b. 1868, Dornum, Germany
d. 1949, New York, New York

Ed Gallagher and Al Shean (real name: Alfred Schoenberg) were a famous comedy team who starred on vaudeville and the musical stages of the twenties. They composed the hit song "Mister Gallagher and Mister Shean" (1922), which they premiered in the *Ziegfeld Follies of 1922.* The team split permanently in 1925.

Sammy Gallop
b. 1915, Duluth, Minnesota
d. 1971, Hollywood, California

Sammy Gallop was a songwriter in the 1940s and 1950s. His best-known hits were 1941's "Elmer's Tune," 1943's "Holiday for Strings," 1946's "Shoofly Pie and Apple Pan Dowdy," and 1955's "Wake the Town and Tell the People."

Kim Gannon
b. 1900, Brooklyn, New York
d. 1974, Lake Worth, Florida

Kim Gannon (real name: James Kimble Gannon) was a lyricist of popular songs during the forties and fifties. His best-known lyrics are 1942's "Moonlight Cocktail," 1943's "I'll Be Home for Christmas," and 1953's "Under Paris Skies."

Joe Garland
b. 1903, Norfolk, Virginia

Joe Garland is famous for composing a couple of jazz-oriented tunes for big bands. He composed 1939's "In the Mood" and Les Brown's theme, "Leap Frog." Otherwise, Garland is best known as a sideman, musical director, and arranger.

Judy Garland
b. 1922, Grand Rapids, Michigan
d. 1969, London, England

Judy Garland (real name: Frances Gumm) was famous for her role of Dorothy in 1939's *The Wizard of Oz,* but she did much more in her career than star in one motion picture. During her teenage years, she was the darling of several movie musicals, several of them costarring Mickey Rooney. One of her first song hits was "You Made Me Love You," which she sang to a photo of Clark Gable in *Broadway Melody of 1938.* Garland began her recording career in 1936 when she made "Swing Mr. Charlie" and "Stompin' at the Savoy" with the Bob Crosby orchestra. Her first million seller came with 1939's "Over the Rainbow" from *The Wizard of Oz.* It was not until 1954 that she next had a million-selling hit; it was "The Man That Got Away" from her film *A Star Is Born.* Her only other gold record came with the double album *Judy at Carnegie Hall* in 1961.

Garland led a troubled and turbulent life, particularly in the fifties and sixties, when she was in ill health.

Liza Minnelli, Garland's daughter by director Vincente Minnelli, has become a star of major proportions.

Betty Garrett
b. 1919, St. Joseph, Missouri

Betty Garrett performed in several movie musicals in the forties and fifties. She also had a starring role in the 1946 Broadway musical *Call Me Mister.* She married entertainer Larry Parks. In 1946's *Call Me Mister,* she introduced "South America, Take it Away."

Clarence Gaskill
b. 1892, Philadelphia, Pennsylvania
d. 1947, Fort Hill, New York

Clarence Gaskill had a very limited output of songs, but now and then he composed a hit. His most remembered songs are 1919's "Sweet Adeline," 1924's "Doo-Wacka-Doo," 1927's "I Can't Believe That You're in Love with Me," and 1931's "Prisoner of Love."

William Gaxton
b. 1893, San Francisco, California
d. 1963, New York, New York

William Gaxton (real name: Arturo Antonio Gaxiola) was the star of several Broadway musicals in the twenties and thirties. His most famous role was as President Wintergreen in the George Gershwin Pulitzer prizewinning musical *Of Thee I Sing.* In addition to his musical activity on Broadway, Gaxton appeared in several Hollywood movie musicals: *Fifty Million Frenchmen* (1931), *Best Foot Forward* (1943), and *Diamond Horseshoe* (1945). Gaxton introduced famous popular songs in several Broadway musicals. He had major roles in *The Music Box Revue of 1922,*

A Connecticut Yankee (1927), *Fifty Million Frenchmen* (1929), *Of Thee I Sing* (1932), *Anything Goes* (1934), and *Leave It to Me* (1938).

Janet Gaynor
b. 1907, Philadelphia, Pennsylvania
d. 1984, Palm Springs, California

Janet Gaynor (real name: Laura Gainer) sang and danced in a costarring role with Charles Farrell in the 1929 movie musical *Sunny Side Up,* in *Happy Days* and *Society Blues* in 1930, and in *Delicious* in 1931. Gaynor and Farrell were the top movie team of the early thirties. Gaynor demanded more serious roles in later years.

George Gershwin
b. 1898, Brooklyn, New York
d. 1937, Hollywood, California

George Gershwin was one of the greatest composers of the first half of the twentieth century in both serious and popular music. In the history of music many geniuses have died at young ages, cutting their productive lives short. Such was the case of Gershwin. He died at age thirty-eight, having composed for only a little more than twenty years. All that he was able to accomplish in those brief years is absolutely remarkable. Gershwin is, of course, in the Songwriters' Hall of Fame.

Gershwin began at age fifteen as a pianist, an accompanist (for Nora Bayes and Louise Dresser,) and a song plugger. He became staff composer for the Harms Publishing Company in 1917 and produced his first major hit, "Swanee," in 1918.

His most illustrious Broadway musical scores were *Lady Be Good* (1924), *Oh, Kay!* (1926), *Funny Face* (1927), *Strike Up the Band* (1928), *Girl Crazy* (1930), *Of Thee I Sing* (1931, first musical to receive the Pulitzer Prize) and *Porgy and Bess* (1935). He composed the serious jazz concerto *Rhapsody in Blue* for Paul Whiteman's Aeolian Hall concert in 1924. *Rhapsody in Blue, An American in Paris* (1928), and *Porgy and Bess* (1935) were the crowning achievements of his musical career.

Gershwin collaborated with several lyricists, but most often with his brother, Ira.

Some of his most famous popular songs prior to 1930 include 1918's "Swanee"; 1922's "Stairway to Paradise"; 1924's "Somebody Loves Me," "Oh, Lady Be Good!," "Fascinating Rhythm," and "The Man I Love," which was a hit years later; 1926's "That Certain Feeling," "Someone to Watch over Me," "Do-

Do-Do,'' and ''Clap Yo' Hands''; 1927's '' 'S Wonderful''; 1928's ''How Long Has This Been Going On?,'' ''Oh Gee, Oh Joy'' and ''I've Got a Crush on You,'' which was most popular in 1930; and 1929's ''Liza.''

In the thirties Gershwin contributed ''Strike Up the Band,'' ''I Got Rhythm,'' ''Bidin' My Time,'' ''But Not for Me,'' and ''Embraceable You'' (1930); ''Of Thee I Sing'' and ''Love Is Sweeping the Country'' (1932); ''Summertime,'' ''I Got Plenty o' Nuttin','' ''It Ain't Necessarily So,'' ''I Loves You, Porgy,'' ''Bess, You Is My Woman Now,'' and ''A Woman Is a Sometime Thing'' (1935); ''A Foggy Day,'' ''Nice Work If You Can Get It,'' ''Shall We Dance?,'' ''Let's Call the Whole Thing Off,'' and ''They Can't Take That Away from Me'' (1937); and ''Love Is Here to Stay'' and ''Love Walked In'' (1938), the songs he was working on when he died.

Ira Gershwin
b. 1896, New York, New York
d. 1983, Beverly Hills, California

Ira Gershwin, brother of George Gershwin, whose outstanding lyrics were an integral part of many of the most popular songs of the twenties and thirties, continued to write long after his brother's death in 1937. Ira's early efforts with his brother were penned under the pseudonym of Arthur Francis because he did not want to capitalize on his brother's blossoming career. The 1924 Broadway production *Lady, Be Good!* brought Ira recognition.

He wrote many of his most famous songs in collaboration with his brother, but he also collaborated with such top composers as Jerome Kern, Harold Arlen, Harry Warren, Burton Lane, Kurt Weill, and Aaron Copland.

Ira's most famous song lyrics with composers other than George were 1930's ''Cheerful Little Earful,'' which he wrote with lyricist Billy Rose and composer Harry Warren for the revue *Sweet and Low;* 1936's ''I Can't Get Started,'' which was introduced by Bob Hope and Eve Arden in the revue *Ziegfeld Follies of 1936;* 1944's ''Long Ago and Far Away,'' the biggest hit he ever had in any one year, written with Jerome Kern for the wartime movie musical *Cover Girl;* and 1954's ''The Man That Got Away,'' which he wrote with Harold Arlen for the movie musical *A Star Is Born.*

Although Ira Gershwin was associated with some of Hollywood's most famous songs, only three of his lyrics won Oscar nominations (1937's ''They Can't Take That Away from Me,'' 1944's ''Long Ago and Far Away,'' and 1954's ''The Man That Got Away''), and none ever won. Ira, like his brother, is a member of the Songwriters' Hall of Fame.

Tamara Geva
b. 1907, St. Petersburg, Russia

Tamara Geva (real name: Sheversheieva Gevergeva) married choreographer George Balanchine in Europe when she was dancing with the Monte Carlo Ballet. She came to Broadway in the Russian revue *Chauve Souris.*

Geva is most remembered for her role in the 1936 Broadway musical *On Your Toes.* She (along with Clifton Webb) also introduced ''Louisiana Hayride'' in the 1932 revue *Flying Colors.*

She should not be confused with the Tamara who starred in 1933's *Roberta* and was killed in an air crash in Lisbon, Portugal, in 1943. That Tamara did not use a surname.

Georgia Gibbs
b. 1920, Worcester, Massachusetts

Georgia Gibbs (real name: Fredda Gibson, born Gibbons) was a popular singer from the late thirties through the fifties. She sang on *Your Hit Parade* in 1937 and 1938 and again in the early forties under the name Gibson. In 1942 she adopted the name Georgia Gibbs. She recorded often in the late forties and fifties, scoring hits with 1952's ''Kiss of Fire'' and 1955's ''Tweedle Dee'' and ''Dance with Me, Henry.''

L. Wolfe Gilbert
b. 1886, Odessa, Russia
d. 1970, Los Angeles, California

L. Wolfe Gilbert was a popular song lyricist from the 1910s into the early 1930s. His best-known songs include 1912's ''Waiting for the *Robert E. Lee,*'' 1921's ''Down Yonder'' (revived in 1951), 1924's ''O, Katharina!,'' 1928's ''Ramona'' and ''Jeannine, I Dream of Lilac Time,'' 1930's ''The Peanut Vendor,'' and 1931's ''Green Eyes,'' ''Mama Inez,'' and ''Marta.'' Gilbert was elected to the Songwriters' Hall of Fame.

Terry Gilkyson
b. 1916, Phoenixville, Pennsylvania

Terry Gilkyson studied music at the University of Pennsylvania. After graduation he worked as a folk singer on armed forces radio. His first success as a recording artist was with the Weavers in 1951 on their recording of ''On Top of Old Smokey.'' He composed "Cry of the Wild Goose," which was a hit for Frankie Laine in 1950, and "Marianne," a big calypso hit. "Marianne" was recorded by Gilkyson and the Easy Riders and became a million seller in 1957.

Haven Gillespie
b. 1888, Covington, Kentucky
d. 1975, Las Vegas, Nevada

Haven Gillespie was a songwriter, primarily a lyricist, who was most active in the twenties and thirties. His best-known songs include 1925's "Drifting and Dreaming," 1926's "Breezin' Along with the Breeze," 1934's "Santa Claus Is Comin' to Town," 1938's "You Go to My Head," and 1949's "That Lucky Old Sun." He was elected to the Songwriters' Hall of Fame.

Will Glahe

Will Glahe's claim to fame in the United States was his 1938 recording of "Beer Barrel Polka," which sold a million copies within five years. The recording was made in Germany, with Glahe featured in an accordion solo.

Arthur Godfrey
b. 1903, New York, New York
d. 1983, New York, New York

Arthur Godfrey was one of the top show business personalities in the forties and fifties. His *Arthur Godfrey's Talent Scouts* show gave many newcomers their breaks into the big time. In the late forties he was an extremely popular radio personality. He continued that popularity in television through the mid-fifties. Godfrey's one gold record was 1947's "Too Fat Polka."

Al Goodhart
b. 1905, New York, New York
d. 1955, New York, New York

Al Goodhart composed a few hit songs during the thirties and forties. His only well-known compositions are 1932's "Fit as a Fiddle" and "Auf Wiedersehen, My Dear."

Benny Goodman
b. 1909, Chicago, Illinois

Benny Goodman, one of the all-time great clarinetists and big band leaders, was called the King of Swing. In the summer of 1934 Goodman formed a big band to play in Billy Rose's Music Hall. After mediocre success playing "society music" for dancing, Goodman made a fortunate decision. While playing at the Palomar Ballroom in Los Angeles in 1935, he decided to feature his swing sound rather than the society style. The audience, particularly the young, responded enthusiastically. By early 1936 the swing craze was under way, thanks in large part to Benny Goodman.

When he was ten, his father had sent him to learn music on a borrowed clarinet at Hull House in Chicago. Within two years he was playing the clarinet professionally. In 1925 he was hired by Ben Pollack for his orchestra and played with him for four years. The next few years Goodman free-lanced in New York with various studio recording groups, in pit bands for Broadway shows, and in radio bands.

Gene Krupa joined the Goodman band as drummer in 1935 and was featured in the first extended jazz drum solo in the best-selling recording, "Sing, Sing, Sing" (1936).

Metronome nominated the Goodman band the best band of 1935. Goodman holds the all-time record of twenty-seven awards in *Down Beat*'s annual readers' poll: top swing band in each year from 1936 through 1941 and then in 1943, top or favorite soloist from 1936 through 1941 and again from 1943 through 1947 and 1949, top clarinetist from 1937 through 1939, top quartet in 1938, and top small combo from 1939 through 1942.

Goodman enjoyed great commercial success, particularly between 1936 and 1942, with his trio (Goodman, pianist Teddy Wilson, and Krupa), quartet (Goodman, Wilson, Krupa, and vibraphonist Lionel Hampton), combos (various combinations of quintet, sextet, and septet), and big band. Most of the great jazz instrumentalists played with the Goodman band and then became famous bandleaders. In addition to Krupa and Hampton, Harry James is a notable example; he joined the band in 1937 and left in late 1938.

Goodman's only million-selling recording was "On a Slow Boat to China" in 1948, unless one also counts "Why Don't You Do Right?," which he and his orchestra recorded with Peggy Lee in 1942. Even so, he is famous for several other numbers: his theme song, "Let's Dance" (1935); "Goody Goody" (1936); and "And the Angels Sing" (1939).

The 1956 movie *The Benny Goodman Story* was a big hit and caused several of the Goodman band's numbers to receive renewed popularity.

Mack Gordon
b. 1904, Warsaw, Poland
d. 1959, New York, New York

Songwriters' Hall of Famer Mack Gordon is particularly remembered as the lyricist of several popular songs from the movies of the thirties and forties. In the thirties he teamed with Harry Revel, and in the forties, with Harry Warren.

Gordon's most famous lyrics include 1930's "Time on My Hands"; 1934's "Did You Ever See a Dream Walking?," "Love Thy Neighbor," "Stay as Sweet as You Are," and "With My Eyes Wide Open I'm Dreaming"; 1941's "Chattanooga Choo Choo"; 1942's "At Last," "I've Got a Gal in Kalamazoo," "I Had the Craziest Dream," and "There Will Never Be Another You"; 1943's "My Heart Tells Me" and "You'll Never Know"; 1945's "The More I See You" and "I Can't Begin to Tell You"; 1946's "You Make Me Feel So Young"; and 1947's "Mam'selle."

Jay Gorney
b. 1896, Bialystok, Russia

Jay Gorney (real name: Daniel Jason Gorney) was the composer of the Depression-era hit song "Brother, Can You Spare a Dime?" (1932). Otherwise, he wrote music for several Hollywood movies from the mid-thirties through the forties, but most of the songs proved to be unimportant. "Baby, Take a Bow" from the 1934 movie *Stand Up and Cheer* is one song that escaped anonymity.

Betty Grable
b. 1916, St. Louis, Missouri
d. 1973, Santa Monica, California

Betty Grable (real name: Ruth Elizabeth Grable) was the number one pinup girl for servicemen during World War II. Almost 2 million copies of her famous picture in a white bathing suit were sent to men in the military all over the world. She was a singing and dancing star of several movie musicals in the forties and fifties. Her fabled legs were often displayed in her movies and on pinup calendars.

She married Jackie Coogan in 1937 (divorced in 1940) and received her first real acclaim in the 1939 Broadway musical *Du Barry Was a Lady*. She returned to Hollywood in the forties and became a star in the movie musical *Down Argentine Way*. She married bandleader Harry James in 1943; they divorced in 1965.

Despite her extensive musical activities, there is an odd lack of recordings by her. She made one record with the Harry James band under the name Ruth Haag ("I Can't Begin to Tell You").

Glen Gray
b. 1906, Roanoke, Illinois
d. 1963, Plymouth, Massachusetts

The Orange Blossom Band was renamed the Casa Loma Orchestra after it had played an engagement at the Casa Loma Hotel in Toronto in 1928. The band was reorganized in 1929, and Glen Gray (real name: Glen Gray ["Spike"] Knoblaugh) became president and leader, but he did not actually front the group until 1937. Pee Wee Hunt, Kenny Sargent, Red Nichols, and Bobby Hackett were members of the band at various times. The band began to attract considerable attention in the early thirties and had a big record of "Sunrise Serenade" in 1939. Other popular recordings include "I Cried for You," "Sleepy Time Gal," and "Smoke Rings," the band's theme song.

Jerry Gray
b. 1915, Boston, Massachusetts

Jerry Gray (real name: Jerry Graziano) composed some of the Glenn Miller orchestra's biggest hits. He began arranging for the Artie Shaw band in the late thirties and for the Miller group by the early forties. He was responsible for the arrangement of "Begin the Beguine" that was Shaw's first major hit.

Gray's most famous compositions include "A String of Pearls" and "Pennsylvania 6–5000."

Kathryn Grayson
b. 1922, Winston-Salem, North Carolina

Singer Kathryn Grayson (real name: Zelma Kathryn Hedrick) starred in several movie musicals in the 1940s and 1950s. Her operatic soprano voice was particularly suited for the songs from *Show Boat, Rio Rita, The Desert Song, The Vagabond King,* and *The Toast of New Orleans* with Mario Lanza and as opera singer Grace Moore in *So This Is Love*. As beautiful as her clear voice was for operatic numbers, she was also very capable on popular numbers.

Bud Green
b. 1897, Austria

Bud Green was a popular song lyricist, particularly during the twenties and thirties. His best-known lyrics include 1924's "Alabamy Bound," 1928's "That's My Weakness Now," 1937's "Once in a While," 1938's "The Flat Foot Floogee" and "More Than Ever," and 1944's "Sentimental Journey."

John Green
b. 1908, New York, New York

John, or Johnny, Green is especially important as the composer of the hit song "Body and Soul" and as an arranger, a conductor, and the musical director for several significant Hollywood films.

Green's hit popular songs include 1928's "Coquette," 1930's "Body and Soul" and "I'm Yours," 1931's "Out of Nowhere," 1933's "I Wanna Be Loved" and "I Cover the Waterfront," and 1934's "Easy Come, Easy Go." He is a member of the Songwriters' Hall of Fame.

Louise Groody
b. 1897, Waco, Texas
d. 1961, Canadensis, Pennsylvania

Louise Groody began her show business career as a cabaret dancer. She had a major role in 1921's *Good Morning, Dearie* and graduated to Broadway stardom in 1925 in *No, No, Nanette,* in which she introduced "I Want to Be Happy" and "Tea for Two" and in 1927's *Hit the Deck,* in which she introduced "Sometimes I'm Happy."

Walter Gross
b. 1909, New York, New York

Walter Gross is most famous as a pianist and composer of the 1947 hit "Tenderly," a million seller for Rosemary Clooney in 1952. As an executive of Musicraft Records, he was the conductor, arranger, and/or pianist on many recording sessions.

H

Connie Haines
b. 1922, Savannah, Georgia

Connie Haines (real name: Yvonne Marie Jamais) is best known as vocalist with the Tommy Dorsey orchestra. She began singing as a child and worked with bands in Miami in the late thirties before her break into the big time. She sang with Harry James for a few months, and about this time she changed her name. She joined the Dorsey band in 1940 and stayed for two years. After she had left the band, she sang as a single and recorded occasionally.

One of her most remembered discs was "Oh, Look at Me Now" with Tommy Dorsey and his orchestra and Frank Sinatra in 1941.

Bill Haley
b. 1925, Highland Park, Michigan
d. 1981, Harlingen, Texas

Bill Haley was one of the most famous of the early rock and roll personalities. He is often given credit for starting the rock and roll craze with his recordings of "Shake, Rattle and Roll" and "Rock Around the Clock" in 1954. Haley and his Comets had sold more than 60 million records by the beginning of the seventies. The collective sales of "Rock Around the Clock" alone have been estimated to be more than 22 million. Haley's only other million seller came in 1956 with "See You Later, Alligator."

Jack Haley
b. circa 1901, Boston, Massachusetts
d. 1979, Los Angeles, California

Jack Haley is probably best known for his role as the Tin Man in the 1939 movie classic *The Wizard of Oz,* but he also appeared in several Broadway musicals and in more than thirty movies. In his early career he was a singer and dancer in vaudeville. Other than his role in *The Wizard of Oz,* his most important contribution to popular music was introducing "Did You Ever See a Dream Walking?" in the movie *Sitting Pretty* in 1933.

Adelaide Hall
b. 1895, Brooklyn, New York

Adelaide Hall starred in the 1920s in several all-black revues, including *Shuffle Along* (1921), *Runnin' Wild* (1923), and *Blackbirds of 1928,* in which she introduced "Diga Diga Doo" and "I Can't Give You Anything but Love." After extensive touring she settled in Europe in 1936. She came back to Broadway in 1957 for a role in *Jamaica.*

Juanita Hall
b. 1901, Keysport, New Jersey
d. 1968, Bay Shore, New York

Juanita Hall (real name: Juanita Long) was famous for her role as Bloody Mary in 1949's *South Pacific,* in which she introduced "Bali Ha'i" and "Happy Talk." She had important roles in 1954's *House of Flowers* and 1958's *Flower Drum Song,* but she never experienced the success of *South Pacific.* She re-created her roles in the movie versions of *South Pacific* and *Flower Drum Song.*

Wendell Hall
b. 1896, St. George, Kansas
d. 1969, Mobile, Alabama

Wendell Hall, the Red-Headed Music Maker, composed and popularized the 1923 hit "It Ain't Gonna Rain No Mo'." His recording, on which he accompanied himself on a ukulele, sold more than 2 million copies.

Stuart Hamblen
b. 1908, Kellyville, Texas

Stuart Hamblen is particularly well known in the western and gospel music field. His best-known popular songs are "This Ole House," a million seller for Rosemary Clooney in 1954, and "It Is No Secret," popularized by Jo Stafford in 1951.

Nancy Hamilton
b. 1908, Sewickley, Pennsylvania

Nancy Hamilton was a singer and actress in several Broadway shows, but she is most famous as the lyricist of the 1940 song "How High the Moon," which became a million-selling recording for Les Paul and Mary Ford in 1951.

Oscar Hammerstein II
b. 1895, New York, New York
d. 1960, Doylestown, Pennsylvania

Other than Irving Berlin, Oscar Hammerstein II was the most prolific lyricist of all time. Hammerstein collaborated with several excellent composers, but his association with Richard Rodgers is best known. He had previously collaborated with Jerome Kern, Sigmund Romberg, Rudolf Friml, George Gershwin, and Vincent Youmans. He is, of course, a member of the Songwriters' Hall of Fame.

Hammerstein was born into a show business family. His father was manager of the historic Victoria vaudeville theater in New York, and his grandfather had been an important opera impresario and theater builder.

Hammerstein's first success came when he teamed up with lyricist Otto Harbach to write for Broadway shows in the twenties. They were first moderately successful and then greatly so. After Lorenz Hart and Richard Rodgers had ended their partnership, Hammerstein and Rodgers formed the most successful partnership in Broadway history.

The list of hit songs credited to Oscar Hammerstein II is filled with some of the greatest lyrics written from the twenties through the fifties. His best-known songs of the twenties include "Rose Marie" and "Indian Love Call" from *Rose Marie* (1924); "Sunny" and "Who?" from *Sunny* (1925); "The Desert Song," "One Alone," and "The Riff Song" from *The Desert Song* (1926); "Make Believe," "Why Do I Love You?" "Ol' Man River," "Bill," "Can't Help Lovin' Dat Man," and "You Are Love" from *Show Boat* (1927); "Lover, Come Back to Me," "Softly, as in a Morning Sunrise," "One Kiss," "Wanting You," and "Stout-Hearted Men" from *The New Moon* (1928); and "Why Was I Born?" from *Sweet Adeline* (1929).

In the thirties Hammerstein continued to produce numerous hits, as yet without Rodgers. His hits of the thirties were: "I've Told Ev'ry Little Star" and "The Song Is You" from *Music in the Air* (1932), "When I Grow Too Old to Dream" from the movie *The Night Is Young* (1935), "I'll Take Romance" from the film *I'll Take Romance* (1937), and "All the Things You Are" from *Very Warm for May* (1939). He did not team up with Rodgers until 1943. His pre-Rodgers hit of the forties was "The Last Time I Saw Paris" (1940, interpolated into the 1941 film *Lady, Be Good!*, but written as an independent number).

The first Broadway musical for the Rodgers and Hammerstein partnership was the fantastically successful *Oklahoma!* Through the rest of the forties Hammerstein's most famous song lyrics were "Oklahoma!," "People Will Say We're in Love," "The Surrey with the Fringe on Top," and "Oh What a Beautiful Mornin'" from *Oklahoma!* (1943); "If I Loved You," "June Is Bustin' Out All Over," and "You'll Never Walk Alone" from *Carousel* (1945); "It Might as Well Be Spring" and "It's a Grand Night for Singing" from *State Fair* (1945); "A Fellow Needs a Girl" and "The Gentleman Is a Dope" from *Allegro* (1947); "Some Enchanted Evening," "Bali Ha'i," "Younger Than Springtime," "I'm Gonna Wash That Man Right out of My Hair," "This Nearly Was Mine," and "There Is Nothin' Like a Dame" from *South Pacific* (1949).

Hammerstein's most memorable lyrics from Broadway musicals of the fifties are "Getting to Know You," "Shall We Dance?," "We Kiss in a Shadow," "I Whistle a Happy Tune," "Hello, Young Lovers," and "Something Wonderful" from *The King and I* (1951); "No Other Love" from *Me and Juliet* (1953); "Everybody's Got a Home but Me" and "All at Once You Love Her" from *Pipe Dream* (1955); "Do I Love You Because You're Beautiful?" and "In My Own Little Corner" from the television musical *Cinderella* (1957); "Love, Look Away," "I Enjoy Being a Girl," and "You Are Beautiful" from *Flower Drum Song* (1958); and "The Sound of Music," "Climb Ev'ry Mountain," "My Favorite Things," "Maria,"

"Edelweiss," and "Do-Re-Mi" from *The Sound of Music* (1959).

James F. Hanley
b. 1892, Rensselaer, Indiana
d. 1942, Douglaston, New York

James F. Hanley composed several hits from 1917 to 1940, but only a few are still remembered. His best-known songs are "Indiana" (1917), "Rose of Washington Square" (1919), "Second Hand Rose" (1921), "Just a Cottage Small" (1925), and "Zing! Went the Strings of My Heart" (1935).

Otto Harbach
b. 1873, Salt Lake City, Utah
d. 1963, New York, New York

Songwriters' Hall of Fame lyricist Otto Harbach was an important writer for several Broadway musicals. Many of his greatest successes were in collaboration with Oscar Hammerstein II. He also wrote with some of popular music's greatest composers, including Jerome Kern, George Gershwin, Rudolf Friml, Vincent Youmans, and Karl Hoschna.

Harbach's most memorable song lyrics are "Cuddle Up a Little Closer" (1980); "Every Little Movement" (1910); "Sympathy" (1912), "The Love Nest" (1920); "Rose Marie" and "Indian Love Call" (1924); "No, No, Nanette," "Sunny," and Who?" (1925); "The Desert Song," "One Alone," and "The Riff Song" (1926); and "Smoke Gets in Your Eyes," "The Touch of Your Hand," and "Yesterdays" (1933).

E. Y. ("Yip") Harburg
b. 1898, New York, New York
d. 1981, Los Angeles, California

Yip Harburg was an important lyricist of popular songs, especially in the thirties and forties. He wrote for several important Broadway musicals and independently. His chief collaborators were composers Harold Arlen and Jay Gorney. Harburg was elected to the Songwriters' Hall of Fame.

Harburg's best-known songs are "Brother, Can You Spare a Dime?" and "April in Paris" (1932); "It's Only a Paper Moon" (1933); "You're a Builder Upper" and "Let's Take a Walk Around the Block (1934); "Over the Rainbow" (1939 Academy Award winner); "Happiness Is Just a Thing Called Joe" (1943); and "How Are Things in Glocca Morra?," "Old Devil Moon," and "Look to the Rainbow" (1947).

The Harmonicats
Jerry Murad
Al Fiore
Don Les

This harmonica group was formed in 1944 and rose to fame with the 1947 million-selling recording of the 1913 Fred Fisher song "Peg o' My Heart." It was their only major hit.

Phil Harris
b. 1906, Linton, Indiana

Phil Harris is particularly associated with novelty songs that he made famous. He was also a bandleader and a radio, movie, and television personality. He joined the Jack Benny radio show in 1936 and stayed with it for ten years. From 1947 through 1954 he costarred with his wife, Alice Faye, on a radio show.

Harris's only million-selling record came with the 1950 hit "The Thing." He later did some voices for Disney cartoons, most notably as Baloo the Bear in *The Jungle Book,* in which he sang the Academy Award nominee "The Bare Necessities."

Lorenz ("Larry") Hart
b. 1895, New York, New York
d. 1943, New York, New York

Larry Hart was one of the greatest lyricists for Broadway musicals, particularly in the successful partnership with Richard Rodgers which began in 1919 and continued into the early forties. Hart was several years older than Rodgers. He had already been writing when he met Rodgers, then a student at Columbia University. The team's first real success came with the score for the 1925 revue *Garrick Gaieties.* They wrote primarily for the Broadway stage but did try writing for the movies during the thirties.

Hart was an eccentric, and his life-style always conflicted with Rodgers's, but somehow they managed to work together to produce some of the most sophisticated lyrics and the most brilliant music that the stage has ever seen. The 1948 film *Words and Music* was based on the Rodgers and Hart partnership.

Hart's most famous song lyrics from the twenties are "Manhattan" (1925), "The Blue Room" and "Mountain Greenery" (1926), "Thou Swell" and "My Heart Stood Still" from *A Connecticut Yankee* (1927), "You Took Advantage of Me" from *Present Arms* and "My Lucky Star" from *She's My Baby* (1928), and "With a Song in My Heart" from *Spring Is Here* (1929).

His best-remembered lyrics from the thirties are "Ten Cents a Dance" and "Dancing on the Ceiling" (dropped from the show, popularized in 1932) from *Simple Simon* (1930); "I've Got Five Dollars" from *America's Sweetheart* (1931); "Isn't It Romantic?," "Mimi," and "Lover" from the movie *Love Me Tonight* (1932); "My Romance," "Little Girl Blue," "The Most Beautiful Girl in the World," and "There's a Small Hotel" (dropped from the show, used in *On Your Toes,* 1936) from *Jumbo* (1935); "Blue Moon," which went through several transformations before it became popular in 1935; "Babes in Arms," "Where or When," "The Lady Is a Tramp," "My Funny Valentine," and "Johnny One Note" from *Babes in Arms* (1937); "I Married an Angel" from *I Married an Angel* and "This Can't Be Love" and "Falling in Love with Love" from *The Boys from Syracuse* (1938); and "I Didn't Know What Time It Was" from *Too Many Girls* (1939).

Little happened in the early forties before Rodgers and Hart split, but Hart's famous lyrics from the forties include "Bewitched, Bothered and Bewildered" and "I Could Write a Book" from *Pal Joey* (1941).

Always the eccentric as far as life-style was concerned, Hart's health weakened and he caught pneumonia. He died shortly after *A Connecticut Yankee* opened.

Hart is, of course, a member of the Songwriters' Hall of Fame.

Erskine Hawkins
b. 1914, Birmingham, Alabama

Erskine Hawkins is a trumpeter who led a swing band in the thirties and forties. He composed "Tuxedo Junction," which became a major hit for Glenn Miller (1940).

Dick Haymes
b. 1916, Buenos Aires, Argentina
d. 1980, Los Angeles, California

Dick Haymes was one of the most popular male singers in the forties and fifties. He began his singing career at age sixteen. Hired by Harry James in 1940 to replace Frank Sinatra, he began to achieve recognition. He switched to the Benny Goodman band in 1942 and toured with the Tommy Dorsey orchestra in 1943, once again following Sinatra.

His biggest boost came in 1943, when he replaced Buddy Clark on a network radio program and began to rival Bing Crosby and Sinatra for popularity. His first million-selling record was 1943's Academy Award winner, "You'll Never Know," from the movie *Hello, Frisco, Hello.* His career got another boost in 1944 in the movie *Irish Eyes Are Smiling* (his film debut), when he played composer Ernest R. Ball. In the next few years he made several movies, appeared often on network radio, especially *Your Hit Parade,* and had a successful recording of "Little White Lies" (1948).

Haymes formed his own production firm in the mid-fifties and continued to perform in nightclubs and television.

Ray Heatherton
b. 1910, Jersey City, New Jersey

Ray Heatherton was the star of the 1937 Broadway musical *Babes in Arms* and had a supporting role in 1930's *The Garrick Gaieties.* He was a popular radio singer during the thirties and sang with several of the important bands of the day. His daughter Joey is a prominent movie and television personality.

Horace Heidt
b. 1901, Alameda, California

Horace Heidt was a popular bandleader in the thirties and forties. His band, billed both as Horace Heidt and his Musical Knights and as the Brigadiers, was at its peak of popularity in the late thirties and early forties. In the late fifties Heidt retired from music.

Heidt and his Musical Knights had a million-selling recording in 1941 with "Deep in the Heart of Texas" and in 1952 with comedian Johnny Standley for "It's in the Book."

Florence Henderson
b. 1934, Dale, Indiana

Florence Henderson first came to Broadway in 1952's *Wish You Were Here.* She starred in 1954's *Fanny.* Henderson played Edvard Grieg's wife, Nina, in the Hollywood version of *Song of Norway* in 1970. In recent years she played the mother on the *Brady Bunch* television series.

Ray Henderson
b. 1896, Buffalo, New York
d. 1970, Greenwich, Connecticut

Ray Henderson was an important composer of popular songs, particularly in the twenties and thirties and especially when he teamed with Lew Brown and Buddy De Sylva from 1926 through 1930.

Henderson's greatest early hits include 1923's "That Old Gang of Mine," 1924's "Alabamy Bound," 1925's

"Five Foot Two, Eyes of Blue," and "I'm Sitting on Top of the World" and 1926's "Bye Bye Blackbird."

In collaboration with De Sylva and Brown, he composed 1926's "Birth of the Blues" and "Black Bottom"; 1927's "Good News," "The Best Things in Life Are Free," "The Varsity Drag," and "It All Depends on You"; 1928's "You're the Cream in My Coffee" and "Sonny Boy"; 1929's "Button Up Your Overcoat" and "My Lucky Star."

After De Sylva had left the team, Henderson and Brown continued together for several years. Henderson's major songs after 1930 include 1931's "The Thrill Is Gone" and "Life Is Just a Bowl of Cherries." Although he wrote consistently through the early forties, he did not have the success he had enjoyed earlier.

Victor Herbert
b. 1859, Dublin, Ireland
d. 1924, New York, New York

Victor Herbert was one of the greatest operetta composers for the Broadway stage. He was trained in classical music in Europe and was a virtuoso cellist. He and his wife, an operatic soprano, came to the United States in 1886. She sang at the Met briefly, and he played in the pit orchestra and performed as a cello soloist. His first composing success came with the Broadway show *The Serenade* (1897), and his first song to become a hit was "Gypsy Love Song" from *The Fortune Teller* (1898).

Herbert's best-known songs prior to the twenties include "Toyland" from *Babes in Toyland* (1903); "Kiss Me Again" from *Mlle. Modiste* (1906); "In Old New York" and "Every Day Is Ladies' Day to Me" from *The Red Mill* (1906); "Rose of the World" from *The Rose of Algeria* (1908); "Ah! Sweet Mystery of Life," "I'm Falling in Love with Someone," and "Italian Street Song" from *Naughty Marietta* (1910); "Sweethearts" from *Sweethearts* (1913); and "Thine Alone" from *Eileen* (1917).

His most memorable songs from the twenties include "When the Right One Comes Along" from *Ziegfeld Follies of 1920* and "A Kiss in the Dark" from *Orange Blossoms*. "Indian Summer," which Herbert wrote as a piano piece in 1919, was revived in 1939 as a song and achieved considerable popularity.

Several earlier operettas, which were made into successful movies in the thirties and early forties, were *Mlle. Modiste, Babes in Toyland, Naughty Marietta,* and *Sweethearts*.

Woody Herman
b. 1913, Milwaukee, Wisconsin

Clarinetist Woody Herman was one of the top bandleaders from the mid-thirties into the seventies. By age eight he was a vaudeville trouper. At nine he was billed as "The Boy Wonder of the Clarinet." At fourteen he began working in local bands. Stints with the bands of Tom Gerun, Harry Sosnick, and Isham Jones followed. When Jones retired in 1938, Woody conducted the Jones orchestra until he assumed complete control in 1941. His band was one of the most important groups in the forties.

Herman's million-selling recordings were "At the Woodchopper's Ball," which he recorded in 1939, and "Laura," the theme of the film *Laura,* which he and his orchestra waxed in 1945. Herman formed Mars Records in the fifties. His band, sometimes called Herman's Herd, was voted the best band of 1949 and appeared in several movies in the forties.

Edward Heyman
b. 1907, New York, New York

Ed Heyman is famous as a lyricist of several popular song hits from the thirties and forties. His first hit came in 1930 with "Body and Soul" which he wrote in collaboration with lyricists Robert Sour and Frank Eyton and composer John Green. Heyman's other hit songs include 1931's "Out of Nowhere," 1932's "Through the Years," 1933's "I Cover the Waterfront," 1934's "You Oughta Be in Pictures" and "Easy Come, Easy Go," 1937's "Boo-Hoo," 1948's "Bluebird of Happiness," and 1952's "When I Fall in Love."

Al Hibbler
b. 1915, Little Rock, Arkansas

Singer Al Hibbler has been blind since birth. He rose to fame with Duke Ellington's band but left in 1951 for a career as a single. He had good success with the song "He" and a million seller with "Unchained Melody" in 1955. Afterward he remained active but never had another million seller.

Hildegarde
b. 1906, Adell, Wisconsin

Hildegarde Loretta Sell, known simply as Hildegarde, was a singer and pianist in nightclubs and on radio, primarily during the forties. Her biggest hit was her theme song, "Darling, Je Vous Aime Beaucoup," which was written by her manager Anna Sosenko, in

1935. Hildegarde also had good success with 1940's "The Last Time I Saw Paris" and 1944's "I'll Be Seeing You."

Billy Hill
b. 1899, Boston, Massachusetts
d. 1940, Boston, Massachusetts

Billy Hill was a famous composer of several western-flavored popular songs particularly in the thirties. His first big hit was "The Last Round-Up" in 1933. Hill's other leading songs include 1934's "Wagon Wheels," 1936's "Empty Saddles," "The Glory of Love," and "In the Chapel in the Moonlight." In most instances Hill wrote both words and music for his songs.

Bob Hilliard
b. 1918, New York, New York
d. 1971, Hollywood, California

Bob Hilliard was an important lyricist of popular songs from the mid-forties into the sixties. His best-known songs include 1947's "Civilization," 1948's "Careless Hands," 1949's "Dear Hearts and Gentle People," 1950's "Dearie," 1951's "Be My Life's Companion," 1952's "Bouquet of Roses," 1954's "Every Street's a Boulevard in Old New York," and 1956's "Moonlight Gambler" and "Our Day Will Come."

Harriet Hilliard
b. circa 1912, Des Moines, Iowa

Harriet Hilliard (real name: Peggy Lou Snyder) was vocal soloist with the band headed by her husband, Ozzie Nelson, in the thirties. She joined the Nelson band in 1932, and she and Ozzie were married in 1935. They were often on radio and occasionally in movies. She introduced "Says My Heart" in the movie musical *The Coconut Grove* (1938). Starting in 1944, the Nelsons starred in a radio show, and in 1968 they starred on television as Ozzie and Harriet. Singer Ricky Nelson is their son.

Louis Hirsch
b. 1887, New York, New York
d. 1924, New York, New York

Composer Louis Hirsch was active in popular music from 1907 until his death in 1924. His most famous song from the period covered by this book is 1920's "The Love Nest" from the stage show *Mary*.

Al Hoffman
b. 1902, Minsk, Russia
d. 1960, New York, New York

Al Hoffman composed several excellent popular songs during the thirties, forties, and fifties. He grew up in Seattle, went to New York in 1928, and began composing in 1930. His best-known songs include 1931's "Heartaches"; 1932's "Auf Wiedersehen, My Dear" and "Fit as a Fiddle"; 1934's "Little Man, You've Had a Busy Day"; 1944's "Mairzy Doats"; 1947's "Chi-Baba, Chi-Baba"; the score for the 1949 Disney cartoon *Cinderella*, which included "A Dream Is a Wish Your Heart Makes" and "Bibbidi-Bobbidi-Boo"; 1950's "If I Knew You Were Comin' I'd ave Baked a Cake"; 1954's "Papa Loves Mambo"; 1955's "Hot Diggity" and "Allegheny Moon"; and 1958's "Hawaiian Wedding Song."

Billie Holiday
b. 1915, Baltimore, Maryland
d. 1959, New York, New York

Billie Holiday (real name: Eleanor Gough) was memorialized in the 1972 movie *Lady Sings the Blues*, which was loosely based on her life story. Nicknamed Lady Day, Holiday began to draw attention in recordings with Teddy Wilson's all-star combo in 1935. She recorded under her own name in 1936, with Count Basie in 1937 and 1938 and with Artie Shaw in 1938. By the late forties her talent had deteriorated primarily because of drug problems.

Libby Holman
b. 1906, Cincinnati, Ohio
d. 1971, Stamford, Connecticut

Torch singer Libby Holman is identified with 1929's "Moanin' Low," 1930's "Body and Soul," and "Something to Remember You By." Her first big success on Broadway came in *The Little Show*, in which she introduced "Moanin' Low," and she quickly followed with 1930's *Three's a Crowd*, in which she introduced "Body and Soul" and "Something to Remember You By." In 1934's *Revenge with Music*, she introduced "You and the Night and the Music." By the end of the thirties her career had faded.

Bob Hope
b. 1903, London, England

Bob Hope (real name: Leslie Townes Hope) is an American institution even though he was not born in this country. He grew up in Cleveland, experimented with boxing as a career, and became a song and dance man in vaudeville. His first roles on Broadway were bit parts before he attracted attention in 1933's *Roberta*. Greater success followed in the 1936 *Ziegfeld Follies*, in which he introduced "I Can't Get Started," and *Red, Hot and Blue*, in which he first presented "It's De-Lovely." He began his incredible career in films in *The Big Broadcast of 1938* and introduced the song that has become his theme, "Thanks for the Memory." Hope and Bing Crosby starred with Dorothy Lamour in a series of *Road* films.

Hope is especially known for his tours overseas to entertain servicemen. His TV appearances since the fifties have been numerous, mostly in specials, often recounting Christmas tours to entertain troops. He, of course, is noted as a comedian, but he has sung creditably in his many movies. In addition to "Thanks for the Memory," he introduced the 1948 Academy Award winner "Buttons and Bows," which he and Jane Russell performed in *The Paleface*.

Lena Horne
b. 1917, Brooklyn, New York

Singer Lena Horne became very popular in the forties and has continued to perform into the eighties. In 1981 a Broadway revue, *Lena Horne: The Lady and Her Music Live on Broadway*, honored her and the music associated with her.

She started her singing career at age sixteen in the chorus at the famous Harlem nightclub the Cotton Club. Her first Broadway appearance came in *Lew Leslie's Blackbirds of 1939*. In the early forties she was a singer with Charlie Barnet and his orchestra. Her first movie role was a small part in 1942's *Panama Hattie*, but the recognition she gained there led to other movies (still mostly small parts or cameo appearances). In 1943 she appeared in the movie version of *Cabin in the Sky*; *Stormy Weather*, which starred some of the country's top black entertainers; *I Dood It*, in which she played herself and sang "Taking a Chance on Love"; *Thousands Cheer*, a revue of big-name stars to entertain the soldiers in which she performed "Honeysuckle Rose"; and *Swing Fever*. Horne was featured in 1944's *Broadway Rhythm*, in which she sang "Brazilian Boogie" and "Somebody Loves Me" and in *Two Girls and a Sailor*, in which she performed "Paper Doll." She had cameo roles in 1946's *Ziegfeld Follies*, in which she sang Ralph Blane and Hugh Martin's "Love"; 1947's *Till the Clouds Roll By*, in which she sang Jerome Kern's "Can't Help

Lovin' Dat Man" and "Why Was I Born?"; and 1948's *Words and Music*, in which she sang Rodgers and Hart's "The Lady Is a Tramp" and "Where or When." She was a guest star in 1950's *Duchess of Idaho*, singing "Baby, Come Out of the Clouds," and in 1956's *Meet Me in Las Vegas*, in which she sang "If I Can't Dream." She was also seen in 1969's nonmusical film *Death of a Gunfighter*.

Horne returned to Broadway in 1957 to star in the musical *Jamaica*.

Eddy Howard
b. 1914, Woodland, California
d. 1963, Palm Desert, California

Singer Eddy Howard first drew national attention when he sang with Dick Jurgens's band in the late thirties. During his work with Jurgens's group, he popularized two of his own compositions: "My Last Goodbye" and "Careless." He led his own band in the forties and fifties. Howard's first big hit came in 1946 with "To Each His Own," which became a million seller. His other big hit was 1951's "Sin," which had sold a million copies by 1956. Ill health caused him to retire for a few years in the early fifties, but he rebounded with a reorganized band in 1954 and remained active into the early sixties.

Pee Wee Hunt
b. 1907, Mount Healthy, Ohio

Pee Wee Hunt (real name: Walter Hunt) played trombone in several bands in the late twenties but began to find fame when he became an original member of the band that became the Casa Loma Orchestra. He was featured vocalist, trombonist, and vice-president of the group for sixteen years. He left the band in 1943 and, after a few years of different jobs, organized his own band in 1946. He and his orchestra had a fantastic hit in 1948 of 1914's "Twelfth Street Rag." Hunt's only other million seller was 1953's "Oh."

Herman Hupfield
b. 1894, Montclair, New Jersey
d. 1951, Montclair, New Jersey

Herman Hupfield did not write a large number of hits, but he managed to produce at least one quality song that will survive.

It was 1931's "As Time Goes By," which was featured in the 1943 movie *Cassablanca* and became an all-time hit. Other songs by Hupfield include "Let's Put Out the Lights" and "When Yuba Plays the Tuba."

SELECTED BIOGRAPHICAL SKETCHES

Walter Huston
b. 1884, Toronto, Canada
d. 1950, Beverly Hills, California

Actor Walter Huston (real name: Walter Houghston) starred in only one Broadway musical, 1938's *Knickerbocker Holiday,* in which he introduced the popular standard "September Song." He was primarily known as an actor in Hollywood films, but he also appeared in vaudeville and in dramatic plays.

Betty Hutton
b. 1921, Battle Creek, Michigan

Singer and actress Betty Hutton (real name: Elizabeth June Thornburg) was a prominent star of several movies in the forties. Her forte was comedy and novelty numbers.

She started out with her sister, Marion Hutton, singing with Vincent Lopez and his orchestra in the late thirties. In 1940 Betty Hutton starred in the Broadway musical *Two for the Show* and had a small part in *Panama Hattie,* but it was not until her first movie musical, *The Fleet's In,* in 1942 that she became a national star. She performed "Build a Better Mouse Trap" and "Arthur Murray Taught Me Dancing in a Hurray" in that film. Also in 1942 came *Star Spangled Rhythm,* which was variety show fare to entertain servicemen. She stole the show in 1943's *Happy Go Lucky,* in which she performed the novelty "Murder He Says," and costarred as Bob Hope's fiancée in *Let's Face It.*

By 1944 Hutton was earning $5,000 a week for her movie roles, as she appeared in *Here Come the Waves,* in which she played both sisters in a singing act, *And the Angels Sing,* and *The Miracle of Morgan's Creek.* Her most important role to this point in her career came in 1945's *Incendiary Blonde,* in which she portrayed entertainer and speakeasy owner Texas Guinan and sang "It Had to Be You" and "Ragtime Cowboy Joe." She also appeared in the variety show film *Duffy's Tavern* in 1945. In 1946's *The Stock Club* Hutton performed one of her famous novelty numbers, "Doctor, Lawyer, Indian Chief." She also made *Cross My Heart* in 1946, but that was not nearly as important as 1947's *The Perils of Pauline,* her best role to date. She next starred in 1949's *Red, Hot and Blue,* which had nothing in common with the 1936 Cole Porter Broadway musical of the same name.

Perhaps Hutton's juiciest role came in the 1950 film version of Irving Berlin's Broadway musical *Annie Get Your Gun,* and the studio wasted no time in capitalizing on her success. It turned out *Let's Dance,* with

Hutton and Fred Astaire, also in 1950. Maybe because of the hectic schedule of movie musicals, she had to have a growth removed from her vocal cords, but that hardly slowed her down. In 1952 she made *Somebody Loves Me,* based on the lives of vaudeville stars Blossom Seeley and Benny Fields. She also starred in the nonmusical *The Greatest Show on Earth* in 1952 and in 1957's *Spring Reunion.*

Marion Hutton
b. 1919, Little Rock, Arkansas

Marion Hutton (real name: Marion Thornburg) is the older sister of Betty Hutton. After the sisters had worked with Vincent Lopez's band, Marion joined Glenn Miller in 1938. She stayed with the Miller band until it disbanded in 1942. After that she worked as a single in clubs, theaters, radio, and movies. She remained active until the fifties, when she appeared only occasionally. She married bandleader Vic Schoen and settled in California.

I

Ink Spots
Orville ("Happy") Jones, bass:
b. 1905, Chicago, Illinois
d. 1944, Chicago, Illinois
Billy Kenny, tenor: b. 1915 d. 1978
Charlie Fuqua, bass
Ivory ("Deek") Watson, tenor

The Ink Spots were porters at New York's Paramount Theater when they were discovered by an agent who arranged for them to record their first big hit, "If I Didn't Care," in 1939. They had several big hits and became famous for talking choruses. They had a million-selling disc with Ella Fitzgerald of "Into Each Life Some Rain Must Fall" in 1944. Their other gold records came in 1946 with "To Each His Own" and "The Gypsy." Jones died in 1944 of a brain hemorrhage and was replaced by his brother, Herb.

Burl Ives
b. 1909, Hunt Township, Illinois

Burl Ives is primarily known as a folk singer. It was not until the late thirties that he began to make his mark in the entertainment industry, and then World War II came along to interrupt his budding career in radio and in the New York theater. During his service stint, however, he was a member of the female chorus of Irving Berlin's *This Is the Army.* After his release from the military Ives got a radio series. In the late forties he became nationally famous as an actor in films. His national exposure in the movies probably helped him reach a wide audience with his folk songs.

J

Harry James
b. 1916, Albany, Georgia
d. 1983, Las Vegas, Nevada

Harry James came from a circus family. His father, the circus bandmaster, taught him the trumpet. The family finally settled in Beaumont, Texas, where Harry attended school. At fifteen he left Beaumont for a job in a band. His first important band post came with Ben Pollack in 1935. Then, in 1937, he joined the Benny Goodman band as featured trumpet soloist. In 1938 Goodman lent James $42,000 to organize his own band. The James orchestra specialized in the blues, boogie woogie, and, of course, trumpet showpieces.

The band's first million seller was its showy theme song, "Ciribiribin," an 1898 Italian tune arranged in big band style with a flashy trumpet part. That recording came in 1939, as did "Two O'Clock Jump," another James specialty.

In the forties the band was at its peak of popularity. James and the band signed a movie contract and appeared in 1942's *Springtime in the Rockies*, in which they performed "I Had the Craziest Dream," with the band's vocalist, Helen Forrest; *Private Buckaroo*, in which they teamed with the Andrews Sisters on "Don't Sit Under the Apple Tree"; and *Syncopation*, in which they performed their 1941 million seller "You Made Me Love You." In 1946 James starred in *Do You Love Me?* and *If I'm Lucky*.

In 1942 James and his band had million-selling recordings of "Easter Parade," "I Had the Craziest Dream," with vocal by Helen Forrest, and "I've Heard That Song Before," backed by "Moonlight Becomes You," with vocals by John McAfee and Helen Forrest. In 1943 they backed Frank Sinatra on the million seller of "All or Nothing at All." Vocalists at different times also included Dick Haymes.

James married the popular film star Betty Grable in 1943; she was his second wife (Louise Tobin was the first). They were divorced in 1965.

After the decline of the big bands James and his group continued to perform occasionally. In the early fifties James had a short-lived TV show. The group has survived and continues to perform the arrangements that made it one of the giants of the era.

Joni James
b. 1930, Chicago, Illinois

Singer Joni James (real name: Joan Carmello Babbo) was particularly popular during the fifties. She began as a dancer but switched to singing. Her biggest hits include 1952's "Why Don't You Believe Me?," 1953's "Your Cheatin' Heart," and "Have You Heard?," and 1955's "How Important Can It Be?"

Gordon Jenkins
b. 1910, Webster Groves, Missouri
d. 1984, Malibu, California

Composer, arranger, and conductor Gordon Jenkins is probably best known as conductor of his orchestra, which has made numerous recordings and has backed many illustrious artists on recordings.

In 1947 Jenkins had his first million seller with "Maybe You'll Be There," which he and his orchestra and chorus recorded with a vocal by Charles La Vere. In 1948 they backed Dick Haymes and Four Hits and a Miss for a million seller of 1930's "Little White Lies." Patty Andrews's 1949 million seller of "I Can Dream, Can't I?" was backed by Jenkins's orchestra and chorus. In 1950, they recorded the number one hit of the year with "Goodnight, Irene," with the folk singers the Weavers.

In addition to his recording, Jenkins has written several popular hits, including 1934's "P.S. I Love You" and 1943's "San Fernando Valley."

Howard Johnson
b. 1887, Waterbury, Connecticut
d. 1941, New York, New York

Lyricist Howard Johnson started his musical career as a pianist for theaters in Boston. Then came a job as a staff writer for a New York publishing house. His most famous lyric was for Kate Smith's theme song, 1931's "When the Moon Comes over the Mountain." The Songwriters' Hall of Fame elected Johnson for membership.

Arthur Johnston
b. 1898, New York, New York
d. 1954, Corona del Mar, California

Songwriters' Hall of Fame member Arthur Johnston is primarily remembered for the songs he composed for movie musicals in the thirties. His most popular hits include 1931's "Just One More Chance," 1934's "Cocktails for Two" and "My Old Flame," and 1936's "Pennies from Heaven."

Johnnie Johnston
b. 1914, St. Louis, Missouri

Singer Johnnie Johnston performed frequently in the forties over radio, in movies, and on recordings.

Al Jolson
b. 1886, St. Petersburg, Russia
d. 1950, San Francisco, California

Billed as "The World's Greatest Entertainer," Al Jolson (real name: Asa Yoelson) was one of the most charismatic personalities of show business from the early 1910s through the mid-1930s. After a few years of relative obscurity his career zoomed again with the release of two motion pictures: *The Jolson Story* (1946) and *Jolson Sings Again* (1949).

Jolson's father trained him to become a synagogue cantor, but he gave up that career to sing popular music. He almost always appeared in blackface on stage, often as Gus, a servant. He appeared in numerous Broadway musicals but rarely, if ever, sang anything that was written for the show. At a particular moment in each performance Jolson would step to the edge of the stage, drop his characterization, and sing whatever songs he chose to perform that evening.

Jolson also starred in the first part-sound movie, *The Jazz Singer*, in which he performed several of his favorite songs. The first words he uttered in the film were his favorite expression, "Folks, you ain't heard nothin' yet!"

Some of the famous hits identified with Jolson (generally because he introduced and popularized them) are 1918's "Rock-a-Bye Your Baby with a Dixie Melody" and "My Mammy," 1919's "Swanee," 1921's "April Showers," 1922's "Toot, Toot, Tootsie!," 1924's "California, Here I Come," 1925's "I'm Sitting on Top of the World," 1928's "Sonny Boy" and "There's a Rainbow 'Round My Shoulder."

Jolson married Ruby Keeler in 1928, but they were divorced in 1939.

Allan Jones
b. 1908, Scranton, Pennsylvania

Singer Allan Jones starred in several movie musicals and appeared on radio often during the thirties and forties. He gained national attention in the mid-1930s, when he introduced "Alone" in the Marx Brothers film *A Night at the Opera*. He costarred with Jeanette MacDonald in the movie version of Rudolf Friml's *The Firefly* in 1937. In the late thirties and forties he re-

mained active on radio. His career waned during the fifties, but he continued to perform.

His son Jack is also a popular singer.

Isham Jones
b. 1894, Coalton, Ohio
d. 1956, Hollywood, California

Bandleader Isham Jones had one of the most successful bands in the period just before the big band era. In addition, Jones composed a few hits that have become standards, especially 1924's "I'll See You in My Dreams" and "It Had to Be You." He is a member of the Songwriters' Hall of Fame.

Jones and his orchestra with feature trumpeter Louis Panico had a recording of "Wabash Blues" in 1921 that sold nearly 2 million copies over the years.

Spike Jones
b. 1911, Long Beach, California
d. 1964, Los Angeles, California

"The King of Corn," Spike Jones (real name: Lindley Armstrong Jones) was famous for his novelty band, billed as Spike Jones and his City Slickers. They mostly performed parodies of popular hits, using pistols, cowbells, saws, whistles, cheers, clinking glasses, etc., to create their zany arrangements.

Jones and his crew gained national attention in 1942 with their rendition of "Der Fuehrer's Face," which made fun of Adolf Hitler. Their next million seller came with "Cocktails for Two" in 1944. A 1946 burlesque of "Glow-Worm" and the 1948 comedy Christmas song "All I Want for Christmas" were also million sellers.

Louis Jordan
b. 1908, Brinkley, Arkansas

Critic Leonard Feather suggests that teenage pop grew out of rock, which grew out of rhythm and blues, which grew out of the music of Louis Jordan. During the forties he was one of the big names in popular music.

Jordan and his Tympany Five had a recording of "Is You Is or Is You Ain't My Baby?" in 1944 that sold a million or more copies through the years. In 1945 their recording of "Caldonia (What Makes Your Big Head So Hard?)" continued the string of eventual million sellers. In 1946 they had two big sellers with "Beware, Brother, Beware" and "Choo Choo Ch'Boogie." Jordan's fifth and last million seller came in 1949 with "Saturday Night Fish Fry."

Dick Jurgens
b. 1910, Sacramento, California

Bandleader Dick Jurgens fronted a very successful sweet-style band that was popular in the late thirties and forties.

K

Irving Kahal
b. 1903, Houtzdale, Pennsylvania
d. 1942, New York, New York

Irving Kahal wrote several successful popular song lyrics in the twenties and thirties. His most famous songs include 1928's "Let a Smile Be Your Umbrella," 1929's "Wedding Bells Are Breaking Up That Old Gang of Mine," 1930's "You Brought a New Kind of Love," 1931's "When I Take My Sugar to Tea," 1936's "The Night Is Young and You're So Beautiful," and 1938's "I Can Dream, Can't I?" and "I'll Be Seeing You." Kahal is a Songwriters' Hall of Fame member.

Gus Kahn
b. 1886, Coblenz, Germany
d. 1941, Beverly Hills, California

Lyricist Gus Kahn is one of the most important writers of popular songs from the early years of this century through the twenties. He collaborated with Egbert Van Alstyne, Walter Donaldson, Isham Jones, and several other noteworthy composers. The 1951 movie musical *I'll See You in My Dreams* was based on Kahn's life and hits. Kahn was elected to the Songwriters' Hall of Fame.

Some of his most famous lyrics include 1916's "Pretty Baby," 1922's "Carolina in the Morning," "My Buddy," and "Toot, Toot, Tootsie!," 1924's "I'll See You in My Dreams," "It Had to Be You," and "The One I Love," 1925's "Yes Sir, That's My Baby," 1928's "Love Me or Leave Me" and "Makin' Whoopee!," 1931's "Dream a Little Dream of Me," 1936's "San Francisco," and 1941's "You Stepped out of a Dream."

Kitty Kallen
b. 1922, Philadelphia, Pennsylvania

Singer Kitty Kallen was particularly active in the forties and early fifties. Her most famous big band jobs were with Jimmy Dorsey and Harry James. During the early fifties her singing career faltered for a while, but it was revived with the 1954 hits "Little Things Mean

a Lot" and "In the Chapel in the Moonlight." Kallen's first big disc, "Besame Mucho," was recorded in 1943 with Jimmy Dorsey; she shared the vocal with Bob Eberly.

Bert Kalmar
b. 1884, New York, New York
d. 1947, Los Angeles, California

Songwriters' Hall of Fame member, lyricist Bert Kalmar, who collaborated almost exclusively with composer Harry Ruby, wrote several hit songs for Hollywood movies and also contributed to several Broadway musicals in the twenties. Kalmar's best known hit lyrics include 1923's "Who's Sorry Now?," 1928's "I Wanna Be Loved by You," and "I Love You So Much," 1930's "Three Little Words," and 1931's "Nevertheless." His last hit came in 1951 with "A Kiss to Build a Dream On," which came about twenty years after his previous hit.

Helen Kane
b. 1908, New York, New York
d. 1966, Jackson Heights, New York

Singer Helen Kane was known as the Boop-Boop-de-Doop Girl. Her rendition of "I Wanna Be Loved by You," with her occasional interpolations of a squeaky "boop-boop-de-doop" was one of the classics of the late twenties. The Betty Boop cartoons imitated Kane's style.

Bronislaw Kaper
b. 1902, Warsaw, Poland

Composer Bronislaw Kaper wrote a few hits for the movies beginning in the mid-thirties. His best-known hits are 1936's "San Francisco" and 1953's "Hi-Lili, Hi-Lo."

Buddy Kaye
b. 1918, New York, New York

Lyricist Buddy Kaye was particularly active in the forties and fifties. His biggest hit was 1945's "Till the End of Time," which he and Ted Mossman wrote to a melody by classical composer Frédéric Chopin. Kaye also wrote special material for nightclub acts for several stars, wrote for cartoon series, and later became a record producer.

Sammy Kaye
b. 1910, Rocky River, Ohio

Bandleader Sammy Kaye led a very successful sweet-style band during the thirties and forties. They continued to thrive into the fifties and sixties, but not quite to the earlier extent. Kaye's slogan was "Swing and Sway with Sammy Kaye."

Kaye and his orchestra had major hits with 1941's "Daddy," 1942's "There Will Never Be Another You," and 1950's "Harbor Lights." He and his band backed Don Cornell on the 1950 hit "It Isn't Fair."

Ruby Keeler
b. 1910, Halifax, Nova Scotia

Dancer and singer Ruby Keeler starred in several movie musicals in the thirties, mostly with Dick Powell. She married Al Jolson in 1928, while she was appearing in Broadway musicals. She began her movie career in 1933 in *Forty-second Street*. She followed that gigantic success with starring roles in *The Gold Diggers of 1933* and about ten other movie musicals by the early forties. She divorced Jolson in 1939, remarried, and went into semiretirement. She came out of retirement to star in the 1970 revival of *No, No, Nanette* on Broadway.

Gene Kelly
b. 1912, Pittsburgh, Pennsylvania

Gene Kelly is one of the most famous and gifted dancers Hollywood has ever featured. His acrobatic dance routines were some of the best ever filmed. Although he is not a great singer, he, like fellow dancer Fred Astaire, has a distinctive singing style that could sell a song.

His early training was on Broadway, where he starred in the 1941 musical *Pal Joey*. He began his movie career in 1942. Over the next several years, he starred in more than thirty movies, notably 1945's *Anchors Aweigh*, 1949's *On the Town*, 1951's *An American in Paris*, 1952's *Singin' in the Rain*, and 1954's *Brigadoon*.

Hal Kemp
b. 1905, Marion, Alabama
d. 1940, Madera, California

Hal Kemp (real name: James Harold Kemp) led a sweet-style band during the thirties. He had organized a band while he was in college, and most of the members had continued with the group when it went professional in 1927. Some of Kemp's most famous hits include "Got a Date with an Angel," which featured a vocal by drummer Skinny Ennis and saxman Saxie Dowell's nonsense songs "Three Little Fishies" and "Playmate."

Kemp was killed in an auto accident on the way to an engagement in San Francisco in late 1940.

Jimmy Kennedy

British songwriter Jimmy Kennedy is best known for the songs he produced in the mid-thirties and forties. His biggest hits include 1935's "Isle of Capri" and "Red Sails in the Sunset," 1937's "Harbor Lights," 1939's "South of the Border," 1940's "My Prayer," and 1953's "April in Portugal."

Charles Kenny
b. 1898, Astoria, New York
d. 1978, Vancouver, Canada

Composer-lyricist Charles Kenny collaborated with his brother, Nick, on several popular songs during the thirties and forties. Their most famous work includes 1931's "Love Letters in the Sand" and 1938's "There's a Gold Mine in the Sky."

Nick Kenny
b. 1895, Astoria, New York
d. 1975, Sarasota, Florida

Lyricist Nick Kenny collaborated with his brother, Charles, to write several popular songs in the thirties and forties. Nick was also a well-known poet and radio columnist for newspapers. (See Charles Kenny, above, for important songs.)

Walter Kent
b. 1911, New York, New York

Composer Walter Kent was most active as a writer of popular songs in the thirties and forties. He wrote 1941's "The White Cliffs of Dover" and 1943's "I'll Be Home for Christmas."

Stan Kenton
b. 1912, Wichita, Kansas
d. 1979, Los Angeles, California

Bandleader Stan Kenton was particularly associated with progressive jazz. After high school he played piano in clubs and worked in radio and as a studio musician. Kenton formed his band in 1940. It won awards as the top band of 1947, 1950, 1951, and 1952. From 1948 Kenton ceased ballroom work to concentrate on concerts and recordings of progressive jazz. His only major recording successes were 1945's "Tampico" and the 1946 novelty song "Shoofly Pie and Apple Pan Dowdy.'' His theme song was ''Artistry in Rhythm.''

Jerome Kern
b. 1885, New York, New York
d. 1945, New York, New York

Jerome Kern was one of the most important composers in popular music history. He wrote his first complete score for a Broadway musical in 1911. Kern and some other composers and lyricists experimented with American subjects for musicals in the small Princess Theater in New York. His first big hit came with ''They Didn't Believe Me'' from *The Girl from Utah* in 1914. Several other shows in the late 1910s and early 1920s led the way for the tremendously important *Show Boat* in 1927 and then for 1933's *Roberta*. By the end of the thirties Kern had composed his last Broadway musical.

He wrote the score for the 1936 Fred Astaire and Ginger Rogers movie musical *Swing Time* and concentrated on that genre in the late thirties and early forties.

Kern's hit output was prolific; some of his most popular hits include 1920's ''Look for the Silver Lining,'' 1925's ''Who?,'' 1927's ''Ol' Man River,'' and ''Can't Help Lovin' Dat Man,'' 1933's ''Smoke Gets in Your Eyes,'' and ''Yesterdays,'' 1935's ''Lovely to Look At,'' 1940's ''All the Things You Are,'' 1941's ''The Last Time I Saw Paris,'' and 1944's ''Long Ago and Far Away.''

The 1946 movie musical *Till the Clouds Roll By* was based on Kern's life and featured many of his most famous hits. He was inducted into the Songwriters' Hall of Fame.

Pee-Wee King
b. 1914, Abrams, Wisconsin

Pee Wee King (real name: Frank King) is most famous in the country music field. However, he wrote several hits that were covered by main-line pop artists and became major hits. They include 1948's ''Tennessee Waltz,'' 1951's ''Slow Poke,'' and 1952's ''You Belong to Me.''

Lisa Kirk
b. 1925, Brownsville, Pennsylvania

Singer and actress Lisa Kirk was active during the forties and fifties. Her biggest role was in 1949's *Kiss Me Kate*. Otherwise, she is best known for her nightclub appearances.

Ted Koehler
b. 1894, Washington, D.C.
d. 1973, Santa Monica, California

Lyricist Ted Koehler, a Songwriters' Hall of Fame member, was very active in the thirties and forties. His most frequent collaborator was composer Harold Arlen. Koehler's best-known lyrics include 1931's ''Wrap Your Troubles in Dreams'' and ''Linda,'' 1932's ''I Gotta Right to Sing the Blues,'' 1933's ''Stormy Weather,'' and 1934's ''Let's Fall in Love.''

André Kostelanetz
b. 1901, St. Petersburg, Russia
d. 1980, Port-au-Prince, Haiti

André Kostelanetz was most famous as an orchestra conductor. He came to the United States from Russia in 1922 and worked as an accompanist for and a coach of opera singers. He appeared on radio as a conductor in the early thirties. In recent years he concentrated on recording work, composing, and arranging. He adapted a Peter I. Tchaikovsky theme into the 1939 hit ''Moon Love.''

Alex Kramer
b. 1903, Montreal, Canada

Alex Kramer is most famous for the 1944 song ''Candy,'' which he wrote. In the forties he was a staff composer for a New York publishing firm. In the late forties he and his wife formed their own publishing business.

Kay Kyser
b. 1906, Rocky Mount, North Carolina

Kay Kyser was one of the most successful bandleaders in the thirties and forties. He formed his first band while he attended the University of North Carolina. By the mid-thirties his band was firmly established as one of the most popular groups. His radio show, *Kay Kyser's Kollege of Musical Knowledge,* in the late thirties and forties was particularly popular. Kyser and his band appeared in several movies from the late thirties through the mid-forties.

Kyser's million-selling discs include 1939's ''Three Little Fishies''; 1942's ''Praise the Lord and Pass the Ammunition,'' ''Strip Polka,'' ''Who Wouldn't Love You?,'' and ''Jingle, Jangle, Jingle''; and 1948's ''Woody Woodpecker'' and a revival of 1928's ''When You're Smiling.''

Mike Douglas was one of the singers with Kyser's band. Kyser retired in the early fifties.

L

Frankie Laine
b. 1913, Chicago, Illinois

Singer Frankie Laine (real name: Frank Paul Lo Vecchio) got his big break in early 1946 and gained national fame with his 1947 million-selling recording of "That's My Desire." In the thirties and early forties he worked at odd jobs and had a few minor singing jobs. Laine also appeared in a few low-budget films in the late forties and early fifties.

The other eight Laine million sellers are 1949's "Mule Train" and "That Lucky Old Sun"; 1950's "Cry of the Wild Goose"; 1951's "Jezebel" and "Jalousie"; 1952's "High Noon"; 1953's "I Believe"; and 1957's "Moonlight Gambler."

Burton Lane
b. 1912, New York, New York

Burton Lane was an important composer of popular songs for Broadway shows and movies from the early thirties through the mid-sixties. His biggest Broadway successes were 1947's *Finian's Rainbow* and 1965's *On a Clear Day You Can See Forever*.

Lane's best-known songs include 1933's "Everything I Have Is Yours" and "Says My Heart," 1941's "How About You?," 1947's "Feudin' and Fightin'," and "How Are Things in Glocca Morra?," and 1965's "On a Clear Day You Can See Forever." Lane is a member of the Songwriters' Hall of Fame.

Frances Langford
b. 1913, Lakeland, Florida

Frances Langford (real name: Frances Newbern) was a popular singer and actress in the thirties and forties on radio, in the movies, and on records. She got her break when Rudy Vallee heard her sing on a Tampa, Florida, radio show and helped her get started in big-time show business. One of her successes came in the 1935 film *Every Night at Eight,* in which she introduced "I'm in the Mood for Love." She sang with Louis Armstrong on several records.

Mario Lanza
b. 1921, Philadelphia, Pennsylvania
d. 1959, Rome, Italy

Mario Lanza (real name: Alfred Arnold Cocozza) was most famous for 1951's "Be My Love," which he introduced in the Hollywood movie musical *Toast of New Orleans* (1950) and for his portrayal of Enrico Caruso in *The Great Caruso* (1951). He sang primarily operatic arias or popular songs in that style. His voice was dubbed for Edmund Purdom's in 1954's movie version of *The Student Prince.* Lanza succumbed to weight problems and died of a heart attack.

Grace La Rue
b. c. 1882
d. 1956, Burlingame, California

Grace La Rue starred in several Broadway musicals and revues from the early 1900s until the late twenties.

Gertrude Lawrence
b. 1898, London, England
d. 1952, New York, New York

Gertrude Lawrence (real name: Gertrude Alexandria Dagmar Lawrence-Klasen) began entertaining in English music halls as a youngster. She made her Broadway debut in 1924's *Charlot's Revue.* Starring roles followed in 1926's *Oh, Kay!,* but her biggest roles came in 1941's *Lady in the Dark* and 1951's *The King and I.* The 1968 movie *Star!,* with Julie Andrews in the leading role, was based on Lawrence's career.

Jack Lawrence
b. 1912, Brooklyn, New York

Jack Lawrence primarily wrote lyrics for songs but occasionally composed the music as well. Most of his songs were produced from the early thirties to the fifties. Lawrence was also a good singer and appeared on several radio shows.

His most famous songs include 1932's "Play, Fiddle, Play," 1939's "If I Didn't Care" and "All or Nothing at All" (popularized in 1943), 1945's "Symphony," 1943's "Linda" and "Tenderly" (popularized in the mid-fifties), 1954's "Hold My Hand," and 1956's "The Poor People of Paris."

Peggy Lee
b. 1922, Jamestown, North Dakota

Peggy Lee (real name: Norma Jean Engstrom) began singing on radio in North Dakota at age sixteen. Her break came when she sang with Will Osborne's band in late 1940. In 1941 she joined Benny Goodman's band and adopted her stage name. Before she left the Goodman band in 1943, she appeared in a couple of films and recorded several songs with it. She married guitarist Dave Barbour in 1943, and they teamed up to write 1948's big hit: "Mañana." In later years she appeared in several films, recorded steadily (often with considerable jazz influence), and frequently appeared on TV.

Alan Jay Lerner
b. 1918, New York, New York

Lyricist Alan Jay Lerner was born into wealth. His father founded the Lerner women's clothing chain. Lerner is primarily noted as the collaborator with composer Frederick Loewe on several successful Broadway musicals and the Academy Award-winning movie musical *Gigi*. Lerner also collaborated with Kurt Weill (1948's *Love Life*), Burton Lane (1965's *On a Clear Day You Can See Forever*), and André Previn (1969's *Coco*). (See Frederick Loewe, page 215, for the Lerner and Loewe collaborations.) Lerner is a member of the Songwriters' Hall of Fame.

Hal Le Roy
b. 1912, Cincinnati, Ohio

Hal LeRoy (real name: John LeRoy Schotte) was primarily known as a dancer, but he sang occasionally. He appeared in vaudeville, in nightclubs, in films, and on Broadway. His chief claim to popular music fame is helping to introduce 1935's "Zing! Went the Strings of My Heart" in the revue *Thumbs Up*.

Al Lewis
b. 1901, New York, New York

Al Lewis, who wrote mostly lyrics and occasionally music, is best known for the songs he wrote from the twenties to the fifties. His most famous hits include 1933's "You Gotta Be a Football Hero," 1940's "Blueberry Hill," and 1941's "Rose O'Day."

Morgan Lewis
b. 1906, Rockville, Connecticut

Composer Morgan Lewis (full name: William Morgan Lewis, Jr.) primarily collaborated with lyricist Nancy Hamilton on songs for the Broadway stage. Their most famous collaboration was "How High the Moon," written in 1940 for *Two for the Show* and popularized by Les Paul and Mary Ford in 1951.

Sam M. Lewis
b. 1885, New York, New York
d. 1959, New York, New York

Songwriters' Hall of Fame member Sam Lewis was a lyricist who wrote several popular hits from 1912

through the thirties. He most often collaborated with Joe Young, but he also wrote with several other noted composers. His most famous lyrics include 1925's "Dinah," "Five Foot Two, Eyes of Blue," and "I'm Sitting on Top of the World"; 1926's "In a Little Spanish Town"; and 1929's "I Kiss Your Hand, Madame."

Ted Lewis
b. 1892, Circleville, Ohio
d. 1971, New York, New York

Clarinetist, bandleader, and entertainer Ted Lewis (real name: Theodore Leopold Friedman) enjoyed a successful sixty-year career in show business. His trademarks were a worn and battered top hat and his opening line, "Is ev'rybody happy?"

Winnie Lightner
b. 1901, New York, New York
d. 1971, Sherman Oaks, California

Comedienne, singer, and dancer Winnie Lightner (real name: Winifred Hanson) was noted for her roles on the Broadway stage of the twenties. By the mid-thirties her career had waned.

Beatrice Lillie
b. 1898, Toronto, Canada

Comedienne Beatrice Lillie was a star in Broadway musicals, in the movies, and over radio primarily from the mid-twenties through the forties. She came to America with the *Charlot's Revue of 1924*. After that big hit she performed in revues, in vaudeville, and on radio, as well as in a half dozen movies from the late twenties. Her last film role was in 1967's *Thoroughly Modern Millie*.

Sidney Lippman
b. 1914, Minneapolis, Minnesota

Composer Sidney Lippman's most famous songs were produced during the forties and fifties. They are 1949's " 'A'—You're Adorable" and 1951's "Too Young." He most often collaborated with lyricist Sylvia Dee.

Jack Little
b. 1900, London, England
d. 1956, Hollywood, Florida

"Little" Jack Little was a popular singer on radio during the twenties, one of the first performers to become popular because of his exposure on that medium. In addition to his singing, he composed several songs, notably 1924's "Jealous" and 1932's "In a Shanty in Old Shanty Town." In the thirties he led a band, and in the forties he worked as a single. After that he became a disc jockey, then disappeared from the public eye.

Jay Livingston
b. 1915, McDonald, Pennsylvania

Composer Jay Livingston produced several popular songs, particularly for the movies. He often collaborated with lyricist Ray Evans. Livingston's best-known compositions include 1946's "To Each His Own"; 1948's Academy Award winner, "Buttons and Bows"; 1950's Academy Award winner, "Mona Lisa"; 1950's "Silver Bells"; 1956's Academy Award winner, "Que Será Será"; and 1957's "Tammy." In addition, Livingston has been very active writing television theme songs. He was elected to the Songwriters' Hall of Fame.

Jerry Livingston
b. 1909, Denver, Colorado

Composer Jerry Livingston (real name: Jerry Levinson) wrote several popular hits from the thirties into the fifties. He formed his own publishing company in the forties and began writing for Hollywood films in the late forties. In the late fifties he composed several successful TV show theme songs, including *Caspar, the Friendly Ghost* and the *Bugs Bunny* theme.

His most famous hits include 1933's "Under a Blanket of Blue" and "It's the Talk of the Town," 1944's "Mairzy Doats," 1947's "Chi-Baba, Chi-Baba," and 1955's "Wake the Town and Tell the People." He also composed the score for the 1949 Disney feature-length cartoon *Cinderella,* which included several popular successes.

John Jacob Loeb
b. 1910, Chicago, Illinois

John Jacob Loeb is most famous as the writer of 1928's "Masquerade," 1937's "Boo-Hoo" and "A Sailboat in the Moonlight," and 1945's "Seems Like Old Times." He most often collaborated with Carmen Lombardo, and Guy Lombardo and his Royal Canadians often introduced his songs.

Frank Loesser
b. 1910, New York, New York
d. 1969, New York, New York

Songwriters' Hall of Fame member Frank Loesser was one of this country's major hit writers. In the early part of his career he primarily wrote lyrics, but later he wrote both lyrics and music.

Loesser's biggest hits include 1938's "Says My Heart," "Small Fry," "Heart and Soul," and "Two Sleepy People"; 1939's "Bubbles in the Wine" (Lawrence Welk's theme); 1942's "I Don't Want to Walk Without You," "Jingle, Jangle, Jingle," and "Praise the Lord and Pass the Ammunition"; 1947's "I Wish I Didn't Love You So"; 1948's *Where's Charley?,* which introduced "Once in Love with Amy" and several other hits, and "On a Slow Boat to China"; 1949's Academy Award-winning song, "Baby, It's Cold Outside"; 1950's *Guys and Dolls,* which introduced "A Bushel and a Peck" and several other outstanding songs; 1952's "Anywhere I Wander"; 1956's *The Most Happy Fella,* which introduced "Standing on the Corner"; and 1961's *How to Succeed in Business Without Really Trying.*

Frederick Loewe
b. 1904, Berlin, Germany

Composer Frederick Loewe settled in America in 1924. He is primarily identified with lyricist Alan Jay Lerner and the musicals they have written for the Broadway stage. They collaborated on seven Broadway musicals and one movie musical. Their greatest hit was 1956's *My Fair Lady,* but several others were also very successful. Their other Broadway hits include 1947's *Brigadoon,* 1951's *Paint Your Wagon,* and 1960's *Camelot.* Lerner and Loewe also wrote for films, notably for 1958's *Gigi,* the winner of nine Academy Awards, including best picture of the year. Loewe is a member of the Songwriters' Hall of Fame.

Ella Logan
b. 1913, Glasgow, Scotland
d. 1969, San Mateo, California

Singer Ella Logan (real name: Ella Allan) was a Scottish singer who was best known for her role as Sharon in the 1947 stage musical *Finian's Rainbow.* She had appeared in several films and in Broadway shows from the early thirties. After her triumph in *Finian's Rainbow,* she never played Broadway again.

Carmen Lombardo
b. 1903, London, Canada
d. 1971, Miami, Florida

Guy Lombardo's brother Carmen played lead saxophone and often sang with the Royal Canadians during the thirties. He also arranged or composed several of their major hits.

Guy Lombardo
b. 1902, London, Canada
d. 1977, Houston, Texas

Guy Lombardo formed a band with three of his brothers, Lebert, Victor, and Carmen, which they called Guy Lombardo and his Royal Canadians. With the slogan ''The Sweetest Music This Side of Heaven'' and ''Auld Lang Syne'' as its theme song, the Lombardo band was probably as commercially successful as any musical group ever. It became famous over television playing for the New Year's Eve celebrations.

Julie London
b. 1926, Santa Rosa, California

Singer and actress Julie London was particularly noted as a singer during the mid-fifties. Her low-voice styling was very distinctive. Her 1955 recording of ''Cry Me a River'' launched her singing career, which in turn boosted her movie career. In 1947 she married actor Jack Webb, but later she divorced him and married pianist and composer Bobby Troup. She recently appeared in the TV series *Emergency*.

Johnny Long
b. 1916, Newell, North Carolina
d. 1972, Parkersburg, West Virginia

Johnny Long led a popular dance band in the thirties and forties. It was most famous for its rearrangements of standards, such as the up tempo version of ''In a Shanty in Old Shanty Town,'' with the band singing takeoff lyrics.

Vincent Lopez
b. 1898, Brooklyn, New York
d. 1975, Miami Beach, Florida

Pianist Vincent Lopez led a sweet-style band that was popular in the twenties and early thirties. Their most notable hit was ''Nola.'' Even after the sweet bands had waned in popularity, Lopez continued to appear on radio, television, and ballrooms. He discovered singer Betty Hutton.

Jimmie Lunceford
b. 1902, Fulton, Missouri
d. 1947, Seaside, Oregon

Jimmie Lunceford gave up a job as athletic director of a Memphis, Tennessee, high school to form a band in the late twenties. It became one of the great hot jazz bands of the thirties and forties. Lunceford was on the road with the band when he suffered a fatal heart attack.

Art Lund
b. 1915, Salt Lake City, Utah

Art Lund (real name: Art London) gained fame as a vocalist with the Benny Goodman band in the forties. He left Goodman in 1942 but returned in 1946. As a single in 1947 he recorded the hit ''Mam'selle.'' He had a starring role in 1956's *The Most Happy Fella*, but by the sixties his career had faded.

Abe Lyman
b. 1897, Chicago, Illinois
d. 1957, Beverly Hills, California

Bandleader Abe Lyman had a very successful radio show in the thirties and forties. Lyman quit the music business in the late forties and opened a restaurant. He also helped write the music or lyrics for several popular songs, including 1923's ''I Cried for You'' and 1926's ''After I Say I'm Sorry.''

Vera Lynn
b. 1917, London, England

Singer Vera Lynn is most famous in the United States for her 1952 hit ''Auf Wiederseh'n, Sweetheart.''

M

Jeanette MacDonald
b. 1901, Philadelphia, Pennsylvania
d. 1965, Houston, Texas

Singing star Jeanette MacDonald is most famous for the operetta-style movie musicals she made with Nelson Eddy in the thirties. She began costarring with Eddy in 1935's *Naughty Marietta,* but their most famous collaboration was 1936's *Rose Marie.* MacDonald was married to actor Gene Raymond.

Gordon MacRae
b. 1921, East Orange, New Jersey

Singer Gordon MacRae is particularly remembered for the movie musicals he made in the fifties. His break into the big time came in 1942, when he began singing with Horace Heidt's band. MacRae had a featured part in the 1946 Broadway musical *Three to Make Ready.* He is particularly remembered for his movie roles in 1955's *Oklahoma!* and 1956's *Carousel.* He remained active in several phases of show business into the seventies.

MacRae had a million-selling recording of "I Still Get Jealous" in 1947 and, with Jo Stafford, had million sellers with "Say Something Sweet to Your Sweetheart" in 1948 and "Whispering Hope" in 1949.

Herb Magidson
b. 1906, Braddock, Pennsylvania

Herb Magidson wrote several important songs in the 1930s and 1940s. His best-known hits include the first Academy Award-winning song, 1934's "The Continental"; 1938's "Music, Maestro, Please"; 1939's "How Long Has This Been Going On?"; and 1950's "Enjoy Yourself—It's Later Than You Think."

Matt Malneck
b. 1904, Newark, New Jersey

Matt Malneck led a successful orchestra in the thirties and forties. He also composed several songs during the thirties, mostly with lyricist Johnny Mercer.

David Mann
b. 1916, Philadelphia, Pennsylvania

Songwriter Dave Mann's best-known hit is 1941's "There! I've Said It Again." Mann did a lot of arranging for singers like Frank Sinatra and Ella Fitzgerald and for radio, television, and movies.

Gerald Marks
b. 1900, Saginaw, Michigan

Gerald Marks's most famous compositions include "All of Me" and "Is It True What They Say About Dixie?" He was also a successful bandleader.

Johnny Marks
b. 1909, Mount Vernon, New York

Composer-lyricist Johnny Marks's most famous song is "Rudolph the Red-Nosed Reindeer."

Everett Marshall
b. 1901, Lawrence, Massachusetts

Singer Everett Marshall was particularly popular during the mid-thirties. He sang in a couple of movie musicals and a few Broadway musicals.

Dean Martin
b. 1917, Steubenville, Ohio

Singer and actor Dean Martin (real name: Dino Crocetti) was singing in nightclubs when he teamed up with comedian Jerry Lewis in the mid-forties. They became stars of several movies, with Martin playing straight man to Lewis. The pair broke up in 1957. Martin achieved wide recognition with his *Dean Martin Show* on television in the seventies.

Martin's most famous recordings include 1953's "That's Amore," 1955's "Memories Are Made of This," 1958's "Return to Me," and "Volare," and 1964's "Everybody Loves Somebody."

Freddy Martin
b. 1907, Springfield, Ohio
d. 1983, Newport Beach, California

Freddy (sometimes spelled Freddie) Martin learned to play the drums in an orphanage band and added the saxophone while he was a student at Ohio State University. He formed his own professional band in 1932. Martin's orchestra had a deep ensemble sound because of his lead tenor saxophone. His biggest hits were 1941's "Tonight We Love" and 1946's "Symphony."

Hugh Martin
b. 1914, Birmingham, Alabama

Composer Hugh Martin teamed with lyricist Ralph Blane on several successful songs for Broadway and Hollywood. Their best-known collaborations include "Buckle Down, Winsocki," "The Trolley Song," "The Boy Next Door," and "Have Yourself a Merry Little Christmas." Most of Martin's songs came from 1941 through 1964.

Mary Martin
b. 1913, Weatherford, Texas

Broadway star Mary Martin is most famous for her leading roles in the musicals *South Pacific* and *The Sound of Music*. She first made an impression when she introduced "My Heart Belongs to Daddy" in 1938's *Leave It to Me*. Other Broadway successes include 1943's *One Touch of Venus* and 1966's *I Do! I Do!*

Martin also starred in a very successful production of *Peter Pan* for television and appeared in about a dozen movies.

She is the mother of Larry Hagman, who is starred as J. R. Ewing in the long-running TV series *Dallas*.

Tony Martin
b. 1914, Oakland, California

Tony Martin (real name: Alvin Morris) began his career as a saxophone player and singer for a band in

San Francisco. After a radio broadcast he was offered and accepted a job in a band at the Chicago World's Fair in 1933. After that he went to Hollywood, where he acted and sang in numerous movie musicals. Martin's only million-selling record was 1946's "To Each His Own."

Al Martino
b. 1927, Philadelphia, Pennsylvania

Singer Al Martino (real name: Alfred Cini) had his first million-selling record with "Here Is My Heart" in 1952. Thirteen years later he had his other million seller with "Spanish Eyes." Martino became more successful in Europe than he was in America.

Frankie Masters
b. 1904, St. Mary's, West Virginia

Frankie Masters led a very successful sweet-style band in the thirties and forties. He also collaborated with Johnny Burke and Kahn Kaene on the 1939 hit "Scatterbrain."

Joseph McCarthy
b. 1885, Somerville, Massachusetts
d. 1943, New York, New York

Lyricist Joseph McCarthy wrote several hit songs from about 1910 through the thirties. He collaborated on the Broadway musicals *Irene* (1919), *Kid Boots* (1924), and *Rio Rita* (1927). His hit lyrics include 1913's "You Made Me Love You," 1918's "I'm Always Chasing Rainbows," 1919's "In My Sweet Little Alice Blue Gown," and 1927's "Rio Rita."

McGuire Sisters
Christine: b. 1929, Middleton, Ohio
Dorothy: b. 1930, Middleton, Ohio
Phyllis: b. 1931, Middleton, Ohio

The McGuire Sisters, from Middleton, Ohio, were one of the most successful female vocal groups in America in the early fifties. They hit the big time in 1954 with their recording of "Goodnight, Sweetheart, Goodnight." Their cover version of "Sincerely" in 1955 was a million seller and brought them even more fame and fortune. Their recording of "Moonglow and the Theme from *Picnic*" in 1956 also became a gold record. "Sugartime," a 1956 song that went gold in 1958, closed out their million sellers.

Jimmy McHugh
b. 1894, Boston, Massachusetts
d. 1969, Beverly Hills, California

Songwriters' Hall of Fame member Jimmy McHugh had a very prolific career as a composer of popular songs. In the early part of his career he collaborated with lyricist Dorothy Fields. Later he worked with several other important lyricists, including Harold Adamson, Johnny Mercer, Ted Koehler, and Ned Washington. Many of his hits were written for the movies or the stage.

McHugh's best-known hits include 1924's "When My Sugar Walks down the Street," 1928's "I Can't Give You Anything but Love," 1930's "Exactly Like You," and "On the Sunny Side of the Street," 1931's "Cuban Love Song," 1933's "Don't Blame Me," 1935's "I'm in the Mood for Love," and 1944's "A Lovely Way to Spend an Evening."

In the fifties McHugh organized the Jimmy McHugh Polio Foundation and Jimmy McHugh Charities. He also organized his own publishing company.

James Melton
b. 1904, Moultrie, Georgia
d. 1961, New York, New York

James Melton was one of the operatic tenors who were able to perform popular songs successfully. He is primarily remembered for the songs he introduced in several movie musicals during the late thirties and early forties, especially "September in the Rain."

Johnny Mercer
b. 1909, Savannah, Georgia
d. 1976, Bel-Air, California

Johnny Mercer got his break in big-time show business when he won a singing contest sponsored by Paul Whiteman. When the Rhythm Boys left the Whiteman orchestra, Mercer was hired as their replacement. In addition to his singing, he often wrote material for the band. After Whiteman came stints with Benny Goodman and Bob Crosby. By this time Mercer had created enough attention to garner a contract to write for films. At first he served as lyricist for other composers, but eventually he wrote both lyrics and music. He is a member of the Songwriters' Hall of Fame.

Mercer was a leading lyricist from the thirties into the sixties and remained active until his death in 1976. He also appeared on radio frequently and recorded often.

Mercer's most famous hits include 1933's "Lazybones," 1934's "P.S. I Love You," 1936's "I'm an Old Cowhand," 1937's "Too Marvelous for Words," 1938's "Jeepers Creepers," "Hooray for Hollywood," and "You Must Have Been a Beautiful Baby," 1940's "Fools Rush In," 1941's "Blues in the Night," 1942's "Tangerine," and "That Old Black Magic," 1945's "Ac-cent-tchu-ate the Positive," "Dream," "Laura," and "On the Atchison, Topeka and the Santa Fe," 1946's "Come Rain or Come Shine," 1951's "In the Cool, Cool, Cool of the Evening," 1955's "Something's Gotta Give," 1959's "I Wanna Be Around," 1961's "Moon River," 1963's "Charade," and 1962's "Days of Wine and Roses." Mercer wrote more than 1,000 songs, making him, along with Irving Berlin and Oscar Hammerstein II, one of the most prolific songwriters of all time.

Mabel Mercer
b. 1900, Staffordshire, England
d. 1984, Pittsfield, Massachusetts

Singer Mabel Mercer came to the United States in the late thirties and often appeared in intimate New York nightclubs. She remained active into her seventies.

Ethel Merman
b. 1909, Astoria, New York
d. 1984, New York, New York

One of Broadway's major performers from the thirties into the fifties, Ethel Merman (real name: Ethel Zimmerman) was famous for her loud, belting style of singing. Although she also performed on radio, in movies and on television, she gained her fame on the Broadway stage. She began her career in 1930's *Girl Crazy,* in which she introduced "I Got Rhythm." Over the next thirty years she starred in more than a dozen musicals and appeared in fifteen movies. Some of her most famous starring roles came in 1934's *Anything Goes,* 1946's *Annie Get Your Gun,* and 1950's *Gypsy.* She continued to perform until shortly before her death.

Bob Merrill
b. 1921, Atlantic City, New Jersey

Composer Bob Merrill wrote several hits from the late forties through the late sixties. In his early career he specialized in novelty songs. Some of his best-known hits include 1953's "Doggie in the Window," 1950's "If I Knew You Were Comin' I'd 'ave Baked a Cake," 1961's "Love Makes the World Go 'Round," and 1964's "People." He composed the scores and wrote

the lyrics for several Broadway musicals, notably 1964's *Funny Girl.*

Merry Macs
Joe McMichael
Ted McMichael
Judd McMichael
Cherry MacKay

Three brothers and one female made up the Merry Macs, which began performing in the early thirties but did not reach prominence until the late thirties and early forties. The female member changed often during the early forties.

George Meyer
b. 1884, Boston, Massachusetts
d. 1959, New York, New York

George Meyer composed several popular songs and a few hits from 1909 through the 1940s. His best-known hits include 1917's "For Me and My Gal" (which was revived in 1942), 1924's "Mandy," and 1942's "There Are Such Things."

Joseph Meyer
b. 1894, Modesto, California

Composer Joseph Meyer's successes include 1922's "My Honey's Lovin' Arms," 1924's "California, Here I Come," and 1925's "If You Knew Susie." He composed songs through the forties but never had hits as big as those from the twenties. The Songwriters' Hall of Fame honored Meyer with membership.

Ray Middleton
b. 1907, Chicago, Illinois
d. 1984, Panorama City, California

Ray Middleton's most famous Broadway roles were in 1933's *Roberta* and in 1946's *Annie Get Your Gun,* in which he played Frank Butler. After several minor movie roles he succeeded Ezio Pinza in *South Pacific* in 1950.

Glenn Miller
b. 1904, Clarinda, Iowa
d. 1944

Glenn Miller was one of the most famous bandleaders of the big band era. His forte was arranging, and his unique clarinet-lead sound became what the public wanted to hear in the last years of the thirties.

Miller's million-selling recordings include 1939's

"Little Brown Jug," "In the Mood," "Sunrise Serenade," and his theme song, "Moonlight Serenade"; 1940's "Pennsylvania 6-5000" and "Tuxedo Junction"; 1941's "Chattanooga Choo Choo"; and 1942's "I've Got a Gal in Kalamazoo" and "American Patrol." The sound track album for the 1954 movie *The Glenn Miller Story* (originally a ten-inch disc, expanded in 1956 to a twelve-inch LP) had become a million seller by 1968.

Miller exerted a great influence on the popular music of the late war years by directing an air force band and broadcasting on radio in the United States and Great Britain. The band was later headquartered in England. In 1944 Miller disappeared on a flight to Paris. His band continued to perform under the leadership of some of the other members.

Marilyn Miller
b. 1898, Evansville, Indiana
d. 1936, New York, New York

Marilyn Miller (real name: Mary Ellen Reynolds) was probably the most popular singer and actress of the Broadway stage of the twenties. She began appearing in vaudeville with her parents and toured the country for several years. She then performed in New York revues and graduated to musical comedy stardom in 1920's *Sally,* in which she introduced "Look for the Silver Lining." Other successes followed in 1925's *Sunny,* 1928's *Rosalie,* in which she first performed "Who?," and 1933's *As Thousands Cheer,* in which she introduced "Easter Parade."

Mitch Miller
b. 1911, Rochester, New York

Mitch Miller is probably best known for his *Sing Along with Mitch* albums and TV series in the late fifties and early sixties. He became director of the Mercury and later Columbia Records pops division. In that capacity he gave many new singers their starts, often conducting or producing their recording sessions.

Miller's first million seller was 1955's revival of the Civil War song "The Yellow Rose of Texas." He and his orchestra accompanied Guy Mitchell on million sellers of "The Roving Kind" and "My Truly, Truly Fair" in 1951 and "Pittsburgh, Pennsylvania" in 1952. Other gold records for Miller and his orchestra include 1957's "March from *Bridge on the River Kwai,*" the 1958 albums *Sing Along with Mitch, Christmas Sing Along with Mitch,* and *More Sing Along with Mitch,* the 1959 albums *Still More Sing Along with Mitch* and *Party Sing Along with Mitch,* and the 1960 albums *Sentimental Sing Along with Mitch* and *Memories Sing Along with Mitch.*

Mills Brothers
Herbert, b. 1912, Piqua, Ohio
Harry, b. 1913, Piqua, Ohio
Donald, b. 1915, Piqua, Ohio

The three brothers from Piqua, Ohio, the Mills Brothers, were a very successful singing group from the early thirties through the seventies. At times an older brother, John, joined the group to play guitar or sing bass.

One of the Mills Brothers' biggest hits came with "Paper Doll," the top hit of 1943. Other successes were 1944's "You Always Hurt the One You Love," 1948's "Lazy River," and 1952's "Glow-Worm," all million sellers. Their versions of "Opus One," "Be My Life's Companion," and "Cab Driver" were also popular.

Irving Mills
b. 1894, New York, New York

Lyricist Irving Mills was a very active songwriter in the twenties and thirties. In addition, he was a publisher (partner in Mills Music and at least four other companies), producer of movie musical shorts and radio shows, bandleader (Mills Blue Rhythm Band), manager for Duke Ellington for a time, and booster of many singers' recording careers, including those of Gene Austin and Rudy Vallee.

As a songwriter Mills's best-known lyrics include 1931's "Mood Indigo" and "Minnie, the Moocher," 1924's "When My Sugar Walks down the Street," 1932's "It Don't Mean a Thing If It Ain't Got That Swing," 1933's "Sophisticated Lady," 1934's "Moonglow," and 1935's "Solitude."

Guy Mitchell
b. 1927, Detroit, Michigan

Guy Mitchell (real name: Al Cernik) was one of the top hit makers of the early fifties. Mitchell signed with Warner Brothers as a child but never became the movie star they expected. He performed with Carmen Cavallaro and his orchestra in the late forties, appeared on *Arthur Godfrey's Talent Scouts,* and signed a recording contract with Columbia Records in 1950. His first million seller came with 1950's "My Heart Cries for You." Other big hits for Mitchell were 1951's "The Roving Kind" and "My Truly, Truly Fair," 1952's "Pittsburgh, Pennsylvania," 1956's "Singing the Blues," and 1959's "Heartaches by the Number."

After the fifties his popularity faded.

SELECTED BIOGRAPHICAL SKETCHES

Sidney Mitchell
b. 1888, Baltimore, Maryland
d. 1942, Los Angeles, California

Lyricist Sidney Mitchell wrote several popular songs and a few hits during the twenties and thirties. His most popular lyric was "You Turned the Tables on Me" (1936).

Vic Mizzy
b. 1916, Brooklyn, New York

Vic Mizzy was a composer of popular songs from the late thirties to the fifties. He is best known for 1945's "My Dreams Keep Getting Better All the Time."

The Modernaires
Hal Dickinson
Ralph Brewster
Chuck Goldstein
Bill Conway

Hal Dickinson was the founder and leader of the Modernaires, who sang with Fred Waring in the mid-thirties and first began to gain national attention when they performed and recorded with Charlie Barnet and his orchestra in 1936. They also worked with Paul Whiteman but were most famous as a prominent feature of Glenn Miller's band in the forties.

The Modernaires' most popular recordings with the Miller band include 1941's "Chattanooga Choo Choo," and 1942's "I've Got a Gal in Kalamazoo," "Juke Box Saturday Night," "Moonlight Cocktail," and "Don't Sit Under the Apple Tree."

The group became a quintet in the mid-forties, when Dickinson's wife, Paula Kelly, joined. Although the personnel changed several times, the group performed often in the forties and fifties and occasionally in later years.

James V. Monaco
b. 1885, Fornia, Italy
d. 1945, Beverly Hills, California

Composer James V. Monaco wrote numerous popular songs over a period from 1911 through the mid-forties. His most famous hits include 1912's "Row, Row, Row," 1913's "You Made Me Love You," 1938's "I've Got a Pocketful of Dreams," and 1945's "I Can't Begin to Tell You." He wrote several songs for Bing Crosby movies in the thirties and forties. Monaco was elected to the Songwriters' Hall of Fame.

Marilyn Monroe
b. 1926, Los Angeles, California
d. 1962, Brentwood, California

The sex symbol of the fifties Marilyn Monroe (real name: Norma Jean Baker) was not particularly known for her musical accomplishments. She did, however, star in the movie musical *Gentlemen Prefer Blondes* (1953), in which she performed some songs with costar Jane Russell.

Vaughn Monroe
b. 1911, Akron, Ohio
d. 1973, Stuart, Florida

Singer and bandleader Vaughn Monroe began his musical career as a trumpeter with Austin Wylie's orchestra. Monroe organized his own band in 1940 and was leader and vocalist. After 1953 he was strictly a soloist. His greatest period of popularity was from the mid-forties into the early years of rock and roll.

Some of Monroe's most popular recordings were 1941's "Racing with the Moon," his theme song; 1945's "There! I've Said It Again"; 1947's "Ballerina"; and 1949's biggest hit, "Riders in the Sky."

By the late fifties he had dropped out of the music business. He returned again in the sixties and was semiactive until his death.

Ricardo Montalban
b. 1920, Mexico City, Mexico

Ricardo Montalban is most famous as a movie and television star, but he did perform the Academy Award-winning song "Baby, It's Cold Outside" with Esther Williams in 1949's *Neptune's Daughter*. Their recording from the sound track became a million seller. He also starred in the Broadway musicals *Seventh Heaven* (1955) and *Jamaica* (1957) and the movie musicals *Fiesta* (1947), *On an Island with You* (1948), and *Two Weeks with Love* (1950). In recent years he has starred on television on *Fantasy Island*.

Art Mooney
b. Lowell, Massachusetts

Bandleader Art Mooney jumped into popularity with his 1947 recording of 1927's "I'm Looking over a Four Leaf Clover," which featured the banjo playing of Mike Pingatore. Mooney continued to revive oldies with a 1948 recording of 1926's "Baby Face" and 1934's "Bluebird of Happiness." In 1955 he and his orchestra garnered their last gold record with "Honey Babe," which had been written for the movie *Battle Cry*. They also accompanied Barry Gordon in 1955's "Nuttin' for Christmas," which sold a million copies. By the late fifties Mooney's popularity had declined.

Grace Moore
b. 1901, Jellicoe, Tennessee
d. 1947, Copenhagen, Denmark

Singer Grace Moore starred in Broadway musicals, in movie musicals, and on radio in the thirties. By the forties her popularity peak had passed, but she remained active until her death in an airplane crash. The 1953 movie *So This Is Love* was based on Moore's life.

Dennis Morgan
b. 1910, Prentice, Wisconsin

Singer and actor Dennis Morgan (real name: Stanley Morner) is known for his work in several movie musicals in the forties and fifties. The movie that brought him stardom was 1940's *Kitty Foyle*. His most famous movie musicals include 1944's *Shine On Harvest Moon* and *The Desert Song*, 1947's *My Wild Irish Rose*, 1948's *Two Guys from Texas*, 1949's *It's a Great Feeling*, and 1951's *Painting the Clouds with Sunshine*.

Helen Morgan
b. 1900, Danville, Illinois
d. 1941, Chicago, Illinois

Torch singer Helen Morgan was immortalized in *The Helen Morgan Story*, a 1957 movie which starred Ann Blyth (Gogi Grant did the singing). Morgan was particularly popular as a singer in the twenties and thirties. She began on Broadway in the 1925 edition of *George White's Scandals*, but her biggest part was as Julie La Verne in the 1927 and 1932 productions of *Show Boat*, in which she introduced "Bill." She played the role in the 1936 movie version as well. She also introduced "Why Was I Born?" in 1929's *Sweet Adeline*.

In the late twenties she opened a nightclub, The House of Morgan. She continued to perform through the mid-thirties, appearing in several movies and on radio.

Russ Morgan
b. 1904, Scranton, Pennsylvania
d. 1969, Las Vegas, Nevada

Russ Morgan led a very popular band in the thirties and forties and composed several songs that it popularized. Morgan's first jobs in music were as a pianist in local clubs. Then he became well known as an arranger for some of the best-known big bands. With the aid of Rudy Vallee, Morgan formed his own band in the mid-thirties, using the slogan "Music in the Morgan Manner." His group appeared often on radio in the late thirties.

Morgan's most famous composition was 1944's "You're Nobody till Somebody Loves You" (popularized by Dean Martin in the fifties). His band's biggest hit came in 1949 with "Cruising down the River." In the fifties and sixties Morgan continued to lead the band on a part-time basis.

Patricia Morison
b. 1915, New York, New York

Singer Patricia Morison starred in the 1949 Broadway musical *Kiss Me Kate*. She also appeared in numerous low-budget films in the late thirties and forties and occasionally on TV in the fifties.

Ella Mae Morse
b. 1924, Mansfield, Texas

Ella Mae Morse is primarily known as a jazz vocalist, but she recorded with Freddie Slack's orchestra in the early forties and introduced a few hits. She appeared in four movies in the mid-forties. She retired for a time but returned in the fifties.

George Murphy
b. 1902, New Haven, Connecticut

George Murphy was a famous dancer, actor, and singer during the 1930s and 1940s. His first featured role on Broadway was in *Roberta* (1933). His movie career began in 1934 and included more than fifty films and almost twenty movie musicals. When his work in films began to wane in the fifties, he entered politics. He was elected senator from California in 1964 and was defeated for reelection in 1970.

N

Lionel Newman
b. 1916, New Haven, Connecticut

Lionel Newman wrote the 1948 hit "Again." He was a noted arranger and musical director for Hollywood films from the late thirties through the fifties.

Ray Noble
b. 1903, Brighton, England
d. 1978, London, England

Composer Ray Noble was the first British bandleader to become successful in the United States, where he came in 1934. He became the arranger and musical director of the Radio City Music Hall in New York City. He also hired Glenn Miller to organize his band and to arrange charts for it. The Noble band was particularly successful in the late thirties and early forties. In the late thirties he began to concentrate on radio work. He served as music director for several famous radio shows, notably the Edgar Bergen and Charlie McCarthy show from 1941 into the 1950s.

Noble's only million-selling record came in 1941 with a revival of 1909's "By the Light of the Silvery Moon," with vocalist Roy Lanson. Noble's most famous compositions include 1931's "Goodnight, Sweetheart," 1932's "Love Is the Sweetest Thing," and 1934's "The Very Thought of You."

Ramon Novarro
b. 1899, Durango, Mexico
d. 1968, Hollywood Hills, California

Ramon Novarro was a famous star of silent and early sound films. He sang in several movie musicals, including 1929's *The Pagan,* in which he introduced "Pagan Love Song." His star roles had become scarce by the mid-thirties.

Donald Novis
b. 1906, Canada
d. 1966, Norwalk, California

Singer Donald Novis was a popular radio personality in the thirties. He also had a good role in the 1935 Broadway musical *Jumbo.* He retired in the forties but returned in a short time. He retired again in 1963, after he had worked for a time at Disneyland.

O

Ben Oakland
b. 1907, Brooklyn, New York

Composer Ben Oakland was particularly active in the thirties and forties. His best-known compositions are 1937's "I'll Take Romance" and 1947's "I'll Dance at Your Wedding."

Helen O'Connell
b. 1920, Lima, Ohio

Helen O'Connell is particularly famous as a singer with the Jimmy Dorsey orchestra from 1939 through 1943. She recorded often with the band and sang on the Dorsey recordings of the hits 1941's "Amapola," and "Green Eyes," and 1942's "Tangerine." She left Dorsey in 1943 and sang on radio for a short period. During the rest of the forties she remained relatively inactive. When she returned to show business in the fifties, she often appeared on television.

George Olsen
b. 1893, Portland, Oregon
d. 1971, Paramus, New Jersey

George Olsen was the leader of an important pre-swing band. His organization was featured in several Broadway shows and in vaudeville. Its biggest hit was 1926's "Who?," which it discovered when it played for the musical *Sunny.* Olsen's recording is reputed to have become a million seller (accurate records were not kept in those early years of the recording industry). Olsen led the orchestra for more than thirty years, but his most productive years were from 1923 to 1934. His theme song was "Beyond the Blue Horizon."

Original Dixieland Jazz Band
Nick La Rocca, leader, cornet,
  b. 1889, New Orleans, Louisiana
  d. 1961, New Orleans, Louisiana
Larry Shields, clarinet,
  b. 1893, New Orleans, Louisiana
  d. 1953, Los Angeles, California
Eddie Edwards, trombone,
  b. 1891, New Orleans, Louisiana
  d. 1963, New York, New York
Henry Ragas, piano
Tony Sbarbaro, drums,
  b. 1897, New Orleans, Louisiana
  d. 1969, Forest Hills, New York

The Original Dixieland Jazz Band was one of the principal groups that was responsible for popularizing jazz in the late 1910s and the 1920s.

The Orioles
Sonny Til, b. 1925 d. 1981
George Nelson, d. late 1960's
Alexander Sharp, d. c. 1959
Johnny Reed
Tommy Gaither, d. 1950

The Orioles worked around the Baltimore area until they got their break on *Arthur Godfrey's Talent Scouts* show, which gave them enough exposure to garner a recording contract and nightclub appearances on the rhythm and blues circuit. Their only million-selling recording was 1953's "Crying in the Chapel."

Harry Owens
b. 1902, O'Neil, Nebraska

Composer and bandleader Harry Owens was known for popularizing Hawaiian music in the United States during the thirties and forties. His most famous composition was 1937's Academy Award winner, "Sweet Leilani."

P

Patti Page
b. 1938, Tulsa, Oklahoma

Patti Page (real name: Clara Ann Fowler) was a popular nightclub, television, and recording singer, who was particularly popular during the fifties. Her first million-selling recording came with the 1949 recording of 1934's "With My Eyes Wide Open I'm Dreaming."

Page began her career as a hillbilly singer on radio, but she quickly broke away to become a top entertainer in clubs and on records. She hit the big time with 1951's "Tennessee Waltz."

Other gold records garnered by Page include 1950's "All My Love"; 1951's "Mockin' Bird Hill," "Would I Love You," "Detour," and "Mister and Mississippi"; 1952's "I Went to Your Wedding"; 1953's "Doggie in the Window" and "Changing Partners"; 1954's "Cross over the Bridge"; 1956's "Allegheny Moon" and "Old Cape Cod"; and 1958's "Left Right out of Your Heart."

In addition to her singing, she appeared in the film *Elmer Gantry* (1960).

Mitchell Parish
b. 1900, Shreveport, Louisiana

Lyricist Mitchell Parish has been one of the most distinguished writers in the business. He specialized in adding lyrics to preexisting music. He is a Songwriters' Hall of Fame member. Some of his most famous hits include 1929's "Star Dust," 1933's "Sophisticated Lady," and "Stars Fell on Alabama," 1934's "Hands Across the Table," 1939's "The Lamp Is Low" and "Deep Purple," and the English-language version of 1958's "Volare."

Frank Parker
b. 1906, New York, New York

Singer Frank Parker (real name: Frank Ciccio) was a popular radio vocalist during the thirties and forties. He sang in a couple of movie musicals in the mid-thirties and in the Broadway musical *Follow the Girls* (1944).

Tony Pastor
b. 1907, Middletown, Connecticut
d. 1969, Old Lynne, Connecticut

Tony Pastor (real name: Antonio Pestritto) was most famous as a tenor saxophonist and singer with Artie Shaw's orchestra in the late thirties. He led his own band in the forties and fifties.

Les Paul
b. 1916, Waukesha, Wisconsin

Les Paul (real name: Leslie Polfuss) and his wife, Mary Ford, recorded several popular hits in the early fifties. Paul was also widely known as a jazz guitarist and for the musical sound effects and overdubbing (multiple recordings) experiments he developed.

Les Paul and Mary Ford's most famous recordings include 1951 recordings of "Mockin' Bird Hill," "How High the Moon," and "The World Is Waiting for the Sunrise" and "Vaya con Dios," the number one hit of 1953.

The Penguins
Curtis Williams, b. 1935, Los Angeles, California
Cleveland Duncan, b. 1935, Los Angeles, Calforina
Dexter Tisby, b. 1936, Los Angeles, California
Bruce Tate, b. 1935, Los Angeles, California

The Penguins were an early rhythm and blues quartet that achieved national attention with their 1954 classic recording of "Earth Angel" just before the advent of rock and roll. The Penguins were discovered and managed by Buck Ram, who also discovered the Platters.

Frank Perkins
b. 1908, Salem, Massachusetts

Composer Frank Perkins did not write many songs, but he managed at least one hit with 1934's "Stars Fell on Alabama." He worked primarily as an arranger for a publishing firm from the late twenties through the mid-thirties. Later he composed, arranged, and conducted for films and, later still, for television.

Edith Piaf
b. 1915, Belleville, France
d. 1963, Paris, France

Edith Piaf was a top-rung French cabaret singer, who had a million-selling recording in the United States of "La Vie en Rose" in 1950.

Piaf lost her sight when she was less than three years old but was cured at a religious shrine at the age of seven. Most of her childhood she spent traveling through the countryside with her father, a circus performer. She began to make her own way at fifteen by singing in the streets of Paris. Piaf soon became a great attraction in Parisian nightclubs.

She assisted Louiguy in writing "La Vie en Rose" in 1946. She also had great success with the singing group Les Compagnons de la Chanson and the song they introduced, "Les Trois Cloches (The Three Bells)," which was popularized in the United States by the Browns in 1959.

The Pied Pipers
John Huddlestone
Chuck Lowry
Clark Yokum
Jo Stafford, b. Coalinga, California

The Pied Pipers started in 1937 with seven men and a woman but eventually became a quartet. They began to get national recognition on Tommy Dorsey's radio program in the late thirties. Their first gold record came in 1942, when they, Dorsey, and his orchestra backed Frank Sinatra on "There Are Such Things." Johnny Mercer signed them to Capitol Records, and they often backed him in recordings. In 1945 they had a million seller with "Dream," recorded with Paul Weston's orchestra. "My Happiness" (1948) was also a million seller; it featured June Hutton, who had replaced Jo Stafford after she went solo in 1945.

Maceo Pinkard
b. 1897, Bluefield, West Virginia
d. 1962, New York, New York

Composer Maceo Pinkard's most famous works include 1925's "Sweet Georgia Brown," 1926's " 'Gimme' a Little Kiss, Will 'Ya' Huh?," 1927's "Here Comes the Show Boat," and 1930's "Them There Eyes."

Ezio Pinza
b. 1892, Rome, Italy
d. 1957, Stamford, Connecticut

Ezio Pinza was best known as a Metropolitan Opera bass-baritone who starred as Emile de Becque in the 1949 musical *South Pacific* (he played the same role in the movie). After a very successful career in opera, Pinza introduced "Some Enchanted Evening" and "This Nearly Was Mine" in *South Pacific*.

He also starred as César in the 1954 musical *Fanny*.

The Platters
Tony Williams, b. 1928, Roselle, New Jersey
David Lynch, b. 1929, St. Louis, Missouri
Paul Robi, d. 1981, New Orleans, Louisiana
Herbert Reed, b. Kansas City, Missouri
Zola Taylor, b. Los Angeles, California

The Platters were discovered by songwriter and producer Buck Ram, who may have formed the group in 1953 and was then managing the Penguins. Ram refused to allow the Penguins to sign with Mercury Records unless the Platters were also given a contract. The Penguins had one hit, 1954's "Earth Angel," while the Platters were one of the most successful rhythm and blues groups throughout the fifties.

The Platters' string of gold records began in 1955 with "Only You." They had even more success in 1956 with "The Great Pretender" and "My Prayer," both in the top ten hits of the year. Revivals of 1944's "Twilight Time" and 1933's "Smoke Gets in Your Eyes" became gold records in 1958.

Tony Williams left the group in 1961 to go solo. He was replaced by Sonny Turner. By the mid-sixties only Herb Reed was left from the original group.

Lew Pollack
b. 1895, New York, New York
d. 1946, Hollywood, California

Composer Lew Pollack wrote several hit songs in the twenties and thirties. His best-known works include 1927's "Charmaine," "Diane," and "Miss Annabelle Lee" and 1934's "Two Cigarettes in the Dark." Pollack was elected to the Songwriters' Hall of Fame.

Cole Porter
b. 1891, Peru, Indiana
d. 1964, Santa Monica, California

One of the greatest composer-lyricists of all time, Cole Porter was born into wealth, the grandson of a lumber magnate. He attended Yale, where he led the glee club and wrote football songs. After matriculating at the Harvard Law School, he transferred to the music school. His first Broadway music score, *See America First* (1916), was a flop.

Porter spent most of the twenties in Europe and did very little serious writing until the end of the decade. During this time he was very much the playboy, flitting from Paris to the Riviera to Venice and occasionally back to the United States.

In 1928 E. Ray Goetz persuaded Porter to write the music for the Broadway musical *Paris*, which was to star Goetz's wife, Irene Bordoni. This was the turning point of Porter's career. *Paris* introduced the hit "Let's Do It." For the remainder of the twenties and the thirties, Porter was busy writing show after show (and hit after hit), including 1929's *Fifty Million Frenchmen* ("You Do Something to Me"), 1930's *Wake Up and Dream* ("What Is This Thing Called Love?"), and *The New Yorkers* ("Love for Sale"), 1932's *Gay Divorcée* ("Night and Day"), 1934's *Anything Goes* ("All Through the Night," "Anything Goes," "Blow, Gabriel, Blow," "I Get a Kick Out of You," and "You're the Top"), 1935's *Jubilee* ("Begin the Beguine" and "Just One of Those Things"), 1936's *Red, Hot and Blue* ("It's De-Lovely"), 1938's *Leave It to Me* ("Get out of Town" and "My Heart Belongs to Daddy"), and 1939's *Du Barry Was a Lady* ("Friendship"). As if he were not busy enough, he found time to write film scores for 1936's *Born to Dance* ("I've Got You Under My Skin" and "Easy to Love") and 1937's *Rosalie* ("Rosalie" and "In the Still of the Night").

In the forties Porter's work was divided between films and stage musicals. Hollywood productions of the decade included *The Broadway Melody of 1940* ("I Concentrate on You"), 1941's *You'll Never Get Rich*, 1943's *Something to Shout About* ("You'd Be So Nice to Come Home To"), and 1944's *Hollywood Canteen* ("Don't Fence Me In"). *Night and Day*, his film biography, appeared in 1946.

Broadway productions of the decade included 1940's *Panama Hattie* (film version, 1942), 1941's *Let's Face It* (film version, 1942), 1943's *Something for the Boys* (film version, 1944), 1944's *Mexican Hayride* (film version, 1948, "I Love You") and *Seven Lively Arts*, and 1948's *Kiss Me Kate* (film version, 1953). *Kiss Me Kate* was Porter's recognized masterpiece, with such songs as "Wunderbar," "Too Darn Hot," and "So in Love."

In the fifties Porter produced musical scores for Broadway's 1950's *Out of This World*, 1953's *Can-Can* ("I Love Paris"), and 1955's *Silk Stockings* (film version, 1957). He wrote songs for the films *High Society* (1956, "True Love") and *Les Girls* (1957).

Porter was noted for his sophisticated, clever lyrics and brilliant melodies supported by complicated, beautiful harmonies. He was, of course, elected to the Songwriters' Hall of Fame.

Dick Powell
b. 1904, Mountain View, Arkansas
d. 1963, Hollywood, California

Dick Powell was one of the most popular stars of the movie musicals of the thirties. He became a star in the 1933 film *Forty-second Street,* introducing the title song and several others in that production. He costarred in several movie musicals with Ruby Keeler and Joan Blondell.

In the late thirties he was also very active on radio. In the mid-forties he had a very popular radio mystery show, *Richard Diamond—Private Detective*. After the thirties Powell's music career took a back seat to his acting (generally tough guy roles) and his dramatic work on radio. He remained active as head of Four Star Television until his death of cancer.

Eleanor Powell
b. 1910, Springfield, Massachusetts
d. 1982, Beverly Hills, California

Eleanor Powell was a famous actress and dancer in several Broadway musicals and movies. By age thirteen she was in Gus Edwards's Kiddie troupe during summer vacation. Her Broadway career started in the late twenties and lasted until the mid-thirties, when she left New York for stardom in Hollywood.

Her screen debut was in *George White's Scandals of 1935,* in which she showed critics and the movie audiences her considerable dancing talent. Her dancing featured a heel-and-toe style that was more sophisticated than most ordinary tap dancing. Next came a starring role in *Broadway Melody of 1936* opposite Robert Taylor; she introduced the Nacio Herb Brown-Arthur Freed song "Broadway Rhythm" in this movie musical. In the next several years she was very busy. Other movie musicals included *Born to Dance, Broadway Melody of 1938, Rosalie* (one of the top box-office attractions of 1937–38), *Honolulu, Broadway Melody of 1940* with Fred Astaire, *Lady Be Good, Ship Ahoy, Thousands Cheer, I Dood It, Sensations of 1945,* and 1950's *The Duchess of Idaho.*

In the mid-forties she married actor Glenn Ford and retired. She came back in the fifties for a television series. After a divorce from Ford in 1959, she staged an elaborate nightclub act that was well received.

Perez Prado
b. 1918, Mantanzos, Cuba

Perez Prado formed his own band in Mexico in 1948 and began to popularize the mambo beat. The mambo began to get more attention in the United States in 1954 (see "Mambo Italiano," page 159, and "Papa Loves Mambo," page 159). Prado and his orchestra had their first million seller in 1955 with "Cherry Pink and Apple Blossom White." They followed that success with a second gold record, "Patricia," in 1958.

R

Ralph Rainger
b. 1901, New York, New York
d. 1942, Palm Springs, California

Songwriters' Hall of Fame member Ralph Rainger was one of Hollywood's most prolific composers in the thirties and early forties. He primarily collaborated with lyricist Leo Robin. Prior to his Hollywood work, Rainger wrote for a few Broadway shows, producing the hit "Moanin' Low" for 1929's *The Little Show*. Others of Rainger's famous hits were 1934's "June in January" and 1937's "Thanks for the Memory."

John Raitt
b. 1917, Santa Ana, California

John Raitt got his first starring role on Broadway in 1945's *Carousel*. As Billy Bigelow, he introduced the very difficult "Soliloquy" and the romantic duet "If I Loved You." After several artistic successes in the next few years Raitt achieved another major Broadway success in 1954's *The Pajama Game*. As Sid Sorokin, the new superintendent of the Sleep Tite Pajama Factory, he introduced the top hit of 1954, "Hey There."

Raitt's daughter, Bonnie, followed her father into the popular music field and has had some success as a country-rock singer.

Erno Rapee
b. 1891, Budapest, Hungary
d. 1945, New York, New York

Composer Erno Rapee is primarily remembered for a few songs he wrote in the late twenties as motion-picture theme songs. He collaborated with Lew Pollack to write 1927's "Charmaine" and "Diane" and 1928's "Angela Mia."

Johnnie Ray
b. 1927, Dallas, Oregon

Is it possible for a deaf person to sing? Ask Johnnie Ray. Despite his handicap, Ray became one of the top singers of the early fifties.

Ray signed a recording contract with Columbia in June 1951 and soon scored with the back-to-back hits "Cry" and "The Little White Cloud That Cried." From that beginning he was labeled "The Cry Guy" or "The Prince of Wails." He also starred in the 1954 musical *There's No Business Like Show Business*. By the end of the fifties he continued to tour and work in theatrical productions of Broadway musicals in various theaters around the country, but his great popularity had dwindled.

He has spent many years and given countless performances working for his fellow deaf.

Andy Razaf
b. 1895, Washington, D.C.
d. 1973, North Hollywood, California

Lyricist Andy Razaf (real name: Andrea Paul Razaf-keriofo) was the son of a Madagascar nobleman. He collaborated with several composers during the twenties and thirties to write some famous songs. His best-known hits include 1929's "Ain't Misbehavin'," "Honeysuckle Rose," and "S'posin'," and 1932's "Keeping out of Mischief Now."

Harry Revel
b. 1905, London, England
d. 1958, New York, New York

Harry Revel composed several hit songs for the movie musicals of the thirties. He collaborated with lyricist Mack Gordon on several hits. Revel came to the United States in the late twenties, met Mack Gordon, and formed their songwriting team. Their partnership began with several unsuccessful Broadway shows, but they began to achieve notable success in the movies about 1933.

Some of his most famous hits include 1933's "Did You Ever See a Dream Walking?," 1934's "With My Eyes Wide Open I'm Dreaming," and "Stay as Sweet as You Are."

Debbie Reynolds
b. 1932, El Paso, Texas

Debbie Reynolds (real name: Mary Frances Reynolds) grew up in Burbank, California, and signed a movie contract in the late forties, after she had been discovered by a talent scout in the Miss Burbank beauty contest.

One of her most famous roles was in 1952's *Singin' in the Rain,* but she also had good success in 1950's *Three Little Words* and *Two Weeks with Love.* In the next several years she starred in numerous movie musicals. In 1957 she starred in *Tammy and the Bachelor* and had a major hit with the movie's theme song.

She married Eddie Fisher in 1955 and divorced him in 1959. During their marriage they parented Carrie Fisher, who has gained considerable fame for her roles in the *Star Wars* films.

Reynolds starred in the 1972 revival of the 1919 Broadway musical *Irene.*

Harry Richman
b. 1895, Cincinnati, Ohio
d. 1972, Hollywood, California

Harry Richman (real name: Harry Reichman) was one of the top vocalists in the twenties and thirties. He had a debonair image and robust theatrical singing style.

Richman achieved stardom in *George White's Scandals of 1926.* In the rest of the twenties he appeared in several Broadway shows and in top nightclubs. He was noted for introducing or popularizing 1926's "The Birth of the Blues," 1930's "Puttin' on the Ritz," and 1931's "I Love a Parade." During the thirties he continued to appear on Broadway and also acted in a few movies. In the late thirties he was often heard on radio. By the mid- to late forties he was only semiactive. He performed occasionally into the early sixties.

Michael Riley
b. 1904, Fall River, Massachusetts

Mike Riley was the coleader of the Riley-Farley Band, which popularized the late thirties hit "The Music Goes 'Round and 'Round." The band performed long after the hit but never had another major success.

Tex Ritter
b. 1906, Panola County, Texas
d. 1974, Nashville, Tennessee

Tex Ritter was one of the most popular western movie stars of the late thirties and forties. He began his film career in 1936 and made more than fifty westerns.

Musically he sang the theme song of the 1952 film *High Noon* on the sound track of the film.

He was the father of John Ritter, the television actor, who appeared for several years on *Three's Company.*

Allan Roberts
b. 1905, Brooklyn, New York
d. 1966, Hollywood, Florida

Allan Roberts was best known for his 1944 hit song "You Always Hurt the One You Love." He usually collaborated with Doris Fisher.

Leo Robin
b. 1900, Pittsburgh, Pennsylvania

Lyricist Leo Robin was a prolific writer of popular songs from the mid-twenties into the fifties. He collaborated with composer Ralph Rainger. (See Rainger, page 227.)

Some of Robin's most famous lyrics include 1927's "Hallelujah!," 1929's "Louise," 1930's "Beyond the Blue Horizon," 1931's "Prisoner of Love," 1934's "June in January," and 1937's "Thanks for the Memory." Robin is a member of the Songwriters' Hall of Fame.

Richard Rodgers
b. 1902, New York, New York
d. 1979, New York, New York

Richard Rodgers was one of the most famous and most prolific composers of popular songs. He collaborated with lyricist Lorenz ("Larry") Hart from 1919 until 1943, when he began his association with Oscar Hammerstein II. Rodgers and Hammerstein wrote together until Hammerstein's death in 1960. Rodgers continued to write, producing both lyrics and music for 1962's *No Strings* and collaborating with Stephen Sondheim on 1965's *Do I Hear a Waltz?* and with Martin Charnin on 1970's *Two By Two.* Rodgers was inducted into the Songwriters' Hall of Fame.

Most of Rodgers's songs were written in a dramatic context, for movies and especially for Broadway musicals. The list of his successful shows and songs is lengthy. Some of them are 1927's *A Connecticut Yankee* ("Thou Swell"), 1929's *Spring Is Here* ("With a Song in My Heart"), 1937's *Babes in Arms* ("My Funny Valentine"), 1941's *Pal Joey* ("Bewitched, Bothered and Bewildered"), 1943's *Oklahoma!* ("People Will Say We're in Love" and "Oh, What a Beautiful Mornin'"), 1945's *Carousel* ("You'll Never Walk Alone"), 1949's *South Pacific* ("Some Enchanted Evening"), 1951's *The King and I* ("Hello,

Young Lovers'' and "Getting to Know You"), 1957's *Cinderella* (television show), 1958's *Flower Drum Song* ("I Enjoy Being a Girl"), and 1959's *The Sound of Music* ("Climb Ev'ry Mountain").

Ginger Rogers
b. 1911, Independence, Missouri

Dancer and film star Ginger Rogers (real name: Virginia Katherine McMath) was one of the most popular performers in the movie musicals of the thirties and forties, particularly when she costarred with Fred Astaire.

She grew up in Fort Worth, Texas. After she had left Texas, she had a minor role in a Broadway show in the late twenties, followed by small roles in a few movies in the early thirties. She first teamed up with Astaire in 1933's *Flying down to Rio*. The duo were not the stars of the film but were an instant hit. Then came eight costarring roles in films that have become classics of the genre.

Over her career Rogers appeared in more than seventy films, both musical and dramatic. She won an Oscar for her role in the 1940 film *Kitty Foyle*.

She was primarily noted as the ideal dancing partner for Astaire, but she also sang and introduced or helped introduce several popular classics: 1933's "Carioca," 1934's "The Continental," 1935's "I Won't Dance" and "Cheek to Cheek," 1932's "Night and Day," 1936's "The Way You Look Tonight" and "A Fine Romance," and 1937's "They Can't Take That Away from Me."

Roy Rogers
b. 1912, Cincinnati, Ohio

Cowboy star Roy Rogers (real name: Leonard Slye) became the king of the cowboys. He was first successful as a member of the Sons of the Pioneers, but he left the group in 1937 for a career as a single. He starred in 1938's *Under Western Stars* and became one of the most successful singing cowboys. He made more than 100 films. He married his frequent costar, Dale Evans, in 1947. Rogers had a very popular radio show for about ten years, and he and Evans had a top-rated television series in the early fifties. In recent years they have been very active in charity work.

Sigmund Romberg
b. 1887, Nagykanizsa, Hungary
d. 1951, New York, New York

Songwriters' Hall of Fame member composer Sigmund Romberg wrote several operettas that were very successful on Broadway and then as movies. His most famous operettas were 1917's *Maytime*, 1921's *Blossom Time*, 1924's *The Student Prince in Heidelberg*, 1926's *Desert Song*, 1928's *The New Moon*, and 1935's *May Wine*.

Romberg came to the United States from Hungary in 1909. After a few odd jobs in music he managed to get several compositions published and was hired by the Shubert brothers to write the 1914 Broadway show *The Whirl of the World*. His most successful operettas were written in the twenties, but they received renewed success in the mid-thirties, when the movie versions were released (many costarred the king and queen of the operetta-style movie, Nelson Eddy and Jeanette MacDonald).

The 1954 movie *Deep in My Heart* was based on the life of Romberg and featured many of his most famous songs.

Harold Rome
b. 1908, Hartford, Connecticut

Harold Rome is a noted composer and lyricist best remembered for his songs from several Broadway shows. His first stage musical was 1937's *Pins and Needles*, which was presented by members of the International Ladies' Garment Workers' Union. Other important musicals were 1946's *Call Me Mister*, 1952's *Wish You Were Here*, 1954's *Fanny*, 1959's *Destry Rides Again*, and 1962's *I Can Get It for You Wholesale*.

Ann Ronell
b. Omaha, Nebraska

Composer Ann Ronell did not write a large number of songs that have become hits. Her most famous hit was 1933's "Who's Afraid of the Big Bad Wolf?" Most of her work consisted of writing movie background music and conducting sound track music.

Mickey Rooney
b. 1920, Brooklyn, New York

One of the most famous entertainers, Mickey Rooney (real name: Joe Yule, Jr.) may be short (only five feet), but he has never been short on energy and talent. He was one of the top box-office movie stars of the late thirties and forties, especially when he costarred with Judy Garland.

Rooney has been married many times and has always been the butt of many jokes about that area of his life.

His first really important role, which brought him stardom, was in 1937's *Thoroughbreds Don't Cry*. He also began the popular *Andy Hardy* films in 1937. The late thirties and forties brought several major movie musicals, including 1939's *Babes in Arms*, 1940's *Strike Up the Band*, 1941's *Babes on Broadway*, and 1948's *Girl Crazy*.

Rooney starred in several nonmusical dramatic films for Hollywood and recently for television. He has remained active in the business, costarring with Ann Miller in a recent Broadway show, *Sugar Babies*.

Billy Rose
b. 1899, New York, New York
d. 1966, Jamaica, West Indies

Billy Rose was a successful lyricist, producer, nightclub owner, and theater owner. One of his marriages was to superstar comedienne Fanny Brice. His most productive period as a songwriter came during the twenties. After that he concentrated on his many other business ventures.

Some of his most famous lyrics include 1923's "Barney Google," "That Old Gang of Mine," and "You've Got to See Mama Every Night," 1924's "Does the Spearmint Lose Its Flavor on the Bedpost Overnight?," 1925's "A Cup of Coffee, a Sandwich and You," 1926's "Tonight You Belong to Me," 1927's "Me and My Shadow," 1928's "Back in Your Own Backyard" and "There's a Rainbow 'Round My Shoulder," 1929's "Great Day," "More Than You Know," and "Without a Song," 1930's "Cheerful Little Earful," "Would You Like to Take a Walk?," and "It Happened in Monterey," 1931's "I Found a Million Dollar Baby," and 1933's "It's Only a Paper Moon." Rose is a member of the Songwriter's Hall of Fame.

David Rose
b. 1910, London, England

Composer David Rose is most famous for the hits he has composed for the orchestra he conducts. His 1943 "Holiday for Strings" and his 1962 "The Stripper" were major hits.

In the early part of his career he was primarily an arranger for several of the big bands, notably for Benny Goodman's band. In the late thirties he was musical director for the Mutual Broadcasting network. By the late forties he had begun a long relationship with comedian Red Skelton as orchestra leader on his radio and then television series ("Holiday for Strings" was the show's theme).

Rose also wrote or arranged several musical scores for Hollywood films, including 1959's *Operation Petticoat* and 1960's *Please Don't Eat the Daisies*.

Vincent Rose
b. 1880, Palermo, Italy
d. 1944, Rockville Centre, New York

Composer Vincent Rose was particularly active as a songwriter in the twenties. His most popular hits include 1920's "Whispering," and "Avalon," 1923's "Linger Awhile," and 1940's "Blueberry Hill." Rose organized an orchestra in 1904 and successfully led that group into the forties. Rose was elected to the Songwriters' Hall of Fame.

Lanny Ross
b. 1906, Seattle, Washington

Lanny Ross was particularly popular as a radio singer in the thirties and forties. He was called the Troubadour of the Moon. He starred in a couple of movies and sang in the 1943 movie musical *Stage Door Canteen*. By the early fifties he was less prominent in show business.

Shirley Ross
b. 1915, Omaha, Nebraska

Shirley Ross is most famous for the duet she sang with Bob Hope in the movie musical *Big Broadcast of 1938*, "Thanks for the Memory," which won the Academy Award for best song. She and Hope followed that success with the duet "Two Sleepy People" in *Thanks for the Memory* (1938). Otherwise, Ross acted and sang in several other movies, was vocalist with some of the big bands, made guest appearances on radio shows, and starred in the 1940 Broadway musical *Higher and Higher*.

Harry Ruby
b. 1895, New York, New York
d. 1974, Woodland Hills, California

Harry Ruby was a successful composer of popular songs with lyricist Bert Kalmar. The 1950 movie *Three Little Words* was based on their songwriting partnership and the hits they produced.

Some of Ruby's most famous melodies include 1923's "Who's Sorry Now?," 1931's "Nevertheless," 1928's "I Wanna Be Loved by You," 1930's "Three Little Words," and 1951's "A Kiss to Build a Dream On."

Ruby wrote very little after Kalmar died in 1947.

Ruby was sometimes called the world's greatest baseball fan because he spent so much time watching the game.

Bob Russell
b. 1914, Passaic, New Jersey

Lyricist Bob Russell (real name: Sidney Keith Russell) was particularly active in songwriting in the forties and fifties. He also wrote music for several movies.

His best-known hits include 1941's "Frenesi" and "Maria Elena," 1943's "Don't Get Around Much Anymore," and 1947's "Ballerina." Russell is a member of the Songwriters' Hall of Fame.

Jane Russell
b. 1921, Bemidji, Minnesota

Actress Jane Russell introduced several popular songs in some of her films between the mid-forties and the late sixties. This buxom beauty's movies were very popular at the box office in the fifties.

Since the sixties she has sung in a gospel quartet with some other former female stars, has made some religious recordings, has done some television commercials, and has worked in Broadway musicals, mostly in road show companies.

S

Arthur Schwartz
b. 1900, Brooklyn, New York
d. 1984, Kintnersville, Pennsylvania

Composer Arthur Schwartz wrote several popular songs with lyricist Howard Dietz that have become classics. Schwartz also collaborated with Dorothy Fields, Frank Loesser, and Leo Robin on occasion. Among Schwartz's most famous songs from Broadway shows are 1929's "I Guess I'll Have to Change My Plans," 1930's "Something to Remember You By," 1931's "Dancing in the Dark" and "I Love Louisa," 1932's "A Shine on Your Shoes" and "Louisiana Hayride," 1934's "You and the Night and the Music" and "If There Is Someone Lovelier Than You," and 1937's "I See Your Face Before Me." He also wrote a few film scores and "They're Either Too Young or Too Old" for the 1943 movie *Thank Your Lucky Stars* and "That's Entertainment" for the 1953 movie version of the 1931 Broadway musical *The Band Wagon*. Schwartz was elected to membership in the Songwriters' Hall of Fame.

Vivienne Segal
b. 1897, Philadelphia, Pennsylvania

Singer and actress Vivienne Segal (real name: Sonia Segal) was the romantic lead in the operettas *The Desert Song* (1926) and *The Three Musketeers* (1928), but she turned to comedy in *Pal Joey* (1940). She introduced "The Desert Song" in the operetta and "Bewitched, Bothered and Bewildered" in *Pal Joey*.

Ben Selvin
b. 1898
d. 1980, Roslyn, New York

Violinist, bandleader and record company executive Ben Selvin started his career in about 1905. Beginning in 1919, he made more recordings than anybody else in the world. He made 9,000 under approximately forty different names for nine different companies. His recording of "Dardanella" in 1920 sold more than 6 million copies on various labels. When he retired at sixty-five, RCA presented him with a gold disc.

Artie Shaw
b. 1910, New York, New York

Clarinetist Artie Shaw (real name: Arthur Arshawsky) and his orchestra were very popular in the mid-thirties. Along with Benny Goodman, Shaw was considered one of the best clarinet players of the swing era. He was very temperamental and often seemed to be feuding with his fans. In 1939 he left the country in a protest against the jitterbug dancing craze.

Shaw started his career at fifteen, playing saxophone in the pit band at New Haven's Olympic Theater. He then held a succession of jobs, including one with Red Norvo's band. In the early thirties he was a radio musician in New York, and in 1935 he took part in New York's first swing concert at the Imperial Theater, where he performed an original jazz piece.

He formed his band soon after, but it did not rise to great popularity until his recordings brought him national fame in the mid- to late thirties. Sales of all of Shaw's recordings total more than 43 million. His gold discs include 1938's "Begin the Beguine," backed by "Indian Love Call," "Nightmare," and "Back Bay Shuffle"; 1939's "Traffic Jam"; 1940's "Frenesi," "Star Dust," and "Summit Ridge Drive"; and 1941's "Dancing in the Dark."

Oscar Shaw
b. 1889, Philadelphia, Pennsylvania
d. 1967, Little Neck, New York

Singer Oscar Shaw (real name: Oscar Schwartz) was an important leading man in the Broadway musicals of the 1910s and 1920s. He introduced "Ka-lu-a" in 1920's *Good Morning, Dearie* and "Do-Do-Do" in 1926's *Oh, Kay!*

Wini Shaw
b. 1910, San Francisco, California

Wini Shaw, a sexy torch singer, introduced "Lullaby of Broadway" in the movie musical *Gold Diggers of 1935.*

Dinah Shore
b. 1917, Winchester, Tennessee

Dinah Shore (real name: Frances Rose Shore) was one of the top female singers from the early forties through the late fifties.

While attending Vanderbilt University, she sang on Nashville radio, using the song "Dinah" as her theme song. She adopted the song's title as her stage name and later legally made it her name.

She left for New York in 1937, sang on radio for a while, and then went back to college to get a degree in sociology. She signed a contract to sing with Ben Bernie's orchestra in 1939, just as the band began a fill-in engagement on network radio. Within a short time she was nationally famous. By 1944 she had her own radio program, and she grew even more popular in recordings, movies, and television. Shore won innumerable awards, including top vocalist on radio and records of 1941. She had a top-rated television series from the mid-fifties into the early sixties. After a period of relative inactivity she has had a nationally syndicated talk show in recent years.

Dinah Shore's million-selling recordings include "Blues in the Night" (1941) and "Buttons and Bows," 1948's Academy Award winner.

Her musical movies include 1943's *Thank Your Lucky Stars,* 1944's *Follow the Boys* and *Up in Arms,* 1945's *Belle of the Yukon,* and 1952's *Aaron Slick from Punkin Crick.* Her voice also appeared in the Disney cartoons *Make Mine Music* (1946) and *Fun and Fancy Free* (1947) and the Jerome Kern screen biography, *Till the Clouds Roll By* (1946).

Carl Sigman
b. 1909, Brooklyn, New York

Composer-lyricist Carl Sigman's most popular songs include 1947's "Ballerina" and "Civilization," 1948's "Enjoy Yourself—It's Later Than You Think," 1949's "Careless Hands," 1950's "My Heart Cries for You," 1951's "It's All in the Game," 1953's "Ebb Tide,"

1954's "Answer Me, My Love," and 1957's "Till." Sigman is a member of the Songwriters' Hall of Fame.

Nina Simone
b. 1933, Tryon, North Carolina

Singer and songwriter Nina Simone (real name: Eunice Waymon) trained at New York's Juilliard School of Music and began her professional career playing and singing in jazz clubs in New York City and Philadelphia. She signed a recording contract in 1959 and released a million-selling single of "I Loves You, Porgy" from Gershwin's *Porgy and Bess.*

Frank Sinatra
b. 1915, Hoboken, New Jersey

Frank Sinatra (real name: Francis Albert Sinatra) was to the mid-forties what Elvis Presley and the Beatles were to later generations: a superstar, a charismatic entertainer.

Sinatra began his rise to fame when he was hired to sing with Harry James's band in 1939. He stayed with James for only a short time before he joined Tommy Dorsey's band. He left the Dorsey group in 1942 and began to cause volcanic sensations among bobby-soxers in 1943. In the late forties he appeared often on radio, including stints on *Your Hit Parade,* and he starred in several movies. *Anchors Aweigh* in 1945 established his credentials as a motion-picture actor (and he danced much better than one would have imagined in some fancy footwork with Gene Kelly). He also starred in 1949's *On the Town,* one of the first movies to be shot on location instead of in a studio.

In the early fifties Sinatra confined his appearances to nightclubs and television. Then, in 1953, he won an Oscar for his acting as Maggio in the film *From Here to Eternity.* His other film credits are numerous; some of his most famous motion-picture appearances include 1954's *Young at Heart,* 1955's *The Tender Trap* and *Guys and Dolls,* 1956's *High Society,* 1957's *Pal Joey* and *The Joker Is Wild,* and 1960's *Can-Can.*

He has recorded often, primarily for Columbia and for Capitol, until he formed his own company, Reprise. Sinatra's million-selling recordings include 1942's "There Are Such Things" (with Tommy Dorsey and his orchestra and the Pied Pipers), 1943's "All or Nothing at All," 1944's "White Christmas," 1953's "Young at Heart," 1955's "Love and Marriage," and "Learnin' the Blues," 1957's "All the Way," 1922's "Chicago" in 1957, 1966's "Strangers in the Night," 1967's "Somethin' Stupid" (with daughter Nancy), and 1969's "My Way."

Noble Sissle

See Eubie Blake, page 174.

Walter Slezak

b. 1902, Vienna, Austria
d. 1983, Flower Hill, New York

Walter Slezak is known today for his acting roles in movies, but he began his career on Broadway as a romantic lead. He introduced "I've Told Every Little Star" in 1932's *Music in the Air*. He also starred as Panisse in 1954's *Fanny*.

Beasley Smith

b. 1901, McEwen, Tennessee

Beasley Smith has been an important figure in the Nashville music scene since the thirties as a bandleader, composer, and record executive. His best-known songs include "Night Train to Memphis" and 1949's "That Lucky Old Sun." In recent years he has been a publisher and arranger for Dot Records.

Harry Smith

b. 1860, Buffalo, New York
d. 1936, Atlantic City, New Jersey

Songwriters' Hall of Fame member Harry Smith wrote more than 120 Broadway musicals, making him one of the most prolific lyricist-librettists of all time. Many of his biggest triumphs came before 1920, so this book does not deal with them, but he was still active during the twenties and early thirties. He wrote "The Sheik of Araby" for 1921's *Make It Snappy*.

Kate Smith

b. 1909, Greenville, Virginia

Kate Smith (real name: Kathryn Elizabeth Smith) is an extremely famous singer and occasional actress from just before and during World War II. She started her career on Broadway in 1926's *Honeymoon Lane* and followed with 1930's *Flying High*. After that she performed in vaudeville and in theaters across the country until she started her own radio show. She was particularly popular as a radio personality, and the exposure got her a movie contract. She sang her theme song, "When the Moon Comes over the Mountain," in 1932's *The Big Broadcast*. She became a national personality when she starred in the 1933 film *Hello Everybody*. Smith was always rather large, which hindered her screen career, but she continued to appear in films, although seldom as part of the main plot. She appeared in 1937's *The Hit Parade,* which was a va-

riety show with a large roster of stars. Next came a cameo appearance in 1941's *The Great American Broadcast,* and she sang "God Bless America" in the movie version of *This Is the Army* in 1943.

She introduced Berlin's "God Bless America" on her radio program in November 1939. Her performance of the number became so famous that she is almost exclusively associated with it.

Her only million-selling disc was 1941's "Rose O'Day," but it is difficult to believe that over the years her "God Bless America" has not passed the million mark.

Ted Snyder

b. 1881, Freeport, Illinois
d. 1965, Hollywood, California

Songwriters' Hall of Fame member Ted Snyder was perhaps most famous as the person who gave Irving Berlin his start by hiring him in 1909 as staff pianist for his publishing company. But he also wrote the hits "The Sheik of Araby" (1921) and "Who's Sorry Now?" (1923).

Sons of the Pioneers

Bob Nolan, b. 1908, Canada
**   d. 1980, Costa Mesa, California**
Leonard Slye (changed name to Roy Rogers),
**   b. 1912, Cincinnati, Ohio**
Tim Spencer, b. 1908, Webb City, Missouri
**   d. 1974**

The group known as the Sons of the Pioneers was one of the leading western vocal (and instrumental, since its members also played guitars) aggregations of the mid-thirties. Other members were added to the original three.

When Leonard Slye became Roy Rogers, left the group, and became the king of the cowboys, the Sons of the Pioneers often appeared and performed in his films. They also appeared on radio often, especially on the Roy Rogers radio series.

Bob Nolan composed the group's most famous songs: 1934's "Tumbling Tumbleweeds" and 1948's "Cool Water."

Ann Sothern

b. 1909, Valley City, North Dakota

Ann Sothern (real name: Harriette Lake) appeared in more than fifty movies from 1934 through 1953. Her first starring role was in 1934's *Let's Fall in Love*. Then followed a succession of movie musicals through the thirties and early forties. By the early fifties her movie career had faded, so she turned to television and starred in the *Ann Sothern Show* for several years.

Jo Stafford
b. 1920, Coalinga, California

Jo Stafford was one of the most popular female vocalists of the mid-forties and fifties. She formed a trio with her sisters and began singing on radio in the mid-thirties. She joined the Pied Pipers in 1937 and remained with them for seven years, at which time she left to try it as a soloist. While with the Pied Pipers, she recorded the million-selling disc of "Dream" (1946). After she had left the group, she performed often on radio and recorded regularly.

In 1947 she recorded a hick version of "Temptation" with Red Ingle and the Natural Seven. The disc label billed her as "Cinderella G. Stump." The hillbilly parody was her first solo million seller. Other gold records came with 1948's "Say Something Sweet to Your Sweetheart," which she recorded with Gordon MacRae and the Starlighters, and 1949's "Whispering Hope," a recording of the gospel favorite with Gordon MacRae and the Paul Weston orchestra. Her first million seller in the fifties was 1951's "Shrimp Boats." In 1952 "You Belong to Me," "Early Autumn," and "Jambalaya" were successful. "Make Love to Me" (1954) finishes out the list of Stafford million sellers; she had sold 25 million disc units by the mid-fifties.

Kay Starr
b. 1922, Dougherty, Oklahoma

Kay Starr (real name: Katherine Starks) was born on an Indian reservation in Oklahoma. When her family moved to Memphis, she sang with jazz violinist Joe Venuti's band (at age fifteen). She left Venuti to join Bob Crosby's band, which carried her to New York. There she recorded with Glenn Miller, but she rejoined Venuti and spent two years with Charlie Barnet's band before embarking on a solo career. Her first recording contract was with Capitol, but she also recorded with Victor in the mid-fifties. She had two big hits with 1952's "Wheel of Fortune" and 1956's "Rock and Roll Waltz."

John Steel
b. circa 1900
d. 1971, New York, New York

John Steel is primarily remembered for introducing "A Pretty Girl Is Like a Melody" and "The Girl of My Dreams" in the *Ziegfeld Follies*. He sang in the *Follies* in 1919, 1920, and 1921 and in *The Music Box Revue* of 1922 and 1923.

Max Steiner
b. 1888, Vienna, Austria
d. 1971, Hollywood, California

Composer Max Steiner wrote mostly music for films. Beginning in the late twenties, he scored hundreds of films and became famous for some of the themes he composed. His most popular music includes "Tara's Theme" from *Gone with the Wind* (1939) and "Theme from *A Summer Place*" (1959).

Sam H. Stept
b. 1897, Odessa, Russia
d. 1964, Hollywood, California

Composer Sam Stept wrote several hits during the thirties and forties. His best-known melodies include 1928's "That's My Weakness Now," 1931's "Please Don't Talk About Me When I'm Gone," and 1942's "Don't Sit Under the Apple Tree."

He came to the United States from Russia in 1900 and grew up in Pittsburgh. He led a dance band in the early twenties and did not begin composing until the late twenties.

Slam Stewart
b. 1914, Englewood, New Jersey

Slam Stewart (real name: Leroy Stewart) was most famous as the partner in the Slim and Slam novelty act. He teamed with Slim Gaillard in 1938. Their best-known hit song was 1938's "The Flat Foot Floogee."

Al Stillman
b. 1906, New York, New York

Lyricist Al Stillman wrote several hits in the 1940s and 1950s. Stillman's best-known lyrics were 1940's "The Breeze and I," 1942's "Juke Box Saturday Night," 1952's "I Believe," 1955's "Moments to Remember," 1956's "No, Not Much!," and 1957's "Chances Are."

Herbert Stothart
b. 1885, Milwaukee, Wisconsin
d. 1949, Los Angeles, California

Herbert Stothart composed songs for the stage and movies. He began in 1920 and wrote most of his hits before the mid-thirties. His most famous songs include 1928's "I Wanna Be Loved by You," and 1931's "Cuban Love Song."

Jule Styne
b. 1905, London, England

Jule Styne is a leading composer of music for movies and Broadway from the 1940s through the 1960s. Styne is a member of the Songwriters' Hall of Fame. He came to the United States from his native London as a small boy and studied music in Chicago.

His most successful Broadway musicals were *Gentlemen Prefer Blondes* (1949), *Bells Are Ringing* (1956), *Gypsy* (1959), and *Funny Girl* (1964).

He composed "I Don't Want to Walk Without You" for the 1941 movie musical *Sweater Girl*, "I've Heard That Song Before" for the 1943 movie musical *Youth on Parade*, "I'll Walk Alone" for the 1944 movie musical *Follow the Boys* and "Saturday Night Is the Loneliest Night in the Week" and "It's Been a Long, Long Time" in 1945, "Let It Snow, Let It Snow, Let It Snow" (1946), and "Five Minutes More" for the 1946 movie musical *The Sweetheart of Sigma Chi.* He wrote "The Things We Did Last Summer" (1946), "Papa, Won't You Dance with Me?" for the 1947 musical *High Button Shoes,* "It's Magic" for the 1948 movie musical *Romance on the High Seas,* and 1949's "Diamonds Are a Girl's Best Friend" for the musical *Gentlemen Prefer Blondes.*

In the fifties his biggest hits were 1954's Academy Award winner, "Three Coins in a Fountain"; 1956's "The Party's Over" and "Just in Time" for the musical *Bells Are Ringing;* and "Everything's Coming Up Roses" for the 1959 musical *Gypsy.*

In the sixties he wrote "Make Someone Happy" for the 1960 musical *Do Re Mi,* "The Second Time Around" for the 1961 movie musical *High Time,* and "People" for the 1964 musical *Funny Girl.*

Kay Swift
b. 1905, New York, New York

Composer Kay Swift wrote the score for the 1930 Broadway musical *Fine and Dandy,* which introduced the title song. She also wrote "Can't We Be Friends?" for the revue *The Little Show* (1929). She wrote several other songs, some of which were minor hits.

Marty Symes
b. 1904, Brooklyn, New York
d. 1953, Forest Hills, New York

Marty Symes was active as a lyricist in the thirties and forties. His most famous lyrics include 1933's "Under a Blanket of Blue," and "The Talk of the Town."

T

William Tabbert
b. 1921, Chicago, Illinois
d. 1974, Dallas, Texas

Singer William Tabbert's chief claim to popular music fame was introducing "Younger Than Springtime" in 1949's *South Pacific* and "Fanny" in 1954's *Fanny.*

Tamara
b. 1907, Poltava, Russia
d. 1943, Lisbon, Portugal

Singer Tamara (real name: Tamara Drasin) introduced "Smoke Gets in Your Eyes" and "The Touch of Your Hand" in 1933's *Roberta* and "I'll Be Seeing You" and "I Can Dream, Can't I?" in 1938's *Right This Way.* She died in an airplane crash on a trip to entertain servicemen during World War II.

Shirley Temple
b. 1928, Santa Monica, California

Shirley Temple was probably the most popular child star the motion-picture industry has ever known. She and her films were top box-office attractions during the thirties and forties.

She was enrolled in dancing school when she was three. She began her film career in bit parts in *Baby Burlesks* shorts that spoofed hit films. In 1934 she became a star, singing "Baby, Take a Bow" in *Stand Up and Cheer.* Next came one of her most famous roles in *Little Miss Marker.* She made more than twenty other films in the thirties.

When she grew up, she did not sustain her former popularity, so she left the business in the late forties. She married actor John Agar in the mid-forties but later divorced him. She married television executive Charles Black in 1950.

In recent years she has been active in politics and served in the United Nations and as a U.S. ambassador.

Some of the songs she introduced include 1934's "On the Good Ship Lollipop," 1935's "Animal Crackers in My Soup," and 1934's "Baby, Take a Bow."

Fay Templeton
b. 1865, Little Rock, Arkansas
d. 1939, San Francisco, California

Fay Templeton was a particularly famous singing star on the Broadway stage from the late 1880s to the early

1910s. Her contribution to the music of the eras covered in this book was the introduction of "Yesterdays" in 1933's *Roberta*.

Norma Terris
b. 1904, Columbus, Kansas

Singer and actress Norma Terris (real name: Norma Allison) made her contribution to popular music history by introducing "Make Believe," "Why Do I Love You?," and "You Are Love" in 1927's *Show Boat*.

The Three Suns
Al Nevins, guitarist
Morty Nevins, accordionist
Artie Dunn, organist, vocalist

This trio was most popular in the late forties and early fifties. Its most famous hits include 1947's "Peg o'My Heart" and 1951's "Twilight Time."

Harry Tierney
b. 1890, Perth Amboy, New Jersey
d. 1965, New York, New York

Composer Harry Tierney collaborated primarily with lyricist Joseph McCarthy on several hit Broadway musicals. Tierney's hit songs include "In My Sweet Little Alice Blue Gown" from *Irene* (1919) and "Rio Rita" and "The Ranger's Song" from *Rio Rita* (1927). Tierney was elected to the Songwriters' Hall of Fame.

Dmitri Tiomkin
b. 1899, Ukraine, Russia
d. 1979, London, England

Composer Dmitri Tiomkin was famous for the themes he wrote for several important films.

Tiomkin came to the United States with his wife, who was a ballet dancer. She did some brief film work in Hollywood. During this time Tiomkin scored several minor films. Most of his most famous film compositions came during the fifties and sixties. Some of his best-known songs include 1952's "High Noon," 1954's "The High and the Mighty," 1956's "Friendly Persuasion," and 1960's "The Green Leaves of Summer."

Charles Tobias
b. 1898, New York, New York
d. 1970

Charles Tobias was most active as a songwriter from the mid-twenties into the fifties. Although he was primarily a lyricist, he occasionally wrote the music, too.

Some of his best-known lyrics include 1941's "Rose O'Day," 1942's "Don't Sit Under the Apple Tree," 1946's "The Old Lamplighter," and 1963's "Those Lazy Hazy Crazy Days of Summer."

Mel Tormé
b. 1925, Chicago, Illinois

Mel Tormé is a very versatile entertainer: He sings jazz, plays drums and piano, and is an actor, a composer, and an arranger. His most famous song creation is 1946's "The Christmas Song," but he also had good success with 1945's "A Stranger in Town." Some called Tormé "the Velvet Fog" because of his soft style of singing.

Arthur Tracy
b. 1903, Kamenetz, Russia

"The Street Singer," Arthur Tracy, was one of the first singers to be popularized by the medium of radio. As a boy he had worked as a strolling street singer. Later he appeared in vaudeville, and in the mid-twenties on radio. The movie *Pennies from Heaven* was very loosely based on Tracy's career.

Merle Travis
b. 1917, Rosewood, Kentucky

Country and western singer Merle Travis is famous as a performer and composer. He composed 1947's "Smoke, Smoke, Smoke That Cigarette" and 1955's "Sixteen Tons." He was particularly active in country music in the forties and fifties.

Orrin Tucker
b. 1911, St. Louis, Missouri

Orrin Tucker conducted his orchestra in ballrooms and concerts in theaters all over the United States during the thirties. They also appeared on the radio version of *Your Hit Parade* for a year. His most famous recording was a 1939 disc of "Oh, Johnny, Oh Johnny, Oh!"

Sophie Tucker
b. 1884, Russia
d. 1966, New York, New York

Show business legend Sophie Tucker (real name: Sonia Kalish) first began singing in her father's café in Hartford, Connecticut, in 1905. She married Louis Tuck (later changed to Tucker for her stage name) in 1906. Her first appearance in the *Ziegfeld Follies* came in 1909. By 1914 she was earning top money. Over her long career Tucker appeared on the stage, in movies, on radio and television, and on recordings.

She became known as the Last of the Red-Hot Mamas because of her risqué songs. Some of her most famous songs include her theme, "Some of These Days" (1910), and "My Yiddishe Momme" (1925).

Roy Turk
b. 1892, New York, New York
d. 1934, Hollywood, California

Lyricist Roy Turk wrote most of his famous songs in the twenties and early thirties. His best-known lyrics include 1926's " 'Gimme' a Little Kiss, Will 'Ya' Huh?" 1928's "I'll Get By," 1931's "Walkin' My Baby Back Home," "Where the Blue of the Night Meets the Gold of the Day," and "I Don't Know Why."

V

Rudy Vallee
b. 1901, Island Pond, Vermont

Rudy Vallee is an all-time great entertainer as singer, actor, and bandleader. He was a singing idol in the late twenties and early thirties. He was to that era what Frank Sinatra was to the teenagers of the forties and what Elvis Presley was to the fifties.

Vallee formed his first band while attending Yale. After leaving college, he formed the Yale Collegians, which opened at the Heigh-Ho Club in New York in early 1928. Up to this point he had left the singing up to others, confining his efforts to leading the band and playing saxophone. But at the Heigh-Ho Club the manager expressed distaste for the band's singer, and Vallee became the last-minute replacement. His voice was thin and weak, so he used a megaphone to amplify it. The gimmick may have been the decision or the stroke of fate that propelled him to fame and fortune. Even though he had to change the band's name to the Connecticut Yankees because Yale alumni objected to the university's name being associated with a nightclub band, Vallee's career zoomed.

He starred in the 1929 movies *The Vagabond Lover* and *Glorifying the American Girl*. He began a network radio program from the Heigh-Ho Club (his greeting "Heigh-ho everybody" became almost as famous as the megaphone) also in 1929. He was particularly important and heard from often in the thirties and to a degree in the forties, after which his fame waned. He made a comeback in the fifties, more as a comedian than as a singer. He had an important role

in the 1961 Broadway musical and the 1967 movie version of *How to Succeed in Business Without Really Trying*. In addition, he was the composer of or lyricist for several popular songs: 1929's "Deep Night" and "I'm Just a Vagabond Lover," and 1930's "Betty Co-ed."

Van and Schenck
Gus Van b. 1887, Brooklyn, New York
    d. 1968, Miami Beach, Florida
Joe Schenck b. 1891, Brooklyn, New York
    d. 1930, Detroit, Michigan

The comedy team of Van and Schenck often performed novelty songs and patter as part of their routines. They were featured in the 1919, 1920, and 1921 editions of the *Ziegfeld Follies*.

James Van Heusen
b. 1913, Syracuse, New York

Songwriters' Hall of Fame composer James ("Jimmy") Van Heusen (real name: Edward Chester Babcock) wrote several important popular songs from the late thirties into the sixties. Many of them were written for films. He collaborated primarily with Eddie De Lange, Johnny Burke, and Sammy Cahn. Van Heusen established his own publishing house in 1939.

Some of his most famous hits include 1939's "Darn That Dream," 1940's "Imagination," 1942's "Moonlight Becomes You," 1943's "Sunday, Monday or Always," 1944's "Swinging on a Star" and "It Could Happen to You," 1945's "Aren't You Glad You're You?" 1947's "But Beautiful," 1955's "The Tender Trap" and "Love and Marriage," 1957's "All the Way," 1959's "High Hopes," 1960's "The Second Time Around," 1963's "Call Me Irresponsible," and 1967's "Thoroughly Modern Millie."

Billy Vaughn
b. 1919, Glasgow, Kentucky

Orchestra director Billy Vaughn had his first big hit recording with the 1955 recording of "Melody of Love." In the early fifties Vaughn was singing with the vocal quartet the Hilltoppers. After a few discs he became musical director of Dot Records. His own singles and albums—particularly "Melody of Love," 1957's "Sail Along Silvery Moon," 1958's "La Paloma," and 1961's "Wheels"—proved to be very successful. He and his orchestra also backed the Fontane Sisters on their 1954 million seller of "Hearts of Stone" and Pat Boone on five of his 1957 million sellers.

Gwen Verdon
b. 1925, Culver City, California

Dancer, singer, and actress Gwen Verdon starred on Broadway in several musicals from the early fifties to the present day. Her most famous Broadway hits include 1955's *Damn Yankees,* 1959's *Redhead,* 1966's *Sweet Charity,* and 1975's *Chicago.*

Albert Von Tilzer
b. 1878, Indianapolis, Indiana
d. 1956, Los Angeles, California

Composer Albert Von Tilzer (real name: Albert Gumm) was an important songwriter from the early 1900s into the 1920s. He was the younger brother of composer Harry Von Tilzer.

Some of Albert Von Tilzer's most popular songs include 1908's "Take Me out to the Ball Game," 1910's "Put Your Arms Around Me, Honey," and 1920's "I'll Be with You in Apple Blossom Time." Both the Von Tilzers, Albert and Harry, were elected to the Songwriters' Hall of Fame.

W

Bea Wain
b. 1917, New York, New York

Singer Bea Wain is best known as the vocalist with the Larry Clinton band during the late thirties. She sang with Fred Waring before she joined Clinton's group. She gained fame with Clinton's orchestra when they popularized 1934's "Deep Purple," and 1938's "My Reverie." She left the band in 1939 to work as a single. Although she continued singing for many years, she never regained her former popularity. She married radio announcer Andre Baruch.

Jimmy Wakely
b. 1914, Mineola, Arkansas
d. 1982, Los Angeles, California

Jimmy Wakely is best known as a singing cowboy in several films. His biggest record hits were mostly "honky-tonk, cheating" songs. He broke the mainstream pop barrier when he teamed with singer Margaret Whiting for several recordings. Thier duet of "Slipping Around" became a million-seller in 1949. Wakely's singing might be called a combination of a country Bing Crosby and a high-brow Gene Autry.

Fats Waller
b. 1904, New York, New York
d. 1943, Kansas City, Missouri

Pianist, singer, and composer Fats Waller (real name: Thomas Waller) was particularly popular and wrote most of his songs in the late twenties and thirties. His most famous compositions are 1929's "Ain't Misbehavin' " and "Honeysuckle Rose."

Ain't Misbehavin', a Broadway musical, celebrated the music Waller wrote and sang during his days in the Harlem of the late twenties and thirties. The show won the Tony Award for the year's best musical for 1978. Waller was elected to the Songwriters' Hall of Fame.

Charles Walters
b. 1911, Pasadena, California

Singer, dancer, actor, choreographer, and director Charles Walters's chief claim to popular music fame was singing "Just One of Those Things" and dancing to "Begin the Beguine" in 1935's *Jubilee.* In 1938 he became a choreographer and later a Hollywood director.

Fred Waring
b. 1900, Tyrone, Pennsylvania
d. 1984, Danville, Pennsylvania

Fred Waring and his brother formed their first musical group in 1916, a quartet called Waring's Banjazzatra. His Collegians were particularly popular during the twenties. He expanded his band to include a glee club, which became well known on radio in the mid-thirties and on television in the late forties.

Fred Waring and his Pennsylvanians' million-selling discs include 1942's "Twas the Night Before Christmas" and an album of Christmas songs in 1946. They combined with Bing Crosby for the 1947 million seller of "Whiffenpoof Song."

In addition to his musical endeavors, he was an inventor (the Waring Blender) and manufacturer. He also founded the Shawnee Press to publish the arrangements the Pennsylvanians performed and was very active for many years in sponsoring workshops for choral directors.

Harry Warren
b. 1893, Brooklyn, New York
d. 1981, Los Angeles, California

Composer Harry Warren was one of the most successful writers of popular songs from the early twenties through the fifties. He collaborated with lyricists Al Dubin (1928–39), Johnny Mercer (1938–39), and Mack Gordon (1940–45). Many of his best-known tunes were written for films and he won three Academy Awards (1935, 1940, and 1946).

Some of Warren's most famous hits include 1930's "Cheerful Little Earful" and "Would You Like to Take a Walk?," 1931's "You're My Everything" and "I Found a Million Dollar Baby," 1932's "You're Getting to Be a Habit with Me," and "Forty-second Street," 1933's "Gold Digger's Song (We're in the Money)," 1934's "I'll String Along," and "I Only Have Eyes for You," 1935's "Lullaby of Broadway," 1937's "September in the Rain," 1938's "Jeepers Creepers," and "You Must Have Been a Beautiful Baby," 1941's "Chattanooga Choo Choo," 1942's "There Will Never Be Another You" and "I've Got a Gal in Kalamazoo," 1943's "I Had the Craziest Dream" and "You'll Never Know," 1945's "On the Atchison, Topeka and Santa Fe," and 1954's "That's Amore." Warren is a member of the Songwriters' Hall of Fame.

Ned Washington
b. 1901, Scranton, Pennsylvania
d. 1976, Los Angeles, California

Lyricist Ned Washington wrote several hits, primarily for Broadway shows and for films. The best-known ones include 1932's "I'm Getting Sentimental over You," and "Smoke Rings," 1933's "A Ghost of a Chance," 1940's "When You Wish upon a Star," 1946's "Stella by Starlight," 1950's "My Foolish Heart," 1952's "High Noon," and 1954's "The High and the Mighty." The Songwriters' Hall of Fame elected Washington to membership.

Ethel Waters
b. 1896, Chester, Pennsylvania
d. 1977, Chatsworth, California

Singer Ethel Waters's blues recordings were particularly popular among jazz connoisseurs, but she became better known to a wider public when she introduced "Dinah" at the Plantation Club in New York, "Heat Wave" in 1933's *As Thousands Cheer,* "Stormy Weather" in a Cotton Club revue, and "Cabin in the Sky" and "Taking a Chance on Love" in 1940's *Cabin in the Sky.* She also appeared in several films and in concerts.

Mabel Wayne
b. 1904, Brooklyn, New York

Songwriters' Hall of Fame member Mabel Wayne was most active as a composer of popular songs from the mid-twenties into the fifties. Her best-known songs include 1930's "It Happened in Monterey," 1934's "Little Man, You've Had a Busy Day," and 1940's "I Understand."

The Weavers
Pete Seeger, b. 1919, New York, New York
Lee Hayes, b. 1914, Little Rock, Arkansas
Fred Hellerman, b. 1927, Brooklyn, New York
Erik Darling, b. 1933, Baltimore, Maryland

Originally the Weavers sang urban folk music about social problems and unpopular causes. They hit the big time in 1950, when they recorded the number one hit of the year with Gordon Jenkins and his orchestra. They followed that success in 1951 with a million seller of "On Top of Old Smokey," adding Terry Gilkyson and Vic Schoen's orchestra.

Clifton Webb
b. 1891, Indianapolis, Indiana
d. 1966, Beverly Hills, California

Actor, singer, and dancer Clifton Webb (real name: Webb Parmelee Hollenbeck) is best remembered for the twenty films he made, particularly the Mr. Belvedere roles he played.

From his mid-teens Webb was a leading man and dancer in several Broadway musicals. In 1928's *Treasure Girl* he introduced "I've Got a Crush on You," in 1929's *The Little Show* he introduced "I Guess I'll Have to Change My Plan," and in 1933's *As Thousands Cheer,* he introduced "Easter Parade." His last musical on Broadway was in 1938, after which he turned to Hollywood.

Joan Weber
b. 1936, Paulsboro, New Jersey

Singer Joan Weber's only million-selling recording was a 1954 disc of "Let Me Go, Lover!" She was discovered by Mitch Miller, who was artists' chief at Columbia Records at the time.

Paul Francis Webster
b. 1907, New York, New York
d. 1984, Beverly Hills, California

Lyricist Paul Francis Webster wrote several major hit songs, most of them for movies from the mid-thirties through the sixties. Several of his songs were Academy Award nominees or winners. Webster is a member of the Songwriters' Hall of Fame.

Some of his best-known songs include 1932's "Masquerade," 1933's "My Moonlight Madonna," 1934's "Two Cigarettes in the Dark," 1941's "I Got It Bad," 1951's "The Loveliest Night of the Year," 1955's "Love Is a Many-Splendored Thing," 1956's "Friendly Persuasion," 1957's "April Love," 1960's "The Green Leaves of Summer," and 1965's "The Shadow of Your Smile" and "Somewhere My Love" (Lara's theme from *Doctor Zhivago*).

Ted Weems
b. 1901, Pitcairn, Pennsylvania
d. 1963, Tulsa, Oklahoma

Bandleader Ted Weems's group of musicians was particularly popular in the twenties and thirties. He continued to be active through the early sixties.

Million-selling recordings by Weems and his orchestra include a 1923 disc of 1918's "Somebody Stole My Gal," 1929's "Piccolo Pete," 1933's "Heartaches" (recorded in 1933, revived in 1947), and a 1947 recording of 1918's "Mickey."

Kurt Weill
b. 1900, Dessau, Germany
d. 1950, New York, New York

Composer Kurt Weill was a very successful writer for the German stage before he came to America. He composed *The Rise and Fall of the City of Mahagonny* in 1927 and *The Threepenny Opera* in 1928. When Weill's works, which were often attacks on the social and political life in Nazi Germany, were not allowed to be performed, Weill and his wife, Lotte Lenya, escaped to Paris, then to London and to New York in 1935. He became an American citizen in 1943. His first success in the United States was with 1938's *Knickerbocker Holiday*, which introduced "September Song." His other successful Broadway shows were 1941's *Lady in the Dark*, 1943's *One Touch of Venus*, 1947's *Street Scene*, and 1949's *Lost in the Stars*. His *Threepenny Opera* was revived on Broadway in 1952 and 1954; "Mack the Knife" came from these updated versions. The Songwriters' Hall of Fame honored Weill by inducting him into the society.

George Weiss
b. 1921, New York, New York

Songwriter George Weiss wrote a few big hits in the forties and fifties. He primarily collaborated with Bennie Benjamin on music and lyrics. His most famous songs include 1946's "Oh, What It Seemed to Be," 1952's "Wheel of Fortune," 1956's "Mr. Wonderful," and "Too Close for Comfort."

Lawrence Welk
b. 1903, Strasburg, North Dakota

Lawrence Welk formed his first band in 1925 and began to play on radio in South Dakota. In the next several years the band became very popular in the midwestern states. In the early fifties Welk began a weekly television series that was broadcast nationally over ABC. In syndication, his show continues on many stations.

Believe it or not, Welk has had only one million-selling recording, and that was "Calcutta" in 1961.

Marcy Westcott
b. Chicago, Illinois

Singer Marcy Westcott starred in two Rodgers and Hart Broadway musicals: 1938's *The Boys from Syracuse* and 1939's *Too Many Girls*. She introduced "This Can't Be Love" and "I Didn't Know What Time It Was."

Paul Weston
b. 1921, Pittsfield, Massachusetts

Paul Weston studied economics in college but became famous as a music arranger. He was hired by Rudy Vallee at the peak of Vallee's popularity. Weston later arranged music for Tommy Dorsey. He has written for several films and is an executive with Capitol Records. He and his orchestra have appeared often on television and have backed such famous recording artists as his wife, Jo Stafford, Doris Day, Gordon MacRae, and the Pied Pipers.

George White
b. 1890, New York, New York
d. 1968, Hollywood, California

George White is primarily remembered for the *Scandals* revues that he presented, which rivaled the *Ziegfeld Follies* in popularity. In addition, he produced several nightclub revues and some films and wrote lyrics for several songs with composer Cliff Friend.

Paul Whiteman
b. 1890, Denver, Colorado
d. 1967, Doylestown, Pennsylvania

Paul Whiteman had the most popular orchestra during the twenties, featuring sweet, lush arrangements with a danceable beat. Called the King of Jazz, Whiteman began his career in symphonic work but left that field to play popular music in 1919. His symphonic orchestra soon began to attract major attention with engagements at the best hotels and with several early recordings. Whiteman organized the concert at Aeolian Hall in New York at which George Gershwin's *Rhapsody in Blue* was premiered.

Whiteman and his Orchestra starred in the 1930 film *The King of Jazz,* which was dedicated to him. They also were popular radio personalities and introduced several new talents, among them the Rhythm Boys (Bing Crosby's start in the business).

Million sellers for Whiteman's band include 1920's "Whispering," backed by "The Japanese Sandman"; 1922's "Three o'Clock in the Morning"; and 1923's "Linger Awhile."

Jack Whiting
b. 1901, Philadelphia, Pennsylvania
d. 1961, New York, New York

Singer, dancer, and actor Jack Whiting appeared in many Broadway musicals from 1922 through the mid-fifties. He had the pleasure of introducing a number of songs that proved to be moderate hits, but only "You're the Cream in My Coffee," from 1928's *Hold Everything,* became a major hit.

Margaret Whiting
b. 1924, Detroit, Michigan

Margaret Whiting, daughter of composer Richard Whiting, was a popular singer during the late forties and early fifties. Her first professional success came with "That Old Black Magic" as vocalist with Freddie Slack's orchestra. More success came in 1943 with "My Ideal." With Billy Butterfield's band in 1944, she helped popularize "Moonlight in Vermont," her first million seller. Her second million seller came in 1948 with "A Tree in the Meadow." Then, in 1949, she teamed with country and western singer Jimmy Wakely for a million seller of "Slipping Around." After that her career waned, although she has continued to perform.

Richard Whiting
b. 1891, Peoria, Illinois
d. 1938, Beverly Hills, California

Composer Richard Whiting was most active as a songwriter during the twenties and thirties. Many of his songs were written for films during the thirties. Whiting was elected to the Songwriters' Hall of Fame.

Some of his best-known hits include 1920's "The Japanese Sandman," 1921's "Ain't We Got Fun?," 1925's "Sleepy Time Gal," 1926's "Breezin' Along with the Breeze," 1928's "She's Funny That Way," 1929's "Louise," 1930's "My Ideal" and "Beyond the Blue Horizon," 1932's "You're an Old Smoothie," 1934's "On the Good Ship Lollipop," 1936's "When Did You Leave Heaven?," 1937's "Too Marvelous for Words," and 1938's "Hooray for Hollywood."

Esther Williams
b. 1923, Los Angeles, California

Actress Esther Williams was the swimming star of several movies from the early forties through the early fifties. Her only famous song hit was the 1950 Academy Award winner, "Baby, It's Cold Outside," which she introduced in a duet with Ricardo Montalban in *Neptune's Daughter.*

Frances Williams
b. 1903, St. Paul, Minnesota
d. 1959, New York, New York

Singer Frances Williams (real name: Frances Jellinek) introduced one important popular hit, "As Time Goes By," in the 1931 production *Everybody's Welcome.*

Hank Williams
b. 1923, Georgiana, Alabama
d. 1953, Oak Hill, West Virginia

Country singer and composer Hank Williams (real name: Hiram King Williams) was named to the Country Music Hall of Fame in 1961. He also was inducted into the Songwriters' Hall of Fame. Williams formed his first band at age thirteen. He cut his first record in 1946 with Sterling Records and switched to MGM in 1947. He recorded many of his songs in a relatively brief period of time.

The 1953 film *Your Cheatin' Heart* was based on Williams's life and included most of his great songs. His son, Hank, Jr., recorded all the songs on the sound track and has continued into the eighties as a country music star.

Roger Williams
b. 1925, Des Moines, Iowa

Pianist Roger Williams (real name: Louis Wertz) was a particularly popular recording artist during the late fifties and early sixties. After he had received a doctorate in music from Drake University, he moved to New York. After some studies in jazz at Juilliard, he won an *Arthur Godfrey's Talent Scouts* show. Williams was signed by Kapp Records and recorded the album *The Boy Next Door* in 1954. Shortly after that he recorded his first big hit, "Autumn Leaves." His other major hit single was 1958's "Till."

Tex Williams
b. 1917, Ramsey, Illinois

Country singer Tex Williams suddenly became a national personality when his recording of 1947's "Smoke, Smoke, Smoke That Cigarette" became a big hit. He had begun to perform in his childhood in Illinois. In 1947 he formed the Western Caravan band, which became very successful, particularly in Southern California. Williams and singer Merle Travis penned the song that made Williams famous. Williams appeared in many films during the forties.

Bob Wills
b. 1905, Groesbeck, Texas
d. 1975, Fort Worth, Texas

Originator of the western swing band style, country singer Bob Wills had his biggest national hit in 1940 with his "San Antonio Rose." He was named to the Country Music Hall of Fame in 1968.

Meredith Willson
b. 1902, Mason City, Iowa
d. 1984, Santa Monica, California

Composer Meredith Willson (real name: Robert Meredith Reiniger) began his professional music career as a flutist in John Philip Sousa's band in 1919. Next came stints with the New York Philharmonic and as musical director for ABC. His Broadway musicals *Music Man* (1957), *The Unsinkable Molly Brown* (1960), and *Here's Love* (1963) were very successful. He wrote a few songs that were popular hits before his Broadway debut: 1941's "You and I" and 1950's "May the Good Lord Bless and Keep You."

Charles Winninger
b. 1884, Athens, Wisconsin
d. 1969, Palm Springs, California

Charles Winninger was primarily a comedy actor, but he introduced the hit "I Want to Be Happy" in 1925's *No, No Nanette.* He was married to singer and actress Blanche Ring. Winninger also appeared in several films.

P. G. Wodehouse
b. 1881, Guildford, England
d. 1975, Southampton, New York

P. G. Wodehouse was an important lyricist for Broadway musicals in the late teens and twenties. His most popular lyrics include 1917's "Till the Clouds Roll By" and 1927's "Bill."

Harry Woods
b. 1896, North Chelmsford, Massachusetts
d. 1970, Phoenix, Arizona

Composer Harry Woods wrote most of his popular songs during the twenties and thirties. His first big hit was 1926's "When the Red, Red Robin Comes Bob, Bob, Bobbin' Along." Others of his best-known songs include 1927's "I'm Looking over a Four Leaf Clover," 1931's "When the Moon Comes over the Mountain," and 1933's "Try a Little Tenderness."

Robert Wright
b. 1914, Daytona Beach, Florida

Bob Wright, who worked exclusively with Chet Forrest, is primarily known for borrowing music from classical composers and transforming them into popular hits in Broadway musicals. Wright and Forrest transformed Edvard Grieg's life and music into 1944's *Song of Norway* and Aleksandr Borodin's music into the songs for 1953's *Kismet.*

Allie Wrubel
b. 1905, Middletown, Connecticut
d. 1973, Twentynine Palms, California

Composer Allie Wrubel wrote several popular songs in the thirties and forties. His best-known hits include 1938's "Music, Maestro, Please" and 1947's "Zip-a-Dee-Doo-Dah." He did a lot of work with Disney studios in the late forties. Wrubel was inducted into the Songwriters' Hall of Fame.

Y

Jack Yellen
b. 1892, Poland

Songwriters' Hall of Fame lyricist Jack Yellen was a prolific writer of popular songs during the twenties and thirties. His main collaborator was composer Milton Ager. The two were partners in the publishing firm of Ager, Yellen and Bornstein.

Yellen's best-known lyrics include 1915's "Alabama Jubilee," and "Are You from Dixie?," 1924's "Hard-Hearted Hannah," 1927's "Ain't She Sweet?" and 1929's "Happy Days Are Here Again."

Vincent Youmans
b. 1898, New York, New York
d. 1946, Denver, Colorado

Vincent Youmans was one of the most famous composers of popular songs in the twenties and early thirties. Many of his most famous hits were premiered in Broadway musicals. Youmans's career was shortened when he contracted tuberculosis and entered a Denver sanitarium in 1934. Although he was able to leave the sanitarium periodically, his later musical endeavors were minimal.

Some of his most famous musicals and songs include 1923's *The Wildflower* ("Bambalina"), 1925's *No, No, Nanette* ("Tea for Two"), *Hit the Deck* ("Sometimes I'm Happy"), 1929's *Great Day* ("More Than You Know" and "Without a Song"), and the 1933 movie musical *Flying Down to Rio* ("Carioca" and "Orchids in the Moonlight"). Youmans was elected to the Songwriters' Hall of Fame.

Joe Young
b. 1889, New York, New York
d. 1939, New York, New York

Lyricist Joe Young was extremely active as a songwriter from 1911 to the late 1930s. From 1916 to the 1930s, he collaborated on lyrics with Sam M. Lewis. He is a member of the Songwriters' Hall of Fame.

Some of his most famous lyrics include 1918's "My Mammy" and "Rock-a-bye Your Baby with a Dixie Melody," 1919's "How Ya Gonna Keep 'Em Down on the Farm?," 1925's "Dinah," "Five Foot Two, Eyes of Blue," and "I'm Sitting on Top of the World," 1931's "You're My Everything," 1932's "In a Shanty in Old Shanty Town," and "Lullaby of the Leaves," and 1935's "I'm Gonna Sit Right Down and Write Myself a Letter."

Victor Young
b. 1900, Chicago, Illinois
d. 1956, Palm Springs, California

Composer and bandleader Victor Young was an important force in popular music from the early thirties

until his death in 1956. He turned to popular music and composing from concert music in the late twenties. In the thirties he recorded often with his band; in the forties his band usually backed singers. Young moved to the West Coast in the mid-thirties and arranged and composed music for the movie industry.

Some of his most popular songs were 1928's "Sweet Sue, Just You," 1933's "A Ghost of a Chance," and "Street of Dreams," 1946's "Stella by Starlight," 1950's "My Foolish Heart," 1952's "When I Fall in Love," and 1956's "Around the World." He received an Academy Award posthumously for his score for the movie *Around the World in 80 Days*. Young is a member of the Songwriters' Hall of Fame.

Z

Hy Zaret
b. 1907, New York, New York

Lyricist Hy Zaret was most active in the popular song field in the 1940s and 1950s. He collaborated with Alex Kramer and Joan Whitney. His best-known lyric was 1955's "Unchained Melody."

Florenz Ziegfeld
b. 1869, Chicago, Illinois
d. 1932, Hollywood, California

Florenz Ziegfeld was most famous as the producer of the spectacular *Ziegfeld Follies*. He began his show business career managing the strong man Sandow. He later brought European star Anna Held to the United States and managed her career here. They married in 1897 and divorced in 1913, so Ziegfeld could marry actress Billie Burke.

The first *Ziegfeld Follies* was staged in 1907, and the *Follies* appeared yearly through the twenties. They were lavish spectacles that "glorified the American girl." Many of the most popular performers of the day were featured in the casts and many of the best songwriters wrote material for them to present.

The movies *The Great Ziegfeld* (1936), *Ziegfeld Girl* (1941), and *Ziegfeld Follies* (1946) were about Ziegfeld and his girls.

Index of Song Titles

"'Twas the Night Before Christmas," 238
"Tweedle Dee," 164, 197
"Twelfth Street Rag," 136, 206
"Twilight Time," 225, 235
"Twist, The," 171
"Two Cigarettes in the Dark," 75–76, 225, 240
"Two Hearts in Three-Quarter Time," 57
"Two O'Clock Jump," 208
"Two Sleepy People," 69, 96, 178, 215, 230
"Typewriter, The," 149, 168
"Tzena, Tzena, Tzena," 142, 145

"Ukulele Lady," 34, 185
"Unchained Melody," 163, 164, 172, 204, 243
"Undecided," 168, 176
"Under a Blanket of Blue," 215, 235
"Under Paris Skies," 195
"Until the Real Thing Comes Along," 179

"Valencia," 34
"Varsity Drag, The," 41, 204
"Vaya Con Dios," 156, 193, 224
"Very Thought of You, The," 100, 178, 223
"Volare," 217, 224

"Wabash Blues," 20, 209
"Wagon Wheels," 75, 76, 185, 205
"Waiting for the *Robert E. Lee*," 18, 197
"Wake the Town and Tell the People," 164, 195, 215
"Walkin' My Baby Back Home," 57, 168, 237
"Walkin' to New Orleans," 187
"Walk on the Wild Side, A," 184
"Waltzing in the Clouds," 104
"Wang, Wang Blues, The," 11, 13, 20–21, 177
"Wanted," 160–61, 181
"Wanting You," 46, 201
"Washboard Blues," 69
"'Way Down Yonder in New Orleans," 24
"Way You Look Tonight, The," 88, 170, 192, 229
"Wedding Bells Are Breaking Up That Old Gang of Mine," 191, 210
"Wedding of the Painted Doll, The," 47, 176
"We Kiss in a Shadow," 146, 201
"We Mustn't Say Goodbye," 114
"We're in the Money (The Gold Diggers' Song)," 53, 71, 188, 239
"We Three," 103–4
"What a Diff'rence a Day Made," 76
"Whatever Lola Wants," 164
"What Is This Thing Called Love?," 57–58, 226
"What'll I Do?," 30, 68, 173
"What's New?," 176

"Wheel of Fortune," 152, 173, 234, 240
"Wheels," 237
"When a Gypsy Makes His Violin Cry," 185
"When Day Is Done," 185
"When Did You Leave Heaven?," 88, 176, 241
"When I Fall in Love," 204, 243
"When I Grow Too Old to Dream," 85, 201
"When I Take My Sugar to Tea," 62, 191, 210
"When It's Sleepy Time Down South," 61
"When My Baby Smiles at Me," 16
"When My Dreamboat Comes Home," 194
"When My Sugar Walks down the Street," 30–31, 170, 218, 220
"When the Lights Go On Again," 173
"When the Moon Comes over the Mountain," 62, 208, 233, 242
"When the Red, Red Robin Comes Bob, Bob, Bobbin' Along," 37, 242
"When the Right One Comes Along," 204
"When You're Smiling," 212
"When Your Hair Has Turned to Silver," 58, 185
"When You Were Sweet Sixteen," 181
"When You Wish Upon a Star," 104, 239
"When Yuba Plays the Tuba," 206
"Where Is Your Heart," 156
"Where or When," 90, 92, 203, 206
"Where the Blue of the Night Meets the Gold of the Day," 62, 168, 237
"Whiffenpoof Song, The," 88, 183, 238
"Whip-poor-will," 16, 185
"Whispering," 15, 17, 230, 241
"Whispering Hope," 217, 234
"Whispering Serenade, The," 153
"Whispers in the Dark," 92
"Whistle While You Work," 96
"White Christmas," 40, 68, 97, 110, 157, 170, 173, 174, 183, 232
"White Cliffs of Dover, The," 211
"Who?," 34, 201, 202, 212, 220, 223
"Who Am I?," 104
"Who Ate Napoleons with Josephine When Bonaparte Was Away?," 24–25
"Whole Lotta Lovin'," 187
"Who's Afraid of the Big Bad Wolf?," 53, 71, 180, 229
"Who's Got the Pain?," 128
"Who's Sorry Now?," 26, 210, 230, 233
"Who's Your Little Whoozis?," 174
"Who Takes Care of the Caretaker's Daughter—While the

Caretaker's Busy Taking Care?," 25
"Who Wouldn't Love You?," 110, 212
"Why, Baby, Why?," 174
"Why Do I Love You?," 41–42, 201, 236
"Why Don't You Believe Me?," 152, 208
"Why Don't You Do Right?," 198
"Why Was I Born?," 50, 201, 206, 222
"Wilhelmina," 143
"Winter Wonderland," 129, 169
"Wishing," 99, 100
"Wish You Were Here," 152, 192
"With a Song in My Heart," 50, 195, 202, 228
"With My Eyes Wide Open I'm Dreaming," 76, 140, 199, 224, 227
"Without a Song," 50, 190, 230, 243
"Woman Is a Sometime Thing, A," 197
"Woodchopper's Ball," 100, 204
"Woodpecker's Song, The," 104, 167
"Woody Woodpecker Song, The," 134, 212
"Wonderful One," 24
"Wonder Why," 147
"Work with Me, Annie," 162, 171
"World Is Waiting for the Sunrise, The," 17, 148, 193, 224
"Would I Love You," 224
"Would You Like to Take a Walk?," 186, 230, 239
"Wrap Your Troubles in Dreams," 212
"Wreck of the Old 97, The," 33, 183
"Wunderbar," 188, 226

"Yellow Rose of Texas, The," 165, 220
"Yes, Sir, That's My Baby," 11, 34–35, 178, 187, 210
"Yesterdays," 51, 71–72, 201, 212, 236
"Yes! We Have No Bananas," 25, 26
"Yoo-hoo," 185
"You Always Hurt the One You Love," 117, 192, 220, 228
"You and I," 107, 242
"You and the Night and the Music," 76, 186, 205, 231
"You Are Beautiful," 201
"You Are Love," 42, 201, 236
"You Are My Lucky Star," 84, 176, 194
"You Are My Sunshine," 104, 184
"You Belong to Me," 152, 212, 234
"You Belong to My Heart," 125
"You Brought a New Kind of Love to Me," 191, 210
"You Call Everybody Darling," 133
"You Call It Madness," 181, 182
"You Can't Be True, Dear," 121, 137

"You'd Be So Nice to Come Home To," 110, 114, 226
"You'd Be Surprised," 178
"You Do," 133
"You do Something to Me," 50, 226
"You Forgot to Remember," 33
"You Go to My Head," 96, 182, 198
"You Gotta Be a Football Hero," 72, 214
"You Keep Coming Back Like a Song," 126
"You Light Up My Life," 174
"You'll Never Know," 80, 112, 114, 191, 199, 203, 239
"You'll Never Walk Alone," 120, 125, 201, 228
"You Made Me Love You—I Didn't Want to Do It," 107, 130, 196, 208, 218, 221
"You Make Me Feel So Young," 199
"You Must Have Been a Beautiful Baby," 96, 219, 239
"Young and Foolish," 161
"Young at Heart," 161, 232
"Younger Than Springtime," 140, 201, 235
"You Oughta Be in Pictures," 76, 204
"Your Cheatin' Heart," 152–53, 208
"You're a Builder Upper," 202
"You're an Old Smoothie," 67, 176, 185, 241
"You're Breaking My Heart," 140
"You're Driving Me Crazy," 187
"You're Getting to Be a Habit with Me," 53, 63, 67, 188, 239
"You're My Everything," 62, 181, 186, 239, 243
"You're Nobody till Somebody Loves You," 222
"You're the Cream in My Coffee," 46, 204, 241
"You're the Top," 76, 85, 226
"You Said You Loved Me," 186
"You Stepped Out of a Dream," 176, 210
"You Took Advantage of Me," 46, 202
"You Turned the Tables on Me," 88–89, 168, 221
"You've Got to See Mamma Ev'ry Night (or You Can't See Mamma at All)," 26, 182, 230
"You Were Meant for Me," 47, 50, 176, 194
"You Were Never Lovelier," 110–11
"You, You, You," 121, 156–57, 168

Z
"Zing a Little Zong," 151
"Zing! Went the Strings of My Heart," 85, 202, 214
"Zip-a-Dee-Doo-Dah," 120, 133, 242
"Zwei Herzen im Dreivierteltakt," 57

Index of Names

Heyward, DuBose, 81, 82, 84
Hibbler, Al, 164, 204
Hickman, Art, 23
Higgins, Billy, 26
Hildegarde, 82, 102, 115, 204–5
Hill, Al, 162
Hill, Annabelle, 134
Hill, Billy, 68, 75, 76, 85, 86, 205
Hill, Robert, 151
Hill, Ruby, 126
Hilliard, Bob, 130, 138, 205
Hilliard, Harriet, 95, 205
Hilltoppers, 163, 237
Himber, Richard, 142
Hines, Earl, 78, 189
Hirsch, Louis A., 16, 205
Hodges, Johnny, 123
Hodgson, Red, 84
Hoey, Evelyn, 63
Hoffman, Al, 112, 131, 141, 142, 143, 159, 205
Hogan, Louanne, 123, 126
Holiday, Billie, 50, 64, 205
Hollander, Frederick, 92, 134
Holloway, Sterling, 36
Holly, Buddy, 122
Holman, Libby, 14, 48, 54, 56–57, 76, 205
Holmes, Herbie, 186
Holmes, Leroy, 158
Homer, Ben, 125
Hooker, Brian, 33
Hooper, R. S., 49
Hope, Bob, 49, 70, 79, 86, 92, 96, 108, 109, 119, 120, 128, 134, 172, 176, 180, 197, 205–6, 230
Horace Heidt and his Brigadiers, 96, 203
Horace Heidt and his Musical Knights, 104, 151, 203
Horne, Lena, 90, 92, 116, 206
Horton, Vaughn, 148
Horwitt, Arnold B., 161
Hoschna, Karl, 202
Hot Five, 37
Hough, Will M., 131
Hoven, George, 148
Howard, Eddy, 129, 131, 140, 148, 149, 206
Howard, Eugene, 68
Howard, Joe E., 131–32
Howard, Willie, 68
Howard Brothers, 21
Howell, Don, 132
Huddleston, John, 225
Hundley, John, 50
Hunt, Pee Wee, 136, 199, 206
Hunter, Alberta, 35
Hunter, Ivory Joe, 121
Hupfeld, Herman, 58, 64, 206
Huston, Walter, 95, 207
Hutton, Betty, 79, 119, 131, 207, 216
Hutton, Ina Ray, 98
Hutton, June, 225
Hutton, Marion, 108, 124, 173, 207
Hylton, Jack, 38

Idriss, Ramez, 134, 137
Ingle, Red, 71, 234
Ink Spots, 98, 103, 127, 129, 193, 207
Iturbi, José, 125
Ivanovici, J., 130
Ives, Burl, 139, 207–8

Jackson, Mahalia, 154
Jackson, Molly, 113
Jacobs, Al, 158
Jacobs, Jacob, 93
Jaffe, Moe, 31, 114
Jamblan and Herpin, 124
James, Etta, 162

James, Harry, 43, 67, 78, 91, 95, 106, 107, 108–9, 111, 112, 123, 173, 190, 194, 198, 199, 200, 203, 208, 210, 232
James, Inez, 156
James, Joni, 152, 153, 162, 208
James, Paul, 55
Jan and Dean, 143
Jason, Will, 61
Jaynes, Betty, 92
Jenkins, Gordon, 138, 139, 142, 143, 145, 208, 239
Jerome, M. K., 117
Johnson, Arthur, 73
Johnson, Bill, 102
Johnson, Buster, 20–21
Johnson, Chick, 25, 26
Johnson, Christine, 124, 125
Johnson, Edward, 108
Johnson, Howard, 15, 62, 208
Johnson, James P., 12
Johnson, Jimmy, 25
Johnson, Van, 61
Johnson, William, 103
Johnston, Arthur, 87, 208
Johnston, Johnnie, 106, 109, 124, 209
Johnston, Pat, 106
Jolson, Al, 12, 13, 14, 16, 17–18, 23, 24, 27, 31, 32, 35, 37, 39, 40, 42, 45, 46, 48, 79, 81, 86, 104, 107, 119, 130, 168, 183, 185, 188, 209, 211
Jones, Allan, 81, 89, 93, 178, 209
Jones, Claude, 12
Jones, Herb, 207
Jones, Isham, 12, 20, 26, 28, 29, 49, 78, 180, 204, 209, 210
Jones, Jack, 209
Jones, John Price, 38
Jones, Orville "Happy," 207
Jones, Spike, 25, 73, 107–8, 134, 150, 209
Jones, Stan, 139
Joplin, Janis, 18
Jordan, Dorothy, 67
Jordan, Louis, 115–16, 132, 209
Jubilee Singers, 47, 50
Jurgens, Dick, 31, 103, 105, 206, 210

K., J., 165
Kaempfert, Bert, 136
Kahal, Irving, 43, 58, 62, 87, 89, 115, 139, 210
Kahn, Gus, 21, 23, 24, 26, 27, 28, 29, 34–35, 44, 56, 59, 65, 67, 68, 69, 87, 104, 119, 168, 210
Kaihan, Maewa, 135
Kallen, Kitty, 78, 86, 114, 124, 158, 189, 210
Kalmar, Bert, 19, 26, 43, 57, 119, 143, 147, 168, 210, 230
Kane, Helen, 43, 45–46, 210
Kaper, Bronislaw, 87, 154, 210
Karas, Anton, 144
Kaye, Buddy, 125, 126, 134, 210
Kaye, Danny, 119, 120, 130
Kaye, Sammy, 78, 97, 99, 105, 108, 122, 127, 138, 140, 142, 182, 210–11
Kearns, Allen, 41
Keeler, Ruby, 48, 53, 63, 66, 70, 74, 75, 209, 211, 226
Keene, Kahn, 99, 218
Kelly, Gene, 47, 49, 79, 95, 102, 116, 119, 179, 211, 232
Kelly, Grace, 169, 183
Kelly, Patsy, 43
Kelly, Paula, 221
Kemp, Hal, 78, 100, 187, 211
Kemper, Ronnie, 31
Ken Darby Choir, 135, 138

Ken Darby Singers, 110
Kendis, James, 15
Ken Lane Singers, 110
Kennedy, Jimmy, 74, 84, 99, 100, 142, 153, 211
Kenny, Billy, 207
Kenny, Charles, 60, 96, 103, 211
Kenny, Nick, 60, 96, 103, 211
Kent, Walter, 112, 117, 123, 211
Kenton, Stan, 95, 128, 211–12
Kern, Jerome, 12, 16, 19, 34, 38, 39, 40, 41, 42, 50, 52, 64, 66, 70, 71–72, 81, 83, 86, 88, 101, 102–3, 110–11, 116, 117, 119, 123, 126, 129, 186, 197, 201, 202, 212, 232
Keyes, James, 160
Killian, Les, 106
King, B. B., 122
King, Charles, 41, 47, 50, 144
King, Dennis, 12, 28, 30, 34
King, Irving, 33
King, Pee Wee, 136, 148, 149, 152, 170, 212
King, Walter Woolf, 67
King, Wayne, 52, 78
Kirby Stone Four, 153
Kirk, Andy, 78
Kirk, Lisa, 131, 212
Klenner, John, 131
Knight, Evelyn, 139
Knight, June, 81, 83
Koehler, Ted, 21, 55, 59, 63, 64, 69, 70, 117, 212, 218
Kohlman, Churchill, 150
Kollmar, Richard, 98
Kosma, Joseph, 161
Kostelanetz, André, 99, 212
Kramer, Alex, 122, 138, 212, 243
Kresa, Helmy, 133
Krupa, Gene, 57, 87, 93, 198
Kyser, Kay, 78, 97, 99, 100, 101, 103, 108, 109, 110, 127, 128, 136, 137, 212

Lacalle, Joseph M., 104
Lahr, Bert, 46, 97
Laine, Frankie, 41, 55, 119, 121, 133, 139, 140, 141, 151, 154, 184, 198, 213
Lamm, Bob, 132, 182
Lamour, Dorothy, 79, 108, 119, 120, 128, 206
Landry, Art, 12, 21
Lane, Abbie, 183
Lane, Burton, 95, 105, 110, 130, 131, 146, 147, 197, 206, 213, 214
Lane, Ken, 110
Laney, King, 152
Lang, Pearl, 124
Lange, Henry, 22
Lange, Johnny, 139, 143
Langford, Frances, 79, 82, 85, 94, 213
Lanson, Roy, 223
Lanson, Snooky, 144
Lanza, Mario, 119, 145, 147, 149, 199, 213
Lara, Augustín, 125
La Rocca, Nick, 223
La Rue, Grace, 21, 213
Larue, Jacques, 162
Latouche, John, 101
Laurence, Elliott, 132
La Vere, Charles, 208
Lavere, Frank, 155
Lawford, Peter, 119
Lawlor, Mary, 38
Lawrence, Gertrude, 12, 31, 36, 37, 54, 55, 146, 213
Lawrence, Jack, 69, 98, 100, 109, 111, 128, 132, 150, 158, 160, 168, 213

Lawson, Herbert Happy, 17
Laye, Evelyn, 85
Layton, J. Turner, 24
Lecuona, Ernesto, 87, 101, 110
Ledbetter, Huddie "Leadbelly," 142, 147
Lee, Lester, 156
Lee, Peggy, 28, 69, 105, 120, 133, 134, 135, 153, 186, 198, 213–14
Legrand, Michel, 155
Leigh, Carolyn, 161
Lemare, Edwin H., 33
Lemare, Jules, 61
Lennon, John, 187
Lenya, Lotte, 240
Leonard, Harlan, 106
Leoncavallo, Ruggiero, 140
Lerner, Alan Jay, 129, 146, 149, 214, 215
Lerner, Sammy, 86
LeRoy, Hal, 85, 214
Les, Don, 202
Les Compagnons de la Chanson, 225
Leslie, Edgar, 38, 87, 130
Leslie, Lew, 13
Les Paul and Mary Ford, 17, 32, 102, 121, 146, 148, 156, 193, 201, 214, 224
Leveen, Raymond, 96
Levinson, Lou, 150
Levy, Eunice, 162
Lewis, Al, 72, 101, 107, 214
Lewis, George, 37
Lewis, Jerry, 120, 140, 160, 217
Lewis, Jerry Lee, 122
Lewis, Morgan, 102, 214
Lewis, Sam M., 16, 20, 31, 32, 36, 168, 182, 214, 243
Lewis, Ted, 12, 16, 22, 29, 40, 214

Liberace, 115
Lightner, Winnie, 23, 25, 30, 59, 214
Lilley, Joseph J., 108, 131
Lillie, Beatrice, 12, 36, 214
Lilo, 155
Lincke, Paul, 150
Lindeman, Edith, 158
Link, Harry, 84
Lippman, Sidney, 122, 134, 149, 214
Little, Eric, 49
Little, Little Jack, 14, 28–29, 64, 78, 214–15
Little Richard, 122
Livingston, Jay, 123, 129, 134, 143, 215
Livingston, Jerry, 71, 112, 141, 164, 184, 215
Lloyd, Harold, 184
Lochard, Jimmy, 180
Lockhart, Eugene, 17
Loeb, John Jacob, 65, 215
Loesser, Frank, 93, 95, 96, 106, 108, 109, 114, 116, 131, 133, 135, 136, 137, 141, 142, 151, 215, 231
Loewe, Frederick, 214, 215
Logan, Ella, 131, 215
Logan, Harold, 128
Lohner, Fritz, 29
Lomax, John, 142
Lombardo, Carmen, 66, 139, 215, 216
Lombardo, Guy, 12, 36, 42, 52, 56, 61, 66, 67, 78, 99, 104, 113, 128, 129, 136, 139, 141, 144, 169, 173, 215, 216
Lombardo, Lebert, 216
Lombardo, Victor, 216
London, Julie, 162, 216
Long, Johnny, 64, 216